Managing complex mergers

Real world lessons in implementing successful cross-cultural mergers and acquisitions

Edited by
Piero Morosini and Ulrich Steger

FT Prentice Hall
FINANCIAL TIMES

An imprint of Pearson Education

London • New York • Toronto • Sydney • Tokyo • Singapore
Hong Kong • Cape Town • Madrid • Paris • Amsterdam • Munich • Milan

PEARSON EDUCATION LIMITED

Head Office
Edinburgh Gate
Harlow CM20 2JE
Tel: +44 (0)1279 623623
Fax: +44 (0)1279 431059
Website: www.pearsoned.co.uk

First published in Great Britain in 2004

ISBN 0 273 66314 3

British Library Cataloguing in Publication Data
A CIP catalogue record for this book can be obtained from the British Library

10 9 8 7 6 5 4 3 2 1

Typeset by Northern Phototypesetting Co. Ltd, Bolton
Printed and bound in Great Britain by Biddles Ltd, Guildford & King's Lynn

The Publishers' policy is to use paper manufactured from sustainable forests.

Managing complex mergers

Contents

p. 44, 86, 148–158

About the authors

The authors represent a team of key faculty members at IMD (International Institute for Management Development, Lausanne) with strong, direct experience working with M&As, as executive educators, researchers, consultants and/or board members.

PIERO MOROSINI is Professor of Strategy at IMD – International Institute for Management Development, Lausanne. He is a teacher, an author and a speaker in the fields of: mergers, acquisitions and alliances, cross-cultural management and knowledge management. Prior to joining IMD in August 1998, he pursued an international career in strategy consulting and in the financial/banking industries in companies such as: Accenture, Robert Fleming, JP Morgan, and McKinsey & Company.

He has attended graduate studies at The Wharton School, University of Pennsylvania, Philadelphia (1986–88), where he obtained a Ph.D. in Management, an M.A. in Decision Sciences and an MBA, and has graduated in Economics at Universidad del Pacífico, Lima (1984).

He is a Thought Leadership award winner worldwide at the former Andersen Consulting Strategic Services Group in 1997–98, and a Senior Research Fellow at ISVOR FIAT since March 2001. He has previously been a Research Fellow at the Wharton Risk Management Center, Philadelphia (1995–98), as well as at the Strategy Department of the Bocconi University, Milan (1993–94). His work on: cross-cultural management, mergers and acquisitions, strategic alliances and knowledge management has been published in a series of books, book chapters and articles in leading academic journals.

PROFESSOR ULRICH STEGER is Professor of International Management, M&As and Environmental Management. Previously he was a full professor at the European Business School, a guest professor at St Gallen University and a Fellow at Harvard University. Before becoming involved in management education, he was active in German politics. He was Minister of Economics and Technology in the state of Hesse and a member of the German Bundestag. He continues to be a member of the supervisory, advisory and managing boards of several major companies and organizations such as ABB and Volkswagen.

Ulrich Steger has worked with companies and executives on M&A issues throughout his professional career, most recently in his role as director of all DaimlerChrysler in-company executive programmes and research initiatives at IMD, as well as in a series of executive programmes with Allianz Dresdner.

DONALD A. MARCHAND is Professor of Strategy and Information Management. His interests include managing information and knowledge to drive superior business performance, e-business strategy for established companies, demand/supply chain management and the strategic use and deployment of information systems and technology in companies operating in local, regional and global markets.

Professor Marchand is an advisor to senior executives of leading service and manufacturing companies in Europe, North America and the Asia Pacific. He was a principal researcher in IMD's seven-year research programme Manufacturing 2000, and has directed national studies of information technology management in the federal, state and local governments in the US.

JACQUES HOROVITZ is Professor of Service Strategy, Service Marketing & Service Management. He focuses on how to compete through service and improve customer satisfaction, with heavy emphasis on service as a strategy for differentiation, on customer loyalty and on creating a service culture.

He brings to practising managers three sets of experiences. First, he has practised service marketing and management in several executive positions. Second, he has advised the CEOs of over 100 companies throughout Europe on service, having founded, developed and managed a pan-European consulting company with offices in seven countries and 50 consultants. Finally, he has extensively researched service strategies and service quality, relationship marketing, customer bonding and published on it.

PAUL STREBEL is the Sandoz Family Foundation Professor of Strategic Change Management. His main area of activity is strategic change management, espeically high-speed strategy, the anticipation of industry breakpoints, and the design and implementation of change processes, including new compacts (commitments) to support ongoing change.

He has directed a variety of in-company programmes for IMD's business partners and associates and has worked privately, as both a keynote spreaker and a seminar leader, for numerous multinationals, including most recently Bosch, Nokia and several large financial services firms.

VLADIMIR PUCIK is Professor of International Human Resources and Strategy. Before joining IMD, Dr Pucik was Associate Professor and Academic Director of International Programs at The Center for Advanced Human Resource Studies at the ILR School, Cornell University, and a faculty member at the School of Business, University of Michigan. He also spent three years as a visiting scholar at Keio and Hitotsubashi University in Tokyo.

He serves on the advisory boards of several high-technology start-ups and has consulted and conducted workshops for major corporations worldwide, including Allianz, BOC, Citibank, Canon, DaimlerChrysler, Dentsu, DHL, GE, Gillette, Hitachi, Kodak, Nokia, Shell, Sony and UBS. Dr Pucik also teaches regularly in a number of executive development programmes in the US, Europe and Asia.

PETER KILLING is Professor of Strategy. His areas of particular interest are strategy creation and execution, the management of change, and the design and management of acquisitions and alliances. Ideas from his books have influenced the activities of many individual managers and companies, including, to name a few of the larger ones, Exxon, Mobil, Nestlé, *elisa*, Telenor, ICI and Zeneca.

In the alliance area, Professor Killing has written and/or edited four books and several articles, including one in the *Harvard Business Review*. Through teaching and consulting, he has directly impacted the alliance activities of many companies, including DaimlerChrysler, the Ford Motor Company, IBM, British Telecom, the British Post Office, and many companies in the European aerospace industry, including the companies that combined to form EADS.

CHRISTOPHER KUMMER is Scientific Assistant for Strategic Management and PhD candidate at the Institute for Technology and Management of the Technical University, Berlin. He has been a research associate at IMD and the Institute for Technology Management of St Gallen University. His areas of interest are strategic management and organizations, mergers and acquisitions, and e-business.

In addition to internships in various industries, Christopher Kummer has been co-founder and CEO of a Swiss start-up company.

PAUL EVANS is the Shell Chaired Professor of Human Resources and Organizational Development and Professor of Organizational Behavior at INSEAD, where he has led activities in the field of human resource and organizational management since the early 1980s. He is director of INSEAD's executive seminars on Management of People and Managerial Skills for International Business, and he works closely on related programmes in Asia. His research and teaching focuses on leadership, the management of change, and international human resource management. He has a degree in law from Cambridge University, an INSEAD MBA, a Danish business diploma, and a PhD from M.I.T.

Introduction by the editors

ANOTHER BOOK on mergers and acquisitions (M&As)? At the dawn of the new millennium, the number of books and articles and the amount of business media attention devoted to these undertakings has in fact closely paralleled a wave of M&As of hitherto unknown scale and global reach. However, a wide body of evidence gathered by academics, management consultants and company executives strongly suggests that the failure to manage the integration of both partners after the deal is done is behind the dismal track record of most M&As.[1] Nevertheless, it is rather surprising that very few authors have actually presented systematic, pragmatic evidence of what makes M&As successes or failures from the perspective of implementation.

This book presents fresh, substantial and pragmatic evidence on a series of implementation issues that are central to the success or failure of international M&As. Most of the contributing authors are professors at IMD – the leading business school in international executive education – with strong experience as international consultants, business researchers and company executives. The authors have worked directly with executives from high-profile global M&As within a variety of industries, ranging from automotive to financial services, pharmaceuticals to media and entertainment. The resulting wealth of experiences, insights and expertise have been shaped into this book.

The content of the book applies to all types of international M&As that are motivated by the need to combine the significant strategic resources of the joining companies after the deal is done. These typically include technologies, fixed and intangible assets, business knowledge, infrastructural

[1] For examples see:
➢ Morosini, P. *Managing Cultural Differences*, Pergamon, Oxford, 1998
➢ "The Case Against Mergers." *The Economist*, 4 January 1997, (cover story)
➢ "Most Mergers Don't Work." *Business Week*, 30 October 1995; (cover story)

resources and, especially, people. M&A undertakings that are largely motivated by financial risk diversification, entrepreneurial experimentation, exceedingly narrow functional learning and the like are therefore outside the main focus of this volume.

What makes this book different?

In this book we have intentionally departed from the theoretical, reductionist and merely normative views that have so far pervaded the majority of contemporary M&A literature. Rather, our work contains compelling evidence from hard-nosed, pragmatic research that opens minds to new perspectives and dispels commonplace myths behind issues such as whether or not cultural differences need to be detrimental to the performance of cross-border M&As, whether such a thing as "mergers of equals" can in fact be implemented, and whether an M&A can actually be turned into an inspiring – rather than a largely distressing – experience for all employees involved.

From the outset, our aim was to provide path-breaking contributions to managers and practitioners involved in M&A activities internationally, on at least three dimensions. First, we provide new and compelling findings, especially in areas that are highly relevant to M&A implementation. Second, we present these original research findings in a pragmatic, managerial language that we hope reaches a wide, global audience of executives and practitioners involved in M&A. Third, we approach M&A issues from a holistic perspective, which makes them relevant to business executives and practitioners alike, rather than taking the largely analytical and sectoral perspectives that seem to be common to much of the specialized M&A literature.

Behind the diversity of M&A perspectives represented by the various authors, the discerning reader will doubtless recognize some overarching principles at work across all of the book's chapters. Among them are the idea that, particularly from an implementation viewpoint, M&As are to be conceived as *broad*, *continuous* and *holistic* managerial undertakings, rather than narrow, sporadic or purely strategic initiatives. There is also the perspective that cultural and organizational differences between the joining companies are potentially beneficial aspects to be managed by savvy global executives – as opposed to sources of managerial risk or detrimental factors per se. Furthermore, there is the consideration that swift, assertive and hands-on approaches to creating a "common glue" between the joining companies might provide all M&As with the most likely path to value creation and successful performance.

How to read this book

This book consists of nine chapters in three parts. Although they have been ordered based on content, the reader can go directly to any chapter of interest and move at will thereafter from topic to topic.

The first part – "New Perspectives on International M&As" – presents findings that might challenge the reader to adopt a radically different way of assessing, negotiating and, especially, preparing for and implementing M&As in the future. In Chapter 1, Ulrich Steger and Christopher Kummer argue persuasively that – unlike previous M&A waves – M&A activity during the 1980s and the 1990s has not just grown in volume. Rather, the scope of M&A motivations, its key drivers – and therefore its performance implications – have widened beyond recognition both at the firm and the industry level.

However, in Chapter 2, bluntly entitled "Are M&As about creating value?", Piero Morosini looks at the dismal performance record of M&As in the past, and provides evidence suggesting that what really drives "value creation" in *all* M&As is the joining companies' *ability* to develop a strong "common glue" across geographic, cultural and organizational boundaries after the deal is done. Morosini reminds us that neither synergies nor more powerful structural relationships can be obtained in the absence of a lasting "common glue" between the joining companies in the first place. Therefore, how to prepare, undertake and monitor the journey towards building this "common glue" between the M&A partners is of central importance to performance.

The second part of the book is called "Managing the Boundaries" and examines some of the most important dimensions for successful implementation of M&As internationally. In Chapter 3 – "Global M&As: Why do so many fail? How to make them successful?" – Morosini presents the first systematic empirical evidence that national cultural differences are not necessarily detrimental to cross-border M&As, as has so often been argued in the past. Rather, if skilfully handled, these differences can actually enhance performance. Morosini goes on to examine compelling approaches used in large-scale "mergers of equals" and acquisitions in the automotive, pharmaceutical, and media and entertainment sectors, illustrating how to create a "common glue" that turns cultural and organizational differences into advantages.

In Chapter 4, Paul Strebel shows how "Institutional factors are critical in cross-cultural M&As". Avoiding cultural clichés, observes Strebel, is the first step that enables a change of mindset in managers involved in M&A activity. In order to foster a mindset that can cross boundaries, Strebel proposes that managers focus on "institutional factors". These factors are widely overlooked by both executives and practitioners, but Strebel demonstrates how they can be turned into critical enablers of performance in international M&As.

Peter Killing, in Chapter 5, looks at a "Merger of equals: the case of AstraZeneca". Taking this description that was used – and often abused – during the wave of unprecedented "mega-mergers" of the late 1990s and early 2000s, Killing addresses two fundamental questions: What is a merger of equals? and: What does it take to create one? Both queries are answered through a first-hand, insightful account of AstraZeneca, the high-profile pharmaceutical "merger of equals".

In Chapter 6, Jacques Horovitz examines "Some key pitfalls in acquisitions". The pitfalls Horovitz highlights were unearthed as a result of his extensive academic, executive and entrepreneurial experience. They cover the assessment, negotiation and integration phases of international acquisitions, and Horovitz gives powerful, straightforward – but often counterintuitive – advice on avoiding such pitfalls.

The third and last part of this volume – entitled "Key Capabilities for M&A Success" – looks at three corporate aspects which are central to creating a "common glue" between companies involved in an M&A, but which too often are ignored by executives, or at best narrowly treated as functional support to "post-merger integration" initiatives.

In Chapter 7, Steger and Kummer maintain that the "Challenges of governance structures in international mergers and acquisitions" are not about ensuring that a new top executive structure is in place – often reflecting a 50:50 or some other type of balance of power between the joining companies. Rather, the real challenge is about seizing the opportunity to make huge changes and shape an entirely new corporate system that will inform the new company's strategy and align it with its competitive milieu.

Chapter 8 looks at "The human factor in mergers and acquisitions". Vladimir Pucik and Paul Evans demonstrate that the "people challenges" in an international M&A really are about identifying, attracting, developing and retaining a key cadre of managers and leaders who can build a strong esprit de corps and share a common set of aspirations and organizational knowledge. In order to ensure M&A success, integration managers, transition teams and the so-called HR function, must therefore play fascinating, pivotal and often unprecedented roles.

Donald A. Marchand, in Chapter 9, presents evidence that measuring, valuing and managing information, people and IT capabilities – both before and after an M&A deal – are also critical to M&A success or failure. Here, the real issue is not just appraising the joining companies' IT assets and usage – as is usually done during an M&A due diligence. Rather, the challenge is to assess and blend the joining companies' intangible capabilities to manage information, IT and people in ways that create competitive advantages in the marketplace. This is what Marchand refers to as "Information Orientation", a concept that is developed in the context of international M&As, complete with case examples, application frameworks and tools.

Acknowledgements

The editors would like to thank Helga Krapf for her outstanding and diligent co-ordination work through all the stages of the effort leading to the publication of this volume. We also thank IMD President Peter Lorange for supporting our initiative, and Professors Carlos Cordon and John Walsh, as well as Petri Lehtivaara, for making sure this support was translated into timely resources, encouragement and appreciation of our work. We also express our gratitude to Lindsay McTeague and Michelle Perrinjaquet for their meticulous and insightful revisions of the manuscript. Last but not least, we warmly thank the participants on one of the editing author's executive and MBA M&A classes over the past five years – the conception of this book and many of the key ideas in it owe much to the views, comments and experiences participants shared in those unforgettable classes.

Piero Morosini and Ulrich Steger
Lausanne, August 2003

Part One

New perspectives on international M&A

1

M&A activity in the new competitive milieu

By
Ulrich Steger and Christopher Kummer

The life cycle of merger and acquisition waves

THE PHENOMENON OF merger and acquisition (M&A) is hardly new. It has always accompanied the economic activity of modern capitalism. However, five major waves of M&A can be identified, which will be explained shortly.[1]

The industrial revolution resulted in the rapid expansion of industries and firms, leading to an increased likelihood of consolidation during or after the boom. Between 1897 and 1904 we therefore saw a first wave of M&A – 'mergers for monopoly'. Companies intended to gain influence and market power by reaping the benefits of monopolies and economies of scale offered by the adoption of new production techniques. Changes in antitrust laws, the desire to dominate the whole supply chain, and early internationalization were the key drivers of a wave of 'mergers for oligopoly' between 1918 and 1932. The pursuit of diversification was the main driver behind the 'conglomerate mergers' that took place between 1955 and 1975. Soon such conglomerates became targets themselves in what was called the 'era of hostile takeovers and mega deals' in the 1980s. Corporate raiders acquired companies which, as entities, were less valuable than the sum of their parts and broke them up. Since 1992 we have been experiencing a 'global merger' wave in an endeavour to attain critical mass and industry influence on a worldwide scale and meet the growth expectations of capital markets.

The lesson we can draw from historic M&A waves is that each wave has a unique life cycle (see Figure 1.1). A wave usually takes some time to build up, but once the peak is reached, it ebbs quickly. But what causes these waves?

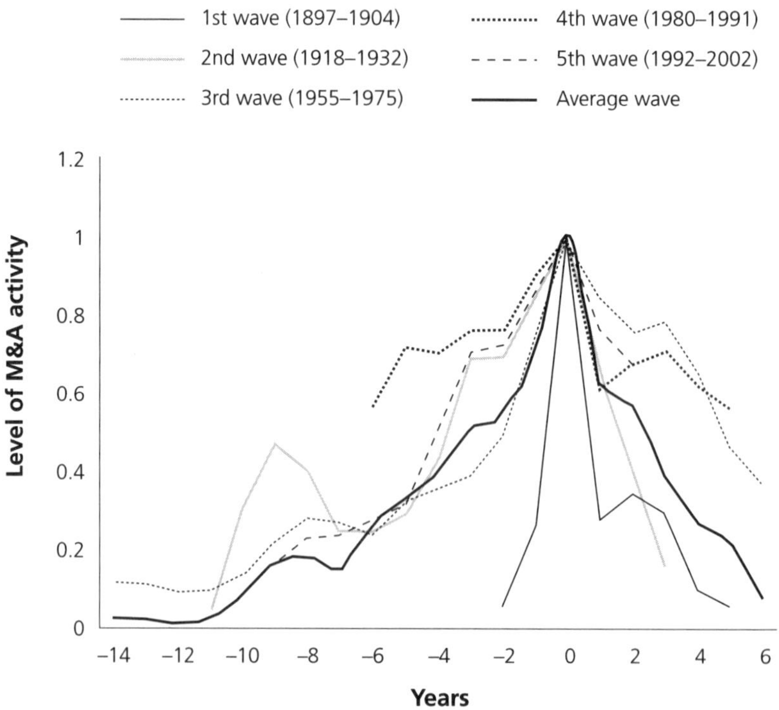

Figure 1.1 ◆ **The life cycle of M&A waves**

Source: Authors' calculations based on Nelson (1959), FTC (1971), and Mergerstat (2003)

The drivers and constraints of M&A activity

Each wave is said to be driven by a few very specific strategic intentions. The factors that cause M&A waves to peak or ebb are manifold. The simultaneous appearance of one factor and high M&A activity does not necessarily imply a strict cause–effect relationship between them. Additionally, each wave is influenced not only by recent trends but also by their development in the past.[2] It is seldom one factor alone that is responsible for the start or end of a wave; rather it is a set of factors that creates favourable or unfavourable conditions. These factors are certainly not independent of each other. Therefore we suggest a holistic approach with a multi-level framework for the analysis of drivers and constraints. This framework is useful for explaining M&A

activity as well as single M&A transactions because it allows multiple factors and motives to contribute to the causes. We will characterize them according to five different levels, from bottom to top (see Figure 1.2):

> It is seldom one factor alone that is responsible for the start or end of a wave

- stakeholders
- firm
- industry
- macro-economy
- society, politics and law.

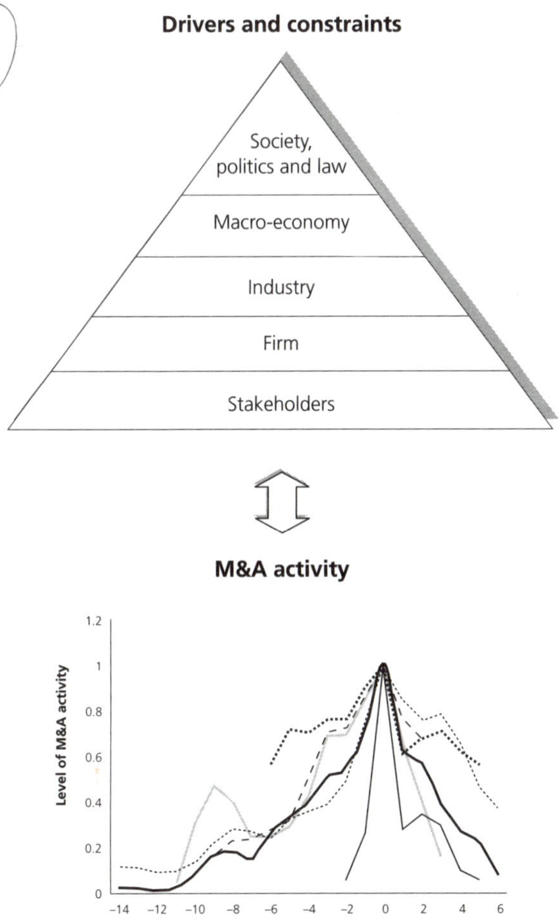

Figure 1.2 ◆ A multi-level framework of the drivers and constraints of M&A activity

Individual stakeholder level

Behind each M&A transaction – directly or indirectly – are stakeholders which are by no means anonymous or secret. When we take a look at a company's environment before, during and after an M&A transaction, we can see a lot of stakeholders (see Figure 1.3). First of all, there is the management of a company and its employees, including unions. The management is supported by an array of service providers, such as investment bankers, management consultants, accountants, lawyers, advertisers and public relations specialists. There are also the shareholders, who decide whether to sell their shares to the acquirer or to engage in a merger, as well as credit grantors and analysts. The credit rating might be subject to a revision. The media and journalists might comment on the transaction. Politicians might contribute to the complex situation. Competitors could complain to antitrust authorities. The transaction might be subject to approval by antitrust authorities anyway. Last, but not least, the transaction might be influenced by customers – who will either be loyal or switch – and suppliers. And because at least two companies are involved in a transaction, the number of people mentioned above roughly doubles. Therefore excellent stakeholder management is one key to mastering M&A.

Within this complex situation each individual follows his or her own agenda and aims. Even if they all act rationally, the M&A transaction will not necessarily be a success – because of divergent interests. But given the high stakes, it cannot be expected that each and every one of these people will act in a rational way, especially not in a dynamic group setting and under enormous stress. Emotions are intense during M&A situations, which are characterized by high information uncertainty and asymmetry between the parties involved. In addition, the uncertainty about personal destiny in a successful transaction is high: why should people take the risk when often they might become victims of their own success? But the economic pressure is sufficiently high that one can easily predict that there will be another M&A wave. We will now analyse the perspectives of stakeholders one by one, starting with those of managers.

The separation of ownership and *management* of companies causes conflicting incentives and raises issues of corporate governance.[3] So managers might not always choose or realize transactions that are advantageous for shareholders. But all hypotheses are far from being proven. The different perspectives of managers and owners have led to the suggestion that managerial myopia causes managers to sacrifice long-term benefits to short-term gains, but it is far from clear whether M&A transactions are short-term or long-term gains.

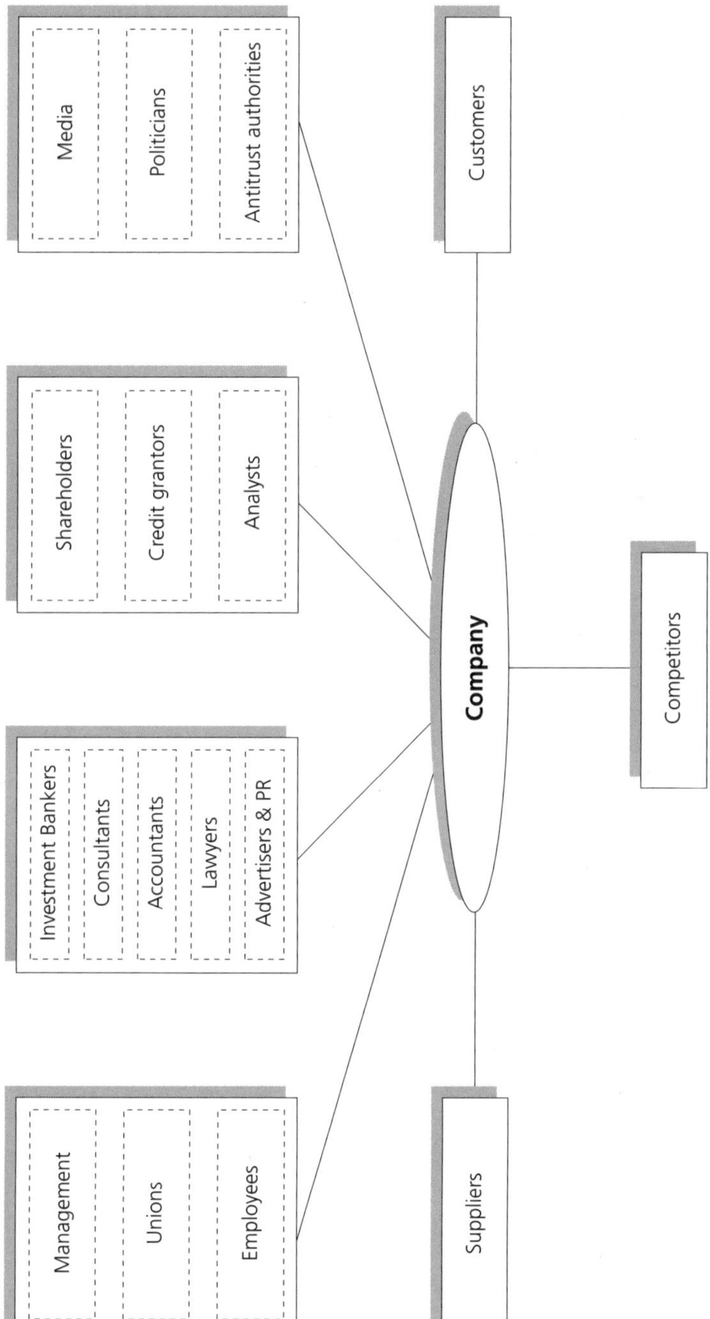

Figure 1.3 ◆ Company and its stakeholders in the M&A environment

Managers might be interested in power and fame, using M&A for 'empire building' – just think of Vivendi, a company that diversified from utilities into telecommunications and media, or Tyco, a diversified manufacturing and service company. They might get carried away by being in the driver's seat, with the chance to reshape a whole company or even industry. Business heroes are needed and stylized by the media. CEOs pay 'irrational' premiums for acquisitions that rise in proportion to the extent of flattering press coverage they receive.[4] The misevaluation of targets might also be caused by managers' hubris.[5] On one hand, this indicates severe corporate governance issues, but when the market realizes this, the stock declines and as a consequence the companies become potential targets. On the other hand, the fear of becoming a target and losing their job contributes to the need to become a consolidator themselves.

Managers might not always choose or realize transactions that are advantageous for shareholders

Another hypothesis claims that M&A helps reallocate resources and enhance efficiency: superior management replaces inferior management, improving the company's efficiency and increasing shareholder value. The market of corporate control should therefore keep management under some control. Excessive free cash flows can seduce managers into favouring investments in less profitable M&A activity in order to keep funds under their control instead of paying them out to shareholders in the form of dividends.[6]

During the diversification period, investment opportunities and managers' choices were supposed to be superior to those of external financial markets and individual investors because managers could elaborate better financial control systems. Management was seen rather as a general capability that could easily be transferred to other companies and industries. Nowadays, external financial markets are regarded as being more efficient. Managing by financial criteria alone is not enough; management capability is seen as being influenced to some extent by industry and sometimes even by firm-specific knowledge. However, managers can become carried away by the chance to apply their managerial skills in other areas, as well as by the opportunity for promotion, with which comes more responsibility but also a higher salary. Large companies can attract new management talent and retain existing managers. M&A is a means of obtaining new management capabilities and industry expertise which are essential when diversifying into new industries. A change in management generations and styles has taken place so that M&A is now a widely accepted way of realizing corporate strategy.

Altogether, the resources invested in preparing an M&A deal are immense. Even if management recognizes that in the end there are few advantages and the transaction is not worth the risk, there is the fear of having missed an opportunity, maybe the chance of a lifetime. The psychological costs of 'walk-away' are tremendous. For the day-to-day business, M&A are exceptions that absorb much management capacity in integration activities so that managers are distracted from daily operations and their usual tasks and firm performance may suffer, even if there is no ill intent.

Employees might benefit from M&A if, for example, a larger company is a more attractive employer and is able to offer new career opportunities, better education and more generous fringe benefits. Yet often restructuring and lay-offs as well as cost cutting follow an M&A, so these potential advantages remain theoretical. Rumours spread and fear paralyzes the frustrated workforce. Usually communication from top management is insufficient. It is not clear who will get which position, and the decision-making processes are often obscure to outsiders. As a result there are groups of losers and winners. Employees think in terms of camps of former employees from one or other company, a labelling which lasts for years. Only close ties to decision makers and networks seem to offer potential for a future career. Unions are also sometimes involved when corporate restructuring takes place, and can mobilize their members, who will readily support protests.

Unions are also sometimes involved when corporate restructuring takes place

Many *professional service providers* are experienced in M&A transactions and help companies to realize their deals. They develop new products and services and try to leverage their knowledge worldwide. They push new management methods and ideas that sometimes turn out to be short-sighted fads. Investment bankers try 'to pitch' a unique opportunity to companies and will also organize the financing of the deal – high provisions and bonuses are enticing. Among these bankers are some stars and teams which change employers quite frequently. Management consultants develop some clever strategy and a strong story for the transaction. They would love to carry out the post-merger integration. So management is pushed by the attitude of 'let's make this deal happen' and might be impressed by a plethora of convincing presentations. Accountants are involved in the due diligence and valuation. Lawyers help prepare the contract and might deal with antitrust issues. Advertisers and public relations specialists support management in communicating the deal. Companies have to sell the transaction externally to the financial community, shareholders and customers as well as internally to employees. Communication costs are even higher when a hostile takeover battle takes place or a new corporate identity is needed.

The advantage of these service providers is their experience with and specialization in M&A transactions. They are not bogged down by the daily business as management is and most do not face any real risks – they benefit even when the transaction turns out to be a disaster. Only when the deal is not done do they suffer a loss of business, so their understandable interest is to make the deal happen. When a combination does fail, there are so many factors that contribute to its failure that blame is not clearly attributable. The service providers may even come out of it with their reputation intact. However, dependence on external service providers is decreasing as managers have become more experienced with M&A and as companies have built up internal M&A departments. In the current M&A recession, the work of these service providers is under tough scrutiny and their margins have fallen dramatically.

Investing in shares has become quite popular and a kind of 'equity culture' has spread, although the bursting of the latest bubble has dampened enthusiasm to some degree. The spread of equity culture is not so much a result of a decrease in the risk aversion of investors as of better usage of the financial spectrum as a whole. Thus investors can reach a better point on the risk-return matrix by either realizing a higher return with the same risk or reaching the same return with less risk. So in an acquisition, the target's *shareholders* are usually not reluctant to sell their shares because the acquirer is paying a premium. Therefore the target's shareholders are always winners in an M&A transaction. However, they might oppose the deal if they will receive stocks instead of cash. They also might not be willing to sell if the offer is below what they paid for their shares or below the initial issue price. That is why in a stock market boom more M&As happen through share swaps. Shareholders might also hold on to their shares for emotional reasons, e.g. the founder or his family are loath to give up their lifetime achievement (as in the 2002 Hewlett-Packard and Compaq merger). In most cases, as the empirical evidence indicates, the acquirer's shareholders suffer as a result of M&A transactions.[7]

> Succession planning in family businesses is becoming an imperative issue

Although diversification nowadays is seen as a dubious reason for M&A, it makes complete sense to diversify by M&A when ownership and management are not separated, i.e. the shareholders are also the managers. These shareholders can then diversify their personal wealth without the need to sell a stake in the company and lose control.

Succession planning in family businesses is becoming an imperative issue, but very often ownership is separated from the management of the company to ensure long-term survival. The 350–year-old Haniel company, ranked No. 11 by turnover in Germany, is a role model.

Fund managers and analysts have a huge impact on management. If institutional investors, e.g. insurance companies, trusts, pension and mutual funds, take over, this usually creates a very different climate and new shareholder activism: switching from a paternal atmosphere to one of pressure for boosting returns. Institutional investors expect higher returns and pay heed to the value of the company.

Politicians are aware of the tremendous consequences and impact of large M&A transactions and often oppose corporate restructuring, especially if layoffs are involved. They may also protect prestigious companies and industries of national importance from being taken over. The influence of the political dimension will be discussed later in more detail on the level of society, politics and law. Antitrust regulators might want to have their say as well, possibly prohibiting the combination. Their decisions are rarely challenged in, and subsequently overruled by, the courts. The advantage of fast growth is negated by the time-consuming, costly and uncertain nature of court proceedings. Nevertheless, some decisions by the European Commission on M&A transactions have been overruled in court.

The needs and goals of all the individuals involved, as well as the advantages and disadvantages to them, are conflicting, even from a rational point of view. What will happen when they behave irrationally? Perhaps surprisingly, it might be a real option to deliberately behave in an irrational way. It is only surprise and sudden moves that give birth to something new. Market forces constantly decrease shareholder value if routine prevails. And we can think of the start of an M&A wave in a similar way – some people try something new and behave countercyclically.

Firm level

Each M&A wave is, of course, only the aggregate of individual M&A transactions. M&A should never be an end in itself, and there are as many reasons put forward for M&A as there are consultants and textbooks on the topic.[8] In general, M&A is meant to help realize corporate strategy and certain strategic intentions. So within corporate strategy M&A plays different roles for company growth and renewal. It is important to understand these differences in order to master the difficulties and address the key issues during the whole M&A process, from strategic fit to post-merger integration. We show that there can also be multiple reasons for M&A transactions on the firm level by characterizing the different types of M&A along two dimensions, namely extension in the scope of business and development of capabilities and skills.

Extension in the scope of business affects the categories, products, markets and even industries. A critical mass can be reached via M&A when scale and realizing cost advantages are essential in order to survive and become more profitable. When this extension is low and businesses overlap, the likelihood of synergies is high. Then the main issue is realizing economies of scale, for example by better capacity management, optimal plant sizes, streamlined manufacturing network and inventory levels, combining secondary functions and back-office, and cutting other overheads. The combined companies can drive down costs faster by taking advantage of the effects of the experience curve as well. M&A can be used to acquire a new customer base. Additionally, there is an opportunity to carry out detailed benchmarking and introduce only the best practices of both companies to enhance operating efficiencies.

If the extension of business is medium, there are either economies of scope or advantages of vertical integration to be exploited. This kind of M&A is a diversification in related fields. Vertical integration can lower transaction costs that stem from information asymmetries and the necessary co-ordination over the firm boundary. The value chain is extended and the combined chain can be streamlined. Economies of scope – or 'one-stop shopping' – can be offered, for instance, when the same raw and semi-finished materials are needed, when production processes and facilities are the same or similar, when the same distribution channels are used or the same customers are targeted, or when complementary products and services are sold. In the banking industry, for example, few banks have succeeded in profitably combining investment banking and traditional lending. Big clients do not seem to care whether banks offer the full range of financial services – they try to select the best provider for each financial service rather than relying on a house banker. 'Cross-selling' efforts with retail banking have not succeeded so far because the issue of whether the customer wants to 'cross-buy', whether the workforce is available and whether channel conflicts have been managed is seldom addressed.

When the extension in the scope of business is high, we can think of it as diversification in mostly unrelated areas. There are almost no cost advantages to be realized. Although in the 1950s and 1960s diversification was seen as a good thing, nowadays diversified companies are less valuable and subject to a 'conglomerate discount'.[9] However, the appraisal of cost advantages is not yet complete. The advantages of M&A are often overestimated and hard to realize. We should be aware that there are also diseconomies of scale and scope. The bigger a company gets, the more bureaucracy is introduced.

The bigger a company gets, the more bureaucracy is introduced

The development of capabilities and skills can be enhanced through M&A transactions. New employees contribute to the knowledge base of the company. A bigger company can also afford larger investments in and long-term development of capabilities and skills, which start-up companies cannot. A larger company allows for greater specialization within the company, with the associated advantages. But a greater degree of specialization also means higher co-ordination costs. Additionally, M&A can lead to 'data-mining' opportunities, i.e. the ability to use different data about customers. It is, however, difficult to realize this opportunity in a sensible way. Nowadays the problem is not so much technical but lies in developing cognitive systems and schemes that really make sense. And even if they are developed, the expected advantages from data-mining will be difficult to realize since new restrictions, namely tougher privacy laws, are on the cards.

Of course the business world is not as clear-cut as the clusters in Figure 1.4 might suggest. Nevertheless, we deem the following archetypes to be extremely useful for focusing on key issues during the M&A process. So we take a look at the different M&A types.

The traditional consolidation M&A is aimed at rationalization, reducing overcapacity and improving competitiveness. Both companies are involved in almost the same business. Pearls on a string M&A take place when large companies absorb many small ones, thereby allowing them to extend their product range and/or regional coverage. The targets are niche players, often still start-ups. Strategic assemblers are companies that grow rapidly in both their capabilities and their business. These assemblers want to become leaders in their respective markets and they frequently make extensive use of often quite expensive transactions, which can be a way into another strategic group within their industry. In the food industry, for instance, we find many examples such as Nestlé and Unilever.

A new industry entrance can be managed through an M&A transaction, when the new capabilities and skills needed are added as the scope of business is extended. Important entry barriers can be torn down. Many transactions in the pharmaceutical industry in the 1980s and 1990s led to the creation of 'life science' companies as previously rather chemical-dominated companies reshaped themselves by adding biotechnology and genetic engineering laboratories. The portfolio turnover – when companies apply portfolio theories that many management consultancies offer – can be attained through many M&A activities. Before becoming an attractive target for Vodafone, Mannesmann transformed itself from a steel and pipe manufacturer to become a leading player in automotive supplies and telecommunications. With a global leap, companies drastically extend their product range and regional reach.

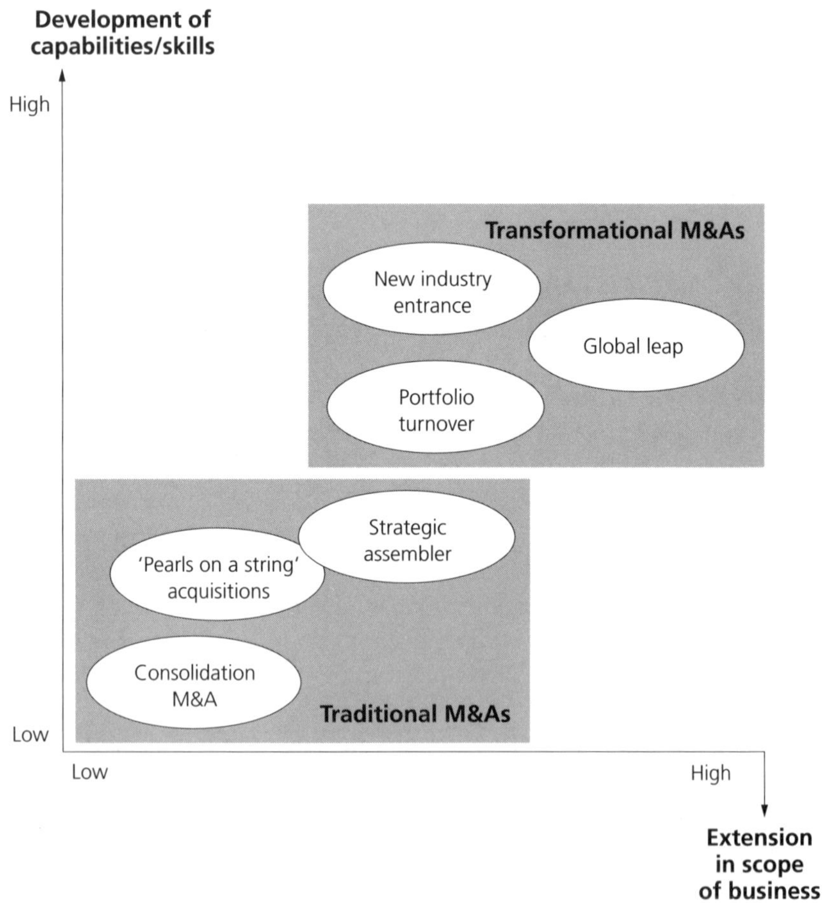

Figure 1.4 ◆ Strategic intentions of mergers and acquisitions
Source: based on Steger (1999), 2

As we can see from the various historic M&A waves, the motives for M&A evolve and change, just as along our dimensions the use of M&A has widened. Hence we distinguish between traditional and transformational M&As. While the traditional types still make sense, there has recently been a shift towards transformational ones. Whereas traditional M&As are about the transfer of capabilities, transformational ones aim more at creating new capabilities. This might be required due to technological breakthroughs (e.g. use of biotechnology in the chemical or pharmaceutical business), the enabling of new business models (e.g. demand chain management) or globalization. Companies run into extreme difficulties if they are not aware of the differences between these M&A types because they have a tremendous impact on all stages of the M&A process, from due diligence to post-merger integration. This is one major reason for the failure of so many M&As. Transformational M&As must be managed in a completely different way because more is at stake – there are more risks than with traditional transactions. Companies that slowly move from one M&A type to another are not aware of the differences. For instance, Norwegian shipbuilder Kvaerner tried to leapfrog to become a global contracting and engineering company through a series of rapid acquisitions, which eventually included the purchase of the UK-based conglomerate, Trafalgar House. Kvaerner moved from a 'string of pearls' to a 'portfolio turnover' acquirer without realizing what difference it made. The old integration method no longer worked; business processes were affected and had to be changed. Furthermore, neither management capacity nor the necessary cash flow could be provided to make the M&As a success.

The old integration method no longer worked; business processes were affected and had to be changed

We see four different ways of handling M&A transactions with regard to the perceived advantage of doing things differently and the perceived advantage of integration (see Figure 1.5).

Most traditional M&As are best served by absorption. The dominant organization will increase its capabilities and competitiveness by the transfer of skills and competencies and the application of 'best practice'. Resources are

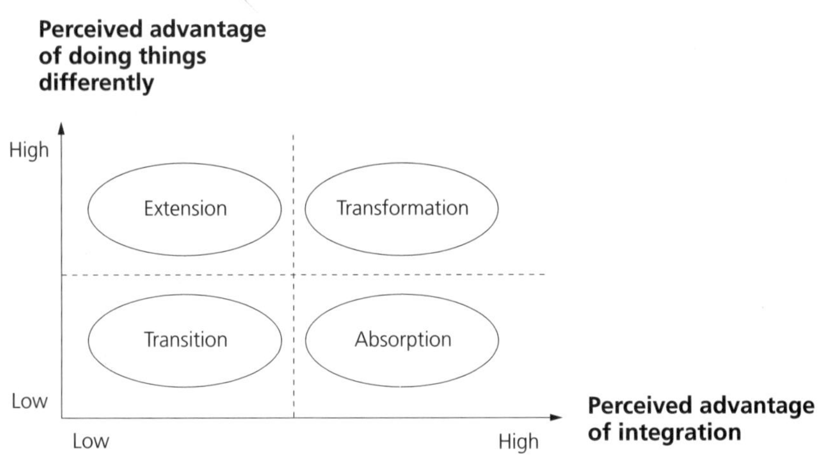

Figure 1.5 ◆ Ways of handling M&A transactions

Source: based on Steger (1999), 3

more efficiently used. Some transactions need little integration, for example those for transition, where acquisitions are added to conglomerates or financial holdings or overcapacity is reduced and only a customer base is added. The extension M&A type is motivated by 'domain exploration' in order to observe and learn a new business. These acquisitions should not be integrated because the different business models usually do not fit. Assembling a brand portfolio follows this logic. A good example is the merger between Guinness' United Distillers and Grand Met's International Distillers & Vintners to form International Distillers Vintners, with one being strong in whisky, gin and cognac, the other in vodka, liqueurs and tequila. The new company is able to counter the rising purchasing power of global retail giants. The transformation type, with a shift to a new technology base, unknown or emerging markets, and a leap in diversity, faces a true dilemma. On the one hand, benefits could be reaped by integration; on the other hand, there are clear advantages in doing things differently. Hence it is necessary to develop new capabilities to cope with the resulting ambiguities and complexities. For example, DaimlerChrysler combined the high research and development (R&D) potential of Daimler that had to be leveraged across a larger base of brands but with the danger of destroying the premium brand positioning of its Mercedes brand.

Industry level

The industry perspective on M&A is quite useful when this knowledge can be put to use for firm-specific M&A activity. The structure-conduct-performance paradigm hypothesizes that market structure determines market conduct, which influences performance. As we can see from the historic M&A waves, some industries are more prone to M&A activity than others. Hence one main characteristic of the phenomenon is its industry specificity. Whereas some industries are regularly subject to transactions, others are not. The degree of industry concentration, in particular, is affected by M&A. Of course, concentration is influenced by other factors as well, e.g. economies of scale, barriers to entry and exit, or the ability of incumbents to keep new entrants from predatory pricing.

But generally the evidence is clear: the more fragmented an industry, the more opportunities for M&A exist. Once the 'game' of M&A has been initiated and activity has significantly picked up, the fear of being left behind spreads and others jump on the bandwagon. They join the consolidation wave, hoping to succeed as consolidators themselves rather than be acquired. Thus the pool of potential M&A candidates is constantly reducing in an industry. As a consequence, M&A activity in an industry is self-energizing.

It is important to think about and look for sudden changes in industry dynamics which may require a strategic move with M&A as a response. These changes occur quickly, and in order to achieve or maintain a leadership position in specific market segments, one should closely watch competitors', suppliers' and customers' moves, such as strategic investments and their patterns and locations, the establishment of strategic alliances, and restructuring with the divestiture of business operations and M&A activities. A Darwinian or evolutionary perspective would see M&A as 'natural selection' – the strong companies acquire the weak ones. This view allows a perspective not only on the individual company but also on the industry as a whole: when only the fittest companies survive, they increase the fitness of their industry.

The stage of evolution of an industry can give an indication of how much M&A activity to expect. At every stage in the life cycle of an industry, i.e. from start to maturity, M&As can be agents for solving the specific problems of companies. In general, M&As help industries to adjust to all kinds of development dynamics and changing competitive paths. When industries are young and entry barriers low, the industry is fragmented and few companies have reached a critical mass. First of all, they merge in order to meet the need for a critical mass, which is hard to achieve. Second, the rise in the number of companies increases the likelihood of M&As as more potential targets and buyers spring up. Third, start-ups sometimes buy competitors that have copied their concept and simply put it to work in other geographical regions. During the expansion phase, capacity can be acquired through M&A.

When maturity is reached and competition is tough, some of the consolidation is achieved via M&A and there is much talk about the 'survival of the endgame'. Overcapacities can be reduced and capacity might even rise as production techniques are optimized. In addition to consolidation M&As, transformational M&As take place in mature industries. There seems to be a U-shaped relationship between capacity utilization and M&A activity. From a business cycle perspective, M&A plays a dual role: during a phase of excess capacity, industry consolidation is driven by M&A, while at peak capacity utilization M&A is used to expand a firm's capacity.[10]

When substitutes pose a threat to one's business, acquiring the potential competitors may be an interesting option, for several reasons. First, the substitute can be withheld from the market and no business is lost. Second, the development of this substitute is under control and a knowledge transfer to one's own business is possible. Third, the substitute can be tried out and if its superiority cannot be kept from the market, one can promote the substitute oneself and influence the process of substitution without losing the market.

For example, some pharmaceutical companies that are active in R&D introduce generics into the market themselves.

M&A balances the power between industries that are connected via the value chain. If suppliers and/or customers combine to form larger entities with more bargaining power, both industries will usually be affected. For example, the retail industry is subject to global consolidation and this affects the consumer goods industry. M&A is a way to evolve into other, more profitable parts of the value chain in order to become full service providers that allow one-stop shopping. For example, technology companies have diversified into services such as consulting. Compaq acquired Digital Equipment Corporation, EDS bought A. T. Kearney, and Cap integrated Gemini Consulting and Ernst & Young Consulting Services. IBM transformed itself from a hardware provider to a comprehensive service company through a string of acquisitions.

M&A balances the power between industries that are connected via the value chain

Furthermore, industries may converge when boundaries blur. Companies think of opportunities to create new business models and change the logic of how the industry works. M&A is an excellent way to do this, but few have succeeded. Examples include deals in which 'old economy' companies acquire ones from the 'new economy', sometimes referred to as merging 'bricks and clicks'. In the past few years, there was widespread belief that digitalization and the Internet would rapidly reshape the media industry. A few examples of players that bet on quick convergence are Vivendi Universal (France), Bertelsmann (Germany) and AOL/Time Warner (USA). In general, only a few have succeeded in realizing a new business model because most have been developed based on new technologies in response to a more complex supply chain and fragmenting customer base.

Macro-economy level

Technology

Changes in technology are the most dynamic sources of change in the whole economy.[11] As competition becomes tougher, innovation is a far more powerful weapon than price.[12] So technology also has a great impact on M&A activity. Its role is threefold: technology can be the initiator, the enabler and the aim of M&A.

As we can see from the historic M&A waves, just as new production techniques, innovations in communication and innovative materials acted as initiators for M&A during the industrial revolution, now – during the information revolution – information technology (IT) is having similar effects. In addition, the time span between invention and innovation is shortening dramatically and the pace of technological developments is accelerating. The euphoric outlook and forecasts of some new technologies and business models attract so much finance that overcapacity is built up – then later reduced by M&A. The technological advantages of a firm can also be transferred via M&A. Substitutes that become available because of technological advances also initiate acquisitions.

Technology is also an enabler of M&A. It makes a new successful combination possible and reasonable. At the turn of the 20th century, innovation with huge economies of scale made large enterprises competitively superior. M&A enables a better utilization of technology to streamline operations and leverage synergies. Investments in technology and enterprise resource planning systems can be shared by a new, larger company. Knowledge can be made available throughout the company and be leveraged by using IT. So M&A activities can help build competencies and organizational capabilities, eliminating organizational 'bottlenecks'. With technology, it becomes easier to use benchmarking and introduce best practices and allocate centres of excellence worldwide.[13] Integrating different IT systems can, however, be difficult, time-consuming and expensive.

As the life cycle of products and technologies is decreasing, and even customers in developing countries and emerging markets can no longer be satisfied with old technologies, constant innovation is a must. Therefore acquisition of technology is one aim of M&A. Some aspects, such as the acquisition of knowledge, competencies and capabilities, have already been discussed under the firm level as the dimension of the 'development of skills and capabilities'. R&D projects are becoming more expensive and riskier, and only large companies are able to finance these investments and take part in R&D races. M&A can help to increase R&D capacity in order to realize a faster time-to-market, with all its advantages. Nevertheless, safety considerations concerning health and environmental aspects certainly limit how much innovation time can be reduced, and changing government regulations in fact add to it. M&A can be used to tap innovation. Acquiring minor or major stakes in highly innovative small firms helps an established company stay in touch with the latest innovative developments and assess the likelihood of their success. This can also help the company fill gaps in its technology or product portfolio or acquire technology that will become the basis for the next product generation. Especially in the IT industry, M&A is used when products and services can be

Especially in the IT industry, M&A is used when products and services can be copied easily

copied easily. Patents can give some protection, but this is by no means comprehensive.

When M&A is used as a way to gain technology, there are many pitfalls to avoid. Above all, the parties involved should not allow themselves to be too distracted by negotiations and, later on, by integration efforts, otherwise they will be left behind by competitors that are not pursuing M&A activities and are therefore able to concentrate all their efforts on innovation. A further problem is the valuation of highly innovative companies that often have few sales to show. The value of technology is a significant component of the firm's value, but intellectual property such as patents, trademarks, brands and copyrights is difficult to measure and traditional financial analysis tools fail. The most important key to success is retaining and motivating key R&D people. The intrinsic motivation concerning perspectives, visions and culture matters even more than compensation and stock options.

Financial markets

There is a close general relationship between financial markets and the M&A phenomenon.[14] Financial markets and their players have already been characterized as major drivers of M&A activity. M&A is a primary agent in reallocating financial resources: the activity of mergers, acquisitions and divestitures led to the development of a 'market for corporate control'. In particular, the most controversial growth path for M&A – namely diversification in unrelated industries – together with the conglomerate merger wave of the 1960s and 1970s helped to create this market. The transparency and efficiency of this market today is better than ever, for example there are now guidelines on publicizing when certain thresholds in stakes in companies have been reached.

Both financial markets and the market for corporate control, however, have their imperfections. So there is room for the misevaluation of companies and arbitrage, which further fuels M&A activity. In the case of underestimation, the buyer expects owners not to estimate the 'correct' value until the M&A deal has taken place. In the case of overestimation, a company that might be overvalued takes advantage of the situation by engaging in M&A activities through a share swap before investors notice or correct the overevaluation. These misevaluations are possible for corporations that are not listed on the stock markets, as well as those that are. Against all 'wisdom' in textbooks on financial markets, markets are far from being perfect and cannot take everything into account. In the long run, markets are right. But in the short run, misevaluations take place – and they do so in bull as well as in bear markets.

M&A can be pursued as financial investments. Some investors, for example, acquire in order to take advantage of misevaluations or to ameliorate the acquired companies by restructuring them or combining them with other acquisitions or companies that enhance their divisions before spinning them off. For example, in the 1980s and 1990s Hoffmann-La Roche, a Swiss pharmaceutical company, added several companies to its fragrance and flavour business, Givaudan, which was finally floated on the Swiss Stock Exchange.

Dubious financial motives for M&A are diversification, enhancement of earnings per share and prevention of comparability of accounting data, especially when management aggressively pushes the share price in order to cash in its stock options. The individual investor is far better equipped to diversify his or her portfolio than companies, i.e. it can be done more cheaply and easily, as well as taking into account personal risk aversion and preferences. In the 1960s, diversification was welcomed by financial markets because companies, as internal capital markets, were thought to have fewer information asymmetries and were thus deemed to be better investors than financial markets. Playing the price/earnings (P/E) ratio game in order merely to enhance earnings per share (EPS) was quite popular during the third wave. When a company with a high P/E ratio acquires one with a low ratio, the EPS of the acquirer rises – the additional use of convertible debt magnifies this effect.[15] Frequent acquirers can also prevent comparability of the balance sheets and profit statements, so that investors cannot clearly distinguish between the effects of various activities.

Financial markets enable M&A transactions by allowing companies to float large issues of equity or bonds to pay for acquisitions. Interest rates influence M&A activity in at least two ways. Directly, M&A is supported by low interest rates, when it is particularly easy to finance transactions with relatively cheap debt. Some companies have piled up a huge mountain of debt because of an aggressive M&A strategy, as many telecommunication and media companies did in the 1990s. Indirectly, M&A is further affected by interest rates because investors are more likely to invest in shares when interest rates are low, which causes stock market levels to rise. Rising share prices make stocks a more attractive payment method for M&A activities.

Rising share prices make stocks a more attractive payment method for M&A activities

But the relationship between financial markets and M&A is far from being unidirectional; financial markets are also driven by M&A. Stock market levels are also driven by speculation and rumours about M&A. Potential targets, in particular, see their share prices rise because the target's shareholders benefit from acquisitions when they are paid a premium. A favourable condition for M&A is a bull market, which is regarded as a good time to sell. The stock market gives currencies and valuations for M&A deals using stock as a currency. This greatly facilitates M&A deals because there is no need for cash. Payments with stock usually take place when stock prices are high. In general, all major and unexpected disruptions that occur in financial markets, e.g. a downdraft in stock prices, an interest rate shock, a credit crunch or failure of the high-yield bond market, cause the M&A level to shrink. If the stock market is volatile, M&A is increasingly the exit route of choice as both buyers and sellers expect to use volatility to make a good deal.

Players in the capital market, such as investment banks, arbitrageurs and corporate raiders, drive companies into M&A. They try to leverage methods and know-how worldwide to expand their business. Since the very first M&A wave, promoters have encouraged companies to buy one another – and benefit from rising stock prices. Investment banks, in particular, have done their bit to promote M&A activities and develop new products. Their traditional use for general corporate-purpose financing is declining, but event-driven financing is on the increase, e.g. for financing acquisitions. So the high-yield bond market has become increasingly attractive to companies that have found traditional methods of fundraising difficult, and investment banks help them to access this market.

Investment banks must have product expertise, research coverage, a global presence and execution strengths, as well as staffing on a worldwide basis. Nevertheless, investment banks tend to specialize in and focus on strategically important industries, as they have to develop specialized knowledge in their clients' industries. The business is thus becoming more institutional and less personality-driven. As mentioned earlier, many clients have in-house M&A staff, so investment banks need to find ways to deliver more added value. Instead of merely executing deals, they are now part of the discussions, help formulate and implement strategy, search the market for opportunities, generate ideas, and analyze, structure and negotiate deals, which increasingly cross borders. They inform clients about what their competitors across the globe are doing and assist in developing the M&A communication. In the Asian financial crises, governments turned to investment banks for advice, while companies used investment banks as a new source of financing and restructuring expertise. With the boom in M&A, investment banks have prospered. But their leading position is also being challenged: in all profitable industries, new competitors enter the market, so management consultancies and accounting and law firms are all expanding into the M&A business. And once the M&A wave ebbs, the investment banks will shrink, confirming the old economic experience that higher profits carry higher risks, in this case due to the cyclical nature of the industry.

Regional aspects and differences of financial markets are important. In Europe, the euro created the world's second largest capital market, establishing the potential for wider and deeper, more fully developed bond and stock markets and hence financing opportunities in Europe. Investors can no longer focus as much on arbitrage opportunities presented by differences in the various European currencies and interest rates. The euro further homogenizes the economies of the European Union, acting as an 'engine' of economical convergence within Europe.

In Asia, the financial crisis of the 1990s became a catalyst for the development of the region's capital markets, pushing for rationalization, privatizations and liberalization of rules on foreign ownership as overgeared conglomerates failed to find domestic solutions. Importing foreign capital and management skills was a way to survive the crisis. M&A activity increased dramatically as western companies purchased Asian ones or their joint ventures (so-called club deals) as they had a shortage of capital and a chronic need for balance-sheet restructuring. General Electric and its famous former CEO Jack Welch used this opportunity extensively. Nowadays, the market for corporate control is quite a global marketplace, with European conglomerates reinventing themselves and in need of restructuring, and with Asia opening up and even Russia taking part in M&A activities.

M&A activity increased dramatically as western companies purchased Asian ones or their joint ventures (so-called club deals)

Economic development

In general, there is a close statistical significant relationship between gross domestic product (GDP) growth and M&A activity. Waves tend to occur during economic expansion and end when the economy slows down. The most prominent theory about the influence of macro-economic factors on M&A activity is that of 'economic disturbance', where shocks cause discrepancies in the valuation of companies to increase and hence more M&A takes place in the affected industry.[16]

Society, politics and law level

National variations in corporate governance or capital market regulations create a lack of transparency and make it difficult to source, decide about, structure and execute M&A deals. Society influences M&A with the values and beliefs that prevail. In particular, hostile takeovers are regarded as taboo and are still not widely accepted in Continental Europe. Public opinion is an important factor in M&A. First, it influences the way politicians (re)act. Second, it is better not to offend the public, who are, after all, the customer base of merging companies. Demographic development is a factor that should not be neglected in the long run. With societies ageing, important entrepreneurial input and drive from younger people are lost. Where fewer companies are established, some types of M&A that we have discussed might become rarer.

Markets are globalizing rapidly and there are now common customer needs, global suppliers, global customers and global channels, and transferable marketing is possible. But these markets are still subject to localization as a counter-force to globalization, such as localized customer needs, customer preferences for system solutions, local knowledge and expertise, local and national brands, and language. M&A can be a means to cope with both the forces and the counter-forces of globalization. In particular, food and consumer goods companies such as Nestlé and Unilever try to balance forces with a lot of acquisitions.

Another conclusion that can be drawn from historic M&A waves is that M&A activity can flourish only in peace time. Politics influences M&A first on a local basis when it comes under pressure from public opinion or ideologies. For example, when industry restructuring takes place and employees are laid off, politicians may try to influence decisions, sometimes with the help of subsidies or outright acquisition and nationalization of the company being sold off.[17] In response, M&A candidates have themselves begun to use the media, e.g. advertising and the Internet, to influence stakeholders and public opinion. Through the law, politics has directly and indirectly influenced M&A activity in the past, sometimes positively, sometimes negatively.[18] Legislators react to M&A waves by introducing new laws. In general, enacting law has never directly contributed to M&A, but its interpretation and enforcement have. And the resources allocated to the institutions, for example by government, will be a decisive factor in determining how much work they are able to do.

If any M&A activity takes place in highly regulated industries at all, transactions usually happen on a domestic basis, e.g. airlines and the banking industry. But key sectors like telecommunications and utilities have been or are subject to deregulation, liberalization and privatization by governments. Such industries usually become congested with more competitors and therefore concentration decreases at first. After these markets have become used to competition, consolidation takes place between these new competitors, first on a national and then on an international scale. These developments also lead to divestitures and industry restructuring as new regulatory mandates force conglomerates and former monopolists to reduce market power by spinning off assets, which become available as M&A candidates. Many of the formerly state-owned monopolists carry out M&A transactions to compete in other markets, to acquire competencies they lack and to transform themselves from an overburdened bureaucracy to a manageable private company. For example, Deutsche Post AG, the former monopoly in postal services in Germany, made a number of acquisitions before and after its initial public offering in November 2000. Political events such as the reunification of Germany and the privatization of formerly state-owned companies in the planning economy fuel the market for corporate control. Other countries could see more privatization in the near future, especially formerly communist countries where reforms are now taking place.

Tax and accounting considerations are normally not the main reason for an M&A transaction, but they play a role when a deal is executed and decisions about the design and structure of the transaction need to be taken in order to optimize tax burdens. The result of a 'merger of equals' is sometimes a dual-headed group structure, with two CEOs, or two holding companies, or two headquarters, i.e. a 'multi-headquartered' company. These designs are based partly on tax-planning considerations to optimize the tax burden on the act of combination and on dividend flows to shareholders. A dual structure where two merging companies agree to hold stakes in the newly formed entity can help the new company remain in important financial indices and thus prevent share flow-backs. Nevertheless, the clear reaction to such structures shows that financial markets, the public and the media either do not understand them at all or understand them too well. Another example of accounting considerations is the sale of newly acquired technology or brands to a third party from which a licence is bought back.

The result of a 'merger of equals' is sometimes a dual-headed group structure, with two CEOs, or two holding companies, or two headquarters

In some countries there are investment and specific takeover laws. For example, pension funds are becoming increasingly important as institutional investors. When these institutional investors are not allowed to invest in foreign companies or in companies that largely run operations in foreign countries, this may hinder cross-border exchange efforts. The defence mechanisms that companies are allowed to use in order to protect themselves against takeovers vary among jurisdictions. For advertising in takeover battles, special rules exist. There are also rules covering the need to make offers to minority shareholders and how to conduct a squeeze-out.

Legislators, especially antitrust authorities, have introduced regulatory facilities since the first M&A wave a century ago. Their aim is to prevent the creation of monopolies especially, but other collusive behaviour as well. With a higher market power, the company can siphon off monopoly rents. Profits in concentrated industries are relatively higher than in more competitive markets. Concentrated industries permit even implicitly collusive behaviour between the remaining players. Even technology and innovations have implications for antitrust authorities, which also pay heed to the innovation effects of mergers and their merits to society. But a patent is a monopoly on intellectual property. This problem can be solved by granting licences to competitors.

Increased regulatory legislation complicates M&A activities. The multiplication of national procedures for the antitrust review of mergers throughout the world has increased the probability that M&A activities in general, but especially cross-border deals, will be subject to filings and review in multiple jurisdictions. This imposes significant transaction costs, consumes much time, causes high uncertainty and increases the potential of conflicting outcomes. However, countries have started exchanging evidence in antitrust cases and helping each other to obtain evidence – take, fore example, the US and Australia with the International Antitrust Enforcement Act in 1994. In sharp contrast to the dismantling of takeover legislation in small jurisdictions, in Europe and the US time-consuming and painstaking examinations are carried out by the antitrust authorities. However, significant differences remain in various jurisdictions in the areas of tax, accounting and auditing standards, pension provision, corporate and shareholder structures, and regulatory requirements.

This overview outlines the many reasons, contextual circumstances and dynamics that can either promote or hamper M&A, giving some idea of all the complexity involved (which is why investment bankers refer to M&A as the 'king discipline'). The following chapters will deal with specific aspects.

Notes

1 For a more detailed discussion of the different waves of mergers, the interested reader should refer to: mergers for monopoly: Stigler 1951, Macrosty 1907 and Nelson 1959; mergers for oligopoly: Borg *et al.* 1989, Leeth and Borg 2000, and Stigler 1951; conglomerate mergers: Conn 1976 and FTC 1971.

2 Barkoulas *et al.* 1999, 8.
3 Problems of corporate governance that are not raised here will be discussed in Chapter 9.
4 'Mad dogs and mergers', *The Economist*, 13 November, 1997, London.
5 Roll 1986.
6 This is called the 'free cash flow hypothesis'. See Jensen 1988, 28 and Lang *et al.* 1991.
7 Ali-Yrkkö 2002, Agrawal *et al.* 1992, Jensen and Ruback 1983, Mitchell and Stafford 2000, and Tichy 2002.
8 For instance, enumerations of M&A motives can be found in Brealey and Myers 2002, Weston *et al.* 2001, and Weston and Weaver 2001.
9 Berger and Ofek 1995, Lang and Stulz 1994. Further pros and cons of diversification are discussed in the section on financial markets.
10 Andrade and Stafford 1999.
11 Cameron 1997, 10.
12 Chandler 1990, 132.
13 Variations of this centre of excellence are the lead-country concept, key-market subsidiary and global-market mandate.
14 M&A activity correlates with stock market level and interest rate at a statistically significant level. This observation does not hold true for the first and fourth waves, although the stock market levels were high at that time. (Source: authors' calculations based on FTC 1971, Globalfindata 2003, Mergerstat 2003 and Nelson 1959.)
15 For further explanations and example calculations see Gaughan 2002, 35 and Weston *et al.* 2001, 190.
16 Gort 1969.
17 For example, US Congress discussed the introduction of a law that would permit the acquisitions of telecommunication companies in the US by companies that are state-owned. This discussion was initiated by the acquisition of VoiceStream by Telekom, the former monopolist in telecommunications in Germany and still partly state-owned by the German Federal Government.
18 For extensive examples and cases in the United States see Carney 2000.

References

Agrawal, A., Jaffe, J. F. and Mandelker, G. N. (1992) 'The post-merger performance of acquiring firms: a re-examination of an anomaly', *The Journal of Finance*, No. 4, Vol. 47, 1605–1621.

Ali-Yrkkö, J. (2002) 'Mergers and acquisitions – reasons and results', *Keskusteluaiheita* – Discussion Paper No. 792, The Research Institute of the Finnish Economy, Helsinki.

Andrade, G. and Stafford, E. (1999) 'Investigating the economic role of mergers', Working Paper No. 00–006, Division of Research, Harvard Business School, Boston/Massachusetts.

Barkoulas, J. T., Baum, C. F. and Chakraborty, A. (1999) 'Waves and persistence in merger and acquisition activity', Working Papers in Economics No. 396, Department of Economics, Boston College, Chestnut Hill.

Berger, P. G. and Ofek, E. (1995) 'Diversification's effect on firm values', *Journal of Financial Economics*, Vol. 6, 39–66.

Borg, J. R., Borg, M. O. and Leeth, J. D. (1989) 'The success of mergers in the 1920s', *International Journal of Industrial Organization*, No. 1, Vol. 7, 117–131.

Brealey, R. A. and Myers, S. C. (2002) *Principles of Corporate Finance*, 7th edition, New York: McGraw-Hill/Irwin.

Cameron, R. (1997) *A Concise Economic History of the World, From Paleolithic Times to the Present*, 3rd edition, Oxford: Oxford University Press.

Carney, W. J. (2000) *Mergers and Acquisitions – Cases and Materials*, New York: Foundation Press.

Chandler, A. D. (1990) 'The enduring logic of industrial success', *Harvard Business Review*, No. 2, Vol. 68, 130–140.

Conn, R. L. (1976) 'The failing firm: industry doctrines in conglomerate mergers', *Journal of Industrial Economics*, No. 3, Vol. 24, 181–187.

FTC (1971) 'Current trends in merger activity', Statistical Report No. 10, Washington: Bureau of Economics, Federal Trade Commission.

Gaughan, P. (2002) *Mergers, Acquisitions, and Corporate Restructurings*, 3rd edition, New York: Wiley & Sons.

Globalfindata (2003) Dow Jones Industrials Average, http://www.globalfindata.com/trial/ADJIA.csv, Los Angeles.

Gort, M. (1969) 'An economic disturbance theory of mergers', *Quarterly Journal of Economics*, No. 4, Vol. 83, 624–642.

Jensen, M. C. (1988) 'Takeovers: their causes and consequences', *Journal of Economic Perspectives*, No. 1, Vol. 2, 21–48.

Jensen, M. C. and Ruback, R. S. (1983) 'The market for corporate control – the scientific evidence', *Journal of Financial Economics*, No. 1, Vol. 11, 5–50.

Lang, L. and Stulz, R. (1994) 'Tobin's Q, corporate diversification, and firm performance', *Journal of Political Economy*, Vol. 102, 1248–1280.

Lang, L., Stulz, R. and Walkling, R. (1991) 'A test of the free cash flow hypothesis – the case of bidder return', *Journal of Financial Economics*, No. 2, Vol. 29, 315–355.

Leeth, J. D. and Borg, J. R. (2000) 'The impact of takeovers on shareholder wealth during the 1920s merger wave', *Journal of Financial and Quantitative Analysis*, Vol. 35, 217–238.

Macrosty, H. W. (1907) *The Trust Movement in British Industry – A Study of Business Organisation*, London: Longmans, Green, and Co.

'Mad dogs and mergers' (1997) *The Economist*, 13 November, London.

Mergerstat (2003) Mergerstat free reports: M&A Activity, US and US Cross-Border Transactions.
http://www.mergerstat.com/free_reports/free_reports_m_and_a_activity.asp, Santa Monica.

Mitchell, M. and Stafford, E. (2000) 'Managerial decisions and log-run stock performance', *Journal of Business*, No. 3, Vol. 73, 287–329.

Nelson, R. L. (1959) *Merger Movements in American Industry (1895–1956)*, Princeton: Princeton University Press.

Roll, R. (1986) 'The hubris hypothesis of corporate takeovers', *Journal of Business*, No. 2, Vol. 59, 197–215.

Steger, U. (1999) 'The transformational merger', *Perspectives for Managers*, No. 12, Vol. 68, 1–4.

Stigler, G. J. (1951) 'The division of labor is limited by the extent of the market', *Journal of Political Economy*, Vol. 59, 185–193.

Tichy, G. (2002) 'What do we know about success and failure of mergers', Working Paper, Austrian Institute of Economic Research, Vienna.

Weston, J. F. and Weaver, S. C. (2001) *Mergers and Acquisitions*, New York: McGraw-Hill.

Weston, J. F., Siu, A. J. and Johnson, B. A. (2001) *Takeovers, Restructuring, and Corporate Governance*, 3rd edition, Upper Saddle River: Prentice-Hall.

2

Are mergers and acquisitions about creating value?

By

Piero Morosini

MOST STRATEGIC THEORIES that attempt to explain why companies engage in merger and acquisition activity highlight 'financial', 'synergistic' or 'market power' arguments. However, these traditional approaches fall short of explaining the strategic rationale that drove companies in the wave of global M&As during the last two decades of the 20th century. In this chapter, *Piero Morosini* suggests that real competitive advantages are based on the combined knowledge assets and social capabilities that can be created on a global scale as a result of these M&As. Therefore, the central strategic issue for these M&As becomes how to rapidly combine these assets and capabilities across cultural and organizational boundaries. How the merging or acquiring companies move to implement this challenge will shape all other financial, synergistic and/or market power considerations.

Overview

There is nothing better than a good theory to guide an organization's or an individual's pragmatic exploits. This much has been asserted by business thinkers[1] and ancient and modern philosophers alike. Without a good theory informing our practical steps in the 'real world', these pundits argue, our efforts will lack any driving purpose and we will inevitably end up drifting aimlessly in an ever-changing milieu.

This seems to hold particularly true for the field of managerial thought and practice concerning mergers and acquisitions. Indeed, the inordinately high failure rate of global M&As over the last three decades of the 20th century[2] raises a pressing concern: that our conventional theories, and therefore our ability to explain why M&A activity occurs, might have failed as well.

Thus, the issue of why companies engage in M&A activity seems to be more relevant today than ever. Although in the past this issue has been approached from a value-creating perspective, in this chapter I will demonstrate that the conventional arguments utilized to underpin corporate value creation through M&A activity are both deceptive and backed up by little empirical support. In fact, the performance track record of M&As has been so dismal to date that many executives and practitioners legitimately raise the question: are M&As about creating value at all?

Are M&As about creating value at all?

Here I argue that this could indeed be the case. However, I maintain that the only possible way to explain why M&As occur from a value-creating perspective is to look at how the joining companies go about building a series of specific, common, knowledge-based assets and capabilities after the M&A deal is concluded. My research findings suggest that the extent to which this series of assets and capabilities is created determines whether or not the value of the combined company will rise after the M&A deal is done. I will therefore shift the focus of attention from what the conventional value-creating tenets uphold and instead examine:

- under which conditions the merging or acquiring companies can create a common social environment where their combined knowledge assets and capabilities can be smoothly turned into valuable, highly competitive products and services;
- how to go about measuring the merging or acquiring companies' ability to create a series of specific, common, knowledge-based assets and capabilities prior to the deal; and
- how to go about measuring the merging or acquiring companies' journey to creating this series of specific, common, knowledge-based assets and capabilities after the deal.

The concepts developed in this chapter apply to all types of M&As that are motivated by the need to combine the significant strategic resources and assets of the joining companies after the deal is done. These typically include technologies, fixed assets, infrastructural resources and, especially, people. M&A

undertakings largely motivated by financial risk diversification, entrepreneurial experimentation, exceedingly narrow functional learning and the like are therefore beyond the focus of this chapter.

Inadequacy of conventional M&A theories

Most conventional theories explaining M&A activity focus on the strategic and financial effects on the acquiring and/or merging companies. The prevailing arguments fall within two broad categories: value-creating and non-value-creating theories.

Value-creating theories postulate that M&As are pursued in order to maximize the value to shareholders of the combined company. Non-value-creating theories, by contrast, suggest that managers of the acquiring and/or merging companies seek to maximize their own utility at the expense of shareholders, especially when their compensation is tied to the size of the company in terms of revenues or assets.

Value-creating theories of M&A activity predict that the wealth of shareholders of both the bidding and the target (and/or the merging) companies will increase as a result of two main criteria: strategic fit and a more powerful structural relationship between the joining companies. On the one hand, strategic fit occurs when positive synergy potential can be identified between the joining companies, i.e. in the form of economies of scale, economies of scope or market power.[3] On the other hand, a more powerful structural relationship between joining companies stems from the ability to create specific supplier–client–competitor legal liaisons through an M&A transaction, i.e. in the form of horizontal or vertical integration, or through the creation of conglomerate groups.

Non-value-creating theories of M&A maintain that a few months before and after the deal, the wealth of shareholders of bidding (or majority owner) companies will fall, whereas the wealth of the target (or minority owner) companies' shareholders will rise. However, no value will necessarily be created within the combined company as a result of the merger or acquisition.

> No value will necessarily be created within the combined company as a result of the merger or acquisition

Both value-creating and non-value-creating theories of M&A activity have been extensively tested from modern financial and strategic management perspectives. Regarding value-creating theories, evidence produced in the late 1980s and early 1990s overwhelmingly suggests that M&As have failed to significantly improve the performance of the joining companies. Not only have 'strategic fit' benefits such as synergies failed to translate into higher value or better performance results for the joining companies, but structural relationships in the form of horizontal and vertical conglomerates have also been unable to reduce financial risks in ways that will create value for shareholders. Regarding non-value-creating theories, however, the empirical evidence suggests that a transfer of value does take place from the bidding to the target company's shareholders within the first few months following an acquisition. Some of the key early empirical studies supporting this evidence are shown in Figure 2.1.

As a result of this empirical evidence, alternative explanations have been sought as to why M&As occur, ranging from corporate learning and experimentation to emotional and psychological elements such as the hubris and ego that seem to characterize some senior executives in companies undertaking M&A deals. However useful, these alternative paradigms have not necessarily provided positive reasons for M&A activity. Thus, on the one hand, generic claims of learning and experimentation will have to go a long way in order to explain the value of the hefty premiums paid in some of the global mega-mergers we witnessed at the dawn of the new millennium. On the other, an abundance of anecdotal evidence should suffice to establish that the effects of senior executives' hubris and disproportionate egos on M&A activity as a whole have been nothing short of disastrous.[4]

Why are conventional M&A theories inadequate?

In my view, conventional value-creating theories explaining M&A activity show three key drawbacks that prevent them from guiding executives to more successful M&A journeys. These are:

- an emphasis on conceiving discrete rather than continuous strategic benefits for the joining companies;
- a misplaced understanding of what drives value creation for the joining companies' stakeholders;
- a lack of attention to the implementation phase following the conclusion of an M&A deal.

First, as already mentioned, conventional value-creating theories postulate that the value of an M&A to the joining companies' stockholders stems either from a more powerful structural relationship or from a positive synergy potential between the joining companies. On the one hand, more powerful

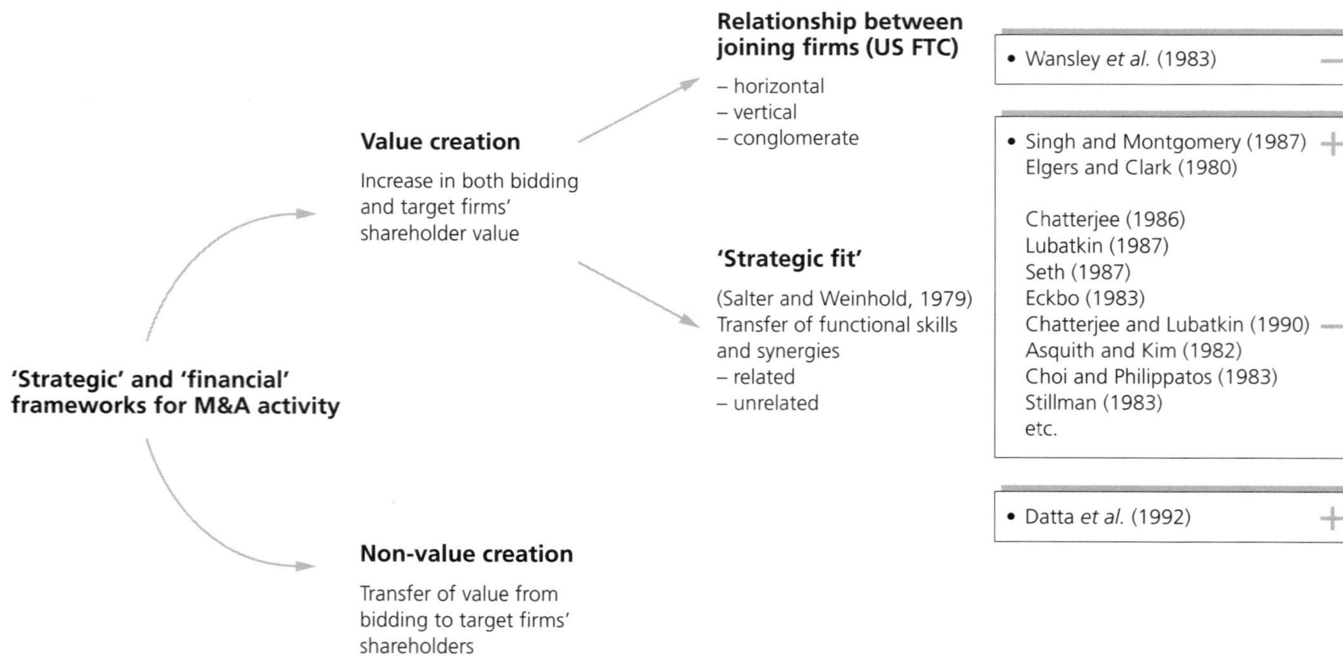

Figure 2.1 ◆ Little empirical support was found for the conventional paradigms explaining M&A activity (late 1980s and early 1990s)

structural relationships between the joining companies are assumed to stem from discrete, legal contracts that allocate property rights in ways that displace market organizations, i.e. in order to develop horizontally or vertically integrated supplier–client–competitor structures or conglomerate groups. However, legal contracts can hardly embody distinctive elements of a company's internal organization such as knowledge sharing, learning or entrepreneurial activity, which can be crucial to its competitive performance. A company is considerably more than a bundle of contracts and M&As are far more complex undertakings than what their contracts say.

On the other hand, according to value-creating M&A theories, positive synergy potential is conceived as stemming from discrete, one-off processes leading to functional skill transfers and/or to the attainment of economies of scale and scope by combining the joining companies' resources. Too often, however, the latter simply involves one-time cost reduction initiatives after the M&A deal is done. Nevertheless, the experience of highly successful M&A players suggests a completely different picture. Following the M&A deal, these successful players approach implementation as a continuous and manageable process that does not end with any post-M&A integration task force but rather in the dynamic blending of the joining companies' key capabilities.[5]

Second, conventional value-creating theories show a misplaced understanding of what exactly drives value creation through M&A for the joining companies' stakeholders. In an M&A, a more powerful structural relationship and/or synergies between the joining companies constitute measurable results rather than value-creation drivers. The real drivers of a company's value to its key stakeholders (its customers, employees, shareholders and others in the social and institutional milieu in which it operates) are the unique ways in which it transforms its tangible and intangible assets and resources into superior, highly competitive products and services. My research findings suggest that a number of specific knowledge-integration mechanisms are crucial for this transformation to take place across all of a company's functional, organizational and cultural boundaries. In the case of M&As, successful merging and acquiring companies have been found to be particularly effective and deliberate at orchestrating such crucial knowledge-integration activities across national and corporate cultural divides during the first two years of the implementation phase.[6]

Third, and closely related to the previous set of arguments, conventional value-creating theories explaining M&A activity generally show a lack of attention to the implementation phase following the conclusion of an M&A deal. Their approaches to understanding post-M&A implementation typically rely on archetypical constructs with labels such as 'absorption', 'assimilation' and 'integration'. Absorption, or assimilation, typically takes place when the acquirer's objective is to consolidate specific assets of the target company in its own corporate realm. Integration usually occurs in the case of acquisitions or mergers – especially the so-called mergers of equals – where the goal is to create an entirely new third company and/or to share the strengths of both joining companies across the board. It is further postulated that under the absorption/assimilation implementation approaches the target company's organizational culture – and often most of its people – do not really matter to the acquirer. By contrast, integration approaches to post-M&A implementation typically involve the creation of a substantially new common culture, or the preservation of separate corporate identities while sharing strengths.

A closer look at successful M&A players gives an entirely different picture. It suggests that it is far more useful for executives to look at what all successful post-M&A implementation approaches have in common than what makes them different. For example, all successful approaches to M&A implementation focus on building 'connective tissue' between the joining companies fast. This tissue will obviously differ according to the joining companies' motivations, i.e. it will be a lot closer to the acquirer's own organizational tissue in the case of consolidating acquisitions and a substantially new corporate tissue in the case of a 'merger of equals'. However, in all cases it is the ability to build this connective tissue fast between the joining companies that seems to set successful M&A players apart from unsuccessful ones. More importantly, this particular ability seems to rely on a well-defined set of organizational mechanisms that have been developed over time and are common to all successful M&A players:

All successful approaches to M&A implementation focus on building 'connective tissue' between the joining companies fast

> *The job [of an 'integration manager' at GE Capital, the financial services arm of US-based General Electric] is to build connective tissue between GE Capital and the new [acquired] organization, tissue that will allow information and resources to pass freely back and forth, tissue that will become self-generating over time. [. . .] An example from a European acquisition illustrates how the integration manager builds connective tissue. After completing the acquisition, the business leader asked the integration manager to quickly introduce the new company to GE's integrity policy. At GE, integrity is [. . .] a detailed requirement meant to ensure that every employee understands what constitutes proper and improper ways of doing business. [. . .] To avoid [a negative] reaction [within the acquired company's managers] the integration*

manager [together with a small group of the acquired company's managers] decided that its own managers (rather than GE's people) should introduce the policy at a series of all-employee meetings. They introduced those meetings by saying, 'One of the benefits of belonging to GE is that they have made explicit the principles of integrity that we have always followed in our company but that we never had the resources to write down. And here they are . . .' [. . .] That may seem like a small matter, but the accumulation of such small matters can destroy the connective tissue between companies. The job of the integration manager is to keep that tissue growing.[7]

A dedicated role and a highly structured approach to leading the building of connective tissue between the joining companies; the introduction of clear, non-negotiable elements such as the acquirer's 'integrity policy' as a key element of this tissue; an emphasis on face-to-face communication mechanisms to build connective tissue between the joining companies; an open, tolerant corporate culture on the part of the acquirer; and flexibility on both sides to gain the buy-in of the acquired company's employees early on – these are all factors that characterize GE Capital's approach to integrating acquisitions.

Another example of consolidating acquisitions further illustrates the interplay of all these elements. Clear success factors for [Internet networking giant] Cisco's M&A management, based in Silicon Valley, include the awareness that it acquires technology through people, the use of its own leading corporate vision and purpose as a tool to attract others, and a corporate culture that is conducive to both accepting 'acquired' people and introducing them into Cisco's own culture. Cisco's CEO John Chambers says: 'If you do not have a culture that quickly embraces the new acquisition, then the odds are high that your acquisition will fail.'

Cisco has developed a well-structured and regimented approach to integrating acquisitions. Its goal is to get the acquired employees' buy-in and to ship the acquired company's products under the Cisco label within a very short time frame. Following an acquisition deal, Cisco's post-merger integration (PMI) team jumps in quickly to carry out the following steps:

- They assemble a customized package that includes descriptions of Cisco's structure and employee benefits, a contact sheet and an explanation of the importance of the new acquisition.
- The day the acquisition is announced, a human resource team from Cisco travels to the acquired company's headquarters to meet people, set expectations and answer questions.
- Together with the acquired company's management, the PMI team organizes the new entity.

- Typically, two new independent business units are created to manage product-engineering and marketing activities, while sales and manufacturing are integrated into Cisco.
- Back at Cisco, the PMI team introduces the new employees into Cisco's computer system, payroll and stock administration programs.
- Subsequently, the PMI team organizes tailor-made orientation courses. The acquired managers are trained in Cisco's leadership and hiring practices: sales people learn about how to sell Cisco's products and engineers learn about Cisco's project-management practices.

The process takes 30 days. Mimi Gigoux, the PMI team leader in 2000, said: 'I joke that I am going to get companies to the point of do-it-yourself integration, where I just send a videotape of me talking.'[8]

Another example suggests that the same key elements that are conspicuous in the integration of consolidating acquisitions seem to also be at play in the successful integration of a 'merger of equals'. A senior executive involved in the 1997 post-merger integration between Ciba-Geigy and Sandoz, which created Novartis, said:

> *[Novartis] was not about the mechanistic jamming of two companies together, but the creation of an entirely new company which was expected to achieve what neither Ciba-Geigy nor Sandoz could have achieved on their own. That is, to create a global leader, one of the world's largest, most successful life sciences companies. [The first Novartis CEO] Daniel Vasella himself became the leader of the post-merger integration. Together with a group of 300 'global managers' from both merging companies, he moved quickly to create a 'common glue' within Novartis. This meant giving Novartis such things as a common set of business values, one company language, a unified set of performance measurements and management control systems, and common career paths and reward policies for the company's upper and senior executives. [Vasella and his 300 'global managers'] implemented all this through continuous face-to-face communications as well as by introducing the sharing of best-practices, world-class benchmarking processes and re-engineering task forces across the company's diversity of functions and geographies.*

The need for new perspectives to explain how M&As can create value

At this point it should be quite obvious to the reader that new, overarching perspectives capable of explaining why and how M&As create value for the joining companies are urgently needed today. New, more powerful theories than the current ones could guide executives and practitioners towards better M&A choices and results, moving them away from the ill-conceived assumptions and devastating M&A outcomes that have occurred all too often in the past.

New, overarching perspectives capable of explaining why and how M&As create value for the joining companies are urgently needed today

As we have seen, a new value-creating approach to explaining M&A activity should explicitly address the main drawbacks of the conventional M&A theories that have been described. Such an approach should therefore look at M&As as continuous processes rather than one-off events; it should focus on the value-creating knowledge-integration mechanisms that can be implanted following the conclusion of an M&A deal; and it should explicitly address the need to build connective tissue – a 'common glue' – fast between the joining companies. What kinds of approaches that share these characteristics can be found in the management literature and how can they be used to explain the issue of value-creating M&As?

Some scholars of the knowledge-based theory of the firm provide insights that certainly are useful for our purposes.[9] These authors have begun to regard companies as social communities in which groups and individuals transform their expertise into economically useful products and services:

> *The key word in the previous statement is 'social'. In other words, this transformation cannot be achieved by individuals on their own, nor in the absence of a company's organizational principles. Therefore, a company's knowledge is socially constructed, underpinned by the way its human resources are organized. [. . .] Hence, companies generate and sustain competitive advantages by transforming social knowledge into economically useful products and services. Here, the word transforming not only refers to the transferring of already existing expertise but also to the ways in which learning takes place and new knowledge is created within a company's social settings.*[10]

More importantly, the same scholars maintain that any company needs to set in place a common stock of organizational knowledge in order to carry out this transformation continuously and in an efficient and effective way. In other words, this common stock of organizational knowledge is required because it enables the efficient and effective transformation of critical resources into valuable products and services across a company's organizational and cultural boundaries. What constitutes this common stock of organizational knowledge and how does a company go about creating it?

My research findings suggest that this common stock of organizational knowledge is made up of five key execution capabilities:

- *Purposeful leadership* – how a company's key executives, or 'global managers', are attracted, developed, motivated and retained, and to what extent they are managed as a truly global, culturally open and cohesive group.
- *Building blocks* – a company's capability to develop common organizational policies and approaches among its global managers, including such things as a common company language, a set of shared business values, common global career development paths and a common approach to internal reporting and performance measurements.
- *Communication rituals* – a set of routine communication interactions to develop common business values among the company's global manager group.
- *Knowledge interactions* – a set of routine interactions to share existing knowledge and create new knowledge across a company's cultural, organizational and functional boundaries.
- *Cross-boundary rotations* – expatriate and repatriate policies within a company that allow for the continuous rotation of key executives across boundaries.

This set of five execution capabilities together constitutes a company's central connective tissue, its 'common glue'. In turn, this 'glue' is what allows a company to continuously integrate key knowledge and resources across cultural, organizational and functional boundaries and to transform them into superior products and services. A company's 'common glue' is intrinsically unique, as it has typically been developed over time throughout the company's history. More importantly, my research findings highlight that the strength and mutual interaction of all of these five execution capabilities have a significant impact on a company's competitive performance. In other words, I

> A company's 'common glue' is intrinsically unique, as it has typically been developed over time throughout the company's history

found that companies with a strong 'common glue' perform significantly better than their competitors. There appears to exist, therefore, a positive correlation between the strength of a company's 'common glue' and its ability to create value for its stakeholders.[11]

Creating M&A value by building a strong 'common glue'

From a knowledge-based perspective, an M&A is about building a new corporate 'common glue' to replace an old one. If, as the previously described research findings suggest, a strong 'common glue' is required for a company to outperform its competitors, there is no way around building this glue as a result of an M&A. The new 'common glue' that is created must obviously be stronger than the one it replaces in order for the joining companies to perform better and create higher value than they could have achieved separately. These are all simple ideas which, nevertheless, have powerful implications for current M&A activity and its future.

First, companies must look critically at their own 'common glue' as they embark on strategic M&A undertakings. The same execution capabilities that underlie a strong 'common glue' are also critical for any company to be able to cross boundaries and reach out to another company in an M&A integration initiative. Therefore, companies intent on engaging in M&A endeavours should start by asking – and finding an answer to – the question: how strong is our company's 'common glue' in the first place?

Academic and anecdotal sources abound with examples of companies that engage in daring M&A deals on a global scale while lacking the most basic 'common glue' elements, such as a common language between the joining companies' top and senior executives; a common set of worldwide performance control measures and systems; or global personnel policies that facilitate the smooth transfer of key executives across the joining companies. In these kinds of companies, M&A deals often add difficulties to an already complex corporate fabric, in the form of additional performance measurement systems to be managed, more ineffectual expatriate and/or repatriate programmes and, especially in the case of cross-border deals, more languages to be handled as part of day-to-day global management operations.

Second, building a 'common glue' will have substantially different forms and content depending on the type of M&A that is carried out. In the case of a merger of equals (or the acquisition of a complementary company of roughly the same size as the acquirer), the 'common glue' that is created might end up combining elements of both joining companies with entirely new ones. For example, in the case of Novartis, English was chosen as the mandatory common language of the global manager group, although this was different from the main languages utilized by both Ciba-Geigy and Sandoz executives prior to the deal. However, the R&D coordination mechanisms that Novartis set in place largely stemmed from Sandoz.

In the case of consolidating acquisitions, it would be fair to say that the 'common glue' that is created is mostly new for the acquired company – and it tends to resemble the acquirer's 'common glue' in all important aspects. However, this does not mean that building a new 'common glue' within the target company should be conceived as a one-way process, monolithically led by the acquirer's integration managers. As I have described, in my research the most successful consolidating acquirers were invariably those with purposeful leadership around culturally tolerant and highly open business values. This more than anything else made it possible for the acquirers to introduce a new 'common glue' fast within the acquired company's organizational fabric.

For those potential – or current – M&A players whose leadership group embraces a 'common glue' historically built on less open, less tolerant business values, this might indicate the need for a profound change agenda. By contrast, my research findings suggest that, even in the case of consolidating acquisitions, the 'common glue' notion does not sit well with the image of arrogant, overwhelming acquirers which has, perhaps inadvertently, been fostered by some of the conventional value-creating M&A theories.

Third, the need to build a strong 'common glue' fast following an M&A deal raises the crucial issue of how to go about replacing and – perhaps more importantly – creating a 'common glue' which will be substantially new for at least one of the joining companies. This is not an easy issue to address, but clearly it is one of the most critical to M&A success.[12]

There is little doubt that executives involved in M&As have on the whole been a lot better at destroying other companies' 'common glues' than at creating strong new ones. However, this should hardly surprise the reader. Consider even the most basic question around this issue: should building the 'common glue' go fast or slowly after the M&A deal is done? The experience of companies such as GE Capital and Cisco suggests that the answer to this question in the case of consolidating acquisitions should invariably be: 'Go as fast as possible, if not faster.'

> Should building the 'common glue' go fast or slowly after the M&A deal is done?

However, in the case of large-scale mergers of equals or acquisitions involving highly visible players in sizeable industries, such as DaimlerChrysler or Japanese Sony's acquisition of Hollywood-based Columbia Pictures, the answer to this question might not be so straightforward. In these cases, corporate stakes in the surrounding industrial, social and political environment can be very high, making it more complex to assess major post-M&A integration decisions. For example, consider the dilemmas typically involved in deciding whether or not to create one organizational structure following the conclusion of the merger deal. It could be argued that a single organizational structure from the outset will greatly facilitate the creation of a purposeful leadership and common building blocks between the merging companies, all of which are critical to sustain a strong 'common glue' early on. And this is precisely what Novartis did only three months after its 1996 merger deal was made public.

However, DaimlerChrysler – the first truly transatlantic merger – and Sony – after its 1989 acquisition of Columbia Pictures – had to deal with a vastly more challenging industrial and social milieu than Novartis ever did. If, following the conclusion of the deal, either DaimlerChrysler or Sony had moved fast to introduce sweeping changes, these companies could have faced strong, emotionally charged opposition, not only from internal sources but also, especially, from US public opinion as a whole. Fuelling concerns against perceived German or Japanese 'corporate invasions' within the US could have been disastrous at the time these M&As took place. Therefore, the image of 'equality', 'fairness' and 'transparency' had to be upheld at all costs.

What can be done when the industrial and social milieu makes it difficult to build a 'common glue' fast following an M&A deal? And if the ultimate goal is to create a strong 'common glue' after the deal is done, what does this mean for M&As that are implemented under the tenet of 'sharing strengths while keeping our separate identities'? Although these are also difficult issues to address, another look at our previous examples allows us further insights. On the one hand, these examples highlight that building a strong 'common glue' after the M&A deal is done must remain the ultimate goal in spite of early obstacles to implementation. On the other, keeping separate identities might be incompatible with comprehensive knowledge exchanges and the sharing of real strengths between the joining companies, as a number of M&A players have found out the hard way.

Thus, at Novartis, creating a third, new 'common glue' was the only consideration – keeping the old corporate identities was never seriously considered, although these identities stemmed from the merging companies' century-old traditions. By contrast, after a disastrous 'hands-off' acquisition implementation, in the early 1990s Sony decisively moved to amalgamate Columbia Pictures into its own 'common glue'. This meant that the company adopted Sony's management control systems and budgetary policies and it was made part of Sony Pictures Entertainment division. Columbia Pictures saw a performance turn for the better during the mid-1990s.

DaimlerChrysler skilfully refrained from introducing any major changes to the former Chrysler organization immediately following the 1998 merger. However, it organized a highly structured set of post-merger integration task forces during most of 1998 and the first nine months of 1999, which produced real management exchanges between the joining companies and delivered tangible, measurable synergies that exceeded most stock analysts' expectations. Nevertheless:

> *After achieving their early PMI results [it was decided that the former Daimler Benz and Chrysler] were to be managed as separate entities in order to maintain the integrity of their brands and their distinct pre-merger corporate cultures. Therefore, the new company was not to implement a common global management overlay across the former Daimler Benz and Chrysler, no common organizational blueprint, no major know-how exchanges, no single set of global personnel policies and no unified building blocks.*
>
> *In the absence of a strong 'common glue', DaimlerChrysler's attempts to gain competitive advantages by combining both merging companies' strengths were lost along the cultural, functional and organizational divides in place. Interestingly, as a result DaimlerChrysler ostensibly shifted to one cultural environment, with some of former Chrysler's key managerial talent leaving the company during 1999 and 2000. This made the sharing of knowledge across the Atlantic and the building of a common pool of corporate values even more difficult. In 2000 a former US Chrysler manager summarized the situation by saying: 'It is unrealistic to expect a German engineer to learn something from an American.'*[13]

From mid-1999 to the end of 2000, DaimlerChrysler's stock price experienced a steady decline of over 40%, significantly lagging both the industry and its competitors. This trend did not seem to improve during 2001, with the company fighting mounting losses stemming from the former Chrysler side – in the red for the first time in years.

All of the above suggest that M&A integration managers must be able to measure the strength of the 'common glue' that is created over time in order to grasp the degree of M&A implementation success that is being achieved. However, quite surprisingly, my research suggests that M&A integration managers are mostly concerned with measuring traditional synergy results, i.e. typically stemming from one-off cost-cutting initiatives and the like, and only in very few cases do they look at the 'common glue' elements. Even when these elements are recognized as critical, integration managers often lack the knowledge or the ability to measure them in a systematic, explicit fashion. I will therefore address this issue in more detail in the following section.

M&A integration managers are mostly concerned with measuring traditional synergy results

Measuring the journey towards the 'common glue'

A well-known adage in business suggests that it is difficult to manage what you cannot measure. Therefore, M&A integration managers need to develop an approach that allows them to measure the strength and effectiveness of the 'common glue' that is being created in a company and assess it against competitive performance.

In order to develop this approach, I worked with a large sample of global managers from a number of leading multinational companies to identify a series of general attributes that could characterize the five execution capabilities that constitute a company's 'common glue'. Next, I conducted statistical analyses that confirmed that 60 of these general attributes could be used to aptly characterize a company's 'common glue'. A survey and a quantitative scale were subsequently created to measure the strength of a company's 'common glue' along the critical attributes of each of the underlying execution capabilities.

Based on this methodological approach, during the 2000–2002 period I surveyed thousands of global managers from a series of international and multinational organizations and measured the strength of their companies' 'common glue'. The results are illustrated in Figure 2.2. Each dot represents one company but the names have been omitted for confidentiality. The graph demonstrates a strong, positive correlation between a company's 'common glue' and competitive performance, measured along a normalized scale on the horizontal and vertical axes, respectively.

Most of the companies in Figure 2.2 have undertaken significant M&A activity at one time or another. For example, 'Company X', an industrial manufacturing concern, was surveyed about four years after it carried out a cross-border merger of equals. Although the merging companies were 'star performers' within their industry prior to their merger, the survey shows

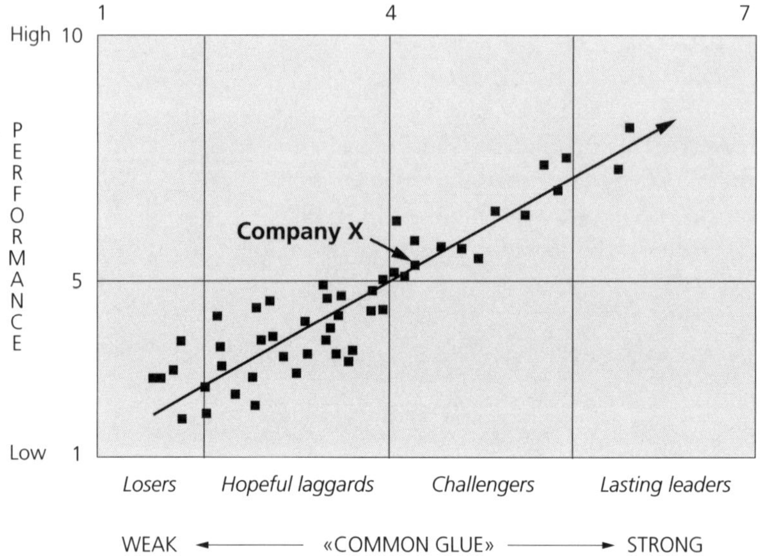

Figure 2.2 ◆ A strong correlation between a company's 'common glue' and its competitive performance

competitive performance – in terms of financial, market growth and innovation performance – barely above average and a relatively weak 'common glue'. These results are placing the company at the bottom of the 'challengers' or at the top of the 'hopeful laggards' group *vis-à-vis* the industry leaders.

A closer look at Company X shows why this is the case. As shown in Figure 2.3, four years into their merger of equals, this company presents fairly solid leadership, building blocks and communication capabilities. However, knowledge interactions and cross-boundary rotations are lagging. Zooming in on the data gathered around these lagging capabilities would reveal that the ability to codify and share knowledge across internal functions and the company's global manager repatriate policies were areas worthy of particular attention. These issues owed as much to the way the merger was managed as to the historical patterns of the merging companies prior to the deal. In fact, one of the merging companies was used to a fairly autonomous divisional structure, with little or no knowledge sharing across divisions, whereas neither of the merging companies had particularly strong repatriate policies and practices.

> One of the merging companies was used to a fairly autonomous divisional structure, with little or no knowledge sharing across divisions

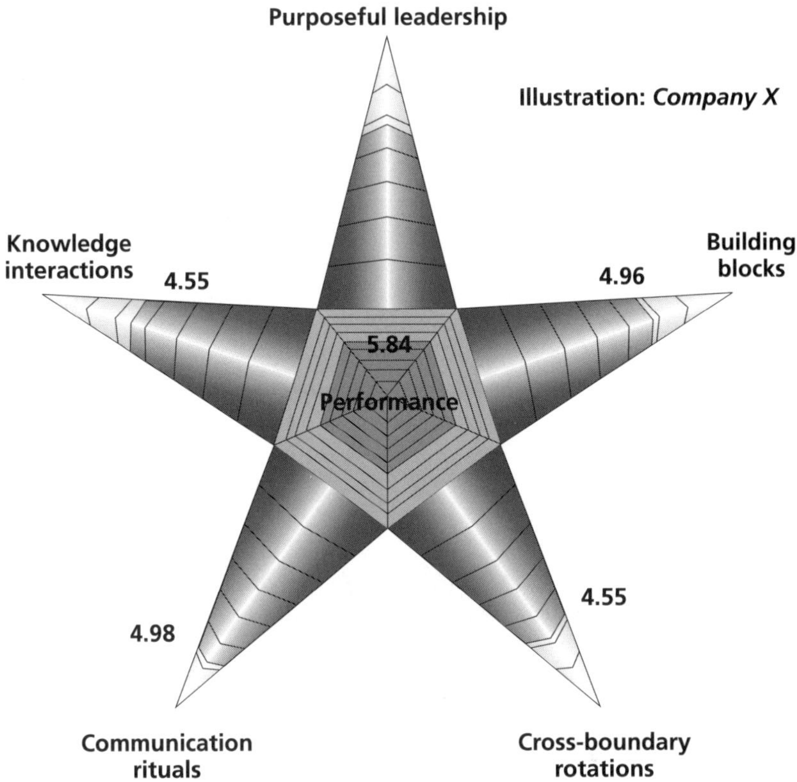

Figure 2.3 ◆ After the M&A deal is done the 'common glue' is measured across the entire set of key capabilities

Four years after their merger of equals both issues are found to be reinforcing each other, making it difficult for this company to smoothly pool its key people and knowledge across boundaries to win new customers. The 'common glue' data suggest that Company X managers should prioritize both of these areas in order to enhance the company's competitive performance. On the one hand, they should start a series of initiatives and processes aimed at facilitating the sharing of key technical and engineering knowledge across functions, divisions and geographies. On the other, they should produce and communicate a unified, global set of repatriate policies so that senior and high-potential managers are not inhibited from spending extended periods abroad for fear of not finding rewarding positions 'back home'.

Company X is halfway on its journey towards building a strong 'common glue' after a major M&A. By building on its existing 'common glue' strengths and closing the gaps that have been identified, it aims to move NE in

Figure 2.2. If it manages to do so, it will have achieved its goal of becoming the industry's global leader in terms of competitive performance, which was one of the key reasons behind its merger of equals.

Best practice: building a new awareness of what makes M&As valuable for your company

Creating real value through M&As is not about attaining financial gains through one-off mechanistic combinations of the joining companies' specific assets and resources. Rather, it is about leading change and effective execution to create a compelling company purpose that drives the blending of both companies' key capabilities into superior, highly competitive products and services.

1 Conventional theories are inadequate to explain how M&As can create value for stakeholders

As evidenced by academic studies and managerial experience, our mainstream value-creating M&A theories have invariably failed to find empirical support. This is because these theories conceive of M&As as leading to discrete, one-off strategic benefits, show an inadequate understanding of what drives value creation for the joining companies' stakeholders and pay little attention to the implementation phase following the conclusion of an M&A deal. New perspectives are therefore needed to explain how M&As can create value for a company's stakeholders.

2 Integrating an M&A is about recreating a social fabric that 'glues' the joining companies together as fast as possible

Knowledge-based theories of the firm suggest that what really drives a company's performance is its ability to transform assets and resources into superior, highly competitive products and services. In addition, these approaches postulate that such ability rests squarely on the specific qualities and nature of a company's social fabric. After an M&A deal is done, the social fabrics of the

> **After an M&A deal is done, the social fabrics of the joining companies typically suffer dramatic alterations**

joining companies typically suffer dramatic alterations. The central issue thus becomes: How to build a new social fabric, connective tissue, a 'common glue' fast between the joining companies?

3 Building a strong 'common glue' between the joining companies is the only way to create real value through M&As

In fact, my research findings suggest that companies with a strong 'common glue' perform significantly better than their competitors. Building a strong 'common glue' between the joining companies therefore becomes paramount for competitive survival after the M&A deal is done. My research findings suggest that this is the case for all types of M&As that are motivated by the need to combine significant strategic resources between the joining companies after the deal. No performance upside should be expected from 'hands-off' integration approaches or from approaches attempting to 'share strengths while maintaining the joining companies' separate identities'.

4 Building a strong 'common glue' within your company constitutes the best platform for future M&A success

The experience of successful M&A players suggests that the same basic execution capabilities inherent in building a strong 'common glue' within a company (a single, purposeful leadership, a set of common organizational building blocks, common communication and knowledge interactions, and one set of policies governing cross-boundary rotations) are also crucial for undertaking successful M&A integration journeys. Therefore, the best place for a company's executives to start such a journey is to ask – and find the answer to – the question: how strong is our company's 'common glue'?

Notes

1 Drucker 1994.
2 As both executives and academics know, although global M&As grew at an unprecedented rate during the last two decades of the 20th century, well over half of them failed (for a comprehensive review of the empirical evidence on M&A performance track record, see Morosini 1998).
3 Thus, M&As are referred to as 'related' transactions whenever there is a relatively

high degree of strategic synergy potential between the joining firms. Conversely, 'unrelated' M&As are those where little or no synergy potential can be found between the joining firms (see Salter and Weinhold 1979).

4 See Chapter 6.

5 Morosini 2001 and and Ashkenas *et al.* 1998

6 Morosini 1998; Haspeslagh and Jemison 1987.

7 Ashkenas *et al.* 1998.

8 Morosini 2001.

9 Kogut and Zander, 1992; Grant, 1996.

10 Morosini 2002, 5.

11 Ibid.

12 Successful approaches to integrating M&As are presented in more detail in Chapter 7.

13 Morosini 2002.

References

Ashkenas, R. N., De Monaco, L. J. and Francis, S. C. (1998) 'Making the deal real: how GE Capital integrates acquisitions', *Harvard Business Review*, 76 (1), 165–77.

Drucker, P. F. (1994) 'The theory of the firm', *Harvard Business Review*, 72 (5), 95–105.

Grant, R. M. (1996) 'Toward a knowledge-based theory of the firm', *Strategic Management Journal*, 17, 109–122.

Haspeslagh, P. C. and Jemison, D. B. (1987) 'Acquisitions: myths & reality', *Sloan Management Review*, 28(2), 53–58.

Hegel, G. W. F. (1979) *Phenomenology of Spirit*, Oxford: Oxford University Press.

Kogut, B. and U. Zander (1992) 'Knowledge of the firm, combinative capabilities, and the replication of technology', *Organization Science*, 3 (3), 383–397.

Morosini, P. (1998) *Managing Cultural Differences: Effective Strategy and Execution Across Cultures in Global Corporate Alliances*, Oxford: Pergamon.

Morosini, P. (2001) 'Managing cross-cultural M&As: today's organizational imperative is how to win in execution', in *International Merger Management – Success Factors of Cross-border Transactions,* Stuttgart: Schäffer-Poeschel.

Morosini, P. (2002) 'Competing on social capabilities: a defining strategic challenge of the new millennium', IMD Working Paper 2002–1, Lausanne: IMD.

Salter, M. S. and Weinhold, W. A. (1979) *Diversification through Acquisition: Strategies for Creating Economic Value*, New York: Free Press.

Zander, U. and Kogut, B. (1995) 'Knowledge and speed of the transfer and imitation of organizational capabilities: an empirical test', *Organization Science*, 6 (1), 76–92.

Part Two

Managing the boundaries

3

Global mergers and acquisitions: why do so many fail? How to make them successful

By
Piero Morosini

CULTURAL AND ORGANIZATIONAL differences arising during the integration phase are often cited as key reasons for the high failure rate of global mergers and acquisitions. However, in this chapter Piero Morosini presents recent research findings suggesting that cultural differences need not be detrimental to the performance of global M&As. Rather, if conveniently handled, these differences can enhance performance. A number of case examples of mega mergers of equals are presented to illustrate these findings, suggesting a set of common implementation principles that can increase your company's post-M&A integration success.

Overview

Ask a group of seasoned international executives the question 'why do so many global M&As fail?' and reasons such as 'national cultural differences', 'different values between the joining companies' and so on will usually feature at the top of their lists. I have received these types of answers over the past five years in the classrooms of the international business school where I teach. The consistency of the responses is quite remarkable, especially if one considers the substantial diversity of nationalities as well as the varied industrial and corporate experiences of these executives.

Are cultural differences that difficult to manage? Could these differences really explain the dismal performance track record of M&As in the past? Or could there be other more significant challenges behind this grim picture? More importantly, how can executives manage all of these challenges and make their companies' future M&A journeys more successful for all relevant stakeholders?

These questions unveil some of the most relevant issues within contemporary global management. Statistics demonstrate that over 70% of all foreign direct investment worldwide during the 1980s and 1990s took the form of M&As. However, as both executives and academics know all too well, the considerable empirical literature over the same two decades suggests that well over half of all M&As fail. Yet this does not seem to have put companies off entering into M&As. Indeed, the amount of value destruction of publicly quoted companies in the US and Europe as a result of M&A activity during the first two years of the new millennium easily surpassed the total value of M&A deals in any given year during the 1980s.

Statistics demonstrate that over 70% of all foreign direct investment worldwide during the 1980s and 1990s took the form of M&As

In this chapter I will look systematically at how national cultural differences affect the performance of cross-border M&As. I will then address the crucial issue of how executives can manage these cultural and organizational differences in ways that will increase the value of the joining companies after the deal is done.

In the following pages I will present findings from the first empirical study linking national cultural differences, execution capabilities and the performance of cross-border M&As. Contrary to established theories, these findings suggest that 'cultural fit' might be far less relevant than a set of specific execution skills to manage across cultural and organizational boundaries following the conclusion of an M&A deal. These research findings suggest that by enacting a set of common implementation principles used by successful M&A players, international executives might reach beyond cultural myths towards more important factors that will increase their chances of M&A success.

In this chapter I will focus on M&As that are motivated by the need to combine the significant strategic assets and resources of the joining companies, as opposed to deals largely motivated by financial risk diversification, financial turnaround, entrepreneurial experimentation and the like. Furthermore, in this chapter the terms 'success' and 'performance' of M&As will refer to whether or not the value of the acquiring and/or merging companies increases after the deal is done. More specifically, the value increases associated with M&As that I have in mind are of an organic nature, resulting largely from things such as mainstream revenue, profitability and/or productivity growth rather than stemming from one-off synergies or speculative financial gains.

M&A failures: are cultural differences to blame?

In the past, many academic theories overwhelmingly highlighted the supposedly detrimental influence of national cultural differences on the performance of cross-border M&As. However, quite astonishingly, until recently these academics had produced no systematic empirical evidence to support their tendency to portray national cultural differences in a consistently negative light. In spite of this, their theoretical claims may well have played on too many executives' innate predispositions, creating the deeply ingrained myth that national cultural differences are to be regarded as detrimental – or at best as risk factors – *vis-à-vis* the performance of cross-border M&As.

In order to empirically test these assumptions, I looked at a representative sample of 400 cross-border M&As that took place between 1987 and 1992. On the one hand, I quantitatively measured the national cultural distance between the acquirer's and the target company's countries of origin using national cultural estimates from a well-known study.[1] On the other, I measured the performance of these cross-border M&As based on the revenue, profitability and productivity growth experienced two years after – as against two years before – the merger or acquisition took place.

I then designed a quantitative multivariate regression model to analyze whether there was any significant correlation between the national cultural distance and the performance of the cross-border M&As in my sample. I introduced a series of other control variables that could also have an impact on M&A performance. These were variables such as the relative size of the M&A, the various industrial sectors in which these M&As took place, whether or not the acquirer and the target company operated in closely related businesses, and the type of execution approaches used during the post-M&A integration period.

> The higher the national cultural distance between the acquirer and the target company, the better the performance results

Contrary to previous managerial theories, I found that the higher the national cultural distance between the acquirer and the target company, the better the performance results. In other words, in my study the cross-border M&As that achieved higher revenue, profitability and productivity growth two years after the deal were those that took place across more different – as opposed to more similar – national cultural divides.

Not only was this the first systematic empirical evidence produced in this field but it also suggested that in the real world things worked in exactly the opposite way from the one most academics (and a good number of executives) expected.[2] Not surprisingly, the question I hear most often when presenting these findings to an audience of (mostly startled) executives is: Why? What is behind these empirical results? Why did the M&As in the survey perform better across more distant national cultural divides?

My research findings suggest that the type of execution approach used during the post-M&A integration period was the most significant factor explaining the differences in performance. In other words, in the sample I studied, *how* the M&As were integrated after the deal was the key to understanding *why* the M&As across more culturally distant countries performed better than the rest. I therefore interviewed a number of executives involved in the more successful M&As in order to look in more detail at exactly how they went about integrating the joining companies. This revealed an insightful picture that is summarized in the following pages.

I will especially focus on case examples of so-called mergers of equals.[3] The learning potential embedded in these kinds of mergers seems to be summed up in the Frank Sinatra song that goes: 'If you can make it there, you can make it anywhere.' There are two main reasons why this might be so. First, large-scale mergers of equals taking place within sizeable, highly visible industries and across diverse national and corporate cultures – such as DaimlerChrysler and Aventis – face uniquely complex and challenging constraints to implementation. These are not only internally driven but also stem from the intensely competitive and emotional reactions that these mergers usually unleash within their surrounding industrial, social and political milieu. Secondly, as hinted at in Chapter 5, I have found that the key implementation principles behind the successful integration of a mega merger of equals are of a general nature that can be applied to all other mergers, as well as acquisitions.

How to integrate a mega merger of equals

The main problem for executives leading the integration in a mega merger of equals is the need to act effectively but in ways that balance contradictory – often seemingly incongruous – criteria. For example, they need to move fast after the deal is done while carefully assessing the implications of crucial organizational decisions. They need to keep an eye on their key customers and markets while carrying out exceedingly demanding integration activities internally. They need to create teams, durable networks and relationships among the merging companies' executives, while breaching wide cultural, functional and organizational divides. They need to create a sense of urgency while maintaining internal stability. The list could go on and on.

So, how to balance these contradictions effectively? How to assess priorities and lead a challenging change agenda within such constraints? How to obtain compelling performance results across cultural and geographic boundaries? Although every merger of equals is unique in many important respects, I have found that most of their integration approaches usually fall within a few well-defined frameworks, which represent fundamentally different ways to address the contradictory challenges of integrating a merger of equals.

A centralized approach to integrating a merger of equals

One approach is to take a radically centralized approach to decision making around a well-defined set of issues. Normally, this option also requires centralized leadership to guide the entire integration effort. The joining firms typically start by quickly forming a small executive committee, usually made up of four or five board members or senior executives from both merging companies. This executive committee then appoints one CEO to lead the new company and agrees with her/him a series of explicit performance targets (usually expressed in challenging stock-earnings growth objectives) within the first three years of the merger.

As a first step, the newly appointed CEO surrounds himself/herself with a small support team of five or ten executives – a group of usually bright, often relatively inexperienced but highly energetic whiz kids. With this support team acting as an advisory board, the CEO then moves to make and implement a series of clear decisions within the first few months of taking charge of the newly merged company.

> **As a first step, the newly appointed CEO surrounds himself/herself with a small support team of five or ten executives**

The CEO then identifies the new company's global managers. In a large-scale merger of equals, this involves selecting a few hundred executives from a pool usually approximating more than 1,000 individuals from both merging companies. This global manager group is singled out early on as the key leadership cadre of the new company.

Next, the CEO concentrates the integration efforts on designing the blueprint of the whole new organization. This blueprint outlines from the beginning how the new company is to be structured. It guides the subsequent integration efforts in a rather rigid, but clear, way. Meanwhile, the CEO appoints suitable global managers for all the key posts, who will subsequently roll out the new detailed organizational design. During the roll-out phase, these global managers will address all relevant integration issues within their areas of responsibility through a series of appointed task forces.

Also within the first few months after the deal has been concluded, the CEO introduces a few distinct organizational 'building blocks' to the company's global manager group. Paramount among these is a book of values, outlining the vision and mission of the new company as well as the code of behaviour and core values that will guide the way of doing business of the new company. Typically, these building blocks also include a common language, a single set of business performance measurements and a common career development path and reward system for the global manager group.

Centralized approaches to post-merger integration also involve launching highly visible, global business initiatives early on, aimed at creating momentum for change as well as building shared values and promoting exchanges between the CEO and key managers. Typical examples of these initiatives include worldwide re-engineering programmes with challenging productivity and efficiency goals as well as holding face-to-face, plenary global manager meetings.

Novartis, the pharmaceutical giant formed in March 1996 from the US$36 billion merger of equals between Ciba-Geigy and Sandoz, illustrates a highly centralized approach to post-merger integration:

> *Together with a dozen key managers, in only nine months Daniel Vasella (the first CEO of Novartis) appointed the company's 300 'global managers' from both merging companies, designed a common organizational blueprint, and set a global re-engineering programme in motion with aggressive financial targets. About two-thirds of Novartis global managers experienced international rotation or job transfers within the first two years of the merger. Building blocks were also established: a common company language (English), three global performance measurements (market share, profitability and return on assets), a unified reporting and control system, a common career policy and performance evaluation for the global managers and a single 'book of values'. The latter highlighted behaviours such as entrepreneurship, self-reliance, integrity and speed. The company's annual budgets became a key tool for bringing some of these values alive, with Vasella stretching his global managers with impossibly high business goals in order to foster proactive, risk-taking behaviour.*[4]

A decentralized approach to blending a 'merger of equals'

The second approach structures the new post-merger organization around key integration areas right from the beginning. A number of task force leaders are typically appointed to address the major integration issues across each functional area. After the task force work, these leaders normally assume formal responsibilities for those areas. However, rather than following a blueprint, this model requires area leaders to come up with their own organizational design. This means that the organizational and managerial structures that the merging companies had in place prior to the deal will usually run parallel to the integration task forces. Typically, few major organizational changes are introduced during the first 12–18 months following the M&A deal and the task forces have concluded their work. Other major decisions, such as identifying the new company's key leadership cadre or codifying the business values of the new organization, usually form part of and follow the recommendations of dedicated integration task forces.

Rather than following a blueprint, this model requires area leaders to come up with their own organizational design

In contrast to the previous model, this approach normally requires more decentralized leadership, with task force leaders reporting to a committee of top executives from both merging companies. A dozen or more executives usually sit on the committee and they appoint not only one (or even two) CEOs but also all of the key top management posts by consensus. In fact, a consensual as much as a decentralized view of decision making across a series of well-structured integration task forces is what characterizes this approach.

Not surprisingly, decentralized post-merger integration approaches seek and usually obtain a 50:50 balance between the joining companies in most important aspects. For example, the top management committee will typically have the same number of executives from each merging company and their positions will clearly aim to balance the distribution of power between the joining organizations. This philosophy will then inform all other crucial integration activities.

In early 1996 Swedish Pharmacia and US-based Upjohn announced their decision to enter into a merger of equals, creating the world's fifth largest pharmaceutical group at the time. The deal took place in the same year as the Novartis merger of equals and within the same industry. However, Pharmacia & Upjohn implemented a typically decentralized merger integration approach that was radically different from that of Novartis. As a former Pharmacia executive noted:

Our executive committee [following the conclusion of the 50:50 merger deal] was made up of 20 people: 10 Swedish executives from Pharmacia and 10 Americans from Upjohn. The CEO was John Zabriskie [former Upjohn CEO] but the chairman of the board was [former Pharmacia CEO] Jan Ekberg. We also made sure that in each of the post-merger integration task forces we had co-leaders from both [merging] companies. The advantage was not only that they produced the post-merger integration plan but that people from our side got to know their people. This was very important because the post-merger steering structure was not easy to design. Upjohn was a very centralized and functionally organized company whereas at Pharmacia we were a decentralized, profit centre-organized company. In the end [in early 1997], we rolled out a new organization based on three PPCs [pharmaceutical product centres] in the US, Sweden and Italy. This structure facilitated the preservation of the corporate identities of the main groups involved in the [1996] merger. Each PPC was given considerable autonomy, with its own R&D, its own operational and its own sales and marketing organizations.[5]

A hybrid, distributed leadership approach to merger integration

Centralized and decentralized approaches to merger integration are schematically represented in Figure 3.1. Each approach has clear advantages but also some important drawbacks. For example, centralized approaches can be fast and display organizational and leadership clarity early on but they can also risk top-down, rash decision-making. Decentralized approaches, by contrast, can be more participative, consensual and thorough but they may end up fostering unclear organizational leadership as well as slow and bureaucratic decision-making.

DaimlerChrysler's post-merger integration approach in the second half of 1998 was an attempt to combine the best of both worlds. It brought together a decentralized management board structure overseeing a series of integration task forces with a centralized coordination team. This approach, which could be called 'distributed leadership', consisted of a management board with a total of 18 members from both merging companies (see Figure 3.2). A subset of eight board members formed the so-called Chairmen's Integration Council (CIC). Small enough to keep track of progress, the CIC oversaw the post-merger integration phase. However, all 18 management board members were directly involved with the integration.

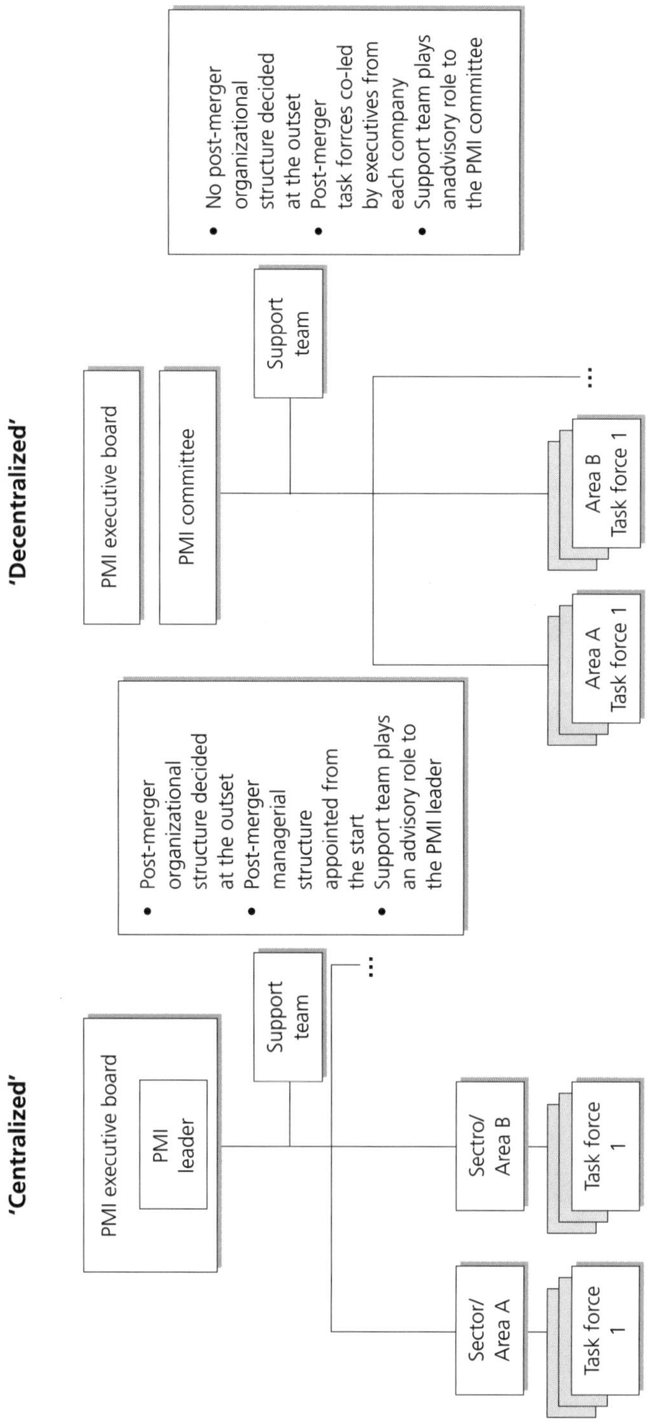

Figure 3.1 ◆ **Post-merger integration (PMI) approaches**

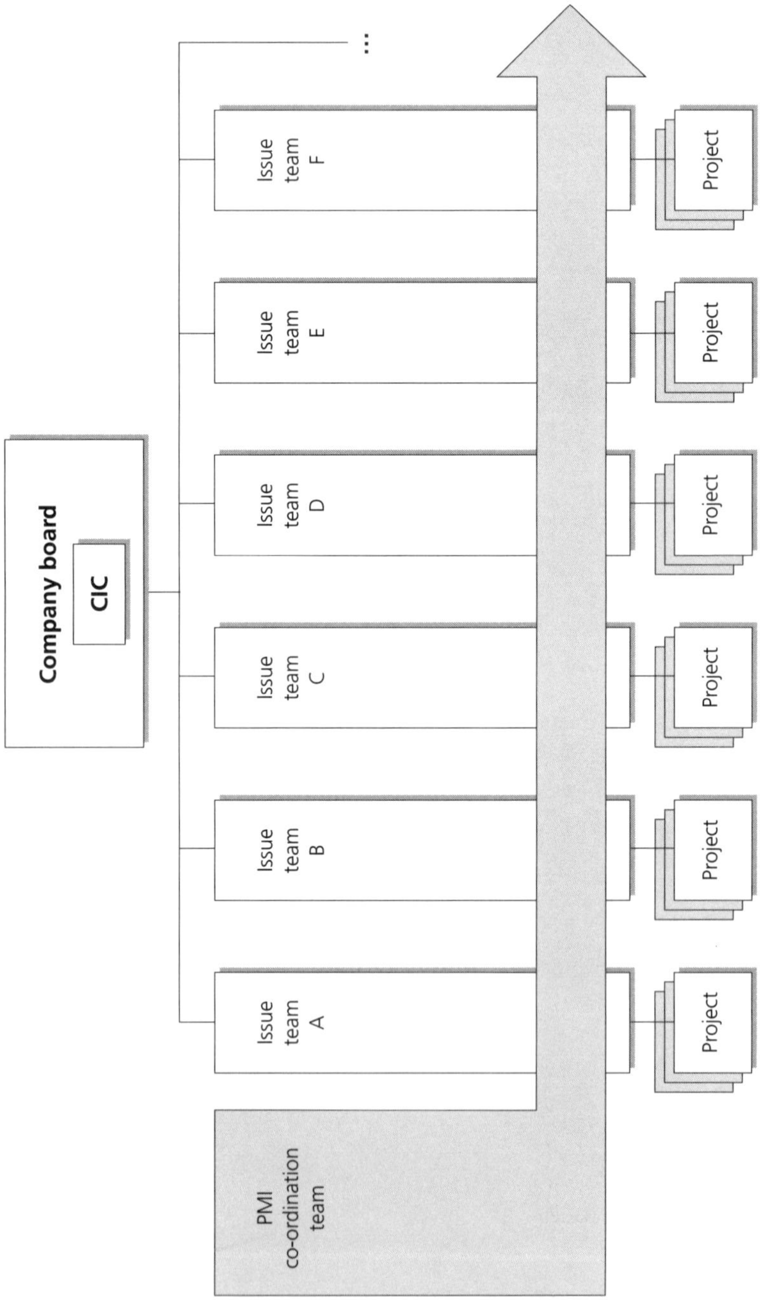

Figure 3.2 ◆ 'Distributed leadership' post-merger integration approach

Each member of the management board (except for the chairmen) was responsible for at least one issue resolution team (IRT). These teams identified and realized the synergies between both companies. There were 12 IRTs grouped around functional topics (for example, purchasing), each jointly run by a management board member from former Chrysler and one from former Daimler Benz, and they reported directly to the CIC. Because of the board members' heavy workload, each IRT had two coordinators in close contact with their counterparts from other IRTs. These coordinators, in addition to a dedicated team of around 10 individuals, formed the so-called post-merger integration team. The PMI team supported and helped monitor the whole integration process. Altogether the distributed leadership integration structure included around 50 dedicated individuals. This relatively small coordination structure in turn oversaw more than 100 integration projects that involved hundreds of managers across the organization.

These coordinators, in addition to a dedicated team of around 10 individuals, formed the so-called post-merger integration team

The IRT leaders were given autonomy to staff their teams, organize their task forces into projects and carry out activities inside both companies. One PMI team member said:

> *The IRT leaders could choose their team members as they wanted. Their choices were always reasonable and there were no big surprises overall. But it is often more important that the people you choose are individuals you feel very comfortable working with, and not just pick the absolute best guys in some technical aspect. You know from the outset that you will have to deliver very tough financial targets under a strict time frame. So life is going to become kind of stressful inside the team at certain points.*[6]

By devising a distributed leadership approach to integration, DaimlerChrysler clearly sought to involve the board members directly in a fairly decentralized fashion, but also to maintain high individual accountability under a central coordination structure. In addition, the PMI team coordinated efforts between IRTs, while leveraging areas that were expected to be common and standard to the whole company, such as overall integration strategy, business culture and certain IT and management information areas.

Which is the best post-merger integration approach?

'It all depends', goes the typical answer from senior executives, 'on the objectives of the merger, on the national and corporate cultures of the merging companies, on their specific industrial contexts, on the macro-economic environment, etc.' However, my research findings suggest an entirely different response to this question. They suggest that the abundance of mergers of equals and similar undertakings that we have witnessed in the past provides enough empirical evidence for us to discern a number of clear patterns.

To put it simply, after looking at a large, representative sample of mergers of equals over the 1990–2000 decade, it is possible to identify very few that most M&A academics and practitioners would agree to classify as 'successful'. However, all mergers of equals that have been identified as successful so far carried out a clearly centralized approach to post-merger integration.

This pattern is illustrated in Figure 3.3. Some of the successful mergers of equals took on a clearly centralized approach to post-merger integration from the very beginning. This was the case with Novartis, which as early as

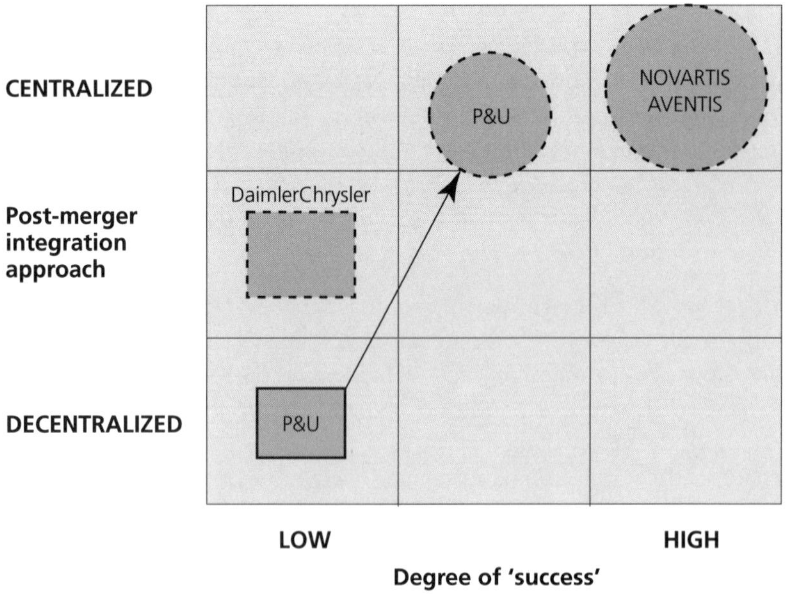

Figure 3.3 ◆ Merger of equals: do decentralized PMI processes ever make sense?

1998 – two years after the merger deal between Ciba-Geigy and Sandoz was announced – was widely regarded as a truly successful merger of equals based on stock earnings, revenue, productivity and profitability growth criteria.

By contrast, an unprecedented and disastrous decline in the company's stock value followed the 1996 implementation of the former Pharmacia & Upjohn's post-merger management structure. The three highly autonomous regional pharmaceutical product centres that were created were widely regarded as preserving the separate identities of the merging companies but at the same time adding to the difficulty of coordinating resources effectively across critical areas such as R&D, supply operations and sales forces. CEO John Zabriskie was forced to resign as a result of the negative stock market reactions to (former) Pharmacia & Upjohn's new organization and a new CEO, Fred Hassan, was appointed in mid-1997. The key points of the new CEO's agenda were to:

- reduce the company's executive committee from 20 to 5 individuals;
- introduce a competence criterion rather than 'balance of nationalities' for appointing the five executive committee members;
- implement a centralized organization for global R&D, manufacturing and supply operations;
- consolidate all pharmaceutical activities under a centralized global management group;
- introduce a single corporate culture and one company headquarters based in New Jersey.

As shown in Figure 3.3, in response to Hassan's agenda, one year after the conclusion of the merger deal the former Pharmacia & Upjohn carried out a dramatic managerial U-turn in order to espouse a decidedly centralized integration approach. The company's performance improved significantly during 1998 and 1999, and the following year it entered into another merger of equals, with US-based Monsanto, to create the new company Pharmacia.

In the global automotive industry, DaimlerChrysler's stock price experienced a steady decline of over 40% from mid-1999 to the end of 2000

In the global automotive industry, DaimlerChrysler's stock price experienced a steady decline of over 40% from mid-1999 to the end of 2000, significantly lagging its main competitors. However, this concealed the fact that DaimlerChrysler's hybrid approach to integrating its May 1998 merger of equals was in fact quite successful. The PMI task force organization leading the merger integration activities exceeded its target of delivering US$1.4 billion in savings, and this was achieved ahead of time. As a result, the company's PMI organization was disbanded in mid-1999, scarcely more than a year after it had been formed.

However, unlike the former Pharmacia & Upjohn, after its first year of post-merger task force integration activities DaimlerChrysler did not move to a more centralized merger integration approach. On the contrary, it deliberately persevered in maintaining an organizational structure that preserved the separate identities of the merging companies. This decision by DaimlerChrysler leadership aimed to 'maintain the integrity of the merging companies' brands and their distinct pre-merger corporate cultures'.[7] However controversial, as a result of this decision the company did not implement a common organizational structure nor a unified global leadership group across the former Daimler Benz and Chrysler. Consequently, few of the expected engineering and product design know-how exchanges between the merging companies actually materialized between 1999 and 2002.

Does this mean that decentralized approaches never make sense?

The empirical evidence I have looked at over the 1990–2000 period spells out a clear case in support of centralized approaches to post-merger integration. However, in the real world company leaders often maintain that it is not always possible to enact a centralized post-merger integration agenda within the context of a merger of equals. Their reasons are compelling. Not only do mega mergers of equals often create unprecedented expectations and anxiety within the merging companies' internal constituencies but they can also give rise to strong reactions – often highly emotionally charged – among the most diverse parties across the broader industrial, social and political milieu. As a result, these company leaders maintain, the space for decision making and executing mergers of equals can be dramatically constrained after the conclusion of the deal.

The same seems to apply to sizeable cross-border acquisitions, as aptly summarized by an executive involved in the 1989 purchase of Hollywood-based Columbia Pictures by Japanese Sony:

> *Although we [at Sony] had expected some strong reactions when we acquired the movie studios in the US, in retrospect I can say that we were a bit surprised at how strong these reactions really were. In a way, Columbia Pictures represented an important part of the American culture and this was seen by*

some as falling into foreign hands. In some instances, our acquisition – just as other Japanese companies' acquisitions in the US at the time [in the late 1980s and early 1990s] – was actually described as some kind of threat. And these circumstances made our [post-acquisition integration] efforts extremely challenging. Now [in mid-1996] the whole situation has changed. [. . .] We are not perceived so much as a threat any more because we Japanese also have our problems.[8]

Sony adopted an extremely hands-off approach to integrating its Columbia Pictures acquisition in the first four years after the deal was concluded. However, in 1994 Sony suddenly switched to a much more centralized decision-making approach *vis-à-vis* its Hollywood studio acquisitions. The head of Sony's film division was fired and the company's budgeting and cost-control policies were rapidly implemented in Columbia Pictures.

These kinds of situations raise the question: when are company executives actually justified in adopting decentralized approaches to post-M&A integration? The M&A experiences of the former Pharmacia & Upjohn as well as Sony suggest that, after the deal is done, decentralized, highly autonomous integration approaches might provide an ideal transition and breathing space whenever the internal and environmental conditions surrounding the integration work are initially fraught with myriad potentially explosive factors. However, after this transitional period is over, a centralized integration approach should definitely follow. This was achieved by both Sony and Pharmacia & Upjohn (but not by DaimlerChrysler).

However, there is a major problem with this 'transitional' integration approach. In fact, unless the merging companies and the surrounding industrial and macro-economic environment are experiencing prosperous times, the cost of implementing the transition can become prohibitively high. In 1994, only four years after its acquisition of Columbia Pictures, Sony announced a write-off of US$3.2 billion to cover losses associated with its movie studio acquisitions. This raised Sony's investments in Hollywood to a total of US$8 billion according to estimates made in 1996 – substantially more than the company had ever anticipated. Similarly, over 30% of the market value of the former Pharmacia & Upjohn evaporated during its disastrous 1996 'transitional' year. Although from late 1997 it went a long way towards recovering from the share price downturn, the company may never have recovered from the market share and commercial opportunities lost early on following the conclusion of the merger deal.

There is a major problem with this 'transitional' integration approach

Thus, after all, even within the most explosively charged corporate milieu, a transitional framework might end up becoming a far too costly alternative to quickly implementing a centralized approach for post-M&A integration. This seems to have been the conclusion reached by Kuwait Petroleum Corporation (KPC), the main shareholder of Aventis, the pharmaceutical giant created after the 1998 merger of equals between Hoechst AG and Rhône-Poulenc S.A.

Centralized owners and decentralized managers at Aventis

After the three-way merger between a German, a US and a French company that created Hoechst-Marion-Roussel (HMR) in 1995, Richard Markham, a former senior executive at Hoechst AG, memorably observed:

> *There is a multiplying effect of three countries times three different companies with three different histories.*[9]

Aventis was to introduce a vastly larger multiplying effect – four countries times six companies with at least seven different histories. It was created after the December 1998 merger of equals between HMR and Rhône-Poulenc-Rorer (RPR). The latter company was the result of a 1990 merger between French Rhône-Poulenc and US-based Rorer Group Inc., and it had acquired British Fisons in 1997.

The scale of Aventis was immense. It had assets worth €40 billion and annual sales of €18 billion combined in the pharmaceutical and agricultural sectors. The public announcement of the deal marked the first step of a three-stage merger that would end in a full-scale link-up between HMR and RPR within three years (see Figure 3.4). The companies knew each other and already had a joint venture, Centeon, in the plasma proteins business. They wanted to extend the experiment to their other pharmaceutical and agricultural businesses and pool their resources for future profitability and growth. As an RPR executive observed: 'Both companies wanted to test the water before deciding to take the final plunge.'

> 'Both companies wanted to test the water before deciding to take the final plunge'

It was decided to form a 50:50 joint venture by the middle of 1999 as soon as the merging companies received approval from the regulatory authorities. The two parts were to be known as Aventis Hoechst and Aventis Rhône-

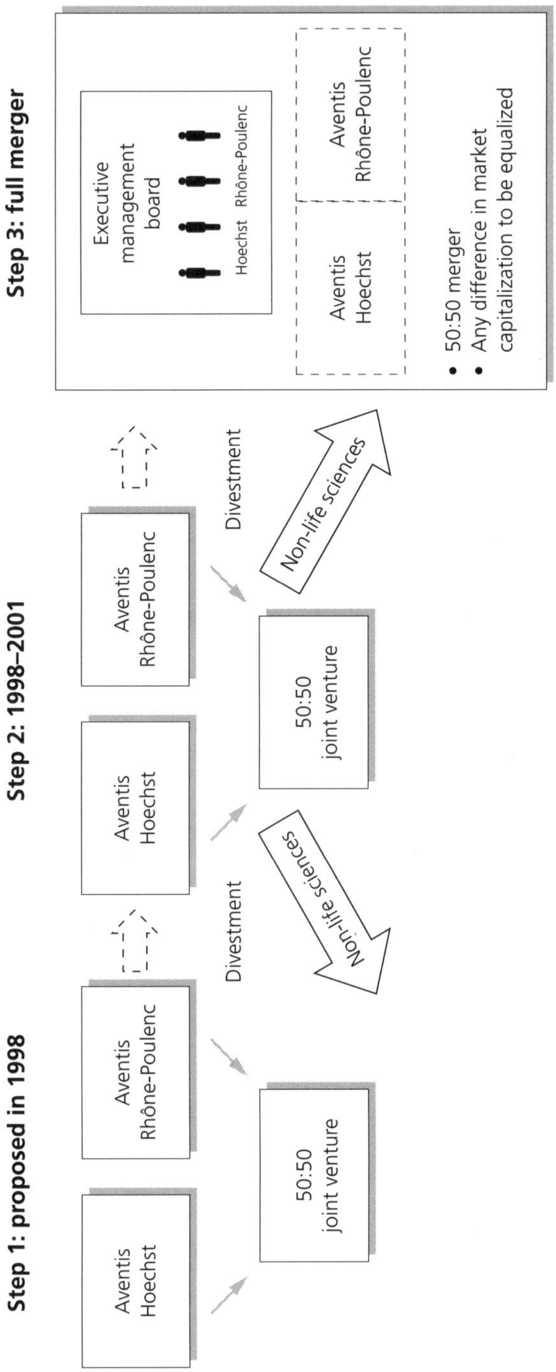

Figure 3.4 ◆ Aventis: the three-step merger process preposed in 1998

Poulenc and were to be listed on the stock markets. The companies would operate in this way for 2–3 years and meanwhile divest all their non-life sciences businesses. The new company was to be run by a four-member executive management board, two each from former HMR and RPR. It would also have a 10-member supervisory board with equal representation from both companies (see Figure 3.5).

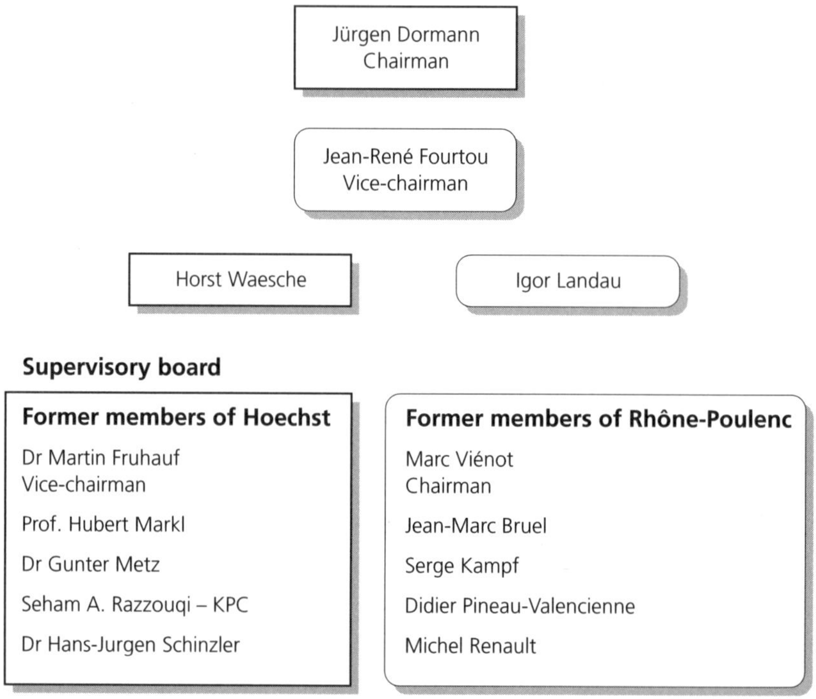

Figure 3.5 ◆ Aventis: management board and supervisory board

However, on February 16 1999 Sheik Saud Nasser al-Sabah, KPC's chairman and Kuwait's oil minister, told a news agency that the oil company had reservations about 'Hoechst's plans to join with Rhône-Poulenc to form the life sciences operation Aventis'. KPC was the largest shareholder in Hoechst AG (HMR's parent company) with a 24.5% stake and could easily block the merger. Rumours were rife in the press and among analysts that this merger might not go through. Hoechst CEO Jürgen Dormann and other senior Hoechst officials flew to Kuwait for discussions. One of them commented:

> *We had discussions with KPC and are confident we will gain the necessary approval for the merger [of equals with Rhône-Poulenc]. We could not go ahead with it without KPC's support.*

Cultural and organizational differences can create real value after an M&A deal

Although they have usually been regarded as key reasons for most M&A failures worldwide, national cultural differences can enhance performance following a cross-border M&A deal. Successful M&A players across more distant cultural divides suggest that assertive, fast and clear integration approaches are far more beneficial to performance than consensual approaches looking to preserve the joining companies' identities or to balance the companies' stakes at every possible level.

1 There are no 'good' or 'bad' national cultures *vis-à-vis* your own in the world of global M&As, only good and bad managers leading integration

The first systematic empirical study in this area found that M&As across more culturally distant countries performed better than those taking place across closer national cultures. More importantly, these research findings suggest that the type of execution approach carried out during the post-M&A integration period was the most significant factor explaining the differences in performance.

2 Yes, integrating an M&A is complex – but seemingly simple organizational building blocks might make all the difference in the end

The more successful M&A players all had the ability to quickly create a common stock of organizational knowledge between the joining companies after the deal was concluded. This connective tissue, this 'common glue', typically included simple things such as a common language, a unified set of management control policies, and a single purpose and common values for the M&A. The execution ability to implant these simple things fast within a clearly defined global management group from both joining companies is what sets successful global M&A players apart from the rest.

3 Centralized approaches to M&A integration are about building a strong 'common glue' fast between the joining companies

My research findings show that centralized approaches to integrating M&As after the deal is done are more successful than any other alternatives. This is because centralized approaches are faster, more assertive and clearer than the more gradual and consensual decentralized integration approaches. This suggests that the advantages of building a 'common glue' fast between the joining companies is vital to performance after the M&A deal and far offsets any of the disadvantages involved in moving fast and decisively to create it.

4 The art is not in the concept: M&As are about mapping and leading a journey towards building key commonalities between the joining companies

The successful M&A players described in this chapter highlight the importance of moving flexibly, creatively and courageously to chart a journey towards building a common stock of organizational knowledge between the joining companies early on. A compelling purpose, clarity of objectives and sheer managerial courage to undertake this journey are the other ingredients that have proved highly important to successful M&A players.

Notes

1 Hofstede 1980.
2 Morosini *et al.* 1998.
3 Regarding 'mergers of equals', in a previous article I observed: 'This terminology usually means different things to different corporate constituencies. ABB, one of the companies which pioneered the latest wave of 'mergers of equals' during the late 1980s, clearly emphasized the fact that each of the merging companies' shareholders ended up with exactly 50% of the new company's stock. The same was the case of [the former] Pharmacia & Upjohn's merger agreement during the early 1990s. However, in the case of DaimlerChrysler's 'merger of equals' in May 1998, Daimler Benz shareholders owned over 50% of the new company's shares. In this case, although both merging companies were fairly similar in revenue size and profitability, a merger of equals seemingly refers to a managerial willingness to combine both companies' key global strengths and obtain the 'best of both worlds' during the post-merger integration phase' (Morosini 1999). An analogous description of what is meant by a 'merger of equals' is also presented in Chapter 5.

4 Morosini 2002, 16.
5 Interview with author. For a more detailed description of this deal see Morosini 1998.
6 Morosini and Raedler 1999.
7 Morosini 2002.
8 Morosini 1998, 55.
9 Morosini and Khandpur 2002.

References

Hofstede, G. (1980) *Culture's Consequences: International Differences in Work-related Values*, Beverly Hills: Sage Publications.

Morosini, P. (1998) *Managing Cultural Differences: Effective Strategy and Execution Across Cultures in Global Corporate Alliances*, Oxford: Pergamon.

Morosini, P. (1999) 'Mega-mergers: the "real" challenges start after the deal is signed', *Perspectives for Managers*, 63, 7.

Morosini, P. (2002) 'Competing on social capabilities: a defining strategic challenge of the new millennium', IMD Working Paper 2002–1, Lausanne: IMD.

Morosini, P., Shane, S. and Singh, H. (1998) 'National cultural distance and cross-border acquisition performance', *Journal of International Business Studies*, 29 (1), 137–158.

Morosini, P. and Raedler, G. (1999) *DaimlerChrysler: Organizing the Post-Merger Integration*, Lausanne: IMD Case GM 774.

Morosini, P. and Khandpur, D. (2002) *Aventis: An Odyssey of Mergers*, Lausanne: IMD Case GM 1105.

4

Institutional factors are critical in cross-cultural M&As

By
Paul Strebel

TO AVOID THE PITFALLS in cross-cultural mergers, it is essential to focus on the specifics of the institutional experience on each side rather than on clichés about the other side's national culture. To mobilize people across regions and countries behind our objectives, we have to avoid cultural stereotyping and concentrate on the features of enabling institutions (for example, political or economic systems) that enhance value creation, both at the macro and the micro level. This chapter illustrates the dangers inherent in cultural clichés with the experience on both sides of the 1998 Daimler–Chrysler merger and summarizes how, on two levels of activity, managers can usefully apply an institutional perspective.

The first significant event aimed at integrating the Daimler and Chrysler cultures was a dinner for the top managers of the two companies. After dinner, the German CEO, Jürgen Schrempp, led the singing around the piano. To the Americans, he did not seem to fit the stereotype of a reserved German at all. Schrempp, on his side, was surprised at the reticence of the Chrysler executives and their reluctance to let their hair down and especially at how early most of them went to bed. Where was that American 'cowboy spirit', the reputed hallmark of Chrysler's daring culture?

Where was that American 'cowboy spirit', the reputed hallmark of Chrysler's daring culture?

When we see people of other backgrounds behaving differently, we often say to ourselves: 'Why can't they be like us?' We look at them through the lens of cultural stereotypes, our view of their typical behaviour – in effect, cultural clichés. And when they break the clichés, we are disturbed because something strange seems to be going on. Since we know cultures change only slowly, we perceive ourselves to be separated from them by permanent cultural differences. In the worst cases, this leads to dangerous myths about others, resulting in violence and bloodshed. In the business world, it may make it impossible for people to work across boundaries and may doom some organizational arrangements, such as particular mergers, to failure before they are even consummated.

Most people in the street, and hence most managers, focus heavily on clichés that are a caricature of values, beliefs and behaviours (the implicit features) rather than on the institutions (the explicit organizational relationships) associated with a particular culture. For practical business purposes, it is essential to go beyond the clichés and come to grips with the institutional side of culture. Awareness of the behaviour represented by the clichés may help to sensitize you to what to expect in different cultural settings, but usually this awareness reflects an average stereotype and ignores the institutional underpinnings. By contrast, with an institutional perspective, we can more objectively understand the differences in values, beliefs and behaviour between the people on the two sides of a cross-cultural merger.

There are different levels on which managers should avoid clichés and focus on institutional details. On the individual level, this calls for understanding differences in institutional details and experience when negotiating and working with partners from another country. On the global level, by contrast, management has to develop and sustain a global culture that can operate in different institutional settings around the world. For both levels, it is essential to be aware of how institutions interact with values, beliefs and behaviour.

The way institutions interact with values, beliefs and behaviour

The reason 'they behave that way', according to widely accepted theory, is that people are shaped by the commonalities in their life experience to see the world in a certain way. This common cultural experience represents a form of 'collective mental programming'[1] that is reflected in their values, beliefs and behaviours, and is embedded in their institutions. The institutions – that is, the family, religious, educational, political and other organizational relationships – in turn reinforce the ways of thinking and behaving. Table 4.1 shows the relationship between some alternative characteristics of institutions and some behaviour preferences of the corresponding implicit culture.

Table 4.1 ◆ Institutions and preferences

Institutions	Some alternatives	Related preferences
Political systems	Libertarian **vs.** Authoritarian	Individual liberty **vs.** Group cohesion
	Effective bureaucracy **vs.** Ineffective bureaucracy	Play by rules **vs.** Don't play by rules
Legal System	Common **vs.** Legal code	Details **vs.** Principles
	Litigation bias **vs.** Settlement bias	Confrontation **vs.** Compromise
Economic system	Weak **vs.** Strong market regulation	Risk taking **vs.** Risk averse
	Weak **vs.** Strong social security	Non-caring **vs.** Caring
Educational system	Data **vs.** Intuition	Bias to facts **vs.** Opinion
	Analysis **vs.** Action	Process oriented **vs.** Task oriented
Language	Informal **vs.** Formal	Easy **vs.** Difficult contact
	Direct **vs.** Indirect	Clarity **vs.** Ambiguity
Religious practice	Many **vs.** One	Tolerant **vs.** Intolerant
	Worldly **vs.** Other worldly	Money **vs.** Intangibles
Local institutions	Many **vs.** Few	Societal pull **vs.** Family Pull
	Private **vs.** State funded	Independence **vs.** Dependence

Institutions and preferences represent two complementary ways of describing and looking at culture. Preferences in the form of values, beliefs and behaviours can be difficult to pin down, but institutions are a concrete reality of everyday life. They can be observed, documented and described in detail. As opposed to inferred behaviour represented by the clichés, institutions are tangible and changes are more visible.

The differences between institutions provide an objective basis for understanding related differences in implicit culture, like its variation in a single country across ethnic groups and regions. In today's fast-moving technological environment, institutions themselves are increasingly subject to radical change, thereby providing a leading indicator of possible changes in values, beliefs and behaviour.

Institutional details reflect differences in values, beliefs and behaviour

There are two broad categories of institution: those that reflect deep ethnic culture, the practice that makes up family, language and religion; and those that reflect national culture, the practice that makes up educational, economic, legal and political organization. The former predate the emergence of the nation state and change much more slowly than the latter.

The differences between the institutional practice reflecting deep ethnic behaviour and that associated with national culture can be striking. Switzerland, with its German, French and Italian language cantons, provides a clear example. The Swiss as a whole are united by a certain idea of Switzerland that has everything to do with its national institutions. Indeed, the Swiss national culture is difficult to describe, except for those aspects shaped by its geography and institutions, such as neutrality and direct democracy. Yet to set these up as cultural clichés can be seriously misleading. The French-speaking Swiss have the same language as, and an ethnic culture similar to, the French. Many of them have holiday homes in France and spend their holidays there. They love French literature and Parisian theatre, and have some of the best *nouvelle cuisine* restaurants in the world. To get a sense of how to court a French-speaking Swiss, you should ignore the clichés and go to Paris rather than Zurich. Conversely, you would never study French national institutions in order to understand how to do business in French-speaking Switzerland. For business, you should also ignore the clichés, but this time go to Zurich and observe the details of institutional business practice there.

To get a sense of how to court a French-speaking Swiss, you should ignore the clichés and go to Paris rather than Zurich

In large countries, strong regional differences driven by the variety in ethnic subgroups and local institutions make cultural clichés even more unreliable. Europeans sometimes think that the United States is a single market sharing a uniform culture. However, those that see the US in terms of cultural clichés usually pay for it dearly, as Daimler did, because the impact of ethnic groups and local institutions on business behaviour and practice is significant. The difference between Michigan, the home of the US auto industry, and California, for example, is marked. Even within a single region, business cultures can vary sharply. Viewed through the eyes of outsiders, two different business cultures exist side by side in San Francisco and Silicon Valley, despite the fact that they share the same region. The continual networking in Silicon Valley, to exchange ideas, money and talent between people of numerous ethnic backgrounds, had its origins in the first computer societies and is a central part of the Valley culture. By contrast, the financial and corporate world of San Francisco, more heavily influenced by white Anglo-Saxon practices, can sometimes be quite traditional.

Institutional change is a leading indicator of changes in values, beliefs and behaviour

The danger of relying on cultural clichés is especially great when institutions undergo radical change, such as in Germany when the Berlin Wall came down. The east and west *Länder* in Germany shared the same language and culture for 1,000 years and yet, after reunification, the predominance of 40 years of communist institutions over national culture was strikingly evident. Most East Germans were lost in the market system and expressed an open nostalgia for the apparent certainty of the old ways of doing things before the collapse of the Wall. After more than ten years of experience with western institutions, however, the traces of the communist past in people's behaviour are disappearing rapidly. The same observation can be made about China: the market economy shaped values, beliefs and behaviour in Hong Kong, while communism shaped the mainland; today, the market economy is rapidly altering the implicit culture of the mainland.

The new institutional possibilities for the rapid accumulation of wealth are removing one of the historically most important roles of clichés. Traditionally, shared values, beliefs and behaviour, reflected in clichés, have played a big role in the struggle over the distribution of wealth. Since it took a long time to accumulate wealth peacefully, the quickest way of acquiring wealth was to put together an army and take it from somebody else. The attributes of ethnic culture captured by clichés have played the role of highly visible markers in distinguishing enemies from friends ever since people started banding together to protect themselves and occasionally raid wealth from their neighbours. So, in the pantheons of national heroes there is a disproportionate number of generals. Even today, bloody battles over turf and resources continue along some of the fault lines created by contiguous ethnic cultures, especially in the developing world.

Yet with the advance of the industrial and information revolutions, it has become much quicker and far less painful to acquire wealth by creating it through business activity. Maximum wealth creation requires using the best talent available, no matter what the cultural background of the people involved. In periods of rapid growth and wealth creation, talented immigrants are usually welcome, as has been evident in the pursuit of talent by high-growth multinationals across the globe. Those engaged in wealth creation, as opposed to wealth redistribution, are indifferent to national clichés.

The individual level

Clichés are not a good guide to institutional reality, even one's own. Most people believe that their country is unique and somehow better than others. However, everyone is living with a set of institutions that leaves much to be desired. The Europeans, with their emphasis on the quality of life, have a level of tradition, inflexibility, taxation and social welfare that Americans believe is holding them back economically. The United States, with its competitive spirit, has a level of litigation and lawyers, prisoners and guns that Europeans and Asians believe undermines the quality of life. East Asians, with their unquestioning commitment to hard work, have a degree of government involvement and low institutional accountability that Americans and Europeans believe makes it difficult for them to adapt and innovate.

> Everyone is living with a set of institutions that leaves much to be desired

Consider how differences between US and German institutions have affected DaimlerChrysler[2] and how these differ from the prevailing cultural clichés. A misleading cliché at that first DaimlerChrysler get-together of top managers was that Americans are more socially relaxed than Germans. The apparent informality in the widespread use of first names in the US, accompanied by the use of titles and the distinction between the formal and informal 'you' in German, reinforces this view. With the cliché in mind, the Chrysler executives naturally expected their Daimler counterparts to be at least as socially reserved as they were, while the Germans expected the Americans to be more socially relaxed.

If the Daimler executives had focused on the fact that many US managers are socially conservative Republicans, they would not have been surprised at all by the latter's reserved behaviour. There are wide variations in the social behaviour preferred by the members of different political parties in both countries. In the US, there is a divide between Republicans and Democrats, with the former favouring a more conservative approach to social behaviour. In Germany, the divide on social behaviour between Christian and Social Democrats is not as wide as it is with the Greens. Most German managers, however, belong to the main political parties and have a centre-right leaning somewhere between the US Democrats and Republicans.

If the Chrysler people had taken into account the fact that Jürgen Schrempp is a political independent, strongly influenced by his stay in South Africa, they too would have been much less surprised after that first dinner together. And they would have been less inclined to believe the cliché that the Germans are straightforward, not much inclined to subtlety and subterfuge. Jürgen Schrempp claimed long and loud that the union of the two companies was a merger of equals. He went to great lengths to treat Bob Eaton, the CEO of Chrysler, as an equal in terms of the protocol at meetings and conferences and in the initial organizational design. But he insisted that the head office be in Germany, not The Netherlands as some had suggested, and that Daimler come before Chrysler in the name. In addition, it was agreed that Bob Eaton would step down after a maximum of three years. By all accounts, right from the beginning, the Daimler people never intended it to be a merger of equals, except in a public relations sense. Not that they intended to impose the Mercedes culture on Chrysler but rather that Mercedes would be the dominant partner. In November 2000, Tracinda Corp., holding 13.75% of Chrysler's stock owned by Kirk Kerkorian, sued DaimlerChrysler for $8 billion, claiming that the merger had not been a true merger but rather a takeover. Despite having received a premium of at least 28%, Tracinda claimed the premium should have been even higher.

For the Daimler people, the most misleading cliché was that of American flexibility, embodied at Chrysler in the free-form discussion, cross-functional product launch teams, much leaner staffs, personal expenses and broader responsibilities of top managers. The Daimler people discovered that cultural clichés, like flexibility, despite some organizational support, are meaningless in the institutional context of very different business models and the way these respond to fluctuations in market demand. Prior to the merger, Chrysler had its highest profits ever and so much cash on hand that its major private shareholder, Kirk Kerkorian, had been pushing for more dividends for several years already and Daimler paid a premium of 28% over the share price at the time. Barely two years after the merger, in the face of weakening demand, Chrysler was bleeding red ink and was a subject of radical restructuring.

> For the Daimler people, the most misleading cliché was that of American flexibility

When the differences in business model are taken into account, it was not surprising, but rather to be expected, that Chrysler's earnings would be highly sensitive to demand fluctuations in the middle-income US market and, therefore, extremely volatile over a business cycle. Chrysler's low-cost model was based on very high fixed costs relative to variable ones: its factories were rather inflexible, tailored to make single products in high volumes at low cost;

its managers had little international experience and were not keen to move around; its unions were less cooperative than German unions with their experience of *Mitbestimmung**; its product portfolio was highly concentrated on the Ram pickups, the minivans and the Jeep SUVs; and 90% of its sales were in North America.

Another cliché is that Germans are more hierarchical than Americans, as is apparent in the German system of corporate governance with its two-tier board structure and formal labour representation. Yet the Chrysler executives were surprised by the power of the top managers on Schrempp's team, while the Daimler executives were surprised by the lack of management depth on the Chrysler side. This is much less surprising when one takes into account the details of the German system of corporate governance that requires a collective form of decision making. The diluted power of the CEO puts a much greater premium on persuasion than in a US company, where the CEO has the option of a more directive, top-down style. On a German management board, the CEO often has to get the votes of his top managers for key decisions.

In the US, there is the danger of less management depth in the presence of dominant CEOs or COOs, such as the charismatic Lee Iacocca and Bob Lutz at Chrysler. The impact of their commander styles on the depth of management talent was aggravated by the lean management approach that was part of Chrysler's low-cost model. The Daimler people saw the problem only after the top Chrysler people – Bob Lutz, Tom Gale and Tom Stallkamp – had gone.

The cliché about hierarchy is also undermined by sharp differences in hierarchical behaviour across industries in both the US and Germany. On the one hand, the software industry is much less hierarchical in both countries, especially in the US, than companies in older industries. On the other hand, the older industries in Germany are populated by technical specialists with the status of expert in their speciality, to whom even senior managers defer on technical matters. With the hierarchical cliché in mind, the Chrysler people were surprised at the status of Daimler engineers, while the Daimler executives were surprised at the willingness of Chrysler's engineers to submit uncritically to their bosses' views.

With respect to legal systems, the English Channel marks one of the world's biggest legal divides. The US legal system, like that of the UK, is based on common (case) law, whereas the German and Continental European system is based on a civil code (legal principles). The US system encourages much more litigation based on reference to previous cases, whereas the

* Co-determination: unions are represented on the boards of large German companies.

Germans rely more on expert arbitration based on the principles of a legal code. Reflecting these differences, the cliché is that the Germans are slower, more rigid and lost in the intricate principles of their control systems and documentation. Indeed, the Chrysler managers were amazed at the level of detail and the size of the briefing books that the Daimler people brought into their meetings. However, what put the Americans at a disadvantage was the way in which the German CEO's personal style trumped the cultural stereotype: the unexpected speed with which Schrempp and his team pushed the negotiations along and managed to stay a step ahead throughout the deal making.

What put the Americans at a disadvantage was the way in which the German CEO's personal style trumped the cultural stereotype

The US GAAP accounting principles are known for their concern with transparency designed to protect the interests of investors, while Continental European accounting standards are more obscure. With the cliché of greater transparency in mind, Daimler's executives thought that Chrysler's financial statements showed what they were getting. Yet the US GAAP exist in the context of the US legal system, which requires management to protect the rights of existing shareholders to the fullest extent possible. In the case of a corporate merger, this means presenting the financial statements in the most favourable light legally possible. In Chrysler's case, this meant positioning the inventory build-up in the books of the distributors.

More attention to institutional differences in the financial markets would have avoided the gaffe DaimlerChrysler's financial team made when it delivered its first quarterly earnings announcement. Despite warnings from the Chrysler side about the earnings sensitivity of the analysts and institutional investors who drive the US financial markets, the Daimler staff went ahead with its low-key, German-style earnings announcement. DaimlerChrysler surprised the US markets with flat earnings way below expectations and paid for it with a sharply plunging share price and loss of investor confidence for many months.

A pointed institutional detail is the difference in speed limits between Germany and the US and the difference in driving cultures that it reflects. Owing to the absence of a speed limit on many *autobahns*, there is a large market in Germany for cars that handle well at 200 km/h (125 mph); conversely, owing to the strictly enforced 55 mph (88 km/h) limit on US highways, Americans look for cars that are comfortable to drive at moderate speeds. There is less of a mass market in the US for Daimler's sophisticated engineering. A big question is how the Daimler people will respect the difference in driving cultures as they look for commonalities across the two companies in the future. Will Daimler be able to leverage its technology at a lower price point?

The global level

The cliché is that successful global companies have global cultures. The reality is that successful global companies do not negate their home country practices. Rather, they understand which of them are part of their success formula and which are redundant or, over time, counterproductive, as well as which practices from elsewhere should be exploited for growth and grafted onto the corporate culture. Then they go out and hire the people in each country who are willing to work in their culture and they adapt locally to local cultural preferences that do not clash with their core culture.

For example, Nokia's culture reflects numerous Finnish habits that have been part of its successful flexibility and rapid execution: a low degree of hierarchy, informality, modesty and a preference for actions over words. These were among the habits, originally essential for survival in the harsh, sparsely inhabited Finnish countryside not tempered by an aristocracy, which persisted when Finland industrialized. Modesty, in particular, is something that Nokia's US managers have difficulty accepting. There is much joking about this in the company, but the 'Finnish way' prevails.

However, English had to replace Finnish as the corporate language as the company went global and the Finns had to learn to express themselves more verbally. In addition, to keep up with the rapidly evolving industry, Nokia needed even more aggressive and entrepreneurial managers – hence the formation of Nokia Ventures in April 1998 and the acquisition of numerous Silicon Valley start-ups.

Successful global players have a full range of mechanisms for building a common institutional base. This starts with a common company language, unified reporting and control systems, clear global career policies, rotation opportunities and training programmes. Some of these mechanisms can be quite innovative, for example cloning to bring emerging market operations up to speed: senior managers in well-developed markets act as mentors for managers in the country organizations in emerging markets and are measured on how well they nurture them along.

> Successful global players have a full range of mechanisms for building a common institutional base

The real challenge in taking advantage of diversity is to include someone on the team with a very different institutional experience from the others. Bringing a minority American, who has grown up in the suburbs, belongs to the same church, went to a private high school and studied engineering at an Ivy League university, onto a management team of Waspish engineers is unlikely to do much for creative diversity. The same applies to European companies trying to gain a more diverse mix on their management teams. Bringing in an American who has lived in Europe for decades is not the same as having someone on board fresh from the US.

Leading global companies capitalize on different experience not only between but also within countries. They know that differences in professional training, for example, often swamp the differences in attitude and behaviour across countries. Finnish and US software engineers typically feel more professionally comfortable with one another than with their respective compatriots in advertising and promotion. Consequently, to get creative diversity, it is often more important to mix functions and hierarchical levels than national cultures. At Nokia, the best people from the relevant functions are put onto cross-functional teams, even if some of the teams turn out to be mainly Finnish.

Rather than putting multinational team members together in one location, successful global companies are especially good at working with them in their local institutional contexts, often separated by large geographic distances, both internally and as external partners. They usually have a number of high-profile stories that are used to explain to new recruits how these teams work. At Nokia, for example, it is the story of Pertii Kerhonen, a young vice-president at the Camberley R&D facility in England, who coordinated the development of the multi-standard phone with researchers, designers, marketers and production people around the world, including outside suppliers, most of them located far away from Camberley. Today, such team members are linked together by Nokia's intra- and extranet.

Companies that understand the global game take advantage of institutional diversity by drawing directly, on site, on the best institutional practice around the world. Nokia and many others look for Internet start-ups in Silicon Valley, design skills in northern Italy and micro-engineering skills in Switzerland. They do basic software design in India. They assemble electronic hardware in Mexico and set up their call centres in Ireland. They also know how to use lead markets to test out new products, for example new cars in high-income countries without an automobile industry of their own, or consumer electronics in Japan.

However, in taking advantage of diversity and using lead markets, it is important to be aware of how subtle institutional details can make or break the transfer of a practice or product from one location to another. The transfer of the i-mode wireless Internet service, for example, from Japan to the US is being affected by numerous institutional differences. Relative to Americans, the Japanese have many fewer PCs, possibly because their written language

characters are much less keyboard friendly and the Japanese
remains metred and rather expensive. Hence, for most c
tomers the i-mode is the only Internet service they have k
most Japanese commute to work or school by public transport, w...
them ample time to use portable devices of all kinds, especially those with screens that display Japanese characters. Americans, by contrast, drive their cars to work and have PCs at home linked to the net with a flat-rate telephone service, which they use to surf the web to get much richer content than is available over the small screens of the wireless Internet. As a result, transferring the Japanese i-mode to the US will be very difficult.

One of the biggest challenges for DaimlerChrysler will be to capitalize in fact on its institutional diversity. This will require walking the global talk, with deeds to build trust, without which there can be no global culture. Calling the combination a merger in the beginning, when it turned out to be an acquisition, did not help. Nor did it help to say that passports do not matter, given the naming of the company and the location of its head office. And then there is the subtle superiority complex about technology among the Mercedes people, which no amount of politically correct English can hide.[3] Since then, management has worked hard to integrate the cultures, with high-profile seminars and employee exchange programmes. Most of all, it has begun to build trust through the appointment of Dieter Zetsche, the down-to-earth, no-nonsense, but people-sensitive German CEO of Chrysler.

> One of the biggest challenges for Daimler-Chrysler will be to capitalize in fact on its institutional diversity

Effective global managers not only respect other people's institutional experience and cultural preferences, they also act and decide that way. They move easily from one institutional setting to another – Zetsche moves easily back and forth and is increasingly at home on both sides of the Atlantic. If anything demonstrates that cultural clichés are not the key it is Zetsche's increasing success in winning the confidence of the Chrysler people. He, and others like him, know how to capitalize, in a risk-effective way, on institutional diversity and the corresponding variety in behaviour and preferences around the world.

They do this by walking the global talk, avoiding national clichés, focusing on concrete institutional details and treating people as individuals. It involves a proactive approach to cross-cultural management, one that takes advantage of the best institutional practice across ethnic groups, regions and countries, and invites active management of the attendant risks and exploitation of the opportunities.

Notes

1 Hofstede, 1983; Hampden-Turner and Trompenaars, 1993.
2 Vlasic and Stertz, 2000.
3 Hawranek and Kurbjuweit, 2001.

References

Hampden-Turner, C. and Trompenaars, F. (1993) *The Seven Cultures of Capitalism*, New York: Currency Doubleday.

Hawranek, D. and Kurbjuweit, D. (2001) 'Die Drei-Welten AG', *Der Spiegel*, 24 February, No. 9, 96–109.

Hofstede, G. (1983) 'The cultural relativity of organizational practices and theories', *Journal of International Business Studies*, Fall, 75–89.

Vlasic, B. and Stertz, B. A. (2000) *Taken for a Ride: How Daimler-Benz Drove Off With Chrysler*, Chichester: John Wiley & Sons, Ltd.

5

Merger of equals: the case of AstraZeneca

By
Peter Killing

The advantage of a merger of equals, compared to an acquisition, is that there is no premium to be paid – and in our industry acquisition premiums are huge. The other major benefit is that you can start fresh and say, 'What do we want this merged company to be?', and then create it. A merger of equals is a major opportunity for positive change.

The challenge is to integrate two companies in a way that you avoid massive infighting, and at the same time not lose focus on running the business.

I think we have done that.

Sir Tom McKillop, CEO, AstraZeneca

MANY MANAGERS WOULD BE sceptical of Tom McKillop's claim that AstraZeneca, the global pharmaceutical company which resulted from the 1998 combination of Astra of Sweden and Zeneca of the UK, was a merger of equals. This is not because they know AstraZeneca well – it is because they do not think there is such a thing as a merger of equals.

The sceptics argue that, at best, the phrase 'merger of equals' is used by well-intentioned but naïve executives to signal how they intend to try to combine two companies – but the reality of doing so is so daunting that they cannot make it work. At worst, the 'merger of equals' label is seen as a ruse that predators use to calm their target's fears while the deal is done (more cheaply than an acquisition) and the reality of 'being bought' sets in later.

This latter view was confirmed for many by the widely proclaimed ‘merger of equals’ between Daimler-Benz and Chrysler in 1998. A year after the deal, Jürgen Schrempp, CEO of DaimlerChrysler, stated: ‘Me being a chess player, I don’t normally talk about the second or third move. The structure that we have now, where Chrysler (is a division), was always the structure I wanted. We had to go a roundabout way but it had to be done for psychological reasons. If I had gone and said Chrysler would be a division, everybody on their side would have said, “There is no way we’ll do a deal.”’:[1] Jack Welch noted, ‘Jurgen is the perfect guy now that it is established that Daimler took over Chrysler. There has to be one way forward and clear rules. There is,’ he added, ‘no such thing as a merger of equals.’[2]

So, is there any point in trying to create a merger of equals? Clearly Tom McKillop thinks so, and Jack Welch does not. This chapter addresses two questions that will help you decide for yourself. They are:

So, is there any point in trying to create a merger of equals?

1. What is a merger of equals?
2. What does it take to create one?

Our focus is on the creation of AstraZeneca, whose executives have generously given their time to allow IMD to study the merger in depth. Thirty-one interviews were conducted with senior AstraZeneca managers (16 with former Zeneca managers, 15 with former Astra managers) in late 2001 and early 2002. Nanci Govinder, an IMD Research Associate, conducted the interviews.[3]

We hope that there is sufficient information in this chapter for you to come to your own conclusions regarding AstraZeneca, and to decide whether there were aspects of the way in which these two companies were merged that you would like to emulate – or avoid! A brief background of each company is presented below.

Astra: a quick overview

Astra AB, founded in 1913 and situated in Sweden, manufactured pharmaceuticals for the management of diseases in the gastrointestinal (digestive system), cardiovascular (heart disease), respiratory (asthma and lung disease), and central nervous systems, as well as pain control. In 1998 Astra employed close to 25,000 people worldwide and was the 15th largest pharmaceutical company in the world. The company's largest shareholder was Investor AB, controlled by the Wallenberg family of Sweden.

In 1982 Astra, looking for a way to break into the US market, signed a key deal with Merck & Co. Inc., one of the US industry leaders, to market Astra's products in the US. In return for signing the agreement, Astra received a cash payment of $60 million. This agreement gave Merck the US rights to the vast majority of products in Astra's R&D pipeline. The agreement had no termination clause, compelling Astra to provide its products to Merck in perpetuity.

Astra made world headlines in the mid-1990s with its blockbuster drug Losec (Prilosec in the US), which treated acid-associated gastrointestinal disorders. In 1995 it became the biggest pharmaceutical product in the history of the industry, with an estimated worldwide market share of 41% and contributions in excess of 55% of Astra's total revenues in 1998. The patents for Losec would expire during the period 2001–2007.

Zeneca: a quick overview

Zeneca Group plc, formed as a result of a demerger of three Imperial Chemical Industries (ICI) businesses in 1993, was based in London and specialized in pharmaceuticals, agrochemicals and speciality chemicals. By 1997 the revenue from the pharmaceuticals business was as large as the combined revenue of the other two businesses, and pharmaceutical profit was more than 70% of Zeneca's total profit.

Four of Zeneca's major drugs, accounting for a total of 62% of sales, would come off patent between 1999 and 2003. New primary care products in the company's R&D pipeline looked capable of off-setting this potential loss of revenue, but these new drugs would require massive investment in sales and marketing – as new guidelines issued by the US Food and Drug Administration allowed drug companies to advertise prescription drugs in 30–60-second TV commercials, called direct-to-consumer (DTC) advertising. It was an open question as to whether companies the size of Zeneca (and Astra) would be able to afford to compete in DTC markets.

At the time of the demerger, Zeneca plc was floated on the London and New York Stock Exchanges and began trading at about £6 per share. By September 1998, the stock had reached approximately £21. Zeneca employed 31,000 people and ranked as the 21st largest pharmaceutical business in the world in 1997.

What is a merger of equals?

Financial construct

At one level a merger of equals is the combination of two companies in such a way that the shareholders of neither of the predecessor companies hold more than 60% of the new company. Under UK law (AstraZeneca was incorporated in the UK) there are important favourable tax implications for a merger of equals: to be considered one, remaining within the 60:40 envelope is mandatory.

In the case of AstraZeneca, the shareholders of Astra held 46.5% of the new company, those of Zeneca held 53.5%. These percentages were based on the market capitalization of the two companies over the six months prior to the merger, adjusted slightly through negotiation. As the shareholders of both companies will have to approve the merger, one of the first requirements of a merger of equals is that both groups must find the share exchange ratio acceptable.

Perceived equality on Day One

The employees of both companies must also be happy with the deal. If the combination is called a merger of equals and is to be a merger of equals, it needs to *look like* a merger of equals on the day it is formed. In other words, it is critical that the employees of neither company perceive themselves to be 'losers' in the transaction. Their perception will be shaped by the ownership percentages referred to above, but also by the way the top jobs are allocated, the composition of the board of directors, the location of the head office, the corporate language and the equality of sacrifice if, for example, plant closures are announced.

Equality in management positions does not mean, however, that a merger of equals should have joint CEOs or joint chairmen. History suggests that jointly held positions are not a good idea, as they typically lead to confusion, conflict and a slow decision-making process.[4]

History suggests that jointly held positions are not a good idea

In the case of AstraZeneca the chairman, Percy Barnevik, who was then chairman of Investor AB (Astra AB's major shareholder), came from the Astra side, and the CEO from Zeneca. But neither Håkan Mogren nor Sir David Barnes, the CEOs of the merging companies, became the CEO of the merged company. Both stepped aside to become deputy chairmen and gave their support to Tom McKillop, who had previously been the head of Zeneca's pharmaceuticals business. This was viewed by senior managers in the new company as an incredibly strong message of commitment to the merger: these two CEOs of successful companies, both well-known public figures, were willing to step aside to get this deal to happen. This message was reinforced at the first joint meeting of managers, which took place shortly before the announcement of the merger, where the two executives spoke powerfully about the need for the merger, their belief in it and why each was willing to give up the CEO role to make it happen.

AstraZeneca's senior management team and board of directors were created with equal numbers of former Astra and Zeneca candidates. Both sides readily agreed that it had to be this way. As Gunnar Christiani, vice president group human resources[5] at Astra, stated: 'The board and the senior executive team were created with an eye to the political situation – but all appointments below that level were based on merit.'

The head office issue was more difficult as it was decided early on that there would be one head office, not two. The ultimate decision was that the head office would be in the Zeneca Group's former head office in London, while R&D management would be located in Sweden, in Astra's former headquarters. Many of the functions that were not represented in London were located in three major hubs: Södertalje, Sweden, Alderley Park, UK and Wilmington, USA. The possibility of creating a neutral head office had been considered, but McKillop considered it to be an expensive and 'stupid massage' that had no real value. Or to put it another way, the symbolism was not worth the cost. Håkan Mogren commented:

> *Although it was an emotional issue in Sweden, it was clear to us that London made a lot more sense than Sweden as the HQ of the new company. But we told people that the HQ would be small, which it is, and thus a lot of work would still be done in Sweden. And it is good for the Swedish employees to know that I am sitting in London, and that Tom McKillop and I are friends. If stupid ideas come up, I will turn them down. So there is a level of reassurance.*

Equality of opportunity

At the heart of a merger of equals is the concept that there is an equal opportunity for everyone. No employee is branded as superior or inferior because of the company that she or he came from. As quickly as possible, people need to throw off the badge of their ancestry and take up their identification with the new company. Pain – and there will always be some pain – also needs to be shared.

In manufacturing, for example, it was decided that seven plants – all relatively small – would be closed. Four were from Zeneca and three from Astra.

However, providing equality of opportunity to all employees can be much easier to say than to do. AstraZeneca was to be run in English, and for Swedes not proficient in English, language was a handicap. Kjell Johansson, Astra's vice president of manufacturing and logistics,[6] commented:

> *There was not much reaction in the manufacturing group at the beginning in Sweden, as we communicated early that we did not foresee any redundancies there. This took away the uncertainty. People were curious and positive, but as time went on it became negative. There was a feeling in the Swedish operations that power was transferred to the UK and the biggest change was that we all had to speak English. This gave Zeneca people a distinct advantage as they could communicate more convincingly in their mother tongue and persuade us to go along with things.*

The 'creating a new company' mindset

Any merger, but especially a merger of equals, needs to be dynamic and forward looking. You need to move beyond the static questions of 'what is mine and what is yours, and who is winning?' to the dynamic 'what can we create and how can we win in the marketplace with our new company?' Company A is not becoming part of company B, nor is the reverse true: a new company is being created. Tom McKillop was adamant about this:

> *You start with a blank sheet of paper and think about how we can work together, what systems and processes we should use to make this new company a winner. You do not pick one element from company A and one from company B, because instantly you create winners and losers.*

In the opinion of Jonathan Symonds, chief financial officer (CFO) of the Zeneca group,[7] AstraZeneca had 12–15 months to create the new company that Tom McKillop wanted:

> *A merger is like an erupting volcano. Everything turns to lava, and lava is fluid. You can mould it and shape and turn it into new things, but eventually it solidifies. In the period when the lava is molten you have an incredible opportunity to do things differently – take advantage of that situation. Do it carefully, do it sensibly and don't push too far in one direction and demotivate everybody. You have a period of 12–15 months before people say, I've had enough of this and want more certainty.*

Creating the new company

The weekend after Tom McKillop was offered the position of CEO of the new company, he took a long walk in the hills, thinking about how the merger process should be managed. He decided on four principles that should govern the process: *fast, fair, flexible* and *forgiving*. He later added a fifth – *communicate*, to everyone, as often as possible.

Soon after, McKillop created a six-person integration steering committee consisting of himself as chair, Håkan Mogren, David Barnes, Åke Stavling, Jonathan Symonds and Gunnar Christiani. (Three executives were from Astra, three from Zeneca.) Åke Stavling, the former CFO of Astra,[11] was to be the head of the integration team that reported to the steering committee. Stavling said:

> *I created an integration team consisting of five people from each company and selected McKinsey [the international consulting firm] to assist in the integration process, but it was clear that they were there to help, not to run the show.*
>
> *We read all the available literature on mergers in the industry and concluded that we could [either] have a very strong centralized integration committee that would control everything and all the functions would continue operating in the usual mode until the committee came back and imposed their findings on everyone. Or we could let the functions do their own integration and the central integration team would focus on overall corporate and cross-functional issues and coordinate the integration work through regular meetings with key functional representatives. We chose the latter model.*
>
> *Our key objectives were to move fast, deliver the synergies, retain key talent, keep focus on the business, and create a new culture. Tom's widely disseminated merger principles of fast, fair, flexible and forgiving helped us a lot.*

Fast

It is a widely held belief that acquisitions should be integrated quickly, but in a merger of equals, especially when the intent is to create a new organization with a new culture, it was not clear that the organization would accept an emphasis on speed. McKillop explained:

It is a widely held belief that acquisitions should be integrated quickly

> *Percy Barnevik encouraged me to go as fast as humanly possible. Say 'no' to every obstacle that people put in your way, jump them and go quickly. People*

would tell me, 'We can't do this or that – we need three months.' I told them they had a week. That was the theme – go fast to reduce uncertainty. In fact, we completed the legal transaction in 80 working days – including dealing with the antitrust authorities. That was a new record for a major merger.

We started the integration task forces before the deal was finalized. We could not exchange confidential information, so they could only work so far, but we kept the pressure on, and the lawyers kept a close eye on us.

Elizabeth Sozanski, Astra's communications manager in the US,[12] has been through six major restructurings in the pharmaceutical industry. This one, she stated, was the best she has experienced. She said:

In a merger you have two choices: slow and painful, or fast and painful. We chose the latter. Tom's rule was 100% fast, 80% right. You have to realize that in a merger the only question that 99% of the people have is 'what about me?', and that is the question to which there is no answer – at least not at first. The senior managers find out their own positions early, so they are OK, but the sooner that certainty goes all the way from top to bottom the better. If you go too slowly the organization destabilizes.

The disadvantage of acting fast was explained by Michael Rance, Zeneca pharma's head of business development.[13] He was at the heart of the integration team for a year and was the 'last man to leave' the integration office:

In the first year we effectively dismantled the two companies, Astra and Zeneca, but did not truly create a new AstraZeneca. What we first created was R&D, operations, sales and marketing, and so on. People identified more with their functions than with AstraZeneca. During that stage my view, and Tom will disagree, is that the senior executive team was not behaving primarily as a cross-functional team but as functional heads. In the pursuit of speed there was little time to recognize the value of looking at things cross-functionally.

The upside was that it was immensely focused and quick. The downside was that we created functions that still needed to be brought together. We are now working on getting our effective and efficient functions to come together, first and foremost, as an effective and efficient corporation. It's a real challenge, but we are succeeding.

Towards the end of 1999 AstraZeneca carried out an internal survey to see how employees were reacting to the integration process. With regard to speed, 72% of the 1,332 respondents said that the pace was right, 11% said it was too fast and 13% said it was too slow. Although regretting that 'we could not have been twice as fast', McKillop nevertheless seemed satisfied with the pace of the integration. He pointed to the following milestones:

- Legal phase completed in 80 working days.
- New single company operating 40 working days after that.
- Central integration done by end of 1999.
- Worldwide sales forces restructured by end of 1999.
- R&D strategy and prioritized portfolio in place within one year.
- More than half way to delivering $1.1 billion in cost synergies within one year.

Fair

According to consultants, the greatest barriers to a successful integration process are low employee commitment to making the integration work and obstructionism by middle management.[14] Both factors can be greatly alleviated if the employees believe that the merger is being handled fairly. Tom McKillop explained what he meant by 'fair':

> *By fair I did not mean 'one for Astra, one for Zeneca'. But it had to be clear that the criteria used for appointments, etc. were fair and that it was a merger, not a takeover. In fact, at the very top I had to disappoint a lot more Zeneca managers than Astra managers because Zeneca had both a pharmaceuticals management team and the management team for the whole company, whereas Astra was run by an executive group of six people. In the end, the only place where senior people left because they were not offered the job they wanted was in R&D, and those were Zeneca people.*

Because of the lay-offs that are typically associated with a large merger it can be difficult for people to perceive it as being fair. Some are losing jobs, others are losing friends they have worked with. In the case of AstraZeneca, it was anticipated that about 5,000 people would be laid off. Most of t hese losses would be in central staff jobs or in sales and marketing support operations, as the company had two sales operations in many countries. In the previously mentioned 1999 employee survey, 12% of the 1,332 respondents said the process was fair to almost everyone, 74% said it was fair to most people, 10% said it was unfair to most and 1% said it was unfair to almost everyone.

Gunnar Christiani commented on how 'fair treatment' was transferred to action:

> *It was clear to us that the staffing process was the first opportunity for the new company to show that its declared values were real and not just lip service. People were going to look very closely at how we managed the appointments.*

> *Therefore the principles for the process and some 60 questions, based on our values, were posted on the company's intranet. To support the feeling of fairness and comfort we ensured that the candidates always met with interviewers from both companies. Managers were trained in giving bad messages and how to care for the non-successful candidates. Call it luck, but in spite of a wide spread between functions, the top 90 appointments were spread 45/45 between Astra and Zeneca managers.*

Any discussion of fairness in a merger quickly leads to a second question: 'But is it really a merger of equals?' Here are two answers from former Astra employees:

Göran Lerenius, formerly Astra general counsel and secretary to the board:[15]

> *It was definitely a merger of equals in the way that we put the two companies together – there was no one that had the lead. There was a balance in the decision-making process.*
>
> *But we have our HQ in London, we are a British company, and we have a lot of British processes that we did not have before. The finance group is heavily ex-Zeneca. So in London, the British culture dominates – that is natural. But in the marketplaces around the world – including the US – we have a dominance of ex-Astra managers. Astra's brand was so much bigger that it was natural. Ex-Astra is also stronger in R&D.*

Elizabeth Sozanski added:

> *For the most part, yes, it has been a merger of equals. The only area you might think otherwise is the selection of headquarters. Not so much that it's in London but that it is in this Zeneca building. It carries a historical connotation. Had I made the decision, I would have moved to a neutral location to make a symbolic statement that we are starting from scratch. Other than that it was a merger of equals.*
>
> *Two years down the line we don't hear people say we used to do it like this and like that – people identify with AstraZeneca. I think this has happened because we've had some successes as AstraZeneca already. Also, it's a good company, people see more opportunities in the bigger entity, and they watch the leadership's actions and draw their own conclusions – which are positive.*

Flexible

Flexibility in AstraZeneca meant two things. First, because of the emphasis on speed, it was anticipated that mistakes would be made. So managers needed to be willing to change decisions that were shown to be incorrect. So the message to everyone was 'do not seek perfection'. Get it approximately right and change it later if you need to.

The second sort of flexibility was at a personal level. To a surprising extent, managers were willing to engage positively in the merger process when it was not clear what their own future would be. Most thought that they would be offered a job in the new company, but in many cases they did not know what that job would be. As one manager said: 'None of us was prepared to put our own position ahead of doing the right thing for the new company. I know that sounds trite and unbelievable, but it was true.'

Managers needed to be willing to change decisions that were shown to be incorrect

The most extreme example occurred at a meeting of about 40 senior managers from both companies held in late November 1998, just before the deal was announced publicly. McKillop explained why he went ahead with the weekend meeting even though he had been advised by consultants and bankers not to do it:

> *At that point hardly anyone in either company knew about the deal. I wanted to have a wider group of people hash it through and get their thoughts on how it would work. Håkan and David opened the meeting and explained why they thought this was the right thing for the two companies. They did it in a very honest, direct and dignified way – very gracefully. There were no winners and no losers – no sulking. Håkan talked of it as a wedding, with he and David as the godfathers.*
>
> *Håkan and I had talked to a number of people beforehand about their position in the merged company, so some people knew what job they would have if the deal were finalized, but just as many did not. At one point we split into functional pairs, each manager with his or her counterpart, and asked them to critique our plans for the new company. This was risky because in some cases one of these people had a new job and the other was not sure. My gamble was that there would be enough excitement generated over that weekend, that even the people who were disappointed with their new job offer would want to stay. And almost all of them did. We only lost one of that group, and in one other case we had to pay someone a bonus to stay – but that was the only time we did that.*

Forgiving

It is apparent that if you ask people to move fast during the integration process, to make decisions without full information, they will make some mistakes. So then to criticize them for the mistakes would be perverse. Tom McKillop's view that forgiveness must be a part of the merger philosophy makes sense. When asked informally how good he was at forgiveness, he grinned and said: 'Well, I've had to bite my tongue a few times.' He added:

> *Of course we will get things wrong because we are going so fast. We know that. But when they do go wrong let's have no screaming or shouting – and no sense of 'them and us'. We are all part of one company now.*

Elizabeth Sozanski pointed out that it is not just poor decisions that you sometimes have to forgive but also, in fact more often, poor behaviour:

> *The way people behave in a merger is very different to the way they behave in steady state. If you look at Mazlow's hierarchy of needs, in steady state you are operating near the top, but in a merger, your basic level of food and shelter is threatened and you react instinctively. Some people are okay, but others are depressed and some become aggressive. It brings out the best and the worst in people, so you have to be forgiving.*

Communicate, communicate, communicate

There are two major communication challenges in a merger. One is with the outside world, in particular with the shareholders and analysts who are tracking your progress. When AstraZeneca was created, a synergy target of $1.1 billion was announced. The merged company's progress towards the target has to be constantly reported in a way that everyone can understand.

> There are two major communication challenges in a merger

The other need is for communication with your employees. As the pre-deal analysis and negotiations have been highly secret, broad internal communication needs to start the day the merger is announced. In the case of AstraZeneca, the morning the merger was made public, all managers around the world had material to explain why the merger was taking place, background on the two companies, and the key integration and merger issues.

Elizabeth Sozanski said:

> *People who do not know what is going on create their own truths. But good communication can take the edge off the uncertainty and get people focused on*

their jobs. The key is to get the senior people out of their offices – to talk to people and admit they do not know the answers, but to make clear the process that is being used, and to indicate when the answers will be known.

The integration team sent frequent updates on the merger progress via e-mail, personal appearances and a website open to all. The challenge was to get messages all the way through the organization. Barrie Thorpe, Zeneca's director of operations,[16] commented:

One of the points I made to the communications team was not to complicate the communications, as one should not underestimate how long it takes to get all the way down the organization. Keep the core thrust of the communication the same so that people all the way down on the shop floor can understand. We often used web-based tools for communication, but at the end of the day it's about talking to groups of people, being seen, and walking the talk. You can never do enough of that.

Gunnar Christiani was particularly concerned with communications between the two cultures – Astra and Zeneca – and the two nationalities – British and Swedish – that were being brought together:

At the very beginning we distributed literature on multicultural differences so that both nationalities could take a look at each other and enter into a cultural dialogue. We also created a binder with guidelines on how to conduct a cultural dialogue, with information on the values and corporate culture of AstraZeneca, including how each function was interpreting our slogan 'First for Innovation and Value'. This binder was distributed to HR managers worldwide and was posted on the web. 66% of the employees participated in a cultural dialogue, evaluating the past of the two organizations and building the future of AstraZeneca.

Progress to date

Tom McKillop suggested that there were three phases to the AstraZeneca merger once it had been agreed and announced. The first was the integration phase, the second was the transformation phase (which overlapped the integration phase) and the third was the productivity phase, which in 2002 was just getting under way. He commented on the integration phase:

The test in the integration phase is: can we keep the business running well while we are integrating? Normally in mergers there is such an internal focus that you take your eye off the market and lose share. We actually gained share during 1999, while all the other majors lost share. The second major test was whether or not we could keep the R&D projects going – as they were going to be so important to us. All of our high-priority projects were delivered on schedule.

McKillop was not alone in believing that the integration was a success. Of the 1,332 respondents to the 1999 survey referred to earlier, 24% indicated that the integration was being very well managed, 58% said it was being adequately managed, 13% said not very well managed and less than 1% said very poorly managed.

In terms of the transformation phase – creating a new company with a great culture – Tom McKillop was not as happy:

AstraZeneca is still too bureaucratic today. There is still too much middle management fear of letting go. Every month now, after our two-day executive meeting, the notes are communicated to 1,400 managers across the company. The message is: if we can share information so openly, so can they.

A former Astra manager agreed with Tom:

We have still not created the elegant, fast-moving, beautiful animal that we wanted. Nor are we as cost effective as we should be. We have a complex structure, with too many layers in some instances, and are control oriented to a level that is not beneficial.

In addition to continuing to try to make the culture less bureaucratic, Tom McKillop's focus in 2002 was on increasing AstraZeneca's productivity:

We see increasing price pressure ahead and a need for ever-lower costs. And lower costs means we need more productive R&D, sales and marketing. The key is to get more, faster, with less input. We have a programme right now in R&D called 10/10 – which means 10% more output for 10% less input. The key to that is speed and creativity. That is what we will need to win.

But of course speed and creativity are not usually the hallmarks of large companies. So we are back to culture. We need to get rid of the bureaucracy of size. I cannot do it all myself, and I have to be careful not to overload the system. First I was pushing the integration, and then the transformation – and now speed and creativity. But we cannot stop.

The bottom line

As stated at the beginning of this chapter, there is a lot of scepticism about mergers of equals, and there are certainly not many managers who would even think of attempting one, given the well-publicized difficulties of merged companies such as Corus and DaimlerChrysler. But the way Astra and Zeneca came together was well managed and the deal has made a lot of sense for both companies. In fact, the new company gained market share in the 12 months following the merger.

> There is a lot of scepticism about mergers of equals, and there are certainly not many managers who would even think of attempting one

What has set this merger of equals apart from others that have not performed as well? Part of the answer lies in the conditions that existed before the deal was done, part in the negotiation process, and a large part in the implementation itself.

Pre-conditions for success

1 The senior managers of each company strongly believed that the merger made strategic sense. Neither company was a reluctant partner to the deal; in fact each had independently arrived at the conclusion that the other was its 'first-choice' partner. And because of the in-depth work the senior teams had done together on a possible merger several years earlier, there was a high level of commitment to the shared vision for the new company, as well as a high degree of mutual respect between the managers of the two companies.

2 Prior to the merger the senior teams believed that the two company cultures were compatible and that British and Swedish management cultures would prove to be similar. This belief was part of the reason that each company had the other as its first choice partner. There was, for example, some reluctance to tie up with a US company.

The negotiations

1 The negotiations were tough, but the strong belief on both sides that the merged company would be a winner kept everyone at the table when discussions got difficult.

2 The key items – the black box issues – were negotiated as a group rather than one by one. Taken independently, any one of these issues could have been a deal-breaker.

3 Throughout the negotiations there was an emphasis on achieving equity for both sides and a strong recognition that the resulting company had

both to *be* a merger of equals and to look like one, to managers, employees and shareholders.

Implementation

1 Both CEOs stepped down to facilitate the coming together of the two companies. This hugely symbolic act set the tone for the merger and dramatically reduced the propensity for infighting.

2 There was equality in senior management appointments, but it was recognized from the outset that a joint CEO structure – like that at AOL/Time Warner and Corus – would not work. Any type of dual management structure is a trap that has to be avoided, in the author's view.

3 The focus was on both fast integration and building a new company. Tom McKillop's drive to keep everyone looking forward – by making them focus on the new company that they were going to build rather than on the company they had come from – was important in creating a unity of purpose. McKillop avoided a 'best of both' approach, which creates winner and losers, and wherever possible went for a 'let's create what is best for the new company' approach.

4 Tom McKillop's merger philosophy of *fast, fair, flexible* and *forgiving*, combined with an emphasis on communication, was a good one. Most importantly, he clearly demonstrated these principles in his own behaviour, as did, at his urging, the senior managers of the combined company.

As the quotes at the end of this chapter make clear, AstraZeneca is still not quite the company that senior management wanted it to be – size does have its disadvantages. But if you are thinking of a merger of equals for your business, the AstraZeneca story may provide you with insights and inspiration. Creating a merger of equals is not easy, but it is possible, and the benefits can be considerable. If the conditions are right, and you are up to the implementation challenge, go for it.

Notes

1 The Schrempp gambit: the chairman of DaimlerChrysler offers a passionate defence of his strategy and tells Tim Burt and Richard Lambert that he never envisaged the merger as a partnership of equals. *Financial Times*, 30 October 2000.

2 Steering straight with his foot to the floor: Profile Jürgen Schrempp, group chairman DaimlerChrysler, *Financial Times*, 26 February 2001.
3 All quotes of AstraZeneca executives are taken from these interviews. For further details of this merger see IMD case study IMD-3-1088: *Astra + Zeneca: 'Merger of Equals'*, 2002.
4 In October 1999 British Steel and Hoogovens of The Netherlands merged to form Corus. The new company had joint CEOs, one from each company. By all accounts the two men personally got on very well. When they both resigned a little more than a year after the merger Sir Brain Moffat, the chairman, was quoted as saying that the board felt Corus needed 'more urgency, more decision making at a faster pace than before'. He said that 'the two people had to agree on every decision which took an inordinate amount of time'. *Financial Times*, 6 December 2000.
5 Gunnar Christiani: executive vice president, HR, AstraZeneca.
6 Kjell Johansson: vice president, manufacturing for Sweden, Europe and Asia Pacific, AstraZeneca.
7 Jonathan Symonds: CFO, AstraZeneca.
8 Anthony Pottage: vice president, R&D administration, AstraZeneca.
9 Claes Wilhelmsson: executive vice president, R&D, AstraZeneca.
10 Laurent Condomine: vice president, business development, AstraZeneca.
11 Åke Stavling: executive director, business development, AstraZeneca.
12 Elizabeth Sozanski: vice president, internal communications, AstraZeneca.
13 Michael Rance: vice president, corporate affairs, AstraZeneca.
14 A.T. Kearney in Åke Stavling slides.
15 Göran Lerenius: legal counsel, AstraZeneca.
16 Barrie Thorpe: executive vice president, operations, AstraZeneca.

References

Burt, T. and Lambert, R. (2000) 'The Schrempp gambit', *Financial Times*, 30 October, London.

Burt, T. (2001) 'Steering straight with his foot to the floor', *Financial Times*, 26 February, London.

Guerrera, F. (2000) 'Corus's joint executives resign', *Financial Times*, 6 December, London.

Killing, P. and Govinder, N. (2002) *Astra + Zeneca: 'Merger of Equals.'* International Institute of Management Development, Case No. IMD-3-1088.

6

Some key pitfalls in acquisitions

By
Jacques Horovitz

MOST STUDIES DONE ON the performance of acquisitions show that between 50% and 75% of them fail, i.e. fail to provide superior profitability or shareholder value, compared with the situation before or to companies in similar industries that did not acquire businesses. This affects a large chunk of the economy, as in 2000 the total value of mergers and acquisitions worldwide amounted to US$3.5 trillion, 36% up from 1998.

Since for simplicity all of these studies have, of course, concentrated on public companies acquiring other public companies, the failure rate may not apply to large public companies whose development strategy has been based purely on the acquisition of small companies. One such example is ISS, the giant global Danish cleaning services company, which has developed mostly by acquiring small, entrepreneurial local cleaning companies and making them grow to form a full offering for cleaning offices, power plants, subways, hospitals, airports and the like all over the world. In fact, there is a lot to learn from this mode of development, whereby the relative size of the acquirer compared with the acquiree means that the deal is always a success.

> In the mainstream of large domestic or international companies acquiring other large companies, failure happens for two reasons

However, in the mainstream of large domestic or international companies acquiring other large companies, failure happens for two reasons. The first – 'pre-acquisition' – has to do with a lack of understanding of the consequences of the acquisition before it is made ('wrong' decision).

The second – 'post-acquisition' – has to do with an inability to fulfil what was promised in terms of return or to change the course of action quickly and sufficiently when things do not go as planned.

In this chapter, after reviewing each key factor that contributes to pre- and post-acquisition mistakes, we draw some implications to help management improve the score.

Pre-acquisition pitfalls

In the course of participating in acquisitions and observing deals, I have identified several factors, or traps, that contribute to failure:

- the initial assessment is too biased by numbers;
- there is a bias towards making a deal;
- there is a wrong assessment of the acquiree's business model;
- the seller artificially boosts profits; and
- due diligence is not enough for managerial assessment.

1 Initial assessment too biased by numbers

Although presentations to analysts and shareholders often emphasize strategic fit and synergies, much of the time in pre-acquisition analysis and evaluation is spent on numbers. There are two reasons for this: the actors involved and the bias of due diligence.

- The actors involved in an acquisition always include an investment bank or financial advisor of some sort and the chief financial officer of the acquirer (and the acquiree). They have almost unlimited time to spend on the deal while the line managers, including the CEOs, have to run the existing companies. These actors are by nature numbers-oriented and love to run simulations and financial scenarios of post-acquisition combined income statements, balance sheets, price/earnings valuations and the like to justify their time and, in the case of the outsiders, immense fees. I remember attending the meetings of a retail group acquiring another one in another country, and six out of eight members of the team were financial/legal advisors. When the acquiree sat around the table, too, twelve out of sixteen people were there in some sort of financial capacity.

In another instance, as managing director, sometimes accompanied by our chairman, I had meetings with the CEO and team of a potential acquiree with a presence in Europe, the US and Asia to discuss issues, strategies, synergies and organizational mode. We had come to an agreement on all key issues. Then we made the mistake of sending our finance director to close the deal. A month later, the CEO of the potential acquiree said he did not want to go ahead with the deal, not because the price was too low but because the content of the discussion had been so discouraging in terms of the potential fun of working together that he preferred to stay out of it.

In yet another instance, we had asked our advisor, Lazard, to contact the seller's advisor, Goldman Sachs, to arrange a meeting before the formal negotiation on price to make sure we understood each other beyond numbers, i.e. in terms of the organizational arrangement after the acquisition and other soft issues. The meeting did not take place before price negotiations started.

- The bias of due diligence is the second reason that much pre-acquisition evaluation focuses on figures. Although auditors usually present full-scope missions when asked, they are seldom equipped to evaluate a business beyond numbers, legal, fiscal and accounting risks, for which they provide considerable help. They have a hard time evaluating inconsistencies in the business model because their training, in most cases, is in finance/accounting. Their bias is thus in making the numbers talk rather than the hearts and souls of people (see trap 5 below).

  Take a simple issue: the seller's management team is not keen on being bought, but the company has to be sold, either because it is performing badly and needs investments or because the CEO, founder and some shareholders have decided to cash in their investment. Do you think due diligence will uncover this? Is it important to know about it?

  Take a more complex issue: ambiance and management style. Suppose a company is very top down and political. As a result, the creativity of the rank and file and their willingness to contribute will be poor. Is it important to know about this before deciding to acquire or not to acquire? Will due diligence pick it up? We will come back to this issue later on and see how these soft issues can be identified as part of the pre-acquisition phase.

Implications

- Make sure that the team looking at a potential acquisition is not too biased by numbers. Carefully select the composition of the negotiating team and its power balance and specify their role: to assess, to identify risks, to seduce, to foresee potential issues or to make the deal.
- Use street-smart evaluations to complement due diligence. Do it before due diligence (it could save a lot of fees). Do it by listening to customers, front-line employees and suppliers rather than the 'unanimous voice' of the management team.
- Look at the incentive package of the seller's management team and especially into any package linked to their selling the company to determine how much you can trust their 'commitment to the future'.

2 Bias towards making a deal

Richard Branson, chairman of Virgin, once said: 'Business opportunities are like buses, there's always another one coming.' People do not always take this view with acquisitions, however. All too often there is a push to do a deal for the sake of doing a deal.

First of all, contrary to 'pure' rational decision making where one assesses a number of options – pluses and minuses – against a set of criteria, opportunities for acquisitions rarely come at the same time but rather in sequence – especially big ones. So one acquisition can rarely be compared with another. In his book, *My Journal*, Jean-Marie Messier, former CEO of Vivendi Universal, mentions that because of his bias towards deal making, one of his mistakes was to buy companies that were not core to his grand strategy of becoming a giant in communications. He gives some examples such as 'mp3' and a mobile phone company in Morocco and mentions in passing that this could have saved him €3 billion – a trifle!

Another factor has to do with the frame of decision making. Once the initial discussions between CEOs or board members have taken place and informal agreements have been reached, sometimes – purely on the basis of warm vibes and camaraderie over a good dinner – everyone charges ahead, focusing on how to make it happen rather than asking whether the potential acquiree is really a good candidate or the best match. And, of course, in trying to resolve how to make it happen, everyone becomes more and more creative at finding good reasons for why it should happen.

Lastly, there are the egos of CEOs. Many acquisitions start with informal top-level discussions about the great strategic content fit combined with personality matches. Such conversations often end with statements such as, 'I think this makes sense for both our companies. We should definitely pursue it', or 'We should get together. We have a lot in common. We will crush the competition and really be able to become number one in our market. Let's put a team together to make it work'.

Lastly, there are the egos of CEOs

It is difficult, then, for people who go to the same presidents' conferences, often organized by the same investment bankers, or who go to the same operas or ski resorts, to go back on their word.

Implications

- Since socializing cannot be forbidden, in order to avoid a bias towards making a deal, as many qualitative inputs as possible must be brought into the picture for the assessment – without falling into the trap of being too influenced by numbers, as described earlier.
- In addition, one member of the assessment team should play the role of devil's advocate, using the qualitative inputs to ask why the deal should not happen. It may not be enough to avoid all disasters or to prevent the deal, but perhaps it can help reduce some future risks by including extra provisions or conditions in the deal (for example, an extra guarantee for liabilities; conditional pricing; conditional liquidation of shares by the seller, if paid in shares; partial withholding of the sum agreed; and delaying signature until a specific event happens).

3 Wrong assessment of the acquiree's business model

A business model is a model that describes the key activities a company performs to do business, i.e. generate sales, allocate resources, spend money and make a profit. It also describes, within each activity, the key options chosen for doing business, the key ways in which activities are coordinated and, ultimately, the cost structure used for doing business the way it does.

Thus two companies in the same industry may do business completely differently (i.e. have a different business model) because they have chosen to perform their key tasks differently. This may be because they emphasize a different market segment within the industry or because they insist on a different lever to gain competitive advantage (cost, value, etc.), or because they are at different stages in their life cycle (start-up, growth, maturity, decline) or because their geographic market is different.

Often the acquirer believes that whatever works for it (i.e. its business model) should work for the acquiree, only to discover later on, once the deal has been done and the acquirer's business model has been more or less imposed on the acquiree, that it leads to poor results.

Let us look at a few examples of differences in business models:

- The acquirer's business model is based on using satisfied customers as the number one marketing tool to drive more sales, whereas the acquiree spends more money and resources on acquiring customers. One invests more in product quality and customer service, while the other uses mostly promotional advertising and brand. If two such companies get together, the chances are high that the acquirer will reduce advertising in order to spend more on quality of product and on service. Customers previously attracted by brand and promotional advertising will stop buying and it will take some time to get the other model working. Hence a dip in sales and in profit.
- The acquirer is in a mature, or leading, market, hence it overspends on cost control and customer retention. It acquires a company in the same industry with the same product line, but in a country with high demand and growth – that is, in a lagging market, where the need for a product or service and its fulfilment develops later. The acquirer is highly likely to apply its cost discipline when assessing the acquiree before the deal, thus hoping for increased results through cost reduction – and, of course, once the deal is done, it will send in a bunch of financial controllers, whereas what is really needed is additional funding for growth and marketing investments.
- Even similar activities can hide completely different drivers for business success. Take as an example Adidas, which bought Salomon. For both companies, the new product development activity for sports gear and skis alike is important. However, at Adidas new products must be brought to the shops within a year – the same year as the one in which they are developed – whereas for skis it is more like two years, as the first year is used to test the equipment with the pros. Using Adidas's business model would push Salomon to speed up its new product development too much, resulting in poor market introduction. It took some time and some integration for Adidas to understand these differences – fashion vs.

performance, sponsoring by athletes vs. product testing by ski instructors, fast time to market vs. slow time to market, outsourced production vs. in-house production.

- As a last example, let us take cultural differences (or different ways of doing business) between countries. What happened to Disney in Europe is typical of what happens in many cross-border acquisitions. Disney learned the hard way that what it did in Orlando did not necessarily apply in France (or Europe). For instance, travel agents and other travel intermediaries are important in order to get started in Europe (in the US, they were not so essential to sustaining traffic because Disney was known). In addition, people in Europe eat at certain times (in the US, they tend to graze all day). These two examples illustrate differences in marketing and product offering. Since these factors were not taken into account early on, EuroDisney did not make its numbers. An acquirer needs to change its paradigm to see through the acquiree's business model to avoid disappointments later – not easy when you are the acquirer, i.e. the 'dominant' partner in the deal.

What happened to Disney in Europe is typical of what happens in many cross-border acquisitions

Implications

- Try to describe both business models carefully and highlight where there are major differences:
  - In terms of the marketing emphasis – to attract, satisfy and retain customers –- are resources allocated to the same activity?
  - Are both companies (in their markets) in the same life cycle stage? If different, which levers are most useful for each stage?
  - Is the cost structure (fixed vs. variable) and the percentage of costs allocated to all activities roughly the same or markedly different? If different, what are the reasons? Local variables such as wage costs? The desired competitive advantage is different? Key resources used are different (outsourced vs. in-house)?
  - What are the key drivers of success in each activity for each business model?

4 Seller artificially boosts profits

I have rarely seen a company that is selling (except if in deep trouble or in need of cash) that does not try to embellish the most recent numbers.

'Dressing the bride' always involves taking the view that 'the current year is much better than ever before, as the market has finally understood the "superiority" of our concept, our products or our services and all the marketing, R&D and cost-saving investments have finally paid off (thanks to IT, of course!)'. Usually such a speech is followed – after the acquisition – by a speech that in essence says: 'Although the market continues to recognize our superiority, economic conditions plus the competition's sharp reaction to our fantastic and innovative steps forward last year are such that our sales are flat, even slightly decreasing, and we will not make our profit target.'

Certainly, historical data analysis – the use of mobile averages over several years – can give some perspective on the previous year's extraordinary results, but the seller will usually voice many arguments about the 'changed conditions' over the years that make past comparisons invalid.

So only a very fine analysis of the decisions taken during the preceding 9–12 months can reveal how elegantly the bride has been dressed for the purpose of valuation. Month-by-month/year-on-year tracking of resource allocation, hiring and firing, marketing spend, delayed new projects, postponed product launches, R&D spending cuts and short-term disinvestments in marketing support can give some clues as to how severe the freezes have been in order to maximize short-term profits.

To gain greater insight in this respect, it is important to have feedback from people at all levels of the company. They can highlight what has specifically been requested this year that was not asked for before in terms of freezing projects, cutting back on things that have no short-term impact, expanding short-term gains at the expense of long-term customer relationships (price cuts to boost sales, getting rid of unprofitable customers fast instead of thinking of how to serve them profitably, disposing of inventories, short-term expense cutting, etc.).

A good indication of this type of dressing the bride is to ask whether a new bonus scheme has been put in place in the last 12 months, for whom and with what criteria. It will reveal a lot about the existing mindset of the acquiree's senior management team. The mere fact that such a scheme has been put in place recently means that there is a short-term orientation towards maximizing gain. The criteria chosen can indicate whether

The mere fact that such a scheme has been put in place recently means that there is a short-term orientation towards maximizing gain they are to suit decisions taken recently (for example, the first thing the seller's management will receive after the acquisition is a bonus based on these short-term decisions) or whether they depict a genuine drive for the long-term development of strategic advantage. Of course, I am not referring here to the walk-away package, which by its very nature is short term, but to the 'stay and thrive' package, i.e. what senior management will make if they stay.

Implications

- Make sure you can uncover the short-term decisions taken (ask people, look at specific key resources such as inventory and advertising, and look for recently broken patterns in decision making).
- Ask for copies of internal memos and e-mails during the last few months. Interview non-managerial staff to see whether they have observed recent broken patterns (see below on due diligence).
- Alternatively, suggest that you want to link part of the price of the acquisition to repeating this year's fantastic results next year and see the reactions.
- Also, as part of the deal, renegotiate the existing bonus scheme and see the reaction. If there is a lot of resistance, it probably means the seller's team was in for short-term dressing and they are less dedicated to the long-term strategic advantage of their company.

5 Due diligence is not enough for managerial assessment

As mentioned earlier, due diligence is usually carried out by accounting firms to spot potential legal, tax and financial risks, and to identify inconsistencies in the business model and results presented. However, it rarely uncovers the 'soft issues', such as a company's ability to cope with change, to adapt and mobilize its energies and resources around a new objective, or its willingness to accept new directions, or the amount of energy it will take to redirect, to create enthusiasm. Neither does it uncover where the hidden, soft resources such as ideas, hidden talents and shared knowledge lie.

Relying mostly on interviews with senior management, the soft issues of due diligence that are uncovered are more a reflection of what senior management thinks than of reality. And in the due diligence report, the hard issues (tax risks, financial risks and potential liabilities, operating risks) take up most of the space.

Problems can arise due to the limited scope of due diligence, because it is performed by accountants and lawyers, because it is usually commissioned by the acquirer's financial director, who has a bias for numbers, and because of the speed with which it has to be done in order to 'finish' the deal, as most due diligence is performed after an agreement has already been reached on the key components of the deal.

I have often used a simple tool to uncover the soft issues – even prior to an agreement – which can tell a lot about the culture of the organization, its achievements and its soft strengths and weakness. I call it the 'flash survey' (there is an example in Appendix 6.1 on page 134). The key is not so much to answer the questions correctly as to gather inputs from a representative sample of people who are normally not seriously involved in due diligence – such as front-line employees, first-line supervisors and field managers – and to compare their response with top management's rosy picture of reality.

In order to administer the survey and still keep the potential deal intact, it has, of course, to be presented so that it does not say: 'Company X wants to buy us. Please fill in this questionnaire and send it to them.' Rather, it should say something like: 'We are trying to pause and reflect on the direction we should take in the future. We need your inputs – please be as frank as possible. To this end, we have asked XYZ of the ABC consulting company to send you an e-mail flash survey, which you can send back directly to them for confidentiality.'

If you look at the sample flash survey, you will notice that beyond gathering inputs on ambiance, leadership style and competitive advantage for today and tomorrow, it uncovers the key ingredients of the acquiree's corporate culture: its values and behaviour.

Corporate culture is a very important factor in the success or failure of an acquisition. Although it is not always necessary to merge two cultures when a merger or acquisition is completed, it is often important not to keep the acquiree at arm's length. Stand-alone acquisitions can work under certain conditions (we bring them cash to grow; they know how to use it to develop even faster than before), but often the acquirer's culture takes precedence over the acquiree's or, at best, a mix of both is necessary for successful implementation of the continued strategy.

> Corporate culture is a very important factor in the success or failure of an acquisition

If this is the case, it is quite clear that cultural fit is important, as depicted in Figure 6.1.

Figure 6.1 ◆ Cultural fit

Implications

- Go beyond classical due diligence.
- Industry, fiscal, legal and financial expertise is not enough and can even be misleading. Limiting interviews to management is also restrictive.
- Take the temperature at the front line.

Post-acquisition pitfalls

Once the acquisition has been made, there are other possible factors that may prevent the planned advantage of the acquisition from being fully realized. While it is necessary to recognize that things will not always be perfect, being aware of some of the pitfalls means that something can be done sooner rather than later, before the situation becomes too bad.

I deliberately wrote 'acquisitions' and not 'mergers' because I believe that most mergers end up becoming acquisitions. DaimlerChrysler was a merger – who is calling the shots today? Who was sent to the US from Germany? AOL-Warner was a merger. Who has been calling the shots, AOL or Warner? AOL – for too long, in fact. It is easy to see who will call the shots in a so-called merger of equals: who is mentioned first in the name of the combined company? Is it Daimler or Chrysler? AOL or Warner, Astra or Zeneca, Asea or Brown Boveri, Vivendi or Universal? This leads me to the first pitfall post acquisition.

1 Misunderstanding who is the boss

A lack of clarity about who is the boss may arise for several reasons: perhaps because it was not clearly stated before the acquisition; perhaps because in order to get a deal, the acquirer was too soft in defining roles post acquisition, such as who will decide on strategy, resource allocation and priorities; perhaps because the acquirer misjudged the capabilities of the acquiree's management and thus promised a lot of autonomy; perhaps because after the honeymoon the bride is not as pretty as she seemed at first; perhaps because the deal was initially presented to analysts and the press as a merger rather than an acquisition; or perhaps because being unclear about who would be in charge was the only face-saving way the seller could explain the sale to his teams (to whom for so many years he had said, 'We are the best, we will take on the world alone').

For all these reasons, there is a tendency for the acquiree's top management to refer to the acquirer as 'our partners', 'our colleagues', 'our friends at HQ', but not as 'our new boss'. If everything goes well, things could be okay, but if changes need to be made, there will be a lot of resistance. The safest bet is to fire managers if they do not clearly recognize who is boss and make sure their employees undestand the situation as well. There is little hope of changing the acquiree's behaviour fast enough to influence the course of action if this turns out to be necessary.

Yes, the acquirer is the new boss, and anyone who does not accept it should leave. Even for 'stand-alone' acquisitions, there is always some interference from the acquirer, be it in terms of a common reporting system and procedures, participation in management meetings or resource allocation whereby the acquirer acts as a bank (both supplying funding and taking extra cash from one acquisition and putting it into another company in the group).

Even for 'stand-alone' acquisitions, there is always some interference from the acquirer

Since frictions are bound to develop as additional pressures build up on the business, it is best to make sure from day one that it is understood that the acquirer is the boss. End of story.

I remember a discussion with the CEO of one of the world's biggest sporting goods companies. We were exchanging our experiences on post-acquisition management of the team. In the acquisition we had made (more than 6,000 people in ten countries), we had put together a fairly structured post-acquisition action plan and process that included task forces, visioning exercises and the like. The first part of the process consisted of holding a three-day 'listening meeting' with the acquiree's top management (excluding the owner-entrepreneur who, we had agreed mutually, would not be managing his company any longer). During this meeting, the senior executives took it in turns to tell us of their achievements in their particular area, as well as what they were trying to achieve in the month(s) and year(s) to come.

It was obvious after three days of intensive listening and probing that the management team were not up to the challenge, nor did they live up to the expectations they had led us to have before the sale in order to secure a good price. They also kept referring to us as 'our partners, our partners', giving us the feeling that we were just a bank to finance their development rather than having a management role – setting objectives, directions and expectations for performance.

As I described the situation to the CEO of the sporting goods company, he commented that it was amazingly similar to the situation he was now facing which was causing him headaches. 'We bought a very well-known, large global company. They insisted at the time of sale that their name be added to ours for the combined company. At the time, I thought it was a good idea. But after the acquisition, it was transformed into: "You mind your business, we mind ours and, by the way, I have some not such good news – the numbers we forecast before the acquisition are not going to be achieved, by 20%, because of . . ."'

'As I suggested a few changes we could make, my comments were received with cynical irony, as if I did not know what I was talking about and that it was not my role to say what to do. I had to fire the CEO and some of his team fairly quickly.'

Implications

- Manage expectations before the acquisition/merger by clearly defining who is going to do what and who will be the boss.
- If this must stay a little vague in order to get the deal through, set up expectations fairly early but without brutality. You might lose good people who were 'sold' another idea of their role.
- One way to avoid brutality is to include the team in the normal management processes you have: budget meetings, strategic planning meetings, performance review meetings, executive committee, integrating organization, reporting system.
- If the above suggestions do not work and the situation is not rosy, do not hesitate to change management fairly fast and fairly drastically.

2 Being without a replacement team

However desirable it may be to fire managers who are performing poorly and who do not think that the acquirer can bring any value to the business besides cash, you will still have to replace them. Good managers are a scarce resource. Many companies fail to gain additional value from their acquisition because they cannot find suitable people from within to take over a management team that is exhausted after having struck the deal, that perhaps is mistrusted because the numbers afterwards do not match the numbers announced before, or that may be unable or unwilling to adapt to a new culture or management style.

Things become worse when people start to equate culture with country. The acquiree feels that the acquirer's reactions are typical of the way things are managed 'there' and the acquirer typically thinks those guys are a bunch of . . ., which of course is what has led to the company being sold in the first place.

There are generally two sources of replacement (or complementary) management if needed: the acquirer's pool of talent and the second layer in the acquiree's hierarchy. Of course, if this talent has not been identified soon enough (preferably before the acquisition), you do not have a replacement team. You are stuck with what you have and headhunters will not come up with a miracle solution.

Using the existing pool of talent within the acquirer rests on the following three assumptions:

- **a** There is currently some slack in the organization i.e. too much talent compared to the activity level prior to the acquisition.
- **b** There are potential managers who can readily replace those who are going to be assigned to the acquired company without jeopardizing the acquirer's performance.
- **c** There are dedicated teams ready to go and 'fix' problems at acquired companies.

Companies that have used acquisitions as almost their only mode of development are very used to b and c. As already mentioned, the Danish cleaning services giant ISS has developed mostly through acquisitions in each of its businesses (airports, offices, commercial cleaning) and in each country. It has a tough methodology for assessing potential acquirees, and within two weeks of the acquisition being concluded, a new managing director, a new reporting system and new methods for cleaning are in place.

The ISSes or the Ciscos of this world have a system for assigning talent from their own pools or even have dedicated management teams to move in immediately after the deal because acquisition is their major mode of development. However, for most companies, which will make one to five acquisitions in the tenure of their current CEO (two years to prepare plus three years to digest times three acquisitions equals a tenure of 15 years!), this amount of slack is not readily available without taking a toll on current performance.

Alternatively, there might be a pool of talent inside the acquired company at the level just below the one that must be disposed of. The big issue here is how to spot the right people and assess how much trust they have in the acquirer and vice versa. Their level of trust will not be high when they see their boss go after he convinced them that selling the company was a fantastic opportunity (perhaps they are even a little scared). Or the acquirer may not trust people from the acquiree since, after all, they were part of a team that basically lied about future prospects. What about internal politics? Who is good? Who is simply a good PR? Who has been shut down for a long time but is still full of energy to get going?

There might be a pool of talent inside the acquired company at the level just below the one that must be disposed of

If you do not have an alternative team, you have to live with the existing one. And this could involve a minimum of a year's suffering and earnings per share going down. For this reason, it is advisable to think ahead and identify a potential team before the acquisition is concluded. Be prepared with an alternative managing director to take over or a new financial director to give you the kind of information you want, or a replacement marketing director to boost sluggish sales, an R&D director to get new products out again, a production director to fix the production problems . . .

Implications

- An alternative managerial team must be spotted early in order to replace an underperforming management team in the acquired company. This in turn means that you must be sure that seconds-in-command can replace those you will have to appoint at fairly short notice.
- If not, you will have to pool your functions with the seller's organization or part of it so that it can report to one of your existing senior executives. For example, R&D for acquirer and acquiree can be combined under the supervision of the buyer's head of R&D or sourcing activities can be integrated. Similarly, functions such as treasury, accounting and IT can be shared. Of course, this is made easier if product, marketing and distribution channels are related.

3 Being impatient

Because the talent is not always available at the right moment and in the right place, or because organizational integration is difficult to achieve, there is often a period of turmoil ahead. A lack of patience can lead to disasters; taking time and ensuring good timing can lead to satisfactory results. Several issues call for patience, for example:

- The acquirer's top management needs to spend more time than expected on the acquiree to fix the people issue as well as the problems that emerge after the acquisition.
- Learning each other's culture takes time.
- By the time you realize that a team (or part of it) must be replaced or that internal systems need to be replaced, time will have elapsed, results will be poor. It will take time to catch up on projects and on cash flow.
- Getting the synergies working also takes time.

Things do not happen overnight. One of the biggest pitfalls post acquisition is underestimating the amount of time it takes to get things done. Yet most people argue that acquiring a company is a faster way to enter a new market, new country and new activity than developing it from scratch. Yes, it is true on paper. Instantly, your company is in two activities instead of one, in several additional countries. However, it may stay only on paper for a long time before any results are achieved.

If top management has to devote time to the new acquisition, this reduces the available time for the existing business. Can they afford it? Who will hold the fort? Are the people in the existing business autonomous enough to take charge or will this management void create a bottleneck in the existing business by delaying necessary decisions? Is it more advisable to acquire smaller companies (small compared with the acquirer) to avoid total immersion of key top people in case of trouble?

Learning each other's methods is also time consuming. People have to meet, understand the current practice, get the best of both worlds, agree on new operating principles.

In one acquisition in which I was involved, pooling of raw material purchases was identified as a key source of benefits (synergy) in the deal. It took time for people to see what was common or different in what they bought; what their commercial terms were like; how each of the logistics chains and ordering systems worked; what could be supplied together; testing the new system – and rejecting it (especially the acquiree, which felt its local needs were not taken into consideration enough, etc.). All of this took almost three years. Yet at the shareholders' meeting which approved the acquisition, earnings per share looked as if they would reach pre-dilution levels in the first year, thanks to 'quasi-immediate improvement' of the gross margin.

The same goes for understanding each other's culture, not just for the sake of understanding but for the sake of working together, of avoiding mistrust and blaming the other party, of not missing opportunities for cooperation.

One of the reasons for the length of time it takes to absorb an acquisition has to do with the control/reporting system. Before the acquisition, whenever the lawyer asks for a number, he gets it, for a very simple reason – everything has been prepared for the sale. After the acquisition, things do not go as smoothly. The numbers obtained before are not part of the ongoing information system. It takes time to link, develop and reshape the system so that the data requested can be given on an ongoing basis.

One of the reasons for the length of time it takes to absorb an acquisition has to do with the control/reporting system

A few years ago I was asked to audit the management capabilities of a bank which was the result of a merger of two banks. I asked why after seven years they still did not have the same name, the same processes, even the same branding. They told me it was too early. Another year was needed to avoid loss of power, discouraging the teams, mixing systems and procedures. Without going to the extremes of this bank, let's look at the calendar set up by a retail group to forge a common culture in their stores after acquisition.

- **Month 1, 2**: Get a sociologist to take a snapshot of the two cultures. What is common, what is different, where can both agree on common values?
- **Month 3**: Seminar of top management and regional managers to get feedback on the study.
- **Month 3 to 6**: Invitation from the managers in each country to other managers to understand how the others work.
- **Month 7**: Seminar of regional and top managers of the acquiree to present the values and core philosophy of the acquirer, obtain their reactions, adapt and formalize.
- **Month 8 to 12**: Induction programme for all the acquiree's store managers to share the values.
- **Month 8 to 12**: In parallel, prepare some actions for year two to move closer to desired behaviour.

- **Month 12 to 16**: Change 50% of regional and 30% of store managers who in day-to-day operations have not adapted their behaviour. Reinduction of new hires.
- **Month 18**: 'Show, share and learn' seminar on each other's best practices.
- **Month 12 to 24**: In parallel, pilot programmes in country of acquiree to show that it works to use the best practices of the acquirer.
- **Month 18 to 24**: Preparation of three-year plan, with mixed teams of managers taking into account the best practices shown.
- **Month 24 to 36**: First concrete results of shift of paradigm.

Exploiting synergies also takes time. We often talk about start-up synergies and ongoing operating synergies. Start-up synergies have to do with what the combined company can achieve almost instantly: for instance, the buyer has cash, the seller needs cash; the buyer has a new technology, the seller needs it; the buyer has an unexploited brand, the seller needs a new one. However, if these start-up synergies are so obvious and fast to achieve, they have already been taken into account in the price of the company being acquired.

So, most synergies that are relative are the operational ones, i.e. those that will be achieved after the acquisition is made, whether by eliminating duplication of effort (administration, marketing, R&D) or of resources (production, logistics) or by creating economies of scale (buying power). And this does not happen overnight . . . except on paper. Yes, you will see beautiful numbers: X% over margin in buying, elimination of Y factories, one sales force, etc . . . Then, after the acquisition has been done, the real work starts. How much do we each buy from each supplier? Who is going to see them and negotiate? Who is going to decide which raw material to suppress (i.e. who is the new boss in purchasing, how much risk is he willing to take to minimize loss of quality and keep existing reliability of supply, certainty of quantities, etc.?)? Again two to three years may be necessary. In DaimlerChrysler, for instance, they were talking, more than three years after the deal, of having been able to achieve 36 synergy projects out of 50 initially proposed; 28 components had already been bought in common. But go back to the time just after the acquisition. Hell came down on the CEO who promised more profits instantly.

Implications

- Do not show shareholders or analysts an (optimistic) indication of results beyond adding together the two existing profits (and this is already risky) before year three.
- Be prepared to reallocate top management's time to handle potential crisis situations.
- Expect the unexpected in terms of information. Have a spare controller ready to be assigned to the acquired company to get the information the way you want it, when you want it.
- Expect to let 50% or more of management go within the first 18 months if you want cultural integration.

In this chapter we have looked at some of the pitfalls in acquisitions that are not linked specifically to strategy but more to execution, to people issues, to soft issues.

As the saying goes: 'Forewarned is forearmed.' Hope it helps.

Appendix 6.1 Flash survey

1. Describe in three words where Company Y was three years ago.
2. Identify three major accomplishments the company has achieved during the last three years.
3. Determine the three major current strengths of Company Y.
4. Identify three major shortcomings (weaknesses).
5. Characterize in two words the working climate at Company Y.
6. Characterize in two words the management style at Company Y.
7. What values (beliefs) are currently promoted at Company Y?
8. What is your biggest concern today?
9. What excites you most?
10. Describe where Company Y should be tomorrow (in three years) using inspiring words. (What is your dream, with a deadline, for Company Y?)
11. List three key ways Company Y can achieve this dream.
12. Identify five behaviours that must be present to promote the success of this dream.
13. What new values should be particularly developed at Company Y?

Part Three

Key capabilities for M&A success

7

Challenges of governance structures in international mergers and acquisitions

By

Ulrich Steger and Christopher Kummer

AS A RESULT OF THE collapse of some large companies and other scandals, corporate governance has been very much in the news lately. But the issue is far from being new. Therefore we will first describe the key issues of corporate governance, including national differences and the latest trends. Then we will take a look at the dual role corporate governance plays in respect of mergers and acquisitions: on the one hand, it eases or impedes the transaction; on the other hand, it sets critical conditions for the implementation of the integration process. To highlight the role of corporate governance in global M&A, we will conclude with the example of the DaimlerChrysler merger.

Corporate governance issues

Corporate governance is about the allocation of power, assignment of responsibility and consideration of interests by various legal and organizational control mechanisms within the company; it is to a company what a constitution is to a country. In most cases it should ensure that companies are run according to the shareholders' interest. The governance of small and medium-sized companies is less complicated because they are usually managed and owned by founders or families, or they are more transparent. However, the evolution of modern, large corporations and the rise of elaborate management methods led to the separation of ownership and management.[1] With this separation, the question of corporate governance became critical:

how could owners influence and control the company in their interests when professional managers actually ran the company?

Management of large corporations is usually chosen on merit and experience, not according to former succession mechanisms such as family ties or marriage. When companies are seen as a nexus of written and unwritten contracts, contracts made between the company and its managers are necessarily incomplete, as they cannot foresee every eventuality.[2] In addition, there is information asymmetry: the managers have more comprehensive and up-to-date information than the external owners. Managers should behave as shareholders' agents, but their interests might be divergent.[3] Therefore corporate governance should guarantee, through a variety of external and internal control and steering systems such as shareholder meetings, the board of directors or reporting rules, that managers work in the owners' interests. These systems are not without their disadvantages, but the benefits should outweigh the costs.

Management of large corporations is usually chosen on merit and experience, not according to former succession mechanisms such as family ties or marriage

Usually the ultimate power should come from shareholder meetings. Shareholders elect the members of the board of directors. These directors should be responsible for the selection and continuous evaluation of top management. They should also set and control the strategic direction and ensure compliance and transparency.[4] In order to realize this strategic direction, the company might pursue M&A activities, for example, when it wants to acquire new technologies or capabilities and pursue 'pearls on a string' acquisitions.[5] The size of the board determines whether discussions can be held effectively and decisions can be made. The composition of the board should to some extent be diverse. Members should have different qualifications, experiences, perspectives and backgrounds, and there should be a range of generations. In general, all the questions relating to group phenomena and teamwork arise when putting together a board.

When problems with corporate governance issues become obvious – as currently – most people call for simple solutions, such as the appointment of so-called independent directors, as the cure-all.[6] They are not managers of the company, nor do they have a direct business relationship with it, and they usually come from business and academic communities. They often have a reputation to lose, so their sense of responsibility should be quite high. Sometimes there are also age restrictions and a mandatory retirement age for board members. On the one hand, this restriction might be outdated because of demographic shifts and the fitness of elderly people caused by economic progress

Northumbria University
Academic Services
University Library
City Campus
Items borrowed

Title: Managing complex mergers : real world lessons in implementing successful cro
ID: 2005211370
Due: 03/09/2015 23:59

Total items: 1
6/08/2015 16:12

Please keep your receipt as a record of when your books are due for return.
http://capitadiscovery.co.uk/northumbria-ac/
Follow us on Twitter @NULibrary

and improved health. On the other hand, boards seem to have few young people, who could provide an interesting perspective.

The frequency of board meetings also determines to some degree how closely the members can watch the development of the company. In theory, the board leads the company, but in practice the balance between directors and management varies widely. And there is always some leadership from 'bottom to top' – the management can decide what information it gives to the board, how to frame issues and set the agenda. A 2002 IMD survey[7] showed that in more than 70% of responding companies, strategy proposals were presented by the CEO!

An important way to align the interests of owners and management is to have a corresponding compensation scheme. But its design poses many difficulties, above all the question of evaluation. Although it is possible to measure managers' results and hold the CEO/management board accountable, the situation is different with the board, whose members have a more indirect role. In general, board members are rarely evaluated individually. When their performance seems lacking, they are dismissed or simply not re-elected. The underlying question is how much impact the board, the management and especially the CEO really have on the success or failure of the company – especially on the outcome of M&A activities. It is not always clear which things they can influence and which are beyond their control. Human nature is such that success is deemed to be the result of one's own hard work, whereas failures are the fault of the environment and chance.

The time dimension, in particular, has to be taken into account when it comes to compensation because there is a time lag between action and results. Stock options are therefore quite popular for rewarding long-term achievements. However, there should always be a clear and ambitious benchmark for performance. In some cases, management is rewarded when the share price rises a few percent in absolute terms, even when the overall market is performing better than the company. Thus share price developments should be viewed in relation to industry indices or even the share prices of the company's most important competitors. In general, M&A is a way to influence the share price.

There should always be a clear and ambitious benchmark for performance

Board membership is not a full-time occupation, although there is now a clear trend towards having a full-time chairman. The responsibility and accountability of board members is also increasing drastically.[8] Being accountable to shareholders calls for more transparency, which puts more pressure on the board to ensure performance. Yet in order to reach a high degree of transparency, information disclosure is necessary. However, there is a need to balance this with a certain secrecy that is necessary for business reasons.

Only unexpected changes in the business, strategy or organization can influence the share price because existing plans and their outlook have theoretically already been taken into account when calculating shareholder value. M&A is a particularly fast way to make such changes happen. But information that is publicly available will be read not only by investors but also by competitors, as a potential source of competitive intelligence. In addition, information that is given, filed or released is subject to litigation by shareholders. Nowadays, however, shareholder management is only part of the story on corporate governance. Whereas the American/Anglo-Saxon version of corporate governance puts the emphasis on the shareholder issue, the Continental European version understands management much more as a custodian that has to take various stakeholders into account, a view that seems to be increasingly popular in the US, too – some 11% of Anglo-Saxon companies (vs. 3% of Continental European firms) report having a sustainability committee on the board.

Corporate governance models[9]

Corporate governance principles, norms and legal requirements vary significantly from one country to another and from one company to another. Recently all kinds of codes have become quite fashionable, in order to try to set minimum standards for organization (e.g. committees) or transparency through disclosure. International companies that have to meet these requirements should already be familiar, to some extent, with differences in national systems from their various foreign subsidiaries. The differences are the result of specific company laws that require different systems depending on the company's legal form and size; the working of a company, however, does not depend on the legal framework. These laws are often influenced by economic development and various crises such as stock market crashes or other scandals. But a company's corporate governance structure, power allocation and effective control are determined more by its growth history, ownership structure and personalities. In the past, banks in Germany and Japan owned significant stakes in companies and large cross-holdings between companies existed. In the US, by contrast, commercial banks were not allowed to make large investments in non-banking companies. Therefore ownership influence varies: whereas banks tend to be 'captive', individual shareholders can exit more easily. Professional institutional investors, in particular, can put badly managed companies under severe pressure.

Whatever corporate governance is required by legal systems in theory, there are different ways of putting it into practice. There needs to be a 'fit' between corporate governance, on the one hand, and strategy and business environment on the other. So there is no definite right or wrong when it comes to corporate governance structures, but only a match to a greater or lesser extent. Problems occur when there is a mismatch or imbalance between these components, for instance when large investors are not represented on the board of directors. Hence, corporate governance practice is determined by personalities, capital markets, rules and laws, and business model and strategy. But a corporate governance system is by no means a substitute for a sophisticated corporate strategy with detailed content – structure *per se* cannot compensate for a lack of content. In particular, financial management styles cannot replace strategic considerations.

There needs to be a 'fit' between corporate governance, on the one hand, and strategy and business environment on the other

In general, we see the following corporate governance models: owner-dominated, consensus-orientated, checks-and-balances, and CEO-centred (see Figure 7.1). These models can be categorized in terms of the balance between shareholders and management.

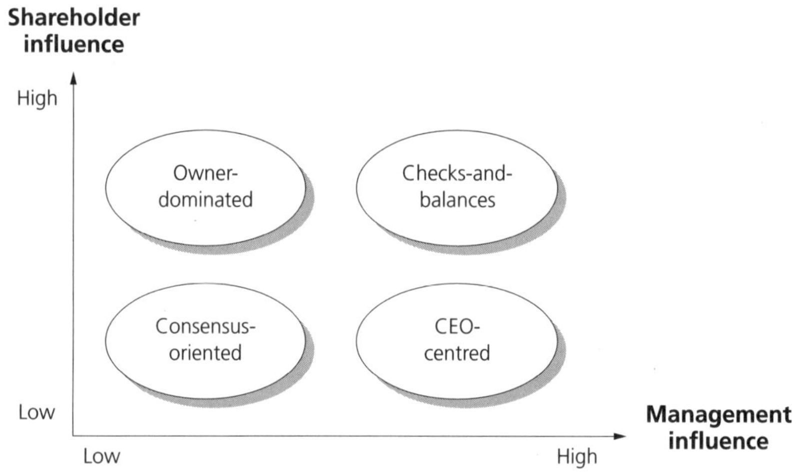

Figure 7.1 ◆ Corporate governance models

- The CEO-centred model is often found in the US – where the role is still frequently combined with that of the chairman of the board – and in France. Here the president/*directeur-général* plays a dominant role, regardless of whether the company has a unitary board structure (with a single administrative board/*conseil d'administration*) or a two-tier structure (with executive committee/*directoire* and supervisory board/*conseil de surveillance*). It allows for quick decisions but tends to be a system with few checks and balances: not many CEOs allow a strong board that can challenge – or even stop – him or her and control the risk of often bold actions.
- The checks-and-balances model is found not only in Germany in two-tier boards (i.e. executive and supervisory) but also in the UK, where the non-executive chairman and the majority of the independent directors define the boundaries within which the CEO and top management team can operate. (For example, at BP in 2002 the unitary board had 11 non-executive and 4 executive members.) In this model, the non-executive directors are also often in charge of evaluating the CEO (and management board) systematically and periodically, as well as initiating the succession of a CEO.
- In the owner-dominated model, a big shareholder or – in privately held companies – the family pull the strings on important issues. The involvement in day-to-day business can vary. The US investor-guru Warren Buffett and the Quandt family at BMW are famous for having instilled in managers the need to have uppermost in their minds the pertinent question: what does our owner think? The Ford family always steps in when things get tough. Others, such as the tycoon-turned-prime-minister Silvio Berlusconi, are known for occasionally becoming embroiled in business details.
- The consensus-orientated model looks at other stakeholders of a company, such as banks, suppliers and customers. Although closer relationships facilitate access to funding and the possibility of a longer-term view, this model is slow when it comes to decision making. The relationship is often also built on a system of cross-shareholdings, a circumstance that international investors in Germany, for example, have long criticized for its lack of transparency. It is also typical in the 'old-boy network' dominated segments of society – typically in emergent markets – where relations of trust, sometimes pushed by societal expectations (e.g. in Asia, inviting important stakeholders on to the board), are still more important than the newly evolving capitalist institutions.

In our survey the majority of companies considered themselves in the checks-and-balances category (see Figure 7.2 for an overview). However, as already mentioned, there is no right or wrong, no superior or inferior model; each is a self-contained corporate governance system, with distinctive strengths but also weaknesses. For example, the checks-and-balances model is most effective in CEO selection and control but often lacks strategic input; in the CEO-centred model it could be the other way around – here quick decision making and strategy implementation are promoted. The suitability of one of these four models to a particular company may therefore change over time, depending on the stage in the company's life cycle and its particular business environment.

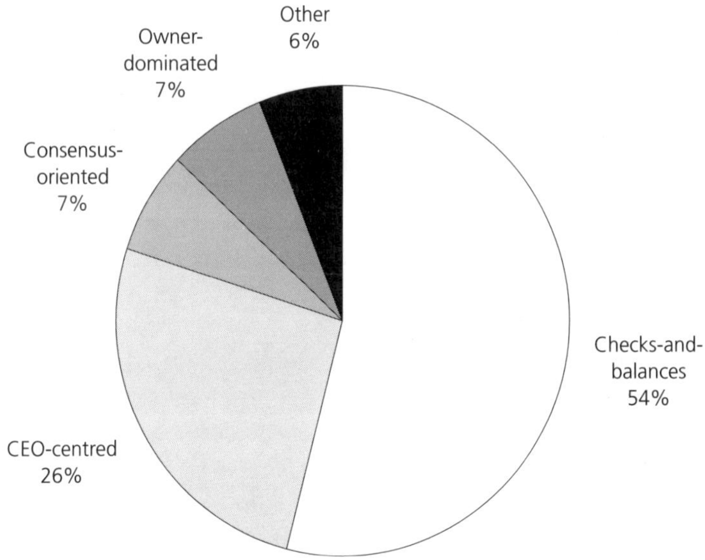

Figure 7.2 ◆ Classification of survey respondents

A company may change the model if the business situation requires it. In one instance, a company changed from a checks-and-balances model – with a separate chairman and CEO, and both an executive and a supervisory board – to a CEO-centred model with a unitary structure when it started to pursue an ambitious M&A growth strategy in a consolidating industry. The need for quick decision making and swift implementation and monitoring of the chosen strategy was better met by the new system with a

> **The fit between company, strategy and corporate governance model is decisive for successful performance**

CEO at the helm who was also an industry insider. The fit between company, strategy and corporate governance model is decisive for successful performance. Whichever corporate governance model prevails, corporate governance plays a central role in the context of M&A.

Corporate governance in the context of mergers and acquisitions

In M&A, corporate governance can play a dual role. On the one hand it can influence the ease with which these transactions are initiated or highlight the barriers. On the other hand, it sets critical conditions for the implementation of the post-M&A integration process and the way the expected benefits are reaped or not.

First of all the 'market of corporate control' keeps badly governed companies in check because companies with inferior corporate governance become potential targets. Potential acquirers see that value creation can easily be realized through the introduction and practice of better corporate governance, and the financial markets' trust can be restored. In effect, the threat of M&A is an effective external control mechanism of management and forces a certain level of corporate governance.

When the board of directors sets the strategic direction of the company, it also implicitly or explicitly decides to some extent about M&A strategies to be pursued by the company. Some strategic goals cannot be realized by organic growth. When shareholders' interests are the primary focus – as in the US style of corporate governance – management must realize every deal that is promising for shareholders (even selling the company, knowing that they will probably lose their jobs). They have to initiate and pursue M&A activities when shareholder value can be created. But they also have to accept takeover offers and refrain from defensive tactics when the share-price premium for the owner is intriguing. Most premiums paid in M&A transactions seem to overestimate advantages, so almost all of the potential value created goes to the target's shareholders. In terms of the success or failure of M&A transactions, the target's shareholders are mostly on the safe side. They gain from a shareholder value point of view because the acquirer pays a premium. In such a situation, it is the task of the board to negotiate a high premium, demanding a share of potential synergies and advantages that the acquirer can realize from the deal. Examples abound, especially in investment banking, telecoms and dot.coms, where acquisitions were clearly overpriced.

However, a board can also reject an offer because it believes in the superiority of its concept (as, for example, in the Mannesmann–Vodafone battle, which was a contest between pure mobile and fixed-net-based telecom strategies). Then it can employ defensive tactics, including looking for a white knight, i.e. another, more suitable acquirer, or installing golden parachutes, i.e. huge payments for management when major changes in ownership occur. However, there are also legal restrictions on the means the board can use. US management does not have to consider what will happen afterwards, as long as shareholder value has been realized; in Europe, corporate governance takes the various stakeholders' interests much more into account, so M&A transactions are much more difficult to realize. This is the difference in theory; in practice, however, boundaries are blurred.

The board of directors has the ultimate responsibility for the company, so therefore its approval is needed for a step as massive as M&A. For major decisions, the shareholder meeting sometimes also decides about these transactions.

M&A transactions can be initiated by each group involved in corporate governance. Owners might consolidate their existing investments in one industry or simply invite management to evaluate the strategic options of M&A activities. The board of directors can conclude from the strategy process that the search for suitable M&A candidates is necessary in order to reach the goals set. Last, but not least, management might approach the board with M&A proposals, sometimes based on pitching by investment bankers.

M&A can help in initiating drastic change management programmes. Such events unfreeze the organization and lift possible inertia. Whole corporate governance traditions and company cultures can be overturned. Many choices about corporate governance are made implicitly, they have evolved over time, or they were made long ago and are outdated. M&A is the opportunity to make huge changes and explicitly choose and shape a new corporate governance system.

> M&A is the opportunity to make huge changes and explicitly choose and shape a new corporate governance system

Corporate governance influences how well the post-merger integration is handled, hence it hinders or supports the reaping of the benefits from M&A. When merging partners have similar corporate governance systems, problems are far smaller than when totally different systems collide. For instance, differences in compensation and reward can sow the seeds of discord. These systems must be changed to be compatible and, in particular, must take into account M&A efforts and results. Transparency is an important factor during the integration process – there is the need to calculate and show synergies, to inform the public about the progress of the integration. So corporate governance is also responsible for the outcome of M&A transactions.

Corporate governance in the United States and Germany

We do not intend to discuss the corporate governance issues and models of the United States and Germany in detail. Rather, we focus on some important features with respect to the merger of Daimler-Benz AG and Chrysler Corporation, which we present as a case study later on. In both countries, the ultimate power for essential and far-reaching decisions lies with the shareholder meeting.

In the United States, corporations are typically run by a so-called unitary board. Hence the board is composed of executive and non-executive board members. The same person often holds the position of chairman of the board and chief executive. US board members are elected by the shareholders annually. Boards meet rather frequently, indicating that they are quite close to what is going on in the company.

In Germany, corporations are governed by a two-tier board system, consisting of management (*Vorstand*) and the supervisory board (*Aufsichtsrat*). No one is allowed to be a member of both boards. The management board is responsible for the day-to-day operations of the company. Corporations with a paid-in capital of more than $3 million require at least two members on the board of management. Management board members' contracts usually run for up to five years. The supervisory board was originally conceived as an institution that was supposed to appoint and control management. As a consequence, members of the supervisory board are not allowed to take part in the running of the business. The company may, however, stipulate in its bylaws that the supervisory board has the right and duty to approve certain categories of management decisions with far-reaching consequences, including, among other things, major acquisitions.

Another important feature of the German board system is the German Co-Determination Act. Half of the members of the supervisory board are elected by the shareholders and half represent the employees. At their annual meeting, shareholders elect members to the supervisory board for the capital side for a period of five years. All employee representatives are voted in by employees – but only German employees are allowed to vote. This discrimination against international employees causes trouble in cross-border mergers in particular. The law stipulates a carefully balanced split between the representatives for blue- and white-collar employees of the company, and it also requires one representative of senior management who is not a board member. As a special twist, the Co-Determination Act also requires that in corporations above a certain size, at least three employee representatives must be delegated to the supervisory board by the industry union. The chairman, who always comes from the capital side, has a casting vote (double vote) should a stalemate arise as a result of the fifty-fifty parity between representatives of the employees and of the capital side.

In accordance with German law, an employees' representative has to be vice-chairman. Besides workers' representation on the supervisory board, a second channel of co-determination exists at the management level, namely the system of works councils. Some observers feel that for practical matters the influence of employees through works councils is much more effective than through supervisory board representation. The chairmen of works councils typically wield great influence and are accordingly courted by management. They are also frequently elected to the supervisory board as employee representatives. In order to make the works council system effective, large companies have to provide fully paid absences for some of the council members. This allows the council to play its role *vis-à-vis* management effectively and to discuss human resource issues. Moreover, some management measures have to be approved by the works councils, such as output-related pay rates, pay structures, hiring and changes in pay. If management and works councils disagree, management can either change its proposal or take it first to an arbitration court and then to the labour court. Although this may sound rather stringent to an outsider, German managers believe that works councils are more flexible than unions.

The chairmen of works councils typically wield great influence and are accordingly courted by management

Case Study: The DaimlerChrysler Merger

The DaimlerChrysler merger is a good 'lead case'[10] for corporate governance issues in the context of M&A because this cross-border deal allows the comparison of two different corporate governance systems and their implications for M&A.

The Daimler perspective

The main architects of the DaimlerChrysler merger were the CEOs – Jürgen E. Schrempp of Daimler-Benz AG and Robert Eaton of Chrysler Corporation. As early as 1995, both firms had evaluated the possibility of establishing a joint venture, codenamed 'Q-Star', to market cars outside their home markets in Europe and the United States. But neither company could agree on personnel and financial issues, so the deal did not go ahead. The same year, Schrempp took over as CEO of Daimler-Benz and implemented a number of far-reaching changes. He saw himself as a protagonist for shareholder value and initiated a cultural change programme to make the employees pay more attention to profitability. The company also sold or liquidated 12 of its unprofitable or non-core subsidiaries. The rather spectacular turnaround substantially strengthened Schrempp's position in the company and *vis-à-vis* the board.

But further consolidation in the automotive industry was inevitable. Although it was the most profitable company in the industry, company growth was limited by the passenger car division, which basically had only one brand – Mercedes-Benz – in the premium sector (this brand was also used for commercial vehicles). So in 1997, in addition to internal strategic studies, Schrempp commissioned a study by an investment bank of ways to remedy the weaknesses of Daimler-Benz. The investment bankers suggested Chrysler and Honda Motors as potential complementary partners based on their product mix and geographic coverage. Since Honda was not considering relinquishing its independence, Schrempp pushed the idea of joining forces with Chrysler.

The investment bankers suggested Chrysler and Honda Motors as potential complementary partners based on their product mix and geographic coverage

From the previous abortive round of discussions, Schrempp had got the distinct impression that Chrysler, as the smallest of the 'Big 3' automakers, was also worried about its size relative to the Big 2, General Motors and Ford. During the North American International Auto Show in Detroit in January 1998, Schrempp approached Eaton with a quite different proposal. In a meeting that lasted only 17 minutes, he proposed a full-fledged merger. The combined company would be the fifth largest automaker in the world, with $132 billion in annual sales. Eaton, who had obviously done similar calculations, promised to let Schrempp know his reaction to the idea within a few weeks. Only a few days after this initial meeting, Eaton called and expressed his interest in further talks about a possible merger.

To avoid any leaks, negotiations were conducted in the strictest secrecy and only a very limited number of people from each company were involved. These few 'insiders' met on February 12 and discussed the state of the industry, as well as possible synergies – identified in R&D, purchasing and manufacturing – that might result from the merger. At the same time, Ford approached Daimler-Benz regarding closer cooperation. Members of the management board met in London with Ford executives to discuss the idea of a possible merger. Ford was trying to expand its share of the premium market, but it later withdrew from the proposed merger because of the veto of the Ford family. However, at this point, the merger talks with Chrysler were quite far along anyway.

External advisers were brought in early as well. On February 17 and 18, investment bankers and corporate lawyers on both sides were included in the meetings, at which various tax, corporate and management issues were discussed. Both parties agreed on the importance of maximizing shareholder value and finding a tax-efficient solution. The post-merger structure should be a merger of equals, which was essential for saving tax on goodwill.

The Geneva Auto Show in early March 1998 was a good opportunity to meet again. Because secrecy was still a major issue, they met in neighbouring Lausanne. The small circle of top executives looked at corporate governance and organizational structures. It soon became clear that, in order to avoid massive tax bills, locating the merged company in Germany was the only option for Chrysler's American and Daimler-Benz's German shareholders. At this time also, a limited number of small working teams were established to work on key issues during March.

On April 7, the management board held its regular weekly meeting and all members were informed about what had been happening over the past few months. At that point, however, the board made no formal decision on the merger. Moreover, Schrempp explained that he had seen a study evaluating the success of attempted mergers, which revealed that total secrecy was essential. At a meeting of Daimler-Benz's management board on April 19, an extensive round of discussions took place. On May 3, it met again and unanimously approved the merger.

Schrempp explained that he had seen a study evaluating the success of attempted mergers, which revealed that total secrecy was essential

Daimler-Benz's supervisory board (see Figures 7.3 and 7.4) normally met only five times a year, but in 1998 it held 11 meetings.

Capital side	**Hilmar Kopper** ***Chairman of supervisory board of Daimler-Benz AG*** Additional board seats: Deutsche Bank AG (Chairman), Mannesmann UI AG (Chairman), Bayer AG, Akzo Nobel NV, Solvay SA, Unilever, Xerox USA	**Martin Kohlhaussen** ***Chairman of management board of Commerzbank AG*** Additional board seats: GKN Automotive International GmbH (Chairman), Bayer AG, Bertelsmann AG, Hochtief AG, Karstadt AG, Schering AG, Winterthur Swiss Insurance
	Birgit Breuel ***Commissioner of World Exhibition EXPO 2000*** Additional board seats: Gruner + Jahr AG, Novartis AG, J.P. Morgan GmbH	**Jean-Marie Messier** ***Director of Compagnie Générale des Eaux*** Additional board seats: Compagnie de Saint-Gobin, LVMH, Srafor Facom, Hava, Canal+, UGC
	John P. Browne ***Group CEO of British Petroleum plc (BP)*** Additional board seats: SmithKline Beecham, Intel Corporation (both non-executive)	**Manfred Schneider** ***Chairman of management board of Bayer AG*** Additional board seats: Allianz AG, Metro AG, RWE AG
	Michael Endres ***Member of the management board of Deutsche Bank AG*** Additional board seats: Deutz AG (Chairman), Heidelberger Printing, Mannesmann ARCOR	**Bernard Walter** ***Chairman of management board of Dresdner Bank AG*** Additional board seats: Degussa AG, Fresenius Medical Care AG, Rheinmetall AG, Rütgers AG, Thyssen AG
	Ulrich Hartmann ***Chairman of management board of VEBA AG*** Additional board seats: Degussa AG (Chairman), Munich RE Insurance (Chairman), RAG AG (Chairman), Hochtief AG, IKB Deutsche Industriebank AG, Henkel KgaA	**Mark Wössner** ***Chairman of management board of Berteslmann AG*** Additional board seats: Gruner + Jahr AG

Figure 7.3 ◆ Capital side of supervisory board of Daimler-Benz AG (1998)

The chairman of the supervisory board, Hilmar Kopper, was officially first informed about the discussions on April 16. He was the former CEO and chairman of Deutsche Bank which, with a stake of 22%, was Daimler-Benz's largest shareholder. Although these details have not been disclosed publicly, it

Employee representation		
	Karl Feuerstein Chairman of the European Daimler-Benz works council	**Helmut Lense** Chairman of the Works Council at the Unterürkheim passenger car plant
	Willi Böhm Member of the Works Council at the truck plant in Wörth	**Walter Riester** Vice President of IG Metall Union
	Manfred Göbels Head of Truck Sales, White Collar Representative	**Manfred Göbels** Chairman of Works Council at Debis AG
	Erich Klemm Chairman of the Works Council at the Sindelfingen plant	**Peter Schönfelder** Member of the Works Council at Daimler-Benz Aeorospace
	Rudolf Kuda Member of the IG Metall Union	**Bernard Wurl** Member of the IG Metall Union

Figure 7.4 ◆ Employee representation on supervisory board of Daimler-Benz AG (1998)

can safely be assumed that Schrempp had revealed general considerations of a merger to Kopper much earlier because the two of them met much more frequently than the supervisory board. On May 4, Schrempp informed Karl Feuerstein (chairman of the European Daimler-Benz works council and member of the supervisory board). Since the merger would not lead to any job losses and the logic behind the merger made sense to Feuerstein, he agreed to the plans. With the leading figures of both benches of the supervisory board – capital side and employee representation – in agreement, Schrempp did not expect much opposition from the other board members. On May 6, the day *The Wall Street Journal* reported on a potential merger between Daimler and Chrysler, the supervisory board met in Stuttgart and was informed of the deal. This meeting did not include a vote but rather a discussion of the reasons behind the move. The actual vote took place on May 14, a week after the deal had been officially announced on May 7.

The Chrysler perspective

With respect to the ownership of the firm, Chrysler had regularly been put under tremendous financial pressure by Kirk Kerkorian, a self-made US billionaire. In 1995, he had even embarked on a bitter takeover battle with the help of Lee Iacocca, the former Chrysler chairman. He later withdrew his bid, but increased his stake to 13.6% of equity. Moreover, Kerkorian constantly fought to increase the maximum limit of equity a Chrysler shareholder could hold – first to 15% and later to 20%. Eaton was strongly opposed to this and publicly accused Tracinda, Kerkorian's investment company, of trying to obtain 'creeping control'.[11] James D. Aljian, a Tracinda executive, represented Kerkorian's views on the Chrysler board. Financial intermediaries increased their influence as well. In order to raise earnings per share, Chrysler started a share buy-back programme. Between 1995 and 1997, Chrysler spent $5.2 billion on repurchasing roughly 22% of outstanding stock. In 1997, the dividend yield on common stock reached 4.5%, equivalent to three times the average for Standard & Poor's (S&P) stocks. Information dissemination to shareholders was considered among the best in the US. As Eaton stated: 'Chrysler is one of the most shareholder-friendly companies in America.'[12]

The Chrysler Corporation board was quite typical of a US corporation. Eaton was chairman of the board as well as chief executive officer. Another executive officer was Robert A. Lutz. In addition, there were ten non-executive directors, from industry and finance. Many of the companies they came from were household names in US business (see Figure 7.5). In a litigious society such as the US, board members are under substantial threat of being sued by shareholders for any wrongdoings on the board. Therefore they are usually particularly careful in handling business and maintain strict confidentiality – a breach of confidentiality or a leak of business information will trigger much more severe sanctions on US board members than on those in any other country.

The Chrysler Corporation board was quite typical of a US corporation

Boards in the United States meet relatively frequently. In 1997, the Chrysler board held 15 meetings (down from 18 in 1996). Eaton informed his board about the merger talks with Daimler-Benz roughly a week after confirming his interest to Schrempp. Thereafter, the Chrysler board was regularly updated on the progress of the talks. The April 7 meeting, when they decided that DaimlerChrysler would be incorporated in Germany, was of particular relevance. After another update on May 5 and 6 with investment bankers and lawyers present, the Chrysler board unanimously approved the merger plans. This meant the green light for the merger from the US side – provided that Chrysler's shareholders also agreed.

Chrysler board

Lilyan Affinito (1982) ***Former President of Maxxam Group Inc.*** Additional board seats: Caterpillar Inc., Jostens Inc., Kmart Corporation	**Kent Kresa (1989)** ***Chairman, President and CEO of Northrop Grumman Corp.*** Additional board seats: Atlantic Richfield Company
James D. Aljian (1996) ***Executive of Tracinda Corporation*** Additional board seats: MGM Grand Inc., Metro-Goldwyn-Mayer Inc.	**Robert A. Lutz (1986)** ***Vice Chairman of Chrysler Corporation*** Additional board seats: Ascom Holdings AG, Silicon Graphics Inc., Northrop Grumman Corp.
Robert E. Allen (1994) ***Retired Chairman of the Board and CEO of AT&T*** Additional board seats: Bristol Myers-Squibb Co., Pepsico Inc.	**Peter A. Magowan (1986)** ***President and Managing General Partner of San Francisco Giants, former Chairman and CEO of Safeway Inc.*** Additional board seats: Caterpillar Inc.,
Joseph Califano, Jr. (1981) ***Chairman and President of the National Center on Addiction and Substance Abuse at Columbia University*** Additional board seats: Authentic Fitness Corporation, Automatic Data Processing Inc., Health Plan Services Inc., Kmart Corporation, Trtavelers Group Inc., Warnaco Inc.	**Lynton R. Wilson (1994)** ***Chairman and Ceo of BCE Inc.*** Additional board seats: Chrysler Canada Ltd., Bell Canada, Bell Canada International Inc., BCE Mobile Commun., Bell-Northern Research Ltd., Northern Telecom Lim., CAE Inc., Tate&Lyle Plc, Teleglobe Inc.
Robert J. Eaton (1992) ***Chairman of the board and CEO of Chrysler Corporation*** Additional board seats: International Paper Company	**John B. Neff (1996)** ***Retired from Wellington Management Company*** Additional board seats: General Accident Insurance, Greenwich Associates
Earl G. Graves (1990) ***Chairman and CEO of Earl G. Graves*** Additional board seats: AMR Corp., Aetna Life & Casualty Company, Federated Department Stores, Rohm & Haas Corporation	**Robert J. Lanigan** ***Retired Chairman of the Board and CEO of Owens-Illinois Inc.*** Additional board seats: Owens-Illinois Inc., Barry Wehmiller Co., The Dun & Bradstreet Corp., Sonat inc., Transocean Offshore Inc., Cognizant Corp.

Figure 7.5 ◆ Board members of Chrysler Corporation (1998)

Source: Chrysler Corporation, Annual Letter to Shareholders 1998

The joint perspective

The initiators and architects of this M&A deal were largely the CEOs, with some involvement of management board members. Corporate governance was a major issue from the very beginning and critical for the merger's success. The conclusions that we can draw from the sequence of events (see Figure 7.6) is that the US board was much more involved, whereas the German board was informed late and only selectively. The way both CEOs managed the timetable of the approval process, and the degree of involvement of the management and supervisory boards, highlight the differences between corporate governance practices in the United States and Germany.

The shareholders had the final decision on the proposed merger. The boards of both companies worked hard to convince them to approve the deal. At extraordinary shareholder meetings of Daimler-Benz AG and Chrysler Corporation the merger decision took place on the same date: September 18, 1998. Both shareholder groups overwhelmingly approved the merger: 99.89% of Daimler-Benz shareholders and 97.5% of Chrysler's.

In a complex, multi-step deal, each Daimler-Benz share was exchanged for one DaimlerChrysler share. In a similar procedure, each Chrysler Corporation share was exchanged at a rate of 1 to 0.62 for each new DaimlerChrysler share. This ratio was equivalent to a premium of 28% over Chrysler's share price on the day the exchange ratio was fixed. The composition of the shareholder body of DaimlerChrysler on November 18 was split equally between US and European shareholders – each group held 44% of the outstanding shares (see Figure 7.7).

The following key modalities of the merger determined the new corporate governance structure. DaimlerChrysler AG is incorporated in Germany. Chrysler's higher standards regarding proximity to shareholders were adopted. Therefore a shareholder committee was set up, including four executives from DaimlerChrysler and the ten shareholders' representatives from the supervisory board. The committee would meet every two months, with the main task of discussing the business strategy and aspects of the financial markets and paying particular attention to share price developments and recommendations from analysts. The approach to dividends in the two companies had been quite different. In accordance with national custom, Chrysler paid a quarterly dividend, whereas Daimler-Benz paid its dividend only once a year. The latter system was adopted for the new company.

Chrysler's higher standards regarding proximity to shareholders were adopted

	January	February	March	April	May	Autumn of '98
Daimler-Benz AG	**January 12:** Schrempp visits Eaton (17 minutes)	**Early February:** Cordes is informed **February 12:** First meeting Schrempp, Cordes, Eaton, Valade **February 17, 18:** Financial advisors enter, Hubbert, Zetsche, Grube	**March 2:** Schrempp, Cordes, Eaton, Valade meet in Switzerland and discuss corporate governance issues	**April 7:** Management board is informed **April 16:** Kopper (head of supervisory board) is informed **April 19:** Detailed explanation to the management board	**May 3:** Management board approves **May 4:** Feuerstein (works council) is informed **May 6:** Supervisory board is informed **May 7:** Merger announcement **May 14:** Daimler-Benz supervisory board approves	**September 18:** Shareholder meeting of Daimler-Benz AG Approval rate: 99,89% **October 26:** Share exchange ends 97% of DB shareholders exchange **November 17:** DCX shares are traded
Chrysler Corporation	**End of January:** Eaton calls Schrempp	**February 5:** Board is informed	**March 5:** Update for board **March 23:** Update for board	**April 7:** Update for board (with bankers) **April 22:** Update for board **April 29:** Update for board (with bankers)	**May 5, 6:** Update for board (with bankers and lawyers) **May 6:** Unanimous approval by the board **May 7:** Merger announcement	**September 18:** Shareholder meeting of Chrysler Corp. Approval rate: 97.5% **November 17:** DCX shares are traded

Figure 7.6 ◆ Timeline of the DaimlerChrysler merger in 1998

Source: DaimlerChrysler AG, company sources

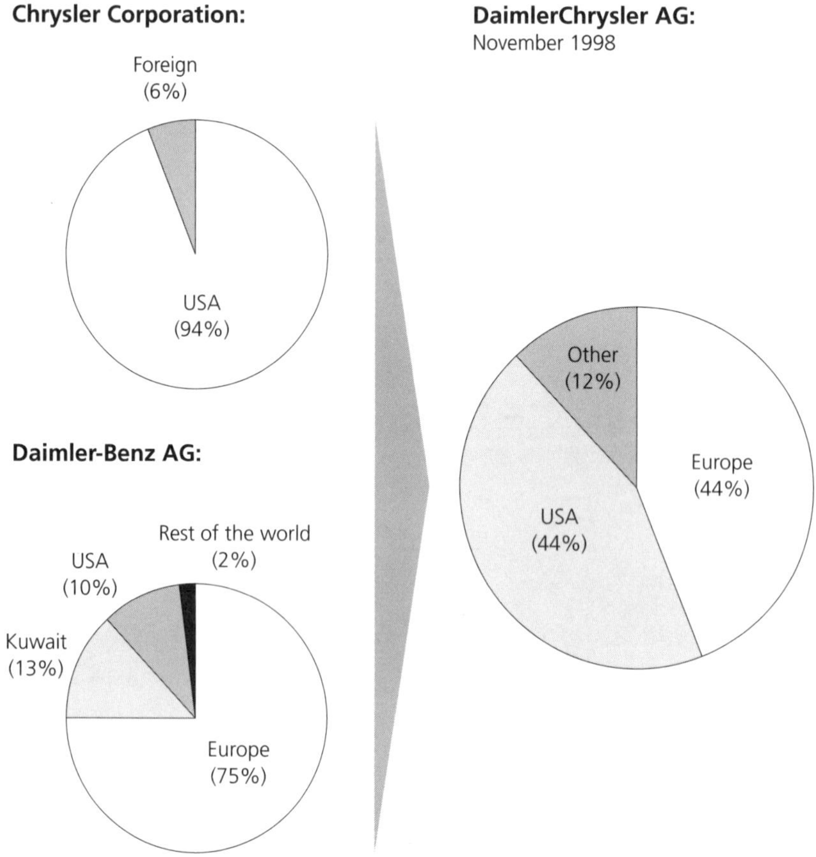

Figure 7.7 ◆ Shareholder structure of DaimlerChrysler AG (1998)
Source: DaimlerChrysler AG

The supervisory board was composed as stipulated by German law with half the members from the capital side and half from the employees representation. The members on the capital side were equally split between former Daimler-Benz and former Chrysler representatives; for the representation of US employees on the board, a particularly sensitive solution was found. Stephen R. Yokich (president of the American United Auto Workers Union) had initially demanded four seats for representatives from Chrysler's US and Canadian facilities. According to German law, the union can claim only three out of ten seats. As the supervisory board could not be enlarged, the German metal workers union, IG Metall, gave up one of its seats to allow Yokich to move in. Daimler-Benz's board of management and Chrysler's top management combined to form DaimlerChrysler's management board with 18 members. Schrempp and Eaton served as co-chairmen of the board.

Much more transparent and sophisticated financial reporting tools were transferred from Chrysler. The differences in absolute amounts and in the structure of compensation at different levels of the two firms varied markedly and were a major problem to be solved.[13] The new compensation package was planned to consist of a basic salary, an annual bonus, a three-year performance plan as a medium-term incentive and stock options as a long-term incentive.

The post-merger integration was handled by an elaborate organization (see Figure 7.8). The structure consisted of the Chairmen's Integration Council (CIC), with a total of eight members, and a ten-member board of management. The integration council oversaw the post-merger integration phase. However, all management board members were involved in the process. Issue resolution teams were jointly run by two members of the management board – one from former Chrysler and one from former Daimler-Benz. These teams were used to identify and realize the synergies between both companies. They reported directly to the CIC. Because of the heavy workload of the board members, each team also had two coordinators who were in close contact with their counterparts from other IRTs. The coordinators formed the so-called post-merger integration team and exchanged their experiences in the integration process. With respect to post-merger integration, the board of directors limited itself to progress reviews.

The coordinators formed the so-called post-merger integration team and exchanged their experiences in the integration process

Apart from the conclusions already drawn, another main characteristic is that there has been a tremendous convergence of both systems. Shareholder standards have been mostly adopted from Chrysler, and stakeholder standards have been adopted from Daimler-Benz.[14] However, the newly merged company had a rough ride, especially when Chrysler ran into huge losses. There were further changes in corporate governance (although they were unrelated to the merger).[15] To date, no merger of a similar size has been realized across borders (although it is debatable whether the 'merger of equals' in fact turned out to be an acquisition, legally it was a merger), probably because many are shying away from the many hurdles that have to be overcome.

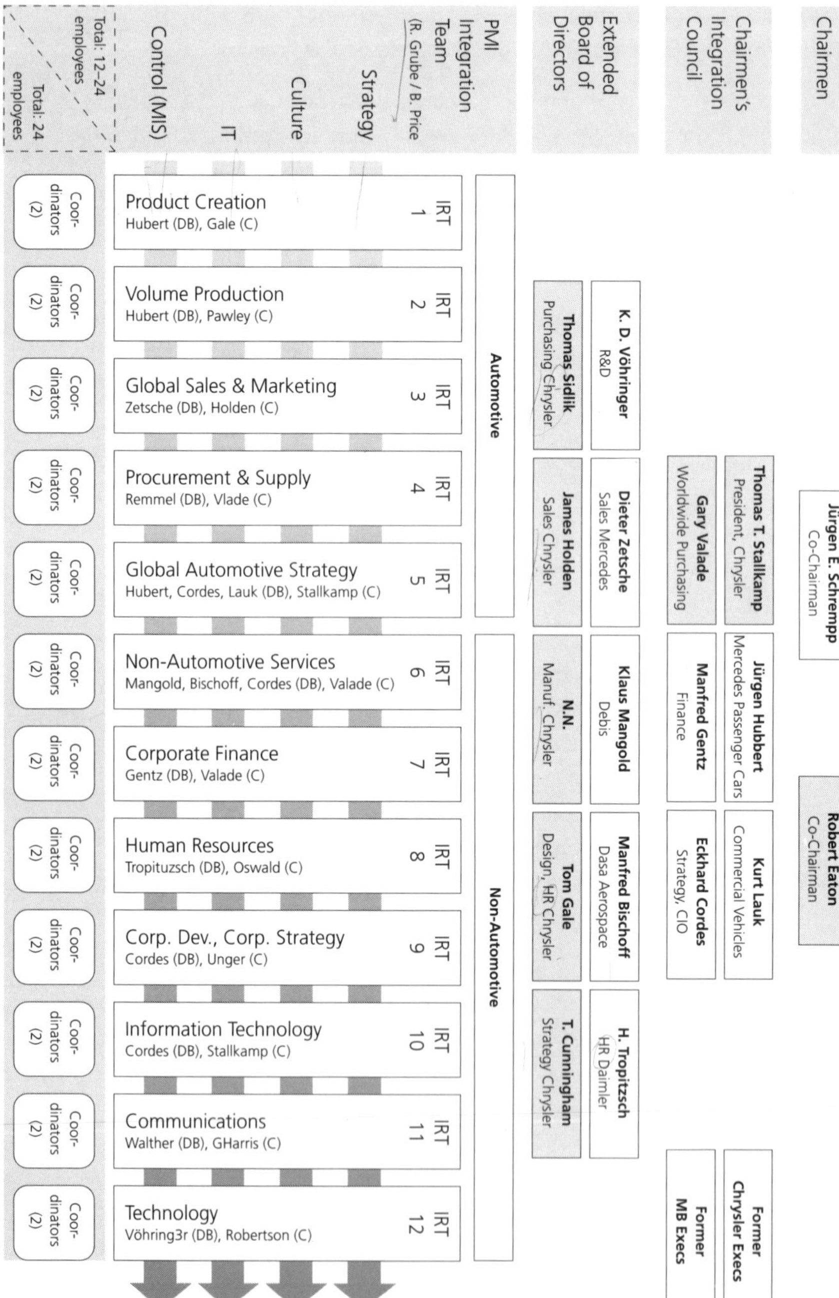

Figure 7.8 ◆ Post-Merger Integration Structure of DaimlerChrysler AG

Source: DaimlerChrysler AG

Notes

1 Berle and Means 1932.
2 Jensen and Meckling 1976.
3 This issue is the subject of the 'principal agent theory' or 'agency theory'. See Fama 1980, Fama and Jensen 1983a and 1983b.
4 NB: this interplay between shareholders, directors and managers varies to a great extent in practice.
5 See Chapter 1.
6 There seems to be a positive impact on shareholder wealth when independent directors are announced, see Rosenstein and Wyatt 1990.
7 A global corporate governance research initiative carried out by IMD in 2002. More than 200 questionnaires, each on boards of directors and investor relations, were analyzed between February and October 2002. In addition, 50 interviews were conducted with CEOs, chairmen and board members of European, US and Asian companies.
8 Cadbury 1999.
9 The models are based on the preliminary results of IMD's global corporate governance research initiative (see Note 7).
10 This case is based on Neubauer, Steger and Rädler 1999a, 1999b and 2000, and Steger and Rädler 1999a and 1999b.
11 Simonian and Waters 1996.
12 Simonian and Waters 1998.
13 For example, in 1997, Eaton earned more than the whole management board of Daimler-Benz put together.
14 Steger 2002, 257 ff.
15 Steger and Rädler 2003.

References

Berle, A. A. and Means, G. C. (1932) *The Modern Corporation and Private Property*, New York: Macmillan.

Cadbury, A. (1999) 'What are the trends in corporate governance? How will they impact your company?', *Long Range Planning*, Vol. 32, 12–19.

Fama, E. F. (1980) 'Agency problems and the theory of the firm', *Journal of Political Economy*, Vol. 88, 288–307.

Fama, E. F. and Jensen, M. C. (1983a) 'Separation of ownership and control', *The Journal of Law and Economics*, Vol. 26, 301–325.

Fama, E. F. and Jensen, M. C. (1983b) 'Agency problems and residual claims', *The Journal of Law and Economics*, Vol. 26, 327–349.

Jensen, M. C. and Meckling, W. H. (1976) 'Theory of the firm: managerial behavior, agency costs and ownership structure', *Journal of Financial Economics*, Vol. 3, 323–329.

Neubauer, F., Steger, U. and Rädler, G. (1999a) *The DaimlerChrysler merger: the involvement of the boards*, IMD – International Institute for Management Development, Case No. IMD-3-0771.

Rosenstein, S. and Wyatt, J. G. (1990) 'Outside directors, board independence, and shareholder wealth', *Journal of Financial Economics*, Vol. 29, 175–191.

Simonian, H. and Waters, R. (1996) 'Chrysler's backseat driver: the battle between Kirk Kerkorian and the car maker over the company's cash is coming to a head', *Financial Times*, 16 January.

Simonian, H. and Waters, R. (1998) 'Unlike fellow travellers', *Financial Times*, 9/10 May.

Sonnenfeld, J. A. (2002) 'What makes good boards great', *Harvard Business Review*, 80 (9), 106–113.

Steger, U. and Rädler, G. (1999a) *The DaimlerChrysler Merger (A): Gaining Global Competitiveness*, IMD – International Institute for Management Development, Case No. IMD-3-0834.

Steger, U. and Rädler, G. (1999b) *The DaimlerChrysler Merger (B): Shaping a Transatlantic Company*, IMD – International Institute for Management Development, Case No. IMD-3-0835.

Steger, U. and Rädler, G. (2003) *Corporate Governance Dynamics at DaimlerChrysler*, IMD – International Institute for Management Development, Case: forthcoming.

Steger, U. (2002) *Corporate Diplomacy: The Strategy for a Volatile, Fragmented Business Environment*, Chichester: Wiley.

8

The human factor in mergers and acquisitions[1]

By
Vladimir Pucik and Paul Evans

THERE IS NO SHORTAGE OF evidence that attention to 'soft' factors or people issues is one of the most critical elements in making acquisition strategy work. Several recent studies have provided evidence that, in addition to institutional issues described in depth in Chapter 4, critical success factors for international M&As are mostly people related, for example retaining key talent, effective communication, selecting the future management team and cultural integration.[2,3,4]

In fact, it is hard to find an acquisition where people issues do not matter. When the objective is to establish a new geographic presence, managing cross-cultural, language and communication issues tops the list of priorities. When the aim is to acquire new technology or to buy market share or competencies, retaining key technical staff or account managers is the principal challenge. When the objective of the deal is consolidation, dealing effectively with redundancies at all levels is the dominant concern.

People issues in planning acquisitions

Without doubt the most important contribution that HR can make during acquisition planning is to ensure that the due diligence process covers all the important human resource management (HRM) considerations, including culture assessment and a human capital audit. Research has shown that cultural compatibility or incompatibility is relevant in many domestic acquisitions and it is probably the most talked-about factor when acquisitions take place across borders. We will come back to this issue in the next section.

Another important component of acquisition planning is making sure that the company has the appropriate leadership team in place. When Renault considered acquiring a 37% stake in Nissan, a big factor in the decision-making process was the knowledge that it had a team of seasoned managers who could be dispatched to Japan to guide the restructuring efforts. In the words of Renault's chairman Louis Schweitzer: 'If I didn't have Mr Ghon [sent to Tokyo by Renault to become president of Nissan], I would not have done the deal with Nissan. That means I sent him in because I had the absolute confidence in his ability.'[25] Contrast this with the Daimler 'merger' with Chrysler, discussed in Chapter 4, which saw three teams of top executives in the first two years after the acquisition.

> Another important component of acquisition planning is making sure that the company has the appropriate leadership team in place

In international acquisitions, human resource strategy cannot be separated from its cultural and social context. Often the company may not have any expertise in the particular country or geographical area, so it is important to plan early how to mobilize the necessary resources to guide the firm through unfamiliar territory. At this early stage it is also important to provide the necessary orientation to the members of the due diligence team, who are likely to be selected for their analytical and technical skills, not for their familiarity with the culture and environment of the target firm.

Some HRM issues may have a direct bearing on the selection of acquisition candidates. What is possible and what is out of bounds? How do you get a quick reading on the quality of human assets before committing resources to full-scale due diligence? Here HR can serve as a valuable resource and a sounding board, providing it has the capacity to obtain and analyze the information. No one can expect HR to have all the information readily available, but in the words of a GE HR manager who participated in planning a number of acquisitions: 'Even if you know the industry, each acquisition is different: different culture, legal framework, management team in place. We are at the table not because we have all the answers, but we certainly know the questions that we have to ask.'

Finally, even at the planning stage it is important to figure out broadly how success will be measured and how to learn from the pending acquisition experience. As the saying goes: 'Success has many fathers, but failure is an orphan.' It is not easy to discover what went wrong after the fact and valuable insights are often lost if they are not recorded in 'real time'. Facilitating the process of knowledge retention is a contribution that HR should be well equipped to handle, starting at the planning stage.

The art of being truly diligent

Getting the strategy right depends very much on doing the homework. Good planning is not possible without good data. Due diligence in an acquisition has two aspects to it. One is, of course, to clarify the legal, financial and business picture. The infrastructure for obtaining this kind of information is well developed, as are the analytic methodologies. The other aspect, equally important but often neglected, is learning about the 'soft' factors influencing the fit between the two organizations, such as the culture and the people practices in the target organization.

In cross-border acquisitions, the due diligence team must be sensitive to the fact that attitudes towards acquisition due diligence vary from country to country

In cross-border acquisitions, the due diligence team must be sensitive to the fact that attitudes towards acquisition due diligence vary from country to country.[6] Under Anglo-Saxon practice, lawyers and their clients expect comprehensive due diligence before the acquisition is completed. In other countries, due diligence may be interpreted as intrusive at best or as a sign of mistrust or bad intentions on the buyer's part. Obtaining information about the people side of the business, such as the quality of the management team, requires particular care.

In cross-border acquisitions, the due diligence team must be sensitive to the fact that attitudes towards acquisition due diligence vary from country to country

The typical list of topics on HR due diligence can easily run to several pages, especially if the acquirer comes from North America (see Table 8.1 for the broad categories of issues to investigate). As time is short, it is important to start with priorities rather than getting lost in technical details. Some items, such as pension plan liabilities, employee grievances and litigation, are checked to protect the company against potential financial exposure. Others, such as talent identification, employee rights to technology, trade secrets and confidentiality, reflect the strategic intent of the acquisition.

Table 8.1 ◆ A human resource due diligence checklist

Organization and management	Compensation/Benefits
Organization charts	Executive compensation
Job title hierarchy	General compensation
Management committees	Incentive compensation
Succession plans	Bonus eligibility
Employment contracts	Stock plans
Employment agreements	Pension Plan
	Coverage
HR policies	Assets and liabilities
Hiring procedures	Non-monetary rewards
Employment documents	
Job descriptions	**Labour relations**
Work rules	
Holiday policy	**Litigations and claims**
Discipline	
Performance management	**HRIS (human resource information systems)**
Early retirement	Employee records
Termination/Severance	

Former employees, industry experts, consultants, executive search firms and a company's customers are usually the best source of information. Cultivating some of these sources on a longer-term basis helps to mediate the constraints of confidentiality. Today web-based search engines can speed up the process of finding information, too. In the first stage, HR due diligence is part of building the overall acquisition roadmap. Once an agreement to acquire or merge has been reached, HR records and interviews with managers in the target company can supplement and verify the assessment.

The transparency and accessibility of this information varies from country to country. Companies often bemoan a lack of information, when in fact the real issue is a lack of familiarity with the local sources of this information. Often information about HR policies is relatively easy to obtain, though the problem is the amount. For example, acquiring a firm in the US may involve reviewing over 20 categories of benefit plans and policies, going back six years to understand all the potential tax liabilities.[7] However, HR due diligence is not just about collecting reams of data in order to avoid potential financial landmines or to be ready to harmonize the policies and practices quickly after the deal, important though these tasks may be. The fundamental purpose is to understand how the HR system impacts on the values, norms and behaviours of the company to be acquired.

To do this well is not easy, even in domestic acquisitions. Less than a third of US HR professionals consider that HR was effective in the due diligence phase of acquisitions.[8] The process of collecting 'soft' due diligence data typically assumes friendly relations between the parties. Often companies believe that this kind of information is not available abroad, especially during the initial planning stage when secrecy and confidentiality are important. Of course, access to information is especially constrained in the case of a hostile acquisition.

Often what is lacking is not information *per se* but discipline and rigour in collecting and analysing the data. Two methodologies can be especially useful here: culture assessment and the human capital audit.

The organizational culture comes out close to the top of the list of factors influencing M&A success, and the importance of understanding the culture of the company to be acquired has been discussed in depth in Chapter 4. Despite this, research has shown that culture assessment is generally not given priority before the deal is done.[9] It is therefore not surprising that culture clashes are so often a source of difficulties after the deal. Depending on the stage of the negotiations and the resources available, cultural assessment can be formal or informal, based on a variety of potential sources such as market intelligence, external data, surveys and interviews. What is important is to have at least a rudimentary framework that helps to organize the issues and draw the proper conclusions.[10]

The human capital audit

There are two dimensions to the human capital audit. One is preventive, focused on liabilities such as pension plan obligations, outstanding grievances and employee litigation, or other employment-related constraints that may impact the acquisition – for example cost of anticipated restructuring. It also includes comparing the compensation policies, benefits and labour contracts of both firms.

The other dimension is focused on identifying talent and in the long run it is probably more critical to the success of the acquisition. There are a number of important facets – ensuring that the target company has the talent necessary to execute the acquisition strategy, identifying which individuals are key to sustaining the value of the deal, and assessing any potential weaknesses in the management team. It is also important to understand the motivation and incentive structure, and to highlight any differences that may impact retention. Finally, understanding the structure of the organization means not just identifying reporting lines but clarifying who is who.

It is also important to understand the motivation and incentive structure, and to highlight any differences that may impact retention

Here are some examples of questions to consider:

- What unique skills do the employees have?
- How does the target's talent compare with the quality of our own?
- What is the background of the management team?
- What will happen if some of the management team leave?
- What is the compensation philosophy?
- How much pay is at risk at various levels of the firm?
- What are the reporting relationships?
- How are decisions made?

Defining the types of skills that people have takes some effort. Many companies therefore ignore the talent question in the early stages of the M&A process, relying instead on financial performance data as a proxy. However, only after a thorough human capital audit can an acquiring company develop strategies to address anticipated problems as early as possible. Significant weaknesses that have been uncovered may call for replacement candidates (external local hires or expatriates) to be ready to step in immediately after closing. And with each replacement there is a potential termination, which again has to be carefully prepared, based on local rules and practice. Other talent might be highly likely to depart. For example, an employee stock option plan may provide for option grants to be fully vested when there is a 'change of control', as after an acquisition.[11] Many valuable contributors thus have no incentive to stay. In such cases, retaining key employees must be considered a 'deal breaker' to be incorporated in the acquisition agreement.[12]

People challenges in post-merger integration

Signing the acquisition contract and the change in ownership triggers changes in organization and leadership. Now is the time to put in place a new organization, appoint new leadership and make sure that key talent is retained – and to manage what is called the 'merger syndrome' (see below). Some changes happen quickly in the months after the closing; others, such as the development of a new culture, need more time to coalesce. A final stage in the acquisition process is the codification and dissemination of learning – what did we learn so next time it can be done faster and better. All these are critical people-related issues.

Most companies use the term 'integration' to describe the post-merger activities designed to bind the acquiring and acquired companies. But what actually happens is assimilation – a process fundamentally different to integration. As when acquisitions are described as mergers, this is another example of how euphemisms are used, sometimes misguidedly, to gloss over the realities.

The logic of assimilation is simple: make the acquired company just like the purchaser, as in absorption acquisitions. However, companies are sensitive to public perceptions of being seen as a foreign bully and they are often hesitant about proclaiming their objective of assimilating the acquired firm, for fear of compromising the deal. But this often creates confusion and mistrust, which will make the assimilation process more difficult. In contrast, GE Capital, the financial services arm of General Electric, offers blunt advice to the management of firms that have been acquired around the world: 'If you do not want to change, don't put yourself for sale.' GE makes it very clear to the acquired company that it now has to play by GE's rules, and it provides a framework in which to do so.

In the case of true integration, the emphasis is on capturing hidden synergies by swapping and leveraging capabilities. Sometimes, the companies may decide to establish a new identity, as with Novartis, which was formed through the merger of Ciba-Geigy and Sandoz in 1996 to create a global life sciences giant. Or the objective may be sharing strengths while maintaining separate identities, as was the publicized strategic intent of DaimlerChrysler described in Chapter 4.

Both approaches to M&A implementation have their merits. The choice of either assimilation or integration depends on the strategic intent behind the acquisition and the desired cultural characteristics of the new organization. Choosing an approach that does not match the strategy or the desired cultural outcome can significantly reduce the value created by the acquisition, if not doom the whole deal. When Deutsche Bank acquired UK-based investment bank Morgan Grenfell in 1989, the strategic intent was to build a global financial powerhouse. However, heavy-handed attempts to assimilate Morgan's aggressive freewheeling entrepreneurs into the bureaucratic and centralized culture of Deutsche simply did not work. In the first two years after the merger, many top-ranking Morgan Grenfell contributors left, destroying the value of the very assets that had made the deal attractive in the first place.

Choosing an approach that does not match the strategy or the desired cultural outcome can significantly reduce the value created by the acquisition

Yet too much caution can be counterproductive. When Japan's Bridgestone purchased US-based Firestone in 1990, it refrained from making significant changes in the organization, even though the acquired company was losing money. Bridgestone did not want to be seen as 'ugly Japanese' taking over a venerable local institution. In reality, many local middle managers were looking forward to the takeover, expecting that their new owners would tackle both the unions and the entrenched old-style top management, but when nothing happened, they left in droves. Faced with growing losses, Tokyo finally moved in several years later to 'clean up the mess'. But it was too late, the company was now too thin on talent. Firestone never fully recovered and today the once powerful brand is on the verge of extinction.

It is also worth noting that companies that are good at assimilation may not be effective integrators. Assimilation and integration require very different organizational routines and mastering both simultaneously is a formidable task. As we will discuss later in greater detail, past experience with acquisitions does not necessarily guarantee success when a company enters unfamiliar territory.

Finally, a complicating factor in international acquisitions is that there are often parts of the organization where a particular approach to the merger makes sense and others where it does not. There are few M&As that fit neatly into the assimilation, integration or other categories. For some countries or regions, or for some parts of the business, a full assimilation may be the best approach; in other parts of the firm, a reverse merger could be a more appropriate strategy. Time and the degree of competition are also important – one cannot search for a perfect partner for ever.

Managing the merger syndrome

Announcing a merger may be fun – for top management. It attracts lots of publicity and senior management can enjoy their time in the spotlight. But lower down in the ranks reactions to this announcement, which often comes like a bolt out of the blue, are different. However well the merger has been planned and prepared, there is always the merger syndrome. At a basic level, this simply reflects the fact that any process of change is stressful.

No matter how the merger is presented in the press, for those who are taken over there is invariably a sense of being losers. Reactions follow the pattern of the shock syndrome people experience following the death of someone close. Initial disbelief and denial are followed by shock, coloured by overreaction ('We are going to lose our jobs') or underreaction ('Oh, it won't change anything'). This leads, in turn, to anger, then individual attempts to bargain or dig one's heels in to take care of oneself, followed ultimately by acceptance. Acceptance itself may take different forms, which can characterize

many successful acquirers is performed by the HR manager assigned to the transition team. But to get on the team requires doing the homework – being proactive is a prerequisite if HR professionals are to be involved.[28]

Perhaps even more important is developing tools to facilitate and speed up the cross-border acquisition process – from due diligence to integration. There is a qualitative difference in the approach to learning here. Acquisition 'best practice' books present scenarios and suggest roadmaps for managers to follow. In contrast, acquisition tool kits provide managers with lists of issues and questions to be addressed at each stage in the acquisition, broad guidelines on what to consider, simple and concise instruments, and sources of advice inside and outside the firm. In repetitive acquisitions, the best practice approach may be sufficient, although most international acquisitions are one of a kind. In all cases, a feedback loop recording what worked, what did not and what can be added is essential.

It is useful to keep in mind that effective learning and a solid track record in implementing acquisitions can sometimes have unintended consequences. Confident that missing skills can always be brought in, the acquiring managers may see outsourcing organizational skills as more attractive than retaining people in order to build those skills internally. This may, however, stifle in-house innovation and experimentation. For example, it has been reported that acquisitions have a negative effect on both R&D intensity (a measure of R&D inputs) and patent intensity (a measure of R&D outputs). Other evidence shows that firms making acquisitions introduce fewer new products into the marketplace.[29] A similar logic may apply to entering new markets via cross-border acquisitions. Firms with successful M&A experience may choose to enter quickly through an acquisition, although the slower, greenfield investment path may give the company more leverage over people-related issues such as organizational culture and workforce composition.

Firms with successful M&A experience may choose to enter quickly through an acquisition

Managing the acquisition process

Regardless of the approach, integrating the acquired company with the new parent is a delicate and complicated process. Who should be responsible for making it happen? After closing, the due diligence team, with its deep knowledge of the acquired company, disbands or goes on to another deal. Meanwhile, the new management team is not yet fully in place. To avoid a vacuum, companies are increasingly turning to dedicated integration managers supported by transition teams to guide the process immediately after the deal has been concluded.

The role of the integration manager

Integration managers are specialists in dealing with transitions. Their role is to make sure that timelines are followed and that key decisions are taken according to the agreed schedule, while removing bottlenecks and making sure that the speed of integration is maintained. They help to engineer the short-term successes that are essential to create positive energy around the merger. They should also champion norms and behaviours consistent with new standards, communicate key messages across the new organization and identify new value-adding opportunities.[30]

An important aspect of the job is helping the acquired company to understand how the new owner operates and what it can offer in terms of capabilities. The integration manager can help the new company take advantage of the owner's existing capabilities and resources, forge social connections, and help with essential but intangible aspects such as interpreting a new language and way of doing things. Acquired companies typically do not know how things work in the corporation that now owns them, and the integration manager can also help the parent to understand the acquired business and what it can offer. This is important because outside the acquisition team, few people in the parent organization are familiar with the capabilities of the acquired unit.

An equally important role for the integration manager is that of information 'gatekeeper' between the two sides, protecting the acquired business from the eager embrace of an owner that could unintentionally undermine what makes the business work. A major source of frustration in many deals is not so much what the parent wants the newly acquired unit to do but what it wants to know. New information requirements must be submitted in a very specific format, and reports are full of incomprehensible jargon – indeed, corporate HR is often the guilty party. When Nokia acquires small high-tech venture companies, one of the rules is that all requests for information from the parent must go to the integration manager. He or she then decides whether and how the unit should comply with the request.

What combination of skills does the integration manager require? First of all, he or she must have a deep knowledge of the parent company – where to get information, who to talk to, how the informal system works. A flexible leadership style is another requirement, since the integration manager must be tough about deadlines and yet a good listener, and able to relate to people at different levels in the organization. Other traits that go with this role are comfort with ambiguity, emotional and cultural intelligence, and the willingness to take risks.[31] An integration manager is not the leader of the business, although these jobs are often stepping stones into a business leadership role.

The responsibilities of the transition team

In most acquisitions, integration teams and task forces support the integration manager. They should have a clear mandate, with targets and accountability for a specific area where integration is required. Since many of these teams are expected to start work the first day after the acquisition has been concluded, identifying potential members should ideally be one outcome of the due diligence process. HR professionals are often key members of the team because many of the team's activities will have implications for human resource policies and practices.

HR professionals are often key members of the team because many of the team's activities will have implications for human resource policies and practices

The specific charter of the transition teams depends on the integration approach discussed above. Overall their role is to take the high-level vision, objectives and synergies and translate them into concrete action. The key priorities, such as business synergies where results can be achieved quickly, should be identified early in the integration planning process so that these specific integration projects can be launched immediately after the deal is closed.

Prioritization is critical. Too many task forces and teams slow things down, creating coordination problems, conflict and confusion. The complexity of DaimlerChrysler's transition structure was one of the reasons why its integration process quickly came to a standstill. The integration projects should focus on those with high-potential savings at low risk, leaving those with greater risk or lower benefits until later. As one experienced M&A manager stated: 'We only attack things that will bring benefits to the business. We do not integrate just for the sake of integrating.'

Another task of the transition team is to spell out the logic of the new business model and translate this into operational targets. This is important in international acquisitions where 'big picture' statements from the corporate centre may not mean much in a different national and business context far away. The transition team should also serve as a role model for how the new organization should act. It should disseminate the shared vision and make sure that practices are appropriately aligned with this. And by facilitating personnel exchange, the transition team can help to develop a better understanding of each other's capabilities.

Who should be appointed to the transition team? The idea of working in what we call a 'split egg' way may be attractive, but here the mixing of line responsibility with transition task force roles often means that neither is done well. Customers do not like to wait until the transition team reaches consensus. On the other hand, integration teams should not be staffed by second-tier managers or by 'losers' in the race for line business jobs – they would not have the credibility to get the job done. So probably the best staffing approach is to appoint up and coming managers, leaving the daily business under the original leadership until the new organization can be put in place.

Transition teams are most effective when members come from both the acquired and the acquiring companies. People who are suited to a transition team usually have a mix of functional and interpersonal competencies (including cross-cultural skills), backed up by strong analytical skills. Having an ability to accept responsibility without full authority and being effective in mobilizing resources across organizational boundaries are two competencies that are especially important and consequently such roles are good development opportunities for those with high potential.

When should HR get involved?

Based on these observations, it may be seen as natural that the HR function should play a significant role in all phases of the acquisition. Yet while this tends to be true during the merger implementation phase, the overall influence that HR has during the whole acquisition process is patchy. In addition many companies have neither the resources nor the know-how to give this HR area the priority it merits.[32]

Although it does not always do so, the human resource function can make a substantial contribution at all stages of the acquisition process. As noted earlier, this depends on the type of acquisition – transformational acquisitions should require far more attention to HRM than traditional acquisitions. But according to a 1997 study conducted by the Conference Board of 88 major corporations in the US and Europe, HR is involved in M&A planning in less than a quarter of responding firms. HR involvement is marginally higher during the negotiation stage, but it is only after the deal has been signed that 80% of the firms see HR as fully engaged. It is obviously not easy for HR to ensure the

> The human resource can make a substantial contribution at all stages of the acquisition process

smooth implementation of the deal when it has had little or no part in shaping it. US-based companies seem to put somewhat more emphasis on getting early HR involvement than their European counterparts.

One reason for 'keeping HR out of the room' is the secrecy surrounding most acquisitions before the bid or agreement is announced. In many companies, communication about pending acquisitions is treated – for commercial and regulatory reasons – as strictly confidential, disseminated on a 'need-to-know' basis. HR is not seen as having that need. A determining factor is whether the top human resource executive is a member of the senior management team and a full participant in the strategy planning process. HR is unlikely to be involved if it is not already perceived as a valuable contributor to strategy development.

During the early stages of the acquisition, it is the responsibility of HR to ensure a sharp focus on people and leadership issues, making sure that transitional organization and teams are in place on day one, fully prepared to deal with the complexities of a cross-cultural deal. The next step is staffing – who will stay and who will go? Here, the ability to rapidly evaluate the talent in the newly acquired organization is essential. It is not easy to assess people quickly in a different culture; most HR professionals find it difficult to trust their experience outside their own cultural milieu.[33] And finally, what kind of policies and practices should be introduced in the acquired organization? HRM provides a subtle control mechanism by which a parent company can influence its acquisition, so the choice of HR approach is intrinsically linked with the overall strategy for integration.

Measuring M&A success

A critical component of the learning process is feedback on the progress the organization has made in reaching the integration goals. The foundation of feedback is measurement. And there is no shortage of measures that can be used to assess the progress on the HRM side of the integration process. Some of these measures focus on key organizational priorities, while others reflect the functional agenda of the HR department:

- *Integration goals*: reorganization and restructuring targets in terms of schedule and cost, including breakdowns for specific business units or geographical areas.
- *Integration of key HR systems*: tracking integration objectives in combining systems for HRIS, compensation, talent development and performance management according to established time frame and budgets.

- *Retention of talent*: retention of acquired talent, success rates for different retention tools, retention rates for specific business units and functions, and cost-effectiveness indicators such as retention/replacement expenses.
- *Best practices:* comparison across organizational units of best practices shared and adopted, including estimation of the impact on revenues, cost or other performance indicators such as customer satisfaction.
- *Employee feedback data:* includes attitude surveys and data from exit interviews.

In complex international acquisitions there are usually too many balls in the air to be able to rely on anecdotes and impressions. Instituting rigorous measurements and having 'real-time' HRM data on the progress of the integration process can prevent costly mistakes. These measures stimulate management to take early corrective action and they establish benchmarks for future acquisitions. Most importantly, they also establish accountability for the people dimension of the acquisition. Without accountability, learning may not get the priority required.

In the long term, the only valid measure of acquisition success is the satisfied customer. Does the acquisition create customer value? From a customer's point of view, has it made sense? If it has not, there is not much chance for long-term growth. When short-term synergies are exhausted, deals that do not create customer value do not have much chance of being sustained. A strong focus on the customer can also help generate the energy to push through the necessary changes. This cuts down on internal politics that divert management attention away from the business. And bear in mind that creating customer value occurs only *after* the deal has been done, which makes post-merger integration such a critical success factor.

In the long term, the only valid measure of acquisition success is the satisfied customer

Summary

For many companies, implementing mergers and acquisitions is still a formidable challenge. The complexity of cross-border deals, due to cultural and physical distance, makes implementation even more difficult. Yet there is little doubt that companies that master the art of international acquisitions will gain significant market advantage, despite caveats regarding some long-term advantages of organic growth. When there is a sound strategy behind the merger, and when the intangible human aspects of an acquisition are seen as just as important as its financial dimensions, acquisitions can become an important tool for gaining a competitive advantage in global markets.

1 Most merger or acquisition failures are linked to problems with post-merger integration. Cultural and people issues consistently rank as one of the main difficulties in executing acquisitions. Do not underestimate the importance of cross-cultural differences, but equally do not confuse culture with poor management.
2 Probably the most consistent predictor of M&A success is past experience in acquisitions. The more the company merges, the better it gets at merging and the stronger the talent and experience are for the next merger. Companies that have solid foundations in HRM and a good track record in managing change also tend to be good at managing acquisitions.
3 There are different strategic logics behind mergers – stand-alone, absorption, reverse merger, 'best of both' and transformation. Each has different implications for the nature of the post-merger integration process. Think about the end state before you start.
4 HR should be involved early in the acquisition planning since the 'soft' aspects of the due diligence process, such as the assessment of culture and people practices in the organization to be acquired, are just as important as the financial analysis.
5 The integration process starts with the creation of a vision and strategy for the combined organization. Clarity in communication about the strategy is an essential foundation for success and the guideline for effective communication is 'play it straight'.
6 However well the acquisition has been prepared, one cannot avoid the merger syndrome – the shock/stress cycle experienced by the 'losers' and the victory cycle experienced by the 'winners'. The 'first hundred days' need to be carefully managed, providing insight, information, involvement and inspiration.
7 Many acquisitions fail because of the loss of key talent, so retention is a key priority. This effort should begin during due diligence so that retention plans can be put in place from the first day of the acquisition. In the long term, retention requires senior management commitment to building personal relationships with the acquired talent.
8 It is important to move with speed. Key decisions about management structure, senior appointments and people's careers should be made as

soon as possible. Uncertainty and anxiety after the acquisition drain energy from the business, increasing the risk of loss of customers.

9 Several steps in the post-merger integration are known to foster success: appoint an integration manager to speed up the process; measure M&A outcomes; assign accountability; secure and celebrate quick wins.

10 Some firms see their competence in making international acquisitions as one of their core capabilities. Their ability to learn from past acquisitions, including the mistakes that are inevitably made, is a distinguishing characteristic.

Notes

1 The content of this chapter is based on Evans P., Pucik, V. and Barsoux, J.-L. (2002) *The Global Challenge*, New York: McGraw-Hill Irwin, 249–296.
2 Kay and Shelton 2000.
3 KPMG 1999.
4 Conference Board 1997.
5 'Renault steers forward', *Wall Street Journal Europe*, 15 February 2001, 31.
6 Chu 1996.
7 Johnson and Rich 2000.
8 Society for Human Resource Management 2000.
9 Angwin 2001.
10 One frequently used assessment tool is the Denison Culture Survey (Denison, Cho, and Young, 2000). For an example of an internally developed instrument, see the Merging Cultures Evaluation Index (MCEI) described in Marks and Mirvis 1998.
11 Some plans allow for employees to cash in immediately after an acquisition is approved by shareholders but before the closing. In such cases, the closing should be made contingent on retention of key staff.
12 In knowledge-intensive acquisitions, it is particularly important to protect the value of the deal from the competitive implications of employee defection. We will discuss specific post-merger retention strategies later, but during due diligence it is essential to clarify who has rights to technology and the know-how – the acquired company or individual employees – and who are the key contributors who should be contractually obliged to remain. When trade secrets and confidential information are important assets of the acquired company, it is wise to tie the closing to no-competition, no-disclosure agreements with key employees.
13 O'Reilly and Pfeffer 2000.
14 Marks and Mirvis 1998.
15 According to research conducted by Krug and Hegerty (2001), the decision of top

managers in an acquired firm to stay rather than leave is correlated with their positive perceptions of the merger announcement.

16 Inkpen, Sundaram and Rockwood 2000.
17 'Torch that sent a deal down in flames' *Financial Times*, 12 April 2000, 22.
18 Marks and Mirvis 1998, 74.
19 Krug and Hegerty 1997.
20 On differences in performance standards across cultures, see Evans, Pucik and Barsoux 2002, 166.
21 Corporate Leadership Council 2000.
22 GE's CAP methodology is discussed in Evans, Pucik and Barsoux 2002, 408.
23 Retention bonus guidelines provide desirable consistency, specifying eligibility, amount, performance criteria, etc. Their effect depends, however, on employees' expectations as well as on labour and tax legislation in the countries involved.
24 Corporate Leadership Council 2000.
25 Krug and Hegerty 2001.
26 Watson Wyatt 1999.
27 Haleblian and Finkelstein 1999.
28 When Citibank top management announced its intention to grow in Europe through acquisitions, senior HR leaders in the region quickly organized an intensive M&A workshop to prepare their key staff for the challenges ahead. Several weeks after the workshop, the bank announced a major deal in Poland – and the local HR manager was there ready to participate fully in the acquisition team.
29 Hitt, Hoskinsson, Ireland and Harrison 1991.
30 Ashkenas, DeMonaco and Francis 1998; Ashkenas and Francis 2000.
31 Ashkenas and Francis 2000.
32 KPMG 1999, 15.
33 To ensure the fairness and objectivity of this process, many companies are turning to outside vendors, usually executive search or HR consulting firms.

References

Angwin, D. (2001) 'Mergers and acquisitions across European borders: national perspectives on preacquisition due diligence and the use of professional advisers', *Journal of World Business*, 36 (1), 32–57.

Ashkenas, R. N. and Francis, S. C. (2000) 'Integration managers: special leaders for special times', *Harvard Business Review*, November–December, 108–116.

Ashkenas, R. N., DeMonaco, L. J. and Francis, S. C. (1998) 'Making the deal real: how GE Capital integrates acquisitions', *Harvard Business Review*, January–February, 165–178.

Chu, W. (1996) 'The human side of examining a foreign target', *Mergers and Acquisitions*, January–February, 35.

Conference Board (1997) 'HR challenges in mergers and acquisitions', *HR Executive Review*, 5 (2).

Corporate Leadership Council (2000) *M&A Talent Management: Identification and Retention of Key Talent during Mergers and Acquisitions*, Washington, DC: Corporate Executive Board, 37.

Denison, D., Cho, H. J. and Young, J. (2000) 'Diagnosing organizational cultures: validating a model and method', IMD Working Paper 2000–9, Lausanne: IMD.

Evans, P., Pucik, V. and Barsoux, J.-L. (2002) *The Global Challenge*, New York: McGraw-Hill Irwin, 166.

Haleblian, J. and Finkelstein, S. (1999) 'The influence of organizational acquisition experience on acquisition performance: a behavioral learning perspective', *Administrative Science Quarterly*, 44 (2), 29–57.

Hitt, M. A., Hoskinsson, R. E., Ireland, R. D. and Harrison, J. J. (1991) 'Are acquisitions a poison pill for innovation?' *Academy of Management Executive*, 5 (4), 22–34.

Inkpen, A. C., Sundaram, A. K. and Rockwood, K. (2000) 'Cross-border acquisitions of U.S. technology assets', *California Management Review*, 42 (3), 50–71.

Johnson, L. and Rich, J. (2000) 'Dealing with employee benefit issues in mergers and acquisitions', *SHRM's Legal Report* (March–April), Arlington VA: Society for Human Resource Management.

Kay, I. T. and Shelton, M. (2000) 'The people problems in mergers', *McKinsey Quarterly* 4, 29–37.

KPMG (1999) *Mergers and Acquisitions: A Global Report – Unlocking Shareholder Value*, Report, New York.

Krug, J. and Hegerty, W. H. (1997) 'Postacquisition turnover among U.S. top management teams: an analysis of the effect of foreign versus domestic acquisition of U.S. targets', *Strategic Management Journal*, 18 (8), 667–675.

Krug, J. and Hegerty, W. H. (2001) 'Predicting who stays and leaves after an acquisition: a study of top managers in multinational firms', *Strategic Management Journal*, 22, 185–196.

Marks, M. L. and Mirvis, P. H. (1998) *Joining forces: making one plus one equal three in mergers, acquisitions, and alliances*, San Francisco: Jossey-Bass, 65–66, 74.

O'Reilly, C. A. and J. Pfeffer (2000) 'New United Motor Manufacturing Inc.: transforming people and systems', *Hidden Value: How Great Companies Achieve Extraordinary Results With Ordinary People*, Boston: Harvard Business School Press, 63–64.

'Renault steers forward' (2001) *Wall Street Journal Europe*, 15 February, 31.

SHRM (2000) 'Making mergers work: strategic importance of people', report by Society for Human Resource Management, Alexandria VA.

'Torch that sent a deal down in flames' (2000) *Financial Times*, 12 April, 22.

Watson Wyatt (1999) 'Watson Wyatt Worldwide's 1998/99 Mergers & Acquisitions Survey', report by Watson Wyatt, Washington DC.

9

Measuring, valuing and managing information, people and IT capabilities: pre- and post-merger and acquisition

By
Donald A. Marchand

THERE IS ONLY ONE TEST of the success or failure of a merger or acquisition: whether or not the value of the acquiring company rises after the deal is done. For publicly held companies, the value is calculated in per-share value increase or decrease. For privately held companies, the value can be measured in company growth and economic value added or EBITDA. M&A remains a popular strategy for growth among senior managers, even when current research shows that about two-thirds of all acquisitions are not immediately value adding for the acquiring company. Of course this is influenced by the anticipated 'synergies' relative to the price of the acquisition. Normally, the higher the price paid for the target, the greater the synergy must be to add value.

Why do so many deals fail or underperform? For the purposes of this chapter, we will examine three primary reasons: First, the acquiring company overestimates the synergies and does not achieve the business benefits anticipated. This could be a function of optimism about the financial returns from the value of the target. Second, the acquiring company overestimates the ability to integrate with the acquisition, which may be more difficult than anticipated because of differences in managerial and people cultures, different business languages and ways of managing information and operating processes, as well as incompatible approaches to IT systems. Deals that are completed for purely financial objectives with no other pre-deal due diligence are particularly susceptible to post-integration problems. Third, and related to the other two reasons, is the hubris factor. The managers pursue a deal with heavy doses of arrogance and optimism that compel them to overestimate the synergies on pre-deal value and post-deal integration.

Deals that are completed for purely financial objectives with no other pre-deal due diligence are particularly susceptible to post-integration problems

So, how does an acquiring company evaluate a target for pre-deal synergies and post-deal integration success? This chapter will address this question by focusing on the synergies that two companies may have related to their information, people and IT practices and the impact that these have on effective information use and business performance. Why are synergies related to information and knowledge use in a company important in M&A?

Valuing the information and knowledge orientation of a company

There are four compelling reasons why managers who are engaged in M&A activities need to carefully evaluate and measure the synergies related to information and knowledge use in a target company as well as in their own.

1 Information and knowledge use drive business performance

First, the way a company uses information and knowledge about customers, products, services, markets and operations is causally linked to business performance. Our research at IMD, conducted since 1997, has demonstrated that a company's effectiveness in using information and knowledge either improves or weakens performance over time.[1] It turns out that the information and knowledge that people in a company act on is critical to its current and future performance. The implication of this finding for M&A analysis is three-fold. First, evaluating the acquiring company's effectiveness in using information and knowledge is required to determine its relative capability to leverage information and knowledge use in a target company. Second, the same evaluation of the target company should be done on a stand-alone basis to determine its potential for business performance improvement over time. Third, once the effectiveness of information and knowledge use has been evaluated in both companies, it is then possible to evaluate the potential for synergies between the two companies. The challenge for the acquiring company is to judge whether the 'present value of the synergies' is worth the premium paid for control: 'an acquisition only enhances value for the buyer if the present value of the cash flow improvement *exceeds* the cost of acquiring the cash flow stream.'[2]

So here we have a fundamental challenge: how can managers evaluate the effectiveness of information and knowledge use relative to performance in the acquiring and target companies?

2 Focus on evaluating information capabilities as well as assets

Since the mid-1990s, managers have tried to value information and knowledge in a company by listing its 'intellectual assets' such as patent rights, R&D spending, products in development or rates of innovation. Although it is important to know what a target company's intellectual assets are, it is difficult to gauge how they are effectively deployed and used. Thus, these intellectual asset assessments have tended to be static pictures of the assets a company possesses at one point in time based on past performance. Translating this asset picture into a calculation of future value has been difficult at best.

Although it is important to know what a target company's intellectual assets are, it is difficult to gauge how they are effectively deployed and used

A more dynamic approach focuses on the business capabilities that managers in a company deploy to use information and knowledge effectively – or ineffectively. Our research has shown that effective information and knowledge use in a company is based on the interaction of three information capabilities – IT practices, information management practices, and the behaviours and values of people in using information and knowledge – which together represent the information orientation (IO) of a company and are directly linked to business performance[3] (see Figure 9.1). Each information capability is necessary, but not sufficient, to improve business performance. To achieve superior business performance, a company's managers must work on all three capabilities to leverage information and knowledge use in their company.

So now we know what to look for in evaluating information use in a company. The information orientation framework (see Figure 9.2) provides a powerful lens for managers to use to evaluate the information, people and IT capabilities in the acquiring and target company alike. In addition, the

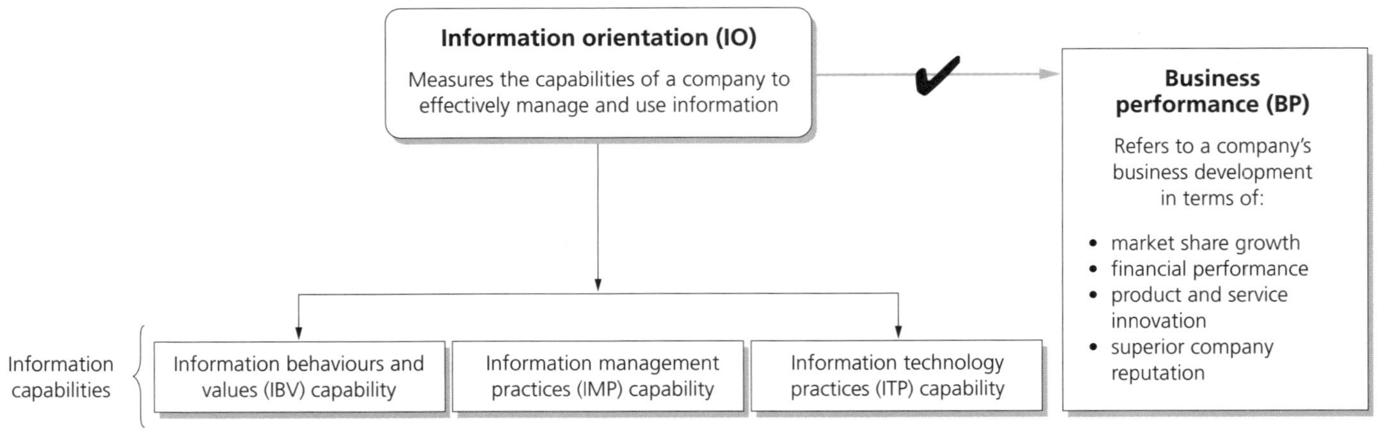

Figure 9.1 ◆ Information orientation linked to business performance

Source: Marchand, Donald A., Kettinger, William J. and Rollins, John D. (2001) *Making the Invisible Visible: How Companies Win With the Right Information, People and IT*, New York and London: John Wiley and Sons.

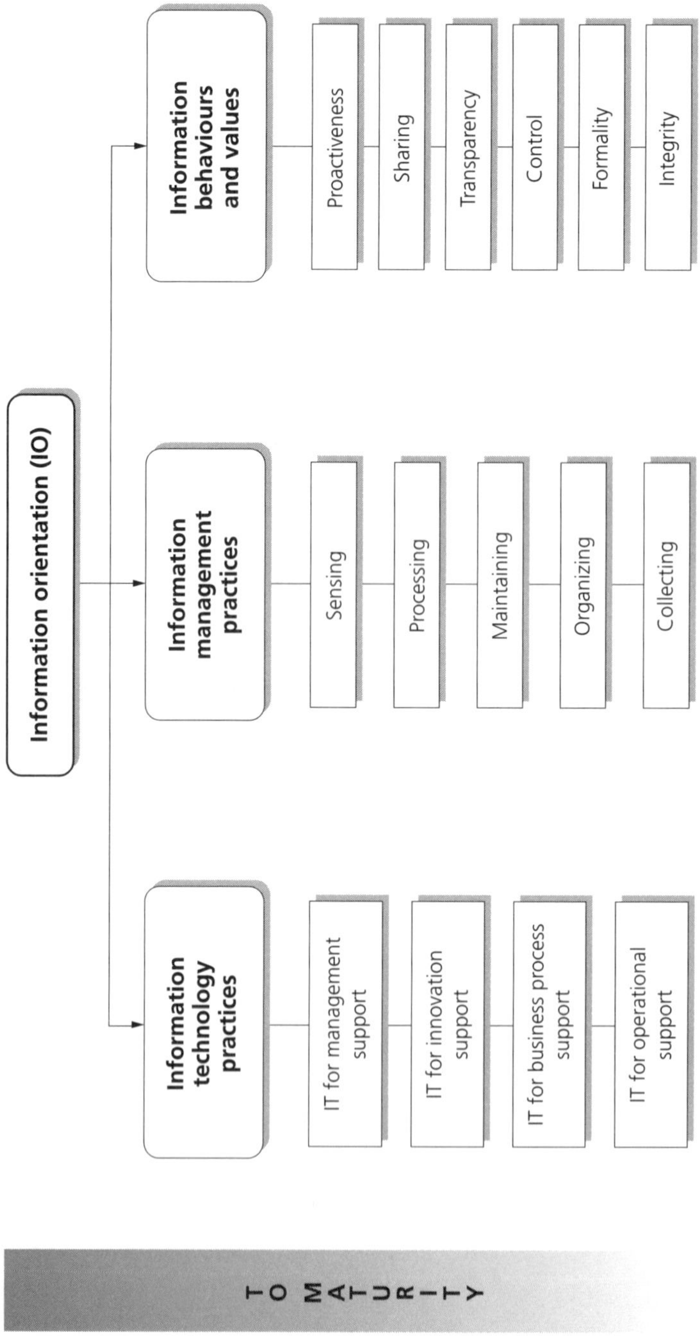

Figure 9.2 ◆ The information orientation maturity framework

Source: Marchand, Donald A., Kettinger, William J. and Rollins, John D. (2001) *Making the Invisible Visible: How Companies Win With the Right Information, People and IT*, New York and London: John Wiley and Sons.

practices and behaviours included in the IO framework can be measured and systematically benchmarked within and across companies. At a minimum, this means that acquiring companies can measure their own information orientation and use external sources of information to evaluate the target company, using the IO framework as a checklist and guide. In the best case, the target company is also measured and evaluated to compare strengths and weaknesses precisely relative to the acquiring company's IO. We will discuss below the M&A implications of knowing the information capabilities of both acquiring and target companies for the success or failure of the deal.

3 Managers' expectations about competing with information in their industry count

The way managers expect to compete with customer, market and operational information in the future is linked to IO.[4] This holds true for both acquiring and target companies. Thus, managers' commitments to build or improve information capabilities in their company are directly linked to their expectations about competing with information in the future.

Valuing 'anticipated synergy' is related to whether managers in either the acquiring or the target company really expect to compete with information and knowledge in the future. These expectations will influence their efforts going forward to improve their information capabilities beyond current levels – or not, as the case may be.

4 Managers' mindsets determine value and business outcomes in M&A

The perceptions of senior managers drive strategic decision making in companies. This is especially true for M&A activity. The valuation of the target company, the price that the acquiring company is willing to pay and the attribution of good will and synergies related to the target company's capabilities are all about the perceptions of key senior managers in the deal. Often these perceptions are translated into assumptions and are interpreted almost as fact. So it is not surprising that the failure of a deal can often be attributed directly to managerial perceptions such as:

- overestimation of synergies;
- overly optimistic appraisals of the ability to integrate;
- overestimation of market potential.

The potential for managerial misperception is particularly high when it comes to attributing value or synergies to information and knowledge use in a company or assessing the extent to which the capabilities to manage information, IT and people are developed. When evaluating the information capabilities of a company, managers tend to focus almost exclusively on IT assets and usage. IT is perceived as a 'hard' factor that can be seen and measured in terms of levels of investment, headcount of technical people and deployment of databases, software, hardware and networks. All these tangible assets can be evaluated in both the acquiring and target companies, unlike the intangible assets related to how people use information and how information is actually managed. Thus, without a perceptual framework and way of measuring these intangible factors, the probability that managers involved in M&A and their advisors will overestimate or underestimate the value and anticipated synergies, including the ability to integrate after the deal has been signed, is very high indeed.

> When evaluating the information capabilities of a company, managers tend to focus almost exclusively on IT assets and usage

If 70–80% of the book value of M&A deals is tied to perceptions about the intangible assets of a company related to information, people, knowledge and IT capabilities, then it is perhaps not surprising that the failure rate of M&As is roughly proportional to the managerial perceptions associated with these less tangible factors. Thus, improving the ability of managers in acquiring and target companies to understand and measure their information, people and IT capabilities relative to business performance could make a substantial contribution to reducing the risk of M&A activity and to providing clearer options for realizing expected value in post-merger integration activities.

Evaluating M&A options for acquiring and target companies

To understand how to evaluate the information capabilities of a company, we will use the cases of eight companies (four acquirers and four targets) with different profiles of information capabilities relative to business performance.[5] Figure 9.3 provides interesting combinations of acquiring and target company capabilities that can be used to examine the probabilities and risks associated with whether and how to proceed with M&A activities. The purpose of this section is to compare the scenarios for pursuing M&A activities and

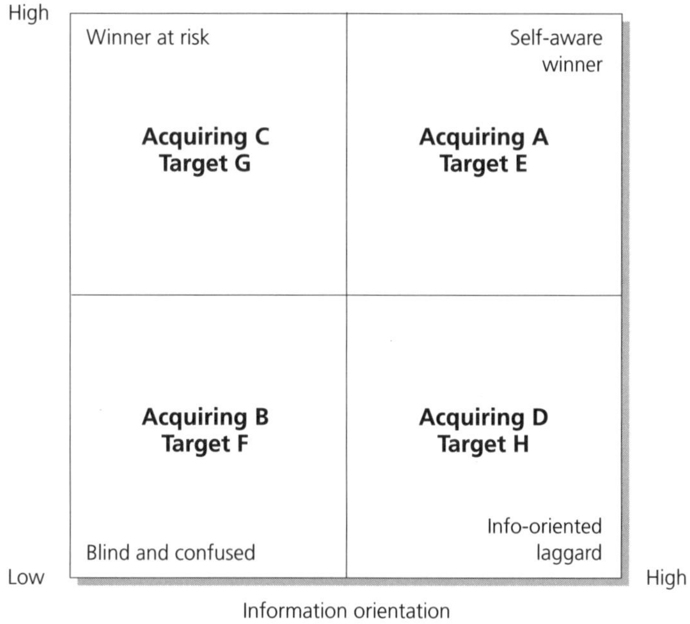

Legend

Self-aware winner
Practices IO to drive high performance

Winner at risk
Delivers good performance now, but lower IO may prevent continued success

Info-oriented laggard
Understands IO, but suffers fundamental weaknesses

Blind and confused
Major business change required

Figure 9.3 ◆ Information orientation to business performance

their probable impacts on acquiring and target companies as well as the likelihood of success and failure in moving forward with the deal.

There are generally four steps to follow in an M&A analysis. We will discuss each step relative to the valuation of information capabilities for each company.

Step 1: Valuing the information capabilities of the acquiring company

This step requires a candid self-appraisal of the information, people and IT capabilities of the acquiring company relative to business performance. Figure 9.4 shows the information orientation dashboards of our eight companies compared with an international index and benchmark developed in our IMD research project.[6] (For simplicity, we use the same IO dashboards for acquiring and target companies, indicating that both companies have similar IO profiles.) If we assume for the time being that the four acquiring companies, A, B, C and D, are in the same industry, then their starting points for considering M&A activity relative to their information orientation and business performance are quite different.

Company A is in the best position to consider M&A activity, since it possesses very good levels of information (its information management practices are in the top 5%), people (information behaviours and values top 5%) and IT capabilities (IT practices top 35%) relative to business performance (top 20%). The key factor in evaluating the success of this company hinges on whether it has also developed post-merger integration competences that will permit it to rapidly integrate target companies into its way of doing business. Without PMI competences, this company risks diluting its information capabilities if it merges with or acquires target companies with lower IO. Conversely, with good PMI capabilities and good business performance, this company is best positioned to merge with or acquire companies that add to its market share growth, business reputation and innovation in products and services.

In contrast, company B is in the worst starting position relative to its information capabilities and business performance. Not only may it lack the financial resources to proceed with deals (business performance bottom 5%), but it also lacks the information (information management practices bottom 5%), people (information behaviours and values bottom 5%) and IT capabilities (IT practices bottom 20%) to merge with other companies in its industry. Its biggest risk is the difficulties it faces in merging its information capabilities with those of the target company. If its PMI activities take too long or prove difficult to execute, this company risks further drops in business performance, which it can ill afford.

Company C appears to be in a good position to proceed financially with M&A based on its good record of past business performance (top 20%), but it lacks the information (information management practices bottom 5%), people (information behaviours and values bottom 35%) and IT capabilities

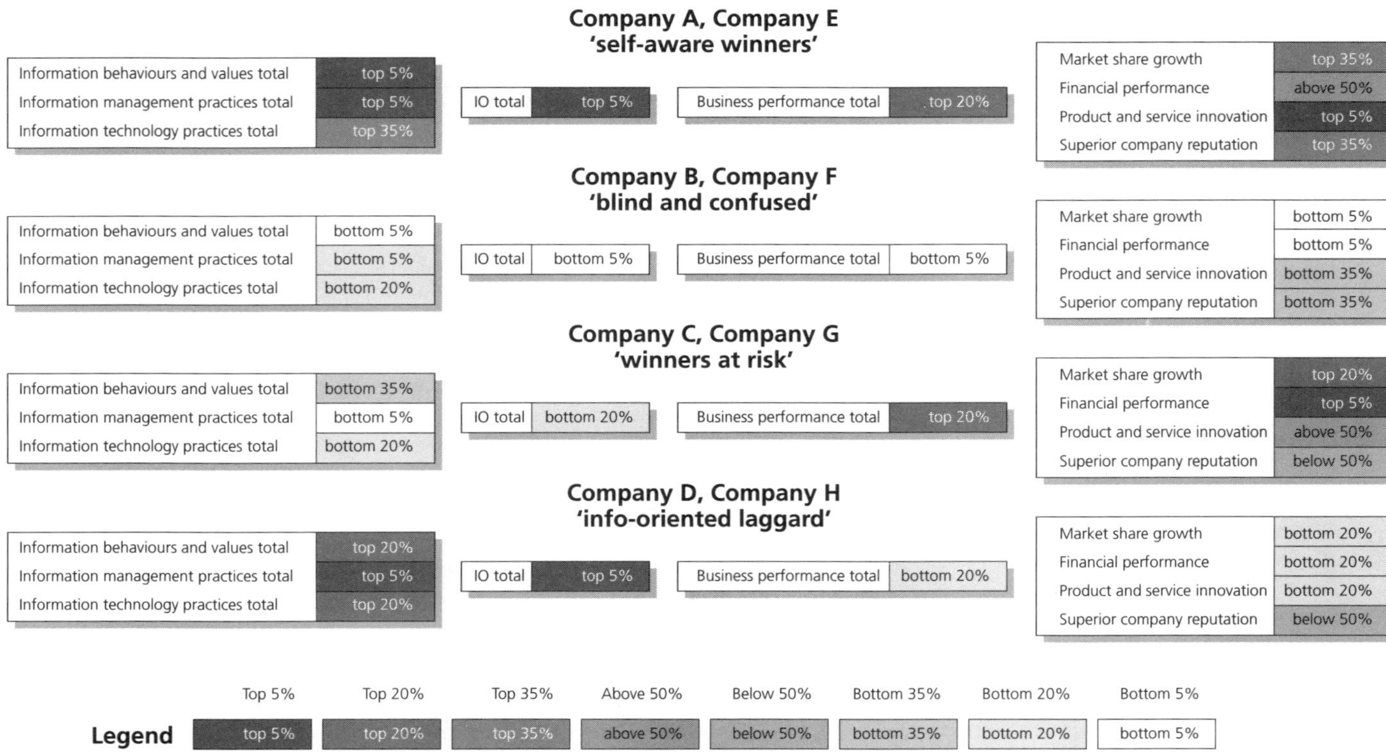

Figure 9.4 ◆ Information orientation dashboards of acquiring and target companies

(IT practices bottom 20%) for effective PMI. This company may be considered a 'winner at risk', since the managers may underestimate the need for good information capabilities in M&A or may overestimate the company's performance, which could lead them to be overconfident about the probable success of their M&A deal-making abilities.

Finally, company D has good information (information management practices top 5%), people (information behaviours and values top 20%) and IT capabilities (IT practices top 20%), but for other business reasons its business performance is low (bottom 20%). Although the company may not be in the best financial position to advance its M&A activities today, its managers have, nonetheless, developed good information capabilities for future success, assuming that the other reasons for poor business performance are addressed. However, this company has the same business risks as company A, since its ability to successfully merge with or acquire other companies depends on its PMI competences.

In the past, managers often under- or overestimated their people, information and IT capabilities since they had no scientifically valid way of indexing and comparing their information capabilities with those of other companies in their industry or across industries. Since these capabilities were difficult to see and accurately evaluate relative to business performance, managers often discovered the real level of these capabilities in their companies *after* the M&A deal had been signed – thus removing the potential to consider the deal in advance with these capabilities in mind.

In the past, managers often under- or overestimated their people, information and IT capabilities

Step 2: Valuing the information capabilities of the target company (without synergy)

The second step in proceeding with an M&A analysis is to evaluate the information, people and IT capabilities of the target company on a stand-alone basis relative to the price of the acquisition. Normally, if this analysis is carried out at all, it is based on public information or informal information gleaned from former employees of the target company or external company analysts. However, evaluating the information practices of a target company becomes increasingly difficult as managers move from IT practices, the so-called hard factors, to information management practices and information behaviours of people, the so-called soft factors.

Valuing the target company's stand-alone information capabilities can also be illustrated by our four dashboards.

As seen in Figure 9.4, company E as a target exhibits a clear track record of focusing on these capabilities (IO total top 5%) to drive its business performance (top 20%). In this case, due diligence would focus on the company's customer or market-facing strategy as well as the public emphasis on having the right information, people and IT capabilities to deliver customer satisfaction, loyalty and innovation in products and services. In this case, the acquiring company could use the IO framework as a checklist to identify clues to the target company's information, people and IT practice maturity.

Publicly available or informal information could also provide some clues to company F's poor information, people and IT practices (IO total bottom 5%) and its poor business performance (bottom 5%). In addition, examining the performance record of the company for signs of poor execution might lead acquiring managers to see deficiencies in IT (bottom 20%), information (bottom 5%) and people practices and behaviours (bottom 5%) such as poor uses of customer or product information between offices of the company or between direct and indirect channels. Thus the symptoms of poor information practices would be evident, even if information about the root causes was not always available.

In target companies E and F, the acquiring company managers could determine strengths and weaknesses in information capabilities using the IO framework as a guide for the due diligence evaluation. However, in the cases of companies G and H, such a qualitative evaluation would be more difficult since the record of business performance points in the opposite direction to IO levels. In company G, the tendency would be to overvalue the target based on its record of good business performance (top 20%), even though its information capabilities are low (IO total bottom 20%). In the case of company H, the tendency is to undervalue the target based on its record of low business performance (bottom 20%), even though it may possess good information capabilities (IO top 5%) for future success.

To overcome these problems of valuation, the acquiring company could request that the target company completes an IO diagnostic to determine the exact levels of its information capabilities relative to business performance.[7] This procedure could be followed when the acquiring company has a range of candidates and can encourage compliance or when the target company believes that proceeding with a more objective evaluation either increases its valuation or permits PMI activities to proceed more effectively. As we will see below, the incentive for using IO diagnostics and benchmarking in M&A

activities may change based on the relative positions of both the acquiring and target companies.

Step 3: Identifying synergies in the capabilities of acquiring and target companies

The third step in M&A analysis is to identify the synergies between the information, people and IT capabilities of the acquiring and target companies. Table 9.1 provides the M&A options for the acquiring companies, A, B, C and D, to evaluate the target companies, E, F, G and H. What we can readily see is the interdependence between the information capabilities and business performance of acquiring and target companies alike.

Table 9.1 ◆ *Valuation options for the information orientation of acquiring and target companies*

Acquiring company	Target company	M&A approach
A	E	High synergy
	F	Rapid merger
	G	Rapid merger
	H	Boost performance
B	E	Reverse acquisition
	F	No deal
	G	High future risks
	H	Buy for information capabilities
C	E	Buy for information capabilities
	F	No deal
	G	High future risks
	H	High future risks
D	E	Boost performance
	F	No deal
	G	High future risks
	H	High future risks

In the case of acquiring company A, the probabilities for success are considerably higher than for all other companies. When A acquires E the two companies can merge their information capabilities and their track records of good business performance for high synergy. Although there are still challenges related to merging IT, information and people practices, there is enough similarity in the IO frameworks of both companies to make this merger of 'equals' a winning proposition for both companies. However, if company A acquires either company F or G with low information capabilities, then company A must possess the PMI competences for a rapid merger to retain its high level of information capabilities. Without PMI competences, company A could face a dilution in information capabilities and business results if the merger takes too long or is poorly managed. Finally, if company A merges with target H, it has the opportunity to boost the performance of the combined companies, since company H brings good information capabilities for the future.

In contrast to company A, company B faces major risks in growing by M&A. In the case of target E, company B's managers must be mature enough to undertake a reverse acquisition, where they adopt the information, people and IT capabilities of company E to boost their poor performance. This process can be difficult, since the acquiring managers must acknowledge that their own company's poor information capabilities must be de-emphasized and divested. For targets F and G there are no real benefits to merging information capabilities, since both are low. In the case of G, company B is buying a track record of good performance in the past but this may perhaps not last, since G lacks the information capabilities required to boost performance in the future. In the case of target H, company B can acquire its more mature information capabilities and perhaps boost future performance, but this assumption is risky since the current performance of both companies is low.

In contrast to company A, company B faces major risks in growing by M&A

In the case of company C, the M&A strategy suggests high risks, except if C buys target company E. In this case, C can acquire the information capabilities of company E, assuming it is willing to de-emphasize or transform its own people and information practices and assume E's IT capabilities. In all other cases, company C faces either a 'no deal', as with company F, or incurs high risks associated with merging when there is low value added or acquiring a target's information capabilities and waiting for a future boost in performance. Since all four targets involve company C in some form of reverse acquisition – for information capabilities or boosting performance, or both – the chances of reaping synergies from these potential deals remain low. In addition, in the case of company C there is the hubris factor, whereby managers may not appreciate the net present value of having low information capabilities today and seeking to acquire new ones from an already successful company to transform in the future. Thus complacency about high current business performance and about building information capabilities may block these managers from future success.

Finally, in the case of company D, the potential for synergy is also mixed. For target company E, the potential to boost information capabilities and performance is quite high. In the case of target company G, there are future risks, since a dilution of information capabilities may occur because the managers of G have been successful thus far without building these capabilities. In the case of target company H, good information capabilities may allow the combined company to break away from past poor performance, but it is not a given and there is a medium to high risk that synergies may not be realized.

Examining the options for M&A related to information capabilities and business performance gives a sobering perspective that identifying the real benefits of M&A and the price of acquiring control of the target company is quite mixed when it comes to valuing the information, people and IT capabilities of companies.

The bottom line is that of the 16 possible merger combinations (shown in Table 9.1), there is only one opportunity (a 6% chance) for a clear synergistic win–win to occur between acquiring and target companies (A and E). There is an additional 12.5% chance that acquiring companies with good PMI skills can achieve success, as is the case when A merges with F or G. There is also a 12.5% chance that a merger will boost performance with increased synergies by combining good IO on both sides (A and H; D and E). By contrast, in 69% of our merger combinations, there are 'no deals', high future risks or the need to engage in difficult reverse acquisitions, where the probability of achieving synergies above the 'walk-away' price – the maximum price for a target that creates value – is very low indeed.

Step 4: Valuing synergies from information capabilities

The fourth step in completing an M&A analysis is to place a value on the anticipated synergy. If the cost of an acquisition is less than the stand-alone value plus the present value of the synergy related to information capabilities, the deal will create shareholder value. However, if our 16 merger combinations are representative of the merger choices available to companies, this outcome has a less than 31% chance of occurring under the best of cases. This means that in 69% of cases, proceeding with an M&A may dilute the value of the acquirer or the target or both, resulting in negative synergies where both companies lose competitive position and erode their already low information capabilities.

Although this analysis of information capabilities in M&A activities may seem pessimistic, the implications for the business strategies of specific companies are not. In the next section, we will discuss five concerns that senior managers must keep in mind when evaluating both the role and value of information, people and IT capabilities in acquiring and target companies.

Implications of information capabilities for competitive strategy

Going strictly by the numbers is risky

The first implication of information capabilities for competitive strategy is that M&A deals completed by senior managers and their advisors for purely financial reasons are the most at risk of failure, since they ignore or downplay both the value and role of intangible factors such as information/knowledge practices, people behaviours and even IT practices in M&A. In this case the problems that arise are two-fold. First, the value of information capabilities is not specifically evaluated in both the acquiring and target companies. Second, unless the acquisition remains stand-alone, the managers of the acquiring company will underestimate or, in the worst case, ignore the PMI competences involving information capabilities required to make a merger successful.

M&A deals in industries such as banking, insurance and financial services are particularly driven by financial rationales that ignore or underestimate differences in information, people and IT capabilities between the acquiring and target companies until after deals have been signed. Thus, before the ink is even dry, the senior managers in these companies become involved in long and tedious processes of merging incompatible information, people and IT capabilities in the two organizations – often diluting the financial rationale for the deal in the first place.

Acquiring but not merging may be safe but costly

The second implication of information capabilities for competitive strategy is that managers who seek to acquire companies but do not successfully merge them dilute value and cost-reduction synergies that are paid for but not captured. In many commodity-based industries, such as cement, paper, pulp and aluminium, the path to global growth requires the acquisition of many local companies. Large companies in these industries tend to measure

> **The result is that many of the acquiring companies remain multi-local across the countries in which they operate**

global growth in terms of tons of products produced. Senior managers in these companies seek acquisitions to increase size and economies of scale, with little or no attention to synergies in information, people and IT capabilities between acquiring and target companies. The result is that many of the acquiring companies remain multi-local across the countries in which they operate.

Although these companies acquire targets with a range of information, people and IT capabilities, they often leave each subsidiary to operate these capabilities independently. As the multi-local company grows into a global group of companies in essentially the same business but with little or no synergies in information capabilities, the price of these duplicative and often incompatible operations is reflected in higher working capital costs for information, people and IT practices across the world. Senior managers often are not aware of the multi-local premium on their operational costs until a competitor comes along that has developed global information capabilities and the right PMI competences to merge local acquisitions and integrate the information, people and IT capabilities in a matter of months rather than years.[8] As competition between multi-local players and a global competitor continues, the operating costs and reduced EBITDA of the multi-local players become more and more of a competitive disadvantage, in some cases eroding the capacity of multi-locals to pay for acquisitions without incurring increased debt.

Poor information capabilities result in lower growth by M&A

Companies that do not build good information capabilities can experience lower growth potential in two ways. As acquiring companies, they are in a poor position to acquire or merge with companies unless they engage in reverse acquisitions with targets that have well-developed information capabilities. Acquiring companies such as B or C are not really in advantageous positions to merge and integrate their information capabilities with others, even if, as with C, they have a record of good business performance. In this case, a company C can afford to acquire targets but dilutes value by not being able to merge with them on a timely basis.

Conversely, target companies that do not develop good information capabilities may attract lower valuation premiums from acquiring companies or may be difficult PMI cases. In either case, if the strategy of the owners or managers of the target company is to attract a higher premium for their company or to grow by merging with a larger and more prestigious global company, then not developing good information, people and IT capabilities dilutes net present value and potential for growth. These targets are less attractive to global suitors unless the global suitor is a multi-local company used to leaving its acquired companies to fend for themselves in local markets.

Good information capabilities coupled with good post-merger integration competences leads to competitive advantage

Companies that develop good information capabilities can achieve competitive advantage by growing through M&A if, and only if, they develop good PMI skills. These competences are required to make sure that acquirers can integrate acquisitions in their way of doing business rapidly and effectively to protect value and to optimize growth through transferring information, people and IT capabilities to local companies.

For example, in 1994, Spain's second largest banking group, Banco Bilbao Vizcaya (BBV), launched a transformation programme in its local retail bank in Spain to cross-sell banking and financial products to customers by developing excellent information, people and IT capabilities.[9] During its first 1,000-Day Programme, BBV increased its business volume by 97.7%, its income before taxes by 131%, its earnings per share by 86.5% and its market capitalization from €4.5 billion to €20 billion. In 1997, BBV launched a second 1,000–Day Programme directed at spending €4 billion on acquisitions in Latin America. In doing so, BBV built a single IT infrastructure among its acquisitions in Latin America and transferred its information and people practices to its acquired banks. In October 1999, BBV merged with Argentaria, a leading Spanish bank in corporate, mortgage and government financial services, to become BBVA, and in less than 13 months expanded its financial product lines by employing the information, people and IT capabilities for cross-selling developed originally in the retail bank. BBVA is ranked among the top 20 global banking institutions in the world, with the largest market share in Latin America. The bank operates under one brand across all products and customers globally.

BBVA is ranked among the top 20 global banking institutions in the world, with the largest market share in Latin America

Although BBVA is well known for its excellence in information capabilities, what is not so well known is its PMI competences. Ironically, these were developed in the late 1990s based on the long and difficult merger between Banco Bilbao and Banco Vizcaya, which took from 1988 into the early 1990s. In order to grow by acquisition first in Latin America and later in Europe,

BBVA senior managers knew that developing PMI competences was critical to their success in rapidly integrating acquisitions into the BBVA way of doing business. Today, BBVA has successfully coupled its excellence in information capabilities with its PMI competences to capture value for acquired banks by rapidly introducing them to the BBVA way of cross-selling financial products and services. In most of its acquisitions, BBVA has taken minority stakes in the acquired bank, but has been able to implement the BBVA way in the target bank to add value and optimize growth in local markets.

A similar example can be found in the cement industry. CEMEX, the third largest cement company globally, developed excellent information, people and IT capabilities in Mexico in the mid-1980s before beginning a series of Latin American and Spanish acquisitions during the early 1990s.[10] As it grew by acquisition, CEMEX learned early on the drawbacks of not having good PMI competences. When it acquired Valencia in Spain in 1992, it took 18 months to integrate the Spanish acquisition into the CEMEX way of leveraging information, people and IT practices. In 2000, when CEMEX acquired Southdown for $2.75 billion in the US, the PMI process was completed in just four months.

Today, CEMEX is the only cement company with a global approach to information capabilities and with rapid PMI competences. Both of its chief competitors are historically multi-local companies that generally do not integrate the information capabilities of acquisitions into their way of doing business and have not developed rapid PMI competences. Thus, CEMEX possesses both cost and value-creating advantages over its two leading rivals in the rapidly consolidating cement industry by leveraging global information capabilities with global PMI competences for growth.

Companies like BBVA and CEMEX represent the top 6% of companies in our analysis, successfully combining excellence in information capabilities with excellence in PMI competences to give them unique competitive advantages over their rivals.

M&A is a not a business result but a strategy for growth and improved business performance

Over recent years, many senior executives have played the M&A game, egged on by advisors who have stood to make huge gains from the deal transaction fees alone. Moreover, many of these deals were rewarded with stock market valuations beyond the imagination of most managers and senior executives. Not unexpectedly, M&A – getting big by whatever criterion was needed in an industry – became an end in itself, perhaps culminating in January 2001 with the merger of AOL and Time Warner. This merger of 'equals' was supposed to lead to unique synergies in the media and online industries. However, it is clear today that the merger not only resulted in multi-billion dollar write-offs but also largely failed to lead to the expected PMI synergies and instead diluted value on all sides.

Treating M&A activities as if they are the business outcome misreads what M&A is all about. M&A is about achieving value and synergies by combining the tangible and intangible assets and capabilities of companies to produce positive financial results and to create future business value through innovation in services and products, superior company reputation and market share growth. At the centre of the valuation challenge is the ability to see, measure and improve the information, people and IT capabilities of both the acquiring and the target company. Focusing on these so-called soft factors today is not merely necessary in M&A activities, it is a critical foundation for business growth and competitive advantage. Perhaps companies like BBVA and CEMEX knew this essential rationale for M&A all along?

Notes

1 Marchand *et al.* 2001a.
2 Mauboussin and Hiler 1998, 10.
3 Marchand *et al.* 2001b, 57–83.
4 Marchand *et al.* 2001a, 209–246.
5 Marchand *et al.* 2001b, 44–45 and 47–51.
6 Ibid. 47–51.
7 The IO diagnostic is available to companies through enterpriseIQ. See www.enterpriseIQ.com for more information.
8 Marchand 2000.
9 Marchand *et al.* 2001b, 4–6.
10 Marchand and Chung 2002.

References

Marchand, Donald A. (2000) 'The IT advantage: competing globally with business flexibility and standardization', in Marchand, D. A. (ed.) *Competing with Information*, London: John Wiley and Sons.

Marchand, D. A., Kettinger, W. J. and Rollins, J. D. (2001a) *Information Orientation: The Link to Business Performance*, Oxford: Oxford University Press.

Marchand, D. A., Kettinger, W. J. and Rollins, J. D. (2001b) *Making the Invisible Visible: How Companies Win with the Right Information, People and IT*, London and New York: John Wiley and Sons.

Marchand, D. A. and Chung, R. (2002) *CEMEX: Global Growth Through Superior Information Capabilities*, IMD – International Institute for Management Development, Case No. IMD-3-1081.

Mauboussin, M. J. and Hiler, B. (1998) 'Let's make a deal: a practical framework for assessing M&A activity', Boston: Credit Suisse First Boston, Volume 4 (Frontiers of Finance), 10.

Index

SMART PUBLIC PROCUREMENT AND LABOUR STANDARDS

Smart procurement aims to leverage public buying power in pursuit of social, environmental and innovation goals. Socially-orientated smart procurement has been a controversial issue under EU law. The extent to which the Court of Justice (ECJ) has supported or rather constrained its development has been intensely debated by academics and practitioners alike. After the slow development of a seemingly permissive approach, the ECJ case law reached an apparent turning point a decade ago in the often criticised judgments in *Rüffert* and *Laval*, which left a number of open questions.

The more recent judgments in *Bundesdruckerei* and *RegioPost* have furthered the ECJ case law on socially orientated smart procurement and aimed to clarify the limits within which Member States can use it to enforce labour standards. This case law opens up additional possibilities, but it also creates legal uncertainty concerning the interaction of the EU rules on the posting of workers, public procurement and fundamental internal market freedoms. These developments have been magnified by the reform of the EU public procurement rules in 2014.

This book assesses the limits that the revised EU rules and the more recent ECJ case law impose on socially-orientated smart procurement and, more generally, critically reflects on potential future developments in this area of intersection of several strands of EU economic law.

Smart Public Procurement and Labour Standards

Pushing the Discussion after *RegioPost*

Edited by
Albert Sánchez-Graells

·HART·
PUBLISHING
OXFORD AND PORTLAND, OREGON
2018

Hart Publishing
An imprint of Bloomsbury Publishing Plc

Hart Publishing Ltd
Kemp House
Chawley Park
Cumnor Hill
Oxford OX2 9PH
UK

Bloomsbury Publishing Plc
50 Bedford Square
London
WC1B 3DP
UK

www.hartpub.co.uk
www.bloomsbury.com

Published in North America (US and Canada) by
Hart Publishing
c/o International Specialized Book Services
920 NE 58th Avenue, Suite 300
Portland, OR 97213-3786
USA

www.isbs.com

HART PUBLISHING, the Hart/Stag logo, BLOOMSBURY and the Diana logo are trademarks of Bloomsbury Publishing Plc

First published 2018

British Library Cataloguing-in-Publication Data
A catalogue record for this book is available from the British Library.

ISBN: HB: 978-1-50991-283-4
ePDF: 978-1-50991-281-0
ePub: 978-1-50991-282-7

Library of Congress Cataloging-in-Publication Data

Names: Sánchez-Graells, Albert, editor, author.

Title: Smart public procurement and labour standards : pushing the discussion after RegioPost / edited by Albert Sánchez-Graells.

Description: Hart Publishing : Portland, Oregon, 2018. | Includes bibliographical references and index.

Identifiers: LCCN 2017050986 (print) | LCCN 2017050499 (ebook) | ISBN 9781509912827 (Epub) | ISBN 9781509912834 (hardback : alk. paper) | ISBN 9781509912810 (ePDF)

Subjects: LCSH: Government purchasing—Law and legislation—European Union countries. | Labor laws and legislation—European Union countries.

Classification: LCC KJE5632 (print) | LCC KJE5632 .S63 2018 (ebook) | DDC 342.24/041—dc23

LC record available at https://lccn.loc.gov/2017050986

Typeset by Compuscript Ltd, Shannon
Printed and bound in Great Britain by CPI Group (UK) Ltd, Croydon CR0 4YY

Acknowledgements

I would like to express my gratitude to the University of Bristol School of Law and to the Faculty of Social Sciences and Law of the University of Bristol for the financial support provided at the start of this project. I would also like to reiterate my gratitude to the contributors to this edited collection, as well as to other colleagues who participated in the workshop but, for different reasons, have not been able to add their voices to this volume. In particular, on this account, I am thankful to Prof Michael Ford QC (Bristol) and to Dr Richard Craven (Leicester). Lastly, I would like to thank the team at Hart Publishing for their patience and support, and for outstanding editorial work. Without their effort, this book would not have been possible.

Albert Sánchez-Graells
Bristol
10 August 2017

Contents

Part III: Labour Law Perspectives of Social Smart Procurement in the EU

List of Contributors

Prof Catherine Barnard, Professor of European Union Law and Jean Monnet Chair of EU Law at the University of Cambridge (Trinity College).

Ms Nina Boeger, Senior Lecturer in Law at the University of Bristol Law School.

Dr Piotr Bogdanowicz, Assistant Professor at the University of Warsaw, and Legal Adviser with Clifford Chance Warsaw.

Prof Roberto Caranta, Full Professor of Administrative Law at the Faculty of Law of the University of Turin, and Visiting Professor of the College of Europe.

Dr Maria Anna Corvaglia, Lecturer in Law at the Birmingham Law School.

Prof ACL Davies, Professor of Law and Public Policy at the Faculty of Law, University of Oxford.

Ms Caroline Nicholas, Senior Legal Officer at the International Trade Law Division of the United Nations Office of Legal Affairs (UNCITRAL Secretariat).

Prof Tonia Novitz, Professor of Labour Law at the University of Bristol Law School.

Dr Lisa Rodgers, Lecturer in Law at the Leicester Law School.

Dr Albert Sánchez-Graells, Reader in Economic Law at the University of Bristol Law School, and Member of the European Commission's Stakeholder Expert Group in Procurement (2015–18).

Ms Abby Semple, Principal Consultant at Public Procurement Analysis and Doctoral Candidate, Department of Politics, University of London (Birkbeck College).

Prof Phil Syrpis, Professor of EU Law at the University of Bristol Law School.

List of Abbreviations

2004 Public Procurement Directive	Directive 2004/18/EC of the European Parliament and of the Council of 31 March 2004 on the coordination of procedures for the award of public works contracts, public supply contracts and public service contracts [2004] OJ L134/114. No longer in force.
2014 Public Procurement Directive	Directive 2014/24/EU of the European Parliament and of the Council of 26 February 2014 on public procurement and repealing Directive 2004/18/EC [2014] OJ L94/65.
2014 Public Procurement Package	The 2014 Public Procurement Directive, together with Directive 2014/23/EU of the European Parliament and of the Council of 26 February 2014 on the award of concession contracts [2014] OJ L94/1, and Directive 2014/25/EU of the European Parliament and of the Council of 26 February 2014 on procurement by entities operating in the water, energy, transport and postal services sectors and repealing Directive 2004/17/EC [2014] OJ L94/243.
Bundesdruckerei	Judgment of 18 September 2014, *Bundesdruckerei*, Case C-549/13, EU:C:2014:2235.
Court of Justice	Court of Justice, ie the higher instance of the Court of Justice of the European Union (CJEU).

Laval	Judgment of 18 December 2007, *Laval un Partneri*, Case C-341/05, EU:C:2007:809.
Posted Workers Directive	Directive 96/71/EC of the European Parliament and of the Council of 16 December 1996 concerning the posting of workers in the framework of the provision of services [1997] OJ L18/1.
PWD Enforcement Directive	Directive 2014/67/EU of the European Parliament and of the Council of 15 May 2014 on the enforcement of Directive 96/71/EC concerning the posting of workers in the framework of the provision of services and amending Regulation (EU) No 1024/2012 on administrative cooperation through the Internal Market Information System ('the IMI Regulation') [2014] OJ L159/11.
RegioPost	Judgment of 17 November 2015, *RegioPost*, Case C-115/14, EU:C:2015:760.
Rüffert	Judgment of 3 April 2008, *Rüffert*, C-346/06, EU:C:2008:189.
TEU	Treaty on European Union [2012] OJ C326/13.
TFEU	Treaty on the Functioning of the European Union [2012] OJ C326/47.

1

Introduction

ALBERT SÁNCHEZ-GRAELLS

I. EDITOR'S NOTE

THIS BOOK IS the result of two years of conversations around the Court of Justice's judgments in *Bundesdrukerei* and *RegioPost*, and the older cases of *Laval* and *Rüffert*, as well as a lengthier set of discussions on the role of European Union (EU) public procurement rules in the promotion of labour and other (environmental, industrial) goals under the umbrella of what is now considered *smart procurement*. The most intense and productive of these discussions took place in the research workshop held at the University of Bristol Law School on 9 May 2016. Most of the contributors to this book took part in the workshop, where we all benefitted from feedback and input from over 30 colleagues from across the EU and European Economic Area (EEA). Other conversations have developed as a result of the workshop or in interactions in other academic conferences, as well as in email exchanges, comments to blog posts and Twitter threats—such is the way of current legal scholarship. The book now brings all these discussions together in one place, and offers the reader the opportunity to join the debate and benefit from the insight and nuance of arguments of the incredibly talented set of scholars who contribute to the book. I am in debt to all of them for their participation in this project and for their commitment to the book, despite the large number of competing demands on their time—especially those heavily involved in public discussions around Brexit.

I am also extremely grateful for the open-mindedness and intellectual honesty that all contributors have demonstrated from the get-go. This is an area of EU economic law where normative considerations tend to carry considerable weight, but where they also tend to remain largely implicit in discussions. Equally, this is an area where normative disagreements can be rather stark, and where it is easy to conflate what scholars would like the law to be with their reading of the relevant sources. In this book, all contributors make an effort to disclose their normative standpoints openly and frankly, and to present the law objectively, which sheds new light on the reasons behind the disagreements, well beyond their technical detail.

Thus, the book will offer the reader not only an extremely detailed analysis of the jurisprudence of the Court of Justice concerning the use of public procurement to enforce labour standards, but also a kaleidoscope of normative understandings of the broader role of public procurement, as well as contrasting visions of the role of the state as a buyer and an employer.

The book is meant to be read as a discussion, both between the reader and the contributors and between the contributors themselves. In that regard, readers are invited to choose their own reading order, and to first concentrate on the contributions addressing aspects closer to their individual concerns, worries or interests. The contributions are interconnected, and cross-references have been included to help the reader navigate them. However, there is no necessary 'better' sequence of arguments and the book is simply organised around the focus of the contributions (as explained below). Attention to detail and nuance is necessary to extract the most from this collection of contributions, as each author holds a specific view on the proper reading of specific passages in the Court of Justice's judgments, or on the relevance of different aspects as either *ratio decidendi* or *obiter dicta*. They also have different views on the implications of the cases in the context of the current policy-making processes, as well as on the likely direction of future developments in this area. This is the reason why this introduction does not provide a summary of the cases under discussion,[1] or a snapshot of the current status of the process of reform of the EU rules on the posting of workers—which would in any event be outdated by the time the reader gets to this point. I would not like to impose *my own* understanding of these issues on the reader, beyond the space confined to my contribution. Rather than that, each author offers his or her own account of both the case law and the current policy-making processes (to the extent he or she considers it appropriate for his or her arguments). The reader should thus have patience in navigating what could superficially seem like relatively repetitive rehearsals of the relevant case law of the Court of Justice and, more importantly, expect to find disagreement and potential contradictions between contributions—in terms both of the interpretation of these sources and of an assessment of their implications. This creates a rich narrative that should allow each reader to reach his or her own position, or to refine it. Ultimately, the book does not aim to offer a conclusion to the debate but

[1] Non-specialist readers, or those not familiar with the details of all cases, may want to (re-)read the following decisions of the Court of Justice: Judgment of 18 December 2007, *Laval un Partneri*, Case C-341/05, EU:C:2007:809; Judgment of 3 April 2008, *Rüffert*, Case C-346/06, EU:C:2008:189; Judgment of 18 September 2014, *Bundesdruckerei*, Case C-549/13, EU:C:2014:2235; and Judgment of 17 November 2015, *RegioPost*, Case C-115/14, EU:C:2015:760. However, their reading is not strictly necessary, as none of the contributions assumes knowledge of the aspects that are relevant to the arguments developed by each of the authors.

simply to contribute to further discussion, to push for a better understanding of the conflicting interests and goals in this area of EU economic law, and to facilitate research-informed policy reform.

II. BOOK STRUCTURE AND OUTLINE

The contributions to the book have been organised in four parts, each addressing a different perspective of the complex issues implicit in the use of public procurement to enforce labour standards. Part I is dedicated to the constitutional and internal market perspectives. Part II looks at the enforcement of labour standards from the perspective of public procurement and market interactions. Part III looks at public procurement as a policy tool from the perspective of employment and labour law. Lastly, Part IV offers perspectives from outside the framework of EU law, and explores the topic in the context of the World Trade Organization (WTO) and United Nations Commission on International Trade Law (UNCITRAL) public procurement regimes.

Part I starts with *Phil Syrpis's* constitutional perspective on *RegioPost*, which focuses on the complex relationships between the 2004 Public Procurement Directive[2] and Article 56 TFEU,[3] as interpreted by the Court of Justice in light of the Posted Workers Directive,[4] in terms of the relationship between primary and secondary law in the EU. His contribution critically assesses the Court of Justice's attempt to elucidate the beginnings of a theory of the relationship between primary and secondary law, clearly lays out the difficulties and internal contradictions in that attempt, and concludes with a plea for the Court to articulate more clearly what is, and what is not, possible for the legislature to achieve via the passage of secondary legislation in the context of the completion of the internal market. From a complementary constitutional perspective, *Piotr Bogdanowicz* then embarks on an analysis of the scope for proportionality assessments under Article 56 TFEU in the Court's case law relating to minimum wage requirements in public contracts (that is, *Rüffert*, *Bundesdruckerei* and *RegioPost*). In particular, he lays out a critical consideration of why proportionality was abandoned by the Court of Justice in *RegioPost*, and reflects on how to apply the proportionality test after *RegioPost*. Importantly, he concludes

[2] Directive 2004/18/EC of the European Parliament and of the Council of 31 March 2004 on the coordination of procedures for the award of public works contracts, public supply contracts and public service contracts (2004 Public Procurement Directive) [2004] OJ L134/114.

[3] Treaty on the Functioning of the European Union (TFEU) [2012] OJ C326/47.

[4] Directive 96/71/EC of the European Parliament and of the Council of 16 December 1996 concerning the posting of workers in the framework of the provision of services (Posted Workers Directive) [1997] OJ L18/1.

that the Court of Justice has now left a door open to discrimination of workers depending on whether their activity is carried out under a public or a private contract, and that this could have not happened if the Court had applied the principle of proportionality in *RegioPost*. In closing this part of the book, *Roberto Caranta* takes a different perspective and looks at this string of case law from the standpoint of the use of judicial precedent and general principles of law by the Court of Justice, paying attention to the inherent tension between civil and common law approaches to the role of the courts that it reflects. His contribution provides some suggestive ideas on how to treat the Court of Justice's case law in a contextualised manner. In my view, taken together, these three contributions offer complementary perspectives on the interaction between primary and secondary EU law and the Court of Justice's difficult exercises in both trying to create some sense of a system, while still carving out space for the adoption of decisions in specific cases in a way that preserves some room for future manoeuvring.

Part II moves on to the assessment of the enforcement of labour standards from the perspective of public procurement and market interactions. *Abby Semple* provides an overview of the evolution of public procurement case law and legislation concerned with the enforcement of labour standards as award criteria or contract compliance conditions, as well as the broader scope that this regulatory system leaves for Member States to pursue labour-orientated policies through public procurement. Her contribution provides a broader background to the use of procurement for environmental and social goals, but focuses on an attempt to clarify the scope for living wages (as a specific instance of a labour standard) to be included in public contracts, both under the current state of EU law and if the proposed revisions to the Posted Workers Directive are adopted. She submits that there are two ways of applying a living wage in public contracts that seem to be in accordance with EU law—one which is immediately effective and another which would apply if the planned changes to the Posted Workers Directive are adopted. In her view, this is reflective of a change of balance between economic and social considerations in the construction of the internal market, as expressed in *RegioPost*. Building on this market perspective, *my contribution* assesses the use of public procurement to enforce labour standards from a competition and state aid perspective, and in particular assesses *Rüffert*, *Bundesdruckerei* and *RegioPost* from an economic perspective. I highlight the potential negative competitive implications that derive from the asymmetrical rules the case law creates for the cross-border and inter-regional provision of services to the public sector. I conclude that, given the current ineffectiveness of the checks and balances theoretically orientated towards the prevention of these undesirable effects, contracting authorities and policy makers would be well advised to abandon their efforts to set partial, incomplete and difficult-to-monitor minimum/living wage requirements for public contracts only. Closing this part, and from a very different perspective on the role of markets in the context of public procurement, *Nina Boeger* considers the normative underpinnings of using procurement to facilitate and support the emergence of new forms of market actors, that is, businesses that set themselves out as value-led enterprises (or 'business for value'). From this standpoint, she characterises procurement as a tool for experimentation in the emergence of new forms of public sector providers that do not necessarily follow the traditional market/charitable provider split, and advocates for a maximum use of the flexibility created by the existing public procurement rules, both at EU level and domestically by Member States (which she analyses in the UK context). She clearly advocates for this use of procurement as a way of nurturing these alternative enterprise forms and, in doing so, transforming the current, dominant form of capitalism. Ultimately, she considers that, while aware of the relevant legal boundaries, public buyers might want to explore ways in which they work creatively within the legal framework to pursue strategies to set up longer-term relationships that socialise public service delivery, relying on the procedural/structural mechanisms of *business for value* enterprises, without exposing themselves to legal risks. On the whole, the contributions to this part show tensions that reflect broader difficult equilibria in the regulation of different aspects of the internal market (goods and services, on the one hand, and labour on the other) in the context of a social market economy. They also highlight the complexity of this area of EU economic law, where the number of overlapping regulatory layers require complex trade-offs.

Part III then places the discussion squarely within the field of employment and labour law, and considers the use of public procurement as a *sui generis instrument* (or surrogate) of regulation. This part offers diverse normative standpoints, and starts with *Lisa Rodgers*' assessment of the use of procurement to enforce labour standards as an instance of 'exception' in the regulation of the internal market, which she considers problematic. Her contribution discusses how labour law has increasingly become part of the general scheme of exception to single market goals, and how this creates a pressure not to allow social considerations that on an independent purposive assessment might be included. She concludes that the new provisions of the 2014 Public Procurement Directive[5] contribute to rather than counteract the tendency at EU level to prioritise economic over social considerations, and that this prioritisation cannot be a valid direction for the future of the EU. In a complementary manner, *ACL Davies* takes up the discussion from the perspective of the use of procurement as an opportunity for the government to reinforce existing public policies through contractual techniques, or to go beyond such policies by acting as a 'model employer'

[5] Directive 2014/24/EU of the European Parliament and of the Council of 26 February 2014 on public procurement and repealing Directive 2004/18/EC [2014] OJ L94/65.

itself. Her contribution defends the idea that governments should be permitted to engage in procurement markets in socially responsible ways. From this perspective, she submits that while the decision in *RegioPost* is to be welcomed for creating greater scope for the use of minimum wage conditions in government contracts, the reasoning in the case falls some way short of a proper understanding of the role of social goals in procurement, with the result that EU law continues to over-regulate this aspect of government activity to the detriment of national autonomy. Next, *Catherine Barnard* continues the discussion from the perspective of the tension derived from the fact that public procurement is premised on the notion of *equal treatment* between bidders, while the treatment of posted workers providing services under Article 56 TFEU has been premised on *differentiation*. In her contribution, she argues that, after considerable experimentation, both the Court of Justice and the EU legislature are moving towards prioritising equal treatment over differentiation in the case of posted workers, at least in respect of the most controversial issue, namely, pay. Further, she submits that this will make the position of contracting authorities in a procurement process easier in terms of process but it may result in the procurement costing more. Lastly, closing this part, *Tonia Novitz* offers a contribution that moves away from individual labour standards to consider the impact of *RegioPost* and other case law of the Court of Justice on the exercise of collective labour rights, with explicit and careful consideration of the idea of 'social dumping' and its implications for 'fair' competition. In her contribution, she examines the peculiar treatment of collective bargaining and procurement under the Posted Workers Directive and case law of the Court of Justice. Considering the scope for 'social dumping', she highlights the problems surrounding the requirement that minimum terms and conditions for posted workers be set by 'universally applicable' collective agreements, particularly in the light of austerity policies that have made such agreements exceedingly rare and unlikely to be given legal effect. On the whole, the four contributions to this part come to stress the tensions that result from the procurement-focused analysis of employment and labour law considerations in *RegioPost*, while they also highlight the scope for reduced friction between these pieces of the puzzle of internal market regulation that could result from a revision of the Posted Workers Directive.

Lastly, Part IV includes two perspectives on the topic from outside or beyond the EU. First, *Maria Anna Corvaglia* considers to what extent the inclusion of domestic requirements aiming at respect for labour standards and at the imposition of minimum wages poses a challenge to the respect of the principle of non-discrimination under both the WTO and the EU procurement frameworks. Her comparative assessment of the rules and requirements derived, respectively, from the WTO Government Procurement Agreement and from EU law shines additional light on the peculiarities of the EU regime. In a complementary manner, in the last contribution to this edited collection, *Caroline Nicholas* offers a comprehensive analysis on the space for labour law and social requirements under the regulatory architecture of the UNCITRAL Model Law on Public Procurement. Her critical considerations also provide a contextual understanding of the regulatory choices implicit in the current EU regime, in particular by stressing potential interactions with the ILO Conventions different from those currently included in the 2014 Public Procurement Package. In my opinion, these two views from the outside enrich the discussion and expand the horizon of regulatory alternatives for any reform of EU law.

Part I

Constitutional and Internal Market Aspects of the Enforcement of Labour Standards through Social Smart Procurement in the EU

2

RegioPost—*A Constitutional Perspective*

PHIL SYRPIS

I. INTRODUCTION

THIS COLLECTION OF essays analyses the *RegioPost* judgment[1] from a range of perspectives. The focus is on the implications for procurement law, and for labour law. Contributors are, in the main, seeking to reflect on the way in which the judgment of the Court of Justice affects the ability of contracting authorities in the Member States to apply social conditions when awarding public contracts. This contribution is rather different, and more limited in scope. My focus is not on the substantive outcome of the case, but instead on its constitutional dimension.

Specifically, I focus on the relationship between the 2004 Public Procurement Directive[2] and Article 56 TFEU,[3] the main Treaty provision on the freedom to provide services. I have written before on the relationship between primary and secondary law in the EU;[4] and this contribution builds on the framework developed there. In *RegioPost*, the Court of Justice attempts to elucidate the beginnings of a theory of the relationship between primary and secondary law. That is to be welcomed. And yet—in part as a result of the impact of the Posted Workers Directive[5] on the interpretation of Article 56 TFEU—the detailed reasoning is constitutionally perplexing.

[1] Judgment of 17 November 2015, *RegioPost*, Case C-115/14, EU:C:2015:760 (*RegioPost*).

[2] Directive 2004/18/EC of the European Parliament and of the Council of 31 March 2004 on the coordination of procedures for the award of public works contracts, public supply contracts and public service contracts (2004 Public Procurement Directive) [2004] OJ L134/114.

[3] Treaty on the Functioning of the European Union (TFEU) [2012] OJ C326/47. For a more specific analysis of the role of proportionality assessments in this context, see the contribution by Bogdanowicz in ch 3 of this book.

[4] P Syrpis, 'The Relationship between Primary and Secondary Law in the EU' (2015) 52 *CML Rev* 461.

[5] Directive 96/71/EC of the European Parliament and of the Council of 16 December 1996 concerning the posting of workers in the framework of the provision of services (Posted Workers Directive) [1997] OJ L18/1.

Moreover, there are significant differences between the approaches adopted by the Court and by its Advocate General, which do not serve to achieve a sense of clarity.

After assessing the constitutional implications of the judgment, I conclude with some reflections on the developing jurisprudence of the Court of Justice in this area, and with a plea to the Court—with Brexit inevitably in mind—to articulate more clearly what is, and what is not, possible for the legislature to achieve via the passage of secondary legislation in the context of the completion of the internal market.

II. THE NATURE OF THE CONSTITUTIONAL PUZZLE

All constitutional legal systems confront issues raised by the relationship between primary and secondary law. Courts the world over are accustomed to dealing with arguments that legislation should be struck down, or interpreted in a particular way, as a result of a conflict with a hierarchically superior, typically constitutional, provision. They seek to find ways to balance strong arguments from democratic and human rights-based perspectives. One of the key questions raised in *RegioPost* is directly relevant to this sort of enquiry. The case, at least in part, concerned the extent to which the passage of secondary legislation (in this case EU law Directives) may have an impact on the case law of the Court of Justice interpreting primary law (primarily, the text of the Treaties).[6]

Ultimately, the 'proper' relationship between primary and secondary law depends on one's assessment of the 'legal' or 'political' nature of the EU's constitutional settlement, and on one's views on the relationship between, and legitimacy of, the judiciary and the legislature at EU level.[7] Most lawyers would, at first blush, assume that there is a simple hierarchical relationship between primary and secondary law, that primary law does and should take priority over secondary law, and that the adoption of secondary legislation should not affect the way in which primary law is interpreted. Political scientists on the other hand, might expect the passage of legislation to have a greater impact on the case law of the Court of Justice.[8] There are strong arguments on both sides.

[6] See also G Davies, 'Legislative Control of the European Court of Justice' (2014) 51 *CML Rev* 1.

[7] See further P Syrpis (ed), *The Judiciary, the Legislature and the EU Internal Market* (Cambridge, Cambridge University Press, 2012).

[8] See further GS Ølykke and A Sánchez-Graells (eds), *Reformation or Deformation of the EU Public Procurement Rules* (Cheltenham, Edward Elgar, 2016) and in particular the contribution by Allerkamp.

In 2015, after surveying a range of cases in which the Court of Justice had to confront the interaction between primary and secondary law, I felt able to conclude only this:

> [T]he presence of secondary legislation is, in certain cases at least, prone to influence the case law of the Court of Justice relating to the interpretation of particular provisions of the Treaties. However, in other cases, it seems that the passage of legislation has no, or next to no, impact on the case law of the Court. There are huge inconsistencies in the Court's approach, and these have important constitutional ramifications.[9]

The Court of Justice's inconsistent approach is, in many respects, unsurprising. It is not at all easy to identify the 'proper' relationship between primary and secondary law. There are many distinctions that are relevant to the analysis, including, in the EU law context, differences between types of secondary legislation (regulations, directives, etc) and differences between legal bases and the legislative procedures they prescribe. It is also pertinent to consider, and this may or may not emerge clearly on the face of the secondary legislation, whether the legislature is aiming simply to afford greater clarity and specificity to the text of the Treaties (to 'put the flesh on the bones' of the Treaty text, as it were), or whether it is aiming to depart, in some way, from the pre-existing law (for example, by seeking to impose some clear limits on the scope of Treaty-based rights).

The most important distinction is the one between total/exhaustive and minimum/partial harmonisation.[10] Where legislation is based on the principle of total harmonisation, secondary legislation will, provided it is lawful, effectively displace primary law. The legality of national provisions will then be dependent solely on their compliance with secondary law (albeit that secondary law may, in this context, be interpreted in the light of primary law). The more difficult situation, exemplified by *RegioPost*, is where secondary legislation is of the minimum standard-setting variety. In these circumstances, primary and secondary law co-exist. Any national provisions must typically comply with both the floor set by secondary legislation and the ceiling set by the Treaties. Thus, it is a combination of primary and secondary law, as interpreted by the judiciary, that determines the extent to which states have freedom to act.

RegioPost provides an opportunity to explore the relationship between primary and secondary law in this complex area in a forensic fashion, and to reflect on the respective roles of the judiciary and the legislature as they combine to craft the internal market.

[9] Syrpis, above n 4, 462.

[10] See M Dougan, 'Minimum harmonization and the Internal Market' (2000) 37 *CML Rev* 853.

III. THE ADMISSIBILITY CHALLENGE

It is not necessary to provide a detailed account of the factual background of the *RegioPost* case here. But it is important to draw attention to the issue of admissibility, and to the way in which the Court of Justice and its Advocate General framed the question posed by the referring court. These issues provide early insights into the constitutional dimension of the case, and to the level of conceptual uncertainty which surrounds their resolution.

The case before the referring court, a Higher Regional Court, in Koblenz, Germany, related to the legality, in EU law, of social conditions in public procurement contracts.[11] The relevant Law of the *Land* of Rhineland-Palatinate (LTTG), to quote from the Court of Justice's summary,

> requires tenderers and their subcontractors to undertake, by means of a written declaration to be enclosed with their tender, to pay staff who are called upon to perform the services covered by the public contract in question a minimum wage laid down in that legislation.[12]

Questions relating to the admissibility of the reference were raised by the municipality of Landau and the German and Italian Governments. They submitted that 'failing a cross-border element, the Court of Justice does not have jurisdiction to rule on the compatibility of the measure at issue in the main proceedings with [the Posted Workers Directive] and/or Article 56 TFEU'.[13] The referring court had asked the following questions:

> Is the first paragraph of Article 56 TFEU, read in conjunction with Article 3(1) of [the Posted Workers Directive] to be interpreted as precluding a national provision which makes it mandatory for a contracting authority to award contracts only to undertakings which undertake, and whose subcontractors undertake, in writing, at the time of submitting the tender, to pay their employees who perform the contract a minimum wage fixed by the State for public contracts only but not for private ones, where there is neither a general statutory minimum wage nor a universally binding collective agreement that binds potential contractors and possible subcontractors?
>
> If the first question is answered in the negative:
>
> Is EU law in the area of public procurement, in particular Article 26 of [the 2004 Public Procurement Directive] to be interpreted as precluding a national provision such as the third sentence of Paragraph 3(1) of the [LTTG] which provides for the mandatory exclusion of a tender if an economic operator does not, at the time of submitting the tender, undertake in a separate declaration to do something which

[11] See Judgment of 3 April 2008, *Rüffert*, Case C-346/06, EU:C:2008:189 (*Rüffert*) and Judgment of 18 September 2014, *Bundesdruckerei*, Case C-549/13, EU:C:2014:2235 (*Bundesdruckerei*).

[12] *RegioPost*, above n 1, para 53.

[13] ibid, para 44.

> he would be contractually obliged to do if awarded the contract even without making that declaration?[14]

It is important to note that, in its first question, the referring court made reference to Article 56 TFEU, 'read in conjunction with' Article 3(1) of the Posted Workers Directive. This indicates its view that the legality of the national law at issue depended on its conformity with primary law (albeit primary law 'read in conjunction with' the Posted Workers Directive) rather than with the 2004 Public Procurement Directive. Indeed, that latter Directive is only mentioned in the second question, which relates to the proportionality of the penalty—specifically the mandatory exclusion of the tender under the LTTG—rather than the legality of the minimum wage stipulation.

Advocate General Mengozzi and the Court of Justice both concluded that the action was admissible. They argued that even in its first question, the referring court should have made reference to the 2004 Public Procurement Directive, and so reframed the question asked.

The Advocate General dealt with the objections to the admissibility of the case by emphasising the fact that 'the national measure at issue is capable of producing cross-border effects'.[15] It was, he states, 'by no means inconceivable' that the call for tenders

> was of interest to a certain number of undertakings established in Member States other than Germany, but that those undertakings did not in the end participate in the procurement procedure for reasons which could be linked to the requirements laid down in Paragraph 3 of the LTTG.[16]

As a result, the Court of Justice has, he argued, the jurisdiction to answer questions relating to the interpretation of Treaty provisions on the fundamental freedoms.

He went on, in what appears to be a separate strand of reasoning (the independent significance of which it is impossible to quantify), to refer to the 2004 Public Procurement Directive. It is, he states,

> primarily the connection between the case in the main proceedings and the provisions of [the 2004 Public Procurement Directive], the applicability of which is not in doubt, which supports my conviction that the objection as to lack of jurisdiction or inadmissibility raised by the Stadt Landau in der Pfalz and the German and Italian Governments must be dismissed.[17]

He concluded that 'it is primarily the conditions governing the application of Article 26 of [the 2004 Public Procurement Directive] which form the

[14] ibid, para 43. There is no discussion of the second question in this contribution. For analysis of that issue, see ch 5 of this book by Semple.
[15] Opinion of AG Mengozzi delivered on 9 September 2015 in *RegioPost*, Case C-115/14, EU:C:2015:566, para 33.
[16] ibid, para 37.
[17] ibid, para 38.

true subject-matter of the interpretation requested by the referring court in its first question'.[18] He explained that

> the applicability of the provisions of [the 2004 Public Procurement Directive] does not depend on the existence of an actual link to the freedom of movement between the Member States; those provisions become relevant as soon as the amount of the contract at issue in the main proceedings exceeds the thresholds for the application of that directive, which, in the case in the main proceedings, it does.[19]

Thus, according to Advocate General Mengozzi, the admissibility of the action depended on a combination of (i) the fact that it is by no means inconceivable that undertakings seeking to provide services in Germany may be deterred by the relevant law, and that therefore there is a cross-border element; and (ii) the fact that Article 26 of the 2004 Public Procurement Directive is clearly applicable on the facts.

The Court agreed with its Advocate General that the question was admissible, and with his focus on the 2004 Public Procurement Directive. It too was able to conclude that 'the referring court asks, in essence, whether Article 26 of [the 2004 Public Procurement Directive] must be interpreted as precluding legislation of a regional entity of a Member State, such as that at issue in the main proceedings'.[20]

However, the Court reached that conclusion via a different route. It was at pains at the outset to establish that it is, in general, able 'to provide the national court with all the elements of interpretation that may be of assistance in adjudicating on the case pending before it, whether or not that court has referred to them in its questions'.[21] It went on to baldly state that

> in order to give a useful answer to the referring court, the first question must in the first place be examined in the light of the provision of EU law that specifically governs it, namely Article 26 of [the 2004 Public Procurement Directive], a provision to which the referring Court, moreover, explicitly refers in its second question ...[22]

The Court went on to explain that as the Directive is applicable, a question not disputed by any of the parties, 'a question of interpretation relating to one of its provisions, in this instance Article 26, is admissible'.[23] This rather overlooks the fact that the referring court had not, in its first question in any event, asked for an interpretation of Article 26 of the 2004 Public Procurement Directive. Nevertheless, the Court, agreeing with the Advocate General, stated that it is by no means inconceivable that undertakings established in other Member States might be interested in participating

[18] ibid, para 43.
[19] ibid.
[20] *RegioPost*, above n 1, para 53.
[21] ibid, para 46.
[22] ibid, para 47.
[23] ibid, para 49.

in the tender process, and that they might be deterred by the obligation in the regional law to comply with the minimum wage imposed.[24] Thus, the Court 'has jurisdiction to give a ruling on Article 56 TFEU'.[25] It chose to add that this jurisdiction (presumably to interpret Article 56 TFEU) exists 'to the extent that the degree of harmonisation envisaged in that directive [presumably the 2004 Public Procurement Directive] so permits', a formulation whose meaning, I confess, escapes me.

The disagreement between the Court and its Advocate General as to the proper framing of the dispute resurfaces in their analysis of the substance of the case, and in particular as regards their treatment of the Posted Workers Directive. It is discussed further in sections IV and V. At this stage, it is sufficient to note two points. First, the question surrounding the applicability of Article 56 TFEU in the context of a dispute all the elements of which are confined within a single Member State, was resolved with reliance on a combination of both the undisputed applicability of the 2004 Public Procurement Directive and the potential deterrent effect of the national law on the provision of cross-border services. Secondly, and more fundamentally, the framework for the assessment of the national law in question was disputed. The national court focused on Article 56 TFEU (read in conjunction with Article 3(1) of the Posted Workers Directive). But its question was reformulated by both the Court of Justice and the Advocate General. In their view, the central question was best seen as relating to the interpretation not of primary law, but of more specific secondary law—Article 26 of the 2004 Public Procurement Directive.

IV. THE ASSESSMENT OF THE LEGALITY OF THE REGIONAL LAW

The question of the referring court, as reformulated, concerned the interpretation of Article 26 of the 2004 Public Procurement Directive. In this section, I explore the relationship between that Article and Article 56 TFEU on the freedom to provide services. As explained in section III, the Court of Justice (and its Advocate General) had no doubt that the Directive was applicable, and that an interpretation of the Directive would assist the national court to determine the legality of the Law of the *Land*. But, as we shall see, questions concerning the relationship between Article 26 of the 2004 Public Procurement Directive and primary law resurfaced in the substance of the judgment. It is argued here that the situation in the *RegioPost* case was complicated by two factors: first, the wording of Article 26, and in particular the fact that it refers, or makes *renvoi*, to 'Union law'; and, secondly, the relationship between Article 56 TFEU and the Posted Workers Directive.

[24] ibid, para 51.
[25] ibid, para 50.

This section first analyses the key paragraphs of the Court's judgment, in so far as they are relevant to the relationship between primary and secondary law. It then considers the nature of the disagreement between the Court of Justice and Advocate General Mengozzi, which has the capacity to shed some further light on the tangled relationship between Article 56 TFEU, the Posted Workers Directive and the 2004 Public Procurement Directive.

A. The Court's Approach

As explained in section III, the key question before the referring court was whether EU law precluded a provision, adopted by the municipality of Landau, that made it mandatory for a contracting authority to award contracts only to undertakings which pay their employees a minimum wage (set out in the LTTG).

The Court of Justice interpreted the referring court's question as one first and foremost concerning the interpretation of Article 26 of the 2004 Public Procurement Directive. Article 26 provides:

> Contracting authorities may lay down special conditions relating to the performance of a contract, provided that these are compatible with [Union] law and are indicated in the contract notice or in the specifications. The conditions governing the performance of a contract may, in particular, concern social and environmental considerations.

The Court had no difficulty in saying that the condition laid down by the municipality was a 'special condition' within the scope of Article 26 of the 2004 Public Procurement Directive;[26] and that it met the criteria of transparency laid down in the Article.[27] Thus, the remaining question was whether the social condition was compatible with Union law.

The Court of Justice began by stating that as Article 26 of the 2004 Public Procurement Directive does not lay down exhaustive rules, the regional law 'may be assessed in the light of the primary law of the EU'.[28] It drew explicit attention to the fact that special conditions relating to the performance of a contract are said, by Article 26, to be permitted only provided that they are compatible with Union law. Paragraphs 57 to 59 of *RegioPost* provide some welcome clarification as regards the relationship between primary and secondary law in the EU. As the Court points out, it is clear that where an EU measure exhaustively harmonises a field, national measures falling within that field 'must be assessed in the light of the provisions of

[26] ibid, para 54.
[27] ibid, para 55.
[28] ibid, para 59.

the harmonising measure *and not* in the light of primary law'.[29] Conversely, where EU measures do not exhaustively harmonise, the legality of national measures is dependent on what is likely to be a complex analysis of primary and secondary law.

At this stage the Court did not, as one might have expected, assess the Law of the *Land* of Rhineland Palatinate with reference to Article 56 TFEU.[30] Instead, and 'in accordance with recital 34 to [the 2004 Public Procurement Directive]', it was necessary to determine whether 'the minimum conditions laid down in [the Posted Workers Directive] are observed in the host member State in respect of posted workers'.[31] From there, the Court carefully distinguished *Rüffert*,[32] before concluding 'that Article 26 of [the 2004 Public Procurement Directive], read in conjunction with [the Posted Workers Directive]', permits the host Member State to lay down a mandatory rule such as that at issue in the main proceedings.[33]

Having reached this conclusion, the Court nevertheless continued, stating that its interpretation of Article 26 of the 2004 Public Procurement Directive 'is confirmed, furthermore, by a reading of that provision in the light of Article 56 TFEU'.[34] The Court did not explain why this extra step was taken, or indeed whether it was necessary to the outcome of the case (though the language used in paragraph 67 of *RegioPost*, that its conclusion is 'confirmed' by the analysis of primary law, suggests that it may not be). All it offers us is the thought that

> [i]t is clear, moreover, from recital 2 to [the 2004 Public Procurement Directive], that the coordinating provisions contained in that directive in respect of public contracts above a certain value must be interpreted in accordance with the rules and principles of the Treaty, including those relating to the freedom to provide services.[35]

In any event, the Court was able, in short order, to hold that the imposition of a minimum wage may prohibit, impede or render less attractive the provision of services; but that it may be justified.[36] In its analysis of justification, the Court again carefully distinguished *Rüffert*. It is worth noting that it drew attention precisely to those features of the law at issue which ensured that it, unlike the collective agreement at issue in *Rüffert*, complied with all

[29] ibid, para 57 (emphasis added).
[30] For an in-depth assessment of this issue, see ch 3 of this book by Bogdanowicz.
[31] *RegioPost*, above n 1, para 60.
[32] ibid, paras 62–65.
[33] ibid, para 66.
[34] ibid, para 67. There are clear parallels with the Court of Justice's approach in *Rüffert*, in which the Court's interpretation of the Posted Workers Directive was, at para 36, 'confirmed by reading it in the light of [Article 56 TFEU]'.
[35] *RegioPost*, above n 1, para 68.
[36] ibid, paras 69–77.

the stipulations in the Posted Workers Directive. The minimum rate of pay imposed was 'laid down by a legislative provision', 'which applied generally to the award of any public contract', and it conferred 'a minimum social protection', since national legislation did not impose 'a lower minimum wage for the postal services sector'.[37]

B. The Disagreement with Advocate General Mengozzi

The Advocate General also centred his analysis on Article 26 of the 2004 Public Procurement Directive. Basing himself on the wording of Article 26 of the Directive,[38] and indeed Recital 34 thereto,[39] he, like the Court, felt that it was necessary to establish whether the requirement in the regional law in question 'is compatible with the relevant provisions of EU law'.[40]

He, however, was 'unpersuaded' as to the applicability of the Posted Workers Directive,[41] and concluded that 'the *renvoi* made to EU law by Article 26 of [the 2004 Public Procurement Directive] relates exclusively to Article 56 TFEU'.[42] This was because, as in the case of *Bundesdruckerei*,

> the case in the main proceedings does not fall within the ambit of any of the measures involving the posting of workers referred to in Article 1(3) of [the Posted Workers Directive]. In particular, for the purposes of performing the public contract for which it tendered, RegioPost, which is established in Germany, did not intend either to rely on an establishment or undertaking within its group which would have posted workers to German territory, or even to use the services of a temporary employment undertaking or placement agency which hires out workers from another Member State in order to have such workers posted to Germany.[43]

He therefore held that while the case falls within the ambit of applicability of the 2004 Public Procurement Directive, and while it is capable of producing cross-border effects and deterring the provision of services by undertakings established in other Member States, it does not fall within the ambit of the Posted Workers Directive.[44]

The Advocate General then analysed Article 56 TFEU. He agreed that the minimum wage legislation imposed 'an additional economic burden that

[37] ibid, paras 75 and 76.
[38] *RegioPost*, Opinion of AG Mengozzi, above n 15, para 49.
[39] ibid, para 48.
[40] ibid, para 50.
[41] ibid, para 52.
[42] ibid, para 60.
[43] ibid, para 53.
[44] For criticism of this aspect of the Opinion, see A Sánchez-Graells, 'AG Opinion Favours Minimum Pay in Public Contracts: Why the CJEU Should Not Follow (C-115/14)', 11 September 2015, at www.howtocrackanut.com/blog/2015/09/ag-opinion-favours-minimum-pay-in.html.

may prohibit, impede or render less attractive the provision of services in Germany',[45] and also that it could be justified. In order to come to this conclusion, the task again was to distinguish *Rüffert*. But the Advocate General could not seek to rely, as the Court had done, on the Posted Workers Directive. His approach therefore could not distinguish *Rüffert* by focusing on the fact that the regional law at issue in *RegioPost*, unlike the one in *Rüffert*, complied with the stipulations within that Directive. Instead, his proposition was that

> the implications of the assessment contained in paragraphs 29 and 39 of the judgment in *Rüffert must now be reconsidered* in the light of Article 26 of [the 2004 Public Procurement Directive], an entirely new provision in EU public procurement law which was not applicable at the time of the facts giving rise to that judgment.[46]

What followed in the Opinion was an analysis of Article 26 of the 2004 Public Procurement Directive, in which the Advocate General emphasised the fact that it explicitly 'authorises Member States to require suppliers which have successfully tendered for public contracts to comply with *special* conditions'.[47] He touched on the limited competence of the *Länder* to lay down general rules on pay, and the requirement, in Article 4(2) of the Treaty on European Union (TEU), for the Union to respect the national identities of the Member States. He was ultimately able to conclude that it is 'perfectly consistent with the powers exercised by the Land of Rhineland-Palatinate that the scope of Paragraph 3 of the LTTG should be confined to workers performing public contracts'.[48] Thus, the law was justified by the objective of protecting workers, and proportionate.[49] Article 56 TFEU did not, therefore, preclude the application of the provision in a situation such as that in the case in the main proceedings.[50]

V. AN ANALYSIS OF THE RELATIONSHIP BETWEEN PRIMARY AND SECONDARY LAW

The exposition of the reasoning of the Court of Justice and Advocate General Mengozzi reveals, more than anything, that the relationship between primary and secondary law is apt to be confusing. The differences in the way in which the tasks facing the referring court and the Court of Justice were conceptualised reveal deep-seated and unresolved questions about the

[45] *RegioPost*, Opinion of AG Mengozzi, above n 15, para 62.
[46] ibid, para 70 (emphasis added).
[47] ibid, para 71.
[48] ibid, para 85.
[49] ibid, para 87.
[50] ibid, para 88.

way in which the task of interpreting EU law is undertaken, in the context of challenges to the legality of national provisions which, in this example, impose social obligations in the context of public procurement processes.

The key Treaty provision is Article 56 TFEU. Its interpretation is contested. There is, in addition, no question that the EU legislature has the competence to adopt secondary legislation in this field. It has in fact adopted a significant amount of harmonisation legislation, of the non-exhaustive variety, as a part of its effort to help complete the internal market.[51] The Posted Workers Directive and the 2004 Public Procurement Directive were the ones which were felt, by the Court of Justice at any rate, to be relevant to the assessment of the legality of the regional minimum wage law. But the relationship between the Treaty provisions and the relevant secondary legislation is, at best, opaque.

In this section, I identify the main points of confusion. My focus is on the nature of the relationship between primary and secondary law in the particular context of Article 26 of the 2004 Public Procurement Directive. But before addressing the relationship between primary and secondary law, it is important to make some observations relating to their respective applicability.

A. The Applicability of Primary and Secondary Law

The *RegioPost* case reveals significant issues in relation to the applicability of both primary and secondary law. The outer reach of the free movement provisions of the Treaties is of course controversial, with academic attention devoted, for example, to the extent to which non-discriminatory rules which hinder trade (or affect market access) should be caught by the free movement provisions, to the horizontal scope of the provisions and to the extent to which they apply to what are termed 'wholly internal situations'. Cases such as *Keck*,[52] *Re Trailers*,[53] *Viking*[54] and *Laval*,[55] and *Zambrano*,[56] have generated a huge volume of academic comment. In *RegioPost*, the broad scope of Article 56 TFEU was confirmed, with the Court of Justice and Advocate General Mengozzi agreeing that the existence of a potential

[51] See, eg, Communication from the European Commission to the European Parliament, the Council, the European Economic and Social Committee and the Committee of the Regions, 'Upgrading the Single Market: More Opportunities for People and Business', 28 October 2015, COM(2015)550.

[52] Judgment of 24 November 1993, *Keck and Mithouard*, Case C-267/91, EU:C:1993:905.

[53] Judgment of 10 February 2009, *Commission v Italy*, Case C-110/05, EU:C:2009:66.

[54] Judgment of 11 December 2007, *The International Transport Workers' Federation and The Finnish Seamen's Union v Viking Line ABP*, Case C-438/05, EU:C:2007:772.

[55] Judgment of 18 December 2007, *Laval un Partneri*, Case C-341/05, EU:C:2007:809.

[56] Judgment of 8 March 2011, *Ruiz Zambrano*, Case C-34/09, EU:C:2011:124.

(or 'not inconceivable') deterrent effect on the provision of cross-border services triggers the application of Article 56 TFEU. But there are some hints, in both the judgment and the Opinion, that the Court might have jurisdiction to answer the questions referred to it simply as a result of the applicability of Article 26 of the 2004 Public Procurement Directive, and independently of the existence of any cross-border element. The threshold for the application of the Directive is a financial one. As we have seen in section IV.A, where the Court applies the 2004 Public Procurement Directive, it interprets the Directive 'in the light of Article 56 TFEU'.[57] Thus, it is possible that the passage of secondary legislation might extend the material reach of primary law; that, as in this case, the principles underlying Article 56 TFEU might guide the interpretation of a Directive in a situation which would not, absent the Directive, fall within the scope of EU law.[58]

The disagreement between the Court and the Advocate General in relation to the applicability of the Posted Workers Directive is also instructive. Clearly, one of the tasks of the Court is to define the scope not only of primary law, but also of secondary law. It has shown itself capable of significant innovation here, for example in the citizenship context.[59] In *RegioPost*, the Court and Advocate General agreed that the 2004 Public Procurement Directive was applicable, and focused their analysis on an interpretation of that provision. But they disagreed in relation to their analysis of the Posted Workers Directive. This had a significant effect on the way in which they reached their conclusions. The Court essentially assessed the legality of the law in question with reference to the Posted Workers Directive. If the Court was right in relation to the applicability of the Posted Workers Directive, its approach is, at the least, explicable. There have, for a number of years, been indications in the case law of the Court that the limits of national autonomy in the field of the provision of services are set by the Court's controversial interpretation of the Posted Workers Directive, rather than by any independent interpretation of the text of Article 56 TFEU.[60] The Court has essentially held, in *Laval* and *Rüffert* for example, that national measures and conditions which go beyond what is envisaged in Article 3 of the Posted Workers Directive breach the Treaties. Thus, in *RegioPost*, the public procurement rules were assessed primarily with reference to Article 26 of the 2004 Public Procurement Directive. That provision allows for social

[57] *RegioPost*, above n 1, para 67.

[58] However, the Court of Justice's case law on the existence of (potential) cross-border interest in the award of public contracts is far from consistent. See the Judgment of 6 October 2015 in *Tecnoedi Construzioni*, Case C-318/15, EU:C:2016:747.

[59] See the examples in the 'avoidance' category in Davies, above n 6, 24–27.

[60] See *Rüffert*, above n 11, para 33: 'As regards the matters referred to in Article 3(1), first subparagraph, (a) to (g), [the Posted Workers Directive] expressly lays down the degree of protection for workers of undertakings established in other Member States who are posted to the territory of the host Member State which the latter State is entitled to require those undertakings to observe'.

conditions to be applied; but only to the extent that they are compatible with Union law. That depends on an interpretation of Article 56 TFEU, which itself depends on an interpretation of the Posted Workers Directive. All this is the result of the combined applicability of the Treaty provision and both relevant directives.

The Advocate General's approach to applicability was very different. He started from the same place—with the applicability of Article 26 of the 2004 Public Procurement Directive—but he was not persuaded in relation to the applicability of the Posted Workers Directive. He therefore read the *renvoi* in Article 26 of the 2004 Public Procurement Directive as a *renvoi* to Article 56 TFEU alone. And, in this particular context, in which he argued that Article 56 TFEU and the 2004 Public Procurement Directive apply and that the Posted Workers Directive does not, he proposed that the implications of *Rüffert* should be reconsidered.

It is of course the case that the task of delineating the outer scope of various laws—be they provisions of primary or secondary law—is difficult. The reach of the Treaty provisions on the freedom to provide services will not necessarily be the same as the reach of directives, which tend to apply only in specific circumstances. Yet in particular where one provision is routinely interpreted in the light of another, and where the relationship between the provisions is (as we shall see) not straightforward, decisions on the applicability or otherwise of particular provisions end up having profound effects on the law.

B. The Relationship between Primary and Secondary Law

The *RegioPost* case raises a multitude of questions that relate to the relationship between primary and secondary law. My key enquiry relates to the extent to which the passage of secondary legislation is apt to influence the case law of the Court interpreting primary law.

The judgment and Opinion reveal that there is no straightforward hierarchy between primary and secondary law. The key finding emerges from paragraphs 57–59 of the judgment. There, the Court stated that 'where a national measure falls within a field that has been exhaustively harmonised at EU level, that measure must be assessed in the light of the provisions of that harmonising measure and not in the light of the primary law of the European Union'. Where, on the other hand, a directive does not lay down exhaustive rules, national legislation 'may be assessed in the light of the primary law of the European Union'. This is undoubtedly helpful, though it does not get us very far. In the internal market context, there is precious little legislation of the exhaustive harmonisation variety. Thus, in order to assess the legality of measures brought about by contracting authorities in the public procurement field, it is necessary to consider not only EU secondary legislation (which does not operate so as to displace primary law), but also EU primary law.

The Court's statement of principle was, it should be said, immediately undermined in its judgment. The Court's consideration of primary law immediately morphed, in paragraph 60, into a consideration of the Posted Workers Directive; and as explained in section IV.A, it only returned later, from paragraph 67, to an independent (or, perhaps more accurately, a superficially independent) analysis of Article 56 TFEU. This reliance on the Posted Workers Directive is constitutionally interesting, especially in the light of the statements in paragraphs 57–59 of *RegioPost*. The Posted Workers Directive is manifestly a provision of secondary, and not primary, law. It is, moreover, not a measure that exhaustively harmonises the field, as the Court itself made clear in *Laval*.[61] Nevertheless, the interpretation of Article 26 of the 2004 Public Procurement Directive ends up depending on the Court's interpretation of primary law; and the Court's interpretation of the relevant primary law provision—Article 56 TFEU in this context—is dictated by, or at least driven by, its interpretation of the Posted Workers Directive.[62] The reality appears to be that it is a rather messy combination of the Court's interpretation of the Treaty text and the Court's interpretation of the relevant secondary legislation, which sets the limits of national autonomy to set social standards in the public procurement context.

It is difficult to be certain of the implications of all this. But if it is right that the Court of Justice is allowing the Posted Workers Directive to drive its interpretation of Article 56 TFEU, and thereby to drive its interpretation of what it is possible for Member States to require of tenderers in the public procurement context, this raises uncomfortable questions about the relationship between the Posted Workers Directive and the 2004 Public Procurement Directive. It should be emphasised how different the Advocate General's approach was. He sought to confine *Rüffert* to its particular context. He was seeking to provide Article 26 of the 2004 Public Procurement Directive with independent meaning; essentially arguing for Article 56 TFEU to be interpreted differently in the posted workers and public procurement contexts. This suggests a rather different relationship between the Posted Workers Directive and the 2004 Public Procurement Directive, but it is an approach likely to run into significant difficulties in those situations which fall within the scope of both pieces of secondary legislation.

[61] *Laval*, above n 55, para 60: 'Nevertheless, [the Posted Workers Directive] did not harmonise the material content of those mandatory rules for minimum protection. That content may accordingly be freely defined by the Member States, in compliance with the Treaty and the general principles of [Union] law.'

[62] See further P Syrpis and T Novitz, 'The EU Internal Market and Domestic Labour Law: Looking Beyond Autonomy' in A Bogg et al (eds), *The Autonomy of Labour Law* (Oxford, Hart Publishing, 2015) at 299–300.

The analysis thus far also serves to make it clear that there is no constitutional hierarchy. Neither primary nor secondary law takes precedence. The Court and Advocate General refer to one being read 'in the light of', or 'in conjunction with' the other; with priority sometimes afforded to primary law and sometimes to secondary law. Where the focus of the analysis is on secondary law (as it was as a result of the way in which the referring court's question was reformulated), it may nevertheless be that it is the interpretation of primary law which is crucial. Conversely, where the focus is on primary law, it may be that the meaning of that law only emerges with reference to secondary law (as in relation to the Court's use of the Posted Workers Directive to identify the limits of national autonomy in the public procurement field). It is, moreover, not clear what relevance, if any, should be attached to the fact that secondary legislation makes *renvoi* either to EU law in general, or to specific provisions of EU law. Both the Court and Advocate General Mengozzi referred to the precise wording not only of Article 26 of the 2004 Public Procurement Directive, but also of various recitals of that Directive which refer to EU law. This question might well be of particular relevance in the public procurement field, in which the successor provision to Article 26 of the 2004 Public Procurement Directive, Article 70 of the 2014 Public Procurement Directive,[63] does not make explicit reference to EU law.

It seems to me that all provisions of secondary law will, and should, be interpreted 'in the light of' the relevant principles of Union law, though there may be some doubt as to which principles apply in particular situations. General references to 'Union law' in secondary legislation are therefore unhelpful, and are not capable of adding anything to the analysis. But references to particular provisions of EU law may be helpful in setting out the relevant context in which interpretation occurs. Thus where, for example, a provision in a Directive makes reference to internal market measures, or social instruments or particular general principles of law, this might, in much the same way as the legal basis for the Directive, serve as a useful signal to the Court to interpret the provision in a particular way.

Many of the difficulties are the result of the lack of clear reasoning on the Court's part. It is typical of the Court's approach to combine various

[63] Directive 2014/24/EU of the European Parliament and of the Council of 26 February 2014 on public procurement and repealing Directive 2004/18/EC (2014 Public Procurement Directive) [2014] OJ L94/65. Art 70 of the 2014 Public Procurement Directive reads as follows: 'Contracting authorities may lay down special conditions relating to the performance of a contract, provided that they are linked to the subject-matter of the contract within the meaning of Article 67(3) and indicated in the call for competition or in the procurement documents. Those conditions may include economic, innovation-related, environmental, social or employment-related considerations.' Art 18(2) does however provide: 'Member States shall take appropriate measures to ensure that in the performance of public contracts economic operators comply with applicable obligations in the fields of environmental, social and labour law established by Union law, national law, collective agreements or by the international environmental, social and labour law provisions listed in Annex X.'

strands of argumentation, and not to make it clear which conclusions flow from which of the strands. For example, as discussed in section III, both the Court and Advocate General Mengozzi agreed that the questions of the referring court were admissible, as a result of (i) the applicability of the 2004 Public Procurement Directive, and (ii) the potential deterrent effect on the cross-border provision of services. But it need not be the case that (i) and (ii) will point in the same direction. It remains unclear whether the Court would have had jurisdiction to answer the questions asked if only one of the two 'tests' produced a positive outcome; or, indeed, what weight we should ascribe to each 'test'. This style of reasoning leaves those seeking to interpret the judgments of the Court with a series of 'what if' questions, resolution of which may well be a long time in coming.

VI. CONCLUSIONS

The intention of this contribution is to provide a constitutional perspective on *RegioPost*. Thus, it should be clear that the aim is not to assess, in substantive terms, the way in which the Court has interpreted Article 56 TFEU in the public procurement context; or to come to a conclusion in relation to the extent to which national and regional minimum wage stipulations are, or should be, permissible under EU law. The main aim of this contribution is to draw attention to the route whereby the Court reaches answers to those substantive questions.

The EU law framework consists of a number of provisions of primary and secondary law. It is abundantly clear that the passage of secondary legislation is apt to affect the nature and form of the argumentation relating to derogations from fundamental freedoms. In some situations, where harmonisation is of the exhaustive type, the effect of legislative intervention is simple; provisions of secondary law essentially displace, or supplant, the provisions of the Treaties. In other situations, things are apt to become much more complicated. In the public procurement field, the legality of social conditions imposed by contracting authorities in the Member States, which seem to be authorised by one piece of secondary legislation, is dependent on the Court's interpretation of Article 56 TFEU, which itself depends on the interpretation of another piece of secondary legislation (which the Advocate General, disagreeing with the Court, argued was not even applicable to the situation in question). Thus, primary and secondary law rules coexist, with the scope of application of each set of rules, the interpretation of those rules and the nature of the relationship between them being contested.

The worrying, if somewhat unsurprising, conclusion is that it is very difficult to know how the type of situation faced by the referring court in *RegioPost* will be conceptualised, let alone decided. This is of concern on many levels. It affects national courts who are seeking to answer questions regarding the limits which EU law imposes on national autonomy. It affects legislators and contracting authorities at the national and the regional level, who may be seeking to promote social and environmental objectives, but who may be anxious about the limits imposed by EU law. The only beneficiaries are the lawyers, whose task it is to craft arguments, of ever-increasing levels of ingenuity, both for and against particular initiatives undertaken at the national or the regional level.

But it is contended here that the most profound effects are encountered by the EU legislature. The result of the obfuscation in the reasoning of the Court is that it is very difficult for the EU legislature to know how it may affect the development of the internal market. Let us assume that the European Parliament, or a group of governments of the Member States, is concerned about the internal market case law of the Court relating to the scope and interpretation of the fundamental freedoms, and that, for example, it is eager to impose some limits on the rights of EU citizens, or keen to make it clear that in the public procurement context, contracting authorities in the Member States are able, under EU law, to insist on certain social or environmental standards. Short of amending the Treaties, it has the competence to enact secondary law. If that secondary law is of the exhaustive type, it will, provided it is lawful, displace the Treaty framework (though exhaustive harmonisation measures are, in this situation, likely to be interpreted in the light of the Treaties). Interventions in, for example, the public procurement field, are however, much more likely to be of the minimum standard-setting variety. Any such interventions will be read in conjunction with, and in the light of, existing primary and, to the extent that it is applicable, relevant secondary law. Their meaning may be emasculated, or avoided, in the ways described by Gareth Davies.[64] However, it is also possible for secondary legislation to shape the way in which primary law is interpreted by the Court. In *RegioPost*, as in *Rüffert*, the Court acknowledged the effect that (its interpretation of) the Posted Workers Directive has on Article 56 TFEU. Moreover, the Advocate General, if not the Court, was of the view that Article 26 of the 2004 Public Procurement Directive was capable of prompting a reconsideration of *Rüffert*, essentially changing the way in which Article 56 TFEU is interpreted.

In the UK, EU lawyers, myself very much included, have been scarred by Brexit. It is more than a little uncomfortable to acknowledge that there is some truth in some of the messages of the 'Leave' campaign, whose lies, and exaggerated claims, are all too easy to mock. The constitutional issue at the heart of *RegioPost* is principally about who has 'control' of the development of the internal market. It is incumbent on the Court of Justice to do better than it has done so far, and to provide a clearer sense of the parameters within which, and the mechanisms through which, the legislature is able to influence the internal market.

[64] See Davies, above n 6.

3

Article 56 TFEU and the Principle of Proportionality: Why, When and How Should They be Applied After RegioPost?

PIOTR BOGDANOWICZ

I. INTRODUCTION

REGIOPOST[1] HAS ALREADY been described in the legal literature as the 'gold standard' for the social protection of workers performing public contracts in the European Union (EU).[2] However, an analysis of the case might indicate that it may in truth be fool's gold. In particular, since the case concerned the free movement of services, it may seem surprising that in this judgment the Court of Justice did not refer to the principle of proportionality.[3] The principle of proportionality constitutes a key element in the justification of restrictions of the fundamental freedoms (such as the free movement of services) that underpin the internal market. The three-step methodology—consisting in the analysis of, first, restriction, then justification and, lastly, proportionality—is also considered to be one of the most predictable and formulaic features of the free movement case law.[4] More importantly, it has been used in the *Rüffert*[5]

[1] Judgment of 17 November 2015, *RegioPost*, Case C-115/14, EU:C:2015:760 (*RegioPost*).

[2] A Brown, 'The Lawfulness of a Regional Law Requiring Tenderers for a Public Contract to Undertake to Pay Workers Performing that Contract the Minimum Wage Laid Down in that Law, Case C-115/14 RegioPost' (2016) 2 *Public Procurement Law Review* NA49.

[3] Which, to stand by references to gold, was first explained by Aristotle in his 'golden mean' theory. See further E Engle, 'The General Principle of Proportionality and Aristotle' in L Huppes-Cluysenaer and NMMS Coelho (eds), *Aristotle and The Philosophy of Law: Theory, Practice and Justice* (Dordrecht, Springer International Publishing, 2013) 266.

[4] N Nic Shuibhne, *The Coherence of EU Free Movement Law. Constitutional Responsibility and the Court of Justice* (Oxford, Oxford University Press, 2013) 24.

[5] Judgment of 3 April 2008, *Rüffert*, C-346/06, EU:C:2008:189 (*Rüffert*).

and *Bundesdruckerei*[6] cases, which anticipated the *RegioPost* judgment and to which the Court itself referred.[7]

This contribution starts by summing up the most relevant conclusions of *Rüffert*, *Bundesdruckerei* and *RegioPost*. With this case law in mind, I focus on the relationships between Article 56 TFEU,[8] the Posted Workers Directive,[9] and the 2004 and 2014 Public Procurement Directives.[10] The foregoing will lead me to the main point of this chapter, that is, a critical consideration of why proportionality was abandoned by the Court in *RegioPost*, and how to apply the proportionality test after *RegioPost*?

II. CASE LAW RELATING TO MINIMUM WAGE IN PUBLIC CONTRACTS

A. *Rüffert*

The issue of national minimum wage laws in the context of public procurement appeared for the first time before the Court of Justice in *Rüffert*. The case concerned a dispute between the contracting authority and a contractor regarding the Law of *Land* Niedersachsen on the award of public contracts. This Law required that certain public contracts be awarded only to contractors who agreed to pay the staff working on such contracts a minimum wage, as prescribed by the 'Buildings and public works' collective agreement at the place where the service is provided.[11] In the case in question, the contracting authority terminated the contract when it became aware of the fact that the contractor's subcontractor, an undertaking established in Poland, paid its workers below the minimum wage laid down by the applicable collective agreement. The case was brought before the German national court, which took the view that the resolution of the dispute

[6] Judgment of 18 September 2014, *Bundesdruckerei*, Case C-549/13, EU:C:2014:2235 (*Bundesdruckerei*).

[7] See, eg, *RegioPost*, above n 1, paras 67 and 70.

[8] Treaty on the Functioning of the European Union (TFEU) [2012] OJ C326/47. Art 56 TFEU states as follows: 'Within the framework of the provisions set out below, restrictions on freedom to provide services within the Union shall be prohibited in respect of nationals of Member States who are established in a Member State other than that of the person for whom the services are intended.'

[9] Directive 96/71/EC of the European Parliament and of the Council of 16 December 1996 concerning the posting of workers in the framework of the provision of services (Posted Workers Directive) [1997] OJ L18/1.

[10] Directive 2004/18/EC of the European Parliament and of the Council of 31 March 2004 on the coordination of procedures for the award of public works contracts, public supply contracts and public service contracts (2004 Public Procurement Directive) [2004] OJ L 134/114; Directive 2014/24/EU of the European Parliament and of the Council of 26 February 2014 on public procurement and repealing Directive 2004/18/EC (2014 Public Procurement Directive) [2014] OJ L 94/65.

[11] On the legal and political context of the case, see C McCrudden, 'The Rüffert Case and Public Procurement' in M Cremona (ed), *Market Integration and Public Services in the European Union* (Oxford, Oxford University Press, 2011) 117, 120–22.

required an interpretation of Article 56 TFEU, referring the preliminary question to the Court of Justice.

Interestingly, following suggestions from the European Commission and a number of Member State governments, the Court of Justice decided to consider in the first place not Article 56 TFEU but the provisions of the Posted Workers Directive. Since a minimum wage requirement was not fixed in accordance with conditions set forth in the Posted Workers Directive, the Court held that Germany was not entitled to impose it.[12] In the view of the Court, such a 'precluding' interpretation of the Posted Workers Directive 'was confirmed by reading it in the light of Article 49 EC [now Article 56 TFEU], since that directive seeks in particular to bring about the freedom to provide services, which is one of the fundamental freedoms guaranteed by the Treaty'.[13] Having said that, the Court applied a three-step test. In the view of the Court:

(a) the national measure was capable of constituting a 'restriction' within the meaning of Article 56 TFEU;[14]
(b) such restriction could be potentially 'justified' by the objectives of ensuring the protection of workers, the protection of independence in the organisation of working life by trade unions and the financial balance of the social security systems;[15]
(c) however, the case-file submitted to the Court did not show that such protection was 'necessary'.[16]

Consequently, the Court ruled that the Posted Workers Directive,

> interpreted in the light of Article [56 TFEU], precludes an authority of a Member State from adopting a measure of a legislative nature requiring the contracting authority to designate as contractors for public works contracts only those undertakings which, when submitting their tenders, agree in writing to pay their employees, in return for performance of the services concerned, at least the remuneration prescribed by the collective agreement the minimum wage in force at the place where those services are performed.[17]

B. *Bundesdruckerei*

In *Bundesdruckerei*, the national court requested from the Court of Justice an additional interpretation of the applicability of Article 56 TFEU and the Posted Workers Directive to the enforcement of labour standards in a

[12] *Rüffert*, above n 5, para 35.
[13] ibid, para 36.
[14] ibid, para 37.
[15] ibid, paras 38, 41 and 42.
[16] ibid, paras 40 and 42.
[17] ibid, para 43.

public procurement setting. The request was made in proceedings between a contractor and a German contracting authority, concerning the obligation, contained in the tender specification relating to a public service contract, to guarantee payment of the minimum wage to the employees of the subcontractor of the contractor, even if the subcontractor was from another Member State (Poland) and its services were also to be rendered in Poland.

Unlike in the situation at issue in *Rüffert*, the Posted Workers Directive was not applicable to the main proceedings. The Court took into account that the contractor did not intend to perform the public contract by posting the employees of its subcontractor to Germany.[18] It held that the 2004 Public Procurement Directive was, however, applicable, since the minimum wage requirement could be classified as a 'special condition relating to the performance of a contract' within the meaning of Article 26 of that Directive. Under this provision, such a condition might be imposed only to the extent it was 'compatible with [Union] law'.[19] The Court then focused on the interpretation of Article 56 TFEU.

The Court referred to *Rüffert*, applied the three-step test and pointed out that the minimum wage requirement constituted a restriction within the meaning of Article 56 TFEU. It might, in principle, be justified by the objective of protecting employees, avoiding 'social dumping' and the penalisation of competing undertakings that grant a reasonable wage to their employees.[20] However, in the view of the Court, this justification could not work since the national legislation was disproportionate.[21]

Consequently, the Court of Justice ruled that in a situation where a contractor intends to carry out a public contract by having recourse exclusively to workers employed by a subcontractor from a Member State other than the contracting authority's, Article 56 TFEU precludes the application by that contracting authority of national legislation which requires that subcontractor to pay those workers a fixed minimum wage.

C. *RegioPost*

This case, like the previous ones, concerned a dispute between the contracting authority and a contractor regarding the obligation, imposed on the contractor and its subcontractors in the context of the award of a public contract for postal services, to undertake to pay a minimum wage to the staff performing the services covered by that public contract.

[18] *Bundesdruckerei*, above n 6, para 25.
[19] ibid, para 28.
[20] ibid, para 31.
[21] ibid, para 34.

In this context, the national court asked for an interpretation of 'Article 56 TFEU read in conjunction with [the Posted Workers Directive]', that is, whether it precludes the national provision's imposing such obligation. In case the answer was negative, the national court asked for an interpretation of Article 26 of the 2004 Public Procurement Directive.

The Court reformulated the questions and answered, in the first place, the question regarding the interpretation of Article 26 of the 2004 Public Procurement Directive. The Court remarked that the Directive did not lay down exhaustive rules in respect of special conditions relating to the performance of contracts, which meant that the national legislation should be assessed 'in the light of the primary law of the European Union'.[22] Then, however, the Court assessed the national legislation not in the light of primary law, eg Article 56 TFEU, but in the light of the minimum conditions laid down in the Posted Workers Directive, an act of secondary law.[23] Following such assessment, the Court held that the minimum wage requirement was compatible with 'Article 26 of [the 2004 Public Procurement Directive], read in conjunction with [the Posted Workers Directive]'.[24] Interestingly, the Court did not stop here but, referring among other things to *Rüffert*, stated that the

> [aforementioned] interpretation of Article 26 of [the 2004 Public Procurement Directive] is confirmed, furthermore, by a reading of that provision in the light of Article 56 TFEU, since that directive seeks in particular to bring about the freedom to provide services, which is one of the fundamental freedoms guaranteed by the Treaty.[25]

The Court then repeated its position taken in *Rüffert* and *Bundesdruckerei*, that a minimum wage requirement may constitute a restriction which may, in principle, be justified by reference to, for example, the objective of protecting workers.[26] One might expect that the next stage of the analysis would be the assessment of the national measure in the light of proportionality. Instead, the Court distinguished situations in *Rüffert* and *RegioPost*. In the former case, it reminded, the collective agreement was applied solely to the construction sector, which did not cover private contracts and had not been declared universally applicable. On the other hand, the minimum rate of pay imposed by the measure in *RegioPost* was laid down in a legislative provision, which, as a mandatory rule for minimum protection, thus applied generally to the award of any public contract in the *Land* of Rhineland-Palatinate, irrespective of the sector concerned.[27]

[22] *RegioPost*, above n 1, para 59.
[23] For in-depth discussion of this aspect, see the contribution by Syrpis in ch 2 of this book.
[24] *RegioPost*, above n 1, para 66.
[25] ibid, para 67.
[26] ibid, paras 69 and 70.
[27] ibid, paras 74 and 75.

D. One Topic, Different Approaches?

At this stage, some preliminary remarks should be made.

First, *the Court reformulates questions received from the national courts.* This may be illustrated by Table 3.1.

Table 3.1: Provisions invoked by the national courts compared with provisions interpreted by the Court

Case	Provision(s) invoked by the national courts	Provision(s) interpreted by the Court
Rüffert	Article 56 TFEU	Posted Workers Directive in the light of Article 56 TFEU
Bundesdruckerei	Article 56 TFEU and Article 3(1) Posted Workers Directive	Article 26 of the 2004 Public Procurement Directive; then Article 56 TFEU
RegioPost	Article 56 TFEU in conjunction with Article 3(1) Posted Workers Directive	Article 26 of the 2004 Public Procurement Directive in conjunction with Article 3(1) Posted Workers Directive; then Article 56 TFEU

Depending on the case, the Court of Justice assessed the minimum wage requirement from the perspective of either Article 56 TFEU, or Article 3(1) of the Posted Workers Directive or Article 26 of the 2004 Public Procurement Directive;[28] however, this was not necessarily the same provision invoked by the national court in the given case. As the Court stated in *Rüffert*, 'in order to give a useful answer, it [was] necessary to take into consideration [other] provisions when examining the question referred for a preliminary ruling'.[29] Consequently, although the national court had requested for an interpretation of Article 56 TFEU, the Court focused on Article 3(1) of the Posted Workers Directive. Similarly, in *RegioPost*, instead of interpreting Article 56 TFEU, 'read in conjunction with Article 3(1) of [the Posted Workers Directive]', in the first place the Court examined the question in light of Article 26 of the 2004 Public Procurement Directive, and only then did it refer to Article 3(1) of the Posted Workers Directive and Article 56 TFEU

[28] Art 26 of the 2004 Public Procurement Directive was not applicable at the time of the facts giving rise to *Rüffert*. The lack of reference to public procurement was, however, criticised by McCrudden, above n 11, 148. See also S Arrowsmith and P Kunzlik, 'Editors Note—the decision in Rüffert v Land' in S Arrowsmith and P Kunzlik (eds), *Social and Environmental Policies in EC Procurement Law. New Directives and New Directions* (Cambridge, Cambridge University Press, 2009) 6–8.

[29] *Rüffert*, above n 5, para 18.

(in that order). The only case where the Court did not reformulate the question was *Bundesdruckerei*, but even here it interpreted provisions that were not invoked by the national court (Article 26 of the 2004 Public Procurement Directive) when it held that one of the acts referred to by the national court (the Posted Workers Directive) was not applicable to the main proceedings.

Secondly, *after reformulating the questions, Article 56 TFEU is not placed centre by the Court*. The common ground of the questions invoked by the national courts was that all courts sought the interpretation of Article 56 TFEU—whether stand-alone (*Rüffert*), together with Article 3(1) of the Posted Workers Directive (*Bundesdruckerei*) or 'read in conjunction with Article 3(1) of the Posted Workers Directive' (*RegioPost*). However, only in *Bundesdruckerei* did the Court made an independent analysis of Article 56 TFEU. In both *Rüffert* and *RegioPost* the Court referred to Article 56 TFEU only to confirm the interpretation of Article 3(1) of the Posted Workers Directive (*Rüffert*) or the interpretation of Article 26 of the 2004 Public Procurement Directive read in conjunction with Article 3(1) of the Posted Workers Directive (*RegioPost*). As noted by Phil Syrpis, 'the Court's interpretation of the relevant primary law provision—Article 56 TFEU in this context—is dictated by its (controversial) interpretation of the Posted Workers Directive'.[30]

Thirdly, *the role of proportionality in Rüffert and RegioPost remains unclear*. This is somehow related to the second point already discussed. In *Rüffert* the Court held that it did not appear from the case-file submitted that the national measure was 'necessary', nor was it 'appropriate' for achieving the legitimate aim recognised by the national legislator. The question may arise: What if the arguments of the Member State concerned were convincing? It seems that this would mean that the minimum wage requirement at issue constituted a justified and proportionate restriction on free movement of services. However, if it did, the interpretation of Article 56 TFEU could not have 'confirmed' the interpretation of Article 3(1) of the Posted Workers Directive. To some extent a similar problem, except that there was no breach of Article 3(1) of the Posted Workers Directive, could have appeared in *RegioPost*, had the Court not abrogated the principle of proportionality. The only case where there was no controversy regarding the application of the principle of proportionality was *Bundesdruckerei*. In this case, however, the Posted Workers Directive did not apply.

Before I focus on proportionality, it is necessary to look at the interaction between Article 56 TFEU and Article 3(1) of the Posted Workers Directive in

[30] P Syrpis, 'EU Secondary Legislation and its Impact on Derogations' in P Koutrakos, N Nic Shuibhne and P Syrpis (eds), *Exceptions from EU Free Movement Law* (Oxford, Hart Publishing, 2016) 278, 286.

the context of Article 26 of the 2004 Public Procurement Directive.[31] In fact, as amply discussed by Phil Syrpis in Chapter 2, this is a broader question about the relationship between primary and secondary law of the EU.

III. IN BETWEEN PRIMARY AND SECONDARY LAW: THE TREATY, THE POSTED WORKERS DIRECTIVE AND THE PUBLIC PROCUREMENT DIRECTIVES

The relationship between EU primary law, such as the Treaties, and secondary law, such as directives, is not expressly laid down in the TFEU. Nevertheless, it is aptly noted that the authors of the Treaties always assumed the existence of a hierarchy of norms.[32] Besides, as specified by Article 1(2) TFEU, the TFEU and the Treaty on European Union constitute the Treaties on which the Union is founded. Thus, primary law is the supreme source of EU law and secondary law is subordinated to it. This emerges from Article 263 TFEU: the Court, which is responsible for securing that primacy, reviews the legality of, among other things, legislative acts, being acts of secondary law, on grounds of 'lack of competence, infringement of an essential procedural requirement, *infringement of the Treaties* or of any rule of law relating to their application, or misuse of powers' (emphasis added). Also, under Article 267 TFEU, the Court has jurisdiction to give preliminary rulings concerning '*the validity* and interpretation of acts of the institutions' (emphasis added) and (only) the interpretation of the Treaties.

National law has to be compliant both with the Treaties and directives, as the case may be. The supremacy of primary law over secondary law does not mean, however, that a national measure has to be assessed in the light of the Treaties in the first turn. According to the settled case law of the Court, 'where a sphere has been the subject of exhaustive harmonisation at [EU] level, any national measure relating thereto must be assessed in the light of the provisions of the harmonising measure and not those of the Treaty'.[33] Advocate General Cruz Villalón called it 'a kind of procedural supersession or "attraction", such that, for the purposes of disposing of a case, the Treaty is superseded as a necessary criterion for assessment in favour of the act of secondary European Union legislation'.[34] In such case, the Court does not declare that the given freedom is inapplicable to the case in question but

[31] C Barnard, 'More Posting' (2014) 43 *Industrial Law Journal* 194; C Barnard, 'To Boldly Go: Social Clauses in Public Procurement' (2017) 46 *Industrial Law Journal* 208.

[32] K Lenaerts and P van Nuffel, *European Union Law* (London, Sweet & Maxwell, 2011) 817.

[33] This formulation was already implied in case law, but it was articulated in the Judgment of 12 October 1993, *Vanacker and Lesage*, Case C-37/92, EU:C:1993:836, and was later confirmed by the Court, inter alia, in its Judgments of 13 December 2001, *DaimlerChrysler*, Case C-324/99, EU:C:2001:682; 11 December 2003, *Deutscher Apothekerverband*, Case C-322/01, EU:C:2003:664; and 14 December 2004, *Radlberger*, Case C-309/02, EU:C:2004:799.

[34] Opinion of AG Cruz Villalón delivered on 19 December 2012 in *Commission v French Republic*, Case C-216/11, EU:C:2012:819, para 35.

rather, on the contrary, confines itself to holding that it is not necessary to carry out an assessment of the freedom in order to dispose of the case. As put by the Advocate General,

> it is for the person alleging consecutively the infringement of an act of secondary legislation and a fundamental freedom to prove that the contested national measure is not subject exclusively to the scope of the act of secondary legislation and that instead it also applies to a sphere outside the scope of the act and covered by the fundamental freedom. Otherwise, a court 'must confine itself' to assessing the national measure 'in the light of the provisions of the harmonising measure and not those of the Treaty,' as the Court of Justice requires.[35]

Interestingly, the judicial interpretation of the Posted Workers Directive is pointed out as an example of secondary law 'taking priority' over primary law.[36] This is not clear from the outset, as the Posted Workers Directive is an instrument of coordination and not of harmonisation. This is explicitly set forth in recital 13 thereof,[37] and is confirmed in the case law of the Court,[38] as well as in the literature.[39] Coordination is considered less radical a method than harmonisation.[40] In *Commission v Germany*, the Court held that since the Posted Workers Directive did not harmonise the material content of mandatory rules for minimum protection set forth in Article 3(1) of the Posted Workers Directive, that content might accordingly be freely defined by the Member States, in compliance with the Treaty and the general principles of EU law, including Article 56 TFEU.[41] The Court took this position in reply to German authorities, who claimed that national provisions 'should have first been examined in light of the Posted Workers Directive, which specifically concerns the posting of workers in the framework of the provision

[35] ibid, para 48. AG Cruz Villalón referred here to the well-established case law of the Court, eg the Judgments of 24 October 2002, *Linhart and Biffl*, Case C-99/01, EU:C:2002:618; 23 January 2003, *Sternbenz and Haug*, Joined Cases C-421/00, C-426/00 and C-16/01, EU:C:2003:46; 24 January 2008, *Roby Profumi*, Case C-257/06, EU:C:2008:35; and 1 October 2009, *HSBC Holdings and Vidacos Nominees*, Case C-569/07, EU:C:2009:594.

[36] P Syrpis, 'The Relationship between Primary Law and Secondary Law in the EU' (2015) 52 *CML Rev* 477.

[37] Recital 13 states as follows: 'Whereas the laws of the Member States must be coordinated in order to lay down a nucleus of mandatory rules for minimum protection to be observed in the host country by employers who post workers to perform temporary work in the territory of a Member State where the services are provided; whereas such coordination can be achieved only by means of [Union] law.'

[38] Judgment of 12 February 2015, *Sähköalojen ammattiliitto ry v Elektrobudowa Spolka Akcyjna*, Case C-396/13, EU:C:2015:86, para 31.

[39] H Verschueren, 'The European Internal Market and the Competition between Workers' (2015) 6 *European Labour Law Journal* 139.

[40] K Kowalik-Bańczyk, 'Komentarz do art. 114' in K Kowalik-Bańczyk, M Szwarc-Kuczer, A Wróbel (eds), *Traktat o funkcjonowaniu Unii Europejskiej. Komentarz. Tom II* (art 90-222) (Warsaw, Wolters Kluwer, 2016) electronic version. She notes, however, that some authors treat these two terms as synonymous.

[41] Judgment of 18 July 2007, *Commission v Germany*, Case C-490/04, EU:C:2007:430, para 19.

of services'.[42] Finally, the Court found that the national law on posting workers was not compatible with Article 56 TFEU, and barely hinted at the Posted Workers Directive. However, few months later, in *Laval*, the Court decided to examine the case 'with regard to the provisions of the Posted Workers Directive interpreted in the light of Article [56 TFEU]'.[43] The exact approach taken by the Court was unclear. The Court started with the assessment of the measure in question under Article 3(1) of the Posted Workers Directive and concluded that minimum rates of pay at issue could not be applied to foreign services since they had not been laid down in accordance with that Article.[44] Then the Court held that 'it is necessary to assess further, the obligations on undertakings established in another Member State which stem from such a system for determining wages with regard to Article 56 TFEU'.[45] However, in subsequent paragraphs, the Court discussed the Posted Workers Directive, not the Treaty. It referred to Article 56 TFEU (and the principle of proportionality) only when it assessed the collective action at issue.[46] For some authors, the clear implication thereof was that 'a national system going beyond the terms of the Posted Workers Directive might nevertheless be compatible'.[47] It should be noted, however, that collective action falls outside Article 3 of the Posted Workers Directive.

So, how do Article 3(1) of the Posted Workers Directive and Article 56 TFEU fit together? Catharine Barnard argues that there are three different models in which Article 3(1) of the Posted Workers Directive can interact with Article 56 TFEU. No single model applies, and different models apply in different situations.[48]

The first model considers that the Posted Workers Directive is an exhaustive harmonisation measure and the review of national rules under Article 56 TFEU is neither permitted nor desirable. The author calls this model 'one bite of the cherry'. She argues that even if the Posted Workers Directive as a whole is not a harmonisation measure, there is a quite small area which is exhaustively harmonised, that is, the regulation as to which national rules (home or host state) apply to the 'terms and conditions of employment' covering the matters specified in Article 3(1)(a)–(g) of the

[42] ibid, para 16.

[43] Judgment of 18 December 2007, *Laval un Partneri*, Case C-341/05, EU:C:2007:809, para 60. In the end, as Hös noted, it was not entirely clear whether the Court was giving a special reading of the Posted Workers Directive in the light Art 56 TFEU, or whether it was rather interpreting Art 56 TFEU with regard to the Posted Workers Directive. See N Hös, 'The principle of proportionality in Viking and Laval: an appropriate standard of judicial review?' (2009) 6 *EUI Working Papers* 25.

[44] *Laval*, above n 43, paras 62–71.

[45] ibid, para 72.

[46] ibid, paras 85–110. Interestingly, some authors argued that the Court had incorrectly applied a proportionality test in *Laval*. See Hös, above n 43, 1–43.

[47] Syrpis, above n 36, 478; P Syrpis and T Novitz, 'The EU Internal Market and Domestic Labour Law: Looking Beyond Autonomy' in A Bogg et al (eds), *The Autonomy of Labour Law* (Oxford, Hart Publishing, 2015) 300.

[48] Barnard, 'More Posting', above n 31, 197–205.

Posted Workers Directive.[49] Interestingly, she implies that 'there are some signs' that the Court followed this approach in *Rüffert*, namely, when the Court said that the interpretation of the Posted Workers Directive is confirmed by reading it in the light of Article 56 TFEU. She concedes, however, that further paragraphs of *Rüffert* suggest that the Court was applying the second model. She calls this second model 'two bites of the cherry'—it consists in a first review under the Posted Workers Directive and then an additional check of the compatibility of the host state's provisions with the Treaty. Barnard argues that this second review under the Treaty does considerable damage to legal certainty, also given the inherently vague notions of justification and proportionality and their application in the discretionary field of social policy—finally resulting in uncertainty.[50] The third model is a variation of the first one. It accepts that the Posted Workers Directive exhaustively harmonises some rules, but within that harmonised space area there is still room for national law to apply. Consequently, it is in respect of these matters that Article 56 TFEU may be applied.[51]

As regards the application of the models, three situations are distinguished: (i) for the areas exhaustively harmonised by the Posted Workers Directive, (ii) for matters falling outside the harmonised areas, and (iii) for matters falling within the Posted Workers Directive but outside the harmonised areas.[52] The main problem with these apparently clear-cut boundaries is that the Court of Justice does not feel restrained by them. If we assume, as Barnard does, that the Posted Workers Directive exhaustively harmonises whichever of the state's rules apply to the 'terms and conditions of employment' as specified in Article 3(1) thereof, then there should be no review of the national rules under Article 56 TFEU (model 1). In contrast, if Article 3(1) of the Posted Workers Directive does not exhaustively harmonise the national rules on minimum rates of pay, the next step should be their review under Article 56 TFEU (model 2). In both the *Rüffert* and *RegioPost* cases the Court reviewed national rules under Article 56 TFEU, which might suggest model 2, but it did so only to 'confirm' its interpretation of the Posted Workers Directive. Even when the Court applied a three-step test in *Rüffert* or a two-step analysis (without proportionality) in *RegioPost*, it is hard to say that this was an independent analysis of the Treaty provisions (as was the case, for example, in *Bundesdruckerei*).[53] In *RegioPost* the Court reformulated the

[49] ibid, 200.

[50] ibid, 199.

[51] ibid, 200 and 202–6.

[52] ibid, 200–5.

[53] Syrpis and Novitz, above n 47, 300. Christopher McCrudden notes that there are two readings of these passages: either the Posted Workers Directive provides a test as to whether a law that was contested as contrary to Art 56 TFEU might be regarded as justified, or the Posted Workers Directive provides a test as to whether there was a breach of Art 56 TFEU itself. He assumes, however, that whichever reading is adopted, it is clear that the Posted Workers Directive constitutes 'a key to determining the acceptability of the contested law under the Treaty'. McCrudden, above n 11, 126. A similar problem appeared in *Laval*; see Hös, above n 43.

question in order to focus on Article 26 of the 2004 Public Procurement Directive, but since that Directive 'does not lay down exhaustive rules in respect of special conditions relating to the performance of contracts' (such as minimum rates of pay), it stated that national rules 'may be assessed in the light of the primary law of the European Union'.[54] However, it then went on to assess the compatibility of Article 26 of the 2004 Public Procurement Directive with the Posted Workers Directive, rather than with Article 56 TFEU. This raises two issues. First, the Posted Workers Directive is not an act of EU primary law, and it is difficult to understand why the Court referred explicitly to primary law but focused on secondary law. It is also unclear why the Court reverted to Article 56 TFEU after the analysis of the Posted Workers Directive was completed. This means that the legality of special social conditions for the performance of public contracts, which seem to be authorised by the 2004 Public Procurement Directive, ends up being dependent on the Court's interpretation of Article 56 TFEU, which itself depends on the interpretation of another piece of secondary legislation.[55]

To make things more complicated, it should be reminded that in *Rüffert* the breach of the Posted Workers Directive was 'confirmed' by the breach of Article 56 TFEU, but the Court suggested that if the case-file submitted to the Court had contained any evidence based on proportionality considerations, the outcome could have been different. What would the judgment in *RegioPost* look like, if the Court had decided to apply the principle of proportionality?

IV. WHY PROPORTIONALITY COULD MATTER IN *REGIOPOST*

Proportionality is considered one of the core principles of EU public procurement law.[56] In general, it requires that the action undertaken be necessary, appropriate (adequate) and proportionate *sensu stricto*.[57] It is called 'an overarching principle of EU law, which must be observed at all times and serves as a corrective standard when assessing the legality of any actions by the authorities'.[58]

[54] *RegioPost*, above n 1, para 59.

[55] Syrpis, above n 30, 286, and in more specific detail in ch 2 of this book.

[56] JM Hebdy and J Meesters, 'The Proportionality Principle in the Dutch Public Procurement Act' (2014) 4 *European Procurement & Public–Private Partnership Law Review* 266.

[57] Such a three-step conventional test is rarely used by the Court, which usually refers to 'necessity' and 'appropriateness'. This was also the case in *Rüffert* and *Bundesdruckerei*. See further on the application of proportionality by the Court, T von Danwitz, 'Thoughts on Proportionality and Coherence in the Jurisprudence of the Court of Justice' in P Cardonnel, A Rosas and N Wahl (eds), *Constitutionalising the EU Judicial System: Essays in Honour of Pernilla Lindh* (Oxford, Hart Publishing, 2012) 372.

[58] HJ Priess, 'The Rules on Exclusion and Self-Cleaning under the 2014 Public Procurement Directive' (2014) 3 *Public Procurement Law Review* 112, 112–13.

However, it appeared in secondary law for the first time in the field of public procurement only in the 2004 Public Procurement Directive, and then in a rather strained form. In recital 2 of its preamble, this Directive stated that 'the award of contracts concluded in the Member States on behalf of the State, regional or local authorities and other bodies governed by public law entities, is subject to the respect of ... *the principle of proportionality* and the principle of transparency' (emphasis added). Besides this recital, the only specific reference to proportionality can be found in provisions concerning requirements pertaining to economic and financial standing and technical and professional ability.[59]

This does not mean that, prior to the inclusion of proportionality in the public procurement directives, the principle of proportionality was not present in the case law of the Court.[60] The *Michaniki* case,[61] as well as other judgments concerning grounds for exclusion from participation in public procurement proceedings, where references to the principle of proportionality are particularly frequent,[62] showed how important this principle may be in public procurement cases. In those cases, the Court applied the said principle even though it was not then included in the public procurement directives. It was sufficient for the Court that proportionality constitutes a general principle of EU law.[63]

The importance of the principle of proportionality was reflected in the new public procurement directives. It is now mentioned in Article 18 of the 2014 Public Procurement Directive, together with other 'principles of procurement', namely equal treatment, non-discrimination and transparency, requiring that '*contracting authorities* shall treat economic operators equally and without discrimination and *shall act in* a transparent and *proportionate manner*' (emphasis added). It also appears in certain specific provisions of the 2014 Public Procurement Directive, for example in Article 19(2) (proportionality of any conditions for the performance of a contract by groups of economic operators, which are different from

[59] See Art 44(2) of the 2004 Public Procurement Directive.

[60] However, to be honest, it was only dealt with briefly thereby. Hebdy and Meesters, above n 56, 266.

[61] See the Judgment of 16 December 2008, *Michaniki*, Case C-213/07, EU:C:2008:731.

[62] See, eg, the Judgments of 3 March 2005, *Fabricom*, Joined Cases C-21/03 and 34/04, EU:C:2005:127; and of 19 May 2009, *Assitur*, Case C-538/07, EU:C:2009:317. The latter case was held a few months after the *Michaniki* case and concerned the interpretation of the previous Council Directive 92/50/EEC of 18 June 1992 relating to the coordination of procedures for the award of public service contracts [1992] OJ L209/1, as amended. The Court recalled that the exhaustive list of grounds for exclusion does not preclude the option for Member States to maintain or adopt substantive rules designed, in particular, to ensure, as regards public contracts, observance of the principle of equal treatment of all tenderers and of the principle of transparency, which constitute the basis of the Directives on procedures for the award of public contracts, 'provided always that the principle of proportionality is observed' (para 21).

[63] T Tridimas, *The General Principles of EU Law* (Oxford, Oxford University Press, 2007) 193.

those imposed on individual participants), Article 42(1) (proportionality of technical specifications), Article 47(3) (proportionality of the extension of the time limits for the receipt of tenders) and in Article 58(1) (proportionality of selection criteria). These provisions only underline the importance of the principle of proportionality, which, as a requirement of a general nature, has to be applied to all actions of contracting authorities, including the application of conditions for the performance of public contracts—now controlled by Article 70 of the 2014 Public Procurement Directive.

The principle of proportionality was applied by the Court both in *Rüffert* and *Bundesdruckerei*. In the latter case proportionality was, in fact, of vital importance for the decision of the Court. The minimum wage at issue was capable of constituting a restriction that might be justified by the objective of protecting employees if only the national measure was appropriate and necessary for achieving that objective. Since it was not appropriate, nor was it necessary to avoid a risk of seriously undermining the balance of the German social security system, the Court considered the national measure disproportionate.

As already mentioned, proportionality also appeared in *Rüffert* where the Court applied the three-step test (restriction, justification, proportionality) in order to 'confirm' its interpretation of the Posted Workers Directive. At first glance, it might seem that the Court would adopt the same approach in *RegioPost*. However, as is known, the Court stopped at the second step of the test—justification by the objective of public interest. The Court recalled *Bundesdruckerei* and held that although the national legislation 'is capable of constituting a restriction within the meaning of Article 56 TFEU',[64] it 'may, in principle, be justified by the objective of protecting workers'.[65] Then, instead of applying the proportionality test, the Court decided to distinguish the national measure reviewed in *Rüffert* from the regulation in question. This helped the Court to handle the main issue, ie that the collective agreement in question was limited to public contracts only. The Court distinguished a collective agreement applying solely to the construction sector, which did not cover private contracts and thus had not been declared universally applicable, from a legislative provision, which 'as a mandatory rule for minimum protection, in principle applies generally to the award of any public contract in the *Land* of Rhineland-Palatinate, irrespective of the sector concerned'.[66] However, as a consequence, not only did the Court not dispel the doubts of the national court,[67] but it also created new ones.

[64] *RegioPost*, above n 1, para 69.

[65] ibid, para 70.

[66] ibid, para 75.

[67] See in particular ibid, para 38, where the referring court considered that 'it would be illogical to interpret Article 3(1) of [the Posted Workers Directive] as meaning that it requires collective agreements setting a minimum wage to be of universal application, including all workers in the sector concerned, whether they be employed in the performance of public contracts or private contracts, while the scope of legislative provisions laying down a minimum wage may be limited to only those workers assigned to the performance of public contracts'.

The main problem with *RegioPost* is that it did not address the issue whether a measure that only applies to public contracts may be regarded appropriate and necessary for the protection of workers. The conclusion of the judgment suggests that it may be regarded as such (otherwise it would have to be considered disproportionate), but since this runs counter to *Rüffert* and *Bundesdruckerei*, the Court should have explained, at least, why employees working in the private sector are not in need of the same wage protection as those working in the context of public contracts.[68] Without such an explanation it is very difficult to argue that the municipality of Landau laid down minimum wage requirements constituting special conditions relating to the performance of a contract in line with EU law, as it was required to do under Article 26 of the 2004 Public Procurement Directive. We simply do not know whether such requirement is compatible with EU law. We cannot just rely on 'the selective applicability of procurement law'[69] and argue that Article 26 of the 2004 Public Procurement Directive would lose its meaning if procurement conditions, which by nature apply to public contracts, would be unjustifiable.[70] This would mean that Article 26 of the 2004 Public Procurement Directive triggers, at the same time, the review of conditions for the performance of public contracts under EU law and justifies laying down these conditions in public contracts.[71]

Had the Court of Justice decided to engage with Article 56 TFEU, it would have had to apply the full three-step test. The lack of the proportionality analysis is a bit strange, since the construction of the judgment itself suggested such a direction (the Court going through two elements of the test: restriction and justification). Only once the third element was applied would we have had a complete picture of the case. It is not an accident that in cases before the Court where Member States invoked the worker protection justification, they lost mainly because the steps taken were not proportionate.[72] This is why I do not agree that 'a national measure that sets minimum rates of pay should generally be assumed [to be] in conformity with Art 56 TFEU'.[73] Other elements are assessed under Article 3(1) of the Posted Workers Directive (such as the

[68] *Rüffert*, above n 5, para 40 and *Bundesdruckerei*, above n 6, para 32. In *RegioPost*, as noted by Francesco Costamagna, not a single word was devoted to this substantive claim made in *Rüffert* and reiterated in *Bundesdruckerei*; see F Costamagna, 'Minimum wage between public procurement and posted workers: anything new after the RegioPost case?' (2017) 1 *EL Rev* 109.

[69] C Kaupa, 'Public Procurement, Social Policy and Minimum Wage Regulation for Posted Workers: Towards a More Balanced Socio-Economic Integration Process?' (2016) 1 *European Papers* 135.

[70] ibid, 136.

[71] This reasoning is equally applicable under Art 70 of the 2014 Public Procurement Directive, even if the general obligation to comply with EU law is not written therein. Cf the contribution by Syrpis in ch 2 of this book.

[72] C Barnard, 'The Worker Protection Justification: Lessons from Consumer Law' in Koutrakos, Nic Shuibhne and Syrpis (eds), above n 30, 106, 116–20.

[73] Kaupa, above n 69.

sources of terms and conditions of employment), others still under Article 56 TFEU (ie restriction, justification, proportionality). Either it is assumed that the Posted Workers Directive exhaustively harmonises whichever of the state's rules apply to the 'terms and conditions of employment' as specified in its Article 3(1), and then a separate review is not needed under Article 56 TFEU, or it should be agreed that Article 56 TFEU is more than a square peg in a round hole.

V. CONCLUSIONS

It is submitted that by its *RegioPost* judgment, the Court of Justice has left the door open for dissimilar treatment of workers carrying out the same activity within the same company (or in different ones), depending on whether the activity is carried out under a public or a private contract.[74] This contribution shows, however, that this could have not happened if only the Court had applied the principle of proportionality. The application of this principle would be in line with the earlier case law of the Court. An alternative scenario for the Court assumes that the Court acknowledges the Posted Workers Directive as the instrument of exhaustive harmonisation of whichever of the state's rules apply to the 'terms and conditions of employment', as specified in Article 3(1) of the Posted Workers Directive. In the absence of this, and the decision to review national rules under Article 56 TFEU, the absence of the proportionality analysis may be considered as a major shortcoming of the *RegioPost* judgment. Unfortunately, it is yet another case which challenges the coherence of the Court's jurisprudence.[75] Paradoxically, a new judgment will be required to clarify the situation.

[74] A Fratini, 'Minimum Wages in the Award of Public Contracts After' in M Crew, PL Parcu and T Brennan (eds), *The Changing Postal and Delivery Sector Towards a Renaissance* (Cham, Springer International Publishing, 2017) 123; A Sánchez-Graells, 'Regulatory Substitution between Labour and Public Procurement Law: The EU's Shifting Approach to Enforcing Labour Standards in Public Contracts' (2018) 24(2) *European Public Law Journal* forthcoming.

[75] On the lack of such coherence in relation to free movement, see Nic Shuibhne, above n 4, 28.

4

Upholding General Principles versus Distinguishing Cases: On the Use of Precedent in EU Public Procurement Law (A Case Study)

ROBERTO CARANTA

It is a basic principle of the administration of justice that like cases should be decided alike.[1]

I. INTRODUCTION

Different jurisdictions treat previous judgments—shortly, precedents—differently.[2]

The approach to precedents in civil law jurisdictions is normally not very structured. Generally speaking, the *stare decisis*—or binding precedent—doctrine is foreign to courts in civil law countries.[3] The situation is well explained by Merryman, pointing out that '[t]he familiar common law doctrine of *stare decisis* ... is obviously inconsistent with the separation of powers as formulated in civil law countries, and is therefore rejected by the civil law tradition. Judicial decisions are not law'.[4] Law is (supposed to be) made

[1] R Cross and JW Harris, *Precedent in English Law*, 4th edn (Oxford, Clarendon Press, 1991) 3.

[2] J Komárek, 'Reasoning with Previous Decisions: Beyond the Doctrine of Precedent' (2013) 51 *American Journal of Comparative Law* 149, 157 ff, whose analysis is much commended to the reader, would rather discuss 'reasoning with previous decisions' as a way to better convey differences in approach; still 'precedent' is considered to be a preferable shorthand.

[3] For an introduction from a common law perspective, see N Duxbury, *The Nature and Authority of Precedent* (Cambridge, Cambridge University Press, 2008) 31 ff.

[4] JH Merryman, *The Civil Law Tradition*, 2nd edn (Stanford, CA, Stanford University Press, 1985) 22; see also ibid, at 29 and 46 ff.

by, and only made by, the elected representatives of the people.[5] This leads civilians 'to stress the importance of very general norms, which are located in the relevant code'.[6]

In practice, of course, courts in civil law jurisdictions (and, as will be seen, the Court of Justice) also tend to 'somehow' follow precedents, especially those emanating from higher courts.[7] Peer pressure plays a role.[8] However, civil law courts tend to treat precedents as if they are showing the way in a very broad manner, enouncing principles rather than laying down specific rules (which again would be contrary to the separation of powers).[9] In the end, principles are found 'not in one case, but in the case-law as a whole'.[10] The somewhat unstructured civil law approach to precedents is reinforced by—and also reinforces—the indifference of (much of) the civil law world to the distinction between ratio decidendi and obiter dicta, which will be clarified below.[11]

Since precedents are often seen as establishing general principles,[12] the indications given by a precedent may then be judged as not tailored to the facts or specific circumstances of some following case.[13] Normally 'a general rule will be more over- and underinclusive than a particular rule'.[14] So the principle is not applied, and in some cases the following judgment may be

[5] P Grossi, *Mitologie giuridiche della modernità* (Milano, Giuffré, 2005) 48 and 135 ff.

[6] ML Wells, 'A Common Lawyer's Perspective on the European Perspective on Punitive Damages' (2010) 70 *Louisiana Law Review* 557, 562; see also ibid, at 573 ff; on codes as sources of principles see also S Whittaker, 'Precedent in English Law: A View from the Citadel' (2006) 14 *European Review of Private Law* 705, 708; the understanding of 'principles' here seems to presuppose a lower level of abstraction compared to how 'general principles' are instead understood in Continental Europe. Lastly, for some historical reasons for the limited relevance of precedents in civil law jurisdictions, including the relevance of scholarly opinions and poor reporting, see A Watson, *The Making of the Civil Law* (Boston, MA, Harvard University Press, 1981) 174 ff.

[7] Merryman, above n 4, 83; see also M Derlén and J Lindholm, 'Peek-A-Boo, It's a Case Law System! Comparing the European Court of Justice and the United States Supreme Court from a Network Perspective' (2017) 18 *German Law Journal* 647, 652 ff.

[8] See, with specific reference to the EU Courts, AH Zhang, 'The Faceless Court' (2016) 38 *University of Pennsylvania Journal of International Law* 71, 112 ff.

[9] For the opposition between 'formally realizable rules' and 'standards or principles' see D Kennedy, 'Form and Substance in Private Law Adjudication' (1976) 89 *Harvard Law Review* 1685, 1687 ff.

[10] Whittaker, above n 6, 741; see also, with reference to the EU Courts, JJ Barceló, 'Precedent in European Community Law' in DN MacCormick and RS Summers (eds), *Interpreting Precedents—A Comparative Study* (Dartmouth, Ashgate, 1997) 407, 428 ff; and MA Jacob, *Precedent and Case-Based Reasoning in the European Court of Justice* (Cambridge, Cambridge University Press, 2014) 84 ff.

[11] This includes the EU courts: Cross and Harris, above n 1, 17; A Arnull, 'Owning Up to Fallibility: Precedent and the Court of Justice' (1993) 30 *CML Rev* 247, 249; Whittaker, above n 6, 741 ff; T Tridimas, 'Precedent and the Court of Justice: A Jurisprudence of Doubt?' in J Dickson and P Eleftheriadis (eds), *Philosophical Foundations of EU Law* (Oxford, Oxford University Press, 2012) 307, 313; see however Barceló, above n 10, 407, 427 f.

[12] Barceló, above n 10, 425.

[13] See again, also for further references, ibid.

[14] Kennedy, above n 9, 1689 ff; see also ibid, at 1697.

seen as establishing a (conflicting) principle. Successive judgments may be seen as championing one of the two (or more) conflicting principles. In the absence of the *stare decisis* doctrine, this may potentially go on forever (and it often goes on for quite a while anyway). The fact that in the EU principles are often seen as an expression of values, politicises—or constitutionalises—the discourse, inevitably making conflicts less tractable.[15]

Precedents are instead taken very seriously in common law jurisdictions. 'The peculiar feature of the English doctrine of precedent is its strongly coercive nature.'[16] However, only *rationes decidendi* are binding.[17] The '*ratio* of a case relates the proposition of law discussed in the judgment or judgments to the facts of the case and to the claims of the parties'.[18] This means that 'the facts of the case form very much more than just a context: they play a crucial role in determining its future force'.[19] Propositions that are not part of the ratio decidendi are simply obiter dicta. They retain (some) persuasive authority but do not bind following courts.[20] Precedents are seen as establishing very specific rules attuned to the special factual situation of the case at hand, rather than declaring broad principles.[21] Different rules may be devised and applied in some following cases if the facts or specific circumstances are different. In sum, 'students of the common law study discrete cases and the facts, reasons, and distinctions courts rely on to resolve them'.[22]

Ultimately, the case law thus developed may paint a very complex picture, difficult to read, if not outright incoherent. Complexity, however, will not normally flow from conflicting guiding principles (or values). It will be due to the inconsistency among specific rules.[23] In the end, 'the growth of the common law is hardly logical and coherent'.[24]

[15] On the link between principles and values, see MW Hesselink, 'Private Law and the European Constitutionalisation of Values' (2016) Amsterdam Law School Research Paper No 2016-26, available at ssrn.com/abstract=2785536.

[16] Cross and Harris, above n 1, 3.

[17] ibid, at 6, who discuss at length the distinction in ch 2. This does not mean that it is always easy to separate rationes and dicta: eg CY Kuek and ES Tay, 'When Obiter Dictum and Minority View Become Ratio Decidendi' (2015) 3 *Malayan Law Journal*, available at ssrn.com/abstract=2710110; P Daly, 'The Signal and the Noise in Administrative Law' (2017) University of Cambridge Faculty of Law Research Paper No 3/2017, available at ssrn.com/abstract=2874310.

[18] Whittaker, above n 6, 718.

[19] ibid; see also Cross and Harris, above n 1, 43 ff.

[20] Whittaker, above n 6, 720.

[21] Even if at times English courts are seen deriving 'wider principles' or 'doctrines' from the case law itself: ibid, at 711; this author's guess from Whittakers' discussion at 728 ff is, however, that the development of these 'principles' is very much conditioned by the specific common law case-by-case approach.

[22] Wells, above n 6, 560; see also Whittaker, above n 6, 711 ff. For a more qualified approach see, however, Cross and Harris, above n 1, 14 ff.

[23] Or for the accretion of multiple exceptions when some 'principle' has been recognised: Whittaker, above n 6, 731 ff.

[24] Wells, above n 6, 568.

It is submitted that keeping in mind the differences between the common law and the civil law approaches to precedents may shed light on the EU case law on the participation in public procurement award procedures by economic operators not relying on a workforce established in the country to which the contracting authority belongs. As discussed in other contributions to this book, that case law spans from *Laval*[25] and *Rüffert*[26] up to and including *RegioPost*.[27] Some of these cases involve the application of the Posted Workers Directive,[28] while others were solved based on the application of TFEU[29] provisions (and their predecessors).[30] The specific public procurement legislation has also featured prominently in the latest case,[31] where the 2004 Public Procurement Directive[32] played a central role.

It is suggested that the perceived clash between principles and/or values (internal market v social considerations) in this line of case law may very much disappear when looking closely at the different facts or specific circumstances of the different cases, such as whether workers were actually posted or not, or whether the minimum salary rules were enacted in legislation or simply provided in collective agreements, and so on. This is true even when factoring in changes in EU public procurement law that took place during the period of creation of this case law.

This contribution will first describe the relevant cases, and then try to present a coherent picture of the case law. It will conclude with some general remarks on how to treat the precedents of the Court of Justice.

II. *LAVAL*: LAYING THE GROUND FOR *RÜFFERT*

Before approaching *Rüffert*, an important precedent giving application to the Posted Workers Directive must be recalled: *Laval*.

25 Judgment of 18 December 2007, *Laval un Partneri*, Case C-341/05, EU:C:2007:809.

26 Judgment of 3 April 2008, *Rüffert*, Case C-346/06, EU:C:2008:189.

27 Judgment of 17 November 2015, *RegioPost*, Case C-115/14, EU:C:2015:760.

28 Directive 96/71/EC of the European Parliament and of the Council of 16 December 1996 concerning the posting of workers in the framework of the provision of services (Posted Workers Directive) [1997] OJ L18/1.

29 Treaty on the Functioning of the European Union (TFEU) [2012] OJ C326/47.

30 For extended discussion of this point, see in particular the contributions by Syrpis and Bogdanowicz in chs 2 and 3 of this book respectively.

31 This does not include the 2014 Public Procurement Directive (Directive 2014/24/EU of the European Parliament and of the Council of 26 February 2014 on public procurement and repealing Directive 2004/18/EC [2014] OJ L94/65), which arguably strengthened the scope for sustainable public procurement: see generally the works in B Sjåfjell and A Wiesbrock (eds), *Sustainable Public Procurement under EU Law* (Cambridge, Cambridge University Press, 2016); see also D Dragos and B Neamtu, 'Sustainable Public Procurement in the EU' in F Lichère, R Caranta and S Treumer (eds), *Moderninsing Public Procurement: The New Directive* (Copenhagen, DJØF, 2014) 301.

32 Directive 2004/18/EC of the European Parliament and of the Council of 31 March 2004 on the coordination of procedures for the award of public works contracts, public supply contracts and public service contracts (2004 Public Procurement Directive) [2004] OJ L134/114.

The case involved the posting of Latvian workers to Sweden. The Posted Workers Directive offers the Member States multiple options in laying down rules to protect posted workers. Under Article 3(1) of the Directive, these rules are laid down by law, regulation or administrative provision, and/or by collective agreements or arbitration awards that have been declared universally applicable under paragraph 8 of the same provision. The last is the case for collective agreements or arbitration awards that must be observed by all undertakings in the geographical area and in the profession or industry concerned. Member States may set up a system for declaring collective agreements or arbitration awards to be of universal application, or decide to rely on a number of indicators, such as the fact that 'the collective agreements or arbitration awards ... are generally applicable to all similar undertakings in the geographical area and in the profession or industry concerned'. In transposing the Posted Workers Directive, Sweden did not provide for minimum rates of pay. Neither did it have at the time a system for declaring collective agreements universally applicable. Lastly, in order to avoid the creation of discriminatory situations, Swedish law did not require foreign undertakings to apply Swedish collective agreements, since not all Swedish employers were bound by a collective agreement.

Laval un Partneri Ltd ('Laval') was a company incorporated under Latvian law and having its registered office in Riga (Latvia). Through a subsidiary, Laval was employing a number of Latvian workers to work on building sites in Sweden. Laval, which had signed collective agreements with the Latvian building sector's trade union, was not bound by any collective agreement involving Swedish trade unions. A number of Swedish trade unions blockaded those building sites in order to put pressure on Laval and force it to sign Swedish collective agreements providing for a higher pay than under the Latvian agreement. Laval sued the trade unions, to have the industrial action declared illegal and get compensation for the loss suffered. The trade unions invoked their right to take collective action, as specified in the national legislation.

The Swedish court wondered whether it was compatible with both the Treaty rules on the freedom to provide services and with the provisions of the Posted Workers Directive for trade unions to attempt to force a foreign undertaking to sign a collective agreement in the host country, when the legislation adopted to implement that Directive did not have any express provisions concerning minimum pay.

The Court of Justice first considered that while the Posted Workers Directive lays down a nucleus of mandatory rules (mainly procedural ones) for minimum protection to be observed in the host country by employers who post workers there, nevertheless it does not harmonise the material content of those mandatory rules. Member States are free to set that minimum content, provided that the Treaty and the general principles of Union law are complied with.[33] It is worth noting that while providing the Member States with multiple alternatives, the Posted Workers Directive defines quite precisely the different procedures through which they can lay down mandatory rules for minimum protection applicable to posted workers.[34]

Indeed, concerning procedural rules, the Posted Workers Directive provides that the mandatory rules are to be established

> either by law, regulation or administrative provision, or by collective agreements or arbitration awards which have been declared universally applicable. Collective agreements and arbitration awards for the purposes of that provision are those which must be observed by all undertakings in the geographical area and in the profession or industry concerned.[35]

In the event that a Member State does not set up a system for declaring collective agreements or arbitration awards to be of universal application, it may still base itself on collective agreements that are either generally applicable to all similar undertakings in the industry concerned and/or which have been concluded by the most representative employers and labour organisations at national level and which are applied throughout the national territory.[36]

Concerning minimum pay, Sweden neither legislated for nor declared any collective agreement of universal application, nor did it decide to base itself on collective agreements applicable at national level, rather leaving pay issues to be negotiated on a case-by-case basis at the place of work.[37] Therefore, according to the Court of Justice, Sweden could not impose a duty to negotiate with domestic trade unions on undertakings availing themselves of posted workers.[38]

Next, the Court of Justice had to assess whether the trade unions were exercising the workers' fundamental right to collective action in a way consistent with the economic rights protected under the Treaty and in accordance with the principle of proportionality.[39] Adopting classic internal market reasoning, the Court held that collective action to force an undertaking to undergo negotiations to be able to operate in another Member State constitutes a restriction on the freedom to provide services.[40] As such, it is

[33] *Laval*, above n 25, paras 58 et seq; see also para 68.
[34] AR Ganesh, 'Appointing Foxes to Guard Henhouses: The European Posted Workers' Directive' (2008) 15 *Columbia Journal of European Law* 123, 137.
[35] See, *Laval*, above n 25, para 64, referring to Art 3(1) of the Posted Workers Directive.
[36] *Laval*, above n 25, para 65.
[37] ibid, paras 67 and 69.
[38] ibid, para 71.
[39] ibid, para 94; see also the analysis by N Reich, 'Free Movement v Social Rights in an Enlarged Union—the *Laval* and *Viking* Cases before the ECJ' (2008) 9 *German Law Journal* 125, 137 ff. Generally, on the issue of proportionality assessements, see the contribution by Bogdanowicz in ch 3 of this book.
[40] *Laval*, above n 25, para 99.

allowed only if it pursues a legitimate objective compatible with the Treaty and is justified by overriding reasons of public interest according to the proportionality test.[41]

Considering that the Union (then Community), along with establishing an internal market, also has a social purpose,[42] the Court of Justice was ready to accept that 'the right to take collective action for the protection of the workers of the host State against possible social dumping may constitute an overriding reason of public interest'.[43] However, the Court held that minimum safeguards for posted worker rights are already embodied in the Posted Workers Directive. In contrast, the absence in Sweden of a clear legislative framework concerning specifically minimum pay, combined with ad hoc negotiations to be carried out building site by building site, would expose undertakings from other Member States to an unacceptable level of uncertainty.[44]

The judgment of the Court in *Laval* may be read as a blueprint for market rights trumping social rights, and it 'aroused strong political reactions'.[45] Coupling it with *Viking*,[46] a case so removed from posted workers and public procurement it needs not concern us here, might reinforce this impression: the two cases have been seen as asserting 'une sorte de primauté des libertés économiques sur les droit sociales'.[47] Or, in plain English, 'The precedence of the economic over the social is pretty clear.'[48] A clash between the fundamental EU freedom to provide services and the right of collective action has also been evoked with reference to both *Laval* and *Rüffert* (to which we shall come soon).[49] Even a less sanguine take acknowledges that *Laval* and *Viking* 'certainly tend to a more "liberal" and less "social" approach by invoking a certain precedence of free movement rights over the fundamental right to strike, despite the "social rhetoric" of the [Court of Justice]'.[50]

Wearing the lenses of a common lawyer constantly focusing on the unique facts of any given case, *Laval* may instead be read as a specific judgment on very special Swedish arrangements combining lack of (any) nationwide

[41] ibid, para 101.
[42] ibid, paras 104 et seq.
[43] ibid, para 103.
[44] ibid, paras 108 et seq.
[45] Reich, above n 39, 127.
[46] Judgment of 11 December 2007, *The International Transport Workers' Federation and The Finnish Seamen's Union v Viking Line ABP*, Case C-438/05, EU:C:2007:772 (*Viking*).
[47] M Manfroni, 'Les divergences de la jurisprudence européenne dans la difficile conciliation entre libertés économiques et droits sociaux' in J Luther and L Mola (eds), *Europe's social rights under the 'Turin process'. Les droits sociaux de l'Europe sous le «processus de Turin»* (Naples, Ed Scientifica, 2016) 157; see also C Barnard, 'The European Court of Justice as a Common Law Court?' (2011) 3 *Neue Zeitschrift für Arbeitsrecht* 122, 124.
[48] C Barnard, 'Social Dumping or Dumping Socialism?' (2008) 67 *CLJ* 262, 264.
[49] Ganesh, above n 34, 131 ff.
[50] Reich, above n 39, 160.

substantive rules on minimum pay with on-site negotiations, which the trade unions were using to achieve results going well beyond the minimum protection offered by the Posted Workers Directive.[51]

For sure, the judgment in *Laval* is not easy to read (if not plainly obscure).[52] One thing that is very apparent is a certain circularity in the Court of Justice's reasoning between primary and secondary law. The Posted Workers Directive was based on the case law giving application to Treaty provisions.[53] In turn, Treaty provisions are now read in the light of the Directive, which is seen as the template to understand what is allowed—or not—by primary law.[54]

III. *RÜFFERT*

Rüffert is the leading case concerning the participation in public procurement award procedures of economic operators not relying on a workforce established in the country to which the contracting authority belongs.

Land Niedersachsen had awarded Objekt und Bauregie a contract for the structural work in the building of a prison. In line with the local legislation on public procurement, the contract contained a declaration regarding payment to employees of at least the minimum wage set in the collective agreement mentioned in a list of sample collective agreements attached to the contract. The contractor used as a subcontractor an undertaking established in Poland, which came under suspicion of having employed workers on the building site at a wage below the minimum wage. *Land* Niedersachsen terminated the contract based, inter alia, on the fact that Objekt und Bauregie had failed to fulfil its contractual obligation to comply with the collective agreement. The contractor went into liquidation, and Mr Rüffert, acting in his capacity as liquidator of the assets of company, brought an action against the *Land*. The referring court doubted the compatibility of the local legislation with the freedom to provide services laid down in what is now Article 56 TFEU (ex Article 49 EC).

Following the Opinion of Advocate General Bot, the Court of Justice decided to rather focus on the Posted Workers Directive.[55] The situation in Germany at the material time was different from the one underlying the *Laval* case (discussed in section II). A mandatory minimum wage had been established at federal level by the Law on the posting of workers, while the

[51] Ganesh, above n 34, 127.

[52] R O'Donoghue and B Carr, 'Dealing with Viking and Laval: From Theory to Practice' (2008–2009) 11 *Cambridge Yearbook of European Legal Studies* 123, 124.

[53] Reich, above n 39, 141.

[54] See also the discussion by Syrpis and Bogdanowicz in chs 2 and 3 of this book respectively.

[55] Opinion of AG Bot delivered on 20 September 2007 in *Rüffert*, Case C-346/06, EU:C:2007:541, paras 61 et seq.

Land legislation on public procurement simply provided that public contracting authorities could award contracts for building works and local public transport services only to undertakings paying the wage laid down in the collective agreements at the place where the service was provided. According to the Court of Justice, the *Land* legislation on public procurement, which did not itself set any minimum rates of pay, could not be considered a law fixing 'a minimum rate of pay, as provided in Article 3(1)(c) of [the Posted Workers Directive]'.[56] Neither could the collective agreements relevant to the contract be said to have been 'declared universally applicable' by the legislation in question.[57] Lastly, according to the Court, the default mechanism for giving effect to collective agreements foreseen by Article 3(8)(2) of the Posted Workers Directive is applicable only where there is no system for declaring collective agreements to be of universal application, which was not the case in the Federal Republic of Germany.[58] Basically, the Court held 'that while the Member States could determine the material content of their minimum wage provisions freely, the procedures to be taken in making such determination' are set by EU law.[59]

Additionally, the Court remarked that a collective agreement such as that at issue in the main proceedings could not meet the requirements of the second subparagraph of Article 3(8) of the Posted Workers Directive, because it was not 'generally applicable to all similar undertakings in the geographical area and in the profession or industry concerned'. Rather it covered

> only a part of the construction sector falling within the geographical area of that agreement, since, first, the law which gives it such an effect applies only to public contracts and not to private contracts and, second, the collective agreement has not been declared universally applicable.[60]

This reasoning was confirmed in the light of Article 56 TFEU (then Article 49 EC).[61] The Court found that legislation such as that at issue in the case may impose on service providers established in another Member State where minimum rates of pay are lower an additional economic burden, and therefore is capable of constituting a restriction within the meaning of Article 56 TFEU.[62] That restriction is not justified by the objective of ensuring the protection of workers. First, the pay provided for in the collective agreements exceeded the minimum rate of pay set in the federal legislation.

[56] *Rüffert*, above n 26, para 24.

[57] ibid, para 25; this is also the starting point for the conclusions of AG Bot: see *Rüffert*, Opinion of AG Bot, above n 55, para 3.

[58] *Rüffert*, above n 26, para 27.

[59] Ganesh, above n 34, 137.

[60] *Rüffert*, above n 26, paras 28 et seq.

[61] Analysing *Rüffert* in *Regiopost*, AG Mengozzi writes of 'the Court's "confirmatory" reasoning relating to Article 56 TFEU'; see Opinion of AG Mengozzi delivered on 9 September 2015 in *RegioPost*, Case C-115/14, EU:C:2015:566, para 69.

[62] *Rüffert*, above n 26, para 37.

Secondly, the minimum did not apply to workers employed in the context of a contract between private parties.[63]

It falls outside the purpose of this short contribution to assess whether the Posted Workers Directive (and/or Article 56 TFEU) could have borne a different interpretation. Suffice it to recall here that Advocate General Bot had opined that the mechanisms in the Directive were aimed at setting minimum standards, the Member States remaining free to set higher standards based on Article 3(7) of the same Directive.[64] Also, the Advocate General considered the national provisions at issue lawful under Article 56 TFEU in so far as he thought them necessary to avoid social dumping.[65]

The judgment is based on a rather close reading of the very specific provisions laid down in the Posted Workers Directive. The Treaty simply reinforces the interpretation given to secondary law provisions.[66] Many commentators preferred instead to frame the discussion in terms of a clash between economic freedom and social rights, with the former being given the upper hand.[67]

The specific legislation on public procurement does not really feature in the judgment. In contrast, Advocate General Bot had referred to Article 23 of Directive 93/37/EEC[68] to support the power of contracting authorities to lay down contract performance conditions transparently, calling for the application of (higher) minimum wages.[69] So much so that the Advocate General concluded his reasoning by stating that

> [s]ince the contract performance condition relating to the minimum remuneration of workers laid down in the disputed provisions ... complies with the principle of non-discrimination on the basis of nationality, and since it complies with the principle of transparency, it must, in my opinion, be considered to be consistent with [Union] law.[70]

IV. *BUNDESDRUCKEREI*

A number of years went by before the Court of Justice had the chance to decide another case involving the participation in public procurement award

[63] ibid, paras 38 et seq; contrast *Rüffert*, Opinion of AG Bot, above n 55, para 128.

[64] *Rüffert*, Opinion of AG Bot, above n 55, paras 81 et seq.

[65] ibid, paras 114 et seq.

[66] See *Rüffert*, above n 26, para 36.

[67] For example, S Robin-Olivier, 'Libre prestation de services, marchés publics et régulation sociale: le droit européen privilégie la concurrence fondée sur le coût du travail' (2008) 44 *Revue trimestrielle de droit européen* 485; J-P Lhernould, 'Illicéité d'une clause sociale dans un appel d'offre de marchés publics: le pot de terre contre le pot de fer?' (2008) 20 *Revue de jurisprudence sociale* 601. The approach is still alive today: Manfroni, above n 47.

[68] Council Directive 93/37/EEC of 14 June 1993 concerning the coordination of procedures for the award of public works contracts [1993] OJ L 199/54.

[69] *Rüffert*, Opinion of AG Bot, above n 55, paras 59 et seq.

[70] ibid, para 135.

procedures of economic operators not relying on a workforce established in the country to which the contracting authority belongs. It was then presented with *Bundesdruckerei*[71] in 2014.

This was again courtesy of a German court. Bundesdruckerei GmbH challenged a clause in the award documents issued by the City of Dortmund, concerning the obligation contained in tendering specifications relating to a public service contract (for the digitalisation of documents and the conversion of data for the urban-planning service) to guarantee payment of a minimum wage to the employees of subcontractors of the tenderer. The required minimum wage was that provided for by legislation of the *Land* to which the public contracting authority belonged. Bundesdruckerei intended to rely on a Polish subcontractor, and all services relating to the performance of the contract were to be carried out in Poland.

The referring court considered the minimum wage requirement to constitute a restriction to trade that could not be justified by an overriding reason in the public interest because the significant disparities between the cost of living in the different Member States made the wage imposed clearly exceed what was required in order to guarantee reasonable remuneration in the light of the cost of living in other countries.[72] The question was framed with reference to both Article 56 TFEU and Article 3(1) of the Posted Workers Directive, but the Court of Justice rightly noted that, unlike in *Rüffert*, the Posted Workers Directive was not applicable because the contract was not to be performed by posting employees of the subcontractor in German territory.[73] Apparently German courts have a knack for getting their EU law referencing wrong.

Keeping in line with Advocate General Bot's Opinion in *Rüffert*, the Court of Justice had no problem in classifying the relevant contract term as a contract performance condition incorporating a social consideration. However, the Court stressed that such a condition, at the relevant time regulated under Article 26 of the 2004 Public Procurement Directive, had to be 'compatible with [Union] law'.[74] This upgraded the question from one about the interpretation of a secondary law instrument to one concerning the Treaty, and more specifically Article 56 TFEU.[75] Relying on *Rüffert*, the Court held that the imposition of

> a minimum wage on subcontractors of a tenderer which are established in a Member State other than that to which the contracting authority belongs and in which minimum rates of pay are lower constitutes an additional economic burden that

[71] Judgment of 18 September 2014, *Bundesdruckerei*, Case C-549/13, EU:C:2014:2235 (*Bundesdruckerei*).

[72] See ibid, paras 18 et seq.

[73] ibid, paras 24 et seq.

[74] ibid, para 28.

[75] ibid, para 29.

may prohibit, impede or render less attractive the provision of their services in the host Member State.[76]

The Court was ready to accept that such a measure might in principle be justified by the objective of protecting employees by avoiding both 'social dumping' and 'the penalisation of competing undertakings which grant a reasonable wage to their employees'.[77] However, and referring again to *Rüffert*, the Court reiterated that a measure applying solely to public contracts would not normally be considered appropriate.[78]

Moreover, and in close adherence to the special facts of the case, in so far as it applied to workers living in a different Member State, the provision was not proportionate to its end.[79] There is indeed no reason why the protection of Polish workers would require them to benefit from a minimum wage set based on the cost of living in Germany.[80] Rather, such a provision deprives Polish companies of their competitive advantage.[81] Not unlike in *Laval*, the application of the German minimum wage provisions in *Bundesdruckerei* would have led to 'protecting and segregating' the national job market from competition.[82]

The discrimination was hitting not just Polish companies, but also Polish workers having a different cost of living (which does not necessarily translate into the quality thereof) who would be deprived of their livelihood. In the end, in *Laval* too it was foreign (in that case Latvian) posted workers losing their jobs.[83]

Bundesdruckerei was considered an easy case, so much so that it was not necessary for the Court of Justice to receive an Advocate General's opinion. The judgment is very short, its merits being discussed in just 13 paragraphs.[84] This did not spare the judgment from criticisms pointing out that solutions more protective of workers' rights (one must assume, German workers) would have been possible.[85]

[76] ibid, para 30; with reference to *Rüffert*, above n 26, para 37.

[77] *Bundesdruckerei*, above n 71, para 31.

[78] ibid, para 32; with reference to *Rüffert*, above n 26, paras 38 et seq.

[79] *Bundesdruckerei*, above n 71, para 33.

[80] ibid; this extends to 'the objective of stability of social security systems', since in no case will the workers burden the German system: ibid, para 35.

[81] ibid, para 34; see also A Brown, 'The Lawfulness of a National Rule Requiring a Subcontractor of a Bidder for a Public Contract to Pay its Workers a Minimum Wage, Even Where the Services Will be Carried Out Exclusively in a Lower-Cost Third Country: Case C-549/13 Bundesdruckerei GmbH v Stadt Dortmund' (2015) 24 *Public Procurement Law Review* NA17, NA20.

[82] See, with reference to *Laval*, Reich, above n 39, 160.

[83] Reich, above n 39, 134; Ganesh, above n 34, 135.

[84] See also Brown, above n 81, NA21.

[85] For example, M Forlivesi, 'La clausola sociale di garanzia del salario minimo negli appalti pubblici al vaglio della Corte di giustizia europea: il caso *Bundesdruckerei*' (2015) 2 *Rivista italiana di diritto del lavoro* 550, 562 ff; E Mazuyer, 'La légitimation de la concurrence salariale entre États membres' (2014) 98 *Revue Lamy droit des affaires* 66, 67 ff.

V. *REGIOPOST*

Somewhat different facts characterise the last instalment of the saga (so far): *RegioPost*. This involves Germany again. This time the Stadt Landau in der Pfalz (Landau in the Palatinate) had asked tenderers and their subcontractors to undertake to pay a minimum wage to the staff performing a public contract for postal services. The request was based on *Land* legislation, which required tenders and their subcontractors to undertake to pay their staff at least the minimum wage set by collective agreements made binding under German federal legislation on the posting of workers, or, in the event that no such agreement was applicable, wages of at least €8.50 gross per hour. RegioPost did not comply and was excluded.

What is worth stressing at the outset is that, unlike in *Rüffert*, in the specific circumstances of *RegioPost*, no worker was to be posted. Nor, unlike in *Bundesdruckerei*, was a foreign subcontractor involved in the performance of a contract that in any case had to be implemented in Germany.[86] Unsurprisingly, some parties to the case objected to the jurisdiction of the Court of Justice. The Court found, however, that since the value of the contract at issue exceeded the threshold set in the 2004 Public Procurement Directive, the contract itself had to be considered as one 'having a certain cross-border interest'.[87] As rightly remarked, this approach makes it easier to determine when the Posted Workers Directive applies, since this depends on the value of the contract. At the same time, the approach extends the applicability of that Directive, and that of the limitations flowing from it, to contracts in reference to which posting is only a possibility, which might never materialise.[88]

On the merits, the Court of Justice considered that the contracting authority's requirement for the payment of a minimum wage amounted to a 'special condition relating to the performance of a contract', which was both publicised *ex ante* and non-discriminatory, as required under Article 26 of the 2004 Public Procurement Directive.[89] To assess whether the condition was also compatible with Union law, as required under the same provision, the Court thought it necessary

> to determine whether, in cross-border situations in which workers from one Member State provide services in another Member State for the purpose of

[86] At least partially. For further discussion, see the contribution by Sánchez-Graells in ch 6 of this book.

[87] *RegioPost*, above n 27, para 51; see also ibid, para 61, holding that the clause at issue might have discouraged economic operators established outside Germany from tendering.

[88] F Costamagna, 'Minimum Wage between Public Procurement and Posted Workers: Anything New after the *RegioPost* Case?' (2017) 42 *EL Rev* 101, 104 ff.

[89] *RegioPost*, above n 27, paras 54 et seq; see also *RegioPost*, Opinion of AG Mengozzi, above n 61, paras 47 e seq.

performing a public contract, the minimum conditions laid down in [the Posted Workers Directive] are observed in the host Member State in respect of posted workers.[90]

Having gone full circle back to the Posted Workers Directive, the Court of Justice deftly distinguished the instant case from *Rüffert* by holding that the German provision now applicable was 'itself laying down the minimum rate of pay'.[91] The Court also disregarded the fact that the provision was—again—applicable to public contracts only, in this instance by holding: first, that the requirement of 'universal application' under Article 3(8) of the Posted Workers Directive referred to collective agreements, not to legislation;[92] and, secondly, that Article 26 of the 2004 Public Procurement Directive was not applicable to private contracts, and therefore contract performance conditions could not be considered contrary to EU law because the scope of the Directive structurally prevented their extension to private contracts.[93] Advocate General Mengozzi elaborated somewhat more on the point, noting that Article 26 of the 2004 Public Procurement Directive on contract performance conditions brought about 'an entirely new provision in EU public procurement law',[94] and that asking for rules imposing the payment of minimum wages in the execution of public contracts to be applicable to all workers would impinge on the federal German constitutional architecture, which does not give the *Länder* the power to rule on private-law working conditions.[95]

The reasoning based on secondary law was then confirmed in the light of Article 56 TFEU.[96] Following *Bundesdruckerei*, the measure at issue was characterised as a restriction on free trade. However, distinguishing *Rüffert*, the measure was found justified by arguing that while in the earlier case 'what was at issue ... was a collective agreement applying solely to the construction sector, which did not cover private contracts and had not been declared universally applicable',[97] the provision relevant in *RegioPost* was 'laid down in a legislative provision, which, as a mandatory rule for minimum protection, in principle applies generally to the award of any public contract in the *Land* of Rhineland-Palatinate, irrespective of the sector concerned'.[98] The distinction based on the legal source setting the minimum

[90] *RegioPost*, above n 27, para 60; AG Mengozzi instead disregarded the relevance of the Posted Workers Directive since no posting of workers was at issue: see *RegioPost*, Opinion of AG Mengozzi, above n 61, paras 53 et seq.

[91] *RegioPost*, above n 27, para 62.

[92] ibid, para 63.

[93] ibid, above n 27, paras 64 et seq.

[94] *RegioPost*, Opinion of AG Mengozzi, above n 61, para 70.

[95] ibid, paras 73 et seq; see also the analysis by Costamagna, above n 88, 109 f.

[96] See also *RegioPost*, Opinion of AG Mengozzi, above n 61, paras 61 et seq.

[97] *RegioPost*, above n 27, para 74.

[98] ibid, para 75; see also *RegioPost*, Opinion of AG Mengozzi, above n 61, paras 73 et seq, where AG Mengozzi stresses that as a matter of domestic constitutional law, a *Land* might not even have the power to legislate on pay conditions for private contracts.

pay was also strengthened by the consideration that while the collective agreement relevant in *Rüffert* set a rate of pay above the minimum laid down in the applicable legislation, in *RegioPost* no other legislative rule was applicable to the workers in the postal sector.[99]

VI. BETWEEN VERY DIFFERENT FACTS AND SOMEWHAT DIFFERENT RULES

Looking at the case law from *Rüffert* to *RegioPost*, one might easily feel disconcerted. The first impression is that of a sudden U-turn, from a very strict internal market approach to the warm embrace of social considerations. That impression may indeed be right.[100] This is not one of the high moments in European integration, and elitist blindness towards social issues is best avoided.[101] In this framework, reform of the Posted Workers Directive is high on some policy makers to-do list.[102] Unlike US courts, the EU courts rarely, if ever, publicly air policy arguments, but this does not mean they are absent from judges' minds.[103]

What is suggested here is that the case law on minimum wages in public procurement cases may—instead, or also—be understood as a series of attempts by the Court of Justice to address different sets of facts in a somewhat changing legal environment. These two aspects will be considered in turn.

The facts of the cases analysed in this contribution could hardly have been more different. And this in many respects. *Rüffert* only involved posted workers; *Bundesdruckerei* did not; neither did *RegioPost*, even if, and this leads to a third factual pattern, they could potentially have been involved. From a different angle, public procurement had a cross-border element in both *Rüffert* and *Bundesdruckerei*. In *Rüffert* those crossing the borders were the workers; in *Bundesdruckerei* the workers were staying put at home and the service was rendered from afar; in *RegioPost* the cross-border element was instead potential, at best.

[99] *RegioPost*, above n 27, paras 74 and 76.

[100] See A Brown, 'The lawfulness of a regional law requiring tenderers for a public contract to undertake to pay workers performing that contract the minimum wage laid down in that law: Case C-115/14 *RegioPost*' (2016) 25 *Public Procurement Law Review* NA49, NA53; and, albeit with a more prudent take, Costamagna, above n 88, 101.

[101] So much so that it even features as an argument in EU constitutional theorisation: C Joerges, 'Unity in Diversity as Europe's Vocation and Conflicts Law as Europe's Constitutional Form' (2013) LEQS Paper No 28, available at ssrn.com/abstract=1723249.

[102] See the contribution by Novitz in ch 11 of this book; see also the position of the newly elected French President, at euobserver.com/political/138020.

[103] This is another aspect on which the EU courts sit on the civil law shores of the common law/civil law divide: as Wells, above n 6, 65–67, remarked, 'Lawyers schooled in the common law tradition take its policy-oriented reasoning for granted.'

These differences alone could easily have vouchsafed different outcomes, at least concerning *Bundesdruckerei*. Intending to have German labour standards applied to Polish workers working in Poland is the next worst thing after requiring the provider of a service to have a business operation in the same region as the contracting authority.[104]

Once the potential posting in *RegioPost* is considered, this case turns into a posted workers case, and in this respect it is very similar to *Rüffert*. Another factual difference immediately kicks in, however, and, as recalled, it was much stressed by the Court. Legislation set the minimum pay in the newest case (*RegioPost*); a collective agreement going beyond the minimum pay set in legislation applied in the earlier case (*Rüffert*).[105]

True, as remarked by Advocate General Mengozzi, in *Rüffert* the Court of Justice found that 'legislation' giving effects to a collective agreement could not be justified as a measure aimed at protecting workers because it applied only to those employed in the delivery of (some) public contracts.[106] Judging on legislation and again referring to *Rüffert*, the Court in *Bundesduckerei* held that

> in so far as it applies solely to public contracts, such a national measure is not appropriate for achieving that objective if there is no information to suggest that employees working in the private sector are not in need of the same wage protection as those working in the context of public contracts.[107]

Referring to legislation did, however, go beyond what was necessary to decide those earlier cases. As was remarked, 'The Court's conclusion in *Rüffert* therefore resulted largely from the specific provisions of the Posted Workers Directive.'[108] Those statements may today be characterised as obiter dicta. Statements made obiter may be departed from, if not outright discarded, in a following case. It has been written that 'distinguishing a precedent means modifying its ratio'.[109] One might also say that distinguishing helps clarify the ratio decidendi, that is, the essential reasons for the decision on these facts, by discarding obiter dicta.[110] Indeed 'ultimately it is for subsequent

[104] Judgment of 27 October 2005, *Contse and Others*, Case C-234/03, EU:C:2005:644.

[105] *RegioPost*, above n 27, paras 75 ff; see also the analysis by Costamagna, above n 88, 81 108.

[106] See *RegioPost*, above n 27, paras 68 et seq, referring to *Rüffert*, above n 26, paras 29 and 39.

[107] *Bundesdruckerei*, above n 71, para 32; see also the analysis by Costamagna, above n 88, 109.

[108] Brown, above n 100, NA54.

[109] Duxbury, above n 3, 27.

[110] R Jennings, 'Judicial Reasoning at an International Court', Speech given 29 January 1991, at the European Institute of the Saarland/Saarbrücken University, at 7, at europainstitut.de/fileadmin/schriften/236.pdf.

judges in later cases to decide on earlier decisions' *rationes decidendi*'.[111] Or, as Marc Jacob has put it, 'Precedents are ... never set in stone but constantly subject to dynamic re-characterisation.'[112]

Some of the relevant EU rules have also changed since *Rüffert* was decided. Before going into these changes, it must be stressed that in the cases at hand, the Court of Justice might appear to be somewhat casual in its dealing with sources, including with the hierarchy of sources. The Posted Workers Directive was indeed based on the Court's case law on the freedom to provide services,[113] but in *Laval* (and *Rüffert*) the Court appeared to be reading Treaty provisions through the Directive, as if the latter was providing the only possible interpretation of the Treaty.[114] In *RegioPost* too, the Court of Justice found its interpretation of the Posted Workers Directive and the 2004 Public Procurement Directive corroborated by (its reading of) the TFEU, rather than the other way round.[115]

A big change in the legal landscape since *Rüffert* was the regulation of contract performance conditions in Article 26 of the 2004 Public Procurement Directive (and now, but with changes which do not need to concern us here, in Article 70 of the 2014 Public Procurement Directive).[116] The new rules did not have any influence in *Bundesduckerei*. Again, it was such a blatant breach of the Treaty provisions on free movement that it could not be saved by secondary law. Article 26 of the 2004 Public Procurement Directive was instead the launch pad used by the Court of Justice in *RegioPost*. The Court relied on the public procurement rules to relax its reading of Article 3 of the Posted Workers Directive, eventually upholding the legality of the German provisions at issue, even though they only applied to public contracts. Reference to the 2004 Public Procurement Directive also allowed the Court to forgo proportionality analysis under Article 56 TFEU, thus setting aside the much criticised 'selectivity' objection, which had featured prominently in both *Rüffert* and *Bundesdruckerei*.[117]

[111] Whittaker, above n 6, 718.

[112] Jacob, above n 10, 83.

[113] Reich, above n 39, 141.

[114] See also the discussion by Syrpis in ch 2 of this book.

[115] See also the discussion by Syrpis in ch 2 of this book; this goes some way towards explaining why the Court in *RegioPost* did not engage in a proportionality analysis, but see the contribution of Bogdanowicz in ch 3 of this book; for a different take, see the contribution by Semple in ch 5.

[116] See the analysis of the new provision in Semple's contribution in ch 5 of this book; see also, including reference to Art 18 of the 2014 Public Procurement Directive, A Wiesbrock, 'Socially responsible public procurement' in Sjåfjell and Wiesbrock (eds), above n 31, 82 ff.

[117] See, also with reference to the even stronger Opinion by AG Mengozzi, Costamagna, above n 88, 109 f.

VII. CONCLUSIONS: HOW TO TREAT THE PRECEDENTS OF THE COURT OF JUSTICE?

One illuminating take on the approach supranational judges have to precedents now deserves full quotation:

> A very important aspect of this process of applying the law must be the question of the use of precedents; and there I feel some difficulty about the way precedents are often used in international law. I feel the doctrine has not been fully worked out. I come from a country where we have a system of binding precedents. But if you have a system of binding precedents you have to think very hard about what is a precedent. Accordingly we try to establish the strict *ratio decidendi* of a case; that is the essential reasons for the decision on these facts, discarding *obiter dicta*, namely the non-essential observations of the court, which may be wise and quotable, but not binding. In the international law field there is no such discipline yet. There is rather a tendency to look at a prior judgment almost as it were a more authoritative academic writing which is to be consulted for nice quotation. This is very well provided an isolated passage of a Judgment is not regarded as being itself binding as a precedent; as if it were a passage from the Holy Writ. Rather should the entire decision, including its factual situation, be consulted when trying to decide ... how far it is proper or necessary to follow precedent.[118]

Indeed, under the common law, dicta alone do not constitute precedents: '[E]ven where a judge does seek to set out the law in a proposition or series of propositions, these words do not themselves have any force except by reference (inter alia) to their relationship to their legal and factual context.'[119]

The Court of Justice is not an international court, it is the (supranational)[120] court of a new legal order.[121] However, and for sure, it is not a common law court. In Merryman's opinion, 'The basic character and the continuing legal development and operation of the European [Union] are the work of people trained in the civil law tradition.'[122] In keeping with its origins, 'Since its establishment, the Court [of Justice] has followed the French tradition of issuing a single, collective, an unanimous judgment without dissents.'[123] The style is highly formal, the tone even 'magisterial'.[124]

[118] Jennings, above n 110, 6.

[119] Whittaker, above n 6, 711 ff; see also Komárek, above n 2, 151 f.

[120] The Court of Justice has been termed 'the most powerful supranational court in the world': Zhang, above n 8, 74.

[121] Judgment of 5 February 1963, *Van Gend en Loos v Administratie der Belastingen*, Case C-26/62, EU:C:1963:1.

[122] Merryman, above n 4, 3.

[123] Zhang, above n 8, 75 and 103 ff; the author also points to the role played by the many *référendaires* who are educated in France and other countries sensible to French influence: ibid, at 94 ff and 108 ff.

[124] Tridimas, above n 11, 308; see also Barceló, above n 10, 411, and, stressing the role played by academics in civil law jurisdictions, Komárek, above n 2, 169.

Coming to the value of precedents, 'the Court is not bound by its previous decisions but in practice it does not often depart from them. A doctrine of binding precedent on common law lines would have been entirely inappropriate in what was originally a court of first and last resort.'[125] Put more succinctly, 'Bred in the civil law tradition, the [Court of Justice] does not adhere the doctrine of binding precedent.'[126]

There are sound reasons for this beyond history and path-dependency. Jan Komárek rightly pointed out that the Court of Justice often acts as a constitutional court probing the legality of legislation, a task not necessarily implying probing factual analysis.[127] This, however, often leads to an inconsistent approach to precedents closely reminiscent of Sir Robert Jennings' words: mere 'quotes' are taken as Holy Writ,[128] or at least as if they were legislative texts.[129] The result may be to obfuscate what coherence might otherwise be found in the case law.[130]

It was submitted here that the case law from *Rüffert* to *RegioPost* would be more readable wearing a common lawyer's lenses. Even limiting the analysis to public procurement law, this is not the only instance in which giving weight to the words and phrases used in a judgment while being oblivious to the special facts of a case has made reading the case law more difficult. An egregious example is given by the *Lianakis* case law.[131] In that case, the contract notice listed among the award criteria the proven experience of the expert on projects carried out over the last three years. This was seen as a violation of the separation between an assessment of the tenderer (and its experience) at an initial stage, and an assessment of the specific advantages of its offer at a later, award stage. Referring to an obiter dictum in *Beentjes*,[132] the Court of Justice, while accepting that EU law does not in theory preclude the examination of the tenderers' suitability and the award of the contract from taking place simultaneously, stressed that the two procedures are nevertheless distinct and are governed by different rules.[133] Thus, in simplified terms, criteria that relate to the tenderer

[125] Arnull, above n 11, 248.

[126] Tridimas, above n 11, 307.

[127] Komárek, above n 2, 153 ff.

[128] The 'magisterial' tone is probably vouchsafing this approach: see Jennings, above n 110, and the quotation cited at n 118. Based on interviews, Zhang, above n 8, 103, claims that 'référendaires have a tendency to strictly adhere to the Court's precedents'; judges might easily feel freer, the point becoming how much any of them really relies on référendaires: ibid, at 92 f.

[129] Komárek, above n 2, 162 f. As Jacob, above n 10, 14, remarks, this may also be attributed to a certain 'industrialisation' of the adjudication process; see also ibid at 95 f.

[130] A frequent criticism is that the practice of single, unanimous judgments impinges on their clarity anyway: see also for further references, Zhang, above n 8, 112.

[131] Judgment of 24 January 2008, *Lianakis and Others*, Case C-532/06, EU:C:2008:40.

[132] Judgment of 20 September 1988, *Beentjes v State of the Netherlands*, Case C-31/87, EU:C:1988:422.

[133] ibid, para 26.

(and its experience) cannot be used for the purposes of the award of the contract. This approach met with resounding criticism, and was not always followed in the Member States. The quality of the performer is obviously relevant in many cases, and may justify a higher contract price.[134] This was arguably the case in *Lianakis*, since the contract was about carrying out a project in respect of the cadastre, town planning and implementing measures, which is in the nature of intellectual services. However, the Court of Justice did not pay any attention to the specific facts of the case at hand, simply repeating dicta found in its precedent. In the end, it took legislation to redress an obvious and unnecessary mistake.[135]

Much has been written on the use of precedents before and by the Court of Justice.[136] It has been argued that 'there is indeed a case law system hiding below the surface of EU law, but the idea of case law has developed beyond its strictest traditional common law roots'.[137] Generally speaking, and it is probably fair to say that its practice is more varied than it appears at first glance,[138] the Court of Justice's approach to precedents does not establish a 'formal relationship' between the facts of a specific case and the authoritative force of the judgment based on those facts. Often the Court of Justice judges on more or less abstract legal issues,[139] and national courts are left to sort out the facts and apply the rule as declared by the Court of Justice.[140]

At times, however, and this is the case with the judgments analysed here, facts are clear enough[141] and the Court of Justice is ready to go into them in detail, including to the extent of distinguishing the case at hand from precedents.[142] Under a 'classical' common law approach to precedents, these differences may by themselves account for what at first sight would otherwise seem to be diverging decisions.[143]

[134] See S Treumer, 'The Distinction between Selection and Award Criteria in EC Public Procurement Law: A Rule without Exception?' (2009) 18 *Public Procurement Law Review* 111; P Faustino Bordalo, 'Evaluation Models in Public Procurement', in M Comba and S Treumer (eds), *Award of Contracts in EU Procurements*, (Copenhagen, DJØF, 2013) 339.

[135] Art 67(2)(b) of the 2014 Public Procurement Directive; true the Court changed course in the Judgment of 26 March 2015, *Ambisig*, Case C-601/13, EU:C:2015:204, but this was based on the changes having taken place at legislative level since *Lianakis* was decided.

[136] A very recent review can be read in Derlén and Lindholm, above n 7, 648 f.

[137] ibid, 686; see, however, the criticism of the methodology followed by these authors by J Frankenreiter, 'Network Analysis and the Use of Precedent in the Case Law of the CJEU—A Reply to Derlén and Lindholm' (2017) 18 *German Law Journal* 687.

[138] Jacob, above n 10, 87 and 125.

[139] See again Komárek, above n 2, 153 ff.

[140] Whittaker, above n 6, 741 ff.

[141] For cases in a different area, see the analysis by Tridimas, above n 11, 314 ff.

[142] See also for more instances Komárek, above n 2, 152 ff; according to Jacob, above n 10, 105 ff, however, this is not often the case.

[143] See section IV.

This is not to be taken to mean that the common law method is by itself, or because of some intrinsic quality,[144] superior to the civil law approach or to the approach being developed by the Court of Justice.[145] The common law approach to law making and interpretation has its own problems:

> Beginning on the 'one case at a time' path, the common law has simply continued along that path. It still develops case by case with little systematic attention to its overall coherence, resulting in a large and disorganized body of decisional law.[146]

Also, having different individual judgments making up the same decision may lead to difficulties in determining the ratio decidendi. Those difficulties are at times intractable, thus making the precedent useless, or rather not even a precedent at all.[147]

However, when trying to make sense of the EU case law, one ignores the special features of each case at one's own risk. This contribution opened with a quotation from the leading English textbook on precedent. The same authors point out that

> [t]here would be no point in setting out many of the remarks of judges insisting on the importance of paying the most scrupulous attention to the facts of the previous cases cited to them. The number of such remarks is legion. The requirement goes to the root of the doctrine of precedent according to which like cases must be decided alike.[148]

Unlike cases may indeed be decided differently.

[144] And also keeping in mind that what is at times presented, is an 'idealised' version of that model: Komárek, above n 2, 170 f.

[145] Derlén and Lindholm, above n 7, 647, are indeed right to stress that the approach of the Court to precedents has evolved during the decades of its existence.

[146] Wells, above n 6, 569; see also ibid, at 571 and 575.

[147] See the illustration in Whittaker, above n 6, 723 ff; the problem seems to be lost on critics of the unanimous judgment approach followed, for instance, by the EU courts.

[148] Cross and Harris, above n 1, 43.

Part II

Procurement and Market Perspectives of the Enforcement of Labour Standards in the EU

5

Living Wages in Public Contracts: Impact of the RegioPost *Judgment and the Proposed Revisions to the Posted Workers Directive*

ABBY SEMPLE*

I. INTRODUCTION

THE IDEA OF including a specified wage requirement in a public contract may appear uncontroversial. A national minimum wage exists in 22 out of 28 Member States of the European Union (EU),[1] although the level at which this is set varies widely.[2] It is certainly possible to require contractors to pay the legal minimum wage in the place where the contract is to be performed, but matters become more complex where either the wage in question is not legally binding on all operators, or where the contract may be performed in whole or part outside of the area where the wage applies. This raises the possibility that bidders who are bound to pay the wage will be competing with bidders who are not. Questions then arise as to whether a requirement on all bidders to pay a designated wage may constitute a restriction on the free movement of goods and services, or conversely whether application of wage requirements only to certain operators (for example, those proposing to carry out the contract in the place where it is tendered) might violate the Treaty principle of non-discrimination.

* I would like to thank Dr Albert Sánchez-Graells and Prof Phil Syrpis of the University of Bristol Law School for comments provided on an earlier draft of this contribution, along with the other participants in the conference which germinated into this book.

[1] Austria, Denmark, Italy, Cyprus, Finland and Sweden are the exceptions.

[2] From €235 per month in Bulgaria to €1,999 in Luxembourg, as of July 2017. Expressed in purchasing power standards (PPSs), this gives a smaller but still significant range of PPS 491 (Bulgaria) to PPS 1,615 (Luxembourg). Source: Eurostat, at ec.europa.eu/eurostat/statistics-explained/index.php/Minimum_wage_statistics.

The 2014 Public Procurement Package[3] seeks to balance free movement and the promotion of competition with the ability—and in some cases duty—to apply social protections within public contracts.

This chapter looks first at the legality of applying living wages[4] in public sector contracts prior to 2016. This analysis draws primarily upon the Court of Justice's interpretation of the 2004 Public Procurement Directive[5] and the Posted Workers Directive[6] in the *Rüffert*,[7] *Bundesdruckerei*[8] and *RegioPost*[9] cases. While these three judgments apply broadly the same approach, in the last two the Court made clear that social protection measures such as minimum wages could in principle be justified even where they restrict free movement of goods and services—and in *RegioPost* it accepted that such social protection measures may be specific to public sector contracts.[10] In *Bundesdruckerei* and *RegioPost*, the Court analysed procurement measures against the Posted Workers Directive, despite its not applying based on the facts of these cases, an approach which may be questioned due to the potential applicability of other EU-derived laws relating, for example, to fixed-term employment and acquired rights. This chapter also considers the impact of Article 3(7) of the Posted Workers Directive, which states that it shall not prevent application of terms and conditions of employment which are more favourable to workers. The Court appears to have interpreted this as only applying where undertakings voluntarily choose to apply more

[3] The 2014 Public Procurement Directive, together with Directive 2014/23/EU of the European Parliament and of the Council of 26 February 2014 on the award of concession contracts [2014] OJ L 94/1, and Directive 2014/25/EU of the European Parliament and of the Council of 26 February 2014 on procurement by entities operating in the water, energy, transport and postal services sectors and repealing Directive 2004/17/EC [2014] OJ L 94/243.

[4] In the UK, the Living Wage Foundation has since 2001 calculated the rate of pay necessary for workers to meet basic needs given prevailing prices, including a small margin for unexpected expenses. The Living Wage has typically been 20–30% higher than the national minimum wage, with the separate London Living Wage being 30–40% higher. Voluntary commitments to pay the Living Wage have been made by some 2,900 private and public sector organisations in the UK. This should be distinguished from the 'National Living Wage' introduced under the National Minimum Wage (Amendment) Regulations 2016, which is the legal minimum for workers aged 25 and over (£7.50 per hour as of April 2017). In other EU countries, wages above legal minima are typically the product of collective bargaining, and are often limited to a particular sector or activity.

[5] Directive 2004/18/EC of the European Parliament and of the Council of 31 March 2004 on the coordination of procedures for the award of public works contracts, public supply contracts and public service contracts (2004 Public Procurement Directive) [2004] OJ L134/114.

[6] Directive 96/71/EC of the European Parliament and of the Council of 16 December 1996 concerning the posting of workers in the framework of the provision of services (Posted Workers Directive) [1997] OJ L18/1.

[7] Judgment of 3 April 2008, *Rüffert*, Case C-346/06, EU:C:2008:189.

[8] Judgment of 18 September 2014, *Bundesdruckerei*, Case C-549/13, EU:C:2014:2235.

[9] Judgment of 17 November 2015, *RegioPost*, Case C-115/14, EU:C:2015:760.

[10] The Court's judgment in this regard was limited to social protection measures laid down by law, regulation or administrative provision. In relation to collective agreements and arbitration awards, there is a requirement of universal or general applicability under Art 3(8) of the Posted Workers Directive.

favourable terms. It naturally leads to the question of whether the living wage can be included as a preference rather than a requirement in tenders, via contract award criteria.

This chapter goes on to examine the current position under the 2014 Public Procurement Package, outlining the impact of the mandatory social clause in Article 18(2) of the 2014 Public Procurement Directive,[11] as well as those recitals that make reference to the Posted Workers Directive and the relevant Treaty principles. In relation to award criteria, I look in particular at the inclusion of trading conditions in Article 67(2)(a) of the 2014 Public Procurement Directive as one of the factors that may be taken into account in the evaluation of tenders. This is derived from the Court of Justice judgment in *Dutch Coffee*,[12] in which it accepted the possibility of award criteria based on fair trade considerations. I argue that as the fair trade criteria considered by the Court included the payment of a wage premium not set out in mandatory or generally applicable measures, award criteria that relate to payment of a living wage may also be justified where they meet the transparency and other requirements for award criteria. I also look at the effect of the proposed changes to the Posted Workers Directive, which would replace the reference to 'minimum rates of pay' with a reference to 'remuneration'—meaning that wage commitments set out in laws, regulations, administrative provisions or eligible collective agreements could be applied even where these do not constitute minimum social protections.

It is worth noting the broader political and economic context in which the Court of Justice has addressed wage considerations in public contracts, which also informed the revision of the Procurement Directives. The Court first examined the relationship between public contracts and the Posted Workers Directive prior to the Eurozone debt crisis, which brought with it severe pressure on Member State budgets as well as diminished trust in national and EU institutions.[13] As austerity constrained public budgets, procurement was increasingly identified as a means of implementing policies that, in more fiscally expansive eras, might have been achieved through direct spending initiatives. For example, considerable emphasis was placed,

[11] Directive 2014/24/EU of the European Parliament and of the Council of 26 February 2014 on public procurement and repealing Directive 2004/18/EC (2014 Public Procurement Directive) [2014] OJ L94/65.

[12] Judgment of 10 May 2012, *Commission v Netherlands*, Case C-368/10, EU:C:2012:284 (*Dutch Coffee*).

[13] See F Roth, F Nowak-Lehmann and T Otter, 'Has the financial crisis shattered citizens' trust in national and European governmental institutions? Evidence from the EU member states, 1999–2010' (2011), available at www.ceps.eu/publications/has-financial-crisis-shattered-citizens%E2%80%99-trust-national-and-european-governmental; K Armingeon and B Ceka, 'The loss of trust in the European Union during the great recession since 2007: the role of heuristics from the national political system' (2014) 15(1) *European Union* 82. Various editions of the Eurobarometer since 2007 also confirm a general decline in trust in both EU and national institutions following the financial crisis.

both at EU and national level, on the ability of public procurement to foster innovation, while at local level the role of public contracts in helping to reduce unemployment and skills shortages regained prominence, having faded in the face of single market orthodoxy in the 1990s and early 2000s.[14] The necessity of addressing the environmental impacts of public contracts also became clearer in the decade after the *Concordia* judgment,[15] which first established the legitimacy of green public procurement. By the time the revision of the Procurement Directives was underway in late 2011, all of the major actors involved in the process[16] appeared to agree upon the legitimacy of including social and environmental considerations in public procurement—although substantial disagreement remained about the scope and means for this, in particular where free movement might be affected. As will be seen in the course of this chapter, these questions are only partially resolved in the text of the 2014 Public Procurement Package.

In parallel, the Posted Workers Directive—intended to determine which employment terms would apply to workers temporarily working in other Member States—came under considerable strain in the period following the 2004 and 2007 enlargements of the Union. There was a 45 per cent increase in the number of posted workers between 2004 and 2007.[17] The basic tension between Member States with high wages and social security costs and newer, poorer members tested the principle of free movement underlying the Posted Workers Directive. Unions and political parties have objected to the 'social dumping' associated with companies using low-cost workers to fulfil contracts while avoiding contributions to the pensions and other entitlements long enjoyed by workers in richer countries.[18] The newer accession states for the most part have supported the right of their companies to rely upon their cost advantages, especially where these companies make social security contributions and pay taxes in their home countries. Court of Justice case law, in particular the *Laval* quartet,[19] served primarily

[14] For discussion of this retrenchment, see C McCrudden, *Buying Social Justice* (Oxford, Oxford University Press, 2007) 330–34. The European Commission was particularly active in bringing infringement proceedings against Member States for use of social and environmental criteria in tenders during this period.

[15] Judgment of 17 September 2002, *Concordia Bus Finland Oy Ab, formerly Stagecoach Finland Oy Ab v Helsingin kaupunki and HKL-Bussiliikenne*, Case C-513/99, EU:C:2002:495 (*Concordia*).

[16] That is, the European Commission, the Parliament and the Member States acting through the Council. The European Court of Justice was also influential on these topics through its case law, as discussed in this chapter.

[17] European Commission, *Impact Assessment regarding reform of the posted workers directive*, SWD (2016) 52.

[18] For discussion of this, see the contribution by Novitz in ch 11 of this book.

[19] See Judgment of 18 December 2007, *Laval un Partneri*, Case C-341/05, EU:C:2007:809 (*Laval*), *Rüffert*, and Judgment of 11 December 2007, *International Transport Workers' Federation, Finnish Seamen's Union v Viking Line ABP et al*, Case C-438/05, EU:C:2007:772 (*Viking*) and Judgment of 19 June 2008, *Commission v Luxembourg*, Case C-319/06, EU:C:2008:350.

to highlight the need for a more comprehensive political settlement that balanced free movement of workers with social protections.

II. RELEVANT LAW PRIOR TO 2016

Three main sources of EU law are relevant to the question of which wage provisions may be enforced in public contracts: the Public Procurement Directives (currently, the 2014 Public Procurement Package), the Posted Workers Directive and the Treaty principles of free movement of goods and services and freedom of establishment, as well as the general principles of transparency and non-discrimination/equal treatment. National law is also relevant inasmuch as both the Procurement Directives and the Posted Workers Directive make direct references to national law on the question of which employment terms must be applied in contracts. Not all public sector contracts are subject to the EU law mentioned, however the Court's case law has created a broad scope of coverage, particularly in respect of the Treaty principles. Even where contracts are excluded from the scope of the Directives, the Court of Justice has held that they may be subject to the Treaty principles if they are of 'certain cross-border interest'. In addition to the free movement of goods and services and freedom of establishment, the Court has applied the principles of non-discrimination/equal treatment and transparency to contracts which are not covered by the Procurement Directives.[20]

A. The Posted Workers Directive

Since 2004, the recitals to the Procurement Directives have referred to the Posted Workers Directive in the context of determining which employment terms may be applied in public contracts. The specific reference to the Posted Workers Directive may be considered surprising, given that only a small number of public contracts involve posting of workers, and various other EU directives, such as those on acquired rights[21] and fixed-term

[20] Amongst others, see the Judgment of 18 November 1999, *Unitron Scandinavia and 3-S*, Case C-275/98, EU:C:1999:567; Judgment of 7 December 2000, *Telaustria and Telefonadress*, Case C-324/98, EU:C:2000:669; and Judgment of 15 May 2008, *SECAP and Santorso*, Joined Cases C-147/06 and C-148/06, EU:C:2008:277. For discussion of the scope of the cross-border interest test, see C Risvig Hamer (ex Hansen), *Contracts Not Covered or Not Fully Covered by the Public Sector Directive* (Copenhagen, DJØF, 2012) 149–58.

[21] Council Directive 2001/23/EC of 12 March 2001 on the approximation of the laws of the Member States relating to the safeguarding of employees' rights in the event of transfers of undertakings, businesses or parts of undertakings or businesses [2001] OJ L82/16. For discussion of the application of acquired rights to public contracts under the Transfer of Undertakings, Protection of Employment (TUPE) Regulations 2006 (SI 2006/246) and the Collective Redundancies and Transfer of Undertakings (Protection of Employment) (Amendment) Regulations 2014 (SI 2014/16), see I Omambala and N Motraghi, 'Implications of Brexit for TUPE in the area of public procurement' (2017) 1 *Public Procurement Law Review* 62.

employment,[22] may also apply—and in some case obligations under these instruments may conflict with the Posted Workers Directive.[23] Keeping in mind that the recitals are not themselves binding but express the intention of the legislator, and so may be used to aid interpretation of the directives, the logic for the specific references to the Posted Workers Directive seems to be as follows. At the time of publishing tender documents (which must include the technical specifications, award criteria, contract clauses, etc), a contracting authority cannot know whether any bidder will seek to rely upon posted workers to carry out the contract. In order to safeguard against this possibility, the terms of the competition and contract must be compatible with the Posted Workers Directive. This logic appears to have been followed by the Court of Justice in the *Bundesdruckerei* and *RegioPost* cases, which did not in fact concern posted workers.[24]

The Posted Workers Directive requires that where workers are temporarily posted from one Member State to another, they are guaranteed certain minimum terms and conditions of employment. In addition to minimum rates of pay, the Posted Workers Directive covers maximum work periods and minimum rest periods; minimum paid annual holidays; conditions for the hiring out of temporary workers; health, safety and hygiene at work; and protective measures with regard to pregnant women or women who have recently given birth, children and young people. On the question of which wage conditions *must* be applied in host states, Article 3(1) of the Posted Workers Directive refers to minimum rates of pay that have been laid down by 'law, regulation or administrative provision', including overtime but excluding supplementary occupational retirement pension schemes. In addition, and in respect of building work only, minimum rates of pay set out in collective agreements or arbitration awards must be enforced in respect of posted workers if the agreements/awards are either universally or generally applicable.[25] The concept of minimum rates of pay is to be interpreted by reference to the law and/or practice of the Member State to which the worker is posted.

However, Article 3(7) of the Posted Workers Directive provides that these minimum conditions shall not prevent the application of terms and conditions of employment more favourable to workers. This clause points to the

[22] Council Directive 1999/70/EC of 28 June 1999 concerning the framework agreement on fixed-term work concluded by ETUC, UNICE and CEEP [1999] OJ L175/43.

[23] For example, under the acquired rights/TUPE framework, employees may be entitled to wages set out in collective agreements which are not universally applicable.

[24] RegioPost did concern postal workers, which is an entirely different matter. The German courts in RegioPost and Bundesdruckerei formulated their references to the Court of Justice in terms of both the Posted Workers Directive and Art 56 of the Treaty on the Functioning of the European Union (TFEU) [2012] OJ C326/47, presumably because of concern about the broader impact of the Rüffert judgment on public contracts.

[25] Art 3(8) of the Posted Workers Directive.

tension at the heart of the Posted Workers Directive: is it about worker protection, or is it about allowing access for posted workers to host state markets? While the answer is undoubtedly 'both', the approach taken by the Court of Justice in the *Laval* quartet of cases (including *Rüffert*) emphasised the latter element, effectively removing the ability of host states to apply higher levels of protection to posted workers. In *RegioPost* the Court appeared more sympathetic to wage protections, but it still purported to review a requirement in a public contract against the provisions in Article 3(1) of the Posted Workers Directive only—implying that if it did not fall within one of the categories set out therein, it could not be applied. More detailed consideration of these cases is given in sections II.B and C.

The interpretation of the term 'administrative provision' in Article 3(1) of the Posted Workers Directive may be significant in any future challenges to living wage policies if, for example, these are adopted by way of governmental circulars or as part of an organisation's standing orders, procurement policy or other non-legislative instruments. The term 'administrative provision' is not defined within the Posted Workers Directive, but the formula 'law, regulation or administrative provision' is frequently used in directives to define the possible means of national implementation. The Court's interpretation of this term in other contexts suggests that administrative measures must be both generally applicable and create mandatory obligations[26]—however, these principles have been applied where administrative measures are used to implement EU law, rather than where they are used by Member States to apply social protections. An administrative provision that is not generally applicable may not always be sufficient to implement a directive—but that does not mean it is not an administrative provision within the meaning of the Posted Workers Directive.

An example of a broader approach to defining administrative provisions can be found in the guidance of the European Commission on implementation of the Strategic Environmental Assessment Directive,[27] which includes the following text:

> Administrative provisions are formal requirements for ensuring that action is taken which are not normally made using the same procedures as would be needed for new laws and which do not necessarily have the full force of law.

[26] See Judgment of 30 May 1991, *Commission v Germany*, Case C-361/88, EU:C:1991:224, in which the Commission challenged Germany's implementation of a directive concerning air pollution by way of an administrative circular. In that case, the Court found that the circular was insufficient to implement the directive because it was neither general nor mandatory. However, this was not put forward as a definition of 'administrative provisions' by the Court—nor has it applied a requirement of generality in its subsequent case law relating to administrative provisions.

[27] Directive 2001/42/EC of the European Parliament and of the Council of 27 June 2001 on the assessment of the effects of certain plans and programmes on the environment [2001] OJ L197/30.

> Some provisions of 'soft law' might count under this heading. Extent of formalities in its preparation and capacity to be enforced may be used as indications to determine whether a particular provision is an 'administrative provision' in the sense of the Directive. Administrative provisions are by definition not necessarily binding, but for the Directive to apply, plans and programmes prepared or adopted under them must be required by them, as is the case with legislative or regulatory provisions.[28]

Must administrative provisions within the meaning of the Posted Workers Directive be generally applicable, or can they apply only to certain types of contract? In relation to collective agreements and arbitration awards, the Posted Workers Directive sets an explicit requirement that these either be universally applicable (where a system for declaring them to be universally applicable exists), or, in the absence of such a system, either (i) generally applicable to all similar undertakings in the geographical area and in the profession or industry concerned or (ii) concluded by the most representative employers' and labour organisations at national level and applied throughout national territory. In contrast, there is no explicit requirement of generality where minimum rates of pay are set out in laws, regulations or administrative provisions—and in *RegioPost* the Court rejected the idea that laws setting minimum wage rates would have to apply generally. It seems clear then that neither under the Posted Workers Directive nor in other areas has the Court held that laws or administrative provisions must be generally applicable in order to be considered as such. The UK courts have also taken a relatively broad view of what constitutes an administrative provision within the meaning of EU law.[29] While this may not extend to requirements set out only in tender documents, procurement policies defined, for example, in governmental circulars or an organisation's standing orders may fall within such a broad interpretation.[30]

B. The *Laval* Quartet

In its 2007–08 term, the Court of Justice delivered four significant judgments dealing with various aspects of the relationship between EU law and collective bargaining rights. The first of these, the *Viking* case,[31] arose out

[28] European Commission, *Guidance on the implementation of Directive 2001/42/EC on the assessment of the effects of certain plans and programmes on the environment* (2003).

[29] In *Walton v The Scottish Ministers* [2012] UKSC 44, and *HS2 Action Alliance and Others v Secretary of State for Transport* [2013] EWCA Civ 920.

[30] For discussion of the possible negative consequences of a broad interpretation in this context, see A Sánchez-Graells, 'Regulatory Substitution between Labour and Public Procurement Law: The EU's Shifting Approach to Enforcing Labour Standards in Public Contracts' (2018) 24(2) *European Public Law forthcoming*, ssrn.com/abstract=2958297.

[31] *Viking*, above n 19.

of the attempted reflagging of a ferry between Finland and Estonia, with the intention of reducing wage costs. The Court held that measures taken by the International Transport Workers Union to prevent this amounted to a restriction on the freedom of establishment under the Treaty. Such a restriction could be justified by an overriding reason of public interest, such as the protection of employees, but only if the restriction was proportionate to the objective pursued. In the *Laval* judgment,[32] delivered one week later, the Court held that attempts by a Swedish trades federation to ensure the application of a local collective agreement to Latvian workers constituted an unjustified restriction on the freedom to provide services. As Sweden lacked both a minimum wage and a mechanism for making collective agreements universally applicable, negotiated wage rates did not fall within the scope of minimum conditions that could be enforced under the Posted Workers Directive. Both judgments were delivered by the Grand Chamber, underlining their political importance in the context of Estonia's and Latvia's recent accession to the EU alongside 10 other central and eastern European countries.[33]

Neither *Viking* nor *Laval* dealt with contracts subject to the public procurement rules;[34] however, the Court had an opportunity to consider this in the *Rüffert* judgment[35] delivered in April 2008. *Rüffert* concerned a works contract which had been terminated by Lower Saxony due to the failure of a subcontractor to comply with minimum rates of pay set out in a collective agreement. Public authorities in Germany are obligated under various regional laws (*Tariftreuegesetze*) to comply with such agreements, and to ensure the compliance of their contractors and subcontractors. The case turned upon the compatibility of this obligation with the Posted Workers Directive and Article 56 TFEU (ex Art 49 TEC) on freedom of establishment. The Court in *Rüffert* held that as the German law in question did not itself fix minimum wage rates but rather referred to collective agreements, which were not universally applicable, Lower Saxony was not entitled to impose the higher rate of pay on posted workers.[36] It observed that imposing higher wage requirements on posted workers had the potential to undermine the competitive advantage of undertakings based in lower-wage Member States and to impede the free movement of services.

[32] *Laval*, above n 19.

[33] Poland, Czech Republic, Malta, Cyprus, Estonia, Latvia, Lithuania, Hungary, Slovakia and Slovenia joined on 1 May 2004; Bulgaria and Romania joined on 1 January 2007.

[34] In *Laval*, Swedish trade unions undertook to blockade construction sites for schools, which were presumably subject to the award of a public contract. However, the case arose out of the actions of the trade union rather than any attempt by a contracting authority to enforce minimum terms and conditions of employment; there is no mention in the judgment of the contract award process.

[35] *Rüffert*, above n 7.

[36] ibid, paras 24–35.

In *Rüffert* the Court interpreted the reference in Article 3(7) of the Posted Workers Directive to 'more favourable conditions' as only allowing the voluntary application of more favourable contractual terms by undertakings in the host or sending state—finding that a Member State could not 'make the provision of services in its territory conditional on the observance of terms and conditions of employment which go beyond the mandatory rules for minimum protection'.[37] This seems to confuse a apecific requirement for delivery of public contracts with a general requirement for provision of services. The Court did not consider case law arising under the Procurement Directives, such as *Beentjes*[38] and *Nord Pas de Calais*,[39] which points to a wider discretion over terms and conditions of employment in the context of public contracts. Criticism of the *Rüffert* judgment emphasised this omission, as well as the Court's failure to consider the equal treatment implications where collective agreements are binding only on domestic contractors, meaning they are at a competitive disadvantage.[40]

In the final case forming part of the 'Laval quartet', *Commission v Luxembourg*, the Court reiterated the view that the purpose of the Posted Workers Directive was to establish 'a nucleus of mandatory rules for minimum protection to be observed in the host country by employers who post workers there',[41] rather than to allow for full enforcement of national rules.

These cases alerted unions and other bodies to a heightened risk that EU law would undermine collective agreements and conditions of employment in richer Member States. The European Parliament adopted a resolution in 2008 directly challenging the Court's Posted Workers Directive jurisprudence, and calling upon the Commission to adopt new legislation safeguarding the rights of workers.[42] The PWD Enforcement Directive,[43] adopted in 2014,

[37] ibid, para 33.

[38] Judgment of 20 September 1988, *Beentjes v State of the Netherlands*, Case C-31/87, EU:C:1988:422.

[39] Judgment of 26 September 2000, *Commission v France*, Case C-225/98, EU:C:2000:494 (*Nord Pas de Calais*).

[40] C Barnard, 'Procurement law to enforce labour standards' in G Davidov and B Langille (eds), *The Idea of Labour Law* (Oxford, Oxford University Press, 2013) 256. See also S Arrowsmith and P Kunzlik (eds), *Social and Environmental Policies in EC Procurement Law: New directives and new directions* (Cambridge, Cambridge University Press, 2009) 1–8; and C McCrudden, 'The Rüffert Case and Public Procurement' in M Cremona (ed), *Market Integration and Public Services in the European Union* (Oxford, Oxford University Press, 2011) 117. McCrudden highlights the legal and political background to the case both within Germany and at EU level, as well as the trade union reaction to the ruling. He argues that the Court did not adequately consider the effect of the Procurement Directives and relevant case law, and that as both the Posted Workers Directive and the Procurement Directives embody political compromises between the Treaty freedoms and social protections, the two must be placed on equal footing in resolving cases such as *Rüffert* (ibid, at 130–33).

[41] *Commission v Luxembourg*, above n 19, para 24.

[42] *European Parliament resolution of 22 October 2008 on challenges to collective agreements in the EU* (2008/2085(INI)).

[43] Directive 2014/67/EU of the European Parliament and of the Council of 15 May 2014 on the enforcement of Directive 96/71/EC concerning the posting of workers in the framework

did not achieve this aim—it provides for more uniform application of the minimum working conditions enforceable under the Posted Workers Directive, but does not attempt to redefine the scope of enforceable conditions as interpreted by the Court. However, the proposals put forward by the Commission in 2016 to amend the Posted Workers Directive would allow for more comprehensive application of host-state employment terms, as discussed in section III.E.

C. *Bundesdruckerei* and *RegioPost*

In 2014, the *Bundesdruckerei* case appeared to confirm the Court of Justice's approach of treating designated wage requirements in public contracts as a restriction on trade. At the same time, the judgment also highlighted the possibility of justifying such restrictions based on social protection factors. In a contract for the provision of data services, the City of Dortmund included a requirement for all tenderers and their subcontractors to pay at least the hourly rates set by the *Tariftreuegesetze*. The applicant objected on the basis that it proposed to perform the contract using workers based in Poland. The Court of Justice held that imposition of a minimum wage on subcontractors based in another Member State could in principle be justified based upon the objectives of protecting employees and preventing social dumping.[44] However, it found that in the circumstances, given that the minimum wage in question applied only to public sector contracts and bore no relation to the cost of living in Poland, it was disproportionate.[45] The wording of the operative part of the judgment is confined to cases in which

> a tenderer intends to carry out a public contract by having recourse exclusively to workers employed by a subcontractor established in a Member State other than that to which the contracting authority belongs.[46]

This suggested that the situation might be different if a contractor intended to rely in part or entirely on workers based in the Member State where the wage rate applied—a factual situation which arose in *RegioPost*.[47]

In 2013, the City of Landau advertised a tender in the *Official Journal of the European Union* for the provision of postal services. As part of their tender, bidders were required to submit a declaration on their own behalf and on behalf of any proposed subcontractors, guaranteeing to

of the provision of services and amending Regulation (EU) No 1024/2012 on administrative cooperation through the Internal Market Information System ('the IMI Regulation') [2014] OJ L159/11.

[44] *Bundesdruckerei*, above n 8, para 31.
[45] ibid, paras 32–34.
[46] ibid, para 36.
[47] *RegioPost*, above n 9.

pay employees involved in delivery of the service at least €8.70 per hour. This was in accordance with a requirement for public contracts set out in regional legislation (similar to the law at issue in *Bundesdruckerei*). At the time that the contract was tendered, no national minimum wage applied in Germany; from 1 January 2015, a minimum wage of €8.50 per hour came into effect. RegioPost submitted the declaration in respect of its subcontractors, but not on its own behalf. In response to a request for clarification, RegioPost indicated that it believed the requirement to submit the declaration was contrary to public procurement law. The City of Landau then excluded RegioPost from the competition, and it challenged this decision.

Both Advocate General Mengozzi and the Court in *RegioPost* reached conclusions markedly different from that in *Rüffert* on the question of whether the contracting authority could enforce the wage provision. Advocate General Mengozzi argued that the fact that the wage agreement in question only applied to public sector contracts should not deprive it of its effect in the context of a procurement procedure. He drew an analogy with the ability of contracting authorities to apply environmental conditions regardless of whether these apply in the private sector generally, as established in *Concordia*.[48] He also considered the requirement applied by the City of Landau to be proportionate, inasmuch as it referred specifically to the workers to be employed on the contract at hand and not to all employees of the tenderers.[49] In his view, Article 26 of the 2004 Public Procurement Directive clearly envisioned the use of social clauses such as those relating to minimum wages,[50] and

> Member States must, in my view, be empowered to adopt laws, regulations or administrative provisions which, in the specific context of public contracts, lay down employment conditions, including a minimum rate of pay, for the benefit of the workers who provide services in performance of those contracts.[51]

The Court for its part held that: (i) the 2004 Public Procurement Directive does not preclude legislation that requires tenderers and their subcontractors to undertake, by means of a written declaration, to pay staff performing the services a predetermined minimum wage; and (ii) a tenderer or subcontractor who refuses to provide an undertaking to pay a minimum wage required under legislation may be excluded from a procurement procedure.

Crucially, the Court held that measures capable of impeding the Article 56 TFEU freedom to provide services can, in principle, be justified by the need to protect workers, even if those measures apply only to public sector contracts.[52] In reaching this conclusion, it distinguished in three respects the

[48] *Concordia*, above n 15.

[49] Opinion of AG Mengozzi delivered on 9 September 2015 in *RegioPost*, Case C-115/14, EU:C:2015:566, para 87.

[50] ibid, para 47.

[51] ibid, para 71.

[52] *RegioPost*, above n 9, paras 63 and 70–72.

factual situation in *RegioPost* from that in *Rüffert*. First, in *Rüffert* the wage in question was set down in a collective agreement, not in legislation—and the Court held that the requirement of 'universal applicability' applied only to collective agreements and not to legislation.[53] Secondly, the collective agreement in *Rüffert* applied only to the construction sector, whereas the minimum wage in *RegioPost* applied to all sectors where public contracts were awarded. Thirdly, in *Rüffert* a separate, lower minimum wage already applied in the construction sector, which was set down in legislation, whereas in *RegioPost* the wage rate in question constituted the minimum social protection available to workers.[54] While the *RegioPost* judgment is thus restricted in the scope of wage provisions to which it applies, the Court did not restrict its findings to cases where all of the bidders are located in one country—it specifically rejected the idea that different rules would apply where cross-border bids were made.[55] The judgment thus went most of the way towards establishing the ability of contracting authorities to insist on minimum wage provisions in public contracts where these are set out in legislation (at least), while leaving open the possibility for review of other wage requirements against the Treaty principles of free movement and non-discrimination.

Once the Court had determined that enforcement of such legislation was possible in public contracts under the auspices of Article 26 of the 2004 Public Procurement Directive, it turned to the question of whether a bidder could be excluded for its failure to provide a declaration that it would comply with the minimum wage. It found that given the importance ascribed to complying with mandatory conditions in tenders, including those adopted under Article 26, exclusion of a bidder was both permissible and proportionate. The fact that the bidder was given an opportunity to clarify the reason for not submitting the declaration was considered relevant in this regard.[56] The Court also noted that the minimum wage requirement was 'formulated in a particularly transparent manner in the contract notice and intended to emphasise, from the outset, the importance of compliance with a mandatory rule'.[57]

The 2014 Public Procurement Package sets higher transparency requirements regarding contract performance clauses than its 2004 predecessor, by requiring that full, free, online access to procurement documents is available from the date of publication of a notice,[58] and by requiring that contract

[53] ibid, para 63.
[54] ibid, paras 73–76.
[55] ibid, paras 50–51. The Court also did not seek to distinguish *Bundesdruckerei*, on the basis that that case involved use of a workforce based in another Member State—perhaps leaving open the question of whether it would follow the same approach as it did in *RegioPost* in this situation.
[56] *RegioPost*, above n 9, para 87.
[57] ibid, para 83.
[58] Art 53(1) of the 2014 Public Procurement Directive.

review clauses must be clear, precise and unequivocal in order to justify modifications after contract award.[59] Section III looks at further changes to the 2014 Public Procurement Package, which are relevant to the question of whether, and how, wage commitments may be included in the award of public contracts.

III. CHANGES IN THE 2014 PUBLIC PROCUREMENT PACKAGE AND PROPOSED REVISIONS TO THE POSTED WORKERS DIRECTIVE

The deadline for transposition of the 2014 Public Procurement Package fell on 18 April 2016. The social and environmental aspects of public contracts received considerable attention during the 2011–14 reform process, not least due to the efforts of the committee within the European Parliament charged with reviewing the draft legislation put forward by the Commission.[60] This committee tabled over 450 amendments, many of which aimed to strengthen the ability of contracting authorities to enforce labour laws and collective agreements in public contracts. The Court of Justice also delivered its judgment in *Dutch Coffee*[61] at a critical juncture in this process, leading the Commission and Council to accept that certain social criteria (specifically trading conditions, such as fair trade commitments) could apply in the award of public contracts. The 2014 Public Procurement Package thus has a markedly more 'social' flavour than its predecessors, containing a number of new or enhanced possibilities to enforce or promote labour standards and social inclusion. Relevant provisions include the ability to reserve contracts for sheltered workshops or employment programmes[62] and the 'light-touch' rules applicable to social and other specific services.[63] However, these provisions are almost all optional rather than mandatory—with Member States or contracting authorities choosing whether to apply them. The main exception is found in Article 18(2) of the 2014 Public Procurement Directive,[64] sometimes referred to as the 'mandatory social clause'.

[59] ibid, Art 72(1)(a).

[60] Committee on Internal Market and Consumer Affairs, Rapporteur: Marc Tarabella (BE).

[61] *Dutch Coffee*, above n 12.

[62] Art 20 of the 2014 Public Sector Directive. This provision expands upon a similar reservation under the 2004 Directives, by (i) including programs which address disadvantaged as well as disabled workers, and (ii) reducing the minimum percentage of such workers who must be employed to 30% from 50%. There is also a separate ability under Art 77 of the 2014 Public Procurement Directive to reserve certain contracts for organisations pursuing public service missions.

[63] Title III (Arts 74–77) of the 2014 Public Procurement Directive.

[64] Identical provisions appear in Art 36(2) of the 2014 Utilities Directive (Directive 2014/25/EU) and Art 30(3) of the 2014 Concessions Directive (Directive 2014/23/EU), both included in the 2014 Public Procurement Package.

A. Article 18(2) of the 2014 Public Procurement Directive, the 'Mandatory Social Clause'

While Article 18(2) of the 2014 Public Procurement Directive in itself creates only a general duty upon Member States to ensure compliance with applicable environmental, social and labour law obligations in the performance of public contracts, a number of other provisions within the 2014 Public Procurement Package enable or require contracting authorities to ensure compliance in the context of procurement procedures. The first is the possibility to exclude an operator, where a contracting authority can demonstrate by any appropriate means that that operator has violated one of the applicable obligations referred to in Article 18(2) of the 2014 Public Procurement Directive.[65] In this context, 'applicable' would appear to refer to any obligation that applied to an operator in a place where it was operating. If it referred only to obligations in the place where the contract will eventually be performed, it would confer an undue advantage on operators based outside of that location, and conferring such undue advantages is prohibited under Article 18(1) of the 2014 Public Procurement Directive. It is open to Member States to make exclusion on this grounds mandatory. There is a maximum exclusionary period of three years from the date of the relevant violation,[66] and operators may submit evidence to demonstrate that they have 'self-cleaned'—for example by repaying any wages wrongfully underpaid and taking concrete measures to ensure this was not repeated.[67] Exclusion is also subject to a proportionality requirement, meaning that it must be appropriate to achieve the objective pursued (eg discouraging violations of wage obligations) and not go beyond what is needed to achieve that objective.

A second operative application of Article 18(2) of the 2014 Public Procurement Directive can be found in the general ability for contracting authorities to reject tenders that do not comply with the applicable obligations. This raises the question of how contracting authorities are to satisfy themselves regarding compliance, for example with wage requirements. In *RegioPost* the Court held that an undertaking to pay the applicable wage could be sought both from bidders and any proposed subcontractors.[68]

[65] Art 57(4)(a) of the 2014 Public Procurement Directive.

[66] ibid, Art 57(7).

[67] Under Art 57(6) of the 2014 Public Procurement Directive, economic operators may seek to prove that they have compensated for, clarified and taken concrete technical, organisational and personnel measures to redress any misconduct. Contracting authorities are obliged to take this into account and, if they consider the actions insufficient to allow inclusion in the procedure, to provide a written statement of the reasons for their decision.

[68] *RegioPost*, above n 9, para 84. While *RegioPost* was decided under the 2004 Public Procurement Directive, there is no reason to suppose that such an undertaking could not also be required under the 2014 Public Procurement Package.

To verify working conditions at facilities used to deliver a contract, it would be open to contracting authorities to seek third-party certification,[69] which may include audits.

The third application of Article 18(2) of the 2014 Public Procurement Directive can be found in the provisions relating to the treatment of abnormally low tenders. Very low-priced tenders may be linked to social dumping, but they may also be due to legitimate factors such as efficient working methods. Court of Justice case law on abnormally low tenders has focused on the need to allow bidders an opportunity to explain their pricing prior to making a decision to reject a tender.[70] As the concept of an abnormally low tender is not itself defined in EU law, it is up to Member States or individual contracting authorities to identify tender pricing which requires further explanation. This is made more important by the obligation set out in Article 69(3) of the 2014 Public Procurement Directive to reject abnormally low tenders where the pricing is due to non-compliance with applicable laws or collective agreements.

Lastly, Article 71 of the 2014 Public Procurement Directive addresses the application of environmental, social and labour laws to subcontractors. Article 71(1) contains a rather general statement that compliance by subcontractors with the Article 18(2) obligations is to be ensured by 'appropriate action by the competent national authorities'. However, Article 71(6)(a) goes further, requiring that where joint liability between main contractors and subcontractors is possible under national law, this shall be used to ensure compliance with applicable environmental, social and labour obligations. One reading of this clause is that it means that joint liability, for example for payment of wages in accordance with collective agreements, *must* be applied in *all* contracts where there are subcontractors. Another reading would be that it only applies where the contract already establishes joint liability between contractors and subcontractors. Both the UK (excluding Scotland) and Ireland appear to have taken the latter interpretation, as they have not transposed Article 71(6)(a) of the 2014 Public Procurement Directive.[71] France, on the other hand, has set out specific rules on joint liability in its transposition, which also applies the rules on abnormally

[69] Contracting authorities are able to refer to particular labels or certification schemes where these meet the basic transparency and accessibility requirements specified in Arts 43 and 44 of the 2014 Public Procurement Directive, but must also accept equivalent labels or certificates.

[70] For example, Judgment of 29 March 2012, *SAG ELV Slovensko and Others*, Case C-599/10, EU:C:2012:191, in which the Court of Justice held there was a duty to investigate abnormally low tenders, and the earlier Judgment of 27 November 2001, *Lombardini and Mantovani*, Joined Cases C-285/99 and C-286/99, EU:C:2001:640; and Judgment of 15 May 2008 in *SECAP*, above n 20.

[71] In respect of England, Wales and Northern Ireland, see the Public Contracts Regulations 2015 (SI 2015/102); in respect of Ireland see the European Union (Award of Public Authority Contracts) Regulations 2016 (SI 284/2016).

low tenders to the costs of subcontractors.[72] The compatibility of any of these approaches with the 2014 Public Procurement Directive has not (yet) been challenged before the Court of Justice. Nevertheless, its judgment in *RegioPost* appears to endorse the idea of applying obligations to subcontractors in the same manner as they are applied to main contractors.

The Scottish Regulations implementing the 2014 Public Procurement Directive transpose Article 18(2) by creating an obligation on contracting authorities to include such conditions in public contracts as are reasonably necessary to ensure that contractors comply with applicable environmental, social and employment law and collective agreements.[73] In contrast, the Public Contracts Regulations 2015 for England, Wales and Northern Ireland do not transpose Article 18(2). However, given the other provisions which implement it in practice discussed above (and which are faithfully transposed in the 2015 Regulations), this does not appear to deprive it of its effectiveness. Article 18(2) of the 2014 Public Procurement Directive and the various provisions which allow it to be implemented offer a relatively strong basis for ensuring that social obligations—including the payment of minimum wages—are applied in public contracts. However, the use of the term 'obligations' raises doubt about whether voluntary commitments, such as a living wage, may be applied under the auspices of Article 18(2). Article 18(2) must be read in light of general EU law, and the recitals to the 2014 Public Procurement Package make direct reference to the Posted Workers Directive in this regard, as it may determine which labour laws are applicable to a public contract.

B. Recitals 37 and 98 of the 2014 Public Procurement Directive

The recitals of the three directives included in the 2014 Public Procurement Package, and in particular those of the 2014 Public Procurement Directive, refer to the need for social protection measures in public contracts to be applied 'in accordance' with the Posted Workers Directive, as well as the principle of non-discrimination. The two recitals that refer to the Posted Workers Directive do so in rather different terms. As these may affect interpretation of the substantive provisions of the directives, it is worth quoting them here. The first, recital 37, states:

> it is of particular importance that Member States and contracting authorities take relevant measures to ensure compliance with obligations in the fields of environmental, social and labour law that apply at the place where the works are executed or the services provided and result from laws, regulations, decrees and decisions,

[72] Arts 45 and 134.1 of the *Décret n° 2016-360 du 25 mars 2016 relatif aux marchés publics*.
[73] Public Contracts (Scotland) Regulations 2015 (SI 2015/446), reg 19.

> at both national and Union level, as well as from collective agreements, provided that such rules, and their application, comply with Union law. ... *However, this should in no way prevent the application of terms and conditions of employment which are more favourable to workers.*
>
> ... Such relevant measures should be applied in accordance with [the Posted Workers Directive] and in a way that ensures equal treatment and does not discriminate directly or indirectly against workers and economic operators from other Member States. (emphasis added)

The second, recital 98, states:

> It is essential that award criteria or contract performance conditions concerning social aspects of the production process ... should be applied in accordance with [the Posted Workers Directive], as interpreted by the Court of Justice of the European Union and should not be chosen or applied in a way that discriminates directly or indirectly against economic operators from other Member States or from third countries part[y] to the [WTO Agreement on Government Procurement] or to Free Trade Agreements to which the Union is party. Thus, *requirements concerning the basic working conditions regulated in [the Posted Workers Directive], such as minimum rates of pay, should remain at the level set by national legislation or by collective agreements applied in accordance with Union law in the context of that Directive.* (emphasis added)

At first glance, the italicised provisions appear to contradict each other. While recital 37 specifically endorses the possibility of applying terms and conditions of employment more favourable to workers than those set out in legislation or collective agreements, recital 98 counsels that minimum rates of pay (which surely form part of terms and conditions of employment) should remain at the levels set out in those laws and collective agreements. Both invoke the Posted Workers Directive alongside the principle of equal treatment and the concepts of direct and indirect discrimination. Is it possible to read these two recitals in a way that gives effect to both of them? Inasmuch as the last sentence of recital 98 refers only to 'requirements' remaining at the levels set out in legislation or collective agreements, it may be construed as not limiting award criteria that relate to preferences. *Rüffert*, *Bundesdruckerei* and *RegioPost* all related to mandatory conditions, and it was in this context that the Court appeared to equate public procurement requirements with general conditions of offering services on the market. Given its decisions in the *Concordia* and *Dutch Coffee* cases, it would be more difficult for the Court of Justice to apply this approach to award criteria.

C. Use of Contract Award Criteria Based on Payment of a Living Wage

Can contracting authorities award marks to bidders who commit to pay a living wage? An argument can be made for this based upon the specific wording of the provisions on award criteria in the 2014 Public Procurement Package, as well as the Court's jurisprudence in this area. As a starting point, the Court has long recognised the ability of contracting authorities to develop and apply award criteria that target specific preferences, and that national legislation cannot restrict this choice to certain criteria.[74] In *Concordia*, the Court developed general requirements for award criteria, which have since been written into the directives, requiring that they be linked to the subject matter of the contract in question,[75] advertised in advance and not be such as to confer an unrestricted freedom of choice on the contracting authority. There is also a requirement that cost or price be taken into account in some way, and that award criteria 'ensure the possibility of effective competition'.[76] Beyond this, the Directives provide a non-exhaustive list of considerations that may be taken into account to identify the most economically advantageous tender.

Amongst the list of considerations that may form part of award criteria, the 2014 Public Procurement Package includes 'trading conditions' for the first time. This can be traced directly to the Court's judgment in *Dutch Coffee*, which concerned the application of (inter alia) fair trade criteria in a contract for the supply of tea and coffee. The Court held in that case that 'There is ... nothing, in principle, to preclude [an award] criterion from referring to the fact that the product concerned was of fair trade origin.'[77] The concept of fair trade origin as applied in the case referred to 'products of fair trade origin purchased at a price and under conditions more favourable than those determined by market forces from organisations made up of small-scale producers in developing countries'.[78]

Although the Court upheld the possibility of applying fair trade award criteria, it rejected the Dutch authority's approach of only awarding marks to bidders who held particular labels attesting to compliance with these criteria. It also ruled that several other criteria linked to sustainable purchasing applied in the case lacked the requisite transparency. However, it is clear from both the judgment and Advocate-General Kokott's Opinion that distinguishing between bids based upon fair trade criteria was compatible with the public procurement rules. Given that the reference to 'trading conditions' has now been included in the 2014 Public Procurement Package, might this also extend to criteria related to the payment of a living wage?

While the criteria in *Dutch Coffee* related to a supply contract, and specifically the terms on which goods were obtained from producers, it is

[74] Judgment of 7 October 2004, *Sintesi*, Case C-247/02, EU:C:2004:593.

[75] *Concordia*, above n 15, para 69. For discussion of this requirement see A Semple, 'The Link to the Subject-matter: A Glass Ceiling for Sustainable Public Contracts?' in B Sjåfjell and A Wiesbrock (eds), *Sustainable Public Procurement under EU Law* (Cambridge, Cambridge University Press, 2015) 50.

[76] These requirements are now set out in Art 67 of the 2014 Public Procurement Directive.

[77] *Dutch Coffee*, above n 12, para 91.

[78] ibid, para 73.

difficult to see why a different analysis would apply to a service contract, provided the criteria were linked to the subject matter of the contract in the sense of relating to the specific services being purchased and not the general practices of operators bidding for a contract. It is also difficult to see why criteria relating to a wage premium paid to workers within the EU should be treated differently from a wage premium paid to workers in third countries, given that there is no harmonisation of wages within the EU. An award criterion that assigned a certain percentage of marks for payment of the living wage is also less likely to restrict competition than the type of wage requirement applied in *Bundesdruckerei* and *RegioPost*, as it would not be a mandatory condition for award of contract but rather one factor to be weighed against others, such as cost and quality.[79] From this perspective, a living wage award criterion might also be less effective at achieving the objective of ensuring that a fair wage is paid to all workers on public contracts, but it would be open to the contracting authority to attach a high weighting to this if it chose to.[80]

D. Contract Performance Clauses

The Court has on several occasions endorsed the idea that employment-related matters may be addressed in conditions for contract performance[81]—and Article 70 of the 2014 Public Procurement Directive now specifically refers to this possibility.[82] In *RegioPost*, the Court clearly upheld the idea that a bidder could be excluded for failing to provide a declaration that it would comply with a contract performance condition. However this raises a fundamental question about the distinction between contract performance conditions and technical specifications—the latter being much more tightly regulated under both the procurement directives and international trade agreements to which the EU is party.[83] Given that the effects

[79] In *Concordia*, above n 15, the Court of Justice allowed an environmental criterion under which only one of the bidders achieved full marks, because there was nothing to prevent other bidders from also achieving full marks.

[80] In *EVN and Wienstrom*, the Court of Justice accepted that a contracting authority might attach a weighting of 45% to an award criterion based upon renewable energy production: Judgment of 4 December 2003, *EVN and Wienstrom*, Case C-448/01, EU:C:2003:651.

[81] In *Beentjes* (above 38), *Nord Pas de Calais* (above n 39), and *Dutch Coffee* (above n 12).

[82] The legislative history of Art 26 of the 2004 Public Procurement Directive shows that both more explicit reference to the possibility of including employment-related conditions (proposed by the French and Belgian delegates) and more explicit reference to the requirement that contract conditions must not be discriminatory (proposed by the Commission) were rejected in the course of the negotiation. See J Hebly (ed), *European Public Procurement: Legislative history of the 'Classic' Directive 2004/18/EC* (Alphen aan den Rijn, Kluwer Law International, 2007) 711–26.

[83] Including the WTO Government Procurement Agreement (GPA) and Comprehensive Economic and Trade Agreement (CETA) with Canada. For a discussion of the scope for pursuing socially responsible procurement under these instruments, see A Semple, 'Socially

upon competition of rejecting a tender for non-compliance with a technical specification or contract performance condition are the same, it is not clear why they should be treated differently. On the other hand, if compliance with contract conditions is not verified during the competitive process, this creates problems in terms of transparency and fair competition.

Despite the requirement under the 2014 Public Procurement Package to publish all procurement documents in advance and the more detailed rules governing modifications,[84] it is clear that not all contract terms can be known in advance, as some will be based on the outcome of the competition. This is most obviously the case regarding price, but in cases where award criteria are used to target the living wage as set out in section III.C, it would also be necessary to include any such commitment in the contract if the winning bidder has offered this in its tender. In this case, the Article 70 reference to employment conditions may provide some reassurance that such terms can be enforced under the procurement rules. However, more general reliance on Article 70 to apply mandatory conditions which would not be enforceable under Article 18(2) may subvert the legislative compromise between free movement of goods and services and social protection measures embodied in the 2014 Public Procurement Package.

E. Proposed Changes to the Posted Workers Directive

In March 2016, the Commission published proposals for revisions to the Posted Workers Directive, which would enhance the ability to apply host Member State conditions.[85] This led 11 national parliaments to invoke the 'yellow card' procedure, seeking to stop the proposals on the grounds that they infringed the principle of subsidiarity.[86] The Commission issued a response in which it rejected the subsidiarity argument, on the basis that the posting of workers necessarily involved cross-border transactions which

Responsible Public Procurement under International Trade Agreements: the GPA, CETA and the EU-Ukraine Deep and Comprehensive Free Trade Area' (2017) 12(3) *European Procurement & Public Private Partnership Law Review* 293–309 forthcoming, available at ssrn.com/abstract=2970964.

[84] Set out in Arts 53(1) and 72(1)(a) of the 2014 Public Procurement Directive.

[85] European Commission, *Proposal for a Directive of the European Parliament and of the Council amending Directive 96/71/EC of The European Parliament and of the Council of 16 December 1996 concerning the posting of workers in the framework of the provision of services*, COM (2016) 128 final.

[86] The parliaments were mainly from Member States responsible for sending posted workers: Poland, Romania, the Czech Republic, Croatia, Bulgaria, Estonia, Latvia, Lithuania and Hungary. However, the Danish Parliament also objected, on the ground that the proposal did not make explicit reference to the competence of Member States to define pay and terms and conditions of employment.

were best regulated at EU level.[87] The Commission also rejected the idea that the existing rules were sufficient to create a level playing field between national and cross-border service providers where they carry out work at the same location. Discussions on the draft continued within the Council and the Employment and Social Affairs Committee of the Parliament in the second half of 2016. At the time of writing,[88] the Commission's proposals look likely to win the necessary support within the European Parliament and Council. If they are adopted, the changes would enhance the ability of host states to enforce wage requirements, including in respect of subcontractors.

Given that the 2014 Public Procurement Package permits enforcement of social clauses to the extent that these comply with EU law, and that the Posted Workers Directive is explicitly mentioned in their recitals, the planned reform to the Posted Workers Directive would also expand the scope for socially responsible public procurement under the Directives. Three proposed changes are of particular significance to the discussion here. The first is the replacement of the reference to 'minimum rates of pay' with the broader concept of 'remuneration', an open-ended category that includes all mandatory elements under national laws, regulations and administrative provisions, as well as under collective agreements which are universally or generally applicable.[89] Member States would be obliged to publish all relevant elements of remuneration on a single national website. The second is the extension of the enforceability of terms set out in collective agreements and arbitration awards to cover all sectors, not only building work. The third relates to subcontractors, enabling Member States to enforce the same conditions regarding remuneration in respect of subcontractors as are applied to primary contractors. The combined effect of these changes, if adopted, would be to expand the scope of employment terms that may be included as mandatory conditions in public contracts. The requirement to publish all relevant remuneration terms on a central website would also increase transparency in the application of such terms.

IV. CONCLUSIONS

This chapter has proposed two ways of applying a living wage in public contracts that seem to be in accordance with EU law—one which is immediately

[87] European Commission, *Communication on the proposal for a Directive amending the Posting of Workers Directive, with regard to the principle of subsidiarity, in accordance with Protocol No 2*, COM (2016) 505.

[88] May 2017.

[89] This follows on from the Court's Judgment of 12 February 2015, *Sähköalojen ammattiliitto*, Case C-396/13, EU:C:2015:86. In this case the Court held 'minimum rates of pay' must be calculated on the basis of the pay categories applicable in the host state, and included daily allowances, payments for travelling time and holidays but excluded accommodation and meal vouchers.

effective and another which would apply if the planned changes to the Posted Workers Directive are adopted. The first is through a contract award criterion that either relates directly to the payment by contractors of a living wage to employees involved in the delivery of a contract, or relates to this in combination with other factors linked to the subject matter of the contract and which are clearly defined in the tender documents. The ability to apply such an award criterion is based upon the Court of Justice's jurisprudence in relation to environmental and social award criteria in public contracts, as well as the specific inclusion of trading conditions in the 2014 Public Procurement Package. The second option would only take effect if the reference to 'minimum rates of pay' in the Posted Workers Directive were to be replaced with a reference to 'remuneration', as envisioned in the Commission's proposal. In this case, the Court of Justice's jurisprudence to the effect that pay requirements can only be included in public contracts where these are minimum mandatory conditions in accordance with the Posted Workers Directive would no longer be relevant—because the Posted Workers Directive would no longer make reference to minimum rates of pay. In order to apply a living wage as a mandatory condition for the award of contracts in this context, it would still need to be set out in a law, regulation or administrative provision, or in an eligible collective agreement or arbitration award. In *RegioPost* the Court of Justice confirmed that such laws may be specific to the public sector, and there also does not seem to be a requirement under EU law for administrative provisions to be generally binding on all operators.

Questions such as the application of a living wage in public contracts have been subject to a detailed legal and political bargaining process within the EU. The balance reflected in the 2014 Public Procurement Package and the Posted Workers Directive is neither final nor static—it is subject both the Court of Justice's ongoing interpretation and to legislative change. Despite a return to economic growth across the EU, low wages and high unemployment continue to cause social unrest in many areas, including movement of workers to countries where demand is greater. The Posted Workers Directive is intended to create a 'level playing field' between these workers and those in the host states receiving them, however its interpretation in the *Laval* quartet had the effect of setting a ceiling rather than a floor for working conditions and wages. The proposed revisions look set to change this balance, assuming the necessary support is found in the Council and Parliament. While public procurement cannot and should not be considered as setting general conditions for the provision of services in a market, it does have an impact beyond the immediate needs of the purchaser.[90] For this reason, inclusion of wage terms that reflect the public sector's commitment to addressing low pay is both politically and economically sensible—and, as this chapter has sought to demonstrate, in line with recent EU law.

[90] For extended discussion, see the contribution by Davies in ch 9 of this book.

6

Competition and State Aid Implications of 'Public' Minimum Wage Clauses in EU Public Procurement after RegioPost

ALBERT SÁNCHEZ-GRAELLS

I. INTRODUCTION

AS OTHER CONTRIBUTIONS to this book stress, the use of public procurement for the enforcement of social policies, and in particular for the imposition of labour standards and minimum wage requirements, has been both widespread and controversial in the European Union (EU).[1] The case law of the Court of Justice has been considered restrictive of the possibilities of using public procurement to enforce minimum wage standards in a flexible way. This rigidity has been particularly linked to the *Rüffert* case,[2] and the way in which the Court of Justice linked the possibility of using procurement to enforce labour standards in compatibility with EU law and, in particular, with the Posted Workers Directive.[3]

[1] For an interesting discussion, see A Wiesbrock, 'Socially Responsible Public Procurement. European Value or National Choice?' in B Sjåfjell and A Wiesbrock (eds), *Sustainable Public Procurement under EU Law: New Perspectives on the State as Stakeholder* (Cambridge, Cambridge University Press, 2015) 75. See also Public World, *EU Public Procurement Regulation and Core Labour Standards. A Report for DFID* (2007), at publicworld.org/files/dfid2007.pdf.

[2] Judgment of 3 April 2008, *Rüffert*, Case C-346/06, EU:C:2008:189. For discussion, see R Caranta, 'Sustainable Public Procurement in the EU' in R Caranta and M Trybus (eds), *The Law of Green and Social Procurement in Europe* (Copenhagen, DJØF, 2010) 15, 35–38.

[3] Directive 96/71/EC of the European Parliament and of the Council of 16 December 1996 concerning the posting of workers in the framework of the provision of services (Posted Workers Directive) [1997] OJ L18/1. For criticism of this approach, see C McCrudden, 'The Rüffert Case and Public Procurement' in M Cremona (ed), *Market Integration and Public Services in the European Union* (Oxford, Oxford University Press, 2011) 117.

Subsequent guidance by the European Commission[4] stressed this link by indicating that the relevant EU public procurement rules make it clear that the laws, regulations and collective agreements, at both national and EU level, in force in the areas of employment conditions and safety at work apply during performance of a public contract, *provided such rules, and the way they are applied, comply with EU law*.[5] And, more specifically, the Commission stressed that one example of such compliance with EU law is the need to meet the requirements of the Posted Workers Directive in public procurement involving cross-border situations, where workers from one Member State provide services in another Member State for the purpose of performing a public contract.[6] Remarkably, though, the extent to which 'autonomous' public procurement requirements also applied to the imposition of (minimum) wage conditions through contract compliance clauses—such as the need for them to be linked to the subject matter of the tendered contract[7]—and the contours of the limitations derived from the Posted Workers Directive remained somewhat unclear. This led to subsequent litigation that challenged some interpretations of *Rüffert* and, in particular, to *RegioPost*.[8]

In its much awaited *RegioPost* judgment, the Court of Justice allowed for the imposition of minimum wage requirements as special performance

[4] European Commission, *'Buying Social' A guide on taking account of social considerations in public procurement* (2011).

[5] This guidance was issued in relation to the now repealed Directive 2004/17/EC of the European Parliament and of the Council of 31 March 2004 coordinating the procurement procedures of entities operating in the water, energy, transport and postal services sectors [2004] OJ L134/1 and Directive 2004/18/EC of the European Parliament and of the Council of 31 March 2004 on the coordination of procedures for the award of public works contracts, public supply contracts and public service contracts (2004 Public Procurement Directive) [2004] OJ L134/114. However, this is equally relevant in relation to the new generation of EU public procurement directives: Directive 2014/24/EU of the European Parliament and of the Council of 26 February 2014 on public procurement and repealing Directive 2004/18/EC (2014 Public Procurement Directive) [2014] OJ L94/65 and Directive 2014/25/EU of the European Parliament and of the Council of 26 February 2014 on procurement by entities operating in the water, energy, transport and postal services sectors and repealing Directive 2004/17/EC [2014] OJ L94/243. See recital 37 of the 2014 Public Procurement Directive.

[6] European Commission, above n 4, 46, fn 86.

[7] This was a debatable question under Art 26 of the 2004 Public Procurement Directive, given its silence, but there were good reasons to consider the need for contract compliance requirements to be linked to the subject matter of the contract; see A Sánchez-Graells, *Public Procurement and the EU Competition Rules* (Oxford, Hart Publishing, 2011) 317. This is now clearly a requirement under Art 70 of the 2014 Public Procurement Directive, which explicitly establishes that 'Contracting authorities may lay down special conditions relating to the performance of a contract, provided that they are linked to the subject-matter of the contract'; see A Sánchez-Graells, *Public Procurement and the EU Competition Rules*, 2nd edn (Oxford, Hart Publishing, 2015) 390. For general critical discussion of this requirement, see A Semple, 'The Link to the Subject Matter: A Glass Ceiling for Sustainable Public Contracts?' in Sjåfjell and Wiesbrock (eds), above n 1, 50.

[8] Judgment of 17 November 2015, *RegioPost*, Case C-115/14, EU:C:2015:760.

conditions in contracts covered by the EU public procurement rules.[9] Interestingly, the Court of Justice achieved this result despite deviating from the proposal of Advocate General Mengozzi,[10] who also advocated for more scope for the imposition of minimum wage clauses in public contracts than seemed to result from a strict reading of *Rüffert*, but on different legal grounds (suggesting that the Posted Workers Directive did not provide the relevant framework for the analysis).[11] The case and its implications from the internal market, labour and public procurement perspectives are discussed at length in other contributions to this book. It has been rightly stressed that *RegioPost* is particularly significant for its perceived deviation from the (at least seemingly) restrictive approach to the use of minimum wage requirements in public procurement,[12] which the Court of Justice initially established in *Rüffert* and recently reiterated in *Bundesdruckerei*.[13]

In my view, however, *RegioPost* does not supersede previous case law (that is, both *Rüffert* and *Bundesdruckerei* remain good law), and the apparent deviation from or contradiction with such case law can be primarily explained by virtue of either (i) the different cross-border situations implied in each of these cases—for example, *Bundesdruckerei* was concerned with the cross-border provision of services rather than the posting of workers, whereas in both *Rüffert* and *RegioPost* the provision of the services was purely domestic, at least in functional terms;[14] or (ii) the different applicability of

[9] For discussion, see A Brown, 'The Lawfulness of a Regional Law Requiring Tenderers for a Public Contract to Undertake to Pay Workers Performing that Contract the Minimum Wage Laid Down in that Law: Case C-115/14' (2016) 25(2) *Public Procurement Law Review* NA49–NA55. See also C Kaupa, 'Public Procurement, Social Policy and Minimum Wage Regulation for Posted Workers: Towards a More Balanced Socio-Economic Integration Process?' (2016) 1(1) *European Papers* 127; and F Costamagna, 'Minimum Wage between Public Procurement and Posted Workers: Anything New after the *RegioPost* Case?' (2017) 42(1) *EL Rev* 101.

[10] Opinion of Advocate General Mengozzi of 9 September 2015 in *RegioPost*, Case C-115/14, EU:C:2015:566.

[11] For discussion of AG Mengozzi's *RegioPost* Opinion, see A Sánchez-Graells, 'AG Opinion Favours Minimum Pay in Public Contracts: Why the CJEU Should Not Follow (C-115/14)', 11 September 2015, at howtocrackanut.com/blog/2015/09/ag-opinion-favours-minimum-pay-in.html. See also Brown, above n 9, NA53–NA54.

[12] See EK Sarter, D Sack and S Fuchs, 'Public Procurement as Social Policy? An introduction to social criteria in public procurement in Germany' (2014) *Working Paper Series Comparative Governance* No 1, at uni-bielefeld.de/soz/powi/pdf/WPCG01_Sarter_Sack_Fuchs_Public_Procurement_Aug14.pdf. It is interesting to note that *Rüffert* led to domestic reforms in order to retain the ability to use public procurement for the enforcement of labour standards. See M Blauberger, 'With Luxembourg in mind ... the remaking of national policies in the face of ECJ jurisprudence' (2012) 19(1) *Journal of European Public Policy* 109.

[13] Judgment of 18 September 2014, *Bundesdruckerei*, Case C-549/13, EU:C:2014:2235. See A Sánchez-Graells, 'CJEU continues reducing the scope of minimum wage laws when public contracts are subcontracted (C-549/13)', 19 September 2014, at howtocrackanut.com/blog/2014/09/cjeu-continues-reducing-scope-of.html.

[14] For discussion, see GS Ølykke, 'The Provision on Abnormally Low Tenders: A Safeguard for Fair Competition?' in GS Ølykke and A Sánchez-Graells (eds), *Reformation or Deformation of the EU Public Procurement Rules* (Cheltenham, Edward Elgar, 2016) 146.

the Posted Workers Directive—for example, in *Rüffert* the Court of Justice found the Posted Workers Directive not to cover collective agreements that created non-universal minimum wage requirements, whereas in *RegioPost* the Court of Justice found the Posted Workers Directive to cover an equivalent requirement resulting from a regional law because it did not consider that instrument to be affected by the requirement of universal applicability.[15] Notably, though, *RegioPost* still leaves some unanswered issues,[16] and it also raises important policy questions and opens the door to future legal reform in the event that more intense labour-orientated smart public procurement is sought, which discussion is best saved.

This chapter aims to adopt an analytical angle different from those that precede and follow in this book, to stress some of the economic implications of the Court of Justice case law on the use of public procurement for the creation or enforcement of labour standards. It particularly focuses on the competition-distortive effects of having different rules for cross-border and inter-regional provision of services to the public sector, as well as on the scope for de facto economic protectionism created by the deference provided to the use of Posted Workers Directive-compliant procurement performance clauses to enforce labour standards. The chapter considers some non-labour and non-procurement implications of this line of case law, and the asymmetrical effects that derive from a joint consideration of *Rüffert*, *Bundesdruckerei* and *RegioPost*. It ultimately aims to stress the tensions and possibly undesired consequences that are only visible from that perspective.

In that regard, it is worth emphasising that these cases have important elements in common that make them somehow indistinguishable from a competition and state aid law perspective. First, both *Bundesdruckerei* and *RegioPost* triggered issues of competitive advantage based on differences in wage levels. While *Bundesdruckerei* concerned differences across Member States, *RegioPost* would cover differences across regions of the same Member State. A close assessment of the underlying economic reality will highlight the difficulties derived from this approach where an economic (geographical) definition of the market is adopted. Thus, from an economic perspective, the difference between these two cases is marginal or strictly formal, and the treatment given by the Court of Justice can trigger difficulties in maintaining a level playing field both in public and private markets

[15] For discussion, see C Barnard, 'The Calm after the Storm: Time to Reflect on EU (Labour) Law Scholarship following the Decisions in *Viking* and *Laval*' in A Bogg, C Costello and ACL Davies (eds), *Research Handbook on EU Labour Law* (Cheltenham, Edward Elgar, 2016) 337, 360.

[16] See A Sánchez-Graells, 'Regulatory substitution between labour and public procurement law: the EU's shifting approach to enforcing labour standards in public contracts' (2018) 24(2) *European Public Law* forthcoming, at ssrn.com/abstract=2958297.

due to the exclusionary effects that increased legal barriers and differential treatment may create. Secondly, both *Rüffert* and *RegioPost* are concerned with special minimum wage rules applicable to public contracts (either in a given economic sector, or more generally) but not applicable to the rest of the economy. Upholding the possibility of creating special wage rules *for public contracts only* strengthens the risk of competitive distortion in private markets, mainly through cross-subsidisation or, under certain specific conditions, even predatory pricing. Additionally, the existence of public contracts-specific minimum wage requirements triggers issues of compliance with state aid rules or, at least, of coordination with the general conditions for the granting of state aid for labour promotion purposes. In my view, an overall assessment of these issues leads to the unavoidable conclusion that the Court of Justice has not sorted out all competition and state aid implications of the use of public procurement for the enforcement of labour standards or, more generally, labour policies—which are likely to continue appearing in litigation at the EU level.

II. BRIEF DISCUSSION OF SELECTED ISSUES IN THE *REGIOPOST* JUDGMENT OF PARTICULAR RELEVANCE FOR ITS ECONOMIC ASSESSMENT

RegioPost offers an interesting platform for the analysis of the competition and state aid implications of public procurement case law—specifically, on the use of public procurement for the enforcement of labour standards, but similar considerations would apply in other areas of procurement case law.[17] This particularly derives from the geographical location of the German municipality of Landau, which was the contracting authority concerned in the *RegioPost* litigation. As the concentric lines in the map in Figure 6.1 show, and from the perspective of the EU internal market, Landau is in a geographical location that makes public contracts put out to tender by that municipality particularly susceptible to having cross-border interest for tenderers located in nearby Member States, mainly from France, but also for Belgian, Luxembourg and Dutch tenderers (depending on the geographical dimension of the markets concerned).[18] From the perspective of domestic German markets, contracts put out to tender in Landau will be potentially

[17] For related discussion, see A Sánchez-Graells, 'Competition and State Aid Implications of the *Spezzino* Judgment (C-113/13): The Scope for Inconsistency in Assessing Support for Public Services Voluntary Organisations' (2016) 11(1) *European Procurement & Public Private Partnership Law Review* 31.

[18] For particularly large markets, or for contracts with a strong German language component, it could also attract interest from Swiss, or even Austrian, tenderers.

interesting not only for undertakings based in the *Land* of Rheinland-Pfalz, but also for those based in the neighbouring *Länder* of Saarland, Baden-Württemberg, Hessen, and even from those further away, such as those established in Bayern and Nordrhein-Westfalen, or beyond.

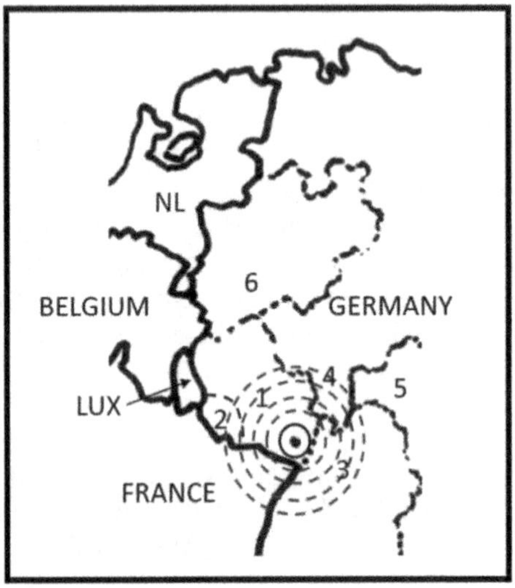

Figure 6.1: Location of Landau and cross-border potential
Source: own elaboration. Key to German *Länder*: (1) Rheinland-Pfalz, (2) Saarland, (3) Baden-Württemberg, (4) Hessen, (5) Bayern, (6) Nordrhein-Westfalen. The location of Landau (in Rheinland-Pfalz) is indicated with a circle.

This situation makes it particularly clear that the rules applicable to the public contracts put out to tender by the municipality of Landau—as the paradigmatic example of a contracting authority putting out to tender contracts of potential cross-border *and* inter-regional interest—can generate effects on the generation of competition for those contracts, as well as on the broader markets affected by the procurement activity of the municipality. This section focuses on the mapping of those effects, and on the consequences of the asymmetry of the rules applicable to the cross-border and inter-regional provision of services to the public sector—which may be particularly relevant for smaller EU Member States, but also for frontier regions.[19]

[19] However, for a puzzling approach to the assessment of the existence of cross-border interest in contracts tendered in this type of geographical circumstances, see the Judgment of 6 October 2016, *Tecnoedi Construzioni*, Case C-318/15, EU:C:2016:747. For discussion, see A Sánchez-Graells, 'Tecnoedi: An Overlooked Distortion of the ECJ's Approach to the Assessment of Cross-Border Interest for Public Contracts? (C-318/15)', 20 March 2017, at howtocrackanut.com/blog/2017/3/20/tecnoedi-an-overlooked-distortion-of-the-ecjs-approach-to-the-assessment-of-cross-border-interest-for-public-contracts-c-31815.

A. Asymmetry between Cross-border and Inter-regional Provision of Services to the Public Sector Leading to Reverse Discrimination of (Domestic) EU Economic Operators

In simplified terms, the rules established in *Bundesdruckerei* and *RegioPost* create an asymmetry between cross-border and inter-regional provision of services to the public sector *solely* on the basis of the Member State in which an economic operator is based. This can be a reasonable criterion for the purposes of preventing social dumping,[20] but such a bright-line distinction between the external and internal borders of a Member State/region within it does not make economic sense where the relevant markets for competition purposes can be geographically defined regardless of those borders (ie where the same market covers several regions in two or more Member States).[21] Thus, in situations where the relevant market spans across regions located in different Member States, the simultaneous application of the *Bundesdruckerei* standard, excluding the possibility of imposing minimum wage requirements on non-domestic bidders, *and* the *RegioPost* standard, allowing for the imposition of minimum wage requirements on domestic tenderers, creates a significant distortion of the undertakings' ability to exploit competitive advantages based on wage differences *solely on the basis of their Member State* of establishment.

In more detail, it is worth recalling that, according to *Bundesdruckerei*, if a service can be provided from a different Member State, it is against EU law to impose minimum wage requirements that apply across the board, that is, regardless of the Member State where performance of the service takes place. As clearly put by the Court of Justice:

> [A] fixed minimum wage corresponding to that required in order to ensure reasonable remuneration for employees in the Member State of the contracting authority in the light of the cost of living in that Member State, but which bears no relation to the cost of living in the Member State in which the services relating to the public contract at issue are performed and for that reason *prevents [economic operators] established in that Member State from deriving a competitive advantage from the differences between the respective rates of pay* ... goes beyond what is necessary to ensure that the objective of employee protection is attained.[22]

[20] See European Commission, *Supporting social responsibility in the economy through public procurement* (2016). For discussion of the competing rationales for EU intervention in domestic labour law and, indirectly, for the justification of restrictions in the creation of a single EU labour market, see P Syrpis, *EU Intervention in Domestic Labour Law* (Oxford, Oxford University Press, 2007) 10–75.

[21] Along the same lines, see A Fletcher and B Lyons, *Geographic Market Definition in European Commission Merger Control*, Study for DG Competition by the Centre for Competition Policy, University of East Anglia (2016) 17–18, at ec.europa.eu/competition/publications/reports/study_gmd.pdf.

[22] *Bundesdruckerei*, above n 13, para 34 (emphasis added).

Conversely, according to *RegioPost*, where the service requires in situ provision, EU public procurement law

> permits the host Member State to lay down, in the context of the award of a public contract, a mandatory rule for minimum protection ... which requires undertakings established in other Member States to comply with an obligation in respect of a minimum rate of pay for the benefit of their workers posted to the territory of the host Member State in order to perform that public contract.[23]

From a technical procurement law perspective, it is worth stressing that *RegioPost* was decided on the basis of Article 26 of the 2004 Public Procurement Directive, but the reasoning is equally applicable to the rules under Article 70 of the 2014 Public Procurement Directive—despite the new drafting of the provision on contract compliance clauses, which introduces two main modifications. First, where Article 26 of the 2004 Public Procurement Directive foresaw that contract compliance clauses had to be 'compatible with [Union] law', Article 70 of the 2014 Public Procurement Directive foresees that they must be 'linked to the subject-matter of the contract within the meaning of Article 67(3)'.[24] However, this cannot be seen as dispensing with the requirement that contract compliance clauses pass a test of legality under EU law. As Advocate General Mengozzi indicated in his *RegioPost* Opinion, Article 26 of the 2004 Public Procurement Directive included a *renvoi* to more general provisions of EU law, which meant that the regional rules imposing compliance with labour standards 'linked to the performance of the public contract, must be compatible with those provisions, including, therefore, with the freedom to provide services guaranteed by the Treaty'.[25] From that perspective, the reference to EU law in Article 26 of the 2004 Public Procurement Directive was dispensable and, consequently, its suppression in the wording of Article 70 of the 2014 Public Procurement Directive cannot in any meaningful way be seen as an impediment to carrying out such an analysis of EU law compatibility—which derives from the principle of supremacy and the system of sources of EU law in any case. Secondly, where Article 26 of the 2004 Public Procurement Directive indicated that '[t]he conditions governing the performance of a contract may, in particular, concern social and environmental considerations', Article 70 of the 2014 Public Procurement Directive now indicates that '[t]hose conditions may include economic, innovation-related, environmental, social or employment-related considerations'. In my view, beyond issues of

[23] *RegioPost*, above n 8, para 66.

[24] Art 67(3) of the 2014 Public Procurement Directive foresees that '[a]ward criteria shall be considered to be linked to the subject-matter of the public contract where they relate to the works, supplies or services to be provided under that contract in any respect and at any stage of their life cycle, including factors involved in: (a) the specific process of production, provision or trading of those works, supplies or services; or (b) a specific process for another stage of their life cycle, even where such factors do not form part of their material substance'.

[25] *RegioPost*, Opinion of AG Mengozzi, above n 10, para 40.

emphasis, the new version of the rule does not alter the legal regime, which is homogeneous across the 2004 and 2014 EU public procurement rules.[26]

Overall, the combined effect of *Bundesdruckerei* and *RegioPost* is that Member States can only impose mandatory minimum wage requirements for the workers posted in their territory for the provision of services under a contract covered by the EU public procurement rules—in compliance with rules adopted respecting the Posted Workers Directive or, more generally, Article 56 TFEU[27] (ie where there is a cross-border interest)—but they cannot do so when the workers need not be based in or posted to that Member State for the provision of the service. From an economic perspective, this is particularly problematic in those cases where alternative modes of provision are possible and the contracting authority has no reason to prefer in situ over remote provision (as was the case in *Bundesdruckerei*). It is also problematic where the choice of one mode of provision over the other is simply predetermining the outcome of the tender, or is otherwise constitutive of an artificial restriction of competition contrary to Article 18(1) of the 2014 Public Procurement Directive.[28] And the same applies in cases of possible hybrid in situ and remote provision (as could have been the case in *RegioPost*). In these cases of alternative or potentially hybrid modes of provision, a further complication derived from the asymmetry between *Bundesdruckerei* and *RegioPost* concerns the assessment of tenders that may seem to be abnormally low due to the potential infringement of the relevant labour standards (ie due to non-compliance with the expected level of minimum/living wage), but which the tenderer can justify on the basis of delocalised alternative or hybrid modes of provision of the services concerned.[29] In these cases, the coordination of the requirements derived from Article 70 with the rules on assessment of apparently abnormally low tenders under Article 69 of the 2014 Public Procurement Directive will be particularly important.

In the specific case of *RegioPost*, it is worth noting that despite the fact that the Court of Justice did not provide much detail in its judgment, the contract put out to tender required in situ provision (of certain parts of the service) within the territory of the contracting authority. In particular, the contract was for the 'collection, carriage and delivery of letters, parcels and packages' in the municipality of Landau.[30] Of course, the contract must also have been for the ancillary activities of sorting and dispatching, which need not necessarily take place in Landau. In that regard, as shown

[26] See Sánchez-Graells, 2nd edn, above n 7.

[27] Treaty on the Functioning of the European Union (TFEU) [2012] OJ C326/47.

[28] For discussion, see A Sánchez-Graells, 'A Deformed Principle of Competition?—The Subjective Drafting of Article 18(1) of Directive 2014/24', in Ølykke and Sánchez-Graells (eds), above n 14, 80.

[29] See Ølykke, above n 14, 146.

[30] *RegioPost*, above n 8, para 19.

in Figure 6.1, it is interesting to stress that Landau is in the German *Länder* of Rheinland-Pfalz, almost at the border with France. Therefore, it would not be inconceivable that a postal operator based in France (eg in Strasbourg) might be interested in the provision of the services, and that it could plan to use its warehouses and sorting facilities in France, so that collection, (partial) carriage and delivery of postal items would take place in Germany (mainly in Landau), but ancillary activities would take place in France. In that case, the combination of the *Bundesdruckerei* and *RegioPost* criteria would be problematic, because the French operator would have to figure out exactly what part of the labour needed to provide the service had to be remunerated at the German minimum wage and what part could be remunerated according to French (assumed) lower wages. Depending on the specifics of the case, the French operator—by having (partial) access to the protection under *Bundesdruckerei*—could derive a competitive advantage from the differences between the respective rates of pay. Conversely, a German operator based in a *Länder* other than Landau's (say, any of the neighbouring *Länder* of Saarland, Baden-Württemberg or Hessen) would not benefit from such protection under EU law,[31] and would thus (in principle) be barred from deriving any benefits from wage differentials across German regions (assuming the minimum wages applicable in those *Länder* were lower than in Rhineland-Palatinate).

In the absence of harmonised rules on minimum wages, the existence of this type of competition based on wage differentials is a crucial element of the internal market—which is recognised in *Bundesdruckerei*. However, given the concentration on the system of allocation of competences underlying the Posted Workers Directive (which precisely aims at reducing the scope for wage competition below the level of domestic minimum wages), *RegioPost* omits this dimension of regulatory competition, and thus creates substantive inconsistency. This situation highlights the existence of an asymmetry between the rules applicable to cross-border and inter-regional provision of services to the public sector, which does not seem to make much economic sense, triggers potential competition distortions (see section III) and which, in any case, triggers issues of *reverse discrimination* of domestic economic operators that do not match a proper conception of a single market.[32]

[31] Potential domestic non-discrimination or equal treatment issues are not taken into consideration for the purposes of this discussion.

[32] The same problem arises in connection with other public procurement rules, such as exclusion requirements; see A Sánchez-Graells, L Butler and P Telles, 'Exclusion and Qualitative Selection of Economic Operators under Public Procurement Procedures. A Comparative View on Selected Jurisdictions' in M Burgi, M Trybus and S Treumer (eds), *Qualification, Exclusion and Selection in EU Procurements*, vol 7 (Copenhagen, DJØF, 2016) 245. For background discussion, see A Tryfonidou, 'Reverse Discrimination in Purely Internal Situations: An Incongruity in a Citizens' Europe' (2008) 35(1) *Legal Issues of Economic Integration* 43. See also D Hanf, 'Reverse Discrimination in EU Law: Constitutional Aberration, Constitutional

B. The Interaction with other 'Smart Procurement' Rules in the 2014 Public Procurement Directive can Result in De Facto Labour-based Domestic Protectionism

Another economic aspect of importance in the analysis of the rules derived from the *Rüffert*, *Bundesdruckerei* and *RegioPost* case law concerns the phases of a public contract to which minimum wage or other labour standards can apply, particularly in view of the growing focus on the analysis of supply chains and the increasing interest of contracting authorities in imposing social requirements beyond the strict scope of the contractual relationship into which they enter with the main contractor.[33] It is worth stressing that these cases have been solely concerned with the execution phase of public contracts. That is, the Court of Justice has ruled on the compatibility with Article 26 of the 2004 Public Procurement Directive of wage requirements applicable to the execution of the specific contract put out to tender by the contracting authority. This is also now clearly within the remit of Article 70 of the 2014 Public Procurement Directive. However, it is worth stressing that other 'smart procurement' rules in that Directive could be used to extend the use of public procurement to impose compliance with (minimum) wage requirements beyond the scope of the specific contract. In particular, this could be problematic in relation to the new rules on life-cycle costing.

It is worth noting that Article 67(3) of the 2014 Public Procurement Directive—which is relevant for the purposes of assessing compatibility of contract compliance clauses with Article 70 of the same Directive (see section II.A)—allows contracting authorities to use award criteria that relate to the works, supplies or services to be provided under that contract in any respect *and at any stage of their life cycle*, including factors involved in (i) the specific process of production, provision or trading of those works, supplies or services, or (ii) the specific process for another stage of their life cycle, even where such factors do not form part of their material substance.[34] Additionally, Article 68 of the 2014 Public Procurement Directive allows contracting authorities to use life-cycle costing as part of their tender assessment methodology, which includes the possibility of imputing the cost of environmental externalities linked to the products, services or works

Necessity, or Judicial Choice' (2011) 18(1) *Maastricht Journal of European and Comparative Law* 29; and P Van Elsuwege, 'The Phenomenon of Reverse Discrimination: An Anomaly in the European Constitutional Order?' in LS Rossi and F Casolari (eds), *The EU after Lisbon. Amending or Coping with the Existing Treaties?* (Berlin, Springer, 2014) 161.

[33] This is also relevant for some aspects of subcontracting policies, but those are not assessed in this chapter. For some discussion, see R Craven, 'Subcontracting Matters: Articles 43 and 71 of the 2014 Directive' in Ølykke and Sánchez-Graells (eds), above n 14, 295.

[34] For discussion of the changes, see S Arrowsmith, *The Law of Public and Utilities Procurement. Regulation in the EU and the UK*, vol 1 (3rd edn, London, Sweet & Maxwell, 2014) 739–47.

during their life cycle, as well as the possibility of taking into account other (direct) costs over the life cycle of the products, services or works, including parts or all of the following costs, regardless of whether they are borne by the contracting authority or other users: (i) costs relating to acquisition; (ii) costs of use, such as consumption of energy and other resources; (iii) maintenance costs; or (iv) end-of-life costs, such as collection and recycling costs. Taken together, these rules could prompt contracting authorities to impose wage requirements not only in the phase of strict execution of the tendered contract, but also in earlier phases (eg imposing the payment of minimum wages down the value chain, including both subcontractors and also suppliers of the main contractor) or after the execution of the contract has ended (eg imposing minimum wages to be paid to workers involved in collection, recycling or disposal, even if that is not undertaken on behalf of the contracting authority but more generally). In these cases, the contours of the subject matter of the contract will likely be litigated again.

Such an expansive approach to the use of (smart) public procurement tools for the enforcement of labour standards would only exacerbate the problems of asymmetry of rules applicable to undertakings based in different Member States. In general terms, and from the perspective of the policy-maker behind the instrumental use of public procurement for labour enforcement, such a strategy could create two sorts of undesirable consequences, which are largely mutually exclusive. First, it could result in the delocalisation of much of the production process to jurisdictions with lower wages, either through subcontracting or through teaming or consortia agreements. And, given the Court of Justice's narrow approach to supporting restrictions on subcontracting,[35] this may be a perverse incentive difficult to counteract. Secondly, and in the opposite direction, in cases where delocalisation is actually not possible, or where the provision of the service requires in situ presence (ie posting of non-domestic workers), an expansive strategy of use of procurement for the enforcement of labour standards beyond the strict execution of the contract would tend to isolate the economy of the region where the (minimum) wage is applicable. Even if this might seem attractive in terms of a de facto strategy of economic protectionism, the contracting authority should be wary of the undesirable medium- and long-term effects of such protectionist policy over its own public procurement expenditure and, more generally, over the competitiveness of the protected industries. Even if those were not relevant (political) considerations, this would trigger significant issues of compliance or compatibility with state aid rules (as discussed in section IV).

[35] See Judgment of 18 March 2004, *Siemens and ARGE Telekom*, Case C-314/01, EU:C:2004:159. See also the Judgment of 27 October 2016, *Hörmann Reisen*, Case C-292/15, EU:C:2016:817.

III. COMPETITION IMPLICATIONS

In section II.A, I stressed the existence of an asymmetry between the rules applicable to the cross-border and inter-regional provision of services to the public sector in terms of the imposition of labour standard-related requirements. While these requirements are not allowed in cross-border provision cases, and assuming their compliance with the requirements of the Posted Workers Directive, they are allowed where the provision of the services requires the posting of workers for in situ provision (either of the whole or of part of the services covered by the contract). This section concentrates on the competition distortions that can result from such asymmetry. The main argument is that the imposition of asymmetrical labour standard (wage) requirements will have negative effects on the access of small and medium enterprises (SMEs) to public procurement, will create internal barriers to inter-regional competition within Member States, and will create the possibility for economic operators engaged in the provision of services for both private and public entities to use the higher wages perceived under public contracts to cross-subsidise activities in the private market, including the possibility of their engagement in predatory practices.

First of all, it seems clear to me that competition will (at the very least, potentially) be distorted in a way that limits SME access to procurement markets.[36] Where the provision of services to the public sector requires the payment of minimum (or living) wages, while the provision of the same services in the private market (of the same jurisdiction, or of another jurisdiction included in the same geographical market) does not, larger undertakings will have a spurious advantage directly derived from their size and their ability to limit the scope of the obligation to pay the specified (higher minimum) wage to the workers directly concerned with the provision of the services to the public sector. Imagine the example of a contract for the provision of cleaning services. An SME with a single team of cleaners will struggle to comply with the wage requirements if that team provides services both to the public sector (eg the city council) and to private sector clients (eg private businesses with offices in the same or the neighbouring building). Even if it were possible under the labour laws of the relevant jurisdiction to set hourly wages linked to the execution of specific contracts (which will not always be the case), this would involve significant red tape for the SME. In that case, it may either decide to specialise in the provision of services to the public sector only (which would be a viable strategy only if this share of the market were sufficient to ensure its financial viability), or it will have to apply the (higher) minimum

[36] This is an important issue to consider, because the revision of the public procurement rules leading to the adoption of 2014 Public Procurement Directive had as one of its core goals enhancing SME access to procurement. For references and a broader discussion, see I Herrera Anchustegui, 'Division into Lots and Demand Aggregation—Extremes Looking for the Correct Balance?' in Ølykke and Sánchez-Graells (eds), above n 14, 125.

wage across the board, thus losing competitiveness (and probably business) in the private part of the market.

If we slightly tweak the example to assess the position of an SME considering entering the public part of the market, it also seems clear that the potential impact of the obligation to pay higher wages not only for the work related to the execution of the public contract, but also across its employment relationships may be a significant deterrent, because it carries a strategic risk associated with a sudden increase in operating costs, which it may not be possible to offset with the financial margin obtainable from the public contract. Conversely, a larger organisation that can have dedicated teams of workers to serve public and private clients independently will be able to avoid this issue.[37] Where the organisation is large enough and well established as a public sector supplier, this may also allow it to compete in ways that represent a cross-subsidy between public and private activities (as discussed below). Generally, the emergence of these asymmetric effects for larger/established undertakings and for smaller undertakings/new entrants carries the risk of entrenching incumbency advantages and reducing competition for public contracts, which ultimately damages the public purse in addition to being a policy skewed against SMEs.[38]

Secondly, and in a related fashion, it also seems clear to me that the existence of the asymmetrical rules will tend to create internal barriers within Member States—and, ultimately, within the EU internal market. The same considerations taken into account above in relation to SMEs apply here, particularly where different regions have different labour standard (wage) requirements applicable to the tendering of public contracts. Small and medium enterprises may be dissuaded by the need to find out the applicable requirements, in addition to the difficulties they may have in complying with those requirements where they have a single workforce involved in the provision of services to contracting authorities in different (minimum wage) jurisdictions. Imagine the case of an IT maintenance company that offers its services to the public sector. It may be based in one region, and thus be familiar with and adjusted to that region's minimum wage requirements. When a contract for the provision of

[37] There is a related issue of discrimination between workers, where the concern would be that workers employed by the same undertaking to perform the exact same tasks could be paid potentially substantially different wages based only on the fact that the ultimate client is public rather than private. Also, one and the same worker may be subjected to pressures to accept different employment conditions for periods where he or she works for public or private clients of the same undertaking. This may even exacerbate the creation of fake self-employment situations in order to circumvent these issues, or exacerbate issues surrounding the use of zero-hour contracts for public work due to its more expensive nature. These may not necessarily be relevant legal issues at EU level or in every Member State, but they seem to be cause for concern more generally. However, these issues exceed the remit of this chapter, and will not be discussed in further detail.

[38] For discussion of incumbency advantages and the benefits of neutralising them, see Sánchez-Graells, 2nd edn, above n 7, 414 ff.

the same services is put out to tender in a different region, it will probably be dissuaded from tendering for it if it has to run the risk of needing to pay higher wages to its employees across the board. This may be the case under relevant labour rules of a given Member State, as the different treatment for posting workers abroad and requiring them to engage in geographical mobility may not allow the undertaking to accommodate two-tier wage levels under single employment contracts, and it may also not be possible to hold more than one contractual relationship between the same employer and employee(s) for these purposes. Overall, then, the same considerations as above apply here, in particular to SMEs. At least from a normative perspective, the fact that the barriers between (public procurement) markets that result from differing (minimum/living) wage requirements may be internal to a single Member State should not drive the analysis and exclude this as a troublesome issue under EU competition law, particularly where the relevant geographic market does not correspond with the geographical boundaries of the different (minimum wage) jurisdictions, because the distortion of competition will trickle down to the 'private' market as well.

Last but not least, it is also foreseeable that the existence of asymmetric wage requirements may allow (large) incumbent public sector suppliers to use their position of strength in the public part of the market to compete aggressively for private business, and in some cases even to benefit from cross-subsidisation of their task force. This may be relevant, for instance, in areas undergoing privatisation, or where innovation may lead to the emergence of potential new suppliers, such as the provision of social and special services under the regime foreseen in Articles 74–77 of the 2014 Public Procurement Directive—which could be particularly problematic in the case of reservation of contracts under Article 77 of that Directive if the beneficiary of the contract reservation then uses the maximum period of exclusivity of three years to engage in the cross-subsidised provision of services in the private sector. The theory would be that, having a secured base of (exclusive or reserved) public contracts ensuring revenue linked to the higher (minimum/living) wage, the incumbent may be in a situation to cross-subsidise between those activities and the services offered to private market users. This could be the case, for example, where the public sector allows for financial margins in proportion to operating costs, which can then provide financial headroom for the undertaking to engage in such cross-subsidy. Similar issues would arise where payments under the public contracts sufficed to cover all indirect costs of public sector suppliers, which would then also be in a position to significantly cross-subsidise the provision of services to the private sector (these would also raise issues under state aid rules, as discussed in section IV). Cross-subsidisation of the provision of services may also be possible where the undertaking is large and organised enough to operate a two-wage tier system within its workforce—for example, creating rota systems where those employees undertaking most of their work for the higher pay of the public sector contracts, also carry out part of the lower-paid private sector (cross-subsidised) contracts. If such a strategy could be sustainably implemented, this would alter competition in the 'non-public market' (which would damage everyone's purse through reduced competition for private contracts, as well as for future public contracts). Some cases could be caught by competition law (and in particular by the prohibition of abuse of dominance based on predation), but this would be highly dependent on market definition and, in any case, riddled with difficulties.

Overall, the main (common) source of potential distortions of competition would derive from the fact that an obligation to pay higher (minimum/living) wages in the execution of public contracts could serve as a publicly-funded barrier to competition for public contracts in that (labour) jurisdiction. Ultimately, incumbent providers would be in a beneficial position, inasmuch as potential entrants, in particular SMEs and/or non-diversified firms, could be deterred due to the increased red tape and strategic risks linked to the cost of their labour. In some circumstances, such incumbent providers could even engage in cross-subsidisation based on the revenue stream obtained from the public contract.

It is worth stressing that these issues are inherent in the fact that different (minimum/living) wage jurisdictions exist within the EU and, thus, to some extent are unavoidable. However, the fact that the *Bundesdruckerei* and *RegioPost* line of case law allows for the asymmetrical application of those requirements to inter-regional competition but not to cross-border competition, and that in any case the analysis undertaken by the Court of Justice is oblivious to the interaction between public sector-only (minimum/living) wage requirements and broader competition for the provision of services to public and private clients, has come to complicate the analysis and to create scope for competitive distortions.[39] In view of these potential competition distortions, where the imposition of labour standards in public contracts does not derive from (regional) law requirements but rather is created by the contracting authority of its own motion—such as in cases of local living-wage requirements—I submit that such a measure, seemingly covered by the umbrella of Article 70 of the 2014 Public Procurement Directive, needs to be subjected to a strict proportionality test to check its compatibility with free movement rules,[40] its link to the subject matter of the contract and its compatibility with Article 18(1) of the 2014 Public Procurement Directive, so that it does not result in an artificial narrowing of competition. In that regard, it is important to stress that, differently

[39] This could have been avoided by the Court of Justice's engaging in a different analysis of the requirements of general application of wage requirements suggested in *Rüffert*. In similar terms, see Costamagna, above n 9, 107–10.

[40] As per *Bundesdruckerei*'s requirements; see *Bundesdruckerei*, above n 13, para 32.

from other *smart* procurement strategies (and most notably environmental goals), labour-orientated public procurement structurally creates barriers to entry into the relevant competition for the public contract (be it a separate market or not), and that it is almost impossible to disentangle its legitimate goals (of prevention of social dumping or exercise of public discretion in terms that signal the behaviour of a *good employer*) from local or regional protectionism—that is, while green procurement can be designed in a way that does not trigger market integration issues, social public procurement is much more difficult, if not impossible, to structure in that way.

Consequently, other than in cases where the labour standards are created by (regional) law—which are saved by the competence split reflected in the Posted Workers Directive—it will be very difficult for contract compliance (wage) clauses to pass the proposed strict proportionality test due to their competition-distortive potential.[41] Where those requirements derive from the enactment of regional (or national) laws, their control can only be left to the general doctrine of *anticompetitive state action*. However, given the extremely limited practical likelihood of the application of the state action doctrine by the European Commission or the Court of Justice in this context, this is not discussed further.[42]

IV. STATE AID IMPLICATIONS

A different, complementary dimension of competition analysis requires an assessment of the use of public procurement for the enforcement of labour standards (and in particular of minimum/living wage requirements) from a state aid perspective—that is, against the general prohibition of state aid in Article 107(1) TFEU. In that regard, it is relevant to note that the 2016 Commission Notice on the notion of State aid[43] has taken the rather maximalist position that where public authorities buy goods or services through tenders that respect EU rules on public procurement, this is in principle sufficient to ensure that the transaction is free of state aid.[44] However, it is also worth stressing that the Notice includes a paragraph that could create difficulties in the assessment of procurement procedures

[41] For further analysis and discussion along these lines, see A Sánchez-Graells, 'Truly Competitive Public Procurement as a Europe 2020 Lever: What Role for the Principle of Competition in Moderating Horizontal Policies?' (2016) 22(2) *European Public Law Journal* 377.

[42] For that discussion, see Sánchez-Graells, 2nd edn, above n 7, 173 ff.

[43] Commission Notice on the notion of State aid as referred to in Article 107(1) of the Treaty on the Functioning of the European Union [2016] OJ C262/1.

[44] European Commission, *State aid: Commission clarifies scope of EU State aid rules to facilitate public investment* (2016), at europa.eu/rapid/press-release_IP-16-1782_en.htm. For discussion, see GS Ølykke, 'Commission Notice on the Notion of State Aid as Referred to in Article 107(1) TFEU—Is the Conduct of a Public Procurement Procedure Sufficient to Eliminate the Risk of Granting State Aid?' (2016) 25(5) *Public Procurement Law Review* 197.

imposing labour (wage) standards—especially if they do not derive from (regional) legislation[45] but are rather created ex novo by the contracting authority on the basis of Article 70 of the 2014 Public Procurement Directive—particularly where they reduce the competitive tension for the contract (see section III), or where they make it difficult to establish that the contracting authority is obtaining a most economically advantageous tender. Indeed, according to paragraph 96 of the Commission Notice on the notion of State aid:

> When public bodies buy assets, goods and services, any specific conditions attached to the tender should be non-discriminatory and *closely and objectively related to the subject matter and to the specific economic objective of the contract.* They should allow for the most economically advantageous offer to match the value of the market. *The criteria therefore should be defined in such a way as to allow for an effectively competitive tendering procedure which leaves the successful bidder with a normal return*, not more. In practice, this implies the use of tenders which put significant weight on the 'price' component of the bid or which are otherwise likely to achieve a competitive outcome (eg certain reverse tenders with sufficiently clear-cut award criteria).[46]

Therefore, the main issue that requires close assessment in that regard is whether the use of the discretion given by Article 70 of the 2014 Public Procurement Directive to contracting authorities in terms of setting their own preferred contract compliance requirements, including requirements to comply with specific labour standards (and, in particular minimum or living wages), is aligned with the requirement that the tender criteria are defined in a way that does not neutralise the relevance given to the price component of the bid (which will be particularly relevant in contracts for the provision of labour-intensive services, such as, for example, security or cleaning services) and/or result in an abnormal (above-market) return for the successful tenderer.[47] In that regard, it is important to consider the ways in which the imposition of (higher) minimum/living wage requirements could result in abnormal returns. This would clearly be the case where the contract included any type of costing method or reimbursement provision based on indirect calculations (of costs, overheads or margins) that took into account the wages payable under the contract, as well as where the contract price

[45] In that case, a further complication would ensue from the fact that the minimum/living wage requirement would derive from a seemingly generally applicable instrument, which could deactivate the prohibition in Art 107(1) TFEU on the basis of its lack of selectivity. On that, see P Nicolaides, 'New Limits to the Concept of Selectivity: The Birth of a "General Exception" to the Prohibition of State Aid in EU Competition Law' (2015) 6(5) *Journal of European Competition Law & Practice* 315.

[46] Commission Notice on the notion of State aid, above n 43, para 96 (emphasis added).

[47] Please note that an assessment of the compatibility of those criteria with the contracting authorities' obligation not to artificially narrow down competition should be carried out under the strict proportionality test mentioned in section III.

was subjected to indexation clauses that increased the minimum/living wage component of the initial contractual cost in a way that did not require the passing on of the additional cost to the workers involved in the execution of the contract (for example, where indexation of public contract prices is independent of indexation for minimum/living wage purposes, and on the assumption that the former is higher than the latter). It would also be the case where the contracting authority does not set up any meaningful process of audit and control of the wage payments made by the tenderer to its workforce throughout the execution of the contract—which would thus allow it to redirect the funds to other uses—or where the minimum wage requirements concerned phases of the life cycle of the contract that the contracting authority has either no way or no intention of verifying.[48]

Where any of these or other issues result in the likely existence of an undue economic advantage for the contractor of the public sector, it will then be necessary to determine whether this state aid can be justified under any of the categories included in the relevant exemption instruments. It will be particularly important to assess compatibility with the different categories of employment-related aid covered by the general block exemption regulation (GBER).[49] In that regard, it is important to note that the GBER only allows some limited types of employment-related aid, including:

(1) aid for the recruitment and employment of disadvantaged workers and workers with disabilities;[50] and
(2) aid orientated towards job creation by SMEs, which must be linked to employment directly created by an investment project, such employment—
  (a) being created within three years of completion of the investment,
  (b) involving a net increase in the number of employees in the establishment concerned, and
  (c) being maintained during a minimum period of three years.[51]

These stringent conditions make it unlikely that, in general circumstances, aid resulting from minimum/living wage conditions in public contracts can be exempted from the prohibition of Article 107(1) TFEU on the basis of the GBER. Additionally, it is important to stress that the GBER does not cover state aid given to maintain jobs, which would be considered operating aid incompatible with Article 107(1) TFEU.

[48] Of course, such lack of intent to verify would in itself create issues in relation to EU public procurement law more generally; see Judgment of 4 December 2003, *EVN and Wienstrom*, Case C-448/01, EU:C:2003:651, para 52.

[49] Commission Regulation (EU) No 651/2014 of 17 June 2014 declaring certain categories of aid compatible with the internal market in application of Articles 107 and 108 of the Treaty [2014] OJ L187/1.

[50] ibid, Art 1(1)(f) and Arts 32 and 33.

[51] ibid, Art 17(5).

Other than exemption under the GBER, any element of state aid derived from minimum/living wage conditions in public contracts could only be exempted as de minimis aid.[52] In that regard, there are two elements to take into consideration. First, that the total amount of aid granted per Member State to a single undertaking shall not exceed €200,000 over any period of three fiscal years.[53] And, secondly, and more importantly, that this applies only to *transparent aid*, ie where it is possible to calculate precisely the gross grant equivalent of the aid ex ante without a risk assessment.[54] Given the complexities in establishing the economic value of the advantage obtainable by any given tenderer as a result of minimum/living wage conditions in public contracts (which would be dependent, at a minimum, on the specific overall contract price offered), and thus the impossibility of determining it in a transparent manner in advance, it would not be possible to consider this type of aid de minimis and thus as exempted from the prohibition of Article 107(1) TFEU.

Overall, from the perspective of the state aid analysis of the compatibility of labour-related contract compliance conditions created by the contracting authority in an exercise of the discretion given by Article 70 of the 2014 Public Procurement Directive, it seems difficult to find ways of exempting aid that results from the creation of an undue economic advantage in relation to compliance with those (higher) minimum/living wage requirements—for example due to indirect mechanisms of calculation of overhead costs or margins, or from price indexation clauses. Thus, contracting authorities seeking to engage in this type of employment-orientated smart public procurement will need to design their contracts, reporting obligations and audit mechanisms in such a way as to ensure that any economic advantage derived from the payment of a higher contractual cost aimed to cover labour costs linked to minimum/living wage requirements is *actually passed through, in full*, to the workers involved in the execution of the contract. Only in those circumstances will they be able to exclude the risk of infringement of the general state aid prohibition in Article 107(1) TFEU.

V. CONCLUSIONS

This chapter has adopted an economic perspective and aimed to assess the main implications of the *Bundesdruckerei–RegioPost* case law on the enforcement of labour law (wage) standards in public procurement. A close assessment of the implications of this body of case law has resulted in the

[52] Commission Regulation (EU) No 1407/2013 of 18 December 2013 on the application of Articles 107 and 108 of the Treaty on the Functioning of the European Union to *de minimis* aid [2013] OJ L352/1.

[53] ibid, Art 3(2).

[54] ibid, Art 4(1).

identification of asymmetries between the rules applicable to the cross-border and the inter-regional provision of services to the public sector, which lead to potential reverse discrimination of (domestic) EU economic operators and to the (regional) fragmentation of markets that economically encompass several (labour) jurisdictions. It has also uncovered risks that the interaction between the contract compliance rules of Article 70 and other 'smart procurement' rules in the 2014 Public Procurement Directive (most notably, those on life-cycle costing) can result in de facto labour requirements-based domestic protectionism. Based on this assessment, the remainder of the chapter has focused on the competition and state aid implications of this body of case law.

The discussion from the competition perspective has concentrated on both the creation of labour (wage) requirements by means of regional laws, as was the case in *RegioPost*, and on instances of independent exercise of administrative discretion under Article 70 of the 2014 Public Procurement Directive to enforce labour standards. Given the clearly anticompetitive risks that derive from the *Bundesdruckerei–RegioPost* approach to the establishment of labour (wage) requirements for public contracts only (either by law, or administrative practice), I have submitted that this should be controlled under a strict proportionality test ultimately justified by the prohibition on contracting authorities' artificial narrowing down of competition for public contracts derived from Article 18(1) of the 2014 Public Procurement Directive. Further, I have expressed that, other than in cases where the labour standards are created by (regional) law—where they are saved by the Posted Workers Directive as interpreted by the Court of Justice in *RegioPost*—it will be very difficult for contract compliance (wage) clauses to pass the proposed strict proportionality test due to its competition-distortive potential. This has also led me to acknowledge the more limited possibilities of subjecting law-based use of public procurement to enforce labour standards to a competition analysis, due to the current limited scope for application of competition law to 'publicly-generated' competition restrictions (ie the anticompetitive state action doctrine).

The discussion from the state aid perspective proved similarly limited in terms of subjection of regional (or national) laws establishing minimum/living wage requirements for public contracts to state aid analysis, not least due to the (likely) lack of selectivity of any such schemes. However, in relation to the use of procurement to further labour law standards without legal back-up—that is, solely on the basis of the exercise of administrative discretion created by Article 70 of the 2014 Public Procurement Directive—I have submitted that there exists the risk of infringement of the general prohibition of state aid in Article 107(1) TFEU in a way that cannot be exempted by either the GBER or as *de minimis* aid. Such risk can only be avoided if contracting authorities seeking to engage in this type of employment-orientated smart public procurement design their contracts, reporting obligations and audit mechanisms in a way that ensures that any economic advantage derived from the payment of a higher contractual price aimed to cover labour costs linked to minimum/living wage requirements is *actually passed through*, *in full*, to the workers involved in the execution of the contract. In my opinion, only in those circumstances will they be able to exclude the risk of infringement of Article 107(1) TFEU.

Overall, then, this chapter has aimed to stress that the line of case law resulting from *Rüffert*, *Bundesdruckerei* and *RegioPost* creates an undesirable situation, because it can result in serious distortions of competition for public contracts, as well as provide opportunities for de facto protectionist policies and administrative practices in ways that competition and state aid law are not necessarily well suited to address—or at least not under current enforcement strategies and settled jurisprudential positions. Consequently, it will be necessary for policy-makers and contracting authorities to understand this potential for competitive distortion and to refrain from using public procurement to enforce labour (wage) standards, except in those limited circumstances where they can be assured that their net effects and costs on the public purse—notably in terms of reduced competition for present and/or future contracts—are exceeded by the benefits derived from those labour rules. This is very unlikely to be the case and, as a consequence, contracting authorities and policy makers would be well advised to abandon their efforts to set partial, incomplete and difficult-to-monitor minimum/living wage requirements for public contracts solely on the strength of the opportunity derived from the expenditure of public funds.

7

Public Procurement and Business for Value: Looking for Alignment in Law and Practice

NINA BOEGER*

I. INTRODUCTION

THE STATE TRADITIONALLY procures from either market actors or charitable providers. If it buys from the market, the tendering process is subject to national and European public procurement law, but if it buys exclusively from charities, some exemptions apply—either as a result of special sectoral regimes,[1] or in order to preserve the constitutional role given to these entities in some jurisdictions.[2] But distinctions have become more complex as new forms of non-charitable enterprise emerge that combine a social mission with an entrepreneurial vision. These organisations are entrepreneurial in the same way as traditional businesses, but also committed to accounting for their impacts (positive and negative) on their stakeholders, internal and external, which set them up to generate societal value rather than exclusively shareholder value. These commitments are embedded in the business, in binding procedural/structural mechanisms that

* Thanks to Albert Sánchez-Graells and the participants in the Workshop 'Public Procurement and Labour Standards—Reopening the Debate after RegioPost' at the University of Bristol Law School on 9 May 2016. Further thanks to Joseph Corkin for extensive discussion over earlier versions of this contribution. Any remaining errors are mine.

[1] See Arts 74–77 (in particular Art 77) of the 2014 Public Procurement Package (Directive 2014/24/EU of the European Parliament and of the Council of 26 February 2014 on public procurement and repealing Directive 2004/18/EC (the 2014 Public Procurement Directive), together with Directive 2014/23/EU of the European Parliament and of the Council of 26 February 2014 on the award of concession contracts [2014] OJ L94/1, and Directive 2014/25/EU of the European Parliament and of the Council of 26 February 2014 on procurement by entities operating in the water, energy, transport and postal services sectors and repealing Directive 2004/17/EC [2014] OJ L94/243).

[2] Judgment of 11 December 2014, *Azienda sanitaria locale n 5 'Spezzino' and Others*, Case C-113/13, EU:C:2014:2440. For critical discussion, see the various contributions to the monographic edition of (2016) 11(1) *European Procurement & Public Private Partnership Law Review*.

are stronger than mere undertakings by management to ensure corporate social responsibility (CSR).

This chapter considers the benefits for the state in procuring from these value-led enterprises, compared to procuring from traditional shareholder corporations. Contracting with them enables the state to establish longer-term relationships for the provision of public goods and services by entrepreneurial actors that will fill gaps in underspecified procurement contracts in line with their commitments to societal value, rather than exploiting them exclusively to generate shareholder value.[3] Consequently, public contracts can be left more open, and their performance demands can be less carefully managed and policed because the state is able to rely on the value-led enterprise's procedural/structural commitments. In terms of the economy more widely, these relationships with value-led enterprises allow the state to nurture a particular form of capitalism and of enterprise that is more sustainable, as it requires less external control than the shareholder corporation because of the internally embedded procedural commitments of the value-led enterprise. Given this is not the dominant form of capitalism now, many value-led enterprises struggle to get a foothold in markets (including public service markets) that are dominated by the shareholder corporation. This chapter considers how the state can resort to public procurement as a way of nurturing these alternative enterprise forms, and in doing so, transform the current, dominant form of capitalism.

Section II of this chapter defines the field of value-led enterprises, distinguishing them from traditional shareholder corporations, both those with and those without voluntary CSR policies. The fundamental distinction, even from shareholder corporations with extensive CSR policies, is that the accountability for their impacts on all internal and external stakeholders (a claim made in many CSR policies) is effected through binding procedural/structural commitments embedded in the value-led enterprises' business model. Section III studies how procuring from them addresses complexity and risk factors at the stage of putting the public contract out to tender and, subsequently, in simplifying the policing and management of its delivery. By contracting with value-led enterprises, the state takes advantage of their entrepreneurialism, yet can at the same time establish longer-term relationships than with shareholder corporations because it can be more confident that their objectives align with its own. These relationships nurture value-led enterprises, which might otherwise struggle to enter markets dominated by shareholder corporations, so that the state creates a win-win situation. Sections IV and V address the question of how public procurement law, and especially EU public procurement law, hinders or enables the emergence of

[3] See also GL Sturgess, *Just Another Paperclip? Rethinking the Market for Complex Public Services—A Report to the Business Services Association* (2017), at bsa-org.com/wp-content/uploads/2017/04/Just-Another-Paperclip-FINAL.pdf.

these relationships, considering in particular whether the law recognises the advantages for the state in these procurement relationships and so facilitates their establishment.

II. BUSINESS FOR VALUE

Traditional shareholder corporations are run to optimise shareholder value. Even in regimes like that in the UK, where managers are not strictly obliged in law to prioritise the interest of shareholders alone in their running of the company,[4] the practice and the ideology of shareholder primacy are widespread.[5] In recent decades, however, these corporations have taken on board the idea that they must improve their governance structures, because serious corporate governance failings have damaged shareholder value and increased economic risk, with widely publicised corporate scandals diminishing public trust in the shareholder-value model.[6]

Putting in place a CSR policy is for many shareholder corporations a direct response to these developments. Voluntary CSR codes enshrine socially and environmentally responsible corporate policies, such as those that relate to renewable energy, emissions or fair trade. Companies with strong CSR policies would often argue they are committed to a wider social purpose than other businesses. However, many commentators contend that these voluntary commitments do not fundamentally change the character of the corporation[7] but are usually linked to a business case for marketing the company as a responsible corporate citizen,[8] which can then be leveraged

[4] The principle of 'enlightened shareholder value' enshrined in s 172 of the UK Companies Act 2006. For discussion, see G Tsagas, 'Section 172 of the Companies Act 2006: Desperate times call for soft law measures' in N Boeger and C Villiers (eds), *Shaping the Corporate Landscape: Towards Corporate Reform and Enterprise Diversity* (Oxford, Hart Publishing, forthcoming).

[5] See Sjåfjell's distinction between shareholder primacy as a social norm and shareholder value as a legal obligation in B Sjåfjell, 'Dismantling the Legal Myth of Shareholder Primacy: The Corporation as a sustainable market actor' in Boeger and Villiers (eds), above n 4.

[6] There are plenty of recent examples, from Enron's accountancy fraud to BP's Deepwater Horizon environmental disaster; widespread tax avoidance including household names Amazon and Starbucks; Railtrack's, the UK train network operator, inadequate health and safety record that led to fatal rail accidents; SportsDirect's poor treatment of its warehouse employees; the deleterious effects of CEO Philip Green's asset stripping of the UK clothing retailer BHS; systematic attempts by 'gig economy' corporations Uber and Deliveroo to side-step employment laws; and so on.

[7] SB Banerjee, 'Corporate Social Responsibility: The Good, the Bad and the Ugly' (2008) 34(1) *Critical Sociology* 51; M Blowfield, 'Corporate Social Responsibility—The Failing Discipline and Why It Matters' (2005) 19(2) *International Relations* 173; N Boeger, R Murray and C Villiers (eds), *Perspectives on Corporate Social Responsibility* (Cheltenham, Edward Elgar, 2008).

[8] J Corkin, 'Misappropriating Citizenship: The Limits of Corporate Social Responsibility' in N Boeger, R Murray and C Villiers (eds), *Perspectives on Corporate Social Responsibility* (Cheltenham, Edward Elgar, 2008).

to generate more profit by selling a business image (eg 'greenwashing' its activities) or for avoiding risks that might potentially destroy shareholder value.[9] More fundamentally, therefore, CSR has been criticised as a 'specific development of neo-liberal ideology that is more of a step backwards from progressive socio-political change rather than a way forward'.[10]

Other businesses have gone further and set themselves up as value-led enterprises (hereafter 'business for value' or 'BfV') that are *categorically* different from shareholder corporations, even those with comprehensive CSR policies, in that their commitments to generating value beyond that to shareholders (return on shareholder investment) are not just fixed in voluntary codes. These commitments are procedurally/structurally embedded into the businesses' constitutions.

For traditional shareholder corporations with CSR policies, shareholders' return on investment, long- or short-term, remains the measure against which the business is assessed, even when socially responsible policies are incorporated into the business's strategy. Shareholder corporations prioritise one type of value (financial value) for the benefit of one particular stakeholder group (the shareholders), even at the expense of wider stakeholders' interests. Business for value enterprises, on the other hand, extend the commitment to generating value to a group of stakeholders wider than purely their shareholders, which is measured not as (short- or long-term) return on investment, but rather as taking full account of the impact of the business, positively and negatively, on its stakeholders. Some are internal to the business (management and employees) and some external, both those directly affected (consumers, suppliers, local communities) and those indirectly implicated (citizens in the welfare state, taxpayers, the environment). Good performance generates value by maximising the positive impact on internal and external stakeholders while limiting negative impacts, with trade-offs to be carefully balanced against each other.

Some activities may impact negatively on certain internal stakeholders (eg cuts to wages or employment conditions imposed on employees). Others impact positively on internal stakeholders, though not necessarily the same group (eg the distribution of profit shares or bonuses to management and/or all or some employees). Some impact positively on certain external stakeholders, for example where the enterprise produces better or cheaper goods and services for the immediate beneficiaries of the business (connected to the business's social mission); while others produce negative impacts on external stakeholders (eg communities, taxpayers, the environment). A BfV enterprise balances the interests of different internal and external stakeholders in

[9] See the examples of corporate scandals, above n 6—where corporate irresponsibility either significantly diminished or entirely wiped out the corporation's shareholder value.

[10] P Fleming and MT Jones, *The End of Corporate Social Responsibility: Crisis and Critique* (London, SAGE, 2013) xii.

these situations by weighing impacts against one another internally (eg how to effect cost savings by cutting salaries or working conditions for workers and/or remuneration packages or bonuses for management, or indeed how each ought to share in the success of the business); external versus internal impacts (the same pay cut may allow the business to reduce prices, benefitting consumers); or one external stakeholder group versus another (eg these consumer benefits may in turn have to be traded off against local communities that are adversely affected by a resulting growth in unemployment).

Procedural measures are built into the business, its governance rules and its constituting document, to ensure that it accounts for the impact of its activities on these stakeholders, internal and external, as well as assessing trade-offs between them. By embedding this commitment procedurally/structurally into its organisation, the BfV enterprise makes it truly binding—more than just a voluntary managerial undertaking—through concrete adjustments to its constitutional documents that can give rise to formal (legal) accountability. For example, constitutional object clauses integrate stakeholder interests and/or commit the business to re-invest surplus for the benefit of its stakeholders; membership (and ownership) of the business includes its stakeholders, not just shareholders; voting rights are democratically allocated rather than based on size of (financial) shareholdings; board membership is adjusted to reflect its stakeholders (including, for example, employees or consumers); and additional reporting commitments may be legally required.

In comparison, CSR policies also refer to responsibilities to wider stakeholders whom they promise to take into account, but the commitment is substantive—a management undertaking—without the formal procedural embedding that ensures compliance. The only accountability for CSR is through the market, and hence the business case is central for CSR policies to succeed. Socially responsible management must increase profits or avoid structural risks that might damage shareholder value in the longer term. Even where stakeholders are consulted on certain issues, decision making rests with a management whose primary commitment is to deliver shareholder value. Business for value enterprises, on the other hand, include binding procedural mechanisms that commit them to consider the impacts on their stakeholders, and by doing so to generate wider societal value, so that value is not fixed ab initio but co-determined by those affected, positively or negatively, by the business.

There is no single BfV format, but rather a continuum of different governance options and constitutional forms. They include cooperatives and mutual business models, businesses that trade as partnerships and associations, social enterprises and community businesses, trading charitable enterprises and some traditional limited companies. Some operate locally, others nationally or internationally. Some are longstanding businesses and others new start-ups. Some accept more commercial restrictions than others.

In the UK, for example, social enterprises have come to be defined as businesses that earn most of their income through trading, but which also enshrine a social (or environmental) purpose and principally reinvest their profits for that mission.[11] Legal formats such as the community interest company[12] or the community benefit society[13] are available to impose an asset lock on the business, a constitutional device that prevents the distribution of residual assets to members and ensures that the public benefit or community benefit of any retained surplus or residual value cannot be appropriated for the private benefit of members.[14] In addition, those community interest companies that are set up as companies limited by shares are subject to a regulated dividend cap, which is calculated as an aggregate limit on the total dividend declared and on the business's ability to carry forward unused dividend capacity. The purpose of this is to ensure that a balance is achieved between attracting investment, on the one hand, and making sure that profits are principally invested for the community benefit on the other.[15]

The idea of social enterprise has made regular appearances in UK policy over the past two decades, but recently the Government has focused on the wider idea of 'mission-led' businesses.[16] It defines these as fully profit-distributing enterprises that identify an intention to have a positive social impact as a central purpose of their business, that make a long-term commitment to deliver on that intention and that report on their social impact to their stakeholders.[17] Rather than an asset lock and dividend cap, the procedural mechanism to protect the BfV character of these enterprises is more flexibly defined. One way of doing so, without going as far as locking in assets or

[11] D Gregory, 'The Politics, Policy, Popular Perception and Practice of Social Enterprise in the 21st Century' in Boeger and Villiers (eds), above n 4.

[12] Companies (Audit, Investigations and Community Enterprise) Act 2004 and Community Interest Company Regulations 2005 (SI 2005/1788), as amended by the Community Interest Company (Amendment) Regulations 2009 (SI 2009/1942) and Community Interest Companies (Amendment) Regulations 2014 (SI 2014/2483).

[13] Co-operative and Community Benefit Societies Act 2014.

[14] Office of the Regulator of Community Interest Companies, *Community Interest Companies: Guidance Chapters*, last updated April 2017, at gov.uk/government/publications/community-interest-companies-how-to-form-a-cic.

[15] S Lloyd, 'Transcript: Creating the CIC' (2010) 35(1) *Vermont Law Review* 31; N Boeger, S Burgess and J Ellison, 'Lessons from the Community Interest Company' in Boeger and Villiers (eds), above n 4.

[16] UK Government, *Mission-led Business Review. Call for Evidence*, May 2016, at gov.uk/government/uploads/system/uploads/attachment_data/file/521927/Mission-Led_Business_Review-Call_for_Evidence.PDF; Advisory Panel's Independent Report on the Review, *On a Mission in the UK Economy*, February 2017, at gov.uk/government/uploads/system/uploads/attachment_data/file/574694/Advisory_Panel_Report_-_Mission-led_Business.pdf.

[17] *Call for Evidence*, above n 16, 2. For discussion see, eg, *Mission-led Business Review: Response from Locality*, at locality.org.uk/wp-content/uploads/Mission-led-businesses-Locality-response.pdf; *Social Enterprise UK—Response to Mission-Led Business Review: Call for Evidence*, at socialenterprise.org.uk/Handlers/Download.ashx?IDMF=4809c576-7264-4545-8e58-7deae1ff67a6. See also D Hunter and N Boeger, 'What is the Point of Business?', 5 December 2016, at legalresearch.blogs.bris.ac.uk/2016/12/what-is-the-point-of-business/.

restricting dividend distribution, is to become a certified B Corporation or 'B Corp'. The B Corp label is not a legal format but a voluntary social certification available to businesses upon application (and payment of a fee) to B Lab, an independent not-for-profit organisation set up for this purpose. B Lab operates internationally, and the B Corp certification is now available in several countries worldwide, including the UK. The idea is that B Corp certification offers an independent assurance that a firm has procedural governance structures in place that commit it not just to its shareholders but to its wider stakeholders and the environment. To obtain the certification, it must have its governance and overall impact on internal and external stakeholders (including workers, communities, environment) assessed by an independent committee of industry experts at least every two years; it must identify in its constitutional document its objective to benefit shareholders *and* to have a positive impact on society and the environment;[18] and it must sign a declaration that sets out the firm's commitment to its stakeholders and the environment.[19]

Social enterprise and mission-led business (such as businesses with a B Corp certification) are not the only structural options for BfV enterprises in the UK. As Ridley-Duff explains, there are other forms of 'solidarity enterprises' that integrate private, mutual and public interests by drawing on the democratic traditions of the cooperative movement[20] but updating them to advance a more open form of cooperativism.[21] Vieta describes the 'new cooperativism' whereby businesses are run by workers and communities. They include a wealth-distribution mechanism to achieve sustainable development goals, with more horizontal labour relations, more egalitarian distribution of surplus, a stronger community orientation and (as with traditional social enterprises) social and/or environmental objectives.[22] As Ridley-Duff points out, whereas 'old cooperativism' confined discussion of a common bond (solidarity) to the social characteristics of a single stakeholder group (workers, consumers, producers, etc), new cooperativism assumes that, provided appropriate institutional arrangements are in place, solidarity can be

[18] In the UK, this requires the adoption of a wording in the constituting document that repeats s 172(1) of the Companies Act 2006, but with some 'small but significant' alterations to satisfy this legal test, according to D Hunter, 'The Arrival of B Corps in Britain: another milestone towards a more nuanced economy?' in Boeger and Villiers (eds), above n 4.

[19] The B Corp Declaration, available at www.bcorporation.net/what-are-b-corps/the-b-corp-declaration.

[20] E Mayo, *The Co-operative Advantage: Innovation, co-operation and why sharing business ownership is good for Britain* (Manchester, Cooperatives UK, 2016).

[21] R Ridley-Duff, 'The Internationalisation of the FairShares Model: where agency meets structure in US and UK company law' in Boeger and Villiers (eds), above n 4; J Laville, 'The Social and Solidarity Economy: A Theoretical and Plural Framework' in J Defourny, L Hulgard and V Pestoff (eds), *Social Enterprise and the Third Sector* (Abingdon, Routledge, 2014).

[22] M Vieta, 'The New Cooperativism' (Editorial) (2010) 4(1) *Affinities: A Journal of Radical Theory, Culture, and Action* 1.

forged between all these stakeholders.[23] Ridley-Duff himself has developed a 'FairShares Model', a constitutional blueprint that a business may adopt, adjusting it to its individual needs, when it sets up as a solidarity enterprise that enfranchises multiple stakeholders. The model may be adjusted to the business's individual needs, regardless of the legal format it chooses to adopt (a limited company, association or society).[24]

Thus, in the UK alone there are different formats for BfV enterprises, and a diversity of governance structures and constitutional models exists. But the commitment to generating value for more than just shareholders, and the concrete procedural/structural guarantees that enshrine this commitment, are what unite all these forms, and what make these businesses categorically different from the traditional shareholder corporation, including those with voluntary CSR policies, which are still ultimately only committed to maximising shareholder value. The business is socialised through that procedural/structural embedding that commits it to deliver wider, societal value, replacing financial value as the exclusive measure of its success.

III. PROCURING FROM BUSINESS FOR VALUE

Many public contracts, especially for larger and more complex public service projects, are incomplete.[25] With limited resources and information, the state cannot predict all the eventualities that may affect contractual performance, and attempting to cover these eventualities in full is complex and costly, especially as some are difficult to quantify or verify. Gaps and ambiguities in these contracts are often not only inevitable, but also beneficial, because the delivery can then be adapted to unforeseen eventualities, and mechanisms for ongoing learning and experimentation built into the contract where services are too complex to pre-specify them fully and too difficult to tie them down contractually in advance. In these circumstances, an important question for the state (in terms of the cost, effectiveness and value-for-money of the contract in question) is to what extent it can rely on providers to fill any gaps and ambiguities in the contract in a way it would have done had it been able to anticipate and/or pre-specify these at the time of entering into the contract.

Shareholder corporations, with or without a CSR policy, respond to contractual uncertainty by exploiting it to maximise their shareholders' return on investment (following the principle of shareholder primacy set out in

[23] Ridley-Duff, above n 21; M Lund, *Solidarity as Business Model: A Multi-Stakeholder Co-operative's Manual* (Kent, OH, Kent State University, 2012).

[24] R Ridley-Duff, *The Case for FairShares: A New Model for Social Enterprise Development and the Strengthening of the Social and Solidarity Economy* (Charleston, CreateSpace, 2015).

[25] OD Hart, *Firms, Contracts and Financial Structure* (Oxford, Clarendon, 1995); OD Hart and J Moore, 'Contracts as Reference Points' (2008) 123 *Quarterly Journal of Economics* 1; Sturgess, above n 3.

section II). Company directors ensure that the corporation complies with regulatory or contractual constraints to the extent that they consider it in the best interest of shareholders not to incur fines, or, in the longer term, not to sully the corporation's reputation when this might impact on its ability to secure future tenders. But to the extent that it serves the interests of their shareholders, they will fill in gaps and ambiguities that arise in the performance of the contract in the interests of their shareholders, even where doing so has negative impacts for public service users, taxpayers, employees, sub-contractors, etc. Public tendering and contract management becomes a zero-sum game between the state and the shareholder corporation, and the further the corporation pulls one way, seeking to exploit uncertainties and ambiguities for shareholder gain, the more the state has to pull back. This forces the state to draft contracts more specifically (with greater complexity); tightening performance measurement and contract monitoring and, if necessary, complaints procedures; or, in extreme cases, setting out punitive measures that include the possibility of excluding providers from future tenders. Transaction costs mount and efficiencies are forgone that might otherwise have been secured with a more flexible contract that allowed for learning in its delivery. Resolving contractual ambiguities or unexpected risks by way of (re)negotiation or, if necessary, judicial interpretation is also costly and time-consuming.

These are resource-intensive measures for the state, requiring skilled personnel and capacity for which, according to the UK National Audit Office (NAO) and others, the state struggles to compete with market actors. Evidence collated by the NAO, for example, documents widespread weaknesses in contract management across all UK government departments as a 'long-standing issue'. The NAO's latest major report into the issue, conducted in 2014 following a string of serious overbilling scandals that involved large corporate contractors, points out that fraud and error, including cases where the provider in question chose to prioritise private profit at the expense of quality and/or integrity, are key consequences of public management weaknesses in circumstances of contractual complexity and uncertainty.[26] Compounding these findings, according to the NAO, is the fact that government departments at all levels currently lack management capacity to effectively address these issues, exposing them to risks, especially vis-à-vis corporate providers with access to considerable resource and expertise to help maximise their own benefit in performing public contracts. Government, the NAO attests, is currently unable to afford 'either to bring in or retain commercial experts to match the combined expertise

[26] National Audit Office, *Transforming Government's Contract Management*, Executive Summary (2014), at nao.org.uk/wp-content/uploads/2014/09/Cabinet-office-cross-government-transforming-governments-contract-management-summary.pdf.

of its contractors'.[27] Meanwhile, according to the House of Commons Public Accounts Committee, certain public services in the UK 'are now dominated by a small number of contractors, and the government is exposed to huge delivery and financial risks should one of these suppliers fail'.[28] The state depends on a handful of shareholder corporations, some of which may be 'too big to fail' and, according to the NAO, 'difficult to live with or without'. But the NAO is concerned that 'the general level of transparency over contractors' cost and profits is limited. The government needs a better understanding of what is a fair return for good performance for it to maintain the appropriate balance between risk and reward.'[29]

Contracts with BfV enterprises offer the state an opportunity to reduce the impact of these constraints because they are not performed to maximise shareholder value alone but respond to uncertainties and ambiguities in any public contract they are committed to delivering, according to their procedural/structural commitment to consider the impacts on their stakeholders. By procuring from BfV, the state can take advantage of their entrepreneurialism and efficiencies as market actors, yet at the same time establish longer-term relationships than with traditional shareholder corporations, because it can be more confident that the objectives of these providers align with its own.[30]

For the state, contracting with BfV enterprises therefore constitutes an alternative model to either full privatisation (where the provider operates for private profit) or reliance on charitable providers (run not for profit and not for trade) in the delivery of public contracts; the advantage of this model being that the state may tap into the entrepreneurship of BfV enterprises as well as their ability to deliver social values by accounting to internal and external stakeholders. Most importantly, where gaps and ambiguities exist in these public contracts, the state can rely on BfV contractors (though not shareholder corporations) to fill them in a way it would have done had it

[27] ibid, 10.

[28] House of Commons Committee of Public Accounts, *Contracting Out Public Services to the Private Sector*, 47th Report of Session 2013–14 (2014), at publications.parliament.uk/pa/cm201314/cmselect/cmpubacc/777/777.pdf?utm_source=rss&utm_medium=rss&utm_campaign=contracting-out-public-services-to-the-private.

[29] National Audit Office, *The Role of Major Contractors in the Delivery of Public Services* (2013) at nao.org.uk/wp-content/uploads/2013/11/10296-001-BOOK-ES.pdf. See also Social Enterprise UK, *The Shadow State: A Report About Outsourcing of Public Services* (2012) 12, at socialenterprise.org.uk/the-shadow-state-a-report-about-outsourcing-of-public-services: 'Even though contracts are a matter of public record, it is usually impossible to find out key details like how much profit is built into each one.'

[30] See K Hall, R Miller and R Millar, 'Public, Private or Neither? Analysing the Publicness of Health Care Social Enterprises' (2016) 18(4) *Public Management Review* 539; L Frith, 'Social Enterprises, Health-Care Provision and Ethical Capital' (2014) 10(2) *Social Enterprise Journal* 105; R Millar, K Hall and R Miller, *Increasing the Role of Social Business Models in Health and Social Care: An Evidence Review*, Public Policy Institute for Wales (2016), at ppiw.org.uk/files/2016/06/Social-Business-Models-in-health-and-social-care.pdf.

anticipated the gap or ambiguity at the time it drafted the contract, relying on the procedural mechanisms that commit the BfV to considering its impacts (value generation) on its wider stakeholders, not just its shareholders. This offers the state the opportunity to simplify public contracts and formulate them in a more open-ended way, incorporating mechanisms for ongoing learning and experimentation on details that are difficult to pre-specify, and to save on its policing and management of the contract's delivery. The state can save on (though not eliminate) risks and reduce the capacity for contracts to go wrong, because it can be more confident that the gaps will be filled in a way that aligns with what it was aiming to achieve in contracting out.

The traditional procurement contract involves a fixing of goods or services to be delivered at a moment in time. Using BfV that incorporates a procedural mechanism which allows for ongoing input from stakeholders right through to the point of delivery of whatever was procured for, sets up a long-term relationship between the BfV enterprise, the state and its stakeholders (widely conceived). It is a radical step away from a traditional privatisation, because the delivery of public contracts by BfV enterprises allows for ongoing collective self-determination in the delivery of public services, via the procedural/structural mechanisms embedded in their business that ensure stakeholders have a say in how the contract is delivered, right through to the point of delivery.[31] The state proceduralises the delivery and evolution of the public contract. It details outcomes (the changes the state wishes to see in the relevant community), but leaves flexibility on issues such as the concrete activities, instruments and stages of delivery, relying on the BfV's procedural guarantees to ensure that performance meets the specified outcomes. These gaps and ambiguities are accepted on the basis that through experimentation and adaptation, the BfV provider can respond to contractual risks and uncertainty (wicked problems or 'unknown unknowns'), taking account of the interests of its stakeholders. Measures in corporate law and corporate governance to enforce the procedural mechanisms internal to the BfV enterprise, are co-opted into the public service model as an additional enforcement safeguard.

Politically, in this model, there is no full transfer from the public to the private realm. Rather, control is transferred from the public realm (the state subject to democratic control) to the societal realm, because the ongoing delivery of the contract is shaped by the society in which the BfV is embedded (via the procedural/structural mechanisms built into the BfV enterprise that ensure it considers the impacts of its business on its stakeholders) and not exclusively by the private interests of its shareholders, with the state 'harnessing the assets and resources of users and communities to achieve

[31] See also UK Government, *Open Public Services White Paper* (2011) at gov.uk/government/publications/open-public-services-white-paper.

better outcomes and lower cost'.[32] In a traditional procurement situation, the state cedes control over contract delivery to market actors (or charitable providers) and seeks to specify goods and services sufficiently tightly to ensure that the contractor delivers what the state needs. In this model, on the other hand, the contract can be deliberately underspecified to allow for some ongoing adaptation, experimentation and learning, and control is ceded not over delivery itself (in the hope that the contract covers all eventualities) but instead to society via the procedural mechanisms that align the delivery of what is being procured for with the interests of all the stakeholders in that delivery, right through to the point of delivery. The model is more accurately a socialisation than a privatisation of a public service, that nevertheless harnesses the entrepreneurialism and market-orientation of the BfV, including its access to capital (although often through social investment rather than capital markets). But it differs also from the charitable provision of public services because, unlike charities, BfV providers are subject to market discipline. Indeed, the state's decision to procure from BfV enterprises provides incentives for charitable providers to become more entrepreneurial and to establish BfV enterprises as trading charities.[33] Doing so also enables charitable organisations to attract the professional talent of those who would otherwise reject working for the voluntary sector.

There is win-win in enabling the state to procure from BfV enterprises while showing these enterprises how they can access more public contracts. Initially at least, BfV relies on the largesse of the state (payment for public service delivery) as a form of incubation, so that by delivering public contracts, BfV forms grow capacity to enable them to deliver private contracts and to participate in and shape the wider economy. By providing this nurturing, a public procurement model that relies on long-term relationships with BfV enterprises therefore not only socialises public service delivery, but also, in the longer term, contributes to the development of new enterprise forms and enables the transition to an alternative form of capitalism that is accountable not for shareholder value but for the impact of economic activity on its stakeholders.

These look like promising possibilities for public procurement, but is there enough flexibility in the legal regime to allow the state to procure in this way? Business for value enterprises depend on public contracts to grow and establish themselves in the wider economy, but the state requires discretion within public procurement rules to be able to target BfV contractors over traditional shareholder corporations where they are presumed by the arguments set out above to have something specific to offer to the delivery

[32] T Bovaird and E Löffler, 'From Engagement to Co-production: How Users and Communities Contribute to Public Services' in V Pestoff, T Brandsen and B Verschure (eds), *New Public Governance, the Third Sector and Co-Production* (Abingdon, Routledge, 2012) 36.

[33] R Ridley-Duff and M Bull, *Understanding Social Enterprise: Theory and Practice*, 2nd edn (London, SAGE, 2015) ch 2.

of public services.[34] Building flexibility into the law, to encourage open-ended procurement and collaboration, and to reward longer-term societal value, improves the chances of BfV enterprises' tendering successfully, but these considerations must be balanced against basic procurement principles, including the need for equal treatment of all tenderers and for transparency.

IV. PUBLIC PROCUREMENT LAW

Unless the state procures exclusively from in-house providers,[35] tendering is subject to national and European public procurement law. The current procurement regulatory framework in England combines policy guidance and detailed legislative provisions, with European Union (EU) and national-level initiatives complementing one another.[36] The primary legal sources are now contained in the 2014 Public Procurement Directive,[37] recently transposed in the Public Contracts Regulations 2015.[38] The rules are detailed and technical and, despite the Government's efforts to supply training materials and information, they are subject to further calls for guidance. They are also subject to ongoing change, driven by evolving European and domestic case law, European Commission communications, and cyclical review of the existing legislation.

National legislation also contains a range of further general and sector-specific rules,[39] which are supplemented by overarching policy guidance. The Government requires all public authorities to attain 'value for money'

[34] See in this context the references at nn 26, 28 and 29, and growing practice- and policy-orientated research into collaborative, co-productive and cooperative approaches to commissioning and procurement, eg J Slay and J Penny, New Economic Foundation, *Commissioning for Outcomes and Co-production* (2014), at neweconomics.org/publications/entry/commissioning-for-outcomes-co-production; T Blume and A Randle, Collaborate and Transition Institute, *Social Value: A Commissioning Framework, Pt 1: Lessons from Lambeth*, at tobyblume.wordpress.com/2013/12/05/social-value-commissioning/, 5 December 2013; D Boyle and M Harris, 'The Challenge of Co-Production' (2009) NEF and NESTA Discussion Paper, at nesta.org.uk/publications/challenge-co-production; H Kippin and A Randle, Collaborate CIC, *From Cooperative Councils to Cooperative Places* (2017), at collaboratecic.com/from-co-operative-councils-to-co-operative-places-4f8ace5e4511.

[35] See Art 12 of the 2014 Public Procurement Directive.

[36] The following discussion focuses on the English (and to some extent UK) context, although parallels with other jurisdictions, where similar national provisions are in place, should be obvious.

[37] Directive 2014/24/EU of the European Parliament and of the Council of 26 February 2014 on public procurement and repealing Directive 2004/18/EC (2014 Public Procurement Directive) [2014] OJ L94/65.

[38] The Public Contracts Regulations 2015 (SI 2015/102) ('the Regulations'). Transposition in Scotland is subject to a different regime.

[39] Recent legislative additions include the National Health Service (Procurement, Patient Choice and Competition) (No 2) Regulations 2013 (SI 2013/500); the Localism Act 2011; the Public Services (Social Value) Act 2012; and the Small Business, Enterprise and Employment Act 2015.

in their public procurement, usually by acquiring goods and services through 'fair and open competition'.[40] Value for money in this context is defined by reference to price, effectiveness and quality, in other words, 'securing the best mix of quality and effectiveness for the least outlay over the period of use of the goods or services bought. It is not about minimising up front prices.'[41] Specific further legal obligations apply to, amongst others, local authorities, which are required by law to attain 'best value' through their commissioning, based on 'a combination of economy, efficiency and effectiveness'.[42]

The purpose of the EU procurement rules is to open up the public procurement market to EU providers, and to ensure its competitiveness so as to maintain the free movement of goods and services in the EU.[43] They also reinforce the UK domestic value-for-money criteria.[44] Authorities are compelled under the Directive, as implemented in the Regulations, to award public contracts on the basis of 'the most economically advantageous tender [MEAT] assessed from the point of view of the contracting authority'.[45] The MEAT may include price or cost, or a price-quality ratio assessed on the basis of qualitative, technical and sustainable (economic, social and environmental) aspects of the tender. These can (subject to certain conditions) include social and environmental factors, which may be considered as performance clauses, selection or award criteria (discussed further below). The assessment may take account of all stages of the life cycle of the product or service in question.

Different procurement rules apply, depending on the type of services, works or supplies that are being contracted for, as well as the overall value of the contract. The full procurement regime set out in the Directive and Regulations—including advertising and publication requirements in the *Official Journal* of the EU and detailed procedures, selection and contract award criteria—applies to contracts above a certain value threshold, unless they qualify for specific exclusions (eg national security). Contracts for social and health services and certain other services, on the other hand, are subject to a more flexible 'light touch' regime, and again only if their value exceeds the relevant threshold (€750,000). The 'light touch' regime leaves the state considerable flexibility in terms of award procedures, but it does

[40] HM Treasury, *Managing Public Money*, Annex 4.6 on Procurement (2013, Annexes revised as at August 2015), at gov.uk/government/uploads/system/uploads/attachment_data/file/212123/Managing_Public_Money_AA_v2_-_chapters_annex_web.pdf.

[41] ibid, para A4.6.3; see also National Audit Office, *Assessing Value for Money* (2017), at nao.org.uk/successful-commissioning/general-principles/value-for-money/assessing-value-for-money/.

[42] UK Local Government Act 1999, s 3(1).

[43] Recital 1 of the 2014 Public Procurement Directive.

[44] Crown Commercial Service, *A Brief Guide to the 2014 EU Public Procurement Directives* (2016), at gov.uk/government/uploads/system/uploads/attachment_data/file/338055/Handbook_Final.pdf.

[45] Public Contracts Regulations 2015, reg 67(1).

require that tenders are advertised and publication of award notices in the *Official Journal*.[46]

Contracting authorities are further required to comply with the basic EU Treaty principles of transparency, equal treatment, non-discrimination, mutual recognition and proportionality whenever they consider that a contract will or might attract interest from suppliers outside the UK. The principles apply to all contracts with a cross-border relevance, including those regulated under the 'light touch' regime, as well as those that fall outside the scope of the Directive and Regulations altogether (eg those that are sub-threshold).[47] In practice, they compel the state to advertise a contract in a way that is commensurate to its scale and value, and to make sufficient information about the contract available, so as to ensure that no disadvantage arises for potential suppliers from other Member States. The Government's position further is that value for money should be attained in all procurement, not just for those contracts covered by the Directive, and that this usually requires some degree of advertising and a competitive tendering process for all, or the great majority of, contracts.[48] Reflecting this position, the Regulations include specific rules that require authorities to advertise all public contracts, including those below the EU thresholds but above certain other thresholds, via the online platform 'Contracts Finder'.[49]

V. FLEXIBILITY WITHIN THE LAW

Despite the level of regulatory detail in the rules, both EU and national public procurement law leave the state with considerable discretion in the substantive design, procedural award and follow-on management of its contracts. The 2014 Public Procurement Directive is complex, reflecting the political differences and compromises that surfaced during its enactment, now embedded in the legal text, but it has succeeded in building further flexibility into the EU economic legal regime to accommodate the state's public interest choices when procuring public goods, works and services. This brief discussion considers the flexibility available within national and EU public procurement law to target the specific advantages of BfV enterprises over shareholder corporations in the delivery of public services, with a focus on three particular aspects: first, on the law's permissiveness regarding substantive criteria and contract specifications; secondly, on structural

[46] Public Contracts Regulations 2015, regs 74–77. A significantly higher threshold applies, see reg 5(1)(d).

[47] Very similar general requirements derive from Art 9 of the UN Convention Against Corruption 2004, adopted by General Assembly Resolution 58/4 of 31 October 2003.

[48] Crown Commercial Service, above n 44, para 8.1.

[49] Available at gov.uk/contracts-finder.

flexibility in the tendering process; and lastly, on the (limited) scope to reserve certain contracts for defined BfV providers.

A. Substantive Criteria

A widely-discussed innovation in the 2014 Public Procurement Directive is its express commitment to 'a better integration of social and environmental considerations in public procurement procedures', where public bodies should be 'allowed to use award criteria or contract performance conditions relating to the works, supplies or services, in all aspects and at any stage of their life cycle, even where such factors do not form part of their material performance'.[50] The assessment of tenders based on the 'most economically advantageous' option, as set out by the Directive and transposed by the Regulations (see section IV), leaves the state a choice between price- or cost-driven procurement, on the one hand, and an assessment that balances cost and quality on the other, where social and environmental considerations are permissible (subject to certain conditions) as selection and award criteria and in contract performance clauses.

Domestic procurement policy and legislation in the UK reinforce the flexibility within these rules. The legislator chose to transpose the full test and to retain its flexibility, rejecting calls that the Directive's transposition should be taken as an opportunity to curtail the state's ability to procure on price alone, and should instead make a cost-quality assessment mandatory.[51] At the same time, to ensure the state maximises value-for-money objectives in what the Cabinet Office describes as 'tight economic times', government guidance encourages public bodies to deliver on their 'best value' obligations by seeking out 'opportunities to secure both the best price and meet the wider social, economic and environmental needs of the community'.[52] These priorities are now enshrined in the Public Services (Social Value) Act 2012, which expressly requires public bodies to consider the economic, social and environmental well-being of the wider community, as opposed to purely commercial value for money, before procuring public service contracts with a value above the EU procurement thresholds.[53] The Act does not impose an obligation to act upon these considerations, but by requiring public bodies

[50] Recital 97 of the 2014 Public Procurement Directive.

[51] See Cabinet Office, *Government Response to the Consultation on UK Transposition of new EU Procurement Directives* (2016) pt 128, at gov.uk/government/consultations/transposing-the-eu-procurement-directives-utilities-contracts-regulations.

[52] Cabinet Office, Efficiency and Reform Group, *Procurement Policy Note: Public Services (Social Value) Act 2012* (first published 20 December 2012 and updated 7 January 2013) 2, at gov.uk/government/publications/procurement-policy-note-10-12-the-public-services-social-value-act-2012.

[53] Public Services (Social Value) Act 2012, s 1(3). For a discussion of the scope and effectiveness of the Act, see N Boeger, 'Reappraising the UK Social Value Legislation' (2017) 37(2) *Public Money & Management* 113.

to reflect on social, environmental and economic outcomes, rather than on narrow commercial service outputs,[54] it encourages an approach to public procurement that builds on dynamic efficiency to generate longer-term value for money in public services. As the New Economics Foundation points out:

> [C]ommissioning for wider public value across the triple bottom line [of economic, environmental and social value] does not necessarily make a service more expensive. It often just requires commissioning for and providing a service in a different way. Even where additional upfront costs are incurred, these should be considered alongside potential cross-departmental and long-term savings which can far outweigh initial investment.[55]

By allowing for social and environmental considerations to be given weight in procurement decisions, public procurement law leaves, at least in principle, flexibility for the state to target the specific advantages that the procedural/structural commitments of BfV enterprises offer. However, the Directive specifies that only social and environmental considerations linked to the subject matter of the contract can be legally considered (provided they are non-discriminatory and in compliance with general EU law).[56] As Semple states, the effect of the latter is 'that specifications, criteria and contract performance clauses must relate to the goods, services or works being purchased, and not concern matters that fall outside the contract at hand'.[57] In particular, any 'criteria and conditions relating to general corporate policy'[58] do not, according to the Directive, constitute legitimate procurement concerns under the EU rules unless they are in some way linked to the subject matter of the contract (ie either to the specific process of production of the goods or services in question, or to a specific process at another stage of their life cycle). Compared to the previous EU regime as derived from the case law of the Court of Justice,[59] the 2014 Public Procurement Directive

[54] The New Economics Foundation proposes definitions that make the difference between outcomes and outputs apparent. It defines outputs as 'a quantitative summary of an activity' that 'tells you an activity has taken place, but it does not tell you what changes as a result'. Outcome, on the other hand, is defined as 'the meaningful and valued impact or change that occurs as a result of a particular activity or set of activities', and may be either achieved 'over a relatively short period of time, or … longer-term in nature.' See J Slay and J Penny, New Economic Foundation, *Commissioning for Outcomes and Co-production* (2014), at neweconomics.org/publications/entry/commissioning-for-outcomes-co-production.

[55] ibid, 22.

[56] Art 67 of the 2014 Public Procurement Directive.

[57] A Semple, 'The Link to the Subject-Matter: A Glass Ceiling for Sustainable Public Contracts?' in B Sjåfjell and A Wiesbrock (eds), *Sustainable Public Procurement under EU Law: New Perspectives on the State as Stakeholder* (Cambridge, Cambridge University Press, 2016) 50, 62.

[58] Recital 97 of the 2014 Public Procurement Directive.

[59] Judgment of 17 September 2002, *Concordia Bus Finland Oy Ab, formerly Stagecoach Finland Oy Ab v Helsingin kaupunki and HKL-Bussiliikenne*, Case C-513/99, EU:C:2002:495; Judgment of 4 December 2003, *EVN and Wienstrom*, Case C-448/01, EU:C:2003:651; and Judgment of 10 May 2012, *Commission v Netherlands*, Case C-368/10, EU:C:2012:284 (*Dutch Coffee*). For discussion of the previous regime, see S Arrowsmith and P Kunzlik (eds), *Social and Environmental Policies in EC Procurement Law: New Directives and New Directions* (Cambridge, Cambridge University Press, 2009).

has extended the requirement in ways that have provoked criticism. Semple, for example, not only criticises the reasoning underlying the Commission's proposals for the extension as 'problematic',[60] but points out further that the application of the requirement encourages, amongst other things, inefficiency and fragmentation in the internal market.[61] Her observations lead Semple to propose that a 'looser version of the test' might eventually emerge by way of judicial interpretation, which could bring it closer to the general review of procurement measures for proportionality.[62]

But even in the light of these concerns, the 'link to the subject matter' requirement is unlikely to present an absolute obstacle for the state when seeking out BfV enterprises that promote the inclusion of, and accountability to, stakeholders involved in or affected by the contract, through to the point of contractual delivery. The current regime still leaves the state flexibility to link the procedural mechanism of a BfV enterprise to the subject matter of contract, and thus to render it a lawful criterion or condition; although it does call for careful drafting of all documentation to ensure that all specifications, criteria and contract clauses are specific to the contractual delivery. In practice, the state must make it absolutely clear that it considers accountability to and input from stakeholders (they may include management, employees, consumers/recipients or those affected by the environmental impact, subcontractors, etc) as an essential part of how the contract is performed; and that these aspects matter directly for the quality and effectiveness of performance of the contract because the state choses to design the contract in an open-ended way, building into it a mechanism for experimentation and adaptation. It is useful for the state to define mechanisms to which it will pay particular attention, for example the composition of management boards or committees that take decisions relating to contract performance; reporting on matters relating to contract performance; reinvestment of surpluses that derive from the contractual performance into matters related to it.

Provided they are well drafted, these criteria or conditions may not be considered too general (a matter of 'general corporate policy') when they target a governance mechanism that impacts directly on decisions and activities during (and specific to) the performance of the contract; especially when, as Semple suggests, there are good arguments for the Court of Justice to continue applying a loose interpretation of the 'link to the subject matter' test.[63] Nor should they be considered discriminatory so as to render them

[60] Semple, above n 57, 61–65.
[61] ibid, 66–70.
[62] ibid, 73–74.
[63] Support for this comes from the loose test on 'link to the subject matter' that the Court applied in the *Dutch Coffee* case, above n 59, upholding the contracting authority's fair-trade stipulations for suppliers to have 'long-term trading relationships' with producers; a matter which, as Semple remarks, 'by definition goes beyond the immediate needs of the contracting authority'. See Semple, above n 57, 59–60.

illegal. Business for value providers, whose structurally embedded mechanisms are more likely to align with at least some of the state's procedural expectations, are probably going to find these types of criteria easier to satisfy than shareholder corporations, and they can be an indirect advantage for BfV enterprises. The more deeply these mechanisms are embedded in the business—where they are a constitutional commitment rather than part of a CSR policy to consult—the more likely is for a potential provider to score highly in relation to these elements of the contract.

But this situation arises directly as a result of the state's structural choice to incorporate elements of proceduralisation into the public contract as a means of delivering best value for its citizens. Faced with these choices, any shareholder corporation is free to make organisational changes, if necessary at a constitutional level, to enhance its chances of convincing the state of its capacity and reliability in delivering these elements of the contract as specified. Shareholder corporations may assume the 'face' of a BfV enterprise by formally putting in place mechanisms for voluntary stakeholder consultations when they perform the contract—essentially as a targeted form of CSR—but these will have to compete against the constitutional guarantees that BfV enterprises offer. To the extent that the former are voluntary undertakings, they offer the state fewer procedural guarantees than the latter in relation to the contractual delivery. But these likely advantages for BfV enterprises over shareholder corporations arise solely because the shareholder corporate model, which businesses adopt by choice, means these competitors are less suited to deliver the specifications of the contract effectively.

B. Procedural Flexibility

The 2014 Public Procurement Directive includes a commitment to supplier diversity by supporting 'the participation of small and medium-sized enterprises in public procurement',[64] and the UK Government has also expressly committed to making the procurement process 'simpler, more open and less bureaucratic—so all businesses, no matter their size, have a chance of success'.[65] One of the measures in place to do this is a provision encouraging public bodies to split contracts into lots; or if they decide not to do so, they must explain why not.[66] While some have argued that the duty to explain is

[64] Recital 2 of the 2014 Public Procurement Directive.

[65] HM Government, *Consultation Document: Making Public Sector Procurement More Accessible to SMEs* (2013), at gov.uk/government/consultations/making-public-sector-procurement-more-accessible-to-smes.

[66] Public Contract Regulations 2015, reg 46.

neither clear nor sufficiently strong,[67] the more important point here is that these rules provide flexibility, which will allow the state to run its public procurement by scaling down contract sizes as far as possible, to attract tenders from BfV enterprises, many of which are smaller organisations and financially dependent on the state's nurturing to scale up their activities. The law makes room for (indeed encourages) procurement bodies to innovate and experiment, particularly to improve supplier diversity by opening up more contracts to smaller organisations, including many BfV enterprises; it is then left to the state to use this flexibility. Other procedural opportunities in the Directive (and the Regulations) underline this point. Pre-tender market engagement, for example, is one way for public bodies to test which aspects of a public contract it may leave underspecified, and the legislation enables this engagement, provided that transparency and equal treatment principles are observed.[68] Preliminary market consultations with suppliers are encouraged, and they give the state the opportunity to publish information to contractors, but also to collect their advice on service designs and procurement procedures. It appears that lack of flexibility in the law is not a hindrance to market engagement, but the state's reluctance to use these opportunities creatively might be.

C. Reserved Contracts

The 2014 Public Procurement Directive (and Regulations) also provides that tenders for certain service contracts (mainly in the social and health sectors) can be reserved, for a limited time, to a mutual and social enterprise that meets defined criteria—a defined form of BfV enterprise.[69] The reservation requires a competition to be published in the *Official Journal* for those services using the 'light touch regime', which allows bids only from enterprises that satisfy the relevant criteria. Reserved contracts cannot be longer than three years, and the state cannot reserve contracts for enterprises that have been awarded a contract within the last three years by the contracting authority concerned. As with procedural flexibility (discussed in section V.B), it is true that these legal provisions make room for the state to experiment, by inviting defined BfV forms to provide public services, and it falls on the state to use creatively any flexibility for which the rules allow. There are practical

[67] For a short critique, expressing the author's regret that contracting authorities were not required to split contracts into lots, see L Olson, 'SME access by splitting contracts into lots', 29 June 2015, at blog.tendersdirect.co.uk/2015/06/29/sme-access-by-splitting-contracts-into-lots/.

[68] Public Contracts Regulations 2015, reg 40.

[69] Public Contract Regulations 2015, reg 77. In addition, the Directive and the Regulations allow reservations for sheltered workshops and employment programmes that involve a proportion of disadvantaged and disabled workers.

difficulties—for example, according to Cooperatives UK, 'there is a risk that enterprises may attempt to pass themselves off as mutuals even if they do not live up to the fundamental characteristics of mutual enterprise. This will need to be addressed in robust guidance for procurers'.[70]

But more fundamental is the question whether this rule really does enable the state to nurture BfV enterprises, as considered in the previous sections. Several commentators are highly sceptical whether the reserved time period of three years suffices to grow the defined enterprises to sustainability (some suggest five years would be more realistic), and question also why organisations already under contract are excluded when their existing provision could be nurtured too.[71] Arguably, the rule does not lose the state anything (there was no express option in law to reserve contracts before), but neither should it be taken for granted that this rule plays a significant role 'in promoting more nurturing partnership arrangements between the social economy and public authorities'[72] in the longer term; unless, of course, the state engages creatively with whatever room it has, to refine the use of reserved contracts and to strengthen the case for how these might be developed as tools that help nurture BfV enterprises more widely.

In sum, recent developments at national and EU level indicate that there is room within public procurement law to facilitate the state's choice to target BfV contractors over traditional shareholder corporations where they are presumed to have something specific to offer to the delivery of public services, provided the state ensures compliance with the relevant procedural rules and principles during the tendering process and when managing the contract. The direction of travel appears to be for procurement law to move away from the traditional conception of competitive tendering that dominated the British (and European) procurement landscape of the 1980s and 1990s, increasingly towards greater permissiveness and rules that give the state more flexibility in developing innovative public service delivery models that are not traditional privatisations. The law has reached a stage where it leaves room to enable the state to support long-term relationships that socialise public service delivery by relying on procedural/structural mechanisms embedded in BfV enterprises, offering the state both the flexibility and the legal tools to do so. Some legal hurdles remain, where further changes could give more flexibility and/or provide greater certainty, and review is likely to be ongoing. But the practical challenge today is arguably to build up both the skill set and the commitment amongst those responsible for public procurement,

[70] Cooperatives UK, *Consultation Response: UK Transposition of new EU Procurement Directives (Public Contracts Regulations 2015)* (October 2014) 3, at uk.coop/sites/default/files/uploads/attachments/uk_transposition_of_new_eu_procurement_directives_public_contracts_regulations_2015_-_co-operatives_uk_response_0.pdf.

[71] ibid, 4.

[72] ibid.

to ensure that they make use of the flexibility available within the legal regime whenever it would be appropriate, and in the citizens' interest, to do so. The law should not be 'a convenient (if not always accurate) excuse' for the state to continue approaches to privatisation that avoid innovation—for example by proceduralising public service models—when it would benefit citizens and taxpayers.[73]

VI. CONCLUSION

This chapter has characterised BfV enterprises as categorically different from shareholder corporations, even those with comprehensive CSR policies, because their commitments to generating value beyond return on shareholder investment are not just fixed in voluntary codes. These commitments are procedurally/structurally embedded into the business, and while there are different formats for BfV (eg B Corps, social enterprises and cooperatives), the commitment to generating value for more than just shareholders, and the concrete procedural/structural guarantees that enshrine this commitment, is what unites all these forms. Section III argued that procuring from BfV enables the state to contract in more open-ended ways, and to set up a long-term relationship between the BfV enterprise, the state and its stakeholders (widely conceived) that allows ongoing input from stakeholders right through to the point of delivery of whatever was procured. Where gaps and ambiguities exist in the contract, the state can rely on BfV contractors (though not shareholder corporations) to fill them in a way it would have done had it anticipated the gap or ambiguity at the time it drafted the contract, relying on the procedural mechanisms that commit the BfV to considering its impacts (value generation) on its wider stakeholders, not just its shareholders.

The BfV is nurtured by the largesse of the state (payment for public service delivery), so that by delivering public contracts, BfV forms grow capacity to enable them to deliver private contracts and to participate in and to shape the wider economy. By providing this nurturing, a public procurement model that relies on long-term relationships with BfV enterprises not only socialises public service delivery, but it can also, in the longer term, contribute to shaping alternative forms of capitalism and of enterprise. Sections IV and V concluded that there is room within public procurement law to facilitate these public service models, though to do so will often require careful

[73] A Davies and R Schon, *Bridging the Divide: Social Entrepreneurs and Commissioners on Public Sector Contracting*, Young Foundation (2013) 10, at youngfoundation.org/publications/bridging-the-divide-social-enterprises-and-commissioners-on-public-sector-contracting/.

drafting. The practical challenge today is arguably to generate enough awareness of the flexibility available within the regime and to encourage the state to use it, developing the skills of procurement officers to do so. Public bodies should be aware of the relevant legal boundaries, but at the same time might explore ways in which can they work creatively within the legal framework to pursue strategies to set up longer-term relationships that socialise public service delivery, relying on the procedural/structural mechanisms of BfV enterprises, without exposing themselves to legal risks.

Part III

Labour Law Perspectives of Social Smart Procurement in the EU

8

The Operation of Labour Law as the Exception: The Case of Public Procurement

LISA RODGERS*

I. INTRODUCTION

THERE ARE A number of rationales for European Union (EU) intervention in (domestic) labour markets.[1] These rationales are not always commensurate. The relationship between labour law and the market is particularly complex. On the one hand, it is possible to see labour law and labour standards as fulfilling a 'market-building' function and furthering market aims.[2] Labour law might act as an institution that creates efficiency and competitiveness through correcting market failures and encouraging cooperation amongst the workforce.[3] On the other hand, labour law and labour standards can be seen as a brake on efficiency, and as acting as a pure 'cost' burden on companies having to implement them. In such an instance, for the setting of labour standards to be a legitimate action, those standards must meet goals that are independent of the market but which are nonetheless desirable.[4] One idea that has been prevalent at EU level is the contribution of labour standards to solidarity and citizenship.[5]

* I would like to acknowledge the support of the University of Leicester in granting me a period of study leave in which to complete the writing of this chapter, and to thank the participants at the 'After Regiopost' conference for very helpful comments on an earlier draft.

[1] P Syrpis, *EU Intervention in Domestic Labour Law* (Oxford, Oxford University Press, 2007) 10. Sypris identifies three distinct rationales for such intervention: integrationist, economic and social.

[2] ibid, 50.

[3] S Deakin, 'The Contribution of Labour Law to Economic and Human Development' in G Davidov and B Langille (eds), *The Idea of Labour Law* (Oxford, Oxford University Press, 2011) 162.

[4] G Davidov, *A Purposive Approach to Labour Law* (Oxford, Oxford University Press, 2016) 55–71.

[5] For information on the relationship between work and citizenship, there is the classic treatise by TH Marshall, 'Work and Wealth' in TH Marshall, *Class, Citizenship and Social Development* (New York, Anchor Books, 1965) 230. A more modern discussion is in J Gordon and RA Lenhardt, 'Rethinking Work and Citizenship' (2008) 55 *UCLA Law Review* 1161.

The argument is that through social inclusion measures, the living standards of all citizens are improved, and individuals are given the chance to participate in and contribute fully to the community.

The inclusion and boosting of 'social inclusion' measures in the recent 2014 Public Procurement Directive[6] might be seen as an example of such an approach. Whilst it is admitted that the Directive is primarily about promoting fair competition in the internal market, the Commission has also promoted the use of the public procurement directives to achieve other, social goals.[7] There are a number of developments in the revised 2014 Public Procurement Directive that attempt to support these 'horizontal' policies. There is a new social clause, under which public authorities will need to ensure compliance with national or EU social and labour rules, applicable collective agreements and international law.[8] This compliance also applies when several subcontractors are involved in the same project. Furthermore, the awarding of a contract will no longer have to depend primarily on price, and contracting authorities can pay more attention to social and labour benefits (whether the working conditions of the contract go beyond legal requirements, are intended to favour the promotion of equality between men and women, or increase the participation of women in the labour market).[9] Furthermore, under the new rules, contracting authorities will be able to restrict some tendering procedures for social enterprises and those offering sheltered workshops, whose main aim is to integrate disadvantaged persons into the labour market.[10]

Some commentators have outlined the benefits that stem from this approach, opening up a new space for labour law and its enforcement.[11] There are, however, concerns that may be raised with this approach: the negative relationship between labour law and the market prevails

[6] Directive 2014/24/EU of the European Parliament and of the Council of 26 February 2014 on public procurement and repealing Directive 2004/18/EC (2014 Public Procurement Directive) [2014] OJ L 94/65.

[7] See the Commission news report on the new Public Procurement Directive: Commission, 'Supporting social responsibility in the economy through public procurement' (9 February 2016), at ec.europa.eu/growth/tools-databases/newsroom/cf/itemdetail.cfm?item_id=8667.

[8] Art 18(2) of the 2014 Public Procurement Directive. For discussion, see the contribution by Semple in ch 5 of this book.

[9] Art 70 of the 2014 Public Procurement Directive. See also Commission, above n 7, para 1, and commentary in R Nielsen, 'Discrimination and Equality in Public Procurement' (undated) 8–9, at arbetsratt.juridicum.su.se/Filer/PDF/klaw46/discrimination.procurement.pdf.

[10] The provisions on social workshops appear in Art 20 of the 2014 Public Procurement Directive. The possibility to reserve contracts for specific types of bidders (other than sheltered workshops) is regulated in Art 77 and only applies to the contracts for social and special services regulated in Art 74 (and Annex XIV).

[11] C McCrudden, *Buying Social Justice: Equality, Government Procurement and Legal Change* (Oxford, Oxford University Press, 2007); S Arrowsmith, 'Horizontal Policies in Public Procurement: A Taxonomy' (2010) 10(2) *Journal of Public Procurement* 149; A Semple, *A Practical Guide to Public Procurement* (Oxford, Oxford University Press, 2015) ch 7.

(labour law is a 'cost' to be borne by the market), whilst at the same time social ideals are not truly independent of market considerations. Labour law and social standards are not independent because they are included as an exception to economic efficiency rules. The value of the exception is therefore not measured against standards of solidarity/worker protection/dignity but against efficiency. The result is that there is a pressure not to allow social considerations, which on an independent purposive assessment might be included.[12] The efficiency paradigm depends on maximising choice to obtain the optimal results. Contractual decisions that 'may' be made on the basis of social considerations therefore potentially mean very little if the efficiency paradigm dominates. Furthermore, the efficiency paradigm dictates that there should be few 'mandatory' social provisions. Where the standards are mandatory, the field of their application is made extremely narrow, given that they are included as a concession, and they act as a break on efficiency. Lastly, labour and social standards are not part of the 'innovative' parts of the new procurement directives but stand in contrast to innovation, efficiency and profit maximisation.

Section II of this chapter discusses how labour law has increasingly become part of the general scheme of exception to single market goals, a position which has only deepened in the wake of the financial crisis. Section III looks at the public procurement directives as an interesting example of this inclusion/exclusion, with reference to the different obligations on contracting authorities at different stages of the product life cycle. Section IV investigates the position of the Court of Justice in interpreting social clauses in the public procurement directives, and the likely trajectory of future claims. Lastly, in section V an overall assessment is made of the contribution of the (social exceptions in the) public procurement directives to the development of labour law as a whole.

II. LABOUR LAW AND THE MARKET IN THE EU

In the earlier years of European integration, it was possible to discern two narratives arising in the promotion of labour law. The first narrative was that labour law was 'market constituting' and would help to achieve the economic aims set out in the Treaties. In the 1970s, there was a particular focus on the development of equality law measures in the employment field, on the understanding that these equality measures would provide

[12] There is a growing literature on the dangers of the spread of the exceptionalism. Some authors describe this as the most important feature of our time. See G Agamben, *State of Exception* (Chicago, IL, Chicago University Press, 2005); A Supiot, *Homo Juridicus: On the Anthropological Function of the Law* (London, Verso, 2007) 51–77.

protection against unfair competition (competition on the basis of low social standards).[13] Several equality directives were enacted, including the directives on equal pay[14] and on equal treatment in the workplace (in relation to sex).[15] Both of these directives were founded on an integrationist logic, under which (sex) equality was sought not in its own right but as means to achieve economic goals. It was thought that the creation of labour standards in the field of sex equality would allow the equalisation of costs and the creation of a level playing field for economic operators.

At the same time, the Social Action Programme of the 1970s introduced the idea of the value of worker protection as an independent goal, and as something to be pursued in its own right. The Social Action Programme followed a meeting of the Heads of State and Government in 1972, at which concerns were raised that economic restructuring across the EU was creating a downward spiral in living and working conditions. The Heads of Government resolved to take more vigorous action in the social field to meet these challenges and protect workers from negative economic consequences. A number of directives were adopted in this vein, including directives on the protection of employees in the event of collective redundancies,[16] transfer of undertakings[17] (now the Acquired Rights Directive (ARD))[18] and the insolvency of the employer.[19] The protective intent of these directives is clearly set out in their preambles. In the Transfer of Undertakings Directive, for example, reference was made in the preamble to the 'economic trends' that were forcing changes in the organisation of work. The risks for workers of these changes made it 'necessary to provide for the protection of employees in the event of a change of employer, in particular to ensure that their rights

[13] L Rodgers, 'Labour Law and Employment Policy in the EU: Conflict or Consensus?' (2011) 27(4) *International Journal of Comparative Labour Law and Industrial Relations* 387, 390.

[14] Council Directive 75/117/EEC of 10 February 1975 on the approximation of the laws of the Member States relating to the application of the principle of equal pay for men and women [1975] OJ L45/19.

[15] Council Directive 76/207/EEC of 9 February 1976 on the implementation of the principle of equal treatment for men and women as regards access to employment, vocational training and promotion, and working conditions [1975] OJ L39/40.

[16] Council Directive 75/129/EEC of 17 February 1975 on the approximation of the laws of the Member States relating to collective redundancies (Collective Redundancies Directive) [1975] OJ L48/29.

[17] Council Directive 77/187/EEC of 14 February 1977 on the approximation of the laws of the Member States relating to the safeguarding of employees' rights in the event of transfers of undertakings, businesses or parts of businesses (Transfer of Undertakings Directive) [1977] OJ L61/126.

[18] Council Directive 2001/23/EC of 12 March 2001 on the approximation of the laws of the Member States relating to the safeguarding of employees' rights in the event of transfers of undertakings, businesses or parts of undertakings or businesses [2001] OJ L 082/16.

[19] Council Directive 80/987/EEC of 20 October 1980 on the approximation of the laws of the Member States relating to the protection of employees in the event of the insolvency of their employer [1980] OJ L283/23.

are safeguarded'.[20] A similar position can be seen in the preamble to the Collective Redundancies Directive, in which it is stated that 'greater protection should be afforded to workers in the event of collective redundancies'.[21]

The clear protective intent of these directives provided considerable benefits to workers when it came to claiming a breach of their rights under the directives at EU level. The Court of Justice consistently referred to this protective intent, and tended to interpret the directives on the side of employees. A good example of this position is provided in the case of *Mølle Kro*,[22] in which the Court interpreted the Transfer of Undertakings Directive widely to conclude that the termination of a lease could constitute a transfer of an undertaking from which protective rights would flow. The Court of Justice was clear on the importance of the protective element of the Directive, which was to 'ensure, as far as possible, that the contract of employment or employment relationship continues unchanged with the transferee, in order to prevent the workers concerned from being placed in a less favourable position solely as a result of the transfer'.[23] Similarly, in *Daddy's Dance Hall*,[24] the Court held that the fact that a transfer took place in two or more stages did not preclude the operation of the Directive.

The 'worker protective' ethos of statutory provision in the 1970s did not survive into the 1980s and 1990s. Instead, labour law became dominated by the idea of 'flexicurity': the promotion of both flexibility (for employers) and security (for employees) in the labour market. Flexicurity involved two important foundational assumptions. The first assumption was that regulation must be sensitive to economic developments and must respond to these demands. It was argued, for example, that flexicurity strategies could help the EU to respond to the pressures on the labour market brought about by globalisation. 'Flexible and reliable contractual arrangements' could be combined with 'comprehensive lifelong learning strategies' and 'active learning policies' that fostered *employment* security. The idea of employment security for workers was interesting.[25] It corresponded with the idea that in the new economy, it was no longer possible to protect individual jobs (job security). The focus of regulation should be the protection of individual development (training, for example) so that individuals could maintain *employment* security over their life cycle.[26] The second foundational

[20] Transfer of Undertakings Directive, Preamble, para 2.

[21] Collective Redundancies Directive, Preamble, para 1.

[22] Judgment of 17 December 1987, *Landorganisationen i Danmark v Ny Mølle Kro*, Case C-287/86, EU:C:1987:573.

[23] ibid, para 25.

[24] Judgment of 10 February 1988, *Tellerup v Daddy's Dance Hall*, Case C-324/86, EU:C:1988:72.

[25] European Commission, 'Towards Fundamental Principles of Flexicurity: More and Better Jobs through Flexibility and Security', COM (2007) 359 final 9.

[26] M De Vos, 'European Flexicurity and Globalization: A Critical Perspective' (2009) 25(3) *The International Journal of Comparative Labour Law and Industrial Relations* 209, 215.

assumption was the idea of balance: that is, both employer and employee needs had to be balanced in order to achieve (economic) progress. The judicious combination of flexibility and security in the labour market was presented as a win-win scenario, providing universal benefits for employers and workers.[27]

The flexicurity agenda fed into the creation of a series of directives concerning atypical work: the Fixed-term Work Directive (FTWD),[28] the Part-Time Work Directive (PTWD)[29] and the Temporary Agency Work Directive (TAWD).[30] The commitment in these directives to the flexicurity agenda was clear. In all their preambles the benefit of the more flexible organisation of work was set out as corresponding both to the 'wishes of employees' and the 'requirements of competition'.[31] Indeed, in the PTWD and the TAWD, the development of these kinds of contracts was actively encouraged. At the same time, the security elements of the equation were met by the promotion of the principle of non-discrimination and improvement in the quality of these forms of work. However, it can be argued that the security elements in the atypical work directives have also become imbued with elements of flexibility, so that their ability to protect workers has been brought into question.[32] For example, in the atypical work directives, a level of flexibility is incorporated into the notion of equal treatment, which is not normally permitted. This is illustrated by the fact that justification is permitted for direct discrimination (as opposed to indirect discrimination), and both the PTWD and the FTWD identify different instances in which justification is recognised. These directives also appear to make little contribution to either job or employment security in practice.[33]

It appears that the adoption of labour law under an economic paradigm (such as flexicurity) can have the function of watering down its protective effects. Labour law is not assessed independently but only in accordance with the needs of efficiency. If there is no belief in the efficiency of labour law as such, it will always lose out in the balancing exercise that ensues. As mentioned, one of the foundational assumptions of flexicurity is belief in the need for balance between economic and social goals. Over time, this 'balancing' has gained increasing importance in its own right, as this balancing

[27] ibid, 216.

[28] Council Directive 1999/70/EC concerning the Framework Agreement on Fixed-term Work concluded by ETUC, UNICE and CEEP [1999] OJ L175/43.

[29] Council Directive 1997/81/EC of 15 December 1997 concerning the Framework Agreement on Part-time work concluded by ETUC, UNICE and CEEP [1988] OJL14/9.

[30] Directive 2008/14/EC of the European Parliament and the Council of 19 November 2008 on temporary agency work [2008] OJ L329/9.

[31] Recital 5 PTWD and FTWD.

[32] M Bell, 'Between Flexicurity and Fundamental Social Rights: The EU Directives on Atypical Work' (2012) 37(1) *EL Rev* 31, 36.

[33] ibid, 38.

mechanism has been increasingly adopted by the Court of Justice as an interpretative technique. For example, the Court of Justice has interpreted protective statutes as necessarily involving an element of 'balancing' employee and employer needs. A most striking example is provided by the relatively recent judgment in *Alemo-Herron*.[34] This case concerned the transfer of employees from a public body to the private sector. Prior to the transfer, the claimants were employed on standard contracts, which provided that their terms and conditions were to be determined according to a local government collective agreement. The transferred employees continued to receive pay increases in line with the collective agreement with the new employer. However, a further transfer occurred, and the new employer argued that it was not bound by any subsequent pay determinations. The Court found for the employer, essentially holding that changes in the collective agreement could not bind the employer because that would interfere with the needs of the employer's business. The argument of the Court was that such business considerations were central to the aims of the ARD, which was concerned not only to safeguard the interests of employees, but also to 'achieve a fair balance' between the interests of employers on the one hand and employees on the other.[35] This case has been cited with approval in subsequent decisions in this field.[36]

Furthermore, the Court of Justice has been increasingly involved in balancing (national) labour law with the fundamental economic freedoms of the internal market. At one time, the Court of Justice denied that the EU economic/social constitutional compromise (and attendant delimitation of those areas deemed within the auspices of national sovereignty) raised any conflict at all in the adjudication of labour rights. In the case of *Rush Portuguesa*, for example, the Court held that in certain areas (outside the EU social competence), national labour laws could not interfere with internal market norms: '[Union] law does not preclude Member States from extending their legislation, or collective agreements entered into by both sides of the industry, to any person who is employed, even temporarily, within their territory, no matter in which country the employer is established'.[37] Furthermore, in *Albany*,[38] the Court found that collective agreements fell outside EU competition rules because those agreements were part of the social sphere allocated to Member States. This position has now changed, with a number of cases displaying the willingness of the Court to enter into this balancing exercise (to the detriment of national labour law).

[34] Judgment of 18 July 2013, *Alemo-Herron and Others*, Case C-426/11, EU:C:2013:521.

[35] ibid, para 25.

[36] Opinion of AG Cruz Villalón delivered on 11 September 2014 in *Österreicherisher Gewerkshaftsbund*, Case C-328/13, EU:C:2014:909, para 54.

[37] Judgment of 27 March 1990, *Rush Portuguesa*, Case C-113/89, EU:C:1990:142, para 18

[38] Judgment of 21 September 1999, *Albany*, Case C-67/96, EU:C:1999:430.

For example, in the case of *Viking*,[39] the Court unceremoniously reconfigured the traditional constitutional compromise. The case concerned the 'reflagging' of a vessel by a Finnish company (Viking) under the Estonian flag, so that it could use an Estonian crew. Collective action was threatened against Viking. Viking sought an injunction against this collective action on the grounds that it interfered with the company's right to establishment under Article 49 TFEU[40] (ex Article 43 EC). Under the original economic/social compromise, national laws concerning collective action fall outside EU competence. They would therefore not be affected by the operation of fundamental economic freedoms established at EU level, such as the right to establishment. However, in the *Viking* case, the Court stated that the regulation of collective action by Member States came within the reach of internal market law:

> It is sufficient to point out that, even if, in the areas which fall outside the scope of the [Union]'s competence, the Member States are still free, in principle to lay down the conditions governing the existence and exercise of the rights in question, the fact remains that, when exercising that competence, the Member States must nevertheless comply with [Union] law.[41]

The case of *Laval*,[42] decided in the same year as *Viking*, confirmed the Court's approach.[43] This case concerned a Latvian company, Laval, which won a contract to build a school in Sweden using Latvian workers. The Swedish construction union wanted Laval to apply a Swedish collective agreement, and Laval refused. The union took collective action, and Laval responded by bringing proceedings against the union, claiming the action was in breach of union law (Article 56 TFEU) and the Posted Workers Directive.[44] The Court found that fundamental freedoms had been breached in this case, following the line of argument pursued in *Viking*. Moreover, the Court found that the Swedish union's action was limited by the operation of the Posted Workers Directive. Under the Posted Workers Directive, each Member State is required to ensure that posted workers receive certain minimum terms and conditions of employment. The terms and conditions are set out in Article 3(1), and include limitations on working time; health, safety and hygiene; protective measures for pregnant women or women who have recently given birth; and equality measures. Minimum rates of pay

[39] Judgment of 11 December 2007, *International Transport Workers' Federation and Finnish Seamen's Union v Viking Line*, Case C-438/05, EU:C:2007:772 (*Viking*).

[40] Treaty on the Functioning of the European Union (TFEU) [2012] OJ C326/47.

[41] *Viking*, above n 39, para 40.

[42] Judgment of 18 December 2007, *Laval un Partneri*, Case C-341/05, EU:C:2007:809.

[43] T Novitz and P Syrpis, 'The Internal Market and Domestic Labour Law: Looking Beyond Autonomy' in A Bogg et al (eds), *The Autonomy of Labour Law* (Oxford, Hart Publishing, 2015) 294.

[44] Directive 96/71/EC of the European Parliament and of the Council of 16 December 1996 concerning the posting of workers in the framework of the provision of services (Posted Workers Directive) [1997] OJ L18/1.

are also included, but are deemed to be 'defined by the national law and/or practice of the Member State to whose territory the worker is posted'. The Court decided that the provisions in the collective agreement were not only unclear, but also went beyond the minimum terms and conditions required by the Directive. This was an unexpected interpretation of the operation of a directive of this kind, as social policy directives had previously been understood as setting minimum standards upon which Member States could improve.[45] It also imposed a wide restriction on the use of collective agreements and the guarantee of collective action, traditionally understood as falling within the competence of Member States.

Finally, the most recent developments in the relationship between EU and domestic labour law can also be seen as a further encroachment by the economic into the social, the spread of the economic paradigm providing a justification for intervention. As a direct consequence of the global financial and economic crisis, a number of Member States requested a bail-out from the EU. Those bail-outs were made conditional on the acceptance by Member States of a Memorandum of Understanding setting out an extensive program of employment and financial reform. As a result, affected Member States have been forced to adopt deregulatory measures that have driven down labour standards. One example is provided by the case of Portugal. In the Technical Memorandum of Understanding between Portugal and the *Troika*, Portugal committed to promoting flexibility and adaptability of human resources in the public administration. This culminated in a number of measures to decrease the labour protections afforded to (public) employees.[46] Furthermore, an indirect consequence of the financial crisis has been the establishment of the Better Regulation Agenda and scrutiny of existing EU labour laws on the basis of their fitness for purpose (efficiency).[47]

III. THE PUBLIC PROCUREMENT DIRECTIVES: THE INCLUSION OF LABOUR AND SOCIAL STANDARDS

It is possible to see the inclusion of labour and social standards in the 2014 Public Procurement Directive as a continuation of developments in labour law more generally at EU level (and EU intervention in domestic labour

[45] C Barnard and S Deakin, 'Social Policy and Labour Market Regulation' in E Jones, A Menon and S Weatherill (eds), *The Oxford Handbook of the European Union* (Oxford, Oxford University Press, 2012) 550.

[46] For example, Law 68/2013, which extended maximum working time for public employees. See the discussion in JMM Boto, 'Some Observations on Public Employment in Europe' (2014) 5(3-4) *European Labour Law Journal* 255, 259.

[47] European Commission Communication from the Commission to the European Parliament, the Council, the European Economic and Social Committee and the Committee of the Regions, *Regulatory Fitness and Performance Programme (REFIT): State of Play and Outlook*, COM (2014) 368 final.

markets). As demonstrated in the previous section, those developments can be analysed in the framework of an increasing dominance of the economic over the social, and the subordination of social considerations within the overall economic paradigm. The inclusion of the labour standards in the 2014 Public Procurement Directive can be seen as a furtherance of this trend, given that the Directive is essentially an economic instrument, and social considerations within that instrument are subordinate to its central economic goals. This section analyses the possible benefits to the labour law project of inclusion in an economic project in this way, as well as the potential dangers and pitfalls of such an approach for labour law and its development. Section IV then looks at the specific context of case law development, and at the particular implications of an increased commitment to labour standards in the 2014 Public Procurement Directive.

A. The Benefits of Inclusion

On the one hand, the inclusion of social and labour aspects in public procurement legislation can be viewed very positively. From the point of view of governments, it represents a win-win situation. Governments can achieve economic and social goals simultaneously, and meet the 'aspirations, expectations and needs of the wider community served by the procurement'.[48] The inclusion of social and labour considerations in public purchasing decisions ensures the accountability of governments to their constituency, and ensures that government money is used to benefit fully the population who have contributed to it. Furthermore, the use of public procurement to meet social and labour law objectives further coincides with the sustainability agenda, which has gained significant traction in recent years. Sustainable procurement practices mean that not only economic and social considerations, but also the current and future needs of the community are balanced. This ensures that resources are used not just for the current generations but for generations to come.[49]

Furthermore, the inclusion of social and labour aspects in public procurement promises to put labour and social law back on the agenda in a legal/political sense. As has already been identified, labour and social law has been subject to deregulatory pressure across the EU in recent years for a number of different reasons. There is the action of the Court of Justice in bringing national labour law under the lens of the internal market, as described in section II. There are also a number of pressures arising directly or indirectly from the financial crisis. Against this deregulatory background,

[48] McCrudden, above n 11, 577.
[49] Semple, above n 11, para 7.02.

it might be suggested that any measures that promote and make visible labour and social law are desirable. The inclusion of social and labour standards might also have beneficial effects in the sense of encouraging the development of corporate social responsibility. The argument proceeds that through the inclusion of social and labour standards in public procurement legislation, companies are encouraged to establish a sense of responsibility, which extends beyond the pure maximisation of profit and towards groups other than shareholders.[50] Through public procurement procedures and decisions, companies become involved in thinking about the communities in which they are founded, and about their wider consumer base. Corporations are encouraged to see costs over a longer-term asset cycle, and to consider the benefits of balancing economic, social and environmental objectives. Indeed, there is a body of literature that suggests that the development of corporate social responsibility successfully enmeshes economic progress and the development of both labour and social standards. By adopting socially responsible practices, corporations can build a favourable public relations profile and thus enhance their consumer base. At the same time, corporate social responsibility improves and enhances human rights, labour rights and labour standards.[51]

At the most progressive end of the corporate social responsibility agenda is the development of social enterprises: 'businesses with shareholder owners that seek to address social problems by combining the dynamism of capitalized for-profit enterprise with the intentionally pro-social orientation of non-profit organisations'.[52] In the social enterprise, the commitment to the social 'mission' is supposedly more foundational, and hence less likely to be ignored or sacrificed to the profit motive. There are certainly ways in which the procurement directives encourage social enterprise. There is a new ability to reserve contracts for health, cultural or social services for competition by enterprises with a public service mission.[53] Interestingly, this latter provision was lobbied for by the UK, where social enterprises are seen as effective means of maintaining the character of public services when they are contracted out.[54] Furthermore, Article 20 of the 2014 Public Procurement

[50] A Voiculescu, 'Another Type of Deficit: Human Rights, Corporate Social Responsibility and the Shaping of the European Union's Linkage Strategy' (2014) 16(1) *European Journal of Law Reform* 770.

[51] L Compa, 'Corporate Social Responsibility and Workers' Rights' (2008) 30(1) *Comparative Labor Law and Policy Journal* 1.

[52] A Page and R Katz, 'Is Social Enterprise the New Corporate Social Responsibility?' (2011) 34 *Seattle University Law Review* 1351, 1361. See also the contribution by Boeger in ch 7 of this book.

[53] Art 77 of the 2014 Public Procurement Directive.

[54] An alternative interpretation of this lobbying activity is that Art 77 enables the Government to pursue its strategy of 'mutualisation' of public services (privatisation through spin-offs). See Chartered Institute of Public Finance and Accountancy, 'Research into the Public Services Mutuals Sector' (February 2017), at www.gov.uk/government/uploads/system/uploads/attachment_data/file/603356/Research_into_the_Public_Service_Mutuals.pdf.

Directive extends the ability of governments to reserve competition for sheltered workshops or employment programmes where at least 30 per cent of the employees are disabled or disadvantaged workers.[55]

However, there are some major problems in the ability of the 2014 Public Procurement Directive to deliver corporate social responsibility, and hence a greater commitment to labour and social standards, by companies over the long term. First of all, recital 97 to the 2014 Public Procurement Directive specifically spells out the fact that contracting authorities should not be allowed to require tenderers to have a certain corporate social or environmental responsibility policy in place.[56] Rather, there must be an assessment of each individual company's capabilities on a case-by-case basis: it is the tender and not the tenderer that is the unit of assessment.[57] This position is reinforced by the reference in the provisions of the 2014 Public Procurement Directive dealing with selection, award and performance criteria to the need for a 'link' to the subject matter of the contract. This implies that contracting authorities are obliged to focus only on the goods, services or works they are purchasing and not on wider corporate practices.[58] Indeed, the pervasiveness of the link to the subject-matter criteria in the 2014 Public Procurement Directive also strengthens the assertion that the Court of Justice will deal with the link to the subject matter strictly and restrictively. This serves to discredit previous case law, which has suggested that in certain circumstances, (award) criteria need not be linked to the subject matter of the contract.[59]

More importantly, the corporate social responsibility agenda shares the problems that have contributed to the deregulatory stance towards labour law/standards outlined in section I. In this agenda, labour and social standards are seen as secondary considerations compared to economic profit. At times of economic stress, therefore, labour and social standards are the first to suffer. Furthermore, the development of corporate social responsibility proceeds on a discretionary and voluntary basis, directed by codes of practice rather than mandatory prescriptions. There is also no monitoring mechanism of these corporate practices, as such, and no effective mechanisms of enforcement, given that standards are self-policed.

Section III.B following will look in more detail at the provisions of the 2014 Public Procurement Directive that relate to labour law and labour

[55] Semple, above n 11, para 7.43.

[56] This recital refers back to the Judgment of 10 May 2012, *Commission v Netherlands*, Case C-368/10, EU:C:2012:284 (*Dutch Coffee*), where this was established.

[57] Semple, above n 11, para 7.48.

[58] ibid, para 7.56.

[59] See, eg, Judgment of 26 September 2000, *Commission v France*, Case C-225/98, EU:C:2000:494. See also the commentary in M Martens and S de Margerie, 'The Link to the Subject-Matter of the Contract in Green and Social Procurement' (2013) 8 *European Procurement and Public Private Partnership Law Review* 1.

and social standards. It will develop some themes of this and the previous section to suggest the weaknesses of public procurement regulation as a means of making a meaningful difference to labour and social standards.

B. The Difficulties of Inclusion: Labour Law as Exception

In the 2014 Public Procurement Directive, labour and social standards are included as an exception to economic rules. This is made clear in the preamble, and in the treatment of the rules relating to labour and social standards in the main body of the Directive. In the opening sections of the preamble, the primary function of the 2014 Public Procurement Directive is set out. Public procurement is stated to be one of the key strategies to push forward the Europe 2020 strategy; it is 'one of the market-based instruments to be used to achieve smart, sustainable and inclusive growth while ensuring the most efficient use of public funds'.[60] The modernisation of the law in this area is deemed necessary to increase the efficiency of public spending, to increase the participation of more small and medium-sized enterprises in the process, whilst at the same time allowing procurers to make better use of public procurement in support of common societal goals. In this formulation, there is no suggestion that there is a connection between societal goals and economic progress: the improvement of social conditions flows from the more efficient use of public funds, but has no economic benefit in and of itself.[61]

This position is reinforced by the specific reference to the inclusion of social and economic criteria in public procurement decisions in recitals 36 to 40 of the preamble. Recital 36 outlines that under normal competition conditions, social enterprises would not usually be able to gain public contracts. However, given the importance of employment and occupation to social integration, specific provisions to reserve contracts for these kinds of businesses are necessary. The further provisions continue in this vein: that labour and social laws are important for social integration but are not of independent economic benefit. They are a side concern:

> [T]he observance of the environmental, social and labour law provisions should be performed at the relevant stages of the procurement procedure, when applying the general principles governing the choice of participants and the award of contracts, when applying the exclusion criteria and when applying the provisions concerning abnormally low tenders.[62]

[60] Preamble to the 2014 Public Procurement Directive, recital 2.

[61] This is discussed further in A Sánchez-Graells, 'Truly competitive public procurement as a Europe 2020 lever: what role for the principle of competition in moderating horizontal policies?' (2016) 22(2) *European Public Law Journal* 377.

[62] Preamble to the 2014 Public Procurement Directive, recital 40.

There is also no attempt to separate the value of social inclusion measures (the reintegration of disabled persons) from the wider benefits to be obtained from the instigation and strengthening of labour laws (dignity, worker protection, etc).

In the main body of the 2014 Public Procurement Directive, the dominance of the economic over the social is also consistently apparent. Article 18(2) sets out the basic principle that in the performance of public contracts, economic operators must comply with applicable environmental, social and labour law obligations established by Union law, national law, collective agreements or relevant international conventions. However, the provisions relating to the duty on contracting authorities to ensure that compliance are set out in discretionary rather than mandatory terms, except where it can be shown that tenders are abnormally low as a result. For example, under Article 57(2) it is stated that contracting authorities 'may' exclude, or 'may be required' to exclude, from the public procurement procedure any economic operator who is in violation of the obligations under Article 18(2). Mandatory exclusion is only effective where the contracting authority can prove that the economic operator has been involved in child labour or trafficking (Article 57(1)). A 'final judgment' is necessary to prove that involvement. The discretionary language is also apparent in relation to the consideration of social/labour aspects as part of contract award or contract performance criteria. In relation to award criteria, contracting authorities have the discretion to consider 'social aspects' as part of their evaluation of the most economically advantageous tender (labour considerations are not specifically mentioned).[63] In relation to performance criteria, contracting authorities 'may' lay down special conditions relating to the performance of the contract, and these 'may' include social or 'employment-related' conditions (the latter being a specific addition to the 2014 Public Procurement Directive in comparison to earlier versions). None of those provisions includes a mandatory consideration of employment standards.

Furthermore, even where the provisions in the 2014 Public Procurement Directive are mandatory, their scope is very narrow. As already mentioned, mandatory exclusion from selection only applies where a contracting authority can prove that the operator has been found guilty of child labour or human trafficking. Mandatory exclusion does not pertain to any of the other obligations under Article 18(2), except where the contracting authority can prove that a tender is priced abnormally low as a result of non-compliance with these obligations. Also, in labour law terms, the scope of Article 18(2) is narrow. In this article, compliance is required with the 'international environmental, social and labour law provisions listed in Annex X'. In Annex X only eight ILO Conventions are mentioned, and there are some

[63] Art 67 of the 2014 Public Procurement Directive.

notable exclusions. Four of those conventions concern child and forced labour, the very worst abuses of labour law. Only four concern more mainstream labour law concerns, and there is no mention at all of the ILO Convention on labour clauses in public contracts.[64] Indeed, it could be argued that a number of ILO Conventions not mentioned in Annex X form part of the culture and legal order of EU Member States, and so should be included as matter of course. Such Conventions might include Convention 81 (labour inspection), Convention 95 (protection of wages), Convention 102 (social security, minimum standards), Convention 138 (minimum age), and Convention 155 (occupational health and safety).[65]

There are further elements in the main body of the 2014 Public Procurement Directive that demonstrate the relegation of labour standards and the dominance of economic considerations. It became clear during the negotiation procedure relating to the Directive that there were many more articles of the 2014 Public Procurement Directive in which social or labour considerations could have been included. This is demonstrated by the response of the European Parliament to the 2011 proposal for a new public procurement directive, drafted during the course of the ordinary legislative procedure. In this response, the rapporteur argued that the Commission's legislative proposal did 'not go far enough, particularly on social aspects'.[66] The rapporteur also suggested that it should be made clear at the outset of the Directive that a central aim of that process was the development of social sustainability. To that end, a new provision was included in Article 2(22), which set out a definition of a 'socially sustainable production process' as 'a production process in which the provision of works, services and supplies complies with health and safety, social and labour law, rules and standards, in particular with regard to the principle of equal treatment in the workplace'. This principle was then referred to in a number of the later provisions.[67] Furthermore, the rapporteur argued that there should be a more comprehensive attempt in the legislation to 'ensure compliance with social standards at *all stages* of the public procurement procedure'.[68] Accordingly, he suggested that the provisions on technical specifications should give more scope to contracting authorities to achieve sustainability objectives. Amendments were made to

[64] Labour Clauses (Public Contracts) Convention, 1949 (No 94).

[65] Labour Inspection Convention, 1947 (No 81); Protection of Wages Convention, 1949 (No 95); Social Security (Minimum Standards) Convention, 1952 (No 102); Minimum Age Convention, 1973 (No 138); Occupational Safety and Health Convention, 1981 (No 155). See E Van den Abeele, *The Reform of the EU's Public Procurement Directives: a Missed Opportunity?*, ETUI Working Paper 2012.11, at ssrn.com/abstract=2202717.

[66] European Parliament, Draft European Parliament Legislative Resolution on the proposal for a directive of the European Parliament and of the Council on public procurement COM (2011) 0896—C7-0006/2012—2011/0438 (COD) 87.

[67] For example, Art 40(1), paras 1–5.

[68] European Parliament, above n 66, 87.

the text of the proposed preamble recital 27 (now 74) to reflect this change, and to the text of Article 40(3)(a) (now Article 42(3)(a)).[69] None of these amendments was included in the final draft.

There is a final area worthy of investigation. One particular innovation in the new 2014 Public Procurement Directive is the idea of life-cycle costing. This is generally considered a more sophisticated cost-assessment technique, which allows tenders to be considered on the basis of qualitative rather than quantitative criteria alone.[70] However, currently, the life-cycle costing extends only to the consideration of environmental externalities,[71] and social and labour law costs may not be taken into account in this process.[72] Although this exclusion is clear, there appears to be little rationale for it beyond the mere relegation of social or labour considerations. Indeed, in the European Parliament rapporteur's amendments, the social sustainable production process was placed alongside life-cycle costing as a consideration in the meeting of the most economically advantageous tender requirement.[73] Likewise, the 2014 Public Procurement Directive introduces a number of instances in which certification of certain standards are required, but this certification only extends to economic and financial standing, quality assurance and environmental standards (apart from in the case of an abnormally low tender).[74] The rapporteur suggested that this system of certification should be extended to proving wider compliance with social or labour law standards, 'defined by Union and national legislation and by collective agreements which apply in the place where the work, service or supply is to be performed'.[75]

It appears, then, from this analysis that although some progress has been made in allowing public authorities to promote a more socially sustainable public procurement process, the provisions of the 2014 Public Procurement Directive have their limitations in this regard, and a much more pervasive and comprehensive approach to the inclusion of social and labour standards could have been taken. However, this minimalist approach is perhaps not

[69] The rapporteur also attempted to strengthen the social aspects of the proposed Directive, by turning the discretionary nature of the provisions relating to the consideration of social and labour standards into mandatory requirements. For example, there was an amendment to the proposed Art 54 (2) (now Art 57(2)) to the effect that where it is established that the tenderer does not comply with its social and labour law obligations, that tenderer should automatically be excluded from the process. However, none of these suggestions was incorporated into the final documents.

[70] Semple, above n 11, para 4.41.

[71] Art 68(1)(b) of the 2014 Public Procurement Directive.

[72] D Dragos and B Neamtu, 'Sustainable Public Procurement: Life-Cycle Costing in the New EU Directive Proposal' (2013) 8(1) *European Procurement & Public Private Partnership Law Review* 19, 25.

[73] The amendment is to the proposed Art 66 (now Art 67) of the 2014 Public Procurement Directive.

[74] Arts 60 and 62 of the 2014 Public Procurement Directive.

[75] Amendment to Art 61(2)(a) (now Art 62) of the 2014 Public Procurement Directive.

surprising given the overall trends at EU level towards the domination of economic over social considerations, and the specific grounding of the 2014 Public Procurement Directive in the Europe 2020 strategy. The problem is that these views are potentially damaging to the labour law project. They are damaging because they suggest that social considerations are of lesser value than economic considerations, to be rejected by discretion rather than having a potential contribution to make to the sustainability of economic investment. The independence of social value is rejected (social value is determined by economic benefit) and labour and social considerations are included as an exception to economic rules. Labour law in particular loses it position: it is included by exclusion.[76]

IV. LABOUR LAW AS EXCLUSION IN THE CASE LAW OF THE COURT OF JUSTICE

An interesting question arises as to how the Court of Justice has treated the operation of the social provisions of the successive iterations of public procurement directives. Of course, no case law has yet arisen on the current formulation of the directives, due to their very recent date of implementation. However, in many respects, the content of the previous incarnations of the 2014 Public Procurement Directive was similar, and so the interpretation of the provisions in previous incarnations could give some indication of the future treatment of social clauses in the current directives. In fact, however, it appears that the case law that has arisen on these social/employment clauses specifically is minimal, and the decisions are not particularly helpful. They suggest that the social and economic aims of the directives are compatible, without fully investigating that compatibility in practice, or the compatibility of those aims with EU law in general. As a result, they suggest an outcome that differs from the treatment of social/labour law clauses in public procurement when wider internal market considerations are taken into account.[77]

The first case of note is that of *Beentjes*.[78] This concerned the legality of a requirement by contracting authorities that contractors employ long-term unemployed persons. The Court of Justice analysed this requirement as a performance condition and held that, as such, this was prima facie compatible with the Public Procurement Directive. However, that condition 'must comply with all the relevant provisions of [Union] law, in particular

[76] Agamben, above n 12.

[77] R Caranta, 'Sustainable Public Procurement in the EU' in R Caranta and M Trybus (eds), *The Law of Green and Social Procurement in Europe* (Copenaghen, DJØF, 2010) 15, 19–26.

[78] Judgment of 20 September 1988, *Beentjes v State of the Netherlands*, Case C-31/87, EU:C:1988:422.

the prohibitions flowing from the principles laid down in the Treaty in regard to the right of establishment and the freedom to provide services'.[79] This meant that the inclusion of this condition must have 'no direct or indirect discriminatory effect on tenderers from other Member States'.[80] The Court did not rule on whether such a criterion would in practice have a discriminatory effect, leaving it for the national court to decide on this matter. Similarly, in the case of *Commission v France* (*Nord-Pas-de-Calais*),[81] the Court was asked to decide whether an award criterion relating to the promotion of employment was in breach of the procurement directive then in force. Again, the Court of Justice held that there was no reason in principle why such a requirement would be incompatible with the directive, provided that it was consistent with 'all the fundamental principles of [Union] law, in particular the principle of non-discrimination flowing from the provisions of the Treaty on the right of establishment and the freedom to provide services'.[82] The Court did not decide the question whether such a criterion was in fact discriminatory, as it stated that this point was not brought before it by the Commission.[83]

It appears that had the question of discrimination been considered by the Court, it would have had little option but to consider these kinds of clauses discriminatory. Local employment clauses by their nature discriminate against tenderers in other Member States and their potential employees, and would in that case fall foul of the principle of non-discrimination in the Treaty.[84] The question is whether such treatment could be justified either under the procurement directives or under wider Treaty provisions. The point concerning justification under the procurement directives has been considered outside the labour context, with some evidence that discriminatory measures could be permitted in some contexts.[85] It appears, though, that it is unlikely that this kind of approach would be taken in the labour context. A number of cases have demonstrated the reluctance of the Court of Justice to uphold local wage clauses where those are imposed in the context of public procurement. For example, the case of *Rüffert*[86] concerned a Lower Saxony law that public building contracts over a certain threshold would be awarded by Lower Saxony public authorities only to those contractors who agreed to respect minimum rates of pay as set out in a collective agreement. The contract was awarded to a German company,

[79] ibid, para 29.

[80] ibid para 36.

[81] Judgment of 26 September 2000, *Commission v France (Nord-Pas-de-Calais)*, Case C-225/98, EU:C:2000:494.

[82] ibid, para 50.

[83] ibid, para 53.

[84] P Oliver, 'When, If Ever, Can Restrictions on Free Movement be Justified on Economic Grounds?' (2016) 41(2) *EL Rev* 147, 167. See also the contribution by Sánchez-Graells in ch 6 of this book.

[85] Judgment of 13 March 2001, *PreussenElecktra*, Case C-379/98, EU:C:2001:160.

[86] Judgment of 3 April 2008, *Rüffert*, Case C-346/06, EU:C:2008:189.

which then subcontracted the work to a Polish undertaking. That undertaking was accused of being in breach of the contract condition by underpaying workers and its contract was terminated. The Polish company challenged the validity of the Lower Saxony law on the basis that it breached Article 49 of the Treaty on freedom of establishment and was also incompatible with the Posted Workers Directive. The Court found that the Posted Workers Directive could not support the Lower Saxony law because it referred to collective agreements that were not 'universally applicable' (as required by Article 3(8) of the Posted Workers Directive). Furthermore, the provisions in the Posted Workers Directive that allowed the 'application of terms and conditions which are more favourable to workers' were not applicable. The law was also in breach of Article 49 and could not be justified.[87]

Rüffert suggested that laws that set compliance with terms and conditions of employment beyond the minimum standards in the Posted Workers Directive would be in breach of EU law.[88] It also suggested that public authorities will not be able to insist on compliance with special labour standards, applicable only to public contractors, at any stage of the procurement process.[89] This position was confirmed in the case of *Bundesdruckerei*.[90] In this case, a Polish company challenged the imposition of minimum wage rates set by Germany in relation to a contract carried out in Poland (where minimum wage rates were lower). The company argued that this minimum wage legislation constituted a restriction within the meaning of Article 56 TFEU. On the one hand, the Court accepted that such legislation could in principle be justified on the basis of the protection of workers and avoiding social dumping. However, the Court found that the measure was disproportionate in this particular case for two main reasons. First, the legislation applied to public contracts only, and there was 'no information to suggest that employees working in the private sector are not in need of the same wage protection as those working in the context of public contracts'.[91] Secondly, the measure bore no relation to the cost of living in other Member States. As the cost of living in Poland was significantly lower than in Germany, the imposition of the minimum wage in this context could not be justified by the legitimate objective of guaranteeing reasonable remuneration in the context of the performance of public contracts.[92]

[87] For example, because the rate of pay guaranteed was even greater than that provided for in national legislation, and the scope of the collective agreement was limited to only part of the construction sector falling within a particular geographical area.

[88] C McCrudden, 'The Rüffert Case and Public Procurement' in M Cremona (ed), *Market Integration and Public Services in the European Union*' (Oxford, Oxford University Press, 2011) 128.

[89] A Koukiadaki, 'The Far Reaching Implications of the Laval Quartet: The Case of the UK Living Wage' (2014) 43(2) *Industrial Law Journal* 91, 101.

[90] Judgment of 18 September 2014, *Bundesdruckerei*, Case C-549/13, EU:C:2014:2235.

[91] ibid, para 31.

[92] Ibid para 18.

Although these judgments were promoted on the basis of preventing discrimination, they were formulated on a particularly economic view of discrimination in the context of the internal market. The idea was that home companies and their workers should not be prevented from participation in the public procurement process by virtue of their nationality. All firms should be able to use their competitive advantage to its best effect. Furthermore, in these cases the Court consistently emphasised the unjust inequality between private sector and public sector workers in terms of wages. It suggested that differential treatment between private and public sector workers was discriminatory and could not be justified. Of course, these judgments do not prevent other kinds of discrimination arising. They suggest that posted workers can be treated less favourably in terms of their working conditions than home-state workers. At the same time, the judgments encourage 'reverse discrimination' against home-state firms.[93] These firms cannot avoid the effect of 'home' labour conditions in the procurement condition, and so will not be able to compete with posting companies. This kind of 'reverse discrimination' is not considered by the courts in this context.

The more recent case of *RegioPost*[94] adopts a potentially more favourable approach to the promotion of labour standards in the context of public procurement and the internal market. This case concerned a legislative provision that laid down a minimum rate of pay for workers engaged on public contracts. It was argued that (following *Rüffert*) this legislative provision could not be applied, since it was discriminatory (it applied to public contracts only) and it was not universally applicable. It was also argued that such a measure was in breach of Article 56 TFEU, in that it constituted an additional economic burden that impeded the freedom of posting companies to provide services in the host Member State. Such an additional burden could not be justified. The Court disagreed. First, it held that the rule in question was universally applicable because there was no other national legislation which imposed a lower wage for the workers under consideration. This could not be brought into question by the fact that the wage applied only to public rather than private sector workers, since such an argument relied on the categorisation in Article 3(8) of the Posted Workers Directive, which was relevant to collective agreements only. Secondly, it held that a condition laying down a minimum rate of pay for public sector workers could justify a breach of Article 56 TFEU in this context. That justification was upheld even though it applied only to public rather than private sector workers, because the limitation of the scope of the national measure was a 'simple consequence' of the fact that there are rules of EU law specific to public procurement.[95]

[93] Koukiadaki, above n 89, 102.
[94] Judgment of 17 November 2015, *RegioPost*, Case C-115/14, EU:C:2015:760.
[95] ibid, para 65.

Although this judgment does suggest a more favourable approach to the imposition of labour standards in public procurement, its impact is likely to be limited for a number of reasons. For a start, it is entirely complicit with the view that the imposition of higher sectoral standards through collective agreements is incompatible with the aims of the internal market (and the public procurement legislation). It is only as a result of accepting this view that it is able to distinguish the *Rüffert* judgment. Furthermore, it does not question the idea that that the Posted Workers Directive should allow only minimum wage standards; it suggests that the relevant law in this case was the minimum wage standard to which the Posted Workers Directive should apply. Of course, both of these positions are reflective of an economic-based assessment of the value (or lack of value) of labour standards and systems. The first position represents a disregard for the importance of collective action in labour law systems.[96] The suggestion is that such collective action is a restraint on economic performance, with no justifiable independent value or benefit for workers. The second suggests that the improvement in wage standards is not something that should be pursued in its own right in the context of the internal market. This position runs counter to certain of the new social provisions of the Lisbon Treaty, which encourage the development of a 'social market economy' and the improvement of living and working standards across the EU. It also runs counter to the principle of the Posted Workers Directive as a directive, a mechanism through which Member States traditionally can go beyond the minimum provisions.[97]

Indeed, there have recently been proposals to amend the Posted Workers Directive in light of the case law described above. It is argued that the Posted Workers Directive has not improved labour standards across the EU, with posted workers on lower rates of pay permitted to undercut local workers on higher wages. It has also contributed to a downward pressure on negotiated terms and conditions, as higher wage rates set by collective agreements will not apply, in the majority of situations, to posted workers. Lastly, the Posted Workers Directive has not contributed to social cohesion, since there is resentment about differential wage rates amongst 'foreign' and local workers.[98] The new proposal suggests a more labour-orientated approach to posted workers, which provides better protection for workers, more transparency, and a 'level playing field between domestic and posting firms while in full respect of Member States' wage-bargaining systems'.[99]

[96] On this point, see the contribution by Novitz in ch 11 of this book.

[97] McCrudden, above n 88, 128.

[98] E Crasta, 'Guten Tag Pet, Reforming the Posted Workers Directive', 10 March 2016, at touchstoneblog.org.uk/2016/03/guten-tag-pet-reforming-the-posted-workers-directive/.

[99] Directorate for Employment, Social Affairs and Inclusion, 'The Commission presents reform of posting of workers—towards a fair and truly European Labour Market (8 March 2016), at ec.europa.eu/social/main.jsp?langId=en&catId=89&newsId=2488&furtherNews=yes.

The proposal suggests that rules on 'remuneration' applied generally to local workers must also be granted to posted workers (including bonuses or allowances). Furthermore, national rules on temporary agency workers must be applied to posted workers, and if the posting exceeds 24 months, the labour law conditions of the Member State will have to be applied.[100]

V. CONCLUSIONS

In the context of the deregulation of labour law across the EU, the added options for the inclusion of labour and social considerations in public contracting might be seen as a welcome development. Employment-related conditions are explicitly mentioned in the 2014 Public Procurement Directive, and contracting authorities are given a greater discretion to evaluate tenders on the basis of their labour and social credentials. There is also a clarification in the 2014 Public Procurement Directive in terms of the stages at which labour and social criteria can be taken into account. Social inclusion measures are given more traction, with greater scope for reserved contracts and preferential treatment of suppliers aiming to ensure the integration of disadvantaged persons into the labour market. It might be suggested that these kinds of measures carry benefits for governments, companies and EU citizens alike. They allow governments to demonstrate accountability in the management of public finance, and achieve economic and social development simultaneously. They allow companies to engage with the sustainability agenda too. This not only improves the local social and working environment, but also contributes to the building of a reputation for a commitment to sustainability which can feed into customer demand.

The problem is that labour and social considerations are a sideshow to the economic aims of the 2014 Public Procurement Directive. The Directive is an instrument designed to further the smooth running of the internal market, and to ensure that public services follow its ethos and rules. It is not an instrument of social development, just as it is not a directive concerned with promoting labour law per se. This carries a number of effects for labour law. First, in very general terms, it means labour law concerns are 'lumped together' with other social aims, which may or may not coincide with labour law's objectives. It also means that, along with other social provisions, labour law is not considered of independent (economic) value. It is incorporated into the 2014 Public Procurement Directive as a concession to economic rules, with the assumption that such a 'cost' may be necessary to achieve other (social) goals. Those social goals are not in themselves defined. This is a disbenefit for the labour law project, given the assertion amongst

100 COM (2016) 128.

many labour lawyers that these kinds of rules not only have economic value, but also serve a number of other goals, not limited to social inclusion. Secondly, in more specific terms, it means that the value of the individual provisions of the 2014 Public Procurement Directive to labour law and social development may be questioned. As labour law is considered secondary to economic aims, there are few provisions in the 2014 Public Procurement Directive making the assessment of labour law credentials mandatory. Moreover, the provisions that are mandatory in relation to the consideration of social/labour conditions are narrowly defined. Only the very worst abuses of labour law, for example, would allow contracting authorities to reject a tender on that basis. It is difficult to see how this would have more than a marginal impact on labour standards across Europe.

It appears that the new provisions of the 2014 Public Procurement Directive contribute to rather than counteract the tendency at EU level to prioritise economic over social considerations. This prioritisation may be in line with the foundations of the EU, but it cannot be a valid direction for its future. The EU is too involved in the 'social' to withdraw now. Indeed, this withdrawal of the EU from its social project is not only of academic concern: it may shape the assessment of its entire legitimacy as a common political goal.

9

Government as a Socially Responsible Market Actor After RegioPost

ACL DAVIES*

I. INTRODUCTION

OVER THE PAST 30 or 40 years, governments around the world have sought to make greater use of the private sector to supply the infrastructure, goods and services required for the achievement of public policy objectives.[1] There is widespread acceptance of the view that it is often more cost-effective to put tasks out to tender, and to rely on the expertise of private firms—subject to competitive pressure when contracts are awarded or renewed—to deliver in accordance with agreed budget targets and quality standards, than to attempt to tackle everything 'in house'. At the same time, there has been a greater focus on taking what might be termed a 'commercial' approach to procurement, in which the government focuses solely on achieving value for money and does not become 'distracted' by other considerations.

Procurement has also become the subject of international and regional regulation, through the United Nations Convention Against Corruption (UNCAC),[2] the Government Procurement Agreement (GPA),[3] and through the EU Treaties and public procurement directives.[4] These regulatory regimes

* I am grateful to the conference participants for a lively discussion and to Albert Sánchez-Graells for his detailed comments on a previous draft of this chapter. Responsibility for any remaining errors and, importantly, the opinions expressed, remains my own. This chapter considers developments up to 19 June 2017.

[1] For ease of explanation, this chapter focuses primarily on central government and does not address in detail the issues surrounding the use by local authorities of social goals in procurement, which can raise complex issues of domestic constitutional law in some countries.

[2] UNCAC (2003), adopted by General Assembly Resolution 58/4 of 31 October 2003, Art 9(1), obliges states to establish a procurement system.

[3] World Trade Organisation, Agreement on Government Procurement (1994), Revised Agreement on Government Procurement (2012).

[4] The current provisions are those of the 2014 Public Procurement Package (Directive 2014/24/EU of the European Parliament and of the Council of 26 February 2014 on public

have sought to open up procurement markets, traditionally dominated by national firms, to competitors from other states. One way in which they have sought to do this, historically at least, is by minimising the discretion of public authorities to do anything other than award the contract to the cheapest bid.

These two broad trends conflict with a much older tradition in public procurement, in which procurement is seen as an opportunity for the government to pursue or reinforce broader public policy objectives.[5] For example, if the government has a policy of promoting equality between men and women, it might include a clause in government contracts requiring contractors to conduct a gender pay gap audit. On this view, procurement is an opportunity for the government to reinforce existing public policies through contractual techniques, or to go beyond such policies by acting as a 'model citizen' itself.

The European Union (EU) has struggled to reconcile these various policy developments. On the one hand, Member State governments spend significant sums of money (around 14 per cent of EU GDP[6]) through procurement, making this area an important component in the creation of the internal market. This has resulted in legislation and judicial decisions seeking to open up national procurement markets to firms from other Member States.[7] On the other hand, several governments have longstanding policies of pursuing social and environmental goals through procurement, and of course the EU itself is not committed to the pursuit of economic objectives to the exclusion of all other considerations.[8] Over time, the procurement directives (and Commission guidance) have become more accepting of the use of procurement for these ends.[9] The *RegioPost* decision[10] is significant for its

procurement and repealing Directive 2004/18/EC [2014] OJ L 94/65 (the 2014 Public Procurement Directive), together with Directive 2014/23/EU of the European Parliament and of the Council of 26 February 2014 on the award of concession contracts [2014] OJ L94/1, and Directive 2014/25/EU of the European Parliament and of the Council of 26 February 2014 on procurement by entities operating in the water, energy, transport and postal services sectors and repealing Directive 2004/17/EC [2014] OJ L94/243). Contracts not governed by the directives may still be subject to Treaty rules, eg, Art 56 of the Treaty on the Functioning of the European Union (TFEU) [2012] OJ C326/47 on the freedom to provide services.

[5] See, generally, C McCrudden, *Buying Social Justice: Equality, Government Procurement, and Legal Change* (Oxford, Oxford University Press, 2007).

[6] European Commission, Public Procurement overview (undated), at ec.europa.eu/growth/single-market/public-procurement_en.

[7] Above n 4. For a historical overview, see S Arrowsmith, *The Law of Public and Utilities Procurement. Regulation in the EU and UK*, vol 1 (3rd edn, London, Sweet & Maxwell, 2014) ch 3.

[8] See, eg, Art 3 of the Treaty on European Union (TEU) [2012] OJ C326/13.

[9] For a detailed history up to 2007, see McCrudden, above n 5, chs 10–14. For more recent developments, see European Commission, *Buying Social: a Guide to Taking Account of Social Considerations in Public Procurement* (2010); European Commission, *Supporting social responsibility in the economy through public procurement*, at ec.europa.eu/growth/tools-databases/newsroom/cf/itemdetail.cfm?item_id=8667&lang=en&title=Supporting-social-responsibility-in-the-economy-through-public-procurement. For analysis of the scope for using the current directives for social purposes, see C Barnard, 'To Boldly Go: Social Clauses in Public Procurement' (2017) 46(2) *Industrial Law Journal* 208.

[10] Judgment of 17 November 2015, *RegioPost*, Case C-115/14, EU:C:2015:760.

recognition of the changing legislative climate and its reversal of a key component of the reasoning in the *Rüffert* decision,[11] which was highly restrictive of the use of public procurement to pursue worker-protective objectives.

In this chapter, I shall seek to defend the idea that governments should be permitted to engage in procurement markets in socially responsible ways. At the very least, governments should be expected to promote compliance with applicable legislation. Arguably, governments should be permitted to pursue policies going beyond this, should they wish to do so, and to act as a role model for the 'good employer' when placing contracts. Importantly, although socially responsible procurement may impose additional costs on firms, these can be reflected in the contract price. Thus, in contrast to other types of government intervention in the market, such as regulation, procurement is distinctive for the fact that the government must pay for its preferences.[12] From this perspective, while the decision in *RegioPost* is to be welcomed for creating greater scope for the use of minimum wage conditions in government contracts, the reasoning in the case falls some way short of a proper understanding of the role of social goals in procurement, with the result that EU law continues to over-regulate this aspect of government activity to the detriment of national autonomy.[13]

II. SOCIAL GOALS IN PROCUREMENT

The use of contracts to further government policies not immediately related to the contract in question is one of the most controversial topics in government contracting.[14] In this section, I explain the controversy and offer a defence of the practice. Although governments may use procurement to enforce a range of different policies, including human rights and environmental standards, I focus on labour standards for ease of explanation.

There are many different examples of labour standards that are, or have been, used in public procurement. These include compliance with minimum wage legislation, or with higher wage requirements set specifically for government contracts, a requirement to have comprehensive race and sex equality policies in place, or an obligation to employ a proportion of long-term unemployed workers in the performance of the contract. A government may use these requirements in different ways at different points in the

[11] Judgment of 3 April 2008, *Rüffert*, Case C-346/06, EU:C:2008:189.

[12] I do not claim that procurement is unique in this regard—state aid shares this characteristic—but space precludes any elaboration of this comparison in the present chapter.

[13] It is worth noting that governments' enthusiasm for social procurement varies widely: see, eg, A Ludlow, 'Social Procurement: Policy and Practice' (2016) 7(3) *European Labour Law Journal* 479.

[14] For a comprehensive account, see McCrudden, above n 5. The discussion here draws on ACL Davies, *The Public Law of Government Contracts* (Oxford, Oxford University Press, 2008) ch 9.

contract's life cycle. During the procurement process, the government may take account of a firm's willingness to comply with social goals (or its past history in this regard) when deciding whether to allow it to bid or whether to award it the contract. Once the contract has been awarded, the government has the option of including social goals as terms of the contract, and using contractual remedies to address any failure on the part of the contractor to comply.

There are two different ways in which the government might seek to use contracts in relation to social policies: to reinforce existing legal requirements, or to enforce requirements that go beyond the current law. The point of the latter is obvious: the government can use the firm's desire to win or retain government business as leverage to enforce higher standards. The former may seem superfluous, since bidders and contractors are already obliged to comply with the general law, but again, the additional leverage generated by the contracting process may be used to make up for shortfalls in the way that the general law is enforced. This is of particular relevance in a country like the UK, where there is no general labour inspectorate and substantial reliance is placed on litigation by individuals as the main method of enforcing labour law, but it also has the more general advantage of reducing the risk that the government appears to be complicit in the contractor's infringements.

The use of social goals in contracting has attracted a great deal of opposition.[15] One concern is that contracts may not be the most efficient way of achieving those goals. For example, it may be cheaper and more effective to tackle unemployment by providing publicly-funded training schemes, rather than by requiring government contractors to hire the unemployed to perform contracts. Another concern is that social policies may give a considerable degree of discretion to those involved in the contract award process. For example, assessing firms' equality policies is a complex task, which does not lend itself to objective criteria. Discretion is a problem because it increases the chances of procurement's being used for 'improper' purposes. International systems of procurement regulation, including the relevant EU directives, have sought to limit governments' ability to use procurement for protectionist purposes: in other words, to favour national firms in their contract award decisions.[16] Historically, the EU regime tried to limit the use of social goals because, by increasing officials' discretion, they might create opportunities for disguised protectionism. Social goals have also been criticised for their potential to act as instruments of oppression by

[15] For an overview see, generally, McCrudden, above n 5, 114–22; and in the context of the cases under consideration in this contribution, A Sánchez-Graells, 'Regulatory Substitution between Labour and Public Procurement Law: the EU's Shifting Approach to Enforcing Labour Standards in Public Contracts' (2018) 24(2) *European Public Law* forthcoming.

[16] Reflecting their basis in internal market law (Art 114 TFEU).

restricting firms' freedom of action, particularly where they go beyond what the general law requires.

However, there are a number of possible justifications for considering social goals in government contracting.[17] The strongest argument for the enforcement of the existing law through procurement is an argument about the Rule of Law and promoting trust in government. Where compliance with particular labour standards is required by law, the government should itself comply with the standards it seeks to enforce against others. It is not unreasonable to expect this to include scrutinising the compliance of its contractors. Of course, one response to this might be to say that the government should rely instead on the normal methods of enforcement in its system of labour law, and work to improve them where they fall short. But there are two reasons to question this. One is that there seems little to be gained by one part of the government machine—a labour inspectorate, for example—pursuing another part of the government machine, such as a contractor, in respect of labour violations. This kind of 'silo' mentality is hardly likely to foster trust in government. Another is that governments are vulnerable to allegations of complicity or hypocrisy if they ignore labour law and other compliance issues in their procurement activities. Again, this has the potential to damage trust in government.

The use of procurement to set standards higher than those laid down by the general law is often justified on the basis that while legislation might be used to set minimum standards across the board, the government might itself wish to behave as a model employer, upholding above-minimum standards in areas such as wages and working time.[18] This sets a good example to other employers, and encourages fair—not just lawful—treatment of workers. Of course, one obvious response to this is that the government—if it believes that the relevant standards are important—should promote legislation to apply them generally, rather than imposing them selectively on contractors. However, this may not be appropriate, for a variety of reasons. For example, the standards in question may be too demanding for some sectors of the labour market (such as a higher minimum wage), or the government may want to build a degree of support for the standards by trying them out before legislating for them (for example, in areas such as equality law or family-friendly policies, where there may be a need to bring about cultural change), or the standards may simply be inappropriate for legislation (for example, in relation to wages where the statutory minimum wage may not be a fair wage for a particular job).

Arguably, a more powerful justification for the practice is to prevent any harm to workers that procurement might otherwise cause. Since government

[17] For a more detailed account, see McCrudden, above n 5, 122–28.

[18] For a detailed account of historical uses of procurement in relation to wages, see ibid, 37–56.

contracts are generally awarded on a competitive basis, firms are likely to find themselves under pressure to cut their costs as much as possible in order to put in an attractive bid. This puts workers' terms and conditions of employment at risk, particularly in labour-intensive services, which are now very commonly put out to tender. Of course, labour law itself acts as a brake on this downward pressure, but in some areas (wages and working time, for example) it may be possible to make substantial cuts in workers' terms and conditions without infringing the law. Governments can avoid the risk of downward pressure on workers' terms and conditions by specifying labour standards in the procurement process. This creates a level playing field on terms and conditions of employment, so that firms are forced to cut costs and compete on other aspects of their bids. Labour standards are 'taken out of competition'. This reasoning underpins much of the International Labour Organisation's (ILO's) work on wage requirements in public procurement.[19]

Of course, one consequence of the use of labour standards in public procurement may be that the practice increases the overall cost of a particular contract. It might do this in one of two ways. One is that firms bidding for the contract might increase their proposed price in order to accommodate the additional costs, for example if they are expected to pay a higher wage to workers performing the contract than they would normally pay. The other is that some firms (particularly smaller ones) might be deterred from bidding for the contract because of the additional complexity of having to meet the standards in question. This would reduce competition for the contract and might lead, indirectly, to the government's having to pay a higher price.

However, there is an important sense in which this apparent disadvantage is, potentially, quite the reverse. When the government asks firms to achieve a particular standard through regulation, the cost of doing so falls on the firm, and must be absorbed by charging higher prices to customers or by reducing profits for shareholders. When the government asks firms to achieve a particular standard in a public procurement contract, the cost of doing so can be passed on to the government.[20] Thus, the government can itself make a decision about whether the benefit of achieving a particular social goal through a contract is worth the expense.[21] This perspective reflects the fact that, nowadays, procurement regulation has moved on from the assumption that the best bid is always the cheapest, at least outside

[19] See ILO Convention 94, Labour Clauses (Public Contracts) Convention, 1949; ILO Recommendation 84, Labour Clauses (Public Contracts) Recommendation, 1949; International Labour Conference, Report III(1B): General Survey concerning the Labour Clauses (Public Contracts) Convention, 1949 (No 94) and Recommendation (No 84) (97th Session, 2008).

[20] Of course, this cost must be paid for through taxation, but addressing the fairness or otherwise of taxation systems is beyond the scope of this chapter.

[21] It may not be possible in every case to identify the *exact* additional cost generated by any particular labour standard, but this is potentially a problem with any requirement a government might lay down in a procurement process.

the context of buying standard goods that are readily available from multiple sources. The 2014 Public Procurement Package permits governments to take into account a range of different features of the bids in order to decide which offers the best *value* in a broader sense, provided that they make clear in advance the criteria they intend to use.[22] Thus, if a government is willing to pay for its preferences, the procurement process enables it to pursue them without any apparent harm to firms.[23] Of course, this does not address the worry that some firms might be deterred from bidding, but this can occur for a variety of reasons and can be tackled in other ways, for example by making sure that any additional social requirements are clearly explained in the bid documents.

To sum up, I have argued that there are several possible justifications for the pursuit of social goals through government contracts. The use of procurement to uphold existing legal obligations enables the government to enforce the law more efficiently and avoid charges of hypocrisy or complicity in relation to infringements of labour laws by contractors. This promotes important Rule of Law values. The use of procurement to promote higher standards than those found in existing legislation enables the government to be a 'model employer' if it chooses to do so, pursuing more ambitious policies in its own activities than those it seeks to impose on the market more generally. It also helps to combat some of the damage that competitive procurement exercises might otherwise do to workers' terms and conditions of employment, by forcing firms to compete for government business by cutting costs in other areas rather than by paring back labour standards to the minimum permitted by law. I noted that although the use of procurement to promote higher standards than those laid down in the general law might increase the cost of some government contracts, that cost is borne by the government itself (and redistributed through taxation) rather than by firms (and their consumers or shareholders).

III. *REGIOPOST* IN CONTEXT

This section examines the *RegioPost* decision in the context of applicable EU directives. I begin by setting out the relevant provisions of the 2004 Public Procurement Directive,[24] which were applicable in *RegioPost* itself.

22 Art 67 of the 2014 Public Procurement Directive.

23 Matters are more complicated in the internal market context, where a labour requirement may remove a competitive advantage enjoyed by a bidder in a Member State with lower labour standards, a point I explore in section IV.B.

24 Directive 2004/18/EC of the European Parliament and of the Council of 31 March 2004 on the coordination of procedures for the award of public works contracts, public supply contracts and public service contracts (2004 Public Procurement Directive) [2004] OJ L134/114.

I then turn to an analysis of the Court of Justice's ruling in *RegioPost*, focusing on the Court's interpretation of the 2004 Public Procurement Directive and the wider EU law context in which the Directive is situated. Lastly, I examine relevant provisions of the 2014 Public Procurement Directive, which has superseded the 2004 Directive, with a view to assessing how the law might continue to develop and what role the *RegioPost* ruling might play in that process.

It is important to note at this stage that social requirements might be addressed in four main ways during the course of a procurement process. These are: (i) excluding potential bidders who have violated labour standards in the past from the opportunity to participate in the procurement process; (ii) including social requirements in the technical specifications of the product to be purchased; (iii) including as one of the award criteria for the contract a bidder's willingness to make a commitment to certain labour standards; and (iv) setting contract terms that require the successful contractor to meet certain labour standards during the performance of the contract. These can blur into each other in some respects, for example (ii) and (iv) where the contract is for services. All four options are regulated by EU law, but with some differences of approach between them.[25] For example, (iv), contract performance conditions, might be argued to occupy a middle position in the EU's regulatory spectrum between a permissive approach to (i), exclusion, and a strict approach to (iii), award criteria. The ruling in *RegioPost* concerns the fourth option—contract performance requirements—so this will be the focus of my discussion.

A. Contract Performance Requirements in the 2004 Public Procurement Directive

The inclusion of labour standards in the contract itself allows the public authority to give a clear signal that compliance with its labour requirements is regarded as an aspect of the performance the contractor is expected to deliver. Depending on the law governing the contract, the public authority may be able to use contractual mechanisms to enforce compliance with those standards. For example, it might be possible to make deductions from payments to the contractor in respect of breaches, or even to terminate the contract for a serious breach.

While this is the most obvious use of contract performance requirements, it is worth noting some blurring with other usages noted at the start of section III. There is some overlap with the contract award process in the

[25] For a detailed analysis of the scope for labour standards at the various stages, see Barnard, above n 9.

sense that (as we shall see) the public authority is generally obliged to publicise the contract performance requirements in advance (either in the contract notice, or in the technical specifications) and contractors will usually be expected to confirm that they are willing to accept the requirements as part of submitting a compliant bid. This may deter some potential bidders from participating in the process. And there is some overlap with the exclusion of bidders in future, since if a bidder wins a contract containing labour clauses but then fails to comply with them, it risks being excluded by the public authority from future competitions. These two features of contract performance conditions are quite important from the public authority's perspective, because their apparently central role—to enable the use of contractual remedies to enforce labour standards—may not always be practical. For example, where the contractor is performing well in other respects and citizens are relying on the service it is delivering, it seems highly unlikely that a public authority would be willing to terminate the contract altogether for a non-egregious labour violation.

The 2004 Public Procurement Directive addressed contract performance conditions in Article 26, as follows:

> Contracting authorities may lay down special conditions relating to the performance of a contract, provided that these are compatible with [Union] law and are indicated in the contract notice or in the specifications. The conditions governing the performance of a contract may, in particular, concern social and environmental considerations.

This provision gave Member States express permission to include social goals among their contract performance requirements. The significance of the word 'special' was not immediately apparent from the text itself, but recital 33 of the 2004 Public Procurement Directive gave a strong indication that Member States were permitted to include conditions that were particular to public procurement contracts and went beyond the reinforcement of generally-applicable labour law:

> [Contract performance conditions] may, in particular, be intended to favour on-site vocational training, the employment of people experiencing particular difficulty in achieving integration, the fight against unemployment or the protection of the environment. For instance, mention may be made, amongst other things, of the requirements—applicable during performance of the contract—to recruit long-term job-seekers or to implement training measures for the unemployed or young persons, to comply in substance with the provisions of the basic International Labour Organisation (ILO) Conventions, assuming that such provisions have not been implemented in national law, and to recruit more handicapped persons than are required under national legislation.[26]

[26] Recitals can be used as an interpretive tool, though the legislative text itself always prevails. See, eg, Judgment of 26 June 2001, *BECTU*, Case 173/99, EU:C:2001:356, paras 37–39; and Judgment of 13 July 1989, *Casa Fleischhandel v BALM*, Case C-215/88, EU:C:1989:331,

Article 26 of the 2004 Public Procurement Directive placed two conditions on the use of contract performance requirements to pursue social goals: they had to be 'compatible with [Union] law' and 'indicated in the contract notice or in the specifications'. The latter was a relatively straightforward transparency requirement, ensuring that potential bidders were aware of the requirements they would be obliged to meet if they won the contract. It enabled bidders to make an informed decision about whether they wanted to bid for the contract at all and, more importantly, about how to price their bid. I shall return to the significance of the latter point below.

The first condition, 'compatibility with [Union] law', was obviously much more complex. Of course, EU law's main focus in the field of public procurement is on promoting the internal market by ensuring a level playing field between bidders from different Member States.[27] Recital 33 of the 2004 Public Procurement Directive accordingly indicated that the key requirement was that contract performance conditions should not be 'directly or indirectly discriminatory'. This is the subject of a substantial body of internal market jurisprudence developed by the Court of Justice, focusing on the nature of the disadvantage suffered by service providers from other Member States and on whether Member States can justify their regulatory requirements as a proportionate means of pursuing a legitimate aim. But the requirement of compatibility with EU law is not confined to internal market law: any aspect of EU law, including labour law, may also be relevant to the assessment.

B. The Ruling in *RegioPost*

Against this background, I now turn to a discussion of the Court's ruling in *RegioPost*. The case concerned the inclusion of a wage requirement as a contract performance condition in a public contract in Germany. The Court's ruling is significant for its choice of legal materials against which to assess the wage requirement's compatibility with EU law, and for its interpretation of the phrase 'special conditions' in Article 26 of the 2004 Public

para 31. The ILO's eight fundamental Conventions are: Freedom of Association and Protection of the Right to Organise Convention, 1948 (No 87), Right to Organise and Collective Bargaining Convention, 1949 (No 98), Forced Labour Convention, 1930 (No 29), Abolition of Forced Labour Convention, 1957 (No 105), Minimum Age Convention, 1973 (No 138), Worst Forms of Child Labour Convention, 1999 (No 182), Equal Remuneration Convention, 1951 (No 100), Discrimination (Employment and Occupation) Convention, 1958 (No 111).

[27] A position powerfully defended against a broader 'efficiency' viewpoint in S Arrowsmith, 'The Purpose of the EU Procurement Directives: Ends, Means and the Implications for National Regulatory Space for Commercial and Horizontal Procurement Policies' (2012) 14 *Cambridge Yearbook of European Legal Studies* 1.

Procurement Directive in the context of its application of the proportionality test to the wage requirement. The Court took the relatively unusual step of departing from one of its earlier decisions, in the *Rüffert* case, and the overall effect of its ruling is to be somewhat more permissive of the use of procurement for social goals.

In *RegioPost*, the town authority of Landau in Germany issued an EU-wide call for bids for a postal services contract. The contract notice stated that the successful bidder would be required to comply with a regional law (known as the LTTG), which set a minimum wage for public contracts. There was no national minimum wage in Germany at the relevant time. Tenderers were required to sign a declaration confirming their willingness to comply with the LTTG. RegioPost protested to the authority that the minimum wage requirement was incompatible with EU law, and submitted a bid without the declaration. The authority warned RegioPost that its bid would be excluded unless it signed the declaration, and gave it two weeks to comply. RegioPost did not submit the declaration and its bid was therefore excluded.

In the ensuing dispute, the question referred to the Court was whether the LTTG was incompatible with EU law and should therefore be disapplied by the national court. The Court began by considering the admissibility of the case.[28] This issue arose because all the bidders were established in Germany, so there was no cross-border element to the case. However, the Court found that the case was admissible because the contract award process was subject to the 2004 Public Procurement Directive, and because there could have been cross-border interest in the contract. It went so far as to suggest that the wage requirement might itself have been responsible for discouraging firms in other Member States from submitting bids.[29]

The central question in the case was, of course, the compatibility of the LTTG with Article 26 of the 2004 Public Procurement Directive. As noted in section III.A, this laid down two conditions: compatibility with EU law and transparency. The Court began by noting that the wage requirement was set out in the contract notice and the specifications, so that the requirement of transparency in Article 26 was met.[30]

The question of compatibility with EU law was assessed in three stages. First, in accordance with recital 33 of the 2004 Public Procurement Directive, the Court satisfied itself that the wage requirement was not directly or indirectly discriminatory.[31] Secondly, the Court considered whether it was

[28] *RegioPost*, above n 10, paras 44–52.
[29] ibid, para 51.
[30] ibid, para 55.
[31] ibid, para 56.

compatible with Article 3(1) of the Posted Workers Directive[32] and, thirdly, the Court assessed whether it was compatible with Article 56 TFEU on the freedom to provide services.[33] The second and third questions occupied the bulk of the discussion.

The relevance of the Posted Workers Directive to the situation was established by reference to recital 34 of the 2004 Public Procurement Directive:

> The laws, regulations and collective agreements, at both national and [Union] level, which are in force in the areas of employment conditions and safety at work apply during performance of a public contract, providing that such rules, and their application, comply with [Union] law. In cross-border situations, where workers from one Member State provide services in another Member State for the purpose of performing a public contract, [the Posted Workers Directive] lays down the minimum conditions which must be observed by the host country in respect of such posted workers.[34]

As the text makes clear, this is intended to be protective of posted workers, highlighting as it does the host state's responsibility and the original intention behind the Posted Workers Directive that it would lay down *minimum* terms and conditions to be applied to such workers.[35] However, in the well-known *Laval* decision, the Court treated the Posted Workers Directive as, in effect, a maximum, with the result that more demanding conditions laid down by a host state for posted workers might fall foul of EU law.[36] This understanding of the Posted Workers Directive clearly underpinned the referring court's question, which was whether the LTTG might have deterred firms established in other Member States from bidding for the contract because of the minimum wage it would have required them to pay to any workers posted to fulfil the contract.[37] This also explains why the Posted Workers Directive was thought to be relevant to the decision, even though the claimant firm (and the other bidders in the case) was established in Germany and thus would not be posting any workers to perform the contract.[38]

32 Directive 96/71/EC of the European Parliament and of the Council of 16 December 1996 concerning the posting of workers in the framework of the provision of services (Posted Workers Directive) [1997] OJ L18/1. For background, see P Davies, 'The Posted Workers Directive and the EC Treaty' (2002) 31 *Industrial Law Journal* 298.

33 See further the contributions by Syrpis and Bogdanowicz in chs 2 and 3 of this book respectively.

34 *RegioPost* para 60.

35 See Art 3(7) of the Posted Workers Directive. For discussion, see ACL Davies, 'One Step Forward, Two Steps Back? The *Viking* and *Laval* Cases in the ECJ' (2008) 37 *Industrial Law Journal* 126, 129; P Syrpis and T Novitz, 'Economic and Social Rights in Conflict: Political and Judicial Approaches to their Reconciliation' (2008) 33 *EL Rev* 411, 416.

36 Judgment of 18 December 2007, *Laval un Partneri*, Case C-341/05, EU:C:2007:809, especially paras 79–81. See further the contribution by Novitz in ch 11 of this book.

37 *RegioPost*, above n 10, para 61.

38 The Advocate General found that the Posted Workers Directive was not relevant for this reason: Opinion of AG Mengozzi delivered on 9 September 2015 in *RegioPost*, Case C-115/14, EU:C:2015:566, paras 53–54, a position defended by F Costamagna, 'Minimum Wage between Public Procurement and Posted Workers: Anything New After the *RegioPost* Case?' (2017) 42 *EL Rev* 101.

In this regard, the Court confirmed that the LTTG was a 'law' prescribing a 'minimum rate of pay' within Article 3(1) of the Posted Workers Directive.[39] There was no other lower rate of pay prescribed by law for the relevant group of workers. One potential difficulty was that the LTTG applied only to public contracts and not to private ones, but the Court noted that the requirement of universal applicability under Article 3(1) and (8) of the Posted Workers Directive applied only to collective agreements,[40] and that Article 26 of the 2004 Public Procurement Directive expressly contemplated that public authorities might set out 'special conditions' applicable only to public contracts.[41]

The Court next turned to an assessment of the wage requirement in the context of Article 56 TFEU on the freedom to provide services, considering the familiar tests: whether there was a restriction, whether it was in pursuit of a legitimate aim, and whether it was justified. The Court decided that the wage requirement was a restriction because it was an 'additional economic burden' for firms established in states with lower rates of pay.[42] But it accepted, following *Bundesdruckerei*,[43] that the aim of protecting workers was legitimate.[44] It then turned to the question of justification.

Here, the national court questioned whether the wage requirement was unjustified in the light of the Court's decision in *Rüffert*, since it applied only to public contracts and not to private ones. It will be recalled that the *Rüffert* case concerned an attempt by a public authority to enforce, in a public works contract, a non-minimum wage contained in a collective agreement applicable only to workers performing public contracts in the construction sector. The Court found that the requirement was not justified under the Treaty, apparently for three reasons: the wage was higher than the legally-binding minimum applicable to posted workers; the collective agreement was not universally applicable in the sense required by the Posted Workers Directive; and it was difficult to understand how the worker protection justification could be invoked to support a requirement applicable only in the public sector.[45] The first two reasons were discussed above: they relate to the Posted Workers Directive and were not applicable on the facts in *RegioPost*. The third reason was potentially applicable in *RegioPost* but the Court simply ignored it, enabling it to find that the wage requirement was justified under Article 56 TFEU. Sánchez-Graells has argued that there is no departure from *Rüffert* because the public/private reasoning was part of the Court's thinking about the universal applicability of the

[39] *RegioPost*, above n 10, para 62.
[40] ibid, para 63.
[41] ibid, paras 64–65.
[42] ibid, para 69.
[43] Judgment of 18 September 2014, *Bundesdruckerei*, Case C-549/13, EU:C:2014:2235.
[44] *RegioPost*, above n 10, para 70.
[45] *Rüffert*, above n 11, paras 23–40.

collective agreement,[46] but this view does not appear to be supported by the judgment in *Rüffert*, which states the proposition in more general terms.[47]

Finally, the Court considered the exclusion of RegioPost's tender by the contracting authority because of its refusal to supply the undertaking that it would comply with the wage requirement. The Court held that this was permitted by Article 26 and recital 34 of the 2004 Public Procurement Directive. It also noted that the requirement to sign the declaration was not burdensome, and that the authority had warned RegioPost that its bid would be excluded if it did not sign the declaration and had given it an opportunity to comply before excluding its bid.

C. Analysis

The *RegioPost* decision is broadly welcome from the perspective of socially responsible procurement, since it accepts that public authorities may lay down contract performance conditions in their contracts that do not apply across the labour market as a whole. Although the Court's reasoning is less than clear in its attempt to 'distinguish' *Rüffert*, it seems likely that its decision in fact reflects the express wording of Article 26 of the 2004 Public Procurement Directive, which was not applicable at the time of the decision in *Rüffert*. This would be rendered ineffective, in the sense that the conditions would not be 'special', if they had to apply beyond the public contract setting.

However, the *RegioPost* decision is likely to prove relatively limited in its effect. One significant factor is the Court's emphasis on the fact that even though the wage requirement did not need to be applicable across the labour market as a whole, it still had to be compatible with the Posted Workers Directive.[48] This meant that it had to be a 'minimum' wage specified in a Posted Workers Directive-compliant measure, in this case, legislation. Thus, the ruling apparently precludes one of the obvious ways in which governments might want to use contract performance conditions: to have a policy of enforcing higher wages for workers performing government contracts where national legislation lays down a minimum wage. This limits governments' ability to use procurement to set a good example, by paying a 'living' wage as opposed to the bare minimum laid down by law, or to specify wages appropriate to the work to be performed, such as a higher rate for skilled work. Of course, matters would be somewhat different if

[46] Sánchez-Graells, above n 15, 15–17.

[47] *Rüffert*, above n 11, para 40. The point is developed more fully by Costamagna, above n 38.

[48] *RegioPost*, above n 10, para 62.

the European Commission were able to secure agreement to its proposed revision of the Posted Workers Directive.[49] This would allow host states greater flexibility to set 'remuneration', not just minimum wages, for posted workers, though this would still have to be done through a Posted Workers Directive-compliant mechanism.

More generally, it is not clear what implications the decision has for terms and conditions that are not listed in the Posted Workers Directive. On one view, since the Posted Workers Directive was treated in the *Laval* case as, in effect, laying down a ceiling, rather than a floor, of rights for posted workers, it should be regarded as exhaustive of the labour standards Member States may specify as contract performance conditions in their procurement contracts. But it is difficult to reconcile this view with recital 33 of the 2004 Public Procurement Directive, which listed a variety of other labour standards not covered by the Posted Workers Directive, such as rights contained in the ILO's fundamental Conventions, and policies such as a requirement to hire the long-term unemployed. This would suggest that other labour standards are also permissible, presumably subject only to their compatibility with Article 56 TFEU. However, this would result in an odd situation in which the Posted Workers Directive acted as a constraint but only on the listed matters, so that a state could include a requirement to hire the unemployed but not an above-minimum wage. Although it is understandable that the Court should seek to reconcile the various elements of EU law with potential relevance to the case before it, this highlights the difficulty of using the Posted Workers Directive for purposes other than those for which it was originally enacted.[50]

Another significant limitation appears not in *RegioPost* itself but in the relationship between *RegioPost* and the Court's earlier ruling in *Bundesdruckerei*. In the latter case, the contracting authority sought to set a wage condition for workers on a public contract for digitising documents. However, this task could be performed remotely and did not require the presence of the workers in the contracting authority's state (Germany in this case). The successful bidder announced its intention to use a subcontractor established in Poland to perform the work, whose workforce would remain in Poland and would not be posted to Germany. It therefore argued that the wage requirement could not be justified. The Court agreed, holding that the wage requirement would prevent the subcontractor from taking advantage of lower wages in Poland when competing for the contract, and that it could not be justified on social protection grounds given that it reflected

[49] Commission, *Proposal for a Directive of the European Parliament and of the Council amending Directive 96/71/EC of the European Parliament and of the Council of 16 December 1996 concerning the posting of workers in the framework of the provision of services*, COM(2016) 128 final.

[50] Though of course these purposes are themselves somewhat conflicted: Davies, above n 32.

the higher cost of living in Germany and was not related to the cost of living in Poland.[51] It should be noted that although the Court's reasoning in *Bundesdruckerei* placed reliance on the *Rüffert* decision, and thus on the idea that it is not justified to apply special requirements in the public sector, it appears that the ratio of *Bundesdruckerei* is capable of surviving the Court's change of approach to that issue in *RegioPost*.[52]

Taking the two rulings together, the most obvious interpretation is that a Member State will only be permitted to specify labour standards where the workers performing the contract will inevitably be doing so on its own territory. Where the workers will be performing remotely—or where there is a *possibility* that the contract could be performed remotely—the Member State will not have that option. The only possible exception to this may be for fundamental rights—such as those contained in the ILO conventions—which might be included regardless of the place of performance, on the ground that such rights are universally applicable.[53] Of course, any attempt to avoid the effect of *Bundesdruckerei* by requiring that the contract be performed in the Member State's territory where this is not essential, is likely to be vulnerable to challenge on the ground that it is discriminatory.[54]

To sum up, then, *RegioPost* takes the important step of recognising that contracting authorities may impose contract performance conditions that are particular to public contracts and are not simply reinforcing the general law applicable also in the private sector. However, it seems that states may only do this in respect of workers who will be performing the contract on their own territory (either as local or posted workers) and not remotely from another Member State. More troublingly, it is unclear which labour rights may be enforced by states as contract performance conditions and, in particular, what the role of the Posted Workers Directive is in answering that question.

D. Contract Performance Requirements in the 2014 Public Procurement Directive

As noted in section III.B, *RegioPost* fell to be considered under the 2004 Public Procurement Directive, which has since been replaced by the 2014 Public Procurement Directive. At first sight, the new Directive looks very similar to the old one, with a clear equivalent to old Article 26 in new

[51] *Bundesdruckerei*, above n 43, para 34.

[52] ibid, paras 32–33.

[53] Listed in n 26 above.

[54] Judgment of 3 December 1974, *Van Binsbergen v Bedrijfsvereniging voor de Metaalnijverheid*, Case C-33/74, EU:C:1974:131.

Article 70. But this masks a significant change in the overall approach, which now has a combination of mandatory and permissive elements.[55]

Article 18(2) of the 2014 Public Procurement Directive makes it mandatory for Member States to ensure that contractors comply with certain provisions of labour law:

> Member States shall take appropriate measures to ensure that in the performance of public contracts economic operators comply with applicable obligations in the fields of environmental, social and labour law established by Union law, national law, collective agreements or by the international environmental, social and labour law provisions listed in Annex X.

It is important to note that this provision does not require Member States to adopt the 'reinforcing' approach to labour legislation in their procurement activities, for example by including compliance with applicable labour law as a contractual obligation. It might be open to a state to argue that the usual enforcement methods applicable in the labour market as a whole—labour inspection, for example—should be regarded as sufficient to secure compliance by its contractors.[56] However, it may encourage some states to consider the 'reinforcing' approach. Perhaps more importantly, by placing this obligation on the Member States, the Directive creates scope for litigation if they fail to take 'appropriate measures', for example in the form of an action by the European Commission against the Member State to enforce compliance with EU law.

There are three points to note about the content of the legal standards to be enforced in this way. First, although the provision refers to EU law, national law and collective agreements, it also makes reference to external standards by requiring compliance with the fundamental ILO conventions listed in Annex X.[57] This provides a set of minimum standards to be applied regardless of their implementation in EU or national law.[58] While some of the ILO standards, notably in relation to equal treatment for men and women,[59] are not likely to be relevant given that there is detailed EU law on

[55] For detailed analysis, see Barnard, above n 9, 235–42.

[56] For example, there is no specific implementation of this provision in the UK: see Public Contracts Regulations 2015 (SI 2015/102), reg 18, which implements Art 18(1) of the 2014 Public Procurement Directive only. There is, however, guidance: Crown Commercial Service, *The Public Contracts Regulations 2015: Social and Environmental Aspects* (2015), at gov.uk/government/uploads/system/uploads/attachment_data/file/558032/20160912socialenvironmentalguidancefinal.pdf.

[57] Above n 26; and see the contribution by Nicholas in ch 13 of this book.

[58] Recital 37 makes clear that Member States may maintain provisions that are more favourable to workers.

[59] Equal Remuneration Convention, 1951 (No 100), Discrimination (Employment and Occupation) Convention, 1958 (No 111).

the subject,[60] requirements relating to freedom of association and collective bargaining (the former not even within the EU's competence[61]) could prove significant in practice in some Member States.[62] Secondly, as one would expect, the national laws and collective agreements to be enforced under this provision must be compatible with EU law. This is made clear in recital 37 of the 2014 Public Procurement Directive. This is important, because it means that Member States cannot rely on this provision to 'get around' restrictions on national law such as those put in place by the Posted Workers Directive. Indeed, the recital contains an express reference to the Posted Workers Directive and to the need to ensure equal treatment of bidders from other Member States. Thirdly, recital 37, after referring to the obligation to ensure compliance with EU and national law and international standards, contains the familiar phrase 'this should in no way prevent the application of terms and conditions of employment which are more favourable to workers'. This is reflective of the fact that EU law generally lays down minimum standards in the labour law context, on which Member States may build. However, Member States' ability to do this in the context of the Posted Workers Directive is, as noted in section III.B, limited by the decision in *Laval*. It remains to be seen what impact—if any—this expression will have in this context.

While Article 18(2) of the 2014 Public Procurement Directive itself does not distinguish explicitly between contracts performed on the territory of the Member State in question and contracts performed remotely, it seems unlikely that it will have any effect on the ruling in *Bundesdruckerei* discussed in section III.C.[63] The reference is to 'applicable obligations' and, with limited exceptions, states do not normally seek to apply their labour laws extra-territorially. This is reinforced by recital 37, which makes clear that the requirement is to ensure compliance with 'obligations ... that apply at the place where the works are executed or the services provided'. This suggests that a contracting authority in Member State A would be obliged to enforce A's minimum wage for contracts being performed within A, but could only insist on compliance with the local law of Member State B where the contract was being performed remotely in B. What would amount to 'appropriate measures' for Member State A to take in relation to the enforcement of the law in Member State B would depend on the facts of the case, but would presumably be less extensive for situations outside the Member State's own jurisdiction.

[60] Arts 153 and 157 TFEU; Directive 2006/54/EC on the implementation of the principle of equal opportunities and equal treatment of men and women in matters of employment and occupation (recast) [2006] OJ L204/23.

[61] Art 153(5) TFEU.

[62] Freedom of Association and Protection of the Right to Organise Convention, 1948 (No 87), Right to Organise and Collective Bargaining Convention, 1949 (No 98).

[63] See discussion at n 51 above.

Another innovation in the 2014 Public Procurement Directive is the inclusion of a provision dealing specifically with subcontractors in Article 71(1):

> Observance of the obligations referred to in Article 18(2) by subcontractors is ensured through appropriate action by the competent national authorities acting within the scope of their responsibility and remit.

This recognises the risk that, in complex supply chains, non-compliance with labour law may occur lower down the chain, and the main contractor may not take effective action to address that non-compliance. It gives contracting authorities some responsibility for securing compliance by subcontractors with applicable EU and national labour law and fundamental ILO norms. However, it is not clear how far that responsibility extends, and the example given in recital 105 is the use of labour inspectorates, so while it is important in principle, the provision may not achieve very much in practice.

These new mandatory provisions sit alongside the old permissive approach, now contained in Article 70 of the 2014 Public Procurement Directive. This is somewhat more specific than old Article 26:

> Contracting authorities may lay down special conditions relating to the performance of a contract, provided that they are linked to the subject-matter of the contract within the meaning of Article 67(3) and indicated in the call for competition or in the procurement documents. Those conditions may include economic, innovation-related, environmental, social or employment-related considerations.

This provision has two obvious similarities with old Article 26. One is the phrase 'special conditions', which was found in *RegioPost* to permit the use of conditions that only applied to public contracts and were not generally applicable in the labour market. This is, of course, somewhat reinforced by the fact that compliance with the general law is now addressed by Article 18(2) of the 2014 Public Procurement Directive, making it even clearer that Article 70 must be concerned with something else. Another is the requirement that contract performance conditions should be announced in advance when the contracting authority invites bids. But the drafting of Article 70 of the 2014 Public Procurement Directive differs from that of Article 26 of the 2004 Public Procurement Directive in two respects. First, there is no reference in the new drafting to compatibility with EU law. However, it seems highly unlikely that this would not be relevant, a view reinforced by recital 104 of the 2014 Public Procurement Directive. Interestingly, though, the recital appears to indicate that contract performance conditions do not require the same level of scrutiny as contract award criteria:

> Unlike contract award criteria which are the basis for a comparative assessment of the quality of tenders, contract performance conditions constitute fixed objective requirements that have no impact on the assessment of tenders. Contract performance conditions should be compatible with this Directive provided that they are not directly or indirectly discriminatory.

Secondly, a new feature of the drafting of Article 70 of the 2014 Public Procurement Directive is the requirement that the conditions be 'linked to the subject-matter of the contract'.[64] This is defined in Article 67(3), in the context of award criteria, as follows:

> Award criteria shall be considered to be linked to the subject-matter of the public contract where they relate to the works, supplies or services to be provided under that contract in any respect and at any stage of their life cycle, including factors involved in:
>
> (a) the specific process of production, provision or trading of those works, supplies or services; or
> (b) a specific process for another stage of their life cycle,
>
> even where such factors do not form part of their material substance.

This is important, because it could have been argued that the 'subject-matter' of a particular contract is simply the goods or services to be provided, and not, for example, the social standards observed in producing those goods or services (a distinction that has been drawn in the World Trade Organisation's (WTO's) dispute settlement jurisprudence in the past).[65] Article 67(3) of the 2014 Public Procurement Directive clarifies that a broader definition including the process of production is in play. However, there is still one limitation, which is that labour standards can only be specified for workers engaged in the performance of the contract. Reflecting the Court's ruling in the *Dutch Coffee* case,[66] the recitals and Commission guidance make it clear that it is not permissible to require the contractor to have general corporate social responsibility policies applicable to all areas of its business.[67]

The 2014 Public Procurement Directive also allows Member States to use social labels at a variety of stages in the procurement process, including as

[64] For a detailed analysis highlighting the risks of a strict interpretation of this provision, see A Semple, 'The Link to the Subject Matter' in B Sjåfjell and A Wiesbrock (eds), *Sustainable Public Procurement under EU Law: New Perspectives on the State as Stakeholder* (Cambridge, Cambridge University Press, 2016) 50.

[65] The classic critique is R Howse and D Regan, 'The Product/Process Distinction—An Illusory Basis for Disciplining "Unilateralism" in Trade Policy' (2000) 11 *European Journal of International Law* 249. For recent analyses of the scope to pursue social and environmental policies within the WTO system, see, eg, H Andersen, 'Protection of Non-Trade Values in WTO Appellate Body Jurisprudence: Exceptions, Economic Arguments, and Eluding Questions' (2015) 18 *Journal of International Economic Law* 383; R Harris and G Moon, 'GATT Article XX and Human Rights: What Do We Know from the First 20 Years?' (2015) 16 *Melbourne Journal of International Law* 176.

[66] Judgment of 10 May 2012, *Commission v Netherlands ('Dutch Coffee')*, Case C-368/10 EU:C:2012:284, [2012] 3 CMLR 11, especially para 103.

[67] Recital 97 of the 2014 Public Procurement Directive. See European Commission, *Contributing to Sustainable Development: The Role of Fair Trade and Non-Governmental Trade-Related Sustainability Assurance Schemes*, COM(2009) 215; *Buying Social*, above n 9; *Supporting Social Responsibility in the Economy through Procurement*, above n 9.

contract award conditions, if certain conditions are met. This is addressed in Article 43. Space precludes a full discussion of this provision here.[68]

The intention underlying the 2014 Public Procurement Directive is clearly to encourage contracting authorities to make greater use of contract conditions to enforce social policies, by making it obligatory for them to concern themselves with contractors' compliance with the general law, and by facilitating their use of additional requirements going beyond the general law. Although *RegioPost* is ostensibly concerned with the interpretation of what is now Article 70, it is arguable that the introduction of Article 18(2) in the 2014 Public Procurement Directive points towards a more generous interpretation of Article 70 than that offered by the Court in *RegioPost*. I elaborate this point in section IV.C.

IV. DISCUSSION

In this section, I seek to draw together the two strands of analysis in this contribution: the discussion of the reasons why a government might seek to use public procurement to pursue social goals, and the discussion of *RegioPost* itself. How might the Court better incorporate the objectives of socially responsible procurement—maintaining consistency across government policy, acting as a model employer or preventing the harm that procurement might otherwise cause—into the Article 56 TFEU proportionality analysis? And what reliance, if any, should be placed on the Posted Workers Directive in this regard?

Of course, one response to this set of questions might be to say that socially responsible procurement is fundamentally incompatible with the internal market rules, so that the only proper response is to exempt this activity altogether from internal market scrutiny by analogy with *Albany*.[69] There is some force in this argument, since there is a profound difference of opinion between the position of the internal market jurisprudence on lower wages as a legitimate source of competitive advantage (discussed further in section IV.A) and, for example, the ILO's view on the matter.[70] However, the Court is reluctant to extend *Albany*, particularly in the internal market context,[71] and has already subjected social goals in procurement to internal market scrutiny, so for pragmatic reasons my focus here will be on ways of reconfiguring the Court's approach to the Article 56 TFEU analysis in this context.

[68] See Barnard, above n 9, 222.

[69] Judgment of 21 September 1999, *Albany*, Case C-67/96, EU:C:1999:430.

[70] Above n 19.

[71] Judgment of 11 December 2007, *The International Transport Workers' Federation and The Finnish Seamen's Union*, Case C-438/05, EU:C:2007:772, paras 48–54. See Syrpis and Novitz, above n 35, 419–20.

A. Legitimate Aim

In the *RegioPost* case, the Court of Justice selected 'worker protection' as the aim being pursued by the contracting authority in setting its minimum wage requirement.[72] At first sight, this is uncontroversial. A minimum wage is well recognised as a basic labour standard, and worker protection has been accepted by the Court in previous case law as a legitimate reason to interfere with free movement.[73] However, I shall suggest here that the focus on worker protection in this context is potentially problematic.

The use of procurement for worker protection attracts the obvious response that it is not an effective means of pursuing that goal because it does not apply to all workers in the labour market. No state would choose procurement as its sole or even principal method of worker protection for precisely this reason. Although the Court in *RegioPost* was able to overcome this by relying on the (different) argument that Article 26 of the 2004 Public Procurement Directive permitted 'special conditions' in public contracts, the relative weakness of the aim may be a factor in the proportionality calculus in future cases.

A better alternative would be for the Court to focus on the justifications commonly given at national level for the use of procurement to pursue social goals—consistency, the 'model employer' argument or preventing the harm that procurement might otherwise cause—and to accept these as legitimate aims at EU level, either instead of, or at least alongside, worker protection. This would offer a much more convincing account of why procurement should be used for social ends even though it protects only a minority of workers.

The consistency argument—that governments should be able to use procurement to enforce labour standards set out in the general law—should extend relatively straightforwardly to the EU level. It will be recalled that this argument is about helping governments to avoid charges of hypocrisy by enforcing labour law not just through labour inspectorates or other specialist mechanisms, but also in their capacity as market actors. Consistency is closely linked to the broader idea of the Rule of Law—that governments should treat like cases alike, and should avoid sudden policy changes that disrupt the lives of citizens[74]—which is one of the founding values of the EU set out in Article 2 TEU. It is unlikely to make much sense to the ordinary

[72] *RegioPost*, above n 10, para 70.

[73] See, eg, Judgment of 23 November 1999, *Arblade*, Case C-369/96, EU:C:1999:575, para 59.

[74] For discussion (in the context of English public law) see, eg, K Steyn, 'Consistency—a Principle of Public Law?' (1997) 2 *Judicial Review* 22; R Clayton, 'Legitimate Expectations, Policy, and the Principle of Consistency' (2003) 62 *CLJ* 93; M Elliott, 'Legitimate Expectation, Consistency and Abuse of Power: the *Rashid* Case' (2005) 10 *Judicial Review* 281.

citizen that the government should enforce standards in one capacity but ignore them in another.

The model employer argument tends to be used to justify the inclusion in government contracts of standards going beyond the requirements of the general law. This is, of course, more controversial, but it can be important for governments for a variety of reasons, including setting standards that are relevant to the contract in question, such as higher wages for skilled workers where the law only enforces a minimum wage. The difficulties with this from the perspective of the Posted Workers Directive were discussed in section III.B, but as a justification for the inclusion of labour standards in a government contract, the argument is quite a strong one. Although EU law encourages the use of standardised requirements in contracts wherever possible, for example in relation to technical specifications, this does not mean that a government is obliged to contract for a standard product where it is not suitable or relevant for its needs.[75] The same should surely be true of labour standards. Indeed, there is a simple method of testing whether the government's use of such standards is legitimate or motivated by protectionism, which is to consider whether it applies the same standards in other contexts. For example, in relation to labour law, it would be possible to compare the treatment of the government's directly-hired staff with its proposed contractual terms for external contractors, subject to appropriate caveats about differences between civil service and other jobs in some states.

The argument about the harm caused by procurement may be more difficult. It will be remembered that the concern here is that, as a competitive process, procurement may exert downward pressure on labour standards as firms try to find ways of cutting their costs and winning government business. By requiring compliance with certain labour standards, governments seek to impose a level playing field on all bidders and thus to take labour standards out of competition. But does this argument work equally well in the EU context?

One potential problem might be that wage differentials already exist in the EU regardless of procurement. The official statistics readily demonstrate wide variations in the average wage between different Member States.[76] In a purely domestic setting with no foreign bidders, which is arguably the context in which the socially responsible approach to procurement has developed, firms face similar labour costs, and it is easier to attribute any drop in standards to the competitive pressure generated by the procurement process itself. In cross-border settings, firms based in other Member States may have lower labour costs for other reasons not related to their participation in a procurement exercise, such as the lower cost of living or average wage in

[75] Art 42 of the 2014 Public Procurement Directive.

[76] See Eurostat, 'Median hourly earnings, all employees (excluding apprentices) by sex', at appsso.eurostat.ec.europa.eu/nui/show.do?dataset=earn_ses_pub2s&lang=en.

the local labour market. On this view, it is much more likely that a state seeking to impose labour standards in a procurement exercise is not in fact aiming to combat the harm procurement might otherwise cause, but instead to pursue a policy of protectionism.

However, the matter does not end there. While EU law allows Member States (and more importantly, economic actors within Member States) to take advantage of differentials to some extent, it does not require those differentials to be maintained over time, and indeed one might expect a long-term effect of the internal market to be a gradual convergence of living standards across the Member States.[77] On that view, while procurement may not always be a source of downward pressure on wages (because differentials already exist for other reasons), the existence of competitive procurement exercises does nothing to encourage any *reduction* in differentials between Member States over time. Why would a firm established in a lower-cost Member State seek to improve the terms and conditions offered to its workers when it can win lucrative contracts in higher-cost Member States by competing on price? Thus, it may still be legitimate for governments to concern themselves with the potential for procurement to have negative social impacts.

To sum up, it can be argued that the reasons often given at domestic level for the pursuit of social goals in procurement are relevant (with some adaptation) at EU level, and are more persuasive as 'legitimate aims' within the proportionality calculus than worker protection. Although social goals in procurement are, of course, worker protective, which is a well-recognised 'legitimate aim', this approach is vulnerable to the charge that social goals in procurement only help a small proportion of workers. While the Court was able to disregard this in the *RegioPost* case, by relying on the Posted Workers Directive and Article 26 of the 2004 Public Procurement Directive, it is always important to have strong legitimate aims to add weight to that side of the proportionality calculus.

B. Disadvantage

A second area of the Court's analysis that is worth unpacking is its approach to the disadvantage allegedly suffered by potential bidders as a result of the inclusion of labour standards in procurement exercises. In assessing this disadvantage, the Court does not distinguish between procurement and other forms of regulatory intervention in the market. While this is consistent with

[77] Of course, there are many and complex reasons why this process is not occurring as quickly as one might hope, one of the obvious ones being that (even with EU free movement rights) workers tend to be less mobile in practice than they are in economic theory, but space precludes a full discussion of this issue here.

the Court's generally broad approach to Article 56 TFEU, it will be suggested here that procurement is a different type of activity and thus might warrant a different analysis. This is relevant because, in any proportionality calculus, there is a balance to be struck between the disadvantage suffered and the government's policy objective, so the extent of the disadvantage is important in determining how 'heavy' the burden of justification on the government might be.

The early cases on the freedom to provide services focused on national measures that discriminated against service providers from other Member States. A classic example is a requirement to have an establishment in a particular state in order to provide services there, which has an obvious discriminatory effect on service providers established in other states.[78] Over time, it has become clear that the Court will subject any rule that restricts access to another Member State's market to scrutiny under Article 56 TFEU, even if it is not directly or indirectly discriminatory. Thus, in *Alpine Investments*, it was found that a prohibition on selling financial services by 'cold-calling' potential customers, which applied equally to national firms and to firms from other Member States, fell to be justified under Article 56 TFEU because it restricted market access, presumably because it deprived firms from other Member States of a means of bringing their products to consumers' attention.[79] The key phrase, from the oft-cited ruling in *Arblade*, is whether the measure in question is 'liable to prohibit, impede or render less advantageous the activities of a provider of services established in another Member State where he lawfully provides similar services'.[80]

This phrase was employed in *RegioPost*, and the Court described the minimum wage requirement as an 'additional economic burden' that fell foul of this test.[81] But why is that the case? It clearly does not 'prohibit' the activities of a provider from another Member State. One possibility might be that it is an impediment. The requirement to pay a minimum wage will, of course, increase the cost to the potential contractor of performing the contract. However, this cost can be passed on to the government when setting the contract price. The transparency requirements already in place in EU law force Member States to announce their requirements in the bid documents, with the result that contractors know the standards they will be obliged to meet and can factor them into the contract price.[82] What the government is doing by requiring a minimum wage is to force bidders to compete on grounds other than wage costs by creating a level playing field

[78] *Van Binsbergen*, above n 54.

[79] Judgment of 10 May 1995, *Alpine Investments v Minister van Financiën*, Case C-384/93, EU:C:1995:126.

[80] *Arblade*, above n 73, para 33.

[81] *RegioPost*, above n 10, para 69.

[82] Arts 48 and 49 of the 2014 Public Procurement Directive.

for this element of the bid. From this perspective, there is no impediment to the provision of services in another Member State, since any additional cost to the service provider will be covered by the government.

Thus, the only possible argument is that the requirement renders the provision of services 'less advantageous'. It does this by removing the opportunity for a firm established in a Member State with lower wage costs to take advantage of that fact when bidding for the contract, by putting in a lower-priced bid and thus increasing its chances of winning the contract. This is inherently quite a limited form of disadvantage—a reduced chance of winning—which should in itself suggest a relatively light justificatory burden for a government pursuing legitimate social policy aims.

Two further factors suggest that the 'reduced chance of winning' may, itself, be somewhat exaggerated. First, the analysis assumes that government contracts are always awarded to the lowest-priced bid, which would make price competition determinative. However, EU law permits use of a 'most economically advantageous tender' approach, in which contracting authorities may take account of a wide range of factors in identifying the winning bid.[83] A level playing field on labour standards only removes one element from the determination of the contract price. The extent to which this element is important in practice will vary from case to case, depending on what proportion of bidders' costs is likely to be made up of wages and other labour costs. Admittedly, some government contracts are for labour-intensive services, where labour costs are likely to be a big component of the contract price, but this is an issue that should be interrogated rather than assumed. Secondly, the assumption appears to be that excluding the competitive advantage of lower labour standards will substantially increase the likelihood of local firms winning the contract, to the exclusion of firms established in other Member States. If correct, that would be an important concern, because the EU's main objective in regulating procurement is to promote the internal market by prohibiting discrimination and removing barriers to market access.[84] However, this may again be an oversimplification. The idea that a level playing field on labour standards will enable a Member State to award contracts to its own national firms ignores all the many other elements of EU regulation of procurement designed to guard against protectionism, such as the requirement to specify the contract award criteria in advance and to apply them in an objective manner.[85]

It is important to recognise that the use of labour standards in public procurement is a preference paid for by the contracting authority, because it is advertised in advance and can be factored into the contract price.

[83] Art 67 of the 2014 Public Procurement Directive.
[84] See Arrowsmith, above n 27.
[85] Above nn 82 and 83.

In that respect, it does not exclude potential bidders from competing. What it may do is to take away a competitive advantage enjoyed by bidders with low labour costs who intended to compete primarily on price. How big a disadvantage that is will vary from case to case. From the perspective of Article 56 TFEU, it is important that the Court takes a realistic approach to the disadvantage suffered by potential bidders, and correctly calibrates the burden of justification on the Member State.

C. Posting

The discussion thus far has focused on two of the basic elements of the proportionality analysis that applies under Article 56 TFEU, without the added complication of the Posted Workers Directive. I offer some brief reflections here on the relevance of the Posted Workers Directive.

Although the discussion of Article 56 TFEU in *RegioPost* by both the Advocate General and the Court focused predominantly on the fact that the wage applied only to workers performing public contracts, both the Opinion and the ruling proceeded on the assumption that it could be characterised as a minimum wage. This assumption is attributable to the perceived need to satisfy Article 3(1) of the Posted Workers Directive, which only allows host states to stipulate a minimum wage for posted workers. Arguably, it was originally envisaged that host states would be able to set higher standards than those laid down in the Posted Workers Directive, but the Court's interpretation in *Laval* discourages this idea: considerable emphasis was placed on firms' need for certainty about the changes they would have to make to workers' terms and conditions of employment when posting them to another Member State.[86]

The relevance of the Posted Workers Directive to the decision in *RegioPost* was contested. Although it was relied upon by the Court, Advocate General Mengozzi regarded it as irrelevant to the decision. This was because it was common ground in the case that RegioPost was established in Germany and intended to use its own German workforce to carry out the contract. It did not have any plans either to use posted workers from another part of its organisation, or to use an agency to source posted workers from another Member State.[87] The Court, by contrast, found that the Posted Workers Directive was relevant because the wage stipulation might have deterred some firms intending to use posted workers to perform the contract from bidding for it.[88] In simple terms, the Advocate General's approach was to consider the applicable law once the contract had been awarded, whereas

[86] See text at n 36 above.
[87] *RegioPost*, Opinion of AG Mengozzi, above n 38, para 53.
[88] *RegioPost*, above n 10, paras 60–61.

the Court's approach was to consider the possibilities at the point at which the contract was being advertised.

The Court's approach might be regarded as a better reflection of the exigencies of the procurement context, in which it is important to be able to advertise clearly in advance the standards that potential bidders will be expected to meet, not least so that they can price their bids appropriately. However, the disadvantage is that it limits states to specifying Posted Workers Directive-compliant standards even when the Posted Workers Directive is not applicable, thus significantly reducing states' capacity to set labour standards for contractors. Indeed, this limitation is potentially much more restrictive than that part of the decision permitting the use of standards specific to government contracts, since it seems highly unlikely that there will be many occasions on which a state is seeking to apply a procurement-specific standard that is at the same time compliant with the Posted Workers Directive.

A preferable alternative—in line with the Advocate General's approach—would be to specify labour standards in the bid documents in terms of the applicable law. Thus, if the contract was performed remotely, contractors would be expected to meet home state standards, and if the contract was performed locally, contractors would be expected to meet local law in full or home state standards plus the local standards permitted under the Posted Workers Directive, depending on whether local or posted workers were to be used to perform the contract. However, even this approach produces odd results. It allows contracting authorities to use the procurement process to enforce the applicable law, but not to set higher standards or to take labour law out of competition in any meaningful sense, and is potentially quite complicated to monitor and enforce.

There are a number of different ways in which this set of issues might be addressed. One is to contest the relevance of the Posted Workers Directive to procurement cases at all. It has often been noted that the Posted Workers Directive is a confused measure, combining some level of worker protection with the pursuit of internal market objectives in accordance with its Treaty basis.[89] Arguably one of its main objectives is to give clarity to firms seeking to post workers as to the labour standards they may be expected to meet. It could be claimed that this is already achieved in the procurement context through the well-established transparency requirements. Another objective is, presumably, to balance worker protection with the maintenance of some competitive advantage for firms. Again, though, as already noted, the procurement context affects this to the extent that the state imposing the labour standards is willing to pay an inflated contract price to cover this, thereby reducing the disadvantage to firms.

Two new developments are also worth considering. One is the 2014 Public Procurement Directive which, as noted, both requires contracting

[89] Davies, above n 32.

authorities to enforce the applicable law under Article 18(2) and permits them to impose 'special conditions' under Article 70. It is at least arguable that this will require the Court to follow the Advocate General's approach in *RegioPost* when applying Article 18(2). If that is so, it is difficult to see how the Court might give meaning to Article 70 without permitting states to go beyond the requirements of the applicable law, even if that might involve requiring higher standards from contractors than would normally be permitted under the Posted Workers Directive. Another is that the European Commission has proposed a revision to the Posted Workers Directive itself, which has not been agreed at the time of writing.[90] Amongst other reforms, this would allow the host state to specify remuneration, not just minimum wages, for posted workers, provided that it did so through a Posted Workers Directive-compatible mechanism as currently defined in Article 3(1) of the Posted Workers Directive. From a procurement perspective, this is significant, because even if it remained the case that states could only specify Posted Workers Directive-compatible labour standards, the Posted Workers Directive itself would be less restrictive, at least in the context of pay.

More generally, it may be worth noting that the Posted Workers Directive and the set of issues raised by *RegioPost* share a common, and quite profound, feature: uncertainty about whether it is the role of EU law to set a floor for labour standards upon which Member States may, at their discretion, build, or to place ceilings on Member States' discretion in this regard. Traditionally, EU labour law has been seen as pursuing a project of setting minimum standards, preventing a race to the bottom but without prohibiting the gradual improvement of working conditions within the EU, by allowing states to maintain existing higher standards or to enact more generous provisions than those laid down in EU directives. More recently, new concerns have emerged to challenge these assumptions, such as the idea of promoting the availability of forms of work that were traditionally regarded as not particularly beneficial for workers, as evidenced by the litigation surrounding the various directives on non-standard forms of work,[91] or preserving some element of competitive advantage in a posting situation, as evidenced by the *Laval* decision in particular. Given how big a change of direction this would be for EU labour law, it is not one that should be undertaken lightly, and particularly not when the relevant directives themselves expressly permit states to set above-minimum standards.[92]

[90] Above n 49.

[91] This has come to light particularly through the case law on the interpretation of the non-regression provisions in these directives, on which see L Corazza, 'Hard Times for Hard Bans: Fixed-Term Work and So-Called Non-Regression Clauses in the Era of Flexicurity' (2011) 17 *European Law Journal* 385; S Peers, 'Non-Regression Clauses: the Fig Leaf has Fallen' (2010) 39 *Industrial Law Journal* 436.

[92] For example, Council Directive 1999/70/EC concerning the framework agreement on fixed-term work concluded by ETUC, UNICE and CEEP [1999] OJ L175/43, Annex, clause 8(1); Art 3(7) of the Posted Workers Directive.

V. CONCLUSIONS AND FUTURE PROSPECTS

RegioPost represents a 'baby step' forward in the use of performance conditions in government contracts to enforce labour standards. It accepts that this may be legitimate even where the standards only apply in the public sector and not across the labour market more generally. However, a significant limitation of the decision appears to be its emphasis on the standard in question as a Posted Workers Directive-compliant minimum wage, even though the Posted Workers Directive was not technically applicable in the case. This may have the effect of constraining states' substantive scope to enforce labour standards by this route. A further limitation is evident from the *Bundesdruckerei* decision, in which the contracting authority was not permitted to enforce a locally-applicable labour standard where the contract was being performed remotely.

The issue of social goals in procurement generates a deep policy clash with EU internal market law. On the one hand, EU procurement law seeks to prevent protectionism and to open up national procurement markets to EU-wide competition. On the other hand, the pursuit of social goals through procurement has traditionally sought to take labour standards out of competition altogether. In the internal market context, this may limit the ability of firms in other Member States, particularly those with lower labour standards, to use the competitive advantage that this gives them to win government contracts in higher-cost Member States. What I have sought to show in this contribution is that it is an oversimplification to present this issue as a straightforward choice between competition and protectionism. Unbridled competition is not and should not be pursued by EU law to the exclusion of all other considerations, a point reflected in the procurement directives and in the *RegioPost* decision itself. And there are legitimate reasons for seeking to enforce, or even improve, labour standards through procurement: to promote consistency across government activities, to promote good labour practices, and to address the downward or at least stagnating pressure on wages and other labour standards competitive procurement might itself generate.

In fact, the truly deep policy problem raised by *RegioPost* but extending far beyond the procurement context is whether it is ever legitimate to treat EU labour law not as a floor of rights on which Member States can choose to build, but as a ceiling limiting their discretion. That is an issue that would benefit from a much fuller discussion by the Court, commentators and policymakers alike.

10

Fair's Fair: Public Procurement, Posting and Pay

CATHERINE BARNARD*

I. INTRODUCTION

THERE HAS ALWAYS been an inherent tension between the principles underpinning public procurement law and those underpinning the Posted Workers Directive.[1] In essence, public procurement is premised on the notion of *equal treatment* between bidders. So, Article 18(1) of the 2014 Public Procurement Directive,[2] the core provision of the Directive, provides: 'Contracting authorities shall treat economic operators *equally and without discrimination* and shall act in a transparent and proportionate manner' (emphasis added). By contrast, the treatment of posted workers providing services under Article 56 TFEU[3] has been premised on *differentiation*: posted workers are not to be treated in the same way as national workers and deliberately so—because posted workers are not similarly situated to national workers (or, indeed migrant workers under Article 45 TFEU). As we shall see, under Article 8(2) of the Rome I Regulation,[4] the contracts of posted workers are usually governed by the law of the home state. Where the pay rates are lower in the home state than in the host state, the bidder intending to use posted workers will have a competitive advantage. This raises problems for a contracting authority conducting a procurement exercise: how to marry the principle of equal treatment required

* Thanks to the editor and to Sjoerd Feenstra for their helpful comments.

[1] Directive 96/71/EC of the European Parliament and of the Council of 16 December 1996 concerning the posting of workers in the framework of the provision of services [1997] OJ L18/1. In this chapter, in order to avoid confusion between the current version and the proposed new version of the Posted Workers Directive, where relevant, reference is made to the 'Posted Workers Directive 96/71'.

[2] Directive 2014/24/EU of the European Parliament and of the Council of 26 February 2014 on public procurement and repealing Directive 2004/18/EC (2014 Public Procurement Directive) [2014] OJ L94/65.

[3] Treaty on the Functioning of the European Union (TFEU) [2012] OJ C326/47.

[4] Regulation (EC) No 593/2008 of the European Parliament and of the Council of 17 June 2008 on the law applicable to contractual obligations (Rome I) [2008] OJ L177/6.

by the 2014 Public Procurement Directive with differentiation required by Article 56 TFEU and the Rome I Regulation. The Posted Workers Directive 96/71 has helped provide some clarity by requiring the host state to apply minimum rates of pay to posted workers, but only where strict conditions have been satisfied. The proposed new Directive[5] goes even further towards equal treatment, at least in respect of pay. Differentiation is, it seems, being tamed.

In this chapter I shall argue that, after considerable experimentation, both the Court of Justice and the legislature of the European Union (EU) are moving towards prioritising equal treatment over differentiation in the case of posted workers, at least in respect of the most controversial issue, namely, pay. This will make the position of contracting authorities in a procurement exercise easier in terms of process, but it may result in the procurement costing more. The argument will be structured as follows. First, the chapter will provide a summary of the conflicting rules at play, and specifically how the requirements of the Posted Workers Directive fit with the EU's procurement rules. Secondly, it will outline the current, vexed position in respect of pay under the Posted Workers Directive, as laid down by Article 3(1)(c), and its interpretation by the Court of Justice. Thirdly, the chapter will consider the changes that may be introduced by the proposed revisions to the Posted Workers Directive, especially in respect of the sensitive issue of pay. The last section contains my conclusions.

II. THE LEGAL ISSUES AT PLAY

A. Migrant versus Posted Workers

One of the first questions facing a contracting authority when considering mandating specific labour standards in the execution of the public contract is who will actually be fulfilling the contract (national or migrant or posted workers?) and which legal regime will apply to the individuals doing the work (home or host state?). Migrant workers moving to work in another Member State on a 'permanent' basis under Article 45 TFEU enjoy *equal treatment* with national workers in the host state. This position reflects Article 8(2) of the Rome I Regulation. Article 8(2) provides:

> To the extent that the law applicable to the individual employment contract has not been chosen by the parties, the contract shall be governed by the law of the country in which or, failing that, from which the employee habitually carries out his work in performance of the contract. The country where the work is habitually carried out shall not be deemed to have changed if he is temporarily employed in another country.

[5] COM(2016) 128 final.

So a Latvian *migrant* worker working in Sweden under Article 45 TFEU will be subject to Swedish law (host state law) in just the same way as a Swedish worker working in Sweden (in both cases Sweden is the country 'from which the employee habitually carries out his work in performance of the contract'). But a Latvian *posted* worker temporarily working in Sweden will remain subject to Latvian law (home state law), since that is the law of the country 'from which the employee habitually carries out his work'. The fact that he is temporarily working in Sweden does not affect this outcome, because 'The country where the work is habitually carried out shall not be deemed to have changed if he is temporarily employed in another country.' In other words, the approach in the case of posted workers is based on *differentiation*. The Court of Justice has supported this view. In principle, it sees the application of national labour law by a host state as a barrier to the provision of services under Article 56 TFEU, and therefore presumptively unlawful, unless the host state can justify the application of its rules and show that they are proportionate.[6]

Yet for many labour law systems this outcome is problematic. The UK and Ireland apply a territorial approach to labour law (other Member States may do so in practice). This means that these states apply their labour law rules to anyone in the territory of the state, irrespective of the capacity in which the individual is in the host state (*qua* national, migrant or posted worker). The individual will be subject to national labour law, provided that he or she falls within the personal scope of the provision (eg he or she is an employee) and the temporal scope of the provision if there is one (eg he or she has completed one year's service to obtain the right). These states therefore do not distinguish between national, migrant and posted workers, and the approach they adopt is one of equal treatment. They take this position in the name of equality, fairness and good industrial relations, albeit, as we shall see, their position may contravene EU law. Their critics might allege protectionism.

For procurement lawyers, the posted workers issue also poses a dilemma. It appears to go against the grain of the equal treatment principle established in Article 18(1) of the 2014 Public Procurement Directive. One way of addressing this is to argue that the position of posted workers and that of national workers are not similar, and so the principle of equal treatment is not engaged. Another way is to say that the application of the equal treatment principle should not undermine the bidder's competitive advantage (through the use of cheaper posted workers). In either case, labour lawyers might not agree.

[6] See, eg, Judgment of 23 November 1999, *Arblade*, Joined Cases C-369/96 and C-376/96, EU:C:1999:575, para 30; Judgment of 25 October 2001, *Finalarte and Others*, Joined Cases C-49/98, C-50/98, C-52/98 to C-54/98 and C-68/98 to C-71/98, EU:C:2001:564, para 31.

The issue of how to treat posted workers becomes particularly difficult in respect of the question of pay. Those conducting a procurement exercise for, say, building works will be motivated in their decision-making, at least in part, by price. In a northern European state, such as Sweden, a contracting authority may have the choice between (i) the bid from an in-state tenderer using national or migrant workers (enjoying equal treatment with Swedish workers in respect of pay and other terms and conditions) paid at Swedish rates, or (ii) one by an out-of-state tenderer using, say, Latvian posted workers, possibly paid at Latvian rates (on this, see section III). Given the pay differentials between Latvia and Sweden, the Latvian bidder may well win. Good news for the Swedish taxpayer (more build for less money), for the Latvian company (winning the contract) and for the Latvian posted workers (more employment), but less good news for the unsuccessful Swedish bidder, its employees and their trade unions (which will cry foul and allege social dumping). This creates a dilemma for the Swedish Government. Should it be opting for the lowest bid (and in so doing save the taxpayer money through cheaper building costs) and incidentally assist the Latvian company, its workers and ultimately the Latvian economy. Or should the Swedish Government be protecting the interests of Swedish workers (who are likely to be voters).[7] Procurement law is clear: economic interests (though the most economically advantageous tender (MEAT)) should prevail over political interest.

But what about the need to ensure that posted workers are protected while working in the higher-cost state? This has become a problem for the Court of Justice too, which has had to hold the ring between the competing interests,[8] and for the EU legislature, which has adopted two Directives in this field: the original Posted Workers Directive 96/71 (with a revision to the Posted Workers Directive now being discussed) and the PWD Enforcement Directive.[9] Meanwhile, the 2014 Public Procurement Directive, with its significantly more 'social' orientation, recognises that the Posted Workers Directive 96/71 may apply to tenders but fails to explain how to accommodate the equal treatment principle on which the procurement rules are premised with the differentiation principle underpinning the notions of posting. It is to this issue that we now turn.

[7] For the French the answer is clear—the latter. See 'Concurrence sociale des travailleurs détachés en France: fausses évidences et réalités' (2016) 171 *Trésor-éco*, at tresor.economie.gouv.fr/Ressources/File/425307.

[8] C Barnard, 'The Worker Protection Justification: Lessons From Consumer Law' in P Koutrakos, N Nic Shuibhne and P Syrpis (eds), *Exceptions from EU Free Movement Law: Derogation, Justification and Proportionality*, (Oxford, Hart Publishing, 2016) 106.

[9] Directive 2014/67/EU of the European Parliament and of the Council of 15 May 2014 on the enforcement of Directive 96/71/EC concerning the posting of workers in the framework of the provision of services and amending Regulation (EU) No 1024/2012 on administrative cooperation through the Internal Market Information System ('the IMI Regulation') (PWD Enforcement Directive) [2014] OJ L159/11.

B. The Interplay between the Posted Workers Directive and the Procurement Directive

It has largely been left to the Court of Justice to work out how the different bits of the legal jigsaw—equal treatment and differentiation—fit together. Three main situations arise, which are considered in turn below.

i. Contract Fulfilled by National Bidder or Out-of-State Bidder Using Labour from the Contracting State

Where an economic operator from either State A or State B wins a contract to provide services/works in State A and will use State A's residents to fulfil the contract, Article 18(2) of the 2014 Public Procurement Directive and Article 8(2) of the Rome I Regulation require the contractor to comply, at a minimum, with State A's labour laws in respect of State A's workers and those workers migrating to State A under Article 45 TFEU.[10] This position is reinforced by Article 69 of the 2014 Public Procurement Directive, which mandates the rejection of an abnormally low tender where the origin of the abnormality is non-compliance with Article 18(2) obligations.

ii. Contract Fulfilled by Out-of-State Bidder Using its Own Labour: Work Performed in Bidder's Own State

Where a bidder in State B wins a service contract in State A but with the work being done in State B, the home state, *Bundesdruckerei*[11] makes clear that the contracting authority in State A cannot insist that State A's labour law rules apply, since this would be contrary to Article 56 TFEU on free movement of services. The 2014 Public Procurement Directive (which was adopted before the decision) does not appear to affect this outcome. Recital 37 says:

> it is of particular importance that Member States and contracting authorities take relevant measures to ensure compliance with obligations in the fields of environmental, social and labour law that apply *at the place* where the works are executed or the services provided and result from laws, regulations, decrees and decisions, at both national and Union level, as well as from collective agreements, provided that such rules, and their application, comply with Union law. (emphasis added)

[10] Recital 37 of the 2014 Public Procurement Directive, first paragraph, which talks about Member States and contracting authorities taking the relevant measures to ensure compliance with the social and labour laws 'at the place where the works are executed or the services provided'.

[11] Judgment of 18 September 2014, *Bundesdruckerei*, Case C-549/13, EU:C:2014:2235.

iii. Contract Fulfilled by Out-of-State Bidder Using its Own Labour: Work Performed in Contracting Authority's Own State

The position is different where a State B contractor wins a contract in State A and plans to bring posted workers with it to fulfil the contract in State A. As we have seen, the position of posted workers working temporarily in another Member State under Article 56 TFEU is, in principle, governed by home state law. However, the case law and now the Posted Workers Directive have mitigated this position somewhat. The case law recognised that host states could apply some of their rules, especially those concerning control measures, to posted workers.[12] The Posted Workers Directive is more prescriptive. It requires *host* states to apply their laws in the areas listed in Article 3(1)(a)–(g) of the Directive, including minimum rates of pay in Article 3(1)(c). The Posted Workers Directive is thus a coordination Directive: it identifies which rules apply in which situations. It does not harmonise 'the material content of those mandatory rules for minimum protection, even though it provides certain information concerning that content'.[13]

The Posted Workers Directive has two purposes. As the Court said in *Laval*,[14] Article 3(1) seeks, first, to ensure a climate of fair competition between national undertakings and undertakings that provide services transnationally, in so far as it requires the latter to afford their workers, as regards a limited list of matters, the terms and conditions of employment laid down in the host Member State by law, regulation or administrative provision, or by collective agreements or arbitration awards, which constitute mandatory rules for minimum protection.[15] The Court continued:

> That provision thus prevents a situation arising in which, by applying to their workers the terms and conditions of employment in force in the Member State of origin as regards those matters, undertakings established in other Member States would compete unfairly against undertakings of the host Member State in the framework of the transnational provision of services, if the level of social protection in the host Member State is higher.[16]

These observations coincide with the services legal basis on which the Directive was based.

The Court in *Laval* then added:

> Secondly, that provision seeks to ensure that posted workers will have the rules of the Member States for minimum protection as regards the terms and conditions of employment relating to those matters applied to them while they work on a temporary basis in the territory of that Member State.[17]

[12] See Barnard, above n 8, for an extensive discussion of the case law.

[13] Judgment of 12 February 2015, *Sähköalojen ammattiliitto*, Case C-396/13, EU:C:2015:86 (the '*ESA* case'), para 31.

[14] Judgment of 18 December 2007, *Laval un Partneri*, Case C-341/05, EU:C:2007:809.

[15] ibid, para 74.

[16] ibid, para 75.

[17] ibid, para 76.

This is the recognition of the social dimension of the Directive. The Court's observations highlight the inherent tension in the Directive: it is a services directive premised on the idea of home state control and thus differentiation, but with a social dimension based on equal treatment, at least in the areas listed in Article 3(1)(a)–(g).

Article 3(1)(a)–(g) of the Posted Workers Directive, as interpreted by the Court of Justice in *Laval* and *Rüffert*,[18] are limited in scope. Given the legal basis of the Posted Workers Directive in the services provisions of the Treaty, these cases demonstrate that the Court saw Article 3(1) as a derogation from the basic rule that *home* state laws apply. Article 3(1) is therefore narrowly construed. This means that a *host* state contracting authority cannot insist that where the contract is being fulfilled by posted workers, they must enjoy all of host state's labour laws; the contracting authority can insist on compliance only with those host state rules listed in Article 3(1)(a)–(g) of the Posted Workers Directive.[19] For this reason, states like the UK, which adopt a territorial approach to labour law, are in breach of the principles in the Posted Workers Directive.

However, *Laval* and *Rüffert* were decided when the 2004 Public Procurement Directive was in force. The 2014 Public Procurement Package has made a difference. In keeping with the EU's objective, first articulated in the Lisbon Treaty, that the EU is a 'social market economy',[20] the 2014 Public Procurement Package is avowedly more social.[21] It has the express objective of making better use of public procurement 'in support of common societal goals', including protection of the environment,[22] promoting innovation, and social inclusion.[23] This change in approach is most clearly demonstrated by the introduction of Article 18(2) into the 2014 Public Procurement Directive. This provides:

> Member States shall take appropriate measures to ensure that in the performance of public contracts economic operators comply with applicable obligations in the fields of environmental, *social and labour law* established by Union law, national law, collective agreements or by the international environmental, social and labour law provisions listed in Annex X. (emphasis added)

[18] Judgment of 3 April 2008, *Rüffert*, Case C-346/06, EU:C:2008:189.

[19] See also Recital 37, second paragraph.

[20] See now Art 3(3) of the Treaty on European Union (TEU).

[21] C Barnard, 'To Boldly Go: Social Clauses in Public Procurement' (2016) 46 *Industrial Law Journal* 208.

[22] Recital 91 of the 2014 Public Procurement Directive says: 'This Directive clarifies how the contracting authorities can contribute to the protection of the environment and the promotion of sustainable development, whilst ensuring that they can obtain the best value for money for their contracts.'

[23] See recitals 47 and 95 of the 2014 Public Procurement Directive; and also European Commission, *Green Paper on the modernisation of EU public procurement policy. Towards a more efficient European Procurement Market*, COM(2011) 15.

Annex X contains reference to the main ILO labour conventions. The introduction of Article 18(2) may be a positive development for the enforcement of labour law.[24]

Recital 37 elaborates on Article 18(2) of the 2014 Public Procurement Directive, part of which was quoted above. It will be recalled that recital 37 provides that it is of particular importance that Member States and contracting authorities ensure compliance with obligations in the fields of social and labour law that result from laws, regulations, decrees and decisions, at both national and Union level, as well as from collective agreements. It continues:

> Equally, obligations stemming from international agreements ratified by all Member States and listed in Annex X should apply during contract performance. However, this should in no way prevent the application of terms and conditions of employment which are more favourable to workers.

Given the pro-social shift of the 2014 Directives, the European Trade Union Confederation (ETUC) has argued that since *Laval/Rüffert* pre-dated the 2014 Public Procurement Package, that case law should be reconsidered.[25] However, the various references to the Posted Workers Directive in the recitals of the 2014 Public Procurement Directive suggest that the EU legislature wished to confirm the case law of the Court of Justice, not reconsider it, albeit that the references to equal treatment confuse the picture. So, for example, recital 37 says:

> The relevant measures should be applied in conformity with the basic principles of Union law, in particular with a view to ensuring equal treatment. Such relevant measures should be applied in accordance with [the Posted Workers] Directive … and in a way that ensures equal treatment and does not discriminate directly or indirectly against economic operators and workers from other Member States.

Recital 98 adds that it is essential that award criteria or contract performance conditions concerning social aspects of the production process relate to the works, supplies or services to be provided under the contract. It continues:

> In addition, they should be applied in accordance with [the Posted Workers Directive], as interpreted by the [Court of Justice] and should not be chosen or applied in a way that discriminates directly or indirectly against economic operators from other Member States … Thus, requirements concerning the basic working conditions regulated in [the Posted Workers Directive], such as minimum rates

[24] See further A Sánchez-Graells, 'Regulatory Substitution between Labour and Public Procurement Law: The EU's Shifting Approach to Enforcing Labour Standards in Public Contracts' (2018) 24(2) *European Public Law* forthcoming.

[25] European Trade Union Confederation, 'New EU Framework on Public procurement: ETUC key points for the transposition of Directive 2014/24/EU' (2014) heading 2.3, at etuc.org/sites/www.etuc.org/files/publication/files/ces-brochure_transpo_edited_03.pdf.

of pay, should remain at the level set by national legislation or by collective agreements applied in accordance with Union law in the context of that Directive.

The repeated references to the Posted Workers Directive suggest that the principle of equal treatment in the 2014 Public Procurement Directive was not intended to trump the carefully balanced approach in the Posted Workers Directive, but the Procurement Directive does not provide much of a steer as to how to square the circle of reconciling principles of equal treatment/host state control, on the one hand, (mainly for national and migrant workers) and home state control for service providers, on the other. The issue is particularly acute in respect of pay.

III. WHAT IS PAY?

A. The Meaning of Pay under the Posted Workers Directive

i. Minimum Rates of Pay as Laid Down by Law or Collective Agreement

Article 3(1)(c) of the Posted Workers Directive says the host state must require the employer to pay '*the minimum rates of pay, including overtime rates*; this point does not apply to supplementary occupational retirement pension schemes' (emphasis added). Article 3(1) makes clear that the minimum rates of pay must be laid down by law, regulation or administrative provision, or, in the case of the building industry, by collective agreement which satisfies the conditions laid down in Article 3(8). So a contracting authority in the UK can insist that a successful bidder who performs the contract using posted workers pay the UK national minimum wage for the under-25s and the national *living* wage for those aged 25 and over, since these are 'laid down by law'.[26] By contrast, in *Rüffert* the Court said that a rate of pay fixed by a collective agreement that applied to public sector contracts only and which had not been declared universally applicable, as required by Article 3(8) could not be justified.[27] This strict reading of Article 3(1) and (8) inclined towards differentiation, not equal treatment.

ii. Voluntary Higher Rates

The position is more complicated in respect of a requirement on the successful bidder to pay the *UK* living wage (not to be confused with the *national*

[26] In his 2015 budget, the Chancellor of the Exchequer announced a 'national living wage'—a 50p increase in the statutory *minimum* pay rate for the over-25s from April 2016, to £7.20 an hour (introduced through amendment to the National Minimum Wage Regulations 2015 (SI 2015/621), at www.legislation.gov.uk/uksi/2015/621/regulation/4/made), followed by a series of stepped increases expected to take the rate above £9 an hour by 2020.

[27] *Rüffert*, above n 18, para 39 cf *RegioPost* below n 35, considered at section III.A.iii below.

living wage). The UK living wage (£8.45 outside London, £9.75 in London) is currently not legally binding,[28] but a significant number of large employers have agreed to pay it, recognising that the cost of living is so high in some areas (for example, Cambridge), workers need to be paid more than the national living wage. So the contracting authority can probably impose a requirement on tenderers to pay the UK living wage in respect of local workers and migrant workers working in the UK under Article 45 TFEU. However, the position may be different in respect of *posted* workers. It may not be possible to require the UK living wage to be paid in respect of posted workers because Article 3(1)(c) of the Posted Workers Directive makes clear that host states can require posting companies to pay the minimum wage only, as laid down by law or collective agreement. This seems to be the intention of recital 98 of the 2014 Public Procurement Directive set out in section II.B.iii.

However, as *Laval* made clear, Article 3(7), first paragraph, of the Posted Workers Directive allows posting companies to pay higher rates of pay if they so choose.[29] While at first sight this seems unlikely, such companies may do so if they think it will (i) strengthen their hand in winning a contract, or (ii) maintain good industrial relations (as in the case of the Lindsey Oil Refinery[30]), or (iii) professionalise the sector (as experience in the cleaning sector has shown[31]). The costs of paying the living wage will, however, be passed on to the contracting authority.

Thus, while voluntary compliance with the UK living wage would satisfy the Posted Workers Directive, a mandatory obligation would not. Yet as Koukiadaki shows,[32] the reality is more complex. Although the UK Cabinet Office has been broadly against the imposition of the UK living wage, for fear of challenge under EU law,[33] the EU, at least pre-*RegioPost*, took a different line. Commissioner McCreevy, in response to a question from Jean Lambert MEP, said '[l]iving-wage conditions may be included in the contract performance clauses of a public procurement contract provided they are not directly or indirectly discriminatory and are indicated in the contract notice or in the contract documents'.[34] The response continues:

> In addition, [living-wage conditions] must be related to the execution of the contract. In order to comply with this last condition, contract performance clauses

[28] See at livingwage.org.uk/. See also the contribution by Semple in ch 5 of this book.

[29] *Laval*, above n 14, para 81.

[30] Barnard, above n 21, 240.

[31] A Koukiadaki, 'The Far-Reaching Implications of the *Laval* Quartet: the case of the UK living wage' (2014) 43 *Industrial Law Journal* 91, 108.

[32] ibid, especially at 106–14.

[33] See also OGC, *Procurement Policy Note—Quarterly Update* (London, OGC, 2009) 4. See also T Ross, 'Downing Street says Boris Johnson's living wage may be "illegal"', 5 November 2012, at telegraph.co.uk/news/politics/9656627/Downing-Street-says-Boris-Johnsons-living-wage-may-be-illegal.html.

[34] European Parliament, 'Answer given by Mr McCreevy on behalf of the European Commission', 11 March 2009, at europarl.europa.eu/sides/getAllAnswers.do?language=EN&

including living-wage conditions must concern only the employees involved in the execution of the relevant contract, and may not be extended to the other employees of the contractor.

In other words, it is possible to impose a requirement to pay the living wage, but the requirement must be linked to the subject matter of the contract (in the broad sense of the phrase).

iii. RegioPost

In *RegioPost*,[35] the Court of Justice returned to the question of whether contracting authorities could prescribe minimum wage requirements, but this time in performance conditions under Article 26 of the 2004 Public Procurement Directive[36] (now Article 70 of the 2014 Public Procurement Directive, which had already been adopted when *RegioPost* was decided) and in the context of a state (*Land*) law that prescribed a minimum hourly wage applicable to companies performing public contracts. This was the first time the Court expressly examined the Posted Workers Directive and 2004 Public Procurement Directive together (in *Rüffert* the Court looked only at the interpretation of the Posted Workers Directive, even though the case arose in the context of a public procurement exercise). The Court upheld the requirement:

> It follows that Article 26 of [the 2004 Public Procurement Directive], read in conjunction with [the Posted Workers Directive], permits the host Member State to lay down, in the context of the award of a public contract, a mandatory rule for minimum protection referred to in point (c) of the first subparagraph of Article 3(1) of [the Posted Workers Directive], ... [ie a minimum wage applicable to public contracts only that was enshrined in regional state law], which requires undertakings established in other Member States to comply with an obligation in respect of a minimum rate of pay for the benefit of their workers posted to the territory of the host Member State in order to perform that public contract. Such a rule is part of the level of protection which must be guaranteed to those workers (see, to that effect, judgment in *Laval un Partneri*, C-341/05, EU:C:2007:809, paragraphs 74, 80 and 81).[37]

However, the Court of Justice did not content itself with a reading of the two Directives. It also verified whether that interpretation of Article 26 of the 2004 Public Procurement Directive could be confirmed by a reading of

reference=P-2009-0922. For discussion in Scotland, see Local Government and Regeneration Committee, Living Wage Enquiry, Scottish Parliament, 21 December 2011, 485.

[35] Judgment of 17 November 2015, *RegioPost*, Case C-115/14, EU:C:2015:760.

[36] Directive 2004/18/EC of the European Parliament and of the Council of 31 March 2004 on the coordination of procedures for the award of public works contracts, public supply contracts and public service contracts (2004 Public Procurement Directive) [2004] OJ L134/114.

[37] *RegioPost*, above n 35, para 66.

that provision in the light of Article 56 TFEU,[38] a necessary exercise since Article 26 did not exhaustively harmonise special conditions relating to the performance of the contract. It found that

> the imposition, under national legislation, of a minimum wage on tenderers and their subcontractors, if any, established in a Member State other than that of the contracting authority and in which minimum rates of pay are lower constitutes an additional economic burden that may prohibit, impede or render less attractive the provision of their services in the host Member State ...[39]

and so constituted a restriction within the meaning of Article 56 TFEU. However, such a national measure could, in principle, be justified by the objective of protecting workers, even though it applied to public contracts only and not to private contracts.

This is a significant departure from the earlier decision in *Rüffert*, not least because the Court recognises the public procurement context in which the rules have been adopted and the fact it did not matter the rules were confined to public contracts. It also shows an increasing willingness by the Court of Justice to recognise the imposition of requirements in respect of minimum rates of pay, and thus equal treatment.

B. Other Allowances

There is a further question. Does the term 'pay' include other allowances? If 'pay' is broadly defined to allow the host state to include not only remuneration such as the minimum wage but also other allowances and benefits, the greater the move towards equal treatment. This means that the posted workers are treated more similarly to national workers. This reduces the potential for 'undercutting' by posted workers (albeit it also reduces the costs savings for the contracting authority). Conversely, if the term 'pay' is narrowly defined and confined only to the actual minimum wage itself then the fewer the requirements the host state can impose on the employer of the posted worker, the greater the differentiation between the treatment of national and posted workers, and the more the out-of-state services provider will have a competitive advantage.

As we have seen, Article 3(1)(c) of the Posted Workers Directive talks of '*the minimum rates of pay, including overtime rates*; this point does not apply to supplementary occupational retirement pension schemes' (emphasis added). Article 3 subsequently provides, 'For the purposes of this directive, *the concept of minimum rates of pay referred to in paragraph 1(c) is defined by the national law and/or practice of the Member State* to whose territory the worker is posted' (emphasis added). This suggests that host Member

[38] For an in-depth analysis of this dimension of the judgment, see the contributions by Syrpis and by Bogdanowicz in chs 2 and 3 of this book respectively.

[39] *RegioPost*, above n 35, para 69.

States have much latitude to define what constitutes 'pay'. However, as the Court of Justice put it in *Isbir*,[40] the task of defining what are the constituent elements of the minimum wage, for the application of the Posted Workers Directive, comes within the scope of the law of the Member State concerned, but 'only in so far as that definition, deriving from the legislation or relevant national collective agreements, or as interpreted by the national courts, does not have the effect of impeding the free movement of services between Member States'.[41] In fact, as we shall see, the Court of Justice has played a considerable role in determining what falls in and out of the definition of 'pay', thereby limiting the Member States' margin of discretion.

Article 3(7), second paragraph, of the Posted Workers Directive also needs to be considered. It was included as part of a compromise between the Portuguese and the Germans. Cryptically, it provides:

> Allowances specific to the posting shall be considered to be part of the minimum wage, unless they are paid in reimbursement of expenditure actually incurred on account of the posting, such as expenditure on travel, board and lodging.

This appears to suggest that while a flat rate allowance, such as a living-away-from-home allowance, does constitute pay, reimbursement of actual expenses does not.

At first the Court of Justice took a strict view as to whether additional payments could be included in the definition of 'pay'. So in *Laval*, for example, the special buildings supplement was not considered pay, nor were a number of insurance premiums.[42] In *Commission v Luxembourg*[43] the Court said the requirement to adjust wages other than the minimum wage automatically to reflect changes in the cost of living was not covered by Article 3(1)(c). In the *ESA* case[44] the Court found that a daily allowance and compensation, both in the form of a flat rate payment, were allowances 'specific to the posting' within the meaning of Article 3(7) and so constituted part of the minimum wage, as was holiday pay, but coverage of the cost of accommodation and meal vouchers did not constitute pay. Similarly, in *STX*[45] the EFTA Court found that overtime pay and a posting allowance were pay if set as a minimum and were transparent, but expenses for travel, board and lodging were not because they were set at a variable rate. In *Isbir*, the Court confirmed that allowances and supplements which are not

> defined as being constituent elements of the minimum wage by the legislation or national practice of the Member State to the territory of which the worker is posted, and which alter the relationship between the service provided by the

[40] Judgment of 7 November 2013, *Isbir*, Case C-522/12, EU:C:2013:711.

[41] ibid, para 37.

[42] *Laval*, above n 14, para 83.

[43] Judgment of 19 June 2008, *Commission v Luxembourg*, Case C-319/06, EU:C:2008:350, para 55.

[44] The *ESA* case, above n 13.

[45] Judgment of 23 January 2012, *STX Norway and Others*, E-2/11 (EFTA Court). See also Case C-396/13 Sähköalojen ammattiliitto EU:C:2015:86.

> worker, on the one hand, and the consideration which he receives in return for that service, on the other, cannot, under the provisions of [the Posted Workers Directive], be treated as being elements of that kind.[46]

So if an employer required a worker to carry out additional work, or to work under particular conditions, compensation had to be provided to the worker for that additional service without it being taken into account for the purpose of calculating the minimum wage.

Part of the confusion in this area is whether an 'addition' or 'subtraction' approach is applied to the notion of pay. Under the 'addition' approach, usually favoured by the host state's trade unions, the host state can specify that pay includes not only the actual minimum wage but also specific allowances. So if the host state minimum pay is €8 an hour, the flat rate living-away-from-home allowance is €4 and the dirty-work allowance is €2 an hour, when added together this gives a total of €14 an hour. So if the minimum wage in Latvia is €3 an hour then the Latvian employer posting a worker to the host state will have to pay an additional €11 an hour (€14 – €3).

Under the 'subtraction' approach, favoured by the posting company, the specific allowances count towards the minimum wage and so are deducted from the total. So using the example above, the sums payable under host state law would be: €8 – €4 – €1 = €3. So the Latvian employer would not have to pay any additional amount, since the minimum wage in Latvia is €3 an hour. When presented in this way, the addition approach comes closer to a full equal treatment model than the subtraction approach. The more recent cases, especially the *ESA* case, point to a shift towards the equal treatment model.

But the equal treatment model does pose a problem for the posting employer. Let us take the situation where the Latvian employer pays €3 an hour in pay and also covers the employees' travel and accommodation. The applicable collective agreement in the host state requires not only a minimum rate of pay, but also a flat rate allowance for living away from home. The posting employer in essence ends up paying twice for the accommodation. This is surely unequal treatment and a restriction on the provision of services.

IV. AMENDMENTS TO THE POSTED WORKERS DIRECTIVE

A. The Amendments

The fact that the Court has been more generous in recognising what constitutes a minimum wage, and has been moving towards more of an equal treatment approach, has not been enough to satisfy receiving states.

[46] *Isbir*, above n 40, para 38.

By a joint letter, Austria, Belgium, France,[47] Germany, Luxembourg, The Netherlands and Sweden called for modernisation of the Posted Workers Directive. They asked for the establishment of the principle of 'equal pay for equal work in the same place' and the setting up of a maximum duration on the limit of a posting, aligning provisions of the Posted Workers Directive with EU Regulation 883/04 on coordination of social security,[48] which provides that a posted worker must remain subject to the legislation of the first Member State, provided that the anticipated duration of such work does not exceed 24 months and that the posted worker is not sent to replace another person.[49] In other words, the Northern Member States were pushing for ever more equal treatment.

The Commission responded with a draft proposal.[50] For our purposes, it contained five important provisions:

(i) In respect of postings exceeding 24 months, the Commission proposed that posted workers be treated like migrant workers, and thus enjoy the principle of equal treatment:

> 1. When the anticipated or the effective duration of posting exceeds twenty-four months, the Member State to whose territory a worker is posted shall be deemed to be the country in which his or her work is habitually carried out.
> 2. For the purpose of paragraph 1, in case of replacement of posted workers performing the same task at the same place, the cumulative duration of the posting periods of the workers concerned shall be taken into account, with regard to workers that are posted for an effective duration of at least six months.

This appears to suggest that posted workers with an expected duration of posting of two years or more must enjoy equal treatment from day one—and thus are treated like migrant workers under Article 45 TFEU.

(ii) The Commission proposed that the reference to 'minimum rates of pay' in Article 3(1)(c) of the Posted Workers Directive be amended to refer to '*remuneration*, including overtime rates; this point does not apply to supplementary occupational retirement pension schemes' (emphasis added).[51]

[47] See, eg, Euractiv, 'France threatens to stop applying EU law on posted workers', 4 July 2016, at euractiv.com/section/social-europe-jobs/news/france-threatens-to-stop-applying-eu-law-on-posted-workers/: 'politicians and unions have blamed the system of seconded or "posted" workers, allowing employers to pay them no more than the minimum rate in the host country, as the cause of job losses in France, particularly in the livestock industry. "The French government is seeking to convince (the EU), and many countries agree, that we need to change. There must be equal treatment upwards to fight social dumping. … If it is not possible to convince … France will not apply this directive."'

[48] Regulation (EC) No 883/2004 of the European Parliament and of the Council of 29 April 2004 on the coordination of social security systems [2004] OJ L166/1.

[49] ibid, Art 12.

[50] COM(2016) 128. See also the contribution by Novitz in ch 11 of this book.

[51] In the original proposal the last sentence of Art 3(1) (which left it to the Member States to define the concept of minimum rates of pay) was deleted (cf Danish yellow card).

(iii) At present the minimum rates of pay must be laid down by law or, in the case of activities in the building industry, by collective agreement. The proposed changes to the Directive remove that building industry qualification in respect of the requirement of pay. In other words, the proposed changes extend to all sectors. So the proposed Directive provides:

> For the purpose of this Directive, remuneration means all the elements of remuneration rendered mandatory by national law, regulation or administrative provision, collective agreements or arbitration awards which have been declared universally applicable and/or, in the absence of a system for declaring collective agreements or arbitration awards to be of universal application, other collective agreements or arbitration awards within the meaning of paragraph 8 second subparagraph, in the Member State to whose territory the worker is posted.

(iv) Given the uncertainty over what constitutes 'pay', the proposed Directive provides:

> Member States shall publish in the single official national website referred to in Article 5 of Directive 2014/67/EU the constituent elements of remuneration in accordance with point (c).

(v) There are also changes proposed to Article 3(9). Reference to Article 5 of the Temporary Agency Workers Directive[52] would allow Member States to derogate from the principle of equal treatment in line with Article 5, while they may already have provided for equal treatment in accordance with the current paragraph 9.

However, the Member States were—and still are—deeply divided by the proposal. Broadly speaking, those in receiving states were in favour, those in sending states were not. Yellow cards were issued by 11 national parliaments,[53] and the matter was reconsidered but the proposal was maintained.[54] In the event, the Ministers of Labour meeting in Council in June 2017 apparently agreed to the second and third proposals but not the first: posted workers will only enjoy full equal treatment in respect of *terms and conditions* after 24 months plus one day. However, crucially, the principle of equal treatment in respect of *pay* will apply to posted workers from day one. So the tortuous case law on what constitutes pay will eventually have to be reconsidered in the light of the broader requirement of remuneration.

[52] Directive 2008/104/EC of the European Parliament and of the Council of 19 November 2008 on temporary agency work [2008] OJ L327/9.

[53] Bulgaria, Croatia, Czech Republic, Denmark, Estonia, Hungary, Latvia, Lithuania, Poland, Romania and Slovakia sent reasoned opinions claiming that the proposal was in breach of the principle of subsidiarity. This triggered the subsidiarity control mechanism (the so-called 'yellow card' procedure). In addition, national parliaments from five Member States (France, Italy, Portugal, Spain and the UK) submitted opinions that the Commission's proposal was indeed compatible with the principle of subsidiarity: europa.eu/rapid/press-release_IP-16-2546_en.htm.

[54] For the Commisison's response, see COM(2016) 505.

But not for a while; a number of states have requested a five-year derogation from the application of the rule. Subsequent discussions have revolved round reducing the maximum duration of posting to 12 months, as well as introducing a reference period of 24 months to calculate this duration and taking into account all periods of posting, including those lasting less than six months. There is also a proposal to incorporate allowances for 'transport, accommodation and meals' into the core set of rights guaranteed to posted workers.

More fundamentally, the European Parliament has made a significant intervention: it says 'The legal basis should be extended, from just provisions concerning the free movement of services, to Article 151 TFEU and points (a) and (b) of Article 153(1) TFEU on workers' rights.'[55] It also notes that Member States are given the autonomy to determine the concept of remuneration on their own territory, but they should ensure that posted workers receive all due entitlements. Double payment of elements constituting the remuneration in the home and the host Member State should be avoided. Further, it says the Directive should not affect the freedom to strike and to conclude collective agreements, and that in order to avoid cascade postings, the same terms and conditions should apply for workers hired by subcontractors or temporary employment undertakings.

Adding Article 153(1)(a) and (b) TFEU as a legal basis would help to shore up the social orientation of the Directive. However, as the preceding discussion has shown, this creates a further tension between the services, host-state orientation of the original version of the original Posted Workers Directive, and thus differentiation of treatment between posted and national workers, on the one hand, and the social orientation of the revisions, and thus equal treatment between posted and national workers, on the other. This sets up the circumstances for a potential challenge to the Directive: if the revisions have both a services and a social legal basis, yet the content is primarily equal treatment-focused and social, does this mean that employers in Eastern European countries might challenge the Directive as being adopted incorrectly on a dual legal basis since one of the objectives of the Directive—guaranteeing a level playing field for foreign service providers—has been overlooked? Or could they argue that this Directive is really about harmonisation of remuneration requirements and therefore Article 153 should not be used because of the exclusion in Article 153(5) TFEU? And how will the proposed amendments to the Directive fit with the PWD Enforcement Directive, which will presumably be used to help enforce the amendments, which only has the services legal basis (Article 53(1) and Article 62 TFEU)?

[55] See at europarl.europa.eu/legislative-train/theme-deeper-and-fairer-internal-market-with-a-strengthened-industrial-base-labour/file-revision-of-the-directive-on-the-posting-of-workers-labour-mobility-package.

B. The Member States' Response

The question of how to manage the posting of workers has become highly politicised, especially in France. Without waiting for the amendments to the Directive, a number of regions in France have, in the name of equal treatment in procurement, the safety of workers and the protection of local jobs, imposed the so-called '*clause Molière*', requiring French to be spoken on building sites.[56] The French Government has declared the rule unlawful.[57] However, President Macron is determined to secure the reforms to the Posted Workers Directive. He has said:[58]

> The differences in living standards create the feeling that people from poorer states with lower incomes pose a threat to people in the richer countries. This feeling played a key role in the Brexit vote and also plays into the hands of extremists in other parts of Western Europe.

He has therefore argued that 'A thoroughgoing solution must be found to correct this absurd directive which creates unemployment, penalises our industry and exacerbates tensions.'[59] However, the Eastern European states, especially Poland (which has half a million Polish posted workers) and Hungary, are standing firm.

V. CONCLUSIONS

This chapter started by highlighting the tensions between the principle of equal treatment in the 2014 Public Procurement Directive and the idea of differentiation underpinning the Posted Workers Directive. We have seen how the Court of Justice has been slowly moving in the direction of supporting a more equal treatment-based approach to posted workers, an approach which has now been strongly endorsed, especially in respect of remuneration, by the legislature in the proposed revision of the Posted Workers Directive. However, equal treatment comes with a risk. Since out-of-state bidders will no longer be able to compete purely on price (through lower wage costs), they may make other cuts in order to retain their competitive advantage. This is already the concern in France, which has threatened to stop applying EU law on posted workers.[60] There are other reports of income for posted workers being 50 per cent less than that usually paid in a

[56] See at www.lefigaro.fr/international/2017/08/21/01003-20170821ARTFIG00261-travailleurs-detaches-la-clause-moliere-l-arme-des-elus-locaux.php.

[57] See at www.lefigaro.fr/conjoncture/2017/05/04/20002-20170504ARTFIG00105-le-gouvernement-declare-la-clause-moliere-illegale.php.

[58] See at www.eurotopics.net/en/184749/macron-vs-the-posted-workers-directive.

[59] ibid.

[60] Euractiv, above n 47.

given place for the same job.[61] In other words, whatever the rules say, many workers are not benefitting from them on the ground. In the work I have done with Amy Ludlow, we found anecdotal evidence that agencies were not paying holiday pay to workers; the holiday pay constituted the profit margin on the job. Employers then rely on the reluctance (of posted/migrant workers) to enforce claims.[62] This raises the question, then, of whether one attempt to create fairness (by legislating to improve the position of posted workers) causes unfairness in another domain (an ever greater incentive for posting companies not to comply with the law). The EU is trying to address this but is facing an uphill battle. Even if the proposed amendments are adopted, the question is whether the Member States can deliver on ensuring effective enforcement and thus guaranteeing genuine equal treatment for posted workers.

[61] R Zahn, *Revision of the Posted Workers' Directive: Equality at Last?* (2016) Working Paper, Centre of European and Transnational Legal Studies Belfast, at strathprints.strath.ac.uk/58911/.

[62] C Barnard and A Ludlow, 'The Enforcement of Rights by EU-8 migrants before Employment Tribunals' (2016) 45 *Industrial Law Journal* 1.

11

Collective Bargaining and Social Dumping in Posting and Procurement

What Might Come from Recent Court of Justice Case Law and the Proposed Reform of the Posted Workers Directive?

TONIA NOVITZ

I. INTRODUCTION

THIS CHAPTER EXAMINES the peculiar treatment of collective bargaining and procurement under posting rules established by the Posted Workers Directive[1] and case law of the Court of Justice. Considering the scope for 'social dumping', the chapter highlights the problems surrounding the requirement that minimum terms and conditions for posted workers be set by 'universally applicable' collective agreements,[2] particularly in the light of austerity policies that have made such agreements (as defined by the Court of Justice) exceedingly rare and unlikely to be given legal effect.

It emerges that while the *ESA* case[3] shows unprecedented sympathy for the engagement of local trade unions in a host state regarding the protection of posted workers' interests, neither that judgment nor that in *RegioPost*[4] makes any significant inroads into the established (and I argue irrational)

[1] Directive 96/71/EC of the European Parliament and of the Council of 16 December 1996 concerning the posting of workers in the framework of the provision of services (Posted Workers Directive) [1997] OJ L18/1.

[2] See ibid, Art 3(1) and (8).

[3] Judgment of 12 February 2015, *Sähköalojen ammattiliitto* (the '*ESA* case'), Case C-396/13, EU:C:2015:86.

[4] Judgment of 17 November 2015, *RegioPost*, Case C-115/14, EU:C:2015:760.

position on collective agreements. This is despite the unrestricted reference to 'collective agreements' and their potential influence in posting to be found in the 2014 Public Procurement Directive,[5] which is not of course the relevant legislation discussed in *RegioPost* but could be expected to be in the contemplation of the Court in cases subsequent to its adoption, if not implementation.[6]

In this respect, the proposals made by the European Commission in 2012 for reform of the priority of economic and social entitlements,[7] and those that followed in 2016 for reform of the Posted Workers Directive[8] as a corrective to 'social dumping', are interesting. The outstanding question, of course, is whether these proposed reforms will be implemented at all. My argument is that even if they are not, the evidence on which the 2016 proposal is based provides the foundation for future litigation and legislation concerning social dumping and posted work. Indeed, the issue of social dumping, while not discussed in depth, is explicit in the impact assessment accompanying the most recent Commission proposals.[9]

This chapter begins by outlining the initial restrictions placed on definitions of 'universally applicable' collective agreements by the Court of Justice in *Laval*[10] and *Rüffert*.[11] It then considers subsequent restrictions on the conclusion and legislative adoption of universally applicable collective agreements promoted by the European Commission in the context of austerity measures, which were deemed appropriate for EU Member States in the aftermath of the financial crisis. The drive for flexibility in labour markets led to a situation where it was difficult to find (and therefore implement) a universally applicable collective agreement in an EU Member State. The consequences for posted workers are addressed in this context. Lastly, attempts at correction of the new status quo by the Court of Justice and by EU legislative organs are also considered.

[5] Directive 2014/24/EU of the European Parliament and of the Council of 26 February 2014 on public procurement and repealing Directive 2004/18/EC [2014] OJ L 94/65 (2014 Public Procurement Directive).

[6] Cf Judgment of 22 November 2005, *Mangold*, Case C-144/04, EU:C:2005:709. Although the approach of the Court of Justice to engagement with the 2014 Public Procurement Directive prior to the requirement for implementation has been uneven; contrast Judgment of 18 December 2015, *Generali-Providencia*, Case C-470/13 EU:C:2014:2469, para 37, and the more cautious approach in the Judgment of 7 April 2016, *Partner Apelski Dariusz*, Case C-324/14, EU:C:2016:214, paras 82–94.

[7] Proposal for a Council Regulation on the exercise of the right to take collective action within the context of the freedom of establishment and the freedom to provide services, COM(2012) 130 final (the 'Monti II Regulation').

[8] Commission Proposal to amend the Posted Workers Directive COM(2016) 128 final.

[9] European Commission, *Commission Staff Working Document, Impact Assessment*, Strasbourg SWD(2016) 52 final ('*Impact Assessment*'), at 10 and 51.

[10] Judgment of 18 December 2007, *Laval un Partneri*, Case C-341/05, EU:C:2007:809.

[11] Judgment of 3 April 2008, *Rüffert*, Case C-346/06, EU:C:2008:189.

II. THE IDEA OF 'SOCIAL DUMPING' AND ITS IMPLICATIONS FOR 'FAIR' COMPETITION

As we shall see, there are indications in the *Laval* judgment and other litigation that 'social dumping' is a legitimate concern of trade unions and the Court of Justice. Trade union action may be lawful where it can be demonstrated to be necessary to prevent social dumping, establishing thereby that the protection of workers is commensurate to the restrictions placed on service providers. However, much depends on what 'social dumping' is to be taken to mean. Generally, the term 'social dumping' has become associated with 'the gaining of unfair competitive advantage within the [Union] through unacceptably low social standards'.[12] Erik Bengtsson similarly defines 'social dumping as the worsening of wages and working conditions, relative to the standard level established by employment regulations or collective agreements in the country or region, pursued by companies to increase their competitiveness'.[13] This issue of the role of low labour standards in gaining a competitive advantage is also present in the definition employed by Daniel Vaughan-Whitehead, that is,

> any practice pursued by an enterprise that deliberately violates or circumvents legislation in the social field or takes advantage of differentials in practice and/or legislation in the social field, in order to gain an economic advantage, notably in terms of competitiveness, the state also playing a determinant role in this process.[14]

The first question is, then, which actors are gaining benefits from and creating the conditions for unfair competition? In this scenario, it may be Member States that seek to attract investment by offering less protective labour laws, leading to what has come to be known as the 'race to the bottom'.[15] Also, employers may be implicated in so far as they take advantage of different legal regimes to pay the lowest wages and allow workers only the most minimal working conditions. It has been suggested by prominent labour lawyers, like Bob Hepple, that the race to the bottom is largely a fiction, since productivity gains lie in increasing wages, as well

[12] Commission Green Paper on European Social Policy, *Options for the Union* COM(93)551 final 17.11.93 at 7; cited by C Barnard, *EC Employment Law*, 3rd edn (Oxford, Oxford University Press, 2006) 56; and by P Syrpis, *EU Intervention in Domestic Labour Law* (Oxford, Oxford University Press, 2007) 41.

[13] E Bengtsson, 'Social Dumping Cases in the Swedish Labour Court in the Wake of Laval, 2004–2010' (2016) 37(1) *Economic and Industrial Democracy* 23, 24; citing M Bernaciek, *Social Dumping: Political Catchphrase or Threat to Labour Standards?* (Brussels, ETUI, 2012) 26.

[14] D Vaughan-Whitehead, *EU Enlargement versus Social Europe? The Uncertain Future of the European Social Model* (Cheltenham, Edward Elgar, 2003) 325.

[15] See B Langille, 'Eight Ways to Think about International Labour Standards' (1997) 31(4) *Journal of World Trade* 27 at 42; discussed also by Syrpis, above n 12, 42.

as working conditions, alongside a stable social policy infrastructure.[16] Therefore, the actors identified by Vaughan-Whitehead[17] will not ultimately follow this path as it is not in their self-interest to do so. However, as we shall see, the financial crisis of 2007 and the austerity policies that followed suggest that, at least in times of economic insecurity, the short-term gains of deregulation by states and cost-cutting by employers may become more attractive to these actors despite their more irrational long-term consequences.[18] This indicates that some protection against that course of action may be desirable, even if it is only likely to arise in times of great economic uncertainty and insecurity.

The second question is what social standards would be regarded as 'unacceptably low'? 'Low-pay competition' has been argued before the Court of Justice as a ground for protection of the German construction industry from foreign competition, but the Court is reluctant to allow Member States to regulate unless 'those rules confer a genuine benefit on the workers concerned, which significantly adds to their social protection'.[19] It is not clear how low the wages have to be, or what employment conditions would be so unacceptable, that state legislation or trade union action protecting workers must be deemed appropriate.

In *Rush Portuguesa*,[20] the first case on 'posted workers' (indeed, which invented the concept of 'posted workers'), there is no ostensible mention of social dumping or unfair competition; instead, the issues are implicit in the case (and much of the commentary). A French undertaking had subcontracted part of the construction of a railway in France to Rush (a Portuguese company), which had brought to France Portuguese workers to do the work required. Portugal was a member of what was then the European Economic Community (EEC) and Rush had entitlements as a service provider under internal market rules, but the workers had no independent rights to freedom of movement under transitional membership arrangements. The Court of Justice found that the service provider was entitled to post these Portuguese workers to perform the work as they did not 'gain access to

[16] B Hepple, *Labour Laws and Global Trade* (Oxford, Hart Publishing, 2005) 13–16.

[17] Vaughan-Whitehead, above n 14.

[18] See R Boyer, 'The Four Fallacies of Contemporary Austerity Policies: The Lost Keynesian Legacy' (2012) 36 *Cambridge Journal of Economics* 283; also Special Issue: The Eurozone Crisis and the Future of European Labour Law (2012) 41(3) *Industrial Law Journal*, especially S Deakin, 'Editorial' at 251–5; and K Armingeon and L Baccaro, 'Political Economy of the Sovereign Debt Crisis: The Limits of Internal Devaluation' (2012) 41(3) *Industrial Law Journal* 254.

[19] Judgment of 25 October 2001, *Finalarte and Others*, Joined Cases C-49/98, C-50/98, C-52/98 to C-54/98 and C-68/98 to C-71/98, EU:C:2001:564, paras 38 and 40–42. See also the brief discussion in Barnard, above n 12, 270.

[20] Judgment of 27 March 1990, *Rush Portuguesa v Office national d'immigration*, Case C-113/89, EU:C:1990:142.

the labour market' of the host state,[21] so that the French *Office national d'immigration* should not fine Rush for breach of the French Labour Code. However, the Court also found that

> [Union] law does not preclude Member States from extending their legislation, or collective labour agreements entered into by both sides of industry, to any person who is employed, even temporarily, within their territory, no matter in which country the employer is established; nor does [Union] law prohibit Member States from enforcing those rules by appropriate means.[22]

In this way, the internal market could not be obstructed, but states could determine what they regarded as appropriate terms of (non-discriminatory) competition between home and foreign service providers. The presumption here would seem to be that equal treatment of local and posted workers is appropriate. Paul Davies viewed this finding as an attempt 'to discourage cross-border providers of services from … a wholesale challenge to the labour law environment of the host country', but also observed that 'the Court's statement did not make clear the reasoning behind this baldly stated conclusion'.[23]

It was assumed by many that this statement in *Rush Portuguesa* was the accommodation written into the Posted Workers Directive. Social dumping was to be prevented by the obligation placed on Member States under Article 3(1) to at least set and enforce a set of minimum labour standards for posted workers, while there was apparently scope to provide greater protections for these workers under Article 3(7). States would be entitled to impose the standards arising from their laws and collective bargaining systems on service providers posting workers to their jurisdiction. That entitlement of states may be understood from other subparagraphs of Article 3 of the Posted Workers Directive to be subject to a more general principle of 'equality of treatment' elaborated on in Article 3(8) and (10) concerning universally applicable collective agreements.[24] Terms and conditions of employment must be non-discriminatory (ie the same as those applicable to internal service providers, as well as those coming from elsewhere in the EU).[25]

[21] ibid, paras 15 and 16.

[22] ibid, para 18.

[23] P Davies, 'Market Integration and Social Policy in the Court of Justice' (1995) 24(1) *Industrial Law Journal* 49, 74.

[24] Such agreements having been a 'tense point of debate' prior to adoption of the Posted Workers Directive. See ibid, 75.

[25] See O De Schutter, 'Transborder Provision of Services and "Social Dumping": Rights-Based Mutual Trust in the Establishment of the Internal Market' in I Lianos and O Ododu (eds), *Regulating Trade in Services in the EU and WTO: Trust, Distrust and Economic Integration* (Cambridge, Cambridge University Press, 2012) 16; and S Evju and T Novitz, 'The Evolving Regulation: Dynamics and Consequences' in S Evju (ed), *Regulating Transnational Labour in Europe: The Quandaries of Multilevel Governance* (Oslo, University of Oslo, 2014) 79–82.

The assumption that Article 3(1) provided minimal protections on which Member States could improve under Article 3(7) was later to be challenged in *Laval*, as we shall see, leaving open the question: how minimal is sufficient? In other words, is the phrase 'social dumping' at all meaningful? The answer to this question is not to be found in the text of the Posted Workers Directive, which does not refer to this term at all.

There are arguably two options. One is to require 'equal pay and equal social protection for the same work', which was the subject of a draft resolution discussed by the European Parliament.[26] In this scenario, allowance would be made for the role of social security, and limits would be placed on maximum periods of posting in order to ensure that longer-term residents from other parts of the EU could be regarded not as merely posted and would be treated on a par with local workers in the host state. This option would follow precedent set by international law relating to migrant workers' rights, which posits this as the default position.[27] It could also be said to follow from the statement of the Court in *Rush Portuguesa*[28] and the emphasis on 'equality of treatment' in Article 3 of the Posted Workers Directive, discussed above. The difficulty with an equal treatment approach, which would entail the same labour standards including rates for posted and local workers, is that pay in some EU Member States is much higher than in others. Imposition of the same local rate of pay on an incoming EU service provider might deprive commercial entities in more recent post-enlargement Member States of their comparative advantage and those states of a valuable source of income.[29] It is, therefore, a solution not likely to win support from those two significant constituencies.[30] This may be why Bengtsson sees

[26] Report on Social Dumping in the European Union (2015/2255 INI), Committee on Employment and Social Affairs, cited in the 2016 *Impact Assessment*, above n 9, 51.

[27] For example, Art 6 of ILO Convention No 97 concerning Migration for Employment (Revised) 1949; Art 10 of ILO Convention No 143 on Migrant Workers (Supplementary Provisions) 1975; and Art 25 of UN International Convention on the protection of the Rights of all Migrant Workers and their Families 1990. This is also the default position for free movement of workers in the EU: Art 45(2) of the Treaty on European Union (TFEU) [2012] OJ C326/13.

[28] *Rush Portuguesa*, above n 20, para 18.

[29] See, for a comparable statement of these concerns, Judgment of 18 September 2014, *Bundesdruckerei*, Case C-549/13, EU:C:2014:2235, para 34: 'By imposing, in such a situation, a fixed minimum wage corresponding to that required in order to ensure reasonable remuneration for employees in the Member State of the contracting authority in the light of the cost of living in that Member State, but which bears no relation to the cost of living in the Member State in which the services relating to the public contract at issue are performed and for that reason prevents subcontractors established in that Member State from deriving a competitive advantage from the differences between the respective rates of pay, that national legislation goes beyond what is necessary to ensure that the objective of employee protection is attained.' See also the contribution by Davies in ch 9 of this book.

[30] See, eg, the special issue, 'The Laval and Viking Cases: Freedom of Services and Establishment v Industrial Conflict in the European Economic Area and Russia' (2009) *Bulletin of Comparative Labour Relations* edited by R Blanpain, who (at xxii) for these reasons considered that '[t]he European Court took the right decision' in *Laval*.

collective agreements as a reference point for the worsening of labour standards, rather than as determinative of whether they are unacceptable.[31]

A second option is that where there is palpable evidence of social harm in the form of labour exploitation, the Court of Justice should be allowed to be cognisant of those concerns, which could affect its findings on the legitimacy of state legislation and trade union action. Further, there is a case for urgent intervention by EU institutions. Indeed, the Commission refers to substantial undercutting of wages by service providers when hiring posted workers, which has depressive effects on wage rates locally, as well as pricing local workers out of jobs they previously expected to do.[32] In other words, posted workers may not 'gain access' to the labour market (in the terms of *Rush Portuguesa*) but may profoundly affect the terms regarding hire of labour in that market. The result is that the Court and EU institutions have the capacity and a duty to act where they see an instance of harm that they can correct by enabling state legislation or trade union action. As we shall see, this residual discretionary power—and arguably moral obligation—can be traced throughout the case law of the Court of Justice from *Laval* onwards, and is referred to in recent legislative proposals. The difficulty is that the scope for action in reliance on this premise remains shrouded in uncertainties. There is, arguably, increasing evidence that action is now required. Yet what can and should be done, and whether this is the role of the Court of Justice or the legislature, remains unclear.[33]

III. THE SCOPE FOR COLLECTIVE BARGAINING FOR POSTED WORKERS UNDER THE *LAVAL* AND *RÜFFERT* CASE LAW

In order to explain the complex demarcation of the legitimate scope of collective bargaining, and to determine what collective agreements can be regarded as enforceable in the context of posting and procurement, it is necessary to outline in some detail the judgments of the Court of Justice in two key cases: *Laval* and *Rüffert*. Together, they demonstrate the high threshold that a trade union in a host state must overcome, if it is to be able to negotiate a collective agreement applicable to workers posted there.

[31] Bengtsson, above n 13, 24.

[32] European Commission, 2016 *Impact Assessment*, above n 9, 13 and 36; see also the extensive research conducted by J Cremers, *In Search of Cheap Labour in Europe: Working and Living Conditions of Posted Workers* (Brussels, CLR Studies: European Institute for Construction Labour Research, 2011).

[33] Regarding the respective roles of the Court and the legislature, see P Syrpis and T Novitz, 'Economic and Social Rights in Conflict: Political and Judicial Approaches to Their Reconciliation' (2008) 33 *EL Rev* 411; also P Syrpis, 'The Relationship between Primary and Secondary Law in the EU' (2015) 52 *CML Rev* 461.

A. *Laval* and Inexcusable Action in Pursuit of an Unenforceable Collective Agreement

In the *Laval* case, a trade union in the host state (namely Sweden) wanted to improve the terms and conditions of workers posted from Latvia, so as to protect the interests of their own Swedish members. This union, which represented workers in Swedish building and public works, Svenska Byggnadsarbetareförbundet operating at a local level, sought to engage the employer in bargaining. The employer, instead, preferred to conclude a collective agreement with a trade union in Latvia, providing for lower rates of pay. In light of this refusal, the local union requested assistance from the union at national level to place pressure on the employer through a boycott of the place of work. This action was supported by sympathy action taken by the Swedish electricians' union, Svenska Elektrikerforbundet, and subsequently by a variety of other unions. The action was enabled by a piece of legislation, known as *Lex Britannia*, which allowed Swedish unions to take industrial action despite a collective agreement concluded by the foreign service provider with another union in another country, although they would not be able to take industrial action during the currency of a Swedish collective agreement covering a Swedish employer.

The employer alleged breach of the principle of free movement of services, and also of the terms of the Posted Workers Directive. In response, the Swedish Government and defendant trade unions argued that the collective action was permissible as the exercise of a fundamental right to strike in pursuance of a legitimate public interest, namely, the protection of workers. The subsequent judgment of the Court of Justice in favour of the employer cast into doubt the capacity for minimum wages (and other work-related benefits) to be set for posted workers by collective bargaining by trade unions in the host state. *Lex Britannia* was seen as discriminatory and itself a breach of EU free movement of services.

Collective bargaining (and the collective action that generated such bargaining) was considered by the Court to be too unpredictable in terms of effect and outcome, creating an unjustifiable barrier to the free movement of service providers. The Court explained that

> collective action such as that at issue in the main proceedings cannot be justified in the light of the public interest objective ... where the negotiations on pay, which that action seeks to require an undertaking established in another Member State to enter into, form part of a national context characterised by a lack of provisions, of any kind, which are sufficiently precise and accessible that they do not render it impossible or excessively difficult in practice for such an undertaking to determine the obligations with which it is required to comply as regards minimum pay.[34]

[34] *Laval*, above n 10, para 110.

That statement was made subject to the proviso that collective action aimed at conclusion of a collective agreement could be permitted 'for the protection of the workers of the host state against possible social dumping' as 'an overriding reason of public interest within the meaning of the case-law which, in principle, justifies a restriction of one of the fundamental freedoms guaranteed by the Treaty'.[35] Indeed, the potential legitimacy of the trade union 'fight against social dumping' was also stressed in the Advocate General's Opinion.[36] However, the scope of 'social dumping' remains nebulous, since what the Court regarded as sufficient to legitimise collective action in support of collective bargaining was not explained.

That collective action and collective bargaining by a host state union might be permitted on the initiative and for the benefit of the posted workers themselves (rather than local workers) does not appear to be contemplated, presumably because this was not relevant on the facts of the *Laval* case. So we do not know what the preconditions would be for legitimate intervention by a host state union on that basis.

Notably, the *Laval* judgment has been controversial and widely criticised. The ILO Committee of Experts on the Application of Conventions and Recommendations (CEACR) was critical of the impact that *Laval* had on the ability of unions to call industrial action which has cross-border effects on the provision of services (in particular, the use made of British Airways of the uncertain legal position established by Court of Justice case law to prevent a strike through the threat of unlimited liability).[37] Further, in relation to Sweden (where the *Laval* dispute arose and where amending legislation was adopted to give effect to the Court of Justice judgment), the CEACR has observed that 'foreign workers should have the right to be represented by the organization of their own choosing and that the organization of their choice should be able to defend its members' interests, including by means of industrial action', and has requested that the Swedish Government review the new legislation with the social partners, so as to enhance the representative capacity of host state unions for posted workers.[38]

[35] ibid, para 103.

[36] Opinion of AG Mengozzi delivered on 23 May 2007 in *Laval*, Case C-341/05, EU:C:2007:291, para 251. Note also ibid, at para 273: 'the collective action, in so far as it sought to impose the rate of pay provided for by the ... collective agreement, would not be disproportionate to the objectives of protecting workers and combating social dumping'. However, application of all the conditions (including social security payments) could be regarded as disproportionate and going 'beyond what was necessary to ensure the protection of workers and to prevent social dumping' (ibid, para 280).

[37] See *Application by the British Air Line Pilots Association to the International Labour Organisation* (2008), para 173. See also ILO CEACR Report on UK compliance with ILO Convention No 87 (2010) 208–09; and ILO CEACR Report on UK compliance with ILO Convention No 87 (2013) 196.

[38] See CEACR Observation adopted 2012 and published 102nd ILO session (2013).

Indeed, CEACR engagement with this issue prefaced and followed the findings of the European Committee of Social Rights (ECSR) that Swedish legislation adopted in response to the *Laval* case was in breach of Article 6(4) of the European Social Charter. The ECSR reached these conclusions on the basis that the new legislation limited possibilities to resort to collective action and subjected 'contravention of the obligation to keep "industrial peace" … to legal sanction and the possibility of economic and even punitive damages'.[39]

Nevertheless, the Court of Justice approach in *Laval* to collective bargaining regarding the terms of posted workers, which was very much focused on the limitations of the Posted Workers Directive, was not reversed, and indeed has had repercussions for public procurement too. It should be noted that, in *Laval*, the Court of Justice took specific note of the limited matters relating to employment of posted workers that a host state could regulate under Article 3(1) of the Posted Workers Directive, alongside limitations of the acceptable modes of regulation. Notably, it was observed by the Court that, under Article 3(1)(b), only 'minimum rates of pay' can be imposed, while in the case at issue the Swedish trade unions were seeking to potentially bargain above a bare minimum.

Attention was paid to the statement prefacing Article 3(1) of the Posted Workers Directive, that terms could be 'laid down' by 'law, regulation or administrative provision', but also by 'collective agreements or arbitration awards which have been declared universally applicable … insofar as they concern' activities listed in the Annex (largely pertaining to the construction industry). In this respect, it is clear that Article 3(1) has to be read in conjunction with Article 3(8), which sets out which 'collective agreements or arbitration awards' have been declared 'universally applicable', that is, those 'which must be observed by all undertakings in the geographical area and in the profession or industry concerned'. In the second paragraph of Article 3(8), it is said:

> In the absence of a system for declaring collective agreements or arbitration awards to be of universal application within the meaning of the first subparagraph, Member States may, if they so decide, base themselves on:
>
> — collective agreements or arbitration awards which are generally applicable to all similar undertakings in the geographical area and in the profession or industry concerned, and/or
> — collective agreements which have been concluded by the most representative employers' and labour organizations at national level and which are applied throughout the national territory

[39] See *Swedish Trade Union Confederation (LO) and Swedish Confederation of Professional Employees (TCO) v Sweden*, Complaint No 85/2012, Decision on admissibility and on the merits, 3 July 2013, para 84. Note that this finding has since been endorsed by the Council of Europe's Committee of Ministers in Resolution CM/ResChS(2014)1, 5 February 2014.

> provided that their application to the undertakings referred to in Article 1(1) ensures equality of treatment on matters listed in the first subparagraph of paragraph 1 of this Article between those undertakings and the other undertakings referred to in this subparagraph which are in a similar position.

Article 3(7) of the Posted Workers Directive states that: 'Paragraphs 1 to 6 shall not prevent application of terms and conditions of employment which are more favourable to workers.' However, this provision was given a very narrow construction, to the point of being almost ignored, on the basis that to do otherwise would 'amount to depriving the directive of its effectiveness'.[40] The emphasis of the Court of Justice was on the element of fair competition ('equality of treatment' of undertakings) inherent in the Posted Workers Directive, rather than the equality of treatment of workers.[41]

States have the option, under Article 3(10) of the Posted Workers Directive, to make legislative provision for regulation of matters outside the terms of Article 3(1), subject to the requirement of 'equal treatment'. Additionally, under Article 3(10), it is possible to apply terms and conditions of employment laid down in the collective agreements or arbitration awards within the meaning of paragraph 8 and concerning activities other than those referred to in the Annex (ie construction and building), again as long as this is done on the basis of 'equality of treatment'.

The problem identified by the Court of Justice in the *Laval* case was that Sweden had not sought to regulate through legislation. Further, the collective bargaining system that operated in the country, which did not require legislative effect to be given to the outcomes of collective bargaining, failed to meet the requirements of Article 3(8) and thereby Article 3(10).[42] Moreover, there was no express Swedish legislation enabling regulation of posted workers' pay above any bare minimum, so this aspect of Article 3(10) could not be satisfied either.

B. *Rüffert* and the Failings of a Sectoral Collective Agreement in a Public Procurement Context

In the case of *Rüffert*, a contract had been awarded to a contractor for structural work in the building of a prison. The award was made subject to compliance with the wage rates set by the collective agreement operative in the place where the work was to be performed.[43] When it became clear that the subcontractor was not paying Polish posted workers the rate to be

[40] *Laval*, above n 10, para 80.

[41] As was observed by commentators at the time of the judgment; eg, ACL Davies, 'One Step Forward, Two Steps Back? The Viking and Laval cases in the ECJ' (2008) 37 *Industrial Law Journal* 126; Syrpis and Novitz, above n 33.

[42] See *Laval*, above n 10, paras 81–85.

[43] *Rüffert*, above n 11, para 11.

paid under the collective agreement (indeed, less than half of this was being paid), the *Land* Niedersachsen terminated the contract and punitive action was taken. After a penalty had been imposed, the appellate court referred the matter brought on appeal to the Court of Justice, suggesting that this obligation to pay the collectively agreed wage operated as an impediment to market access from other EU Member States.[44] The referring court further expressed doubt as to whether the obligation to pay the collectively agreed wage could be justified by overriding reasons of public interest.[45] This was because the wage rates under the applicable collective agreement were significantly higher than 'the minimum wage applicable on the territory of the Federal Republic of Germany', and therefore were not necessary to the protection of workers.[46] Here the ideal of equality of treatment came into conflict with the notion that the bare minimum is what needs to be guaranteed.

The Court of Justice issued its judgment on the basis that it had been conceded that the collective agreement in question had not been 'declared universally applicable' and could not, in any case, be regarded as applicable by virtue of the requirements of the Posted Workers Directive in Article 3(8). Nor could it be said that the minimum wage had been fixed 'by law' under Article 3(1): 'a legislative measure such as the Landesvergabegesetz, which does not itself fix any minimum rates of pay, cannot be considered to be a law, within the meaning of the first indent of the first subparagraph of Article 3(1)'.[47] Moreover, the existence of a mechanism in Germany for the legal extension of collective agreements rendered the second paragraph of Article 3(8) inapplicable.[48] The remainder of the judgment offers guidance as to the application of the second paragraph of Article 3(8) but is, for this reason, to be regarded as obiter.

As regards the potential applicability of this second paragraph, the Court of Justice observed that the collective agreement at issue in *Rüffert* was a local agreement. This would not be a problem per se, were it 'generally applicable to all similar undertakings in the geographical area and in the profession or industry concerned' in accordance with the first indent of the second paragraph of Article 3(8) of the Posted Workers Directive. However, the collective agreement covered only a part of the construction sector in that geographical region, applying only to public and not private contracts, and therefore might be understood not to apply to the entire 'profession or industry':

> In a context such as that in the main proceedings, the binding effect of a collective agreement such as that at issue here covers only a part of the construction sector falling within the geographical area of that agreement, since, first, the law

[44] ibid, para 14.
[45] ibid, para 15.
[46] Opinion of AG Bot delivered on 20 September 2007 in *Rüffert*, Case C-346/06, EU:C:2007:541, para 44.
[47] *Rüffert*, above n 11, para 29.
[48] ibid, para 27.

> which gives it such an effect applies only to public contracts and not to private contracts and, second, the collective agreement has not been declared universally applicable.[49]

The requisite criteria for universality were considered thereby to be missing.

Moreover, although the reasons for this view were not stated, the Court of Justice pronounced that such a 'rate of pay cannot be considered to be a term and condition of employment which is more favourable to workers within the meaning of Article 3(7)'.[50] The undertaking could, of its own accord, sign a local collective agreement, but could not be required to do so in this instance as a condition for bidding for the contract.[51] Certainly, the imposition of such a collective agreement by the local government could not be regarded any more permissible than the coercive behaviour of the Swedish trade unions in *Laval*.

Through this prescriptive treatment in *Laval* and *Rüffert* of the appropriate limits of setting standards for posted workers via legislation or collective bargaining, what had been seen by some as a 'floor of rights' in the Posted Workers Directive came to be seen as a 'ceiling'.[52] If the national measures taken in respect of protection of the rights of posted workers did not fit within the ambit of the precise terms set out in the Posted Workers Directive, they were impermissible, despite the apparent scope in Article 3(7) for a more generous interpretation of the Directive, 'more favourable to workers'. 'Social dumping' seems to be assumed to be concerned with violation of the most minimal wage entitlements and other working conditions; parity of treatment of host state and posted workers is not possible due to the narrow construction of a universally applicable collective agreement.

IV. COLLECTIVE BARGAINING REFORMS IN THE CONTEXT OF AUSTERITY AFTER 2010: OR HOW THE 'UNIVERSALLY APPLICABLE' COLLECTIVE AGREEMENT WAS ERODED

Following the financial crisis, the EU promoted what have broadly come to be described as 'austerity' policies.[53] In specific 'bailout' programmes (for Greece, Portugal, Ireland and Cyprus) and 'financial assistance' programmes (for Hungary, Latvia, Romania and Spain), the provision of

[49] ibid.

[50] ibid, para 32.

[51] ibid, para 34.

[52] E Sjödin, *Notes on the Implementation of the Services Directive in Sweden* FORMULA Paper (2011) 2. See also the contribution by Davies in ch 9 of this book.

[53] See J Peters, 'Neoliberal Convergence in North America and Western Europe: Fiscal Austerity, Privatization, and Public Sector Reform' (2012) 19(2) *Review of International Political Economy* 208; R Torres, 'European Labour Markets in Crisis' (2013) 152 *International Labour Review* 167; and A Stoleroff, 'Employment Relations and Unions in Public Administration in Portugal and Spain: From Reform to Austerity' (2013) *European Journal of Industrial Relations* 1.

monies was conditional on following certain economic policies, designed to reduce state spending (so as to facilitate repayment of sovereign debt) and attract international investment by making labour markets more flexible.[54] These requirements emanated from what came to be known as 'the Troika': the European Central Bank, the European Commission and the International Monetary Fund (IMF). The conditions were set out in Memoranda of Understanding (MoUs) and accompanying letters; but they then became seen as policy prescriptions, which could be applied more generally through ostensibly soft-law EU mechanisms, such as the Europe 2020 Growth Strategy[55] and accompanying Country Specific Recommendations (CSRs)[56] addressed to each individual Member State. The Recommendations are, of course, said to be 'country specific' but have tended to follow a common pattern.[57]

In these attempts to remove the 'rigidities' of labour markets, there have emerged recommendations to bypass trade union participation in wage-setting[58] and to end national level and sectoral bargaining.[59] Trade unions that operate across a country are considered to create wage rigidities—perhaps because they are aware of terms and conditions elsewhere and are skilled in negotiations. So the overarching strategy has been to enable bargaining (i) at the level of the company or enterprise, and (ii) without trade unions.[60]

For example, in Greece, negotiating rights over terms and conditions have been granted to non-union employee groups (or 'associations of persons').

[54] C Barnard, 'EU Employment Law and the European Social Model: The Past, the Present and the Future' (2014) 67 *Current Legal Problems* 199, 230. See also the contribution by Rodgers in ch 8 of this book.

[55] See Communication from the Commission, EUROPE 2020: A strategy for smart, sustainable and inclusive growth, COM(2010) 2020 final.

[56] European Commission, 'Recommendation for a Council Recommendation on the economic policy of the euro area' COM(2015) 992 final, 2.

[57] See at ec.europa.eu/europe2020/making-it-happen/country-specific-recommendations/index_en.htm; although note that for 18 EU states this also involves a macro-economic imbalance procedure under which more stringent demands are made regarding the budgetary deficit. See at ec.europa.eu/economy_finance/economic_governance/macroeconomic_imbalance_procedure/index_en.htm.

[58] In respect of this internal devaluation strategy, see A Koukiadaki and L Kretsos, 'Opening Pandora's Box: The Sovereign Debt Crisis and Labour Market Regulation in Greece' (2012) 41 *Industrial Law Journal* 276, 291–93; also I Szabo, 'Between Polarization and Statism—Effects of the Crisis on Collective Bargaining Processes and Outcomes in Hungary' (2013) 19(2) *Transfer* 205, 211.

[59] Koukiadaki and Kretsos, above n 58, 290; HA Costa, 'From Europe as a Model to Europe as Austerity: The Impact of the Crisis on Portuguese Trade Unions' (2012) 18 *Transfer* 397, 408; and A Trif, 'Romania: Collective Bargaining under Attack' (2013) 19 *Transfer* 227, 231–32.

[60] See S Clauwaert and I Schömann, *The Crisis and National Labour Law Reforms: A Mapping Exercise* (2012) ETUI Working Paper 2012.04; and A Koukiadaki, I Tavora and M Martinez Lucio, *The Transformation of Joint Regulation and Labour Market Policy in Europe during the Crisis: Comparative Project Report* (Manchester/Brussels, University of Manchester/The European Commission, 2014).

The enterprise-level agreements that emerge then can undermine national collective bargaining terms.[61] In Hungary, from January 2013, the Government has given employers what has been described as a 'secret weapon', by entitling 'puppet' works councils to negotiate collective agreements where there is no union.[62]

The Troika has generally opposed centralised national-level collective bargaining, seeing this as insufficiently flexible.[63] In Greece, the national general collective agreement had determined the national minimum wage, while occupational sectoral agreements (national and local) provided for additional higher rates of pay.[64] In order to move towards lower wage levels, and therefore a lower cost base for government, industry and services, new laws allowed occupational and enterprise agreements to bargain down from a nationally set floor. This was compounded by the change to regulation by 'collective agreements', which, as noted above, no longer have to involve trade union representation.[65] Further, the content of the national collective agreement was subject to government intervention in 2012, with new legislation imposing a cut of 22 per cent at all levels, with a further 10 per cent cut for those under the age of 25.[66]

In Portugal, a further development has been the removal of past practice whereby all-important industry-level collective agreements were extended through legislation across an industry.[67] This has been attributed to direct pressure from the Troika, which sees such methods of wage setting as insufficiently flexible.[68]

In Romania, following the €20 billion bailout in 2010, the national collective agreement, which had set minimum rights for the entire Romanian workforce, was undermined. This was achieved by legislation in 2011, which no longer enables cross-sectoral agreements and imposed new requirements in respect of 'representativity'.[69]

In a potent analysis of recent industrial relations trends in 2016, Jelle Visser observed that

> the heaviest losses in bargaining coverage occurred in a subset of ten countries: Romania, Greece, Slovenia, Slovakia, Hungary, Israel, Portugal, Bulgaria, Ireland and Latvia. In each of these countries the decline in bargaining coverage was associated with, or caused by, regulatory change such as the discontinuation of

[61] Neatly summarised in KD Ewing and J Hendy, *Reconstruction after the Crisis: A Manifesto for Collective Bargaining* (Liverpool, Institute of Employment Rights, 2013) 37; and Koukiadaki and Kretsos, above n 58, 291–93.

[62] Szabo, above n 58, 211.

[63] Costa, above n 59, 405.

[64] Koukiadaki and Kretsos, above n 58, 290.

[65] ibid, 291.

[66] ibid, 299.

[67] Ewing and Hendy, above n 61, 37.

[68] Costa, above n 59, 408.

[69] Trif, above n 59, 231–32.

> national agreements and multi-employer bargaining, changes in the rules or policies on extension of sector agreements to non-organized employers, and in the legal treatment of the validity of multi-annual and expired agreements.[70]

It is notable that six of the eight MoU countries are represented here and that, apart from Israel, all are EU Member States. Moreover, Visser points to the shift away from national-level and sectoral bargaining as even more widespread than this, in highlighting measures taken to reduce the incidence of legislative extension of collective bargaining not only in the 'bailout' countries subject to MoUs, such as Greece, Ireland, Portugal and Romania, but also Bulgaria, the Czech Republic, Estonia and Slovakia. Only Germany and The Netherlands took active steps to support and facilitate extension agreement measures.[71] Apart from these two states, there is now a dearth of national- or sectoral-level agreements that could be declared universally applicable, whether in the public or private sector, and few covering both sectors.

V. THE IMPLICATIONS FOR POSTED WORKERS AND THE COURT OF JUSTICE RESPONSE

The reasons for the vulnerability of posted workers are glaring. They live some distance from their home state, where they would know the language, the laws and legal system, and where they may be able to rely on support from a local trade union which can represent them in the workplace and bargain for superior wages. In the absence of such support, isolated in accommodation provided by their employer, without a working knowledge of the national language, a posted worker may find the host state a hostile place, in which it is more difficult to achieve wages comparable to local workers and protection of other rights at work.[72] One solution might seem to be collective representation of the interests of posted workers by trade unions in the host state.[73] However, the narrow definition of a 'universally applicable collective agreement', which was established in the *Laval* and *Rüffert* cases, compounded by the decline following the financial crisis in the types of sectoral bargaining and legislative extension of collective agreements that would enable the existence of a 'universally applicable collective agreement', have left posted workers without that option.

From what little we are told by official Commission sources, in the context of European austerity, the incidence of posted work increased dramatically

[70] J Visser, 'What Happened to Collective Bargaining During the Great Recession?' (2016) 5(9) *IZA Journal of Labor Policy*.

[71] ibid, 6–8.

[72] See Cremers, above n 32.

[73] L Hayes and T Novitz, 'Workers Without Footprints: The Legal Fiction of Migrant Workers as Posted Workers' in B Ryan (ed), *Labour Migration in Hard Times: Reforming labour market regulation?* (Liverpool, Institute of Employment Rights, 2013) 99.

from 2010 onwards, by almost 49 per cent (totalling approximately 1.9 million workers).[74] It would seem that the pressures experienced by employers during the financial crisis had made the employment of flexible cheaper migrant labour much more attractive during this period;[75] and it may have been of assistance to employers that it became progressively less likely that there would be a universally applicable collective agreement to determine their terms and conditions. The Commission has cited evidence that posted workers have a greater likelihood of health and safety incidents. Further, it observes that posted workers tend to earn substantially less than local workers, with reports of income of less than 50 per cent than that usually paid in a given place for the same job. This observation is perhaps reminiscent of the facts of *Rüffert*, where the Court of Justice seemed unconcerned that less than half of the 'going rate' was paid to posted workers, but it is here presented as evidence that pay is unacceptably low, in social dumping terms. This may be due not only to the negative effects on the workers posted, but also to the ability of local workers to find employment when the cost of their labour is so deeply undercut. It has been documented that 'fake' posting has occurred, where workers pretend to be from another EU Member State or are hired through an agency which operates from another EU Member State, so that they can at least get access to local jobs, albeit at substantially lower rates of pay than they could have received for the same work previously.[76]

A crucial question, then, is whether the Court of Justice is willing to take the initiative so as to extend protections for posted workers, whether in terms of the application of collective agreements for their benefit or by reconsidering restrictions on public procurement rules. Arguably, in the *ESA* and *RegioPost* cases, the Court of Justice had the opportunity to reconsider past approaches, but there is little sign of a significant departure from its earlier approach in *Laval* and *Rüffert*.

A. The *ESA* Case: Local Trade Unions in Protection of Posted Workers' Interests

In the *ESA* case,[77] the Court of Justice showed unprecedented sympathy for the engagement of local trade unions in the protection of posted workers'

[74] European Commission, 2016 *Impact Assessment*, above n 9, 13 and 36; and Commission Proposal to amend the Posted Workers Directive, above n 8.

[75] CM Reinhart and KS Rogoff, *From Financial Crash to Debt Crisis* (2010) Working Paper 15795, at nber.org/papers/w15795. See also J Carmassi, D Gros and S Micossi, 'The Global Financial Crisis: Causes and Cures' (2009) 47 *Journal of Common Market Studies* 977.

[76] See Cremers, above n 32.

[77] *Sähköalojen ammattiliitto*, above n 3.

interests. In that instance, 186 Polish workers were hired by ESA under Polish contracts of employment to carry out work at a nuclear power station in Finland. The workers claimed that they were entitled to the minimum wages set by the Finnish collective agreements, and individually assigned their claims to the local Finish trade union, Sähköalojen ammattiliitto, so as to bring these before the host state (ie Finnish) courts. There were two key issues. The first was whether the Finnish trade union could act for the Polish workers in this respect, since Polish law prevents such an assignment of a claim for wages. The second was whether minimum wages could be and were set by the relevant Finnish collective agreements in a way that was acceptable under the Posted Workers Directive. Notably, however, this was not a case involving what could be alleged to be only protectionist action by the local trade union, but was (unlike the facts of *Laval*) activity aimed at the protection of the posted workers themselves on their own initiative.

The assignment point was relatively straightforward. The Court reached its conclusion in favour of assignment on the basis of interpretation of Article 3(1) of the Posted Workers Directive:

> The second subparagraph of Article 3(1) of [the Posted Workers Directive] makes absolutely clear that questions concerning 'minimum rates of pay' within the meaning of the directive are governed, whatever the law applicable to the employment relationship, by the law of the Member State to whose territory the workers are posted in order to carry out their work: in this case, Finland.[78]

As assignment is lawful under Finnish law, the local trade union could pursue the claim for wages on the Polish workers' behalf. Such an approach is consistent with Article 11 of the PWD Enforcement Directive,[79] which also envisages enforcement of claims for wages by local unions. Advocate General Wahl additionally relied on the Rome I Regulation[80] in this respect, which indicates that choice-of-law rules can be determined by 'a more specific choice-of-law rule contained in another EU legal instrument, in accordance with Article 23 of the Rome I Regulation'.[81] He also relied on recital 23 in the preamble to the Rome I Regulation, for the proposition that

> the regulation is by no means oblivious to the need to protect parties that are regarded as the weaker party in the contractual relationship under consideration.

[78] ibid, para 23.

[79] Directive 2014/67/EU of the European Parliament and of the Council of 15 May 2014 on the enforcement of Directive 96/71/EC concerning the posting of workers in the framework of the provision of services and amending Regulation (EU) No 1024/2012 on administrative cooperation through the Internal Market Information System ('the IMI Regulation') (PWD Enforcement Directive) [2014] OJ L159/11.

[80] Regulation (EC) No 593/2008 of the European Parliament and of the Council of 17 June 2008 on the law applicable to contractual obligations ('Rome I') [2008] OJ L177/6.

[81] Opinion of AG Wahl delivered on 18 September 2014 in *Sähköalojen ammattiliitto* (the '*ESA* case'), Case C-396/13, EU:C:2014:2236, paras 50–58.

> To protect such parties, precedence ought to be given to choice-of-law rules that are more favourable to the interests of such parties, rather than to the general rules.[82]

The question, then, was whether this notion of protection of workers might sway the Court as regards setting of minimum wages for posted workers via collective agreements. The crucial issue here was whether certain elements of pay determination established by the collective agreements could constitute 'minimum pay' under Article 3(1) of the Posted Workers Directive. The term 'minimum' was broadly defined, allowing for different forms of pay (such as piecework and hourly pay), and also for differentiations between particular categories of workers according to their skills and qualifications. However, true to the principle of transparency for the service provider stressed in *Laval*,

> if they are to be enforceable against an employer posting workers, the rules on the categorisation of those workers into pay groups which are applied in the host Member State must also be binding and meet the requirements of transparency, which means, in particular, that they must be accessible and clear. It is for the national court to ascertain whether those conditions are met in the case before it.[83]

The Court also found that a daily allowance[84] and compensation for daily travelling time[85] were to be included in the notion of a 'minimum wage'. Additionally, the Court found that 'the pay which the posted workers must receive for the minimum paid annual holidays corresponds to the minimum wage to which those workers are entitled during the reference period'.[86] However, accommodation costs and meal vouchers were not regarded as coming within the compass of the minimum wage as understood to be set in accordance with Article 3(1) of the Posted Workers Directive.[87]

The issue as to whether the Finnish collective agreements met the criteria to be regarded as universally applicable was not considered in the *ESA* judgment. It was, however, an issue discussed briefly in the Advocate General's Opinion. Wahl observed:

> In this case, Elektrobudowa has argued that the Finnish collective agreement system is not transparent given that it allows domestic undertakings to conclude, under certain conditions, alternative collective agreements that take precedence over the one declared universally applicable in the sector concerned. As a consequence, foreign undertakings wishing to provide services in Finland are, in its view, subject to differential treatment that cannot be justified. Indeed, Article 3(8) of

[82] ibid, para 49.
[83] *ESA* case, above n 3, para 44. See also on these issues ibid, paras 36–45.
[84] ibid, paras 46–52.
[85] ibid, paras 53–60.
[86] ibid, paras 69–70.
[87] ibid, paras 61–68.

> [the Posted Workers Directive] expressly provides that minimum standards set by universally applicable collective agreements must be observed by *all* undertakings in the geographical area and in the profession or industry concerned.[88]

The Advocate General recognised that this was not the basis of a reference from the national court and, as such, was not at issue. However, he returned to the complex objectives of the Posted Workers Directive, finding that 'a system such as the Finnish one', which allows domestic undertakings to circumvent a 'universally applicable collective agreement' by concluding another, creates problems for cross-border services, as it then allows for unequal treatment of service providers.[89] A domestic employer could pay wages lower than the minimum wage, whereas an employer established in another Member State could not do so. These observations suggest that the fundamental concern with protection of fair competition between domestic and other EU service providers, which directed the interpretation of the Court of Justice in *Laval*, has not changed, even if both the Advocate General and the Court are sympathetic to the plight of the particular posted workers in the *ESA* case.

B. *RegioPost* and New Options for Protection of Public Sector Labour Conditions?

In *RegioPost*, the Court took a first step away from *Rüffert*, so as to allow legal effect to regional legislation which directly set minimum wages to be applied in the context of public procurement decisions. Notably, there was at that time no collective agreement setting a minimum wage which the legislation was applying, even if it was historically based on collectively bargained rates.[90] This view is consistent with the findings of German academics who argue that the judgment in *Rüffert* must be understood as meaning that Article 3(1) of the Posted Workers Directive does not preclude a legislative provision that lays down a minimum rate of pay, even if it has to be complied with in the performance of public contracts only, 'since the requirement as to universal application does not concern legislative provisions, but only collective agreements'.[91]

RegioPost retreated from the view that differentiation between private and public sector contracts is problematic, in reliance on the specificity of the 2004 Public Procurement Directive.[92] The judgment did, however, stress

[88] *ESA* case, Opinion of AG Wahl, above n 81, para 62.
[89] ibid, paras 63–64.
[90] *RegioPost*, above n 4, para 21.
[91] As discussed ibid, para 37.
[92] Directive 2004/18/EC of the European Parliament and of the Council of 31 March 2004 on the coordination of procedures for the award of public works contracts, public supply contracts and public service contracts [2004] OJ L134/114. No longer in force. See *RegioPost*, above n 4, paras 64–68 and 78.

that *Rüffert* dealt with a different type of measure, namely the setting of a rate of minimum pay by a sectoral collective agreement that was higher than the legally imposed minimum wage.[93] Here, the entirety of the public sector in a given geographical area was covered and the measure was a legal enactment.[94] Moreover, it was relevant that

> that legislative provision confers a minimum social protection since, at the time of the facts in the main proceedings, the [Posted workers law (Gesetz über zwingende Arbeitsbedingungen bei grenzüberschreitenden Dienstleistungen, 'AEntG')] did not impose, nor did other national legislation impose, a lower minimum wage for the postal services sector.[95]

With respect, none of this suggests a likely departure from the approach taken in *Rüffert*. Special requirements continue to apply as regards 'universally applicable' collective agreements that have not been relaxed, despite the increasing rarity of such instruments as a source of norms and the increasingly low wages and poor working conditions of posted workers.

Ultimately, the Court of Justice has failed to make any inroads into the established (albeit irrational) position on the legal effect of collective agreements in the context of posted work. This is despite the unrestricted reference to 'collective agreements' and their potential influence in setting the terms of award of public contracts under Article 18(2) of the 2014 Public Procurement Directive, which is not of course the relevant legislation discussed in *RegioPost* but could be expected to be in the contemplation of the Court.

VI. THE CASE FOR LEGISLATIVE REFORM: NEW POSSIBILITIES FOR COLLECTIVE BARGAINING REGULATION OR JUST EVIDENCE REGARDING SOCIAL DUMPING?

The first attempt to address this situation through legislative reform was made in the draft 'Monti II' Regulation.[96] That instrument was ostensibly designed to promote respect for social rights when exercising economic rights (and vice versa), but the lack of a prioritisation of either set of norms caused dissatisfaction on both sides of the political spectrum and was discontinued following the first use of the 'yellow card' procedure post-Lisbon. Nevertheless, it is interesting in so far as it illustrates the commitment of at least one faction inside the European Commission to the promotion of social welfare and, one may fairly assume, the prevention of 'social dumping'. Of potentially greater significance is the 2016 Commission Proposal for reform of the Posted Workers Directive, which, although also issued a

[93] *RegioPost*, above n 4, paras 73–74.
[94] ibid, para 75.
[95] ibid, para 76.
[96] See n 7 above.

'yellow card', has been kept on the agenda, most probably by virtue of the very compelling evidence of exploitation on which the proposal is based, namely forms of social dumping in the light of the financial crisis discussed in sections II and IV.[97]

A. The Objectives and Abandonment of the Draft Monti II Regulation

The draft 'Monti II' Regulation was concerned with 'A New Strategy for the Single Market'[98] that could re-balance economic and social interests within the EU following the *Laval* case and its parallel concerning industrial action in the context of freedom of establishment, the *Viking* case.[99] Both judgments had stressed the recognition by the Court of Justice of a right to strike under EU law, but in both the economic freedom of the employer had been given priority. Arguably, the narrow definition of collective agreements in *Laval* and *Rüffert* followed from this premise that the free movement entitlements of the employer would, ultimately, prevail.

Drafts of the 'Monti II' Regulation had been leaked before the official version was issued, but the key provision was an exception clause (or 'Monti clause'), which stated that the Regulation would not affect 'the exercise of fundamental rights as recognised in the Member States, including the right or freedom to strike or to take other action covered by the specific industrial relations systems in Member States in accordance with national law and practices'. Then followed Article 2, which stated:

> The exercise of the freedom of establishment and the freedom to provide services enshrined in the Treaty shall respect the fundamental right to take collective action, including the right or freedom to strike, and conversely, the exercise of the fundamental right to take collective action, including the right or freedom to strike, shall respect these economic freedoms.

An earlier leaked draft had said that there would be 'no primacy' between the two, but while that explicit statement was dropped from the final text, this seemed to be implicit here too. The problem, of course, was that this was a profound challenge to what most would consider the primacy of human rights.[100]

Article 3 offered 'alternative dispute resolutions' to be decided by the Member States and social partners at European level, which might resolve

[97] See n 9 above.

[98] See, eg, at ec.europa.eu/internal_market/strategy/docs/monti_report_final_10_05_2010_en.pdf, 68.

[99] Judgment of 11 December 2007, *The International Transport Workers' Federation and The Finnish Seamen's Union*, Case C-438/05, EU:C:2007:772 (*Viking*).

[100] KD Ewing, *The Draft Monti II Regulation: An Inadequate Response to* Viking *and* Laval (2011), at ier.org.uk/sites/ier.org.uk/files/The%20Draft%20Monti%2011%20Regulation%20by%20Keith%20Ewing%20March%202012.pdf.

situations where the clash acknowledged in Article 2 arose, but this was not to 'deprive interested parties from recourse to judicial remedies for their disputes or conflicts if the mechanisms referred to in paragraph 1 fail to lead to a resolution after a reasonable period'. Additionally, an 'Alert mechanism' was placed in Article 4 so that:

> Whenever serious acts or circumstances affecting the effective exercise of the freedom of establishment or the freedom to provide services which could cause grave disruption to the proper functioning of the internal market and/or which may cause serious damage to its industrial relations system or create serious social unrest in its territory or in the territory of other Member States, arise, the Member State concerned shall immediately inform and notify the Member State of establishment or origin of the service provider and/or other relevant Member States concerned as well as the Commission.

How this provision was to operate was unclear, but that did not matter since the Member States swiftly sought to reject the entire proposal. After 12 parliaments adopted 'Reasoned Opinions' objecting to the EU legislative proposal (acting as a 'virtual third chamber'), the Commission decided to withdraw it.[101] So the judicial statements in *Laval* (and *Rüffert*) regarding the scope for collective action, and thereby collective bargaining and collective agreement concerning posted workers, remained determinative. From 2012 to 2016 the expansion in posted work continued apace, without significant protections for workers.

B. Another 'Yellow Card' but No Withdrawal of the 2016 Proposal for Amendment of the Posted Workers Directive

In March 2016, the European Commission made a number of proposals for reform of the Posted Workers Directive, which challenge the now established conventions regarding the relevance of collective agreements to pay and other conditions for posted workers.[102] These have the potential to reflect the significance of changes in contemporary European labour markets, as regards, for example, supply chains. However, on investigation, their content and impact are likely to be very limited. In reality, it would seem that the Commission has its eye on the road transport sector and an Investment Plan for Europe, rather than the maintenance of collective bargaining and the application of terms from collective agreements to posted work.[103]

[101] See I Cooper, 'A Yellow Card for the Striker: National Parliaments and the Defeat of EU Legislation on the Right to Strike' (2015) 22(10) *Journal of European Public Policy* 1406, 1407 and 1421.

[102] See Commission Proposal to amend the Posted Workers Directive, above n 8.

[103] ibid, 3.

First, when a posted worker has spent more than two years in the host country, he or she will cease to be 'temporary' and his or her terms and conditions will no longer be regulated by the Posted Workers Directive. When it is anticipated that the duration of posting will be longer than 24 months, or when the effective duration of posting exceeds 24 months, the host Member State would be deemed to be the country in which the work is habitually carried out. In terms of Rome I, this would mean that 'the labour law of the host Member State will therefore apply to the employment contract of such posted workers, if no other choice of law was made by the parties'.[104] So any collective agreement concluded that would be otherwise lawfully applicable to domestic workers can be applied to the posted worker who either plans to stay, or who has stayed more than two years in the host state. Moreover, such workers would acquire the same entitlements to take industrial action as local workers in respect of their terms and conditions, and a union would be able to call them out on strike on that basis (if such action was otherwise lawful in the host state, for example on the basis of membership or even secondary action permitted there).[105] This would have significance, but still does not affect the apparent bar that *Laval* places on collective action seeking improved terms and conditions for posted workers who intend to stay for less than two years, or who stay for one year and 364 days in the host state. Presumably collective bargaining locally on their terms and conditions, in a way which is at all coercive in relation to the service provider, is not acceptable in so far as it could impose unanticipated costs on a service provider.

Secondly, when a collective agreement has been concluded and made 'universally applicable' by the state, the proposal is that this will set mandatory standards for posted workers in all sectors, not just that of construction.[106] That discretion would no longer merely lie with the Member State under Article 3(10) of the Posted Workers Directive, as it does at present. This innovation seems likely to have limited effect apart from enabling greater 'equality of treatment' in a very few states. (The Commission apparently anticipates only Denmark, Ireland and Luxembourg.)[107]

What is more exciting is the third proposal regarding 'subcontracting chains', whereby Member States will have the option to apply remuneration established at company level and other applicable collective agreements to any subcontractor, even where posting of workers is envisaged.[108] This is explicitly stated to give 'the faculty to Member States to oblige undertakings to subcontract only to undertakings that grant workers certain conditions

[104] ibid 6–7.
[105] Cf *Laval*, above n 10.
[106] ibid, at 7.
[107] 2016 *Impact Assessment*, above n 9, 11–12.
[108] See Commission Proposal to amend the Posted Workers Directive, above n 8, 7–8.

on remuneration applicable to the contractor, including those resulting from non-universally applicable collective agreements'.[109] That capacity would remain subject to proportionality tests and non-discrimination requirements. Yet even so, such a measure would more closely reflect the realities of the labour markets of EU Member States post-austerity measures and the incidence of subcontracting alongside enterprise-based collective agreements.[110]

That proposal can be linked to a further proposed change to the reference to 'minimum rates of pay' in Article 3(1) of the Posted Workers Directive. This term is to be replaced with 'remuneration', suggesting scope for bargaining over and above a bare minimum wage for remuneration composed of a variety of elements, which would be applied equally to employees and subcontractors of a corporate entity. Arguably, this wording also reflects the different modes of pay recognised in the *ESA* case.[111] This would enable the Posted Workers Directive to reflect the more dynamic wage-setting realities in the contemporary labour market.

Attention to 'subcontracting' reinforces the more limited provision in Article 71(6) of the 2014 Public Procurement Directive, which sets out the potential for 'joint liability between subcontractors and the main contractor' and replacement of the subcontractor with the original 'economic contractor' where there is breach of Article 18(2) and therefore grounds for exclusion under Article 57 of the 2014 Public Procurement Directive.

The Commission's proposal regarding the Posted Workers Directive might also seem to be indicative of EU engagement with external international standards relating to supply chains being established in the World Bank by the International Finance Corporation (IFC) Performance Standards (PSs).[112] The risks and impacts of supply chains are to be considered by those seeking IFC funding under PS 1, paragraph 10. Moreover, a key objective of PS2 is 'to protect workers, including vulnerable categories of workers such as children, migrant workers, workers engaged by third parties, and workers in the client's supply chain'.[113] Arguably, though, the IFC PSs do not go as far as the planned revisions to the Posted Workers Directive, because they are not concerned with issues of remuneration or collective representation but rather protection from forced labour, child labour and unsafe working conditions.[114] The limitation implicit in the reform

109 ibid.

110 See above, text accompanying nn 53 to 66.

111 See section V.A.

112 IFC, *Performance Standards on Environmental and Social Sustainability* (2012) at ifc.org/wps/wcm/connect/115482804a0255db96fbffd1a5d13d27/PS_English_2012_Full-Document.pdf?MOD=AJPERES.

113 ibid, PS 2, paras 2 and 4.

114 ibid, PS 2, paras 27–9.

proposed by the Commission is that, by way of contrast, it seems only to be restricted to remuneration, overlooking the often crucial role which trade unions play regarding regulation of working time and, more broadly, health and safety and other employment issues, expressly recognised by the IFC PSs and even Article 3(1) of the Posted Workers Directive.

Lastly, there seems to be a change of emphasis in the recitals of the proposed amended Posted Workers Directive. Whereas recital 5 of the current Posted Workers Directive states 'Whereas any such promotion of the transnational provision of services requires a climate of fair competition and measures guaranteeing respect for the rights of workers', recital 4 of the proposed revision states that 'Almost twenty years after its adoption, it is necessary to assess whether the [Posted] Workers Directive still strikes the right balance between the need to promote the freedom to provide services and the need to protect the rights of posted workers'. Moreover, recital 5 now makes reference to 'equal treatment and the prohibition of any discrimination', which would offer the most extensive constraints on social dumping, having profound effects on intra-state competition regarding services in the EU.

VII. CONCLUSIONS

We shall now have to wait and see whether the Commission's Proposal is adopted. This may depend on how very hostile the EU and its Member States are to standards set by collective bargaining, whether in relation to public or private contracts. It was evident from the initial proposal that the Commission anticipated some opposition, at least until after the implementation of the PWD Enforcement Directive has taken place and very possibly beyond.[115] The response of those national Parliaments that issued a 'yellow card' has made that resistance palpable. However, given the opportunity to review and withdraw the Proposal, the Commission has not done so, but seems likely to press ahead with reforms, perhaps because this body is now fully persuaded that the status quo is unsustainable.[116]

This may be because, unlike the draft 'Monti II' Regulation, the issue of 'social dumping', in the form of widespread unacceptably low labour

[115] Commission Proposal to amend the Posted Workers Directive, above n 8, 5: 'Bulgaria, Czech Republic, Estonia, Hungary, Lithuania, Latvia, Poland, Slovakia and Romania, by a joint letter, have argued that a review of the 1996 Directive is premature and should be postponed after the deadline for the transposition of the Enforcement Directive has elapsed and its effects carefully evaluated and assessed. These Member States have expressed the concern that the principle of equal pay for equal work in the same place may be incompatible with the single market, as pay rate differences constitute one legitimate element of competitive advantage for service providers'.

[116] See ETUC Press Release 'Commission must now press ahead with urgent revision of Posting of Workers Directive', 23 September 2016, at etuc.org/press/commission-must-now-press-ahead-urgent-revision-posting-workers-directive#.WOjHEK2guUk.

standards mentioned so long ago in the *Laval* case, has become pressing. If, indeed, there are problems with significant wage deprivation, industrial accidents and social deprivation among posted workers, the argument that the service provider's free movement rights trump a right to collective bargaining becomes progressively weaker. Further, the risks of impact on terms and conditions of workers already in the host state become a real possibility.

It is possible that protection of posted workers' conditions of employment through collective bargaining was initially deemed inappropriate, and was treated by the Court of Justice restrictively because it was seen to have a protectionist tinge. However, that element of protectionism may not always be present. Compare, for example, the thwarting of Latvian workers' access to jobs in Swedish construction in *Laval* with the assistance meaningfully offered to Polish posted workers to recover wages in the *ESA* case. Indeed, there is increasing evidence of cross-border trade union engagement, so as to collectively address unpaid or excessively low wages. Magdalena Bernaciek, for one, has observed the work of Solidarnosc's international office, which has included putting Polish posted workers in touch with Norwegian trade unions so that they could become members and recover unpaid wages through legal proceedings, but also supporting boycotts by Danish unions in response to the undercutting of wages in otherwise applicable collective agreements.[117]

It may also be possible that Court of Justice's resistance to enforcing collective agreements came out of a fear that this was an attempt to impose a strict 'equal treatment' approach, as opposed to resistance to unacceptably low labour standards. However, there is growing evidence that failure to enable (and enforce) collective bargaining has palpable social effects, which breed forms of insecurity and nationalism that are ultimately destructive of the social fabric of the EU.[118] Even the doublethink of the Commission[119] cannot promote deregulation of collective bargaining so that universally applicable collective agreements are a thing of the past, while requiring such agreements as a precondition of effective regulation of posted workers' terms and conditions. It has become clear that something has to shift. It will be interesting to see whether the legislature has to take the lead, or whether the small shifts in approach evident in the *ESA* and *RegioPost* cases are indicative of recognition by the Court of Justice that changes could be made to its posted workers jurisprudence and treatment of universally applicable collective agreements.

[117] M Bernaciek, 'Polish Trade Unions and Social Dumping Debates: Between a Rock and a Hard Place' (2016) 22(4) *Transfer* 505, 513.

[118] T Novitz, 'Collective Bargaining, Equality and Migration: The Journey to and from Brexit' (2017) 46(1) *Industrial Law Journal* 109. See also Visser, above n 70.

[119] T Novitz, 'The EU and the Right to Strike: Regulation through the Back Door and its Impact on Social Dialogue' (2016) 27(1) *King's Law Journal* 46, 65.

Part IV

Perspectives on Social Smart Procurement Beyond the EU

12

RegioPost *and Labour Rights Conditionality: Comparing the EU Procurement Regime with the WTO Government Procurement Agreement*

MARIA ANNA CORVAGLIA

I. INTRODUCTION

FOLLOWING ITS 'GLOBAL Revolution', the liberalisation of international procurement markets represents a major driver behind the negotiation and the conclusion of a growing number of international trade agreements addressing the regulation of public procurement. International and regional trade agreements have progressively prompted governments to liberalise their procurement markets on a non-discriminatory basis, requiring clear commitments on procurement market access.[1] The World Trade Organisation (WTO) Government Procurement Agreement (GPA) and many Preferential Trade Agreements (PTAs), including the European Union (EU) as a regional trade organisation,[2] share the common objective of the elimination of procurement practices representing non-tariff barriers to cross-border trade flows on the basis of the principle of non-discrimination.

[1] S Arrowsmith, 'National and International Perspectives on the Regulation of Public Procurement: Harmony or Conflict?' in S Arrowsmith and A Davies (eds), *Public Procurement: Global Revolution* (London, Kluwer, 1998) 3.

[2] For the purpose of this analysis, the EU will not be analysed under its constitutional aspects but as a model of regional trade integration, in its most advanced form. It is interesting to note that, according to the latest WTO reserch on the classification of PTAs regulating public procurement, the EU paradoxically belongs to the category of PTAs that does not address the field of government procurement at all in its funding treaties. The EU Treaties do not contain any specific public procurement provisions in their wording; only secondary EU legislation (Directives) expressly mentions and regulates the procurement field. RD Anderson et al, 'Government Procurement Provisions in Regional Trade Agreements: A Stepping Stone to the GPA Accession?' in S Arrowsmith and RD Anderson (eds), *The WTO Regime on Government Procurement: Challenges and Reform* (Cambridge, Cambridge University Press, 2011) 561.

When compared to international regulatory instruments such as the UNCITRAL Model Law,[3] or to the World Bank's Procurement Framework, international trade agreements have traditionally been described as the most intrusive regulatory instruments of procurement regulation, with a great impact on the freedom to include labour clauses in the domestic regulation of public procurement activities.[4] The implementation of labour rights in general, and the enforcement of minimum wages in particular, has proved particularly controversial in the context of the GPA, the plurilateral agreement regulating public procurement in the WTO.[5] The preamble to the revised GPA clarifies that the primary function of the agreement is to establish an 'effective multilateral framework for government procurement, with a view to achieving greater liberalization and expansion of, and improving the framework for, the conduct of international trade'. The goal of the GPA to liberalise the field of public procurement is achieved through the *de iure* and *de facto* implementation of the principle of non-discrimination in the conduct of the procurement activities covered by the GPA commitments.[6]

As highlighted in *RegioPost*,[7] the use of procurement to enforce minimum working conditions has the potential to create conflicts with the fundamental economic freedoms in the EU internal market.[8] As clarified in paragraph 69 of the *RegioPost* judgment, the imposition of respect for minimum wages by national provisions in tenders and subcontracts 'constitutes an additional economic burden that may prohibit, impede or render less attractive the provision of their services in the host Member State ... capable of constituting a restriction within the meaning of Article 56 TFEU'. On a parallel basis, tensions are inevitable between the enforcement of minimum wages in public contracts and the principle of non-discrimination as

[3] For further discussion, see the contribution by Nicholas in ch 13 of this book.

[4] This is further elaborated in MA Corvaglia, *Public Procurement and Labour Rights Towards Coherence in International Instruments of Procurement Regulation* (Oxford, Hart Publishing, 2017).

[5] The WTO regime of procurement regulation was first elaborated in 1979 with the 'Tokyo Round Code on Government Procurement' and then established in the GPA agreement, signed in Marrakesh in 1994 and which entered into force in 1996. P Van Den Bossche, *The Law and Policy of the World Trde Organization. Text, Cases and Materials* (Cambridge, Cambridge University Press, 2005) 53–54. After a long renegotiating process, the last comprehensive revision of the GPA text was agreed at the WTO Ministerial Conference in December 2011, and the 2012 Revised Agreement on Government Procurement formally entered into force in April 2014. RD Anderson, SL Schooner and C D Swan, 'The WTO's Revised Government Procurement Agreement—An Important Milestone Toward Greater Market Access and Transparency in Global Procurement Markets' (2012) 54 *Government Contractor* 1.

[6] BM Hoekman and P Mavroidis, 'Basic Elements of the Agreement on Government Procurement' in BM Hoekman and P Mavroidis (eds), *Law and Policy in Public Purchasing: The WTO Agreement on Government Procurement* (Ann Arbor, MI, University of Michigan Press, 1997) 13.

[7] Judgment of 17 November 2015, *RegioPost*, Case C-115/14, EU:C:2015:760.

[8] B Hoekman, 'International Cooperation on Public Procurement Regulation' in A Georgopoulos, B Hoekman and PC Mavroidis (eds), *The Internationalization of Government Procurement Regulation* (Oxford, Oxford University Press, 2017) 568.

imposed in Article IV GPA.[9] The inclusion of labour considerations alongside the procurement process may imply direct or indirect forms of discrimination in favour of domestic suppliers, potentially in violation of the procurement regulatory architecture established in the GPA. A fundamental regulatory question remains unresolved in the academic discourse on the international trade regulation of public procurement: how can we balance the legitimate goal of ensuring the protection of minimum labour rights in procurement contracts with the objective of the progressive elimination of cross-border discriminatory procurement practices, an object common to all international trade instruments of procurement regulation?

To add to the discussion around this open question, this chapter will site the analysis of the *RegioPost* judgment in a broader and multi-layered framework, establishing a comparative analysis between the EU and the WTO approaches to the regulation of public procurement. Starting from the clarifications reached by the Court of Justice in *RegioPost* on the possibilities for the enforcement of minimum wages in the EU procurement regulatory framework, the chapter will address the regulatory opportunities offered under the WTO regulation of public procurement for the inclusion of minimum labour rights in procurement practices. This comparative exercise will focus essentially on the interpretation of the principle of non-discrimination, a founding principle of both the WTO and the EU regulation of public procurement. The key question this contribution aims to answer is the following: To what extent does the inclusion of domestic requirements aiming at respect for labour standards and at the imposition of minimum wages pose a challenge to respect for the principle of non-discrimination under both the WTO and the EU procurement frameworks? The WTO and the EU provide two different regulatory approaches to this unsettled, open regulatory tension between the enforcement of labour rights and respect for the principle of non-discrimination. The comparative analysis will underline certain regulatory commonalities and the significant divergences between the WTO and the EU interpretations of the principles of non-discrimination in their procurement regulations, as rooted in various regulatory and institutional variables.

This chapter will discuss the differences and the commonalities between the WTO and the EU layers of procurement governance, on the basis of

[9] Art IV GPA defines the standard of of non-discrimination in the WTO regulation of public procurement, articulated in the most favoured nation (MFN) clause and the national treatment principle as explored in section II of this chapter. Art IV:1(a) ensures respect for the national treatment principle, while Art IV:1(b) accords MFN treatment, stating that 'With respect to any measure regarding covered procurement, each Party, including its procuring entities, shall accord immediately and unconditionally to the goods and services of any other Party and to the suppliers of any other Party offering the goods or services of any Party, treatment no less favourable than the treatment the Party, including its procuring entities, accords to: a) domestic goods, services and suppliers; and b) goods, services and suppliers of any other Party'.

the conclusions reached in the *RegioPost* judgment. The analysis will focus on four major aspects of the discussion, first addressing the regulation under the EU procurement system and then analysing the WTO procurement regulation. The standard and the function of non-discrimination will be analysed in both the WTO and the EU regulatory approaches to public procurement, emphasising the challenges posed by the inclusion of minimum working conditions in public contracts. The analysis will then turn to the regulation of production methods and processes in the interpretation of the principle of non-discrimination, highlighting the regulatory divergences between the EU and the WTO in the development of regulation of production and delivery processes in the context of public procurement. The derogations and the exceptions guaranteed for procurement practices in violation of the principle of non-discrimination will then be addressed in both the WTO and the EU procurement systems, particularly exploring the flexibilities offered in the coverage of the plurilateral regulation of public procurement under the GPA. The analysis will be completed by turning to the WTO and the EU treatment of the regulation of transparency and non-discrimination, imposed via special conditions relating to the performance of public contracts, at the centre of the controversies in the *RegioPost* case. Finally, conclusions will be drawn from these findings, seeking to compare the modes of protection in procurement contracts and to emphasise commonalities and differences.

However, shifting the focus of the analysis from the EU to the WTO regulation of procurement, two significant aspects of the *RegioPost* judgment will not be taken into consideration in this comparative study. First, this chapter will not assess the significance of this judgment in light of the previous jurisprudence of the Court of Justice on social clauses in public procurement, particularly its deviation from the more restrictive approach to the use of minimum wage requirements in public procurement established in the *Rüffert*[10] and *Bundesdruckerei*[11] cases. Secondly, the role played by the interpretation of the Posted Workers Directive[12] will not be taken into consideration in the analysis. In the context of the WTO architecture of international trade regulation, the discipline of the transnational provision of services and the movement of people and service providers fall within the regulatory scope of the General Agreement on Trade in Services (GATS), while this chapter will essentially focus on the GPA, the WTO plurilateral agreement regulating public procurement. The reader will find extensive analysis of both issues in previous chapters of this book.

[10] Judgment of 3 April 2008, *Rüffert*, Case C-346/06, EU:C:2008:189.

[11] Judgment of 18 September 2014, *Bundesdruckerei*, Case C-549/13, EU:C:2014:2235.

[12] Directive 96/71/EC of the European Parliament and of the Council of 16 December 1996 concerning the posting of workers in the framework of the provision of services (Posted Workers Directive) [1997] OJ L18/1.

II. THE TENSION BETWEEN NON-DISCRIMINATION AND LABOUR RIGHTS' CONDITIONALITY IN PUBLIC PROCUREMENT

At the core of the controversies in the *RegioPost* dispute—which factual aspects are extensively explored in other chapters of this book—was the obligation imposed on contractors and subcontractors to ensure the payment of minimum wages to their workers, as imposed by the Rhineland-Palatinate's regional legislation, only at level of the *Länder*. In order to be awarded the public contracts for the distribution of postal services, contractors and subcontractors were required to provide proof of the commitment to pay a minimum hourly wage to the workers involved in the execution of the public contracts by submitting written certification.[13]

In line with the previous case law of the Court of Justice, the *RegioPost* judgment reaffirmed that the imposition of certain minimum working conditions, like hourly minimum wages, can represent a distortion of the fundamental freedom of movement of the EU internal market, in this case the freedom to provide services according to Article 56 TFEU.[14] As stated by the Court of Justice in paragraph 69:

> [T]he imposition, under national legislation, of a minimum wage on tenderers and their subcontractors, if any, established in a Member State other than that of the contracting authority and in which minimum rates of pay are lower constitutes an additional economic burden that may prohibit, impede or render less attractive the provision of their services in the host Member State.

The economic burden imposed by the requirement to respect minimum labour conditions may imply direct or indirect forms of discrimination between suppliers competing for the public contract. It potentially clashes with the essence itself of the principle of non-discrimination in international economic law, which aims to guarantee equality of opportunity in the market, without additional requirements or conditionality imposed by national governments.[15]

The main regulatory objective of the GPA is to guarantee respect for the principle of non-discrimination in the procurement practices covered by the threshold and by the Schedule of Commitments agreed between the GPA Signatory Parties.[16] The principle of non-discrimination has two dimensions

[13] F Costamagna, 'Minimum Wage between Public Procurement and Posted Workers: Anything New after the RegioPost Case?' (2017) 42 *European Law Review* 101.

[14] Treaty on the Functioning of the European Union (TFEU) [2012] OJ C326/47.

[15] T Cottier and M Oesch, 'Direct and Indirect Discrimination in WTO and EU Law' in SE Gaines, BE Olsen and KE Sørensen (eds), *Liberalising Trade in the EU and the WTO: A Legal Comparison* (Cambridge, Cambridge University Press 2012) 141.

[16] Only the entities listed as a Signatory Party in Appendix I to the GPA are covered by the GPA Agreement. Annexes 1–3 to that Appendix specify the central and sub-central government entities scheduled by each party, and also specify the minimum threshold values above which a procurement is covered by the Agreement. Annexes 4 and 5 to Appendix I specify each

in the context of the GPA: national treatment and the MFN clause, as set out in Article IV:1 of the Revised GPA. First, Article IV:1(a) aims at ensuring respect for the national treatment principle: each GPA Signatory Party must provide 'treatment no less favourable than the treatment the Party, including its procuring entities, accords to domestic goods, services and suppliers'. Secondly, according to Article IV:1(b), GPA Parties must also accord no less favourable treatment among the GPA Signatory Parties, regardless of the country of origin of the goods and services. Both national treatment and MFN clauses will be granted immediately and unconditionally within the scope of application covered by the agreement, 'to the goods and services of any other Party and to the suppliers of any other Party offering the goods or services of any Party'.[17]

In the GPA, the obligation of non-discrimination is expressed in terms of 'treatment not less favourable'. As uniformly interpreted in other WTO agreements, 'treatment not less favourable' consists of the lack of de jure and *de facto* forms of discriminatory practices.[18] In the WTO regulatory framework, the principle of non-discrimination is not limited to the prohibition of formal and *de jure* discrimination, it also ensures that any discriminatory and protectionist effect of the measure at issue is prohibited in its application, with a prohibition of *de facto* discrimination.[19] *De facto* discrimination usually derives from neutral regulatory provisions, and usually results in the allocation of unfair advantages to national producers or suppliers. To assess the extent of *de facto* discrimination, the evaluation needs to cover the effects and the implications of the regulatory measure and its 'protective nature and purpose', taking into consideration the specific design and structure of the measure on the market.[20] As translated by Arrowsmith

party's covered services and construction services. For an introduction to the issue of the coverage of the GPA, see P Trepte, 'The Agreement on Government Procurement' in PFJ Macrory, AE Appleton and MG Plummer (eds), *The World Trade Organization: Legal, Economic and Political Analysis*, vol I (New York, Springer, 2005) 1138.

[17] For the sake of completeness, it should be reminded that Art 25 of Directive 2014/24/EU of the European Parliament and of the Council of 26 February 2014 on public procurement and repealing Directive 2004/18/EC (2014 Public Procurement Directive) [2014] OJ L94/65 ensures respect for the GPA commitments to non-discrimination in the EU regulation of procurement. Art 25 requires that 'contracting authorities shall accord to the works, supplies, services and economic operators of the signatories to those agreements treatment no less favourable than the treatment accorded to the works, supplies, services and economic operators of the Union'.

[18] The principle of non-discrimination in the WTO legal framework is at the centre of a vast academic production. For a more comprehensive overview of the analysis of the principle of non-discrimination, in both the commitments to national treatment and the MFN obligation, in the different WTO agreements, see WJ Davey, 'Non-Discrimination in the World Trade Organization: The Rules and Exceptions' (2011) 354 *Collected Courses of the Hague Academy of International Law* 317.

[19] Cottier and Oesch, above n 15, 144.

[20] See T Cottier and PC Mavroidis (eds), *Regulatory Barriers and the Principle of Non-Discrimination in World Trade Law* (Ann Arbor, MI, University of Michigan Press, 2000).

in the context of procurement, the interpretation of the principle of non-discrimination necessarily has to take into consideration the relevance of the modification of the conditions for competition resulting from the procurement regulatory measure, 'and to consider how far the condition is justified by reference to the commercial objectives that it seeks to implement'.[21] Unfortunately, the application of the principle of non-discrimination in the field of public procrement has not been fully explored or clarified in the GPA jurisprudence under the WTO dispute settlement mechanism.[22]

In WTO legal terms, the conditionality of labour rights protection imposed alongside the procurement process—like the requirement to respect minimum wages in the *RegioPost* case—have the potential to result in *de facto* discrimination among the different competing suppliers, based on their country of origin.[23] More precisely, this is a *de facto* violation of the national treatment commitment that could represent the most likely scenario resulting from the enforcement of minimum labour standards in the award of procurement contracts.[24] The conditionality regarding respect for labour rights may entail *de facto* discriminatory effects if the requirements for participation in the public tendering process are drafted in a way that is more accessible for national suppliers.[25] The potential *de facto* discrimination associated with the protection of human rights and labour rights in the WTO legal framework of public procurement was the central legal issue in the *US Massachusetts State Law* dispute, but unfortunately never resulted in an official interpretation of a panel report.[26]

[21] S Arrowsmith, *Government Procurement in the WTO* (London, Kluwer, 2003) 163.

[22] The only relevant case addressing the application of the principle of non-discrimination in public procurement is the panel report of the *Trondheim* case, adjudicated under the Tokyo Procurement Code. However, the panel report does not fully elaborate on the implementation of the national treatment per se, but only in the context of the use of a single tendering process. *Norway—Procurement of Toll Collection Equipment for the City of Trondheim*, Report of the Panel adopted by the Committee on Government Procurement on 13 May 1992 (GPR.DS2/R). The case is analysed in M Matsushita, 'Major WTO Dispute Cases Concerning Government Procurement' (2006) 1 *Asian Journal of WTO & International Health Law and Policy* 299.

[23] C McCrudden, 'International Economic Law and Human Rights: A Framework for Discussion of the Legality of "Selective Purchasing" Law Under the WTO Government Procurement Agreement' (1999) 2 *Journal of International Economic Law* 30.

[24] HK Nielsen, 'Public Procurement and International Labour Standards' (1995) 2 *Public Procurement Law Review* 94.

[25] A Davies, 'The National Treatment and Exception Provisions of the Agreement on Government Procurement and the Pursuit of Horizontal Policies' in Arrowsmith and Anderson (eds), above n 2, 433.

[26] The dispute arose from the Commonwealth of Massachusetts State Law prohibiting state procuring authorities from awarding public contracts to suppliers doing business with Myanmar, based on serious human rights violations in that country. The EU and Japan claimed a violation of the non-discrimination principle, as it explicitly did not provide 'to the suppliers of other Parties offering products or services of the Parties immediate and unconditional treatment no less favourable than that accorded to domestic services and suppliers and that accorded to services and suppliers or any other Party'. See EU Request for Establishment of a Panel, *WTO United States—Measure Affecting Government Procurement*, WTDS88/3, 9 September 1998.

However, it is relevant to note that the compliance with labour legal requirements set in national regulations and enforcing the protection of international minimum standards of labour rights protection, applicable in an undifferentiated way to national and foreign suppliers, could be interpreted as mitigating the potential risk of violation of the national treatment principle.[27] In light of the WTO approach to non-discrimination in public procurement, there is a considerable difference between procurement policies that require compliance with national legal requirements and policies that impose criteria that go further than the enforcement of the domestic legal norms, thus implying even further effects to the conditions of competition in the procurement markets.[28] Moreover, the reference to international legal standards in procurement documentation, as, for example, in the International Labour Organisation (ILO) Core Labour Conventions, guarantees respect for the principle of non-discrimination on the basis of the nationality of the suppliers, ultimately avoiding the risk of violation of the national treatment principle.[29] In balancing the protection of minimum working conditions and the principle of non-discrimination, as highlighted in the *RegioPost* case, the role that could be played by ILO Convention No 94 on Labour Clauses (Public Contracts)—aimed at ensuring that workers enjoy wages and working conditions as satisfactory as the conditions normally established in national law—becomes particularly important.[30]

III. THE REGULATION OF PRODUCTION METHODS AND PROCESSES AND THE PRINCIPLE OF NON-DISCRIMINATION

In light of the space that minimum labour rights may or not occupy in the regulation of public procurement practices, another important dimension of the interpretation of the principle of non-discrimination has to be taken into consideration in both the WTO and EU legal frameworks. Attention to working conditions, together with environmental concerns, can also be

A panel report was never released as the dispute was settled at domestic level by a decision of the US Supreme Court, which declared the Massachusetts procurement law to be unconstitutional: *Crosby v National Foreign Trade Council* 530 US 363, 373 (2000). For a detailed analysis, see C Kaufmann, *Globalisation and Labour Rights: The Conflict Between Core Labour Rights and International Economic Law* (Oxford, Hart Publishing, 2007) 177–79.

[27] J Pauwelyn, 'Human Rights in WTO Dispute Settlement' in T Cottier, J Pauwelyn and El Burgi, *Human Rights and International Trade* (Oxford, Oxford University Press, 2005).

[28] S Arrowsmith, 'Horizontal Policies in Public Procurement: A Taxonomy' (2010) 10 *Journal of Public Procurement* 149.

[29] G Marceau, 'Trade and Labour' in D Bethlehem et al (eds), *The Oxford Handbook of International Trade Law* (Oxford, Oxford University Press, 2009) 555.

[30] C McCrudden, *Buying Social Justice: Equality, Government Procurement and Legal Change* (Oxford, Oxford University Press, 2007) 554.

described and framed as fundamental characteristics of production processes and supply methods, which are frequently addressed in public procurement practices. For this reason, it becomes essential to understand to what extent production methods and processes are regulatory features included (or not) in the determination of any discrimination between the goods and the services procured. This is a particularly controversial aspect of the concept of non-discrimination, as respect for labour rights and for minimum working conditions represents an aspect of the production process that has no impact on the final characteristics of the goods and services procured, and which does not necessarily have a strict link with the subject matter of the procrement contract.

The issue of process and production methods (PPMs) has been widely addressed in EU law, and the Court of Justice has often recognised the possibility of imposing restrictions on free movement in the single market on the basis of PPM-based differentiations.[31] However, it is in the context of the EU regulation of public procurement that the PPM issue plays a very prominent role, framed in terms of a 'link with the subject matter of the contract'.[32] If the 2014 Procurement Directive considerably increases the possibility of including labour considerations in the award of public contracts, the enforcement of minimum working conditions in public procurement finds in the link with the subject matter of the contract its most stringent limit under the EU procurement regime.[33] Having a link to the subject matter of the contract represents an essential requirement for the lawfulness of the inclusion of any non-economic criteria in the procurement process, as initially introduced by the Court of Justice judgments in *Concordia Bus*[34] and in *EVN and Wienstrom*[35] in the context of the use of environmental conditionalities in public procurement.[36] The requirement for a link with the subject matter of the contract essentially aims at balancing the legitimate use of public procurement for the enforcement of labour rights with the priority of ensuring efficiency in the conduct of the procurement process itself,

[31] G Davies, '"Process and Production Method"-Based Trade Restrictions in the EU' (2008) 10 *Cambridge Yearbook of European Legal Studies* 69.

[32] Cottier and Oesch, above n 15, 169.

[33] A Semple, 'The Link to the Subject-Matter: A Glass Ceiling for Sustainable Public Contracts?' in B Sjåfjell and A Wiesbrock (eds), *Sustainable Public Procurement under EU Law. New Perspectives on the State as Stakeholder* (Cambridge, Cambridge University Press, 2015) 50, 66–70.

[34] Judgment of 17 September 2002, *Concordia Bus*, Case C-513/99, EU:C:2002:495.

[35] Judgment of 4 December 2003, *EVN and Wienstrom*, Case C-448/01, EU:C:2003:651.

[36] A further interpretation of the requirement of the link with a subject matter of the contract under Directive 2004/18/EC of the European Parliament and of the Council of 31 March 2004 on the coordination of procedures for the award of public works contracts, public supply contracts and public service contracts (2004 Public Procurement Directive) [2004] OJ L134/114, was at the centre of the interpretation by the Court of Justice in the *Dutch Coffee* case. Judgment of 10 May 2012, *Commission v Netherlands*, Case C-368/10, EU:C:2012:284.

thus excluding considerations that fall outside the scope of the contract and which may diverge from the needs of the governmental authorities.

The 2014 reform of the Procurement Directives shed light on a few interpretative issues concerning the requirement for a link with the subject matter, in particularly regarding its definition and its application throughout the procurement process. Recital 97 of the 2014 Public Procurement Directive clarifies that the 'link with the subject-matter of the contract excludes criteria and conditions relating to general corporate policy, which cannot be considered as a factor characterizing the specific process of production or provision of the purchased works, supplies or services'. Article 67(3) of the 2014 Public Procurement Directive also sets out an attempt to define this fundamental requirement.[37] Moreover, one of the most evident regulatory changes effected in the 2014 Public Procurement Package[38] consists in the extension of the requirement regarding the link to the subject matter to all specifications and criteria throughout the entire procurement process, and it is not imposed exclusively at the award stage, as was the case in the 2004 Public Procurement Directive. In the 2014 Public Procurement Directive, the linkage to the subject matter is required not only in the development of award criteria, but also in relation to the technical specifications, selection criteria and contract performance clauses, as well as being imposed on variants and labels.[39]

The interpretation of the link with the subject matter of the contract was not addressed in the *RegioPost* judgment, as adjudicated against the framework set by the 2004 Public Procurement Directive, which imposed this linkage only at the award stage of the procurement process. However, it is interesting to note that the conditionality regarding respect for minimum wages in special conditions for the performance of the contract at the centre of the *RegioPost* dispute, if regulated under Article 70 of the 2014 Public Procurement Directive (instead of the 2004 version), would necessarily have involved scrutiny of this requirement in light of the new regulatory approach to the issue of the subject matter of the contract. It would be interesting to see, in the development of the future case law of the Court of

[37] Art 67 of the 2014 Public Procurement Directive specifies that conditions linked to the subject matter in conformity with the new Directive can be identified 'where they relate to the works, supplies or services to be provided under that contract in any respect and at any stage of their life cycle, including factors involved in: (a) the specific process of production, provision or trading of those works, supplies or services; or (b) a specific process for another stage of their life cycle, even where such factors do not form part of their material substance'.

[38] The 2014 Public Procurement Directive, together with Directive 2014/23/EU of the European Parliament and of the Council of 26 February 2014 on the award of concession contracts [2014] OJ L94/1, and Directive 2014/25/EU of the European Parliament and of the Council of 26 February 2014 on procurement by entities operating in the water, energy, transport and postal services sectors and repealing Directive 2004/17/EC [2014] OJ L94/243.

[39] Semple, above n 33, 61.

Justice on the issue, whether production characteristics concerning respect for human rights or the labour conditions of the workforce could be considered as criteria able to be linked to the subject matter of the contract. Requirements relating to the general ethical sourcing policy followed by the tenderers or the overall management of the suppliers cannot be included in the procurement process, and broad ethical considerations and the possible corporate responsibility policies pursued by the different suppliers remain outside of the evaluation process in the procurement cycle.[40]

In the WTO legal system, the admissibility PPMs and 'non-product related PPMs' (non-PPMs) have gradually assumed a crucial importance in the determination of the standard of non-discrimination.[41] The WTO jurisprudence has vastly elaborated on the crucial importance that the concept of 'likeness' has in defining the terms of comparison between goods and services in order to prove discrimination in WTO law.[42] In the WTO regulatory framework, the prohibition of non-discrimination applies only as far as the concept of 'likeness' applies. If the discrimination between 'like' products, services and service providers represents a violation under WTO law, it is possible to treat differently products that are not 'like'. The PPMs debate directly impacts on the concept of 'likeness'. On the one hand, it seems to be commonly accepted that it is possible to consider non-'like'—and subsequently discriminate against—products on the basis of production methods resulting in a difference in their final characteristics. On the other hand, the possibility of differentiating and discriminating between 'like' goods and services based on process-based measures that do not impact on the final characteristics of the products (non-PPMs) is still highly contested.[43] Production characteristics, like social and environmental concerns, may have a direct or indirect impact on the extent of the discrimination between procured 'like' national and imported products.[44]

The legitimacy of non-PPM considerations is particularly controversial in the interpretation of the standard of non-discrimination in the GPA framework. In defining the standard of non-discrimination in procurement, the wording of Article IV GPA does not refer to the issue of 'likeness' of

[40] R Caranta, 'The Changes to the Public Contract Directives and the Story They Tell About How EU Law Works' (2015) 52 *CML Rev* 391, 418.

[41] For a comprehensive overview see CR Conrad, *Processes and Production Methods (PPMs) in WTO Law: Interfacing Trade and Social Goals* (Cambridge, Cambridge University Press 2011).

[42] RE Hudec, 'The Product-Process Doctrine in GATT/WTO Jurisprudence' in M Bronckers and R Quick (eds), *New Directions in International Economic Law, Essays in Honor of JH Jackson* (London, Kluwer, 2000) 187.

[43] R Howse and D Regan, 'The Product/Process Dinstinction—An Illusory Basis for Disciplinating "Unilateralism " in Trade Policy' (2000) 11 *European Journal of International Law* 249.

[44] S Charnovitz, 'The Law of Environmental "PPMs" in the WTO: Debunking the Myth of Illegality' (2002) 27 *Yale Journal of International Law* 59.

the procured goods, services and suppliers as established in Articles I and III of the General Agreement on Tariffs and Trade (GATT) and, similarly, Article II GATS. Article IV GPA simply prohibits discrimination of 'goods, services and suppliers' and not of 'like' products and services. It has been argued that the notion of likeness is implicit in and self-evident from the GPA provision.[45] However, the lack of a 'likeness' reference in the wording of Article IV clearly shapes the interpretation of 'not less favourable' treatment in public procurement, following a different approach on likeness compared to GATT and GATS. A greater margin of flexibility for the comparative evaluation of discrimination in public procurement practices, focused on the competitive conditions in the market and including other characteristics of the production methods, seems to be granted in the GPA text.[46] The lack of a 'likeness' standard in Article IV GPA significantly undermines the importance of the non-PPM debate, welcoming a more extensive interpretation of non-discrimination compared to other WTO agreements. For all these reasons, the identification of discriminatory effects in the design of the procurement measures—including the possibility to differentiate on the basis of non-PPM concerns like the protection of labour rights—becomes more evident and more interconnected with the provisions regulating the procedural aspects of the procurement process and the transparency of different phases of the award procedure, in both the GPA and the EU Directives.

IV. PERMITTED EXCEPTIONS AND DEROGATIONS FROM THE PRINCIPLE OF NON-DISCRIMINATION

As explored so far, the principle of non-discrimination represents the main limitation on the instrumental use of procurement practices for the implementation of labour rights under international trade instruments regulating procurement. The requirement to respect minimum working conditions, set out in domestic or local regulations, may constitute a violation of the principle of non-discrimination, leading to distortions of the conditions of competition in the public market. However, even if in violation of the WTO principle of non-discrimination or the EU fundamental economic freedoms, it is still possible to justify these discriminatory procurement practices under both these trade regimes.

In the EU framework, the protection of workers' rights has been consistently included in the interpretation of the justifications for restrictions to the

[45] S Lester, B Mercurio and A Davies, *World Trade Law. Text, Materials & Commentary*, 2nd edn (Oxford, Hart Publishing, 2012) 714.

[46] MA Corvaglia, 'Public Procurement and Private Standards: Ensuring Sustainability under the WTO Agreement on Government Procurement' (2016) 19 *Journal of International Economic Law* 607.

internal market fundamental freedoms. The Court of Justice has on various occasions recognised the potential admissibility of discriminatory practices on the basis of considerations of public interest and subject to compliance with the principle of proportionality.[47] According to an established jurisprudence of the Court of Justice,[48] and confirmed in the *RegioPost* judgment,[49] the protection of workers and the improvement of working conditions have been recognised as overriding reasons relating to the public interest, and as mandatory requirements capable of justifying discriminatory procurement measures.[50]

Similarly to the EU framework, procurement measures imposing respect for minimum working criteria may still be in compliance with the GPA regulatory framework even if shown to be discriminatory.[51] The WTO plurilateral regulation allows for the use of procurement practices for the enforcement of labour rights in violation of the principle of non-discrimination in two specific circumstances: (i) if these procurement practices are included in the derogations to the GPA coverage in the Parties' schedules of commitments; and (ii) where included in the scope of application of the agreement, if these discriminatory practices can be still justified under the exceptions in Article III of the revised GPA.[52]

Only a limited list of non-trade objectives are admissible as legitimate justifications for a violation of the non-discriminatory principle under WTO law. Regulatory space for legitimate policy goals is recognised in Article XX GATT—as well as Article XIV GATS for services—to the extent that the necessity of the unequal treatment is proved and the conditions of the introductory clause (the *chapeau*) are met.[53] On a parallel basis, a number of

[47] E Reid, 'Regulatory Autonomy in the EU and WTO: Defining and Defending its Limits' (2010) 44 *Journal of World Trade* 877.

[48] The policy objectives of the protection of workers and protection from unfair competition, in the form of a request for respect for minimum wages, have been recognised as legitimate grounds for derogation from the non-discrimination provisions of the TFEU, in the established jurisprudence that began with Judgment of 18 December 2007, *Laval un Partneri*, Case C-341/05, EU:C:2007:809 and which was more recently developed in *Rüffert* and *Bundesdruckerei* prior to *RegioPost.*

[49] *RegioPost*, above n 7, paras 70 and 71.

[50] R Nielsen, 'Social Rights and Market Freedom in the European Constitution: A Labour Law Perspective' (2007) 44 *CML Rev* 531.

[51] Corvaglia, above n 4, 128.

[52] Art III:2 GPA states that 'Subject to the requirement that such measures are not applied in a manner that would constitute a means of arbitrary or unjustifiable discrimination between Parties where the same conditions prevail or a disguised restriction on international trade, nothing in this Agreement shall be construed to prevent any Party from imposing or enforcing measures: a. necessary to protect public morals, order or safety; b. necessary to protect human, animal or plant life or health; c. necessary to protect intellectual property; or d. relating to goods or services of persons with disabilities, philanthropic institutions or prison labour.'

[53] B Mcgrady, 'Necessity Exceptions in WTO Law: Retreaded Tyres, Regulatory Purpose and Cumulative Regulatory Measures' (2009) 12 *Journal of International Economic Law* 153; L Bartels, 'The Chapeau of the General Exceptions in the WTO GATT and GATS Agreements:

exceptions to discriminatory procurement practices pursuing legitimate policy goals are also offered in the revised GPA.[54] Compared to the EU procurement framework—where the protection of workers' rights has been clearly recognised as a legitimate justification—within the context of the general exceptions in Article III GPA, the justification of discriminatory practices on the basis of consideration of labour rights is still fairly problematic. However, even without an explicit mention of labour standards, three aspects of Article III:2 GPA can be invoked as grounds for the inclusion of labour considerations in the interpretation of the GPA exceptions.

First, the most straightforward reference to labour rights is offered by paragraph (d) of Article III:2 GPA, which allows for discriminatory procurement practices relating to 'goods or services of persons with disabilities, philanthropic institutions or prison labour'. The wording of the provision opens up the possibility of an extensive interpretation of procurement practices, with references to ILO Convention No 159 concerning Vocational Rehabilitation of Employment of Disabled Persons (1983) and to ILO Convention No 29 on Forced Labour (1930). However, it appears to be rather difficult to argue that an extensive interpretation of other ILO core conventions or labour standards, like the reference to minimum working conditions, can be included in the detailed scope of this provision. Secondly, it might be possible to imagine an extensive interpretation of paragraph (b) of Article III:2 GPA, including labour considerations restricting the procurement market as 'necessary to protect human health'. However, the interpretative efforts to assimilate the protection of the physical health with the protection of workers' labour conditions find a major limitation in the unresolved question of the extraterritorial application of WTO general exceptions.[55] Lastly, paragraph (a) of Article III:2 GPA includes protection of 'public morals, order or safety' in the scope of the GPA general exceptions, allowing for the possibility of granting exceptions based on human and labour rights justifications rooted in public morals. Parallel to the moral exceptions included in the GATT and GATS,[56] it has been argued that inclusion of

A Reconstruction' (2015) 109 *American Journal of International Law* 95; T Voon, 'Exploring the Meaning of Trade-Restrictiveness in the WTO' (2015) 14(3) *World Trade Review* 451; H Andersen, 'Protection of Non-Trade Values in WTO Appellate Body Jurisprudence: Exceptions, Economic Arguments, and Eluding Questions' (2015) 18 *Journal of International Economic Law* 383.

[54] Together with the case of defence procurement practices explicitly excluded by Art III:1, derogations from national treatment and MFN rules in the conduct of public award procedures expressly apply to measures necessary to protect public morals or human, animal or plant life or health, or products manufactured by handicapped persons, prison labour or philanthropic institutions, according to Art III:2 GPA. Lester, Mercurio and Davies, above n 45, 710.

[55] L Bartels, 'Article XX of GATT and the Problem of Extraterritorial Jurisdiction. The Case of Trade Measures for the Protection of Human Rights' (2002) 36 *Journal of World Trade* 353.

[56] The interpretation of the notion of 'public morals' inside the WTO regulatory framework has been articulated in the context of Art XX GATT and Art XIV GATS, and in light of the

social considerations, particularly the protection of some basic human rights and labour standards, in the conduct of award procedures could be interpreted as grounded in public morality concerns.[57] Significant uncertainties still remain regarding the interpretation of the notion of 'public morals' inside the WTO regulatory framework, as the idea of public morals entails substantial differences between the WTO member states on the basis of the dominant religious or ethical beliefs to be taken into consideration.[58] Further uncertainties are also linked to the specific interpretation of the idea of public morals in the context of public procurement, as it is necessarily linked to the position of the government as the principal buyer in the market, responsible and accountable for its moral conduct in its choices when spending taxpayers' public money.[59]

However, even if it were possible to include minimum labour rights in the interpretation of the different grounds for exceptions listed in Article III GPA, the legitimacy of the use of general exceptions under the GPA could be called into question. The most difficult aspect to prove is probably the so-called 'necessity test', showing clear similarities with the analysis of the EU proportionality principle.[60] In order to be in conformity with the WTO framework, the regulatory measures have to be shown to be necessary for the realisation of the policy objectives listed as a ground for exception. Parallel to the exceptions provisions in other WTO agreements, Article III GPA requires that the adoption of discriminatory procurement practices be necessary for the achievement of the relevant social and labour policies, and should demonstrate a well-defined link between the policy objective and the regulatory measure adopted for that purpose.[61] Compared with the clear inclusion of the protection of workers' rights under the justifications for violation of the EU internal market fundamental freedoms, the interpretation of the protection of minimum labour rights under the general exceptions in the GPA appears to be particularly problematic. The difficulties in

adjudication of the *US—Gambling* case (*US—Measures Affecting the Cross-Border Supply of Gambling and Betting Services*, Report of the Appellate Body, WT/DS285/AB/R, 7 April 2005) and the more recent *EC—Seal Products* case (*European Communities—Measures Prohibiting the Importation and Marketing of Seal Products*, Report of the Appellate Body, WT/DS400/AB/R and WT/DS401/AB/R, 22 May 2014). For a deeper analysis, see R Howse, J Langille and K Sykes, 'Pluralism in Practice: Moral Legislation and the Law of the WTO After Seal Products' (2015) 48 *George Washington International Law Review* 81.

[57] For a closer study of the relation between general exceptions and human rights, see G Marceau, 'WTO Dispute Settlement and Human Rights' (2002) 13 *European Journal of International Law* 753.

[58] S Charnovitz, 'The Moral Exception in Trade Policy' (1997) 38 *Virginia Journal of International Law* 689.

[59] McCrudden, above n 30, 498.

[60] SE Gaines and BE Olsen, 'Trade and Social Objectives' in Gaines, Olsen and Sørensen (eds), above n 15, 211.

[61] Andersen, above n 53, 383.

defining the grounds for exception and applying the standard of necessity in Article III GPA translated into a widespread preference of the GPA Signatory Parties for excluding from the GPA's coverage their instrumental procurement practices for social and labour policies, rather than justifying them under the GPA general exceptions.

The GPA coverage has a more complex architecture compared to the coverage of the EU Directives, which extend to all procurement contracts above certain financial thresholds.[62] The GPA discipline only extends to the covered procurement activities between GPA Signatory Parties, as stated in Article II:1 GPA. Moreover, as clarified by Article II:4 GPA, coverage is defined by the commitments listed in the seven annexes of Appendix I to the GPA for each GPA Signatory Party.[63] These annexes set out the specification of the threshold values, the lists of each Party's procurement agencies required to comply at central, sub-central and local level, together with the lists of sectorial coverage of goods, services and construction services specified by the GPA Parties. In relation to the use of public procurement for social purposes, the GPA negotiating history shows a clear preference for making use of the flexibilities offered by the GPA, rather than jusfitying discriminatory practices under the GPA general exceptions.[64] The GPA Signatory Parties have traditionally excluded broad procurement programmes targeting objectives of social integration from the scope of application of the GPA committments. To mention just a few examples, Canada excluded from its GPA commitments procurement schemes in favour of small and minority-owned businesses, together with 'any measure adopted or maintained with respect to Aboriginal peoples',[65] and on a similar basis the US established an extensive system of domestic and small-business preferences, as well as broad socio-environmental requirements, exempted from its GPA national treatment commitments.[66]

V. PROCEDURAL REQUIREMENTS UNDER THE WTO AND THE EU REGIMES AND THE CASE OF SPECIAL CONDITIONS FOR THE PERFORMANCE OF PUBLIC CONTRACTS

In the analysis of the strategic use of procurement to enforce labour rights, it is worth remembering that the inclusion of labour clauses is theoretically and

[62] C Maria Cantore and S Togan, 'Public Procurement in the EU' in A Geogopoulos, B Hoekman and PC Mavroidis (eds), *The Internationalization of Government Procurement Regulation* (Oxford, Oxford University Press, 2017) 145.

[63] PC Mavroidis, *Trade in Goods*, 2nd edn (Oxford, Oxford University Press, 2012) 803.

[64] McCrudden, above n 30, 205.

[65] PM Lalonde, 'The Internationalization of Canada's Public Procurement' in Georgopoulos, Hoekman and Mavroidis (eds), above n 62, 300.

[66] CR Yukins, 'US Government Contracting in the Context of Global Public Procurement' in Georgopoulos, Hoekman and Mavroidis (eds), above n 62, 264.

technically possible in all phases of the procurement process, from procurement planning to the final stage of public contract management, even if with different economic and legal implications.[67] What requires close analysis is the legality of the inclusion of the requirement for labour rights' protection in the regulation of each stage of the procurement process, under the different international instruments of procurement regulation.[68] In the context of the international trade regulation of public procurement, the principle of non-discrimination is translated into detailed procedural requirements of fairness and transparency alongside each step of the procurement process. For this reason, the interpretation of the principle of non-discrimination cannot be seen in isolation from the analysis of the regulation of the procedural aspects of the conduct of the procurement process, in both the WTO and the EU regulatory systems.

On the one hand, in the regulatory framework of the TFEU provisions on the fundamental freedoms in the single market, the EU Directives integrate the Treaty provisions applicable to procurement with very detailed regulation of the entire award process of public contracts.[69] The 2014 Public Procurement Package provides considerable clarification and improvement in ensuring more possibilities for the inclusion of social and labour policies in the award of public contracts, offering more flexible award criteria, horizontal performance clauses and more detailed rules on subcontracting.[70] On the other hand, in the GPA, the non-discrimination principle is enforced by a detailed procedural regulation concerning the award process, which is intended to increase transparency and openness in the concrete conduct of the procurement cycle. The transparency provisions and positive commitments set out in the GPA for each stage of the procurement process have been described as a 'proxy for identifying discrimination' in the conduct of the procurement process.[71] However, the relationship between an alleged violation of Article V:1 GPA and respect for the specific transparency and procedural rules has not been fully explored at all in the academic literature, nor in the limited GPA jurisprudence. For example, it is unclear if a violation of Article V:1 GPA necessarily has to be claimed in association with the violation of one of the GPA provisions regarding non-discriminatory and transparent award criteria or technical specifications.

In its analysis of the inclusion of labour rights throughout the procurement process, the *RegioPost* judgment focused attention on the possibility

[67] S Arrowsmith, J Linarelli and D Wallace, *Regulating Public Procurement: National and International Perspectives* (London, Kluwer, 2000) 251.

[68] For a more extensive comparaison between the GPA, the EU Procurement Directives, the UNCITRAL Model Law and the World Bank's Procurement Framework, see Corvaglia, above n 4.

[69] P Trepte, *Public Procurement in the EU. A Practitioner's Guide*, 2nd edn (Oxford, Oxford University Press, 2007) 1.07.

[70] Caranta, above n 40, 391.

[71] Lester, Mercurio and Davies, above n 45, 714.

of including labour rights requirements in the special conditions relating to the performance of the contract, in the context of Article 26 of the 2004 Public Procurement Directive. As suggested by the European Commission, special conditions and performance clauses have been generally described as 'the most appropriate stage of the procedure to include social considerations relating to employment and labour conditions of the workers involved in performance of the contract'.[72] The clear preference for the inclusion of labour considerations at this stage of the procurement process found its original legal ground in recital 33 and Article 26 of the 2004 Public Procurement Directive, and it has been reaffirmed in Article 70 of the 2014 Public Procurement Directive, which adds a specific reference to the possibility of 'employment-related' special conditions. Contrary to the previous case law of the Court of Justice, the *RegioPost* judgment recognised the possibility of including minimum wage requirements—as set in a legislative measure and not in a collective agreement—as fully compatible with EU law, in light of the TFEU free movement of services, the Posted Workers Directive and the 2004 Public Procurement Directive.[73]

Compared to the EU Directives, the GPA offers minimal and less detailed regulation of the performance stage of public procurement contracts. Under the GPA regulatory framework, contracting authorities seem to have substantial freedom to decide the contract conditions to be imposed on the winning tenderers.[74] However, performance conditions cannot derogate from the principle of non-discrimination and transparency. Apart from this fundamental restriction, nothing in the GPA seems to prohibit the use of contract conditions focusing on the production processes and supply methods of the goods and services procured.[75]

Lastly, it is important to point out that, within the discussion of the labour use of procurement in the GPA regulatory framework, the prohibition of offsets in Article IV:6 may also play a considerable role in the analysis of this stage of the procurement process.[76] Contract performance conditions imposing local content requirements may fall within the definition of offsets included in Article I:l GPA as 'measures used to encourage local development or improve the balance-of-payments accounts by means of domestic content, licensing of technology, investment requirements, counter-trade or similar requirements'. For this reason, it should be important to assess to

[72] European Commission, *Buying Social. A Guide to Taking Account of Social Considerations in Public Procurement*, (2010) 44.

[73] McCrudden, above n 30, 490.

[74] L Tosoni, 'The Impact of the Revised WTO Government Procurement Agreement on the EU Procurement Rules from a Sustainability Perspective' (2013) 8 *European Procurement & Public Private Partnership Law Review* 47.

[75] RH Weber, 'Development Promotion as a Secondary Policy in Public Procurement' (2009) 4 *Public Procurement Law Review* 184.

[76] McCrudden, above n 30, 490.

what extent the requirement for respect of minimum labour rights embedded in contract performance may result in de facto offsets, which are always prohibited in the GPA framework.

VI. CONCLUSIONS

The inclusion of minimum working conditions, like respect for minimum wages as highlighted in the *RegioPost* judgment, has been framed in this chapter in terms of a regulatory tension between the principle of non-discrimination, common to WTO and EU procurement regulatory systems, and the priority to ensure respect for minimum labour conditions. Focused on the interpretation of the principle of non-discrimination, the comparative analysis between the EU and the WTO systems of procurement regulation has shown patterns of convergence and considerable divergences regarding the possibilities for the inclusion of minimum labour rights in the award of public contracts. From the comparison of these two international trade instruments of procurement regulation, in light of the discussion fuelled by the *RegioPost* case, the following relevant conclusions can be drawn.

First, the principle of non-discrimination represents the backbone of both the GPA agreement and the EU regulation of public procurement. The concept of non-discrimination, interpreted as fair opportunities and equal conditions of competition, offers a common approach to regulatory coherence between the WTO and the EU systems of procurement governance. Moreover, it is the principle of non-discrimination that has the most substantial impact on the achievement of labour policies in public procurement. The inclusion of labour rights conditionality in the public procurement process is extremely difficult to isolate from the allocation of preference and economic benefits to domestic suppliers, often resulting in a *de facto* violation of the principle of non-discrimination under both the WTO and the EU legal systems.

Secondly, in the context of the interpretation of the principle of non-discrimination, the WTO and the EU provide two divergent approaches to the issue of process and production methods (PPMs). If the consideration of non-PPMs has been more openly accepted in the EU context, the WTO allows differentiations of goods and services only based on production methods that result in a change in the final characteristics of the products. In particular, the PPMs debate plays a crucial role in the EU procurement regulation. Considerations regarding PPMs can be framed in the requirement for a 'link to the subject matter of the contract', which represents the main limitation on the inclusion of social and labour considerations in the procurement cycle in the 2014 Public Procurement Package. In the GPA framework, however, the discussion of non-PPM considerations is undermined by the lack of a likeness requirement in the wording of the GPA prohibition on discrimination, thus allowing a more inclusive interpretation of the prohibition.

Thirdly, even if there are fundamental similarities in its interpretation, explicit exceptions and derogations from the principle of non-discrimination are used differently under WTO and EU law, in order to guarantee the lawfulness of procurement practices enforcing minimum working conditions. On the one hand, the application of the principle of non-discrimination in the GPA categorically excludes the allocation of preferences to domestic producers deriving from the conditionality of labour rights, unless justified under its general exceptions or excluded from its coverage. Due to the difficulties in justifying them under the GPA general exceptions, the Signatory Parties made use of the extensive flexibilities for the exclusion from GPA coverage of procurement practices enforcing labour policies, thus resulting in discriminatory barriers to trade. On the other hand, the EU has not allowed extensive derogations from its the coverage of the 2014 Public Procurement Package, but has granted exceptions to the fundamental freedoms of the internal market on the basis of the protection of workers' rights, under the strict application of the principle of proportionality.

Lastly, the execution phase of public contracts provides considerable opportunities for the enforcement of minimum labour rights without explicitly violating the principle of non-discrimination under both the WTO and the EU regulation of public procurement. Contract performance conditions based on minimum labour standards do not represent discriminatory procurement measures per se, particularly if they are aimed at enforcing labour rights already embedded in national and local measures and applicable to foreign and national suppliers. In the EU procurement regulatory framework, contract performance conditions have been traditionally approached as the preferred stage of the procurement process at which to enforce minimum labour rights, in respect of the requirement for a link to the subject matter of the contract as required under the 2014 Public Procurement Directive. Under the GPA, the contracting authorities have substantial freedom to decide the contract conditions to be imposed on the winning tenderers, without derogating from the principles of non-discrimination and transparency and the prohibition of offsets.

13

A View from Outside the EU: UNCITRAL's Approach to Balancing Economic and Social Considerations in Public Procurement

CAROLINE NICHOLAS*

I. INTRODUCTION

AS WE HAVE seen throughout this book, policymakers within the European Union (EU) and beyond have long been aware of the potential of public purchasing power for the pursuit of 'sustainability policies'—that is, social, environmental and economic policies. The Organisation for Economic Cooperation and Development (OECD) reported in 2013 that 29 per cent of total general government expenditure in its Member States and an average of 12.1 per cent GDP was spent on public procurement.[1] Public procurement can therefore be viewed as a powerful tool for promoting sustainability policies given its scale and because of the opportunities offered by the confluence of governments' regulatory, policy and purchasing activities.[2]

Early efforts to pursue sustainability policies in public procurement at the international level focused largely on environmental issues, such as reducing the carbon footprint of government purchasing, introducing life-cycle costing and so on.[3] Developments have broadened the range of policy objectives

* The views expressed in this chapter are the author's own and are not to be viewed as representing official views of the United Nations, including its Secretariats and members.

[1] OECD, *Government at a Glance 2011* (2011) 148 f, at dx.doi.org/10.1787/gov_glance-2011-en.

[2] C McCrudden, 'Using Public Procurement to Achieve Social Outcomes' (2004) 28 *Natural Resources Forum* 257.

[3] See, eg, S Brammer and H Walker, 'Sustainable Procurement in the Public Sector: An International Comparative Study' (2011)31(4) *International Journal of Operations & Production Management* 452. See, too, the discussions in UNCITRAL: Report of Working Group I (Procurement) on the work of its fifteenth session, A/CN.9/668, paras 82 et seq; Report of

to include innovation[4] and social issues such as improving labour standards,[5] addressing economic empowerment for historically disadvantaged groups,[6] and combatting human trafficking through public procurement and associated supply chains.[7] Indeed, it is now considered an uncontroversial proposition that governments use their public procurement systems to implement sustainability policies including social questions, and so the debate is how they may do so effectively, rather than whether or not public procurement systems should be used in this manner.[8]

This book has considered the limitations on applying labour standards through public procurement in the system of the EU. This chapter will look beyond that system and consider some of the approaches to social policies in public procurement pursued and limitations to be found elsewhere.

II. INTERNATIONAL LABOUR STANDARDS AND THEIR APPLICATION AT THE NATIONAL LEVEL

Promoting fair working conditions has long been a significant policy aspiration at the level of international organisations, including the United Nations, and was included in the 1948 Universal Declaration of Human Rights. The International Labour Organisation (ILO) was established in 1919 to promote 'opportunities for women and men to obtain decent and productive work, in conditions of freedom, equity, security and dignity'.[9] Four categories of rights—freedom of association and collective bargaining, freedom from forced labour, freedom from discrimination and prohibiting child labour—are referred to as core labour standards, and are regulated in

Working Group I (Procurement) on the work of its seventeenth session, A/CN.9/687, paras 53 et seq; Report of the United Nations Commission on International Trade Law, forty-second session, A/64/17, paras 144 et seq, at uncitral.org/uncitral/en/commission/sessions/42nd.html; and Evaluation and comparison of tenders and the use of procurement to promote industrial, social and environmental policies, A/CN.9/WG.I/XV/CRP.2. All UNCITRAL documents with the designation 'A/CN.9 …' are available at uncitral.org/uncitral/en/commission/working_groups/1Procurement.html, unless otherwise noted.

[4] J Edler and L Georghiou, 'Public procurement and innovation—Resurrecting the demand side' (2007) 36(7) *Research Policy* 949.

[5] See, eg, hrprocurementlab.org/wp-content/uploads/2016/06/Public-Procurement-and-Human-Rights-A-Survey-of-Twenty-Jurisdictions-Final.pdf.

[6] See, eg, Broad-Based Black Economic Empowerment programme in South Africa, details of which are available at www.dti.gov.za/economic_empowerment/bee.jsp.

[7] See, eg, OSCE, *Prevention of Trafficking for Labour Exploitation in Supply Chains* (2016) at osce.org/secretariat/290106?download=true.

[8] See, eg, G Quinot, 'The Promotion of Socio-Economic Objectives through Procurement' in G Quinot and S Arrowsmith (eds), *Public Procurement Regulation in Africa* (Cambridge, Cambridge University Press, 2013) 370.

[9] See ilo.org/public/english/download/glance.pdf.

eight international agreements (the fundamental ILO Conventions).[10] These were included in the Declaration on Fundamental Principles and Rights at Work adopted in 1998, at the 86th International Labour Conference, which affirmed

> that all Members, even if they have not ratified the Conventions in question, have an obligation arising from the very fact of membership in the Organization to respect, to promote and to realize, in good faith and in accordance with the [ILO] Constitution, the principles concerning the fundamental rights which are the subject of those Conventions.

Following this approach, Article 18(2) of the 2014 Public Procurement Directive[11] requires EU Member States to enforce suppliers' compliance with these fundamental Conventions (through their inclusion in Annex X to the Directive).

While there have been many expressions of support and endorsement of labour standards including in the 1998 ILO Declaration and more recently in the *Ten Principles of the UN Global Compact*,[12] assessing precisely which standards apply at the national level remains challenging. First, the ILO Conventions as a whole number nearly 200, and include the 1971 Minimum Wage Fixing Convention (No 131), which 'encourages member States which ratify to establish a system of minimum wages', and which, the ILO explains, can be achieved 'either by fixing a single minimum wage of general application or by fixing a series of minimum wages applying to particular groups of workers'.[13] This Convention is not as widely implemented as might be expected: according to the ILO, by the end of 2015, Convention No 131 had been ratified by 52 ILO Member States. It is not in force in all countries of the EU, nor is it included in Annex X to the 2014 Public Procurement Directive.[14]

Secondly, there are varying levels of ratification of the fundamental and other ILO Conventions,[15] and considerable flexibility to adapt the

[10] Freedom of Association and Protection of the Right to Organise Convention, 1948 (No 87); Right to Organise and Collective Bargaining Convention, 1949 (No 98); Forced Labour Convention, 1930 (No 29); Abolition of Forced Labour Convention, 1957 (No 105); Minimum Age Convention, 1973 (No 138); Worst Forms of Child Labour Convention, 1999 (No 182); Equal Remuneration Convention, 1951 (No 100); and Discrimination (Employment and Occupation) Convention, 1958 (No 111). See further at ilo.org/wcmsp5/groups/public/@ed_norm/@declaration/documents/publication/wcms_095895.pdf.

[11] Directive 2014/24/EU of the European Parliament and of the Council of 26 February 2014 on public procurement and repealing Directive 2004/18/EC (2014 Public Procurement Directive) [2014] OJ L94/65.

[12] See unglobalcompact.org/what-is-gc/mission/principles.

[13] See ilo.org/global/topics/wages/minimum-wages/definition/WCMS_439070/lang--en/index.htm.

[14] See ilo.org/dyn/normlex/en/f?p=1000:11300:0::NO:11300:P11300_INSTRUMENT_ID:312276.

[15] See ilo.org/global/standards/introduction-to-international-labour-standards/conventions-and-recommendations/lang--en/index.htm.

Conventions to national circumstances when implementing them at the national level.[16] It is important to note that ratification of a convention does not mean that its provisions apply domestically. When becoming a party to a convention or treaty, national governments commit themselves to carry out all necessary legislative and administrative actions to implement the convention or treaty within the domestic legal order, and how this is done is set by each government and varies from country to country.[17]

Thirdly, some standards are qualitative and others constitute declarations of rights (imposing negative obligations on Member States), so compliance in practice is difficult to evaluate, and enforcement mechanisms are relatively weak.[18] Consequently, there is no single cohesive set of national norms governing labour standards at the international level that can be referred to as *the* standards to be applied.

III. LABOUR STANDARDS IN PUBLIC PROCUREMENT

Labour standards, and social issues more generally, can comprise negative or positive obligations (employers must refrain from using child labour, or must pay a defined minimum wage). Similarly, suppliers in the public procurement context can be required to display positive characteristics (experience) or negative ones (eg that their directors have not been found

[16] The ILO explains that 'For example, standards on minimum wages do not require member states to set a specific minimum wage but to establish a system and the machinery to fix minimum wage rates appropriate to their economic development. Other standards have so-called "flexibility" clauses allowing states to lay down temporary standards that are lower than those normally prescribed, to exclude certain categories of workers from the application of a convention, or to apply only certain parts of the instrument. Ratifying countries are usually required to make a declaration to the Director-General of the ILO if they exercise any of the flexibility options, and to make use of such clauses only in consultation with the social partners. Reservations to ILO conventions, however, are not permitted.' See ilo.org/global/standards/introduction-to-international-labour-standards/international-labour-standards-creation/lang--en/index.htm.

[17] Technically, this is the case with EU Directives: the European Commission explains that a Directive 'is a flexible instrument mainly used as a means to harmonise national laws. It requires EU countries to achieve a certain result but leaves them free to choose how to do so.' See Art 288 of the Treaty on the Functioning of the European Union (TFEU) [2012] OJ C326/47, and the Commission's explanation at eur-lex.europa.eu/legal-content/EN/TXT/?uri=LEGISSUM:l14527. However, transposition in practice involves a high degree of correlation with the Directive's text.

[18] KA Elliot, 'The ILO and Enforcement of Core Labor Standards' (2000) International Economics Policy Briefs 00-6, at piie.com/publications/pb/pb00-6.pdf. The ILO Constitution has routine reporting-and-review processes (under which Member States should explain why they have not ratified a particular convention and describing what they are doing under their national laws to achieve the goals of the convention), and procedures for handling complaints by worker or employer groups or governments regarding another member's compliance. The ILO can investigate and report on non-compliance, a 'name-and-shame' opportunity, and has technical assistance programmes to encourage compliance. However, much of the process effectively requires the cooperation of ILO Member States.

guilty of tax evasion). For the purposes of this chapter, we shall focus on the more challenging positive aspects of social issues in public procurement—negative characteristics more commonly involve the fundamental ILO conditions, and are less likely to be considered discriminatory.

Positive labour standards can be categorised into three broad types. The first comprises nationally-applicable laws or other legal rules on labour standards, such as a minimum wage or series of minimum wages, whether these were introduced to implement international commitments such as the ILO Conventions or as a national policy initiative.

The second is labour standards that seek to go beyond legal minimums, which constitute established policies but do not impose legally binding obligations—such as a voluntary but defined living wage, or a standard that employers must 'refuse to tolerate any unacceptable treatment of employees, such as mental cruelty, sexual or personal harassment or discrimination'.[19]

The third is policies that seek to reward qualitative standards—such as policies promoting greater diversity in recruitment and greater employment of disadvantaged groups in society and the economy.[20]

As regards the first and second categories, suppliers will either meet or fail to meet the requirements concerned, and so they can be described as 'pass/fail issues'. The third category can include a qualitative assessment of a (quantitative or other) condition, for example recognising the extent to which the employer exceeds any applicable legal minimum or a defined benchmark. This distinction—pass/fail or merit-based recognition—has different consequences for the manner in which they may be applied in the procurement context, as discussed in section VI.

Also from a categorisation perspective, labour standards relate to the qualities of the supplier (and its personnel) and not the goods (supplies), construction (works) or services that are being procured. Consequently, the main procurement tools for considering them relate to eligibility (ability to participate) and qualification (conditions of participation) of suppliers—an example would be conditions on the wages paid to all employees of the supplier concerned. Less commonly, the terms of a procurement contract might address the wages paid to the workers on the contract concerned. In limited circumstances, there are also limited ways of including labour standards as merit-based award criteria.[21] As a result, we shall need to conduct an analysis of several elements of the public procurement process.

[19] Included in several commercial codes of conduct between private sector suppliers and participants in their supply chains, on file with the author.

[20] For a detailed discussion of the taxonomy of sustainability policies, see S Arrowsmith, 'Horizontal Policies in Public Procurement: A Taxonomy' (2010) 10(2) *Journal of Public Procurement* 149.

[21] Art 67 of the 2014 Public Procurement Directive allows for award criteria to relate to the *process* of production of goods or delivery of services, which may arguably allow for some labour standards to be included. The more flexible UNCITRAL approach is discussed in section VI.

IV. NON-DISCRIMINATION AND EQUALITY OF TREATMENT IN THE LEGAL FRAMEWORK GOVERNING PUBLIC PROCUREMENT BEYOND THE EU

The concept of non-discrimination involves essentially negative obligations, which operate as constraints (procuring entities are not permitted to select suppliers because they are, for example, below a certain size, located in a particular town, and so on). The concept of equal treatment, on the other hand, is a positive one. A central question of this book is whether policies promoting labour standards breach legal rules mandating non-discrimination among suppliers and/or equality of treatment to suppliers. Applying one or more of the above categories of labour standards can be argued to favour one group of suppliers—those that meet or exceed the standards concerned—and by implication may disfavour or exclude and so arguably discriminate against other potential suppliers, or fail to offer them equal treatment.[22]

A first element of the issue is to identify applicable legal rules on non-discrimination and equality of treatment. In a major work on public procurement policy, Trepte considered three abstract 'models' of public procurement,[23] of which one is an 'international' model. Under this model, national governments are required to follow internationally-agreed principles and procedures, which—although somewhat of a generalisation—tend to focus on integrity issues and trade liberalisation. In the period since Trepte's book was issued, the international model has become the norm, so that states are in practice required to follow a series of international norms and standards when regulating their domestic public procurement activities, as is explained later in this section, the effect of which is to impose constraints on their domestic systems. We have seen that the ILO Conventions described in section II commit ratifying countries to implement legal norms in their domestic system, which involve commitments to other participating countries. Readers in the EU will be familiar with the transposition of EU Directives from this perspective. States outside the EU may not be required to implement EU Directives, but are nonetheless subject to other international agreements posing constraints on the regulation of public procurement at the national level.

The first of these international agreements, and the one with the broadest coverage, is the United Nations Convention against Corruption (UNCAC),

[22] K Karjalainen and K Kemppainen, 'The Involvement of Small- and Medium-Sized Enterprises in Public Procurement: Impact of Resource Perceptions, Electronic Systems and Enterprise Size' (2008) 14(4) *Journal of Purchasing and Management* 230. See also the contribution by Davies in ch 9 of this book.

[23] P Trepte, *Regulating Procurement: Understanding the Ends and Means of Public Procurement Regulation* (Oxford, Oxford University Press, 2004) 63–66.

which came into force in 2005.[24] As at the time of writing (April 2017), UNCAC has 140 signatories and 181 parties.[25] The objectives of UNCAC are to promote, facilitate and support: (i) measures to prevent and combat corruption more efficiently and effectively, (ii) international cooperation and technical assistance, and (iii) integrity, accountability, and proper management of public affairs and property.[26] The text covers public procurement in a single provision, Article 9, in Chapter II (on 'Preventive Measures'), and requires systems to be based on 'transparency, competition and objective criteria in decision-making', which, the article continues, are 'effective, inter alia, in preventing corruption'.[27] Article 9 UNCAC itself is set at the level of principle: for example, it requires systems to 'address ... [t]he establishment, in advance, of conditions for participation, including selection and award criteria and tendering rules, and their publication'.[28] It should be noted, however, that Article 9 contains no express requirement for equal treatment of suppliers, neither is there a general requirement to avoid discrimination.[29] Consequently, UNCAC would not prevent the implementation of sustainability policies even if their effect were discriminatory or that suppliers were not afforded equality of treatment, provided the manner of

[24] The text of UNCAC is available at unodc.org/unodc/en/treaties/CAC/index.html. UNCAC entered into force on 14 December 2005, following the ratification of its text by 30 signatories.

[25] See unodc.org/unodc/en/treaties/CAC/signatories.html.

[26] UNCITRAL, United Nations Convention against Corruption: Implementing Procurement-Related Aspects (2008), at uncitral.org/pdf/english/workinggroups/wg_1/INF.2.pdf.

[27] See UNCAC, Art 9, Public procurement and the management of public finances. Art 9(1) addresses procurement, and Art 9(2) and (3) address the management of public finances. UNCAC's other provisions also have procurement implications, notably those addressing preventive measures (preventive measures include anti-corruption policies, practices and bodies) (Arts 5 and 6), codes of conduct for public officials (Art 8), and public reporting (Art 10).

[28] The full text of Art 9(1) reads as follows: '1. Each State Party shall, in accordance with the fundamental principles of its legal system, take the necessary steps to establish appropriate systems of procurement, based on transparency, competition and objective criteria in decision-making, that are effective, inter alia, in preventing corruption. Such systems, which may take into account appropriate threshold values in their application, shall address, inter alia: (a) The public distribution of information relating to procurement procedures and contracts, including information on invitations to tender and relevant or pertinent information on the award of contracts, allowing potential tenderers sufficient time to prepare and submit their tenders; (b) The establishment, in advance, of conditions for participation, including selection and award criteria and tendering rules, and their publication; (c) The use of objective and predetermined criteria for public procurement decisions, in order to facilitate the subsequent verification of the correct application of the rules or procedures; (d) An effective system of domestic review, including an effective system of appeal, to ensure legal recourse and remedies in the event that the rules or procedures established pursuant to this paragraph are not followed; (e) Where appropriate, measures to regulate matters regarding personnel responsible for procurement, such as declaration of interest in particular public procurements, screening procedures and training requirements.'

[29] It should be recalled that these principles are not directly enforceable under UNCAC but must be implemented at the national level, and states are given flexibility in how to do so, as described in section II.

doing so did not breach the transparency, competition and objectivity principles mandated by Article 9.

The second group of international agreements promotes trade liberalisation and includes measures governing public procurement. Among these agreements, the best known is the World Trade Organisation's (WTO's) Agreement on Government Procurement (GPA).[30] The GPA is a binding plurilateral agreement[31] that seeks to open up markets 'to international competition by preventing States parties from discriminating against suppliers from other States parties, and applying rules of transparency and open competition in procurement'.[32] The GPA has 19 parties covering 47 WTO members (the EU and its 28 Member States are counted as one party),[33] and public procurement activities worth an estimated US$1.7 trillion annually are open to competition among suppliers from GPA parties.[34]

The GPA implements non-discrimination through the right of suppliers located in GPA participating countries to compete on an equal footing with domestic suppliers in the public procurement markets of other GPA parties as regards 'covered' procurement.[35] Thus the GPA requires 'national treatment', meaning that GPA parties must give to foreign suppliers treatment 'no less favourable' than they give to their domestic suppliers (Article III:1(a)) and must ensure that suppliers in all GPA parties are treated no less favourably than domestic suppliers because of their foreign affiliation or ownership, or because their goods and services are of foreign origin. This is a positive obligation, though it arises only where a privilege

[30] See WTO, Agreement on Government Procurement (2016), at wto.org/english/tratop_e/gproc_e/gp_gpa_e.htm.

[31] Meaning that it comprises only those Member States of the WTO that have agreed to be bound by its terms.

[32] C Nicholas, 'Work of UNCITRAL on government procurement: purpose, objectives, and complementarity with the work of the WTO' in S Arrowsmith and RD Anderson (eds), *The WTO Regime on Government Procurement: Challenge and Reform* (Cambridge, Cambridge University Press, 2011) 746.

[33] Consequently, the procurement laws of the EU and its Member States—including the 2014 Public Procurement Directive and national laws—are required to be (and are accepted as compliant by the GPA Committee) with the provisions of the GPA. A further eight states with observer status on the GPA Committee are in the process of acceding to the GPA. See further at wto.org/english/tratop_e/gproc_e/memobs_e.htm.

[34] See RD Anderson et al, 'Assessing the Value of Future Accessions to the WTO Agreement on Government Procurement (GPA): Some New Data Sources, Provisional Estimates, and an Evaluative Framework for Individual WTO Members Considering Accession' (2011) WTO Staff Working Paper ERSD-2011-15, at wto.org/english/res_e/reser_e/ersd201115_e.htm.

[35] Recital 2, which states that 'Recognizing that laws, regulations, procedures and practices regarding government procurement should not be prepared, adopted or applied to foreign or domestic products and services and to foreign or domestic suppliers so as to afford protection to domestic products or services or domestic suppliers and should not discriminate among foreign products or services or among foreign suppliers'. See also the contribution by Corvaglia in ch 12 of this book.

is granted in fact. The GPA also states that parties may not discriminate among goods, services and suppliers of other signatories (Article III:1(b)), a negative obligation.[36] Further, the GPA establishes minimum rules on integrity, transparency and procedural fairness to ensure that the above principles are applied in practice.[37] The GPA approach is broadly reflected in other regional free trade agreements addressing public procurement.[38]

The third type of international agreement arises under the World Bank and other multilateral and regional development banks' (MDBs') lending operations. The MDBs have dedicated procurement rules and procedures,[39] which historically have been used for the procurement of goods, construction and services under MDB-funded projects (effectively displacing local laws, as the loan agreement is concluded as an international agreement). These rules and procedures have also served as the basis for national procurement laws, notably where the MDBs provide technical assistance for law reform in public procurement at the national level. Consequently, the legal frameworks governing public procurement in MDB borrower countries commonly reflect the rules of the MDBs (and will continue to do so as progress towards the use of country systems in public procurement,

[36] There are also 'transitional measures' for developing countries that join the GPA, softening these requirements: see AC Müller, 'Special and Differential Treatment and Other Special Measures for Developing Countries under the Agreement on Government Procurement: The Current Text and New Provisions' in Arrowsmith and Anderson (eds), above n 32.

[37] The procedures in the GPA are also considered to promote value for money in public procurement. See, further, RD Anderson and AC Müller, 'WTO Accession and Accession to the Agreement on Government Procurement (GPA): What Is the Relationship? Why Should WTO Accession Candidates Also Consider GPA Accession? What Are the Pros and Cons?' in O Chiedu and U Dadush (eds), *WTO Accessions and Trade Multilateralism: Case Studies and Lessons* (Cambridge, WTO and Cambridge University Press, 2015); C Nicholas and AC Müller, 'SME Participation in Government Procurement Markets: Legal and Policy Considerations under the WTO Agreement on Government Procurement and the UNCITRAL Model Law on Public Procurement' in T Rensmann (ed), *Small and Medium-Sized Enterprises in International Economic Law* (Oxford, Oxford University Press, 2017).

[38] Other trade associations addressing public procurement include the Asia-Pacific Economic Cooperation (APEC), with its the Non-Binding Principles on Government Procurement, the draft Free Trade Area of the Americas Agreement (FTAAA), the North American Free Trade Agreement (NAFTA), the proposed Trans-Pacific Partnership (TPP, Chapter 15) and the Transatlantic Trade and Investment Partnership (TTIP—see trade.ec.europa.eu/doclib/docs/2015/january/tradoc_153000.3%20Public%20Procurement.pdf).

[39] For the African Development Bank, see Policies and Procedures, at afdb.org/en/projects-and-operations/procurement/resources-for-borrowers/policies-procedures/; for the Asian Development Bank, see Procurement Guidelines, at adb.org/documents/procurement-guidelines?ref=/projects; for the European Bank for Reconstruction and Development, see Procurement Policies and Rules, at ebrd.com/news/publications/policies/procurement-policies-and-rules.html; for the Inter-American Development Bank, see Procurement Policies and Rules, iadb.org/en/projects/project-procurement,8148.html?open_tab=tab-18495; for the World Bank, see Procurement Policies and Procedures, policies.worldbank.org/sites/ppf3/PPFDocuments/Forms/DispPage.aspx?docid=4005.

a key pillar of the aid effectiveness agenda, remains slow).[40] These rules include and implement a core principle that the MDBs will give all eligible bidders from developed and developing countries the same information and equal opportunity to compete in MDB-financed procurement,[41] generally interpreted to mean that domestic suppliers cannot be preferred over foreign ones (indeed, domestic preferences are generally prohibited in MDB-funded procurement). Despite the reference to 'equal opportunity', the obligation is essentially a negative one, not to discriminate against foreign suppliers.

The fourth type of international text on public procurement is not an international agreement per se but a model. The United Nations Commission on International Trade Law (UNCITRAL) has worked in the area of public procurement since the 1980s, and has issued several 'model laws' on the topic, of which the latest (and current version) is the 2011 Model Law on Public Procurement (the 'Model Law').[42] A UNCITRAL Model Law is, as its name implies, a non-binding template—in the instant case, addressing national legislation on public procurement. The Model Law is accompanied by a Guide to Enactment, itself adopted by UNCITRAL at its forty-fifth session, in 2012, which provides background and explanatory information on the policy considerations reflected in the Model Law.[43]

UNCITRAL recognised that the Model Law on Public Procurement would be of limited use unless it was compatible with the other international regimes so far as possible, notably UNCAC and the GPA. In this regard, Article 3 of the Model Law expressly defers to international agreements of the country concerned.[44] Thus, in MDB-funded procurement, and where the MDBs' rules conflict with national rules, the MDBs' rules will prevail; if an enacting state is a GPA party, and a provision were considered to be incompatible with the GPA, the GPA's provision would also prevail.

However, the Model Law is conceived as a template for *national* systems, and so its primary objective, as explained in the Guide to Enactment,

[40] Generally, see S Williams-Elegbe, *Public Procurement and Multilateral Development Banks: Law, Practice and Problems*, (Oxford, Hart Publishing, 2017). As regards the World Bank use of 'Alternative Procurement Arrangements', see worldbank.org/en/projects-operations/products-and-services/brief/procurement-new-framework#APA; for the use of country systems in the IADB, see publications.iadb.org/handle/11319/5852; in Africa, see effectiveinstitutions.org/media/Towards_a_greater_use_of_country_systems_in_Africa.pdf.

[41] See the documents referred to in n 39 above.

[42] The text of the Model Law is found in Annex I to the report of UNCITRAL on the work of its forty-fourth session (Official Records of the General Assembly, Sixty-sixth Session, Supplement No 17 (A/66/17)), and is also available at uncitral.org/uncitral/uncitral_texts/procurement_infrastructure.html.

[43] Para 46 of the report of UNCITRAL on the work of its forty-fifth session (Official Records of the General Assembly, Sixty-seventh Session, Supplement No 17 (A/67/17). The text of the Guide is available at uncitral.org/uncitral/en/uncitral_texts/procurement_infrastructure/2012Guide.html.

[44] See Guide to Enactment, above n 43, 11.

is to ensure 'that the government purchaser will spend public funds with responsibility and accountability, and thus will obtain value for money'.[45] The Model Law uses the familiar principles of economy and efficiency (value for money), maximising participation and competition of suppliers in procurement; assuring integrity, fairness and public confidence in the procurement process; and promoting transparency as the tools for achieving its primary objective.[46]

Reflecting UNCITRAL's overall mandate to promote international trade,[47] the Model Law is also designed to open up public procurement to international competition. Consequently, the Model Law's approach to maximising participation and competition is reflected in a default rule that national and foreign suppliers are not discriminated against in public procurement under systems based on the Model Law. In this regard, the Model Law and GPA are designed to complement each other: use of the Model Law is, indeed, recognised as one manner of meeting the procedural rules of the GPA.[48]

The remainder of this chapter will consider the categories of labour standards and the nature of non-discrimination and equal treatment in the light of these international agreements and texts. It will highlight some provisions in the UNCITRAL Model Law that may grant greater flexibility than in the EU system to apply social policy goals such as labour standards in public procurement, despite a policy-neutral approach to sustainability under the Model Law.

V. THE APPLICATION OF LABOUR STANDARDS UNDER THE UNCITRAL MODEL LAW ON PUBLIC PROCUREMENT (2011)

It should be emphasised that there was no detailed debate on policies on labour standards or social goals as a general policy objective during the

[45] ibid, 35.

[46] For a discussion of the objectives of public procurement regulations, see SL Schooner, 'Desiderata: Objectives for a System of Government Contract Law' (2002) 11 *Public Procurement Law Review* 103.

[47] UNCITRAL has a mandate 'to further the progressive harmonisation and unification of the law of international trade' (General Assembly Resolution 37/106), by the issue of harmonised texts that seek to remove the types of barriers to cross-border commerce that substantive rules can impose. UNCITRAL seeks to harmonise substantive private law rules governing commerce so as, in the procurement context, to reduce the obstacles to bidding for foreign government contracts: as Schooner and Yukins put it, when suppliers bid overseas, they generally 'run headlong into dense and alien procurement regimes', see SL Schooner and CR Yukins, 'Incrementalism: Eroding the Impediments to a Global Public Procurement Market' (2007) 38 *Georgetown Journal of International Law* 529. Harmonised regimes should be more familiar to suppliers in the countries concerned and the legal outcome more predictable, thus encouraging them to compete. See, further, 'Origin, Mandate and Composition of UNCITRAL', available at uncitral.org/uncitral/en/about_us.html.

[48] Nicholas and Müller, above n 37.

conclusion of the 2011 Model Law. Indeed, the deliberations of the Working Group that developed the eventual Model Law[49] demonstrate that sustainability policies were considered mostly through the prism of environmental policies (reflecting then prevailing policy priorities at the international level).[50] The Model Law and accompanying Guide to Enactment also refer to examples of norms originating outside the public procurement system that must be followed in procurement processes nationally, including security clearances, environmental considerations, international labour law and human rights obligations,[51] and United Nations Security Council sanctions or anti-terrorism measures.[52] However, the focus is normative only. Assessing how social policy goals such as labour standards can be implemented in a public procurement system based on the UNCITRAL Model Law therefore requires an application of principles conceived for a broader notion of sustainability.

The main policy direction of the Model Law is that all procurement is conducted using fully open competition unless there is legal authority and justification to do otherwise. The default procurement method is called 'open tendering' (akin to the EU's open procedure), which is based on the notion of unrestricted or non-discriminatory eligibility to participate, irrespective of whether suppliers are domestic or foreign, and other procedural safeguards to ensure competition, transparency and objectivity.[53]

This approach is given effect through express prohibitions against discrimination where eligibility (the right to participate), qualification conditions for suppliers, assessment of responsiveness of tenders and evaluation of tenders are concerned. On eligibility, Article 8, paragraph 2 of the Model Law creates a general rule that the 'procuring entity

[49] UNCITRAL's texts are generally concluded through a Working Group, which is tasked by the Commission with the substantive preparatory work on topics and producing a draft legal text for its consideration. See uncitral.org/uncitral/en/about/methods.html.

[50] See the references in n 3 above.

[51] See Guide to Enactment, above n 43, 79–81, commentary to Art 9 of the Model Law, paras 2 and 7; and ibid, 61, commentary to Art 3 of the Model Law.

[52] See ibid, 54, commentary on 'Preferences on the basis of nationality or the place of origin of the subject matter of the procurement'; ibid, 61, commentary to Art 3 of the Model Law, para 2; ibid, 78, commentary to Art 8, para 2; and ibid, 79, commentary to Art 9, para 8.

[53] The Guide to Enactment explains that the main features of open tendering 'include the unrestricted solicitation of participation by suppliers; a comprehensive description and specification in the solicitation documents of what is to be procured, thus providing a common basis on which suppliers are to prepare their tenders; full disclosure of the criteria to be used in evaluating and comparing tenders and in selecting the successful tender; the strict prohibition against negotiations between the procuring entity and suppliers on the substance of their tenders; the public opening of tenders at the deadline for submission; and the disclosure of any formalities required for entry into force of the procurement contract'; see Guide to Enactment, above n 43, 143, Introduction to ch 3. The Model Law also contains default rules in favour of international participation in any procurement process, and to the effect that prior announcements of procurement proceedings under the Model Law be published internationally and in a language customarily used in international trade (Arts 33 and 13 respectively).

shall establish no ... requirement aimed at limiting the participation of suppliers ... in procurement proceedings that discriminates against or among suppliers ... or against categories thereof'.[54] Article 8, paragraph 1 expressly prohibits limiting eligibility on the grounds of nationality, again as a general rule. As the Guide to Enactment explains, 'the purpose of article 8 is to provide for full, unrestricted and international participation in public procurement': the rule applies equally to domestic suppliers among themselves and as regards domestic versus foreign suppliers.

Article 9, addressing qualification requirements for each procurement procedure, sets out an exhaustive list of criteria that the procuring entity may use in the assessment of qualifications of suppliers. The procuring entity can apply any of the criteria that it considers 'appropriate and relevant in the circumstances of the procurement', subject to a non-discrimination provision in the same terms as in Article 8. These criteria include positive technical, financial and professional qualifications, and that suppliers have paid applicable taxes and social security contributions, and negative characteristics (that they are not insolvent, for example). The purpose of the article is to prevent the qualification procedure from being misused to restrict market access through the use of hidden barriers (at the domestic or international level, or both), and transparency mechanisms ensure that obscure licences and qualifications can be assessed for relevance. This approach provides an example of how the Model Law implements the UNCAC requirements for competition, objectivity and transparency.

The criteria must relate to the standards and processes followed by suppliers generally, rather than to the characteristics of the subject matter of the procurement, and include 'ethical and other standards applicable' in the country concerned, which, the Guide to Enactment notes, can include policies such as the promotion of international labour law and human rights standards, avoiding child labour and the exploitation of labour.[55]

From this perspective, the procurement official must follow any rule of domestic labour law whether the source of the legal rule is national policy or the domestic implementation of international labour or other commitments. Any qualification criterion based on such a legal rule will clearly be 'appropriate and relevant' as well as 'applicable' in the country concerned.

The word 'standards' is not defined in Article 9 of the Model Law, nor further explained in the Guide to Enactment. Elsewhere in the Model Law, references are made to binding rules, to case law and directives of general application, and to the procurement regulations (meaning delegated legislation designed to implement the principles and procedures of the Model Law

[54] This rule operates also to establish a default rule in favour of international participation in any procurement process.

[55] See Guide to Enactment, above n 43, 5, para 11, and ibid, 78, commentary to Art 9, para 2.

at the more detailed level)[56] and to 'other provisions of law'. The choice of the term 'standards' in Article 9 indicates that a less restrictive approach was intended, and the Guide to Enactment explains that corporate social responsibility measures could be included as qualification criteria.[57] Consequently, and with the caveat that this point was not discussed by the Working Group when drafting the Model Law, the better interpretation is that the 'standards' need not have the force of law but they do need to 'apply' in the country concerned. Again, the concept of 'applicable in this State' was not defined, and it does not appear to have been clarified in case law, so there is no definitive view as regards whether norms must be universally applicable in the country concerned, or whether they can be limited in application to, for example, procurement contracts only. Given that the procuring entity may apply any listed qualification criteria that are 'appropriate and relevant' under Article 9, it is submitted that where the application of the standards is not discriminatory in the sense of designed to exclude sectors of the market, such limitations would fall within the flexibility under Article 9.

Thus, the second category of labour standard described in section III—a living wage that is recognised as a benchmark in a country, even if, legally speaking, not a binding one—could be included as a qualification requirement under the Model Law, provided, of course, that its use is not designed to discriminate among suppliers. This approach would also allow for international labour standards that have not been implemented as rules at the national level but which are recognised in an enacting state to be applied in public procurement—following the approach that the 2014 Public Procurement Directive takes in Article 18(2) and Annex X.

While the decision on where to set the balance between procurement and other policy goals under the Model Law is left to enacting states, there was lively debate in UNCITRAL on whether and how to limit the scope of the flexibility conferred in the Model Law. Concerns were expressed that the initially proposed approach was 'excessively broad ..., allowing virtually any policy to be considered as a [sustainability] policy of the State',[58] with the potential to undermine procurement objectives such as value for money. Ultimately, UNCITRAL noted that 'the reference to [these] policies ... was not intended to be open-ended but [to] encompass those set out in the legislation of the enacting State, and those that could be triggered by international regulation'.[59] Although the context for this commentary was United Nations Security Council anti-terrorism measures or sanctions regimes, the point would also apply to any international regulation, including the

[56] See ibid, 62 ff, commentary to Art 4.

[57] See ibid, 8, 'Community participation in procurement', para 25.

[58] Report of Working Group I (Procurement) on the work of its eighteenth session, A/CN.9/690, paras 104–06.

[59] ibid.

ILO Conventions, to the extent that they have been implemented or indeed accepted by the state concerned (for example, if a Convention has been signed but not ratified).

In terms of enforcement, suppliers that do not meet the necessary qualification requirements are disqualified, under the provisions of Article 9, from the procurement procedure concerned. In addition, Article 21 of the Model Law provides 'grounds for the mandatory exclusion of a supplier ... from the procurement proceedings for reasons not linked to qualification or to the content of a [tender]'.[60] The Guide, commenting on the corruption context, notes that the article

> is intended to be consistent with international standards and to outlaw any corrupt practices regardless of their form and how they were defined. Such standards may be found in international instruments, such as the United Nations Convention against Corruption ..., or documents issued by international organizations, such as the Organisation for Economic Co-operation and Development (OECD) and multilateral development banks.[61]

The commentary in the Guide to Enactment adds that the standards

> may evolve over time ... [E]nacting States are encouraged to consider international standards against corrupt practices applicable at the time of the enactment of the Model Law. Some of them may be binding on the enacting State if it is a party to the international instruments concerned.[62]

This logic would, of course, apply equally to other international norms and standards.

In addition to exclusion in the cases of corruption and conflicts of interest, Article 21 also addresses any supplier with an 'unfair competitive advantage'. The Guide to Enactment notes that what would be considered an unfair competitive advantage is an open-ended concept, that it is one for national governments to decide in light of their own circumstances, but that it includes issues of 'fairness' and 'market conditions'. Consequently, where there are binding rules in a country that a supplier does not meet—failing to pay the minimum wage, for example—Article 21 *requires* the exclusion of that supplier on the basis that it has an unfair competitive advantage, even if the qualification criteria did not include a requirement to pay the minimum wage.[63] In this regard, the UNCITRAL provisions are more

[60] Guide to Enactment, above n 43, 109, commentary to Art 21, para 1.

[61] ibid, 110, commentary to Art 21, para 2.

[62] ibid.

[63] Similarly, under the GPA, a party may exclude a supplier on a non-exhaustive list of grounds, including 'acts or omissions that adversely reflect on the commercial integrity of the supplier'. Labour standards are not specifically mentioned, but could be applied; breach thereof could also be considered as a failure of commercial integrity. See, further, Nicholas and Müller, above n 37.

prescriptive than those of the 2014 Public Procurement Directive, which allows Member States flexibility as regards exclusion in case of non-compliance with the ILO Conventions and other norms referred to in Articles 18(2), 56(1), 57(4)(a) and Annex X of the Directive,[64] except in the narrow circumstances foreseen in Article 69(3), which *in fine* requires contracting authorities to 'reject the tender, where they have established that the tender is abnormally low because it does not comply with applicable obligations referred to in Article 18(2)'.[65]

On the other hand, whether non-compliance with non-binding standards such as a living wage can justify exclusion for an unfair competitive advantage under Article 21 is another question that has not been tested judicially or in the literature. It is submitted, albeit side-stepping the issue, that the approach of the Model Law implies a recommendation that any standards to be treated as of general application should be identified in the procurement regulations, an approach that is consistent with the Model Law on other aspects of sustainability policies explained in section VI. This approach would also encourage transparency and objectivity in application, and limit the risk of challenge to that application.

A general non-discrimination rule in almost identical terms to that in Article 9 also expressly applies to the description of the subject matter of the procurement (Article 10),[66] and to the general rules on designing and applying the evaluation criteria that will govern the award of the procurement contract concerned (Article 11). The Model Law is silent on the terms of the procurement contract, beyond requiring that those known at the time of solicitation be disclosed in the solicitation documents, though it is clearly intended that the entire procurement procedure be non-discriminatory in the sense already discussed. There would appear to be no barrier to imposing a code of conduct upon suppliers as part of the procurement contract, as the United Nations does with its own suppliers,[67] which could also require subcontractors and other firms in the supply chain to follow the standards set out in the code, subject again to the caveats discussed earlier in this section. Codes of conduct found in practice include minimum standards,

[64] It should be added that the UNCITRAL Model Law provisions on abnormally low tenders, in Art 20, are limited to performance risks arising from low prices, and not from non-compliance with legal rules on social issues, for example.

[65] See GS Ølykke, 'The Provision on Abnormally Low Tenders: A Safeguard for Fair Competition?' in GS Ølykke and A Sánchez-Graells (eds), *Reformation or Deformation of the EU Public Procurement Rules* (Cheltenham, Edward Elgar, 2016) 146.

[66] Art 10, para 2 states that 'subject to article 8, no description of the subject-matter of a procurement may be used that may restrict participation of suppliers or contractors in or their access to the procurement proceedings, including any restriction on the basis of nationality'. See also Guide to Enactment, above n 43, 53, 'The implementation in practice of socio-economic policies through procurement', para 30.

[67] See UN Supplier Code of Conduct Rev.05 (2013), at wipo.int/export/sites/www/procurement/en/pdf/un_code.pdf.

agreements to comply with legal obligations and in many cases aspirational policies that are not measurable, so this action goes beyond imposing enforceable requirements.

It can therefore be stated that, subject to the general non-discrimination rules, the Model Law would allow labour standards that apply as a matter of law and non-binding standards implementing social policies that are set out in the procurement regulations, or accepted elsewhere as a matter of public policy in the country concerned, as 'appropriate and relevant' qualification criteria, and that those requirements could be imposed as contractual conditions. In other words, foreign suppliers can be required to comply with rules and policies applicable in the procuring country.

VI. EQUALITY OF TREATMENT AND NON-DISCRIMINATION UNDER THE UNCITRAL MODEL LAW

The Model Law's approach to non-discrimination and equal opportunity for suppliers is subtly different from the equivalent provisions implementing the internal market obligations in the EU system. As we have seen, there is no equivalent to the internal market's four freedoms under the Model Law (or, indeed, under the GPA and MDBs' rules), and the freedom to provide services is at the root of the positive obligations inherent in the notion of 'equal treatment' of suppliers.

This conclusion is derived, in addition, from one of the Model Law's objectives, which is to ensure 'fair, equal and equitable treatment' of suppliers. The Guide to Enactment describes this objective as an 'umbrella term used to denote the concept of non-discrimination and objectivity in taking procurement decisions that affect suppliers'.[68] While the Guide to Enactment continues that 'UNCITRAL has decided to include the notion of "equal treatment" in the Model Law to make it clear that this notion is no less part of this objective than it is in other systems that refer expressly to equal treatment', the emphasis is on (negative) non-discrimination rather than (positive) equal treatment.

Indeed, the early editions of the Model Law did not refer to 'equal treatment' of suppliers at all, but to 'fair and equitable treatment'.[69] The 1994 Guide to Enactment explained that 'as a general rule, suppliers ... are to be permitted to participate in procurement proceedings without regard to

[68] See Guide to Enactment, above n 43, 42, 'Providing for the fair, equal and equitable treatment of all suppliers and contractors', para 26.

[69] The UNCITRAL Model Law on Procurement of Goods, Construction and Services (1994). See Official Records of the General Assembly, forty-ninth Session, Supplement No 17 and corrigendum (A/49/17 and Corr.1), Annex I. The text of the Model Law and its accompanying Guide to Enactment are available at uncitral.org/uncitral/en/uncitral_texts/procurement_infrastructure.html.

nationality and that foreign suppliers ... should not otherwise be subject to discrimination',[70] but that states

> may allow for the use of procurement to promote industrial, social or environmental objectives. Such objectives may include the promotion of national industrial development (through the exclusion of foreign suppliers, the granting of preferences and the use of single source procurement in limited circumstances).[71]

Article 6, paragraph 5 of the 1994 Model Law provided that (with exceptions for the above circumstances), 'the procuring entity shall establish no criterion, requirement or procedure with respect to the qualifications of suppliers ... that discriminates against or among [them] or against categories thereof on the basis of nationality, or that is not objectively justifiable'. In essence, therefore, the 1994 Model Law expressly authorised the use of discriminatory tools as exceptions to the default rules on non-discrimination so far as foreign suppliers were concerned, albeit on certain conditions.[72] This approach is also different from that in the 2011 Model Law, which extends the non-discrimination principles to both national and foreign suppliers, so that any criterion that discriminated among domestic suppliers would be prohibited.

When first starting the process to update the 1994 Model Law, UNCITRAL delegates noted that many states were using public procurement systems to achieve national sustainability policy objectives.[73] However, while some participants considered such use appropriate, there was limited enthusiasm for addressing what were described as these '*non-procurement goals*' in the text: *procurement* objectives—such as economy, efficiency, transparency, competition and integrity—should be the primary considerations for a public procurement system, it was stated.[74] The essence of the UNCITRAL approach was that public procurement was an economic activity, and social or other policies were secondary.

Thus, to the extent that any sustainability policy objective might compromise these primarily economic procurement goals (for example, paying

[70] See 1994 Guide to Enactment, above n 69, 51, 'Provisions on international participation in procurement proceedings', paras 24–25.

[71] See Recent developments in the area of public procurement—issues arising from recent experience with the UNCITRAL Model Law on Procurement of Goods, Construction and Services, A/CN.9/WG.I/WP.32, para 52.

[72] In particular, subject to compliance with international commitments.

[73] These policies can be termed socio-economic policies (UNCITRAL) or sustainability policies, and are known more commonly as secondary or horizontal policies (in the EU). For a detailed consideration of the EU context, see S Arrowsmith and P Kunzlik (eds), *Social and Environmental Policies in EC Procurement Law: New Directives and New Directions* (Cambridge, Cambridge University Press, 2009).

[74] See Report of Working Group I (Procurement) on the work of its sixth session (Vienna, 30 August–3 September 2004), A/CN.9/568, paras 94–101, at uncitral.org/uncitral/en/commission/working_groups/1Procurement.html.

higher prices for goods from suppliers that employed the disadvantaged or a living wage), using the public procurement system to implement the policy should be considered exceptional, as explained in the Guide to Enactment to the 2011 Model Law.[75] Consequently, the Model Law is cautious on when procurement can be used to promote the non-economic elements of sustainability policy goals, and a key focus is how to ensure that such uses are transparent.[76] This position can be contrasted with that of the EU under the Europe 2020 Agenda, and the 2016 OECD Recommendation on Public Procurement, which supports the use of 'public procurement as a strategic tool'.[77]

Nonetheless, UNCITRAL recognises that governments can and do use their procurement systems to pursue social and other non-economic sustainability policy goals, and allows exceptions to its general rules for the purpose—notably, the Model Law's non-discrimination provisions explained earlier in this section. In each of Articles 8–11, this general rule is subject to an exception: there can be no discrimination at any stage of the procurement process 'against or among suppliers ... or against categories thereof ... *[e]xcept when authorized or required to do so by the procurement regulations of other provisions of law of this State*' (emphasis added). In other words, what would otherwise be discriminatory requirements can be applied under the 2011 Model Law, in a manner similar to the earlier 1994 version as previously described.

The key safeguard is that legal authorisation is to be provided in laws or regulations (delegated legislation), and the Guide to Enactment notes that policy and implementation guidance on use of the public procurement legal framework should set out clearly where the authorisations are to be found.[78] The objective is to ensure that ad hoc policies of an individual procuring entity—which could distort market access further than the policymakers at the central level intended, and could be used to disguise favouritism—are prohibited.

As the Guide to Enactment further explains, the purpose of this provision is to allow procuring entity, in limited circumstances, and solely in order to promote a government's sustainability policies, to restrict procurement

[75] See Guide to Enactment, above n 43, 4–8, 'Balancing procurement policy expressed in the Model Law and overall objectives and policies of enacting States'; and ibid, 52 ff, 'The implementation in practice of socio-economic policies through procurement', Introduction to Chapter I of the Model Law.

[76] See Report of Working Group I (Procurement) on the work of its sixth session A/CN.9/568, para 101.

[77] The OECD refers to the proper allocation of resources, rather than the most economically efficient allocation of those resources, emphasising that environmental and social issues are included. See, further, at oecd.org/gov/ethics/OECD-Recommendation-on-Public-Procurement.pdf.

[78] See Guide to Enactment, above n 43, 52 ff, 'The implementation in practice of socio-economic policies through procurement', Introduction to Chapter I of the Model Law.

to certain groups of suppliers.[79] Thus the Guide to Enactment notes, for example, that the Model Law allows procuring entities to impose requirements to 'employ local labour or materials ... as qualification criteria under article 9'.[80] While traditionally considered in the context of social and economic development policies (small and medium-sized enterprises (SMEs), minority enterprises, small social organisations, disadvantaged groups, persons with disabilities, etc), an enacting state is therefore authorised to restrict the procurement to those suppliers complying with certain labour standards if it so chooses. Of course, there may be trade-offs among these policies: the additional cost of some labour standards may be such that more vulnerable suppliers are not able to implement them (as the recitals to the 2014 Public Procurement Directive also acknowledge in the context of SMEs and sustainability standards more generally), and the Guide to Enactment contains a detailed discussion of this question.[81]

In terms of ensuring transparency and objectivity in application, the Model Law envisages both mandatory use of sustainability policies (so that procuring entities must apply them) and permissive use (so that procuring entities may apply them). Permissive sustainability criteria—whether labour standards or others—are at greater risk of being considered discriminatory, given an inevitable element of subjectivity in deciding whether or not to apply them in any particular case. The Guide to Enactment therefore recommends that rules or policy guidance from the public procurement agency or other relevant body should identify mandatory criteria and the extent of procuring entities' discretion in applying other criteria, should address the application of the rules in practice, and should advise on techniques to ensure that they are applied in an objective and transparent manner.[82] Furthermore, any sustainability policies that involve exceptions to the general non-discrimination rules are subject to 'rigorous transparency requirements to ensure that the manner in which the policies will be applied in the procurement process is clear to all participants',[83] again to ensure transparency and objectivity in the process and to limit any negative effects on competition.

Recalling the international trade context of the UNCITRAL Model Law, the Guide to Enactment continues that any sustainability policy may be implemented in this way 'only to the extent that the international obligations of the enacting State so permit'.[84] This provision is necessary in light

[79] ibid.

[80] See ibid, 8, 'Community participation in procurement', para 25.

[81] ibid, 4–8, 'Balancing procurement policy expressed in the Model Law and overall objectives and policies of enacting States'.

[82] ibid.

[83] ibid, para 20.

[84] ibid, para 17.

of the obvious risk that the policies may 'have the effect of discriminating against foreign suppliers ..., either because they are so intended or because they have such an effect (for example, where standards imposed are higher than those applying in other States)'.[85] Particular reference is made to the GPA in this context, given the UNCITRAL objective of compliance with the GPA to the extent possible.[86]

As procedures on eligibility, qualification and responsiveness in the Model Law involve 'pass/fail' conditions, exceeding the legal minimum or benchmark concerned cannot be rewarded through these steps in the procurement process. However, higher or qualitative standards on social policies can be addressed in the selection of the winning supplier: that is, in designing and applying evaluation criteria (Article 11). This apparently paradoxical rule in the case of labour standards, which apply to the supplier and not to what is being procured, arises in an exemption to the general rule that the evaluation criteria must relate to the subject matter of that procurement. This general rule, which is similar to the rule in Article 67 of the 2014 Public Procurement Directive, was introduced in the 2011 Model Law as a 'cornerstone to ensure best value for money and [to] assist in curbing abuse'.[87] However, when drafting the provisions concerned, the Working Group noted that applying this requirement to all evaluation criteria would prevent the flexibility to follow sustainability policies that was present in the 1994 Model Law. The issue was considered in the context of environmental criteria, with lengthy debate on whether it would be correct that 'performances in environmental protection' would necessarily relate to the subject matter of the procurement.[88] Concerns were also expressed that the Model Law should not provide that the use of environmental evaluation criteria should be treated as 'an exceptional measure, when in reality it was being done as a matter of practice'.[89] After discussion, the Working Group concluded that while many environmental evaluation criteria would be related to the subject matter of the procurement, and so could be applied as any other criteria, others, such as general procedures for the disposal of waste, might not.

As a result, environmental criteria are included in the illustrative list of 'standard' evaluation criteria in Article 11, but the article separately allows the procuring entity to use what the Guide to Enactment describes as a 'special group of evaluation criteria' to pursue sustainability policies, and

[85] ibid.

[86] ibid, 11–12, 'International context of the Model Law and promotion of international participation in procurement proceedings'.

[87] See Report of Working Group I (Procurement) on the work of its fifteenth session, A/CN.9/668, para 83.

[88] See Report of Working Group I (Procurement) on the work of its seventeenth session, A/CN.9/687, paras 56 and 58.

[89] ibid, para 57.

these policies need not be linked to the subject matter of the procurement. This position is to be contrasted with the use of, for example, social policies under Article 67(2) of the 2014 Public Procurement Directive. In this regard, it is difficult to see how purely social policy goals could be linked to the subject matter of the contract, in that social policies in particular are likely to relate to the supplier, not the goods, construction or services concerned. Recalling that the evaluation criteria we are talking of are not 'pass/fail' requirements (which would determine qualification of suppliers and the responsiveness of their tenders) but non-price, quality criteria, whose assessment can be expressed as a sliding scale under which higher standards are rewarded, under the UNCITRAL Model Law, the procuring entity could set a minimum benchmark for diversity in employment practices as a qualification criterion, and give additional credit for exceeding that minimum in the evaluation criteria. Examples include, for example, credit for the extent to which particular groups of society will be employed or be engaged as subcontractors, and a sliding scale could range from the legal minimum wage to a living wage.[90]

The Model Law's flexibility is subject to several safeguards, reflecting those applying to exemptions from the other non-discrimination provisions described earlier in this section. The first is that these evaluation criteria may include only those 'criteria that the procurement regulations or other provisions of law of this State authorise or require to be taken into account' (Article 11(3)(a)). The reason for this requirement is that sustainability evaluation criteria are considered to be less objective and more discretionary than 'standard' evaluation criteria, and to this extent may pose risks to good procurement practice. Objectivity is therefore assured through restricting the policies to those that can be considered as official policies of the government concerned—and, as previously explained, they could take the form of legally-binding rules or non-binding standards.

The second safeguard is that the use of these criteria is subject to the same stringent transparency requirements and other procedural requirements as all evaluation criteria (so as to reduce the scope for arbitrary decisions). Here, the procuring entity must set out all evaluation criteria in the solicitation documents, their relative weights and how they will be applied in the evaluation process (Article 11, paragraph 5). The evaluation criteria under Article 11, paragraph 4, must also 'to the extent practicable, be objective, quantifiable and expressed in monetary terms [and] aimed at enabling submissions to be evaluated objectively and compared on a common basis'.[91]

[90] This flexibility under the UNCITRAL Model Law, it should be recalled, is not available where qualification (selection) and award criteria need to be separated, such as in the EU following the ruling in the Judgment of 24 January 2008, *Lianakis and Others*, Case C-532/06, EU:C:2008:40. See also the contribution by Caranta in ch 4 of this book.

[91] Guide to Enactment, above n 43, 86, commentary to Art 11, para 6.

Simply put, the evaluation criteria must spell out exactly how much credit will be given for graded or qualitative social standards that exceed any minimum required.

Again, the Guide to Enactment recommends that 'rules or guidance issued by the public procurement agency or other body should direct procuring entities to other relevant laws and rules, so that they are aware of any mandatory socio-economic criteria to be applied and of the extent of their discretion in applying [sustainability] criteria',[92] and that the guidance should extend to how to ensure they are applied in an objective and transparent manner, and how to apply the standards concerned without risk of 'disruptive challenge procedures'.[93] A final safeguard is that the use and manner of use of these exceptional evaluation criteria must be reflected in the record of the procurement proceedings that Article 25 of the Model Law requires for each procurement, allowing for appropriate oversight.

The key feature of the provisions, as we have seen, is that by implication the evaluation criteria do not need to relate to the subject matter of that procurement. Their purpose is clear: they allow governments to implement sustainability policies—and while environmental policies were at the forefront of the Working Group's deliberations, social policies and labour standards can be treated the same way. This flexibility does not appear to be present in the EU system.

This policy approach, it is submitted, is entirely consistent with the negative, non-discrimination stance of the Model Law, and its policy choice to allow enacting states the freedom to decide which sustainability issues to pursue through their public procurement systems. The position can be contrasted with the positive obligations to afford equal treatment to suppliers in the EU system, which, it should be recalled, derive not from the 2014 Public Procurement Directive but from other quasi-constitutional rules of the Union. The right to provide cross-border services under Article 56 TFEU, considered in the series of cases including *RegioPost*,[94] *Rüffert*[95] and *Bundesdruckerei*,[96] does not arise under the UNCITRAL Model Law (and indeed the GPA).

VII. CONCLUSIONS

The UNCITRAL Model Law on Public Procurement contains a variety of procedures permitting the flexible pursuit of social policies in the public

[92] ibid, commentary to Art 11, para 7.
[93] ibid, 87, commentary to Art 11, para 10.
[94] Judgment of 17 November 2015, *RegioPost*, Case C-115/14, EU:C:2015:760.
[95] Judgment of 3 April 2008, *Rüffert*, Case C-346/06, EU:C:2008:189.
[96] Judgment of 18 September 2014, *Bundesdruckerei*, Case C-549/13, EU:C:2014:2235.

procurement systems following the Model Law. These are found in the procedures governing eligibility, qualification requirements and on the evaluation of tenders, and are subject to rigorous objectivity and transparency procedural safeguards designed to minimise the impact on the overarching procurement policy objectives. The de-linkage of social policies (as well as other aspects of sustainability policies) from the subject matter of the procurement contract allows above-minimum compliance to be rewarded in the system. The ability to do so is subject to the safeguards to prevent the use of policies that are intentionally discriminatory (in the sense of deliberately favouring certain groups of suppliers), though it should be emphasised that awarding merit for social policies need not be discriminatory. Whether this approach could be considered to breach pure equal treatment obligations is for others to assess, but where the policies concerned are defined and objectively applied, it is at least arguable that they are no more discriminatory than, for example, setting particular levels of prior experience.

The Model Law does not seek to promote or discourage the pursuit of social policies through public procurement, but it sets out to regulate such action in an effective way, focusing on objectivity, minimising the impact on competition and rigorous transparency mechanisms. This approach is to be considered compliant with the main international agreements governing public procurement, notably the mandatory requirements of UNCAC. Provided that social criteria are applied to all potential suppliers equally, whether they are national or foreign, the flexibility applied should also not offend against the GPA national treatment and non-discrimination rules (though this is a matter that would be considered through the WTO's GPA Committee and dispute resolution mechanisms).

The UNCITRAL approach is also to encourage policymakers to evaluate the success, or otherwise, of their sustainability policies and to avoid policies that may be just politically popular, expensive and/or ineffective. In this regard, the approach also reflects key OECD recommendations that policymakers and those responsible for governance of procurement systems should '[e]valuate the use of public procurement as one method of pursuing secondary policy objectives in accordance with clear national priorities, balancing the potential benefits against the need to achieve value for money', and that procurement systems 'should establish a central listing of all mandatory and recommended goals or requirements regarding secondary policy objectives, with a brief explanation and reference linking to the origin', so that this list can operate as a capacity-building tool, and allow evaluation to enhance efficiency and efficacy of those policies.[97]

[97] See at www.oecd.org/corruption/recommendation-on-public-procurement.htm. See also OECD Public Governance Reviews: The Korean Public Procurement Service Innovating for Effectiveness (2016), especially at 103, and a blog on *Improving Procurement Policy Globally*, at public.spendmatters.eu/2015/10/07/caroline-nicholas-of-uncitral-improving-procurement-policy-globally-part-2/.

Index